August 18-20, 2017
Tacoma, WA, USA

Association for Computing Machinery

Advancing Computing as a Science & Profession

ICER'17

Proceedings of the 2017 ACM Conference on

International Computing Education Research

Sponsored by:

ACM SIGCSE

Supported by:

Oracle Academy, Microsoft, University of California, Riverside, University of Arizona, University of California, Davis, University of Michigan, & zyBooks

**Association for
Computing Machinery**

Advancing Computing as a Science & Profession

The Association for Computing Machinery
2 Penn Plaza, Suite 701
New York, New York 10121-0701

ISBN: 978-1-4503-4968-0 (Digital)

ISBN: 978-1-4503-5672-5 (Print)

Additional copies may be ordered prepaid from:

ACM Order Department
PO Box 30777
New York, NY 10087-0777, USA

Phone: 1-800-342-6626 (USA and Canada)
+1-212-626-0500 (Global)
Fax: +1-212-944-1318
E-mail: acmhelp@acm.org
Hours of Operation: 8:30 am – 4:30 pm ET

ICER 2017 Chairs' Welcome

We welcome you to the thirteenth annual International Computing Education Research Conference, ICER 2017, sponsored by the ACM Special Interest Group on Computer Science Education (SIGCSE). Tacoma, Washington, USA is the host city for this year's conference, with sessions taking place on the downtown campus of the University of Washington Tacoma.

ICER stands as the premier ACM forum for dissemination and discussion of the latest findings in computing education research across the globe. ICER research papers represent significant, rigorous contributions to the field. One hundred eight research papers were submitted, with twenty-nine papers accepted for publication (a 27% acceptance rate) in the conference proceedings in the ACM Digital Library. All papers were double-blind peer reviewed by three members of the review committee. In addition, each paper received a meta-review by a member of the program committee, with the two Program Co-Chairs making final acceptance decisions.

In addition to the research paper presentations, ICER includes Lightning Talk and Poster sessions as a way for ICER attendees to present early results, gain feedback from conference attendees, find collaborators on a topic, and/or spark discussion among conference participants. The conference also serves a vital mentoring and advising role for upcoming discipline-based computing education researchers through the Doctoral Consortium. The Work in Progress workshop is a dedicated one-day workshop for ICER attendees to provide and receive friendly, constructive feedback on research during formative stages of development.

Associated co-located workshops with external sponsorship at ICER 2017 include Social Theory for Computer Science Education, Leveraging Programming and Social Analytics to Improve Computing Education, and Research on Learning about Machine Learning.

We are honored to welcome Wolff-Michael Roth, the Lansdowne Professor of Applied Cognitive Science in the Faculty of Education at the University of Victoria, British Columbia, Canada to present the ICER 2017 keynote address. For the past 30 years, he has been investigating knowing and learning across the lifespan in formal educational, workplace, and leisure settings. His journal and book publications range across several disciplines and fields (natural sciences, research methodology, education, psychology, social studies of science), drawing on a wide spectrum of research methods and theories. Professor Roth's keynote, Minding One's Business, examines where the mind is "located" when people do what they characteristically do. He draws on several empirical examples to exhibit how, when, and where to look to find cognition that is not reduced to the physical body (including brain physiology) or to some non-physical mind and that is not reduced to the individual or social.

ICER's diverse program is the result of the reviewing committee, program committee and conference organizing team's combined effort. We thank all of our volunteers for their hard work in making this year a success. We particularly thank those reviewers willing to step in at the last minute to take on additional reviews. Lastly, we thank our supporters for their generous contributions that will help ensure ICER 2017 will be both successful and memorable for all.

Josh Tenenberg
Donald Chinn
Lauri Malmi
Ari Korhonen
Judy Sheard

Table of Contents

Session: Keynote & Invited Talk

Session 1: Novice Programmers

Session 2: Student Perceptions, Conceptions, Reactions

Session 3: When Things Go Wrong

Session 4: Tool-mediated Learning

Session 10: Outside the Conventional Classroom

Doctoral Consortium

ICER 2017 Conference Organization

General Chairs:	Josh Tenenberg (*University of Washington Tacoma, USA*)
	Donald Chinn (*University of Washington Tacoma, USA*)
	Judy Sheard (*Monash University, Australia*)
	Lauri Malmi (*Aalto University, Finland*)
Program Chairs:	Josh Tenenberg (*University of Washington Tacoma, USA*)
	Lauri Malmi (*Aalto University, Finland*)
Associate Chair:	Ari Korhonen (*Aalto University, Finland*)
Lightning Talks and Posters Chairs:	Katrina Falkner (*University of Adelaide, Australia*)
	Anna Eckerdal (*Uppsala University, Sweden*)
Local Arrangements Chair:	Donald Chinn (*University of Washington Tacoma, USA*)
Doctoral Consortium Chairs:	Ben Shapiro (*University of Colorado Boulder, USA*)
	Jan Vahrenhold (*University of Münster, Germany*)
Work in Progress Workshop Chairs:	Colleen Lewis (*Harvey Mudd College, USA*)
	Sally Fincher (*University of Kent, UK*)
Submission Chair:	Simon (*University of Newcastle, Australia*)
Program Committee:	Tony Clear (*Auckland University of Technology, New Zealand*)
	Quintin Cutts (*University of Glasgow, Scotland*)
	Brian Dorn (*University of Nebraska Omaha, USA*)
	Anna Eckerdal (*Uppsala University, Sweden*)
	Katrina Falkner (*University of Adelaide, Australia*)
	Sally Fincher (*University of Kent, UK*)
	Peter Hubwieser (*Technical University of Munich, Germany*)
	Chris Hundhausen (*Washington State University, USA*)
	Maria Knobelsdorf (*University of Hamburg, Germany*)
	Andy Ko (*University of Washington, USA*)
	Andrew Luxton-Reilly (*University of Auckland, New Zealand*)
	Robert McCartney (*University of Connecticut, USA*)
	Kate Sanders (*Rhode Island College, USA*)
	Carsten Schulte (*University of Paderborn, Germany*)
	Juha Sorva (*Aalto University, Finland*)
Reviewers:	Christine Alvarado (*UC San Diego, USA*)
	Owen Astrachan (*Duke University, USA*)
	Brett Becker (*University College Dublin, Ireland*)
	Andrew Begel (*Microsoft Research, USA*)
	Moti Ben-Ari (*Weizmann Institute of Science, Israel*)
	Jonas Boustedt (*University of Gävle, Sweden*)

ICER 2017 Sponsor & Supporters

Sponsor:

Supporters:

Support for the Doctoral Consortium provided by researchers from the
University of California, Riverside,
University of Arizona,
University of California, Davis,
University of Michigan, and
zyBooks.

Minding One's Business: On the How, When, and Where of Cognition

Wolff-Michael Roth
Faculty of Education
University of Victoria
Victoria, Canada
mroth@uvic.ca

ABSTRACT[1]

Where is the mind when we mind our business, that is, when we do what we characteristically do? Is mind between the two ears and underneath the skull? Is it in the business that has been minded? Or is it somewhere else? A foray into the literature on theories of cognition (knowing, learning) has to be confusing. There is research that looks for mind in neurons and neuronal connections; other studies assume an enacted or embodied mind; others again consider mind to be in society. How we think about cognition has direct implication on when and where we look for it when conducting research, and how we go about teaching a field. If we assume a classical computer metaphor, then learning occurs when information is transferred to the brain (mind) of the learner where it is stored, and lecturing constitutes a main pedagogical modality. If we assume that knowledge is actively constructed when we engage in relevant activities, then one or another student-centered pedagogy will be the method of choice. When the metaphor is the embodied or enactivist mind, then opportunities tend to be provided for students to act with the relevant practical objects.

In this talk, I work through some empirical examples to exhibit how, when, and where to look to find cognition that is not reduced to the physical body (including brain physiology) or to some non-physical mind and that is not reduced to the individual or social. Instead, the physical or mental dimensions, the individual or social aspects, are but manifestations of a thinking body that itself is invisible in the same way as the wave functions in quantum mechanics. *Minding one's business*, i.e., acting so that what is done is intelligible and intelligent, simultaneously is individual and social, sensuous (material, specific) and super-sensuous (ideal, universal). As a result, phenomena commonly searched for in the brain—e.g., remembering, perceiving, knowing a concept, reasoning— manifest themselves, often contradictorily, in different modes and modalities. Some implications are sketched for computing education.

ICER '17, August 18-20, 2017, Tacoma, WA, USA
© 2017 Copyright is held by the owner/author(s).
ACM ISBN 978-1-4503-4968-0/17/08.
http://dx.doi.org/10.1145/3105726.3105747

CCS CONCEPTS

• Social and professional topics → Computing education

KEYWORDS

Theories of cognition; embodied cognition; enactivist cognition

2 BIOGRAPHY

Wolff-Michael Roth is Lansdowne Professor of Applied Cognitive Science in the Faculty of Education at the University of Victoria, British Columbia, Canada. After an MSc in physics, he obtained a PhD from the College of Science and Technology at the University of Southern Mississippi for an investigation on the development of mathematical reasoning in adults. His early experiences include eight years as teacher of science, mathematics, and computer science. For the past 30 years, he has been investigating knowing and learning across the lifespan in formal educational (elementary, middle, high school, and university), workplace (fish culturists, scientists, electricians, pilots, software developers), and leisure settings (environmentalists). His journal publications range across several disciplines and fields (natural sciences, research methodology, education, psychology, social studies of science) and he has drawn on the entire spectrum of research methods (from quantitative to qualitative, and also has modeled human behavior using mathematical models and artificial neural networks) and theories of cognition (information processing, [radical, social] constructivism discursive psychology, phenomenology, cultural-historical psychology). He has received many career and publication awards, elected fellow of the American Association for the Advancement of Science and the American Educational Research Association, and was awarded an honorary doctorate from the University of Ioannina, Greece.

Comprehension First: Evaluating a Novel Pedagogy and Tutoring System for Program Tracing in CS1

Greg L. Nelson
University of Washington
Allen School, DUB Group
Seattle, Washington 98195
glnelson@uw.edu

Benjamin Xie
University of Washington
The Information School, DUB Group
Seattle, Washington 98195
bxie@uw.edu

Andrew J. Ko
University of Washington
The Information School, DUB Group
Seattle, Washington 98195
ajko@uw.edu

ABSTRACT

What knowledge does learning programming require? Prior work has focused on theorizing program writing and problem solving skills. We examine program comprehension and propose a formal theory of program tracing knowledge based on control flow paths through an interpreter program's source code. Because novices cannot understand the interpreter's programming language notation, we transform it into causal relationships from code tokens to instructions to machine state changes. To teach this knowledge, we propose a comprehension-first pedagogy based on causal inference, by showing, explaining, and assessing each path by stepping through concrete examples within many example programs. To assess this pedagogy, we built PLTutor, a tutorial system with a fixed curriculum of example programs. We evaluate learning gains among self-selected CS1 students using a block randomized lab study comparing PLTutor with Codecademy, a writing tutorial. In our small study, we find some evidence of improved learning gains on the SCS1, with average learning gains of PLTutor 60% higher than Codecademy (gain of 3.89 vs. 2.42 out of 27 questions). These gains strongly predicted midterms (R^2=.64) only for PLTutor participants, whose grades showed less variation and no failures.

KEYWORDS
knowledge representation, program tracing, notional machine

1 INTRODUCTION

Programming requires many complex skills, including planning, program design, and problem domain knowledge [47, 48, 74]. It also fundamentally requires, however, knowledge of how programs execute [13, 44, 49, 55, 86]. Unfortunately, many learners still struggle to master even basic program comprehension skills: two large multinational studies show more than 60% of students incorrectly answer questions about the execution of basic programs [45, 56].

Teachers and researchers have attempted to address learners' fragile knowledge of program execution in diverse ways, creating [37, 51, 62, 63, 65] or changing languages [15, 20, 41, 69, 73] and building writing [17, 39, 68] and visualization tools [29, 34, 34, 57, 81, 87, 91]. Pedagogy has also evolved, reordering [23, 61, 80, 84, 85] and changing what is taught [14, 50, 72], refining worked examples [58], explicitly teaching problem solving [48, 61] and program design [27], and exploring a discovery pedagogy [46].

Most of these diverse approaches have been evaluated in a *writing*-focused pedagogical context. People receive instruction on a programming construct's syntax and semantics, practice by writing code, then advance to the next construct (roughly a spiral syntax approach [76]). In contrast, little prior work has explored a *comprehension*-first pedagogy, teaching *program semantics*—how static code causes dynamic computer behavior—*before* teaching learners to write code. Prior work proposes some approaches and curricular ordering [6, 21, 38, 76, 79] but lacks implementations and evaluations on learning outcomes.

This leads us to our central research question: *What effects does a comprehension-first and theoretically-informed pedagogy have on learning program comprehension and writing skills?*

We argue that comprehension-first is not just another pedagogical strategy, but instead requires a new conceptualization of what it means to "know" a programming language. We therefore contribute a theory of program tracing knowledge, derived from abstract control flow paths through a programming language interpreter's execution rules. Based on this theory, we contribute the first comprehension-first pedagogy that teaches and assesses tracing skills for a Turing-complete portion of a programming language, without learners writing or editing code and without requiring them to infer program behavior from input and output. Based on this pedagogy, we built an interactive tutorial, PLTutor, to explore preliminary answers to our research question. We then conducted a formative experimental comparison of PLTutor and a writing-focused Codecademy tutorial, investigating the effects of a comprehension-first pedagogy on CS1 learning outcomes.

2 RELATED WORK

Prior work on *tools* has enabled comprehension-first pedagogy, but has lacked high-quality evaluations of its effects on comprehension and writing. For instance, program visualization can help learners comprehend detailed low-level operations in programs [57] or low-level visual program simulation [81], but these have not been applied in a comprehension-first pedagogy. UUhistle has some technical features that would support a learner independently following a comprehension-focused curriculum (e.g., by choosing from a list of programs with instructor annotations), but that has not been evaluated [81]. Bayman et al. compared the effects of combinations of syntax and semantic knowledge in diagrams on writing

ICER'17, August 18-20, 2017, Tacoma, WA, USA.
© 2017 Copyright held by the owner/author(s). Publication rights licensed to ACM.
978-1-4503-4968-0/17/08...$15.00
DOI: http://dx.doi.org/10.1145/3105726.3106178

and comprehension practice [5]. Computer tutors tried low-level evaluation exercises, but sequenced with writing exercises; this had no benefits for writing skills vs. only having writing exercises [2].

Other work implements a comprehension-first pedagogy but has limitations in their evaluations or the breadth of what they teach. Dyck et al. only assessed writing ability after using a computer-based manual with rudimentary assessments of program tracing [25]. To our knowledge, the only self-contained tool that implements a comprehension-first pedagogy is Reduct [3], an educational game that teaches operational semantics. Its design focuses on engagement, does not include a textual notation, does not cover variables, scope, loops, and nested or ordered statements, and shows some inaccurate semantics for Javascript. Its evaluation also lacks a validated assessment, a pre-test, or comparison to other tools.

Prior *theoretical* work on program comprehension spans both cognitive studies of program comprehension and pedagogical approaches to teaching program tracing. Neither of these areas have a theory for what comprehension knowledge is.

Researchers since the 1970s have theorized about *how* people comprehend code [11, 32, 60, 75, 77]. This research has developed cognitive theories of comprehension processes, describing perception [32, 60], mental structures [11, 19, 55], and novices and experts differences [11, 19, 53, 77]. These theories facilitate questions about perceptual strategies that novices and experts use to comprehend code, what features of code experts use to comprehend code, and what kinds of knowledge experts use. These theories focus on comprehension process and behavior; we contribute a theory that 1) specifies what knowledge people must have to be able to execute these processes and 2) formally connects this knowledge to syntax.

Prior work makes key distinctions between writing, syntax, and semantic knowledge (for example, [5, 32, 52, 54, 77]) but lacks formal connections across levels of semantics knowledge and a principled way to derive it. Mayer divides semantics into micro (statement) and macro (program) levels, and describes *transactions* at a sub-statement level as action, object, and location [52, 54]. However, these natural language descriptions lack connections to the sub-expression parts of the code that causes them.

Berry generated animated program visualizations from operational semantics, a formalism used by PL researchers for proofs and reasoning [7]. We instead propose the knowledge needed to learn program tracing is not the *abstract formal* semantics for a language, but the semantics as actually implemented in a language's interpreter, mapped to a notional machine to facilitate comprehension.

Within CS education, early approaches utilized writing tasks that required program comprehension, focusing on teaching syntax and semantics one language construct at a time, while gaining writing knowledge about the construct [74, 76, 85]. In contrast, around 1980 Deimel et al. [21] and Kimura [38] briefly proposed, without evaluating, a comprehension-first curriculum starting with running programs and looking at I/O to infer semantics. Major literature reviews fail to mention their existence, even since the 1990s [67, 74, 90]. Both of these pedagogies lack a definition of the knowledge learned, making one unable to determine when language features have been fully covered. They also lacked assessment methods beyond I/O prediction, making it hard to give targeted practice, diagnose misconceptions, and correct them with feedback.

3 PROGRAM TRACING KNOWLEDGE

The critical gaps in prior work are in both tools and theory. No theories describe the knowledge necessary for program tracing skills, and no tutorials or visualization tools have been designed or evaluated with a comprehension-first pedagogy. Therefore, in this section, we present a theory of what program tracing knowledge is and build upon it in later sections to inform the design and evaluation of a tutor that teaches program tracing knowledge.

Our first observation about tracing is that inside the interpreter that executes programs for a particular programming language (PL) is the exact knowledge required to execute a program. It just happens to be represented in a notation designed for *computers* to understand rather than people. For example, in many PL courses, students write an interpreter for a calculator language; it reads text such as 2+3 and executes that code. The interpreter contains definitions of execution rules like `if(operator == "+") { result = left + right; }`. We argue that this logic is the knowledge required to accurately trace program execution.

Unfortunately, because this logic is represented as code, it is not easily learned by novices. First, few materials for learning a language actually show the interpreter's logic explicitly. Moreover, even if this logic was visible, novices would not likely understand it because they do not understand the notation that it is written in. This provides a key theoretical explanation for why learning to trace programs is hard—this notational barrier can only be overcome once you understand programming languages, creating a recursive learning dependency.

Execution rule logic, however, is not alone a suitable account of the knowledge required for tracing. Our second claim is that to know a programming language, learners also must be able to *map* these execution rules to the syntax and state that determines what rules are followed and in which situations. Therefore, knowledge of a PL is also the *mapping* between syntax, semantics, and state.

To illustrate this mapping, Table 1 shows an interpreter in pseudocode, showing the three conventional stages of transforming program source code into executable instructions, for a simple JavaScript-like expression x == 0. The first stage translates characters into tokens; the second stage translates tokens into an abstract syntax tree (AST); the final stage translates the AST into machine instructions that ultimately determine program behavior. We argue that learners do not need to understand these stages themselves, but rather that they need to understand *each path* through these stages that map syntax and state to behavior. We show one example of a path underlined in Table 1, which specifically concerns the 0 in our x == 0 expression, showing its translation from character to token to a machine instruction that pushes 0 onto an accumulator stack for comparison to x by the == operator. This simple mapping rule—that a numerical literal like 0 is a token in an expression that results in a number being pushed onto a stack for later comparison—is just one of the execution rule paths; we argue learners must understand all possible paths to know the whole language.

Some rules have one path (for example, the 0 in x==0 only has one in our example language), but some execution rules have multiple control flow paths, depending on the code or runtime state involved. For example, if statements in many imperative languages can optionally include an else statement. If an AST has an else

Stage	Transformation Rule (Pseudocode)	Example Output (input for next row)
1. Tokenize	Any number => Number Operator => Op Variable name => Name	Name(x) Op(==) Number(0)
2. Parse	Parse(*toks*) => *AST*(Parse(*toks$_L$*), Op, Parse(*toks$_R$*)) ELSE *AST*(Number) ELSE *AST*(Name)	*AST*(*AST*(Name(*x*)) Op(==) *AST*(Num(0)))

3. To Machine Code	Code(*AST*) =>
	 IF *AST$_1$* Op(==)*AST$_2$*:
	    Code(*AST$_1$*)
	    Code(*AST$_2$*)
	    DO_EQUALS_OP
	 ELSE IF Number(*n*): PUSH *n*
	 ELSE IF Name: LOOK_UP_AND_PUSH name
		LOOKUP_AND_-PUSH "x"
		 PUSH 0
		 DO_EQUALS_OP

Table 1: An interpreter with pseudocode notation. For input x==0, the example column shows instances of tokens in the 1st row, ASTs on the 2nd, and instructions on the last. An example semantic path is underlined for a PUSH instruction for the number token.

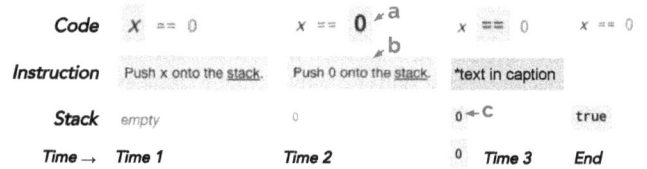

Figure 1: Stepping through three semantic paths covered by the example program x==0. *text is "Pop 0 and 0 off the stack, compute 0==0, and push the result onto the stack".

statement, the mapping is different, because the end of the if block must include a jump past the else block. Learners must understand these syntax-dependent branches in compilation and execution.

We therefore view the set of *all* possible paths through all of the compilation and execution rules in all of a programming language's constructs as the knowledge required to "know" a PL. This symbolic representation preserves the fidelity of the knowledge because we derive the knowledge directly from the interpreter. As we will show, we can then make these abstract paths concrete by presenting programs that cover these paths.

4 PEDAGOGY AND PLTUTOR

In this section we propose a comprehension-first pedagogy that embodies our theory of program tracing knowledge. Our design focuses on helping people learn 1) PL semantics and 2) program tracing skills; our prototype focuses specifically on JavaScript. The central pedagogical strategy in PLTutor is to build upon the experience of using a debugger, but 1) allow stepping forward and back in time, 2) allow stepping at an instruction-level rather than line-level granularity, and 3) interleave conceptual instruction about semantics throughout the program's execution.

Figure 1 shows the experience of using PLTutor to observe program execution over time. For example, Figure 1.a shows the path underlined in the first and second row of Table 1 for the token 0 in x==0, and Figure 1.b shows the third row in Table 1. The change to machine state displays on the next time step (see 0 on top of stack at Figure 1.c). This representation addresses the notational barrier to accessing the information in Table 1. As a side note, for brevity Figure 1 assumes x has value zero (e.g. at first time step).

The next two subsections discuss in detail how our pedagogy (partially implemented in PLTutor) teaches learners both the syntax, state, and semantics mapping and program tracing.

4.1 Programming Language Semantics

Now we theorize how learning may occur within PLTutor's pedagogy. We start with an example in another domain, then return to learning PL semantics. We start from a theory of learning for "a causes b" relationships (also called causal inference). For instance, a child may see a switch flipped then a light goes on, and they may infer the switch caused the light to go on, just from one example. How can this rapid learning occur? A theory of causal inference identifies three key enablers for this learning: *ontology* (differentiating/recognizing entities and their causal types), *constraints* on relationships (how plausible are relationships), and *functional forms* of relationships (from how effects combine and compare, to specific forms like $f = ma$ [28]. For the light example, *ontology* includes a light and a switch as mechanical entities, *constraints* includes closeness in time (switches tend to control things quickly), and *functional form* may include knowing the switch up position activates ("turns on") whatever it controls. With these enablers, causal learning then occurs by *observing examples of the causal relationships* [28].

We theorize learning PL semantics as grasping the *causal relationships* from code to machine behavior. To enable causal learning, our key insight is to convert the abstract path representations from the prior section into a concrete causal visualization, showing the causal relationship between *tokens*, *machine instructions*, and the machine state changes caused by the instructions.

Now we summarize how our pedagogy provides the three key enablers for causal learning, for program semantics; afterwards we will discuss them in a particular implementation (PLTutor). To provide *ontology*, we start learning with conceptual content describing entities (code, instruction, and machine model), show them in the visualization, and explain how to recognize them in the visualization. To provide *constraints* on relationships, we provide conceptual content emphasizing the mechanical relationship (to avoid the "computer as person" misconception [66]; causal learning theory gives us a new lens for why this misconception may be so damaging - having the wrong relationship misleads the causal learning process). We also give *functional forms* via syntax highlights for the token part, text descriptions of the instruction part, and the change in machine model state over each small time step.

To create this causal model, we extract patterns from interpreter implementations. We introduce two abstractions—the *instruction* and the *machine model*—to simplify this knowledge, while retaining fidelity. Typically, paths through the interpreter end with manipulating the state of the program being executed (either by generating machine code or with PL statements (for an implementation hosted in another language)). We encode these state changes as one or more instructions for a machine model (which serves as a model

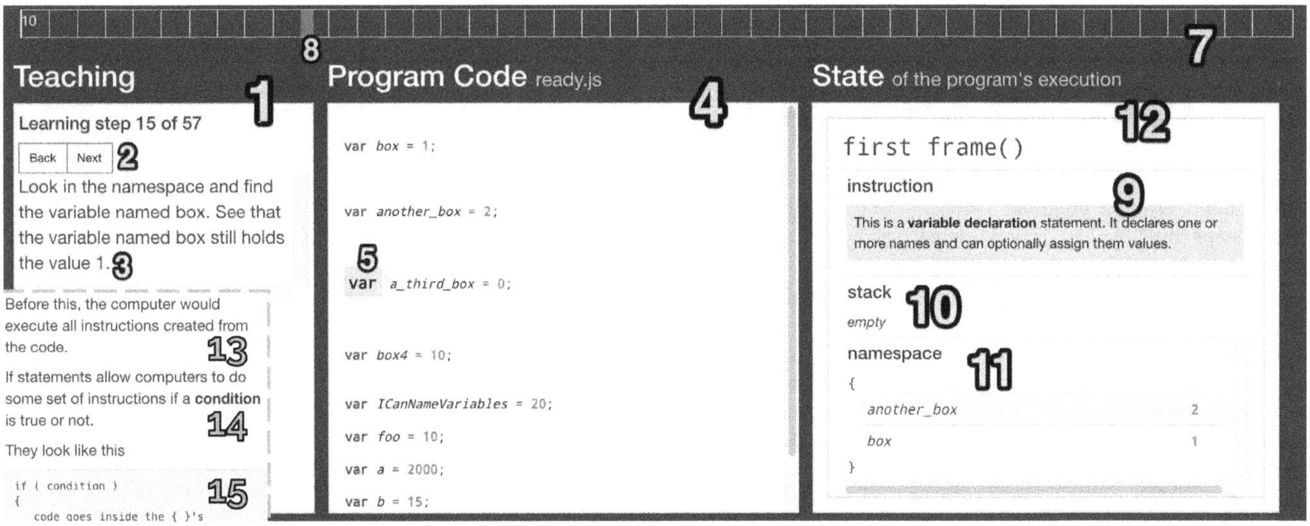

Figure 2: PLTutor showing an early lesson on variables: left, 1) the learning content and assessment area with 2) stepping buttons and 3) conceptual instruction; 4) program code with 5) token-level highlighting to show what caused the instruction; machine model: 7) timeline of instructions executed for the program 8) current step, 9) current instruction's description, 10) stack, 11) namespace, 12) call frame. Lower left inset shows content for conceptual instruction for a later if lesson.

notional machine [24]). The interpreter produces a list of instructions, which are then sent to the machine model. This separates the state of the program's execution entirely into the machine model. Using the machine instruction as a bridge between syntax and state transformation, we can connect the path through the interpreter to machine state changes.

We can also connect instructions back to the code that causes them. These connections follow the semantic path, going back to the program code via the tokens that caused values in them. For example, for the path underlined in Table 1, the PUSH 0 instruction connects to the 0 in the source code via the token Number(0); the LOOKUP_AND_PUSH "x" instruction connects to the x in Name(x).

Figure 2 shows PLTutor, our web-based prototype that visualizes these causal connections. In this figure, PLTutor is visualizing the beginning of a JavaScript variable declaration statement, which is mapped to the *var* keyword in 2.5. The machine state is on the right with the machine instruction shown at 2.9.

In PLTutor, our pedagogy has learners *observe examples of the causal relationships* by stepping forward in time in the program's execution, one instruction at a time. A single step changes the token being highlighted, the current instruction, and machine state. For example, Figure 1 shows three steps for the JavaScript program x == 0. Our prototype supports the full semantics of JavaScript, providing mappings between all constructs in the language and the machine instructions that govern JavaScript program execution.

Within this representation, our pedagogy identifies a unique causal role for the *instruction* between code and the machine model. The instruction *makes visible* the causal relationship between syntax and machine behavior. The instruction also provides *constraints* on relationships between code and machine state changes (a parser generates instructions from code, which is the only way code causes machine behavior). We also designed instructions to provide a set of *functional forms* that simplify and localize relationships; all

instructions only 1) push onto an accumulator stack (either from the literals in the code or the namespace) 2) pop values from the stack, do a local operation only with those values, and push the result onto the stack, 3) set a value in the namespace, 4) pop a value and change the program counter (for conditionals, loops, and functions), or 5) clear the stack (which we map to the ; token). These forms provide further *constraints* on relationships: for example, values from code tokens only change the stack, namespace values only come from the stack, and instructions only come from the code. These constraints and functional forms should help learners' causal inference [28].

Besides this causal role, the instruction also makes visible how a language executes syntax. Without it, stepping through the interpreted program line by line requires understanding how the computer navigates the program code notation. In contrast, stepping through a list of instructions only requires moving forward and backwards through an execution history and comprehending changes to machine state (see Figure 1).

PLTutor also conveys constraints, functional forms, and ontology by showing natural language explanations of the actions instructions are taking. PLT reinforces functional forms by showing an instruction's form as a description filled in with concrete values (see Figure 2.9, which explains how a variable declaration begins). PLT also shows learning content at 2.3 throughout the lesson.

To scaffold causal inference, the curriculum starts with *ontology*, with 5-10 minutes of conceptual instruction about the computer, code, state, the interpreter, instructions, and machine model. It provides ontology by describing the entities and how they are shown in the interface; for example, "The namespace is where variables are stored. This is like a table with two columns...". It also gives constraints on their relationships; for example, "In general, the list of instructions does not change as a computer executes a program." This information also serves as organizing concepts [10].

4.2 Program Tracing

Our theory of program tracing knowledge suggests a general approach for a pedagogy: show a faithful representation of each interpreter path, assess the learners' knowledge of each path, correct misconceptions, and cover all the paths for completeness.

To cover most of the paths, PLTutor uses a fixed, sequenced curriculum of example programs. Instead of stepping through execution steps directly as in prior work, each program has a list of *learning* steps, specifying 1) the learning content or assessment to show and 2) which execution step to show. This decoupling allows the curriculum to navigate anywhere in the program's execution when the learner advances to the next learning step. There are three types of learning steps in the tutorial: *conceptual* steps (show conceptual instructional content), *execution* steps (show an instruction executing), and *assessment* steps (prompt a learner to fill in values, described shortly). Learners advance forward or backward through these steps by clicking the "Back" and "Next" buttons (Figure 2.2) or using keyboard arrow keys. Learners may also drag the bar (Figure 2.8) to scroll through execution steps. On the final learning step of a lesson, a "Next Program" button appears, which navigates to the next program in the curriculum. This contrasts with prior work, in which learners must find and choose a next program for themselves, constructing their own curriculum from a menu [81].

Our pedagogy interleaves these three types of steps (conceptual, execution, and assessment) through a program's execution. To illustrate this, we describe the learning steps for a first lesson for a construct (such as if). These follow a pattern: reference relevant prior knowledge, contrast what is new ("Before this..." see Figure 2.13), present the goal of the construct ("If statements allow...", Figure 2.14), present the syntactic pattern (see 2.15), then scaffold learning strategies ("step through to see how it works", and, later, prompts mental execution "What do you think this next if statement will do? Read through it and think, then step through it."). Where possible, steps introduce constructs with "equivalent" programs, based on similar instructions or state changes. For instance, in our arrays lesson, is_day_free_0=false; is_day_free_1=true; precedes is_day_free = [false, true]; this may help transfer and provide *constraints* for causal inference. After such code, steps show an example path and a low-level assessment (described shortly), then address common misconceptions in turn by: 1) showing learning content against it, 2) executing a counter-example, 3) stepping through code with assessments for the misconception.

Besides the ordering of steps within each program, the stepping interface scaffolds perception of conceptual and execution information. On steps with learning content, learners experience a slight 1-second pause before they can advance, to encourage reading. At key points in the middle of a program's execution, learning steps stop advancing execution to show conceptual instruction. For example, PLTutor pauses in the middle of a condition evaluation to describe what is happening when first learning if statements. Execution steps show causality temporally, and having many steps shows many examples of the causal relationships, as recommended by [28]. Their granular, sub-expression level of detail may help structure inferences from these lower level steps into higher level inferences across multiple steps and lines of code [28].

To aid higher-level causal inferences, PLTutor assesses knowledge of each path at multiple levels. For the single execution step

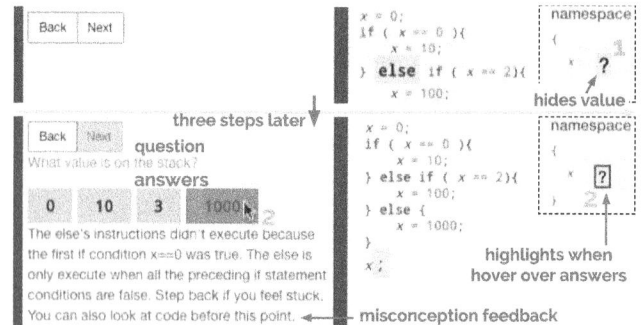

Figure 3: Assessments scaffold state, hiding values with a ? (see 1), so learners mentally execute semantics to answer. The assessment shows three steps later. This allows assessing from the step to multiple line or program level granularity, without requiring navigation restrictions to hide values.

level, it navigates to a step and hides a value for the learner to fill in. Figure 3 shows an assessment across multiple steps. Using value hiding and the learning step's ability to control what execution step is shown, this enables scaffolded assessments, showing some instruction or code navigation, across multiple levels of granularity, including the simple effects of one execution step (done in prior work [82]) to showing the resulting state of many execution steps as if it were one large step. PLTutor also scaffolds links between assessment question phrases and machine state by showing which question to fill in; hovering over any answer shows a box around the corresponding value (see Figure 3.2). It also shows misconception feedback for inaccurate answers (see bottom Figure 3).

In addition to introduction and practice lessons, our pedagogy includes review lessons, which apply constructs together and occur after the end of operators, conditionals, and the loops material. These lessons describe how constructs can be used with each other. They contrast larger "equivalent" code segments, justifying language features by appealing to "good" properties of code like readability, brevity, and ability to modify or reuse. We include these integration lessons to increase retention and motivate learning by showing how constructs are used together for actual problems [10], and to connect knowledge to the design goals of the language.

4.3 PLTutor Limitations

PLTutor only partially implements the principles we have discussed for a comprehension-first pedagogy. It covers all the paths in our JavaScript interpreter except for strings, I/O, objects, some unary and binary operators (like -- and modulus), and error paths (like invalid variable names or syntax errors). For example, we do not show the failing examples required to fully specify variable naming patterns. We expect later writing pedagogy to cover them, and language runtimes make them visible with error messages.

While PLTutor's assessments directly or indirectly cover much of each semantic path, it leaves some out and does not fade scaffolding entirely. It directly assesses machine state changes by having users fill in values in the machine state via linked assessments. It indirectly assesses control flow via simple value changes (which depend on the variable assignment path in earlier lessons); Figure 3 shows one. PLTutor does not assess ontology directly or fully remove scaffolding in its curriculum; for example, it always shows machine state, instruction execution steps, and allows stepping.

Finally, at the time of our evaluation, PLTutor was very much a research prototype. When we evaluated it, it had usability issues and the environment made little effort to engage learners, introducing numerous barriers to sustained engagement and learning.

5 EVALUATION

What effects does a comprehension-first and theoretically-informed pedagogy have on learning code comprehension and writing skills? To investigate, we conducted a formative, block-randomized, between subjects study comparing a comprehension-first tutorial, PLTutor, with Codecademy [16], chosen for its traditional writing-focused spiral pedagogy [76] and quality from 4 years of curriculum refinement. We label the PLTutor condition *PLT* and the other *CC*.

5.1 Method

Our inclusion criteria were undergraduates that had not completed a CS1 course in college and had not used a Codecademy tutorial. We recruited students starting a CS1 class that followed a procedural-first writing pedagogy using Java [72]. Participants came to a Saturday 10:30am–6pm workshop, took a pre-survey and a pre-test, used a tutorial for 4.33 hours, and then took a post-test and post-survey. As a pre/post-test we used the SCS1 [26, 64], a validated measure of CS1 knowledge. Both surveys used validated measures for fixed vs. growth mindset [8] and programming self-efficacy [71]. The pre-survey also measured daytime/chronic sleepiness using the Epworth Sleepiness Scale [4], as prior work argues these affect learning [18, 22, 33, 59, 70].

At the first two lectures and via email, we advertised the study as a chance to excel in the class, potentially biasing towards motivated and at-risk students. Overall, 200 of 988 students responded to an emailed recruitment survey and 90 met our inclusion criteria. Using this survey, we block randomized [31] participants into a condition using hours of prior programming, self-reported likelihood of attendance, age, and gender, then invited subjects. From these blocks, we randomly invited participants from each block, ultimately having 41 attend the workshops. After confirming attendance by email, we sent subjects the room for their condition.

The two instructors of the one day workshops followed a written experimental protocol and coordinated to make any necessary day-of changes jointly. They then showed an introductory SCS1 test directions video, gave the pre-test, then showed video instructions for their condition's tutorial and stated students would have 4 hours and 20 minutes to learn the material. They served lunch during the tutorial period at 1PM. After a 10-minute break following the tutorial, students had 1 hour for the SCS1 post-test and could start the post-survey when done. The instructors then served dinner.

We operationalized learning outcomes by proxying program comprehension with SCS1 score and writing skills with midterm grade. Learning gain (posttest score−pretest score) is noisy because it combines pre and post test measurement error [9]; we also counted per-question and per-individual performance from incorrect on pre-test to correct on post-test (which we call *FT*, for false-to-true), as well as likely prior knowledge as correctly answering a question on both the pre and post test (*TT*, for true-to-true). We defined *learning capacity* for a person as (the # of questions

not left blank)-*TT* and *learning capacity* for each question as (# of people that did not leave the question blank)-*TT*. We defined *LCL*, the % learned that could learn, as *FT* / learning capacity (like normalized gain in [83]).

The SCS1 system randomly lost some tests; we dropped those participants, reducing sample size to 18 in PLT and 19 in CC. We separated novices (operationalized as less than 10 hours of self-reported experience and no prior CS class) from experienced students (had prior CS class or >10 hours of self-reported experience).

5.2 Results

Despite random assignment, we found differences that may have confounded measures of learning gains. We analyzed these and other differences by default with the Wilcoxon rank-sum test for non-normal data. We add and note a t-test when Shapiro-Wilks's normality test had $p > 0.1$ for each group (still has low power for our sample size). Pre-test SCS1 differences between the two conditions were large and marginally significant (CC−PLT mean=1.65, W $p < .111$, t-test $p < 0.058$), but self-reported prior programming experience and mindset did not differ significantly.

While many individuals in both groups achieved higher SCS1 scores, comparing *within* each condition, only PLT's post-scores were significantly different from its pre-scores (p<.0044) (for CC p<.089). Figure 4 shows descriptive statistics; for comparison, students near the end of a CS1 course score from 2 to 20, $m = 9.68, SD = 3.5$ [64]. Comparing conditions, PLT had higher individual *FT*, with Cohen's d=.59 (p<.12, t-test p<.075); for *learning gain*: Cohen's d=.398 (p<.41, t-test p<.24); for the % learned that each person could learn (*LCL*): d=.34 (p<.39, t-test p<.31). To control our analysis for other variables, we tried to fit post-score with linear and binomial generalized linear models, but residuals strongly violated modeling assumptions.

When we consider the specific questions in the SCS1, PLT outperformed CC on 37% of questions and CC outperformed PLT on 22%, based on between group difference of $\geqslant .1$ in LCL (the % of people who got the question right that did not already get that question right on the pre-test). Figure 5 shows questions sorted from left to right by this LCL difference, with * at bottom for non-overlap of their 95% confidence intervals of the probability p of a binomial distribution estimated from x=FT and n=capacity (Wilson [12]).

CC did better for some code completion (Q18,25,21) and writing conceptual questions (e.g., Q1: When would you not write a for loop... Q6: Imagine writing code for each task - can you do it without conditional operators...). It also did better on topics missing from PLT's curriculum like strings (Q18) and a tracing question with modulus (Q19). In contrast, PLT did better for tracing (Q2,23,3,12,24,14,8), a tracing conceptual question relying on sub-expression detail (Q10), and complex code completion questions (Q13,Q26). PLT also did better on topics missing from CC's curriculum like recursion (Q14 and even Q24 involving strings). PLT also did better on a tracing question with strings that only used array syntax and semantics (Q15).

PLT had less variation and a more normal distribution for later writing outcomes compared to CC (see Figure 4.f, 4.e). Shapiro-Wilks normality test rejected CC's midterm distribution (p<.013) but not PLT's (p=.4723). For PLT, midterm fit a linear model on each of: *learning gain*: (adj-R^2=.6469 (95% CI: .28, .84 by [35, 36])

Mindset	Cond.	Pre-Score	Post-Score	Learning Gain	F to T	LCL	T to F	T to T	Midterm
All	CC	8.26 2.96	10.68 4.63	2.42 3.2	4.68 2.43	.24 .14	2.47 1.58	5.74 3.3	76.11 15.68
All	PLT	6.61 2.09	10.5 4.49	3.89 4.1	6.39 3.15	.29 .16	2.50 1.92	4.11 2.32	77.28 9.03
Growth Novices	CC	6.57 2.51	8.57 2.88	2 3.27	4.57 2.07	.2 .09	2.57 1.72	4 2.52	69.57 19.5
Growth Novices	PLT	6.14 1.57	11 5.89	4.86 4.85	6.71 4.27	.31 .22	1.86 1.07	4.29 2.36	78.57 11.46
Fixed Not novices	CC	9.25 2.83	11.92 5.11	2.67 3.28	4.75 2.70	.26 .16	2.42 1.56	6.75 3.36	79.92 12.32
Fixed Not novices	PLT	6.91 2.39	10.18 3.63	3.27 3.66	6.18 2.40	.28 .12	2.91 2.26	4.00 2.41	76.45 7.62

Axes: 0 9 18 27 | 0 9 18 27 | 0 5 10 | 0 5 10 15 | 0 0.5 1.0 | 0 5 10 15 | 0 5 10 15 30 | 50 70 90

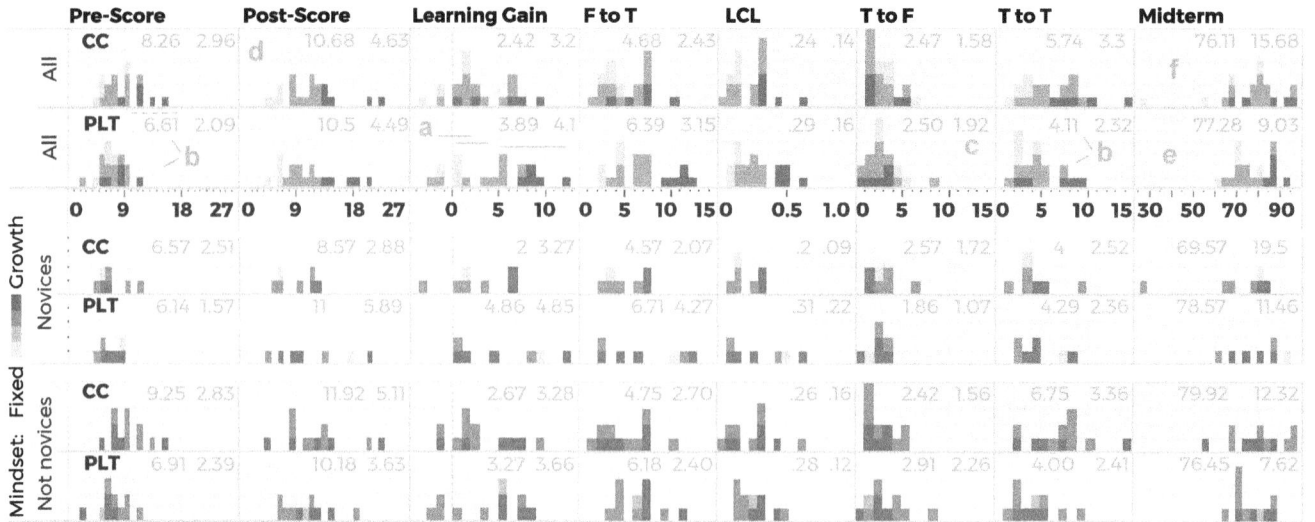

Figure 4: Histograms (with mean then *SD* inside) by condition (top) colored by *post-score* (dark grey: ≥ 13 (about a *SD* above the mean of students finishing CS1 from [64], grey: within a *SD*, light grey for below), then experience (mindset color).

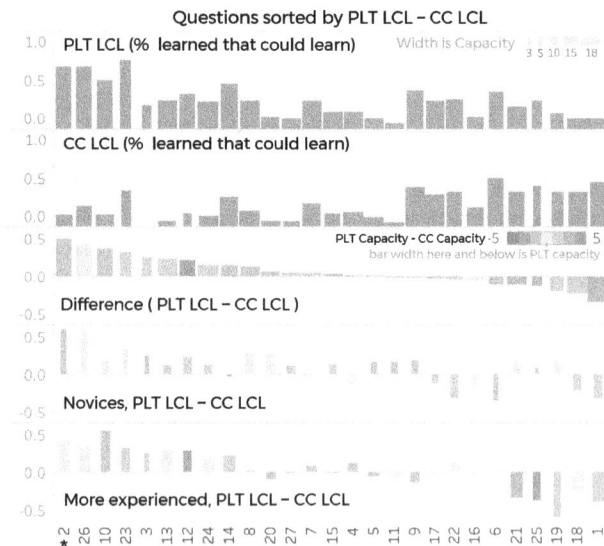

Questions sorted by PLT LCL − CC LCL

PLT LCL (% learned that could learn)   Width is Capacity   3 5 10 15 18

CC LCL (% learned that could learn)

PLT Capacity − CC Capacity -5 ... 5
bar width here and below is PLT capacity

Difference (PLT LCL − CC LCL)

Novices, PLT LCL − CC LCL

More experienced, PLT LCL − CC LCL

Figure 5: Per-question statistics, ordered by PLT's LCL minus CC's LCL. Bar width shows capacity.

p<.00004 residual SE=5.37), *post-score*: (adj-R^2=.5502 p<.00025), *LCL*: (adj-R^2=.53 p<.00037), and *FT*: (adj-R^2=.4983 p<.00064). For CC, only a post-score model had significance (adj-R^2=0.1784, p<.041, SE 14.21). PLT had no midterm failures (vs. 2 in CC). Midterm average did not differ significantly between PLT or CC (see 4.e), or those in the recruitment group that met the inclusion criteria and did not participate, midterm $m = 72.1, SD = 22.1$ (n=38).

To partly check the validity of midterm as a proxy for writing skill, we offered $6 for a photo of the midterm (with per question grades) to those that met the inclusion criteria (90) and got 17. A linear model from total score predicted the writing part (adj-R^2=.85) much better than the other parts (adj-R^2=.61), suggesting total midterm score varies fairly closely with the writing portion.

As a manipulation check, two months after the workshops we offered post-midterm tutoring. In each session, before tutoring, we conducted a think-aloud interview for tracing mental model granularity by prompting learners to "Underline the code as the computer sees it, then describe what the computer does" for Java versions of program B2 & G3 from [78]. Learning gains and midterms mostly increased with more sub-expression tracing (except P5). Two participants (P1 and P2) responded from CC. P1 had 2 TT, 2 FT, and a 54 midterm; her tracing model had some sub-expression (but not for control structures and had an early loop exit error); P2 (2 TT, 6 FT, 79 midterm) was mostly line-level but separated assignment (like y=1+1;) into 3 steps: the left side y, then =, then the rest 1+1;. Four participants (P3 to P6) responded from PLT. Compared to P2, two showed more but non-uniform sub-expression with self-caught misconceptions, P3 (4 TT, 7 FT, 72 midterm) and P4 (5 TT,7 FT, 77 midterm). P5 (8 TT, 12 FT, 86 midterm) had a line level model. P6 had a consistent sub-expression model (3 TT, 11 FT, 85 midterm).

We also asked which tutorial features they remembered, as a gross check on importance or causality. Better learning outcomes mostly increased with more correct and complete feature recall, suggesting they impacted learning. In CC P1 and P2 both recalled writing, exercise feedback, and help; only P2 had the print output. In PLT, P3 recalled learning content and (incorrectly) writing code only, with the stack shown briefly during execution with no stepping controls; the others recalled content, stepping and assessments; for the state display (see right side of Figure 2), P4 had namespace (2.11), P5 had steps bar (2.8), P6 had all except instruction (2.9).

6 THREATS TO VALIDITY

While we made efforts to ensure validity (minimizing confounds, block-randomizing group assignment, measuring confounding factors, avoiding early-riser effects[22], mitigating experimenter bias, etc.), there are still several threats to validity.

Differences between our study and the validation of SCS1 complicate the interpretation of our results. We post-tested within 4.3 hours of the pre-test; a carry-over effect may inflate post-scores (e.g.

remembering questions) [1]. Guessing, especially by novices, may have impacted scores. While the SCS1 is the best publicly available measure, it's validity arguments do not formally generalize i) to novice test takers, ii) in a pretest-posttest context, and iii) as a measure of learning gains. Our measure of writing skills (the midterm) had unknown measurement error and lacks validation.

Motivation differences, participant fatigue, measurement error, unmeasured participant variation, and differences in workshop setting also threaten validity. Internally, instructor variations may favor the Codecademy condition, which had a more experienced teacher. The PLTutor instructor also had to leave the room for 45 minutes to handle a lunch issue. Externally, the study's short duration may create a ceiling effect on learning gains. The study protocol, curricular quality, time-on-task, program domain, and pedagogical and lack of adaptive tutorial features affect results. In particular, in informal interviews, participants reported frustration with repetitive practice in the PLTutor curriculum, which may have reduced engagement and therefore learning.

7 DISCUSSION

We have presented a new theoretical account of program tracing knowledge, a new pedagogy for teaching this knowledge embodied by PLTutor, and empirical evidence of the effects of PLTutor on program tracing and writing skills. These effects included:

- Higher total and question-specific learning gain than Codecademy (overall 37% of questions and 70% for novices).
- Less midterm variation and no failure on the midterm. Learning gains from the tutorial also strongly predicted the midterm, suggesting a strong relationship or shared factors between learning rate in the tutorial and the class.
- More learners who started with low pre-scores had large learning gains (see dark grey in pre-score and TT (likely prior knowledge) in Figure 4.b).

Our study suggests greater learning gains for PLTutor compared to Codecademy. PLTutor matched Codecademy's post-scores even with a significant initial deficit (see Figure 4.b). This might just be mean-reversion for Codecademy (guessing on the pre-test with less luck on the post) but true to false shows little to no difference (see 4.c). The other interpretation is that PLTutor brought its less experienced group to parity with Codecademy (see 4.d); if the writing tutorial was better at teaching program tracing, it ought to have magnified initial differences. PLTutor also had more learning at the question level, doing better on 37% vs. 22% for Codecademy (1.68 times more). Question-level differences might come from sampling error, which is hard to model without item response theory parameters for the SCS1. However, these differences always aligned with curricular differences (no recursion in CC, no strings or modulus in PLTutor) and theoretical explanations—for example, writing did better on 3 out of 9 code completion problems, as did PLTutor for 8 out of 13 tracing problems. This supports the interpretation that our results do not just come from noise or guessing differences, though our small study still has threats to validity.

Our empirically strongest result is that PLTutor normalized midterm outcomes. PLTutor had no failures vs. 2 in CC (see 4.f vs. 4.e). With only one early measurement, in our small study only PLTutor learning gains predicted midterm (adj-R^2 =.64), among the best of work predicting CS1 outcomes (adj-R^2 .44 to .46 [54, 88, 89]), better even than those using mid-course measures like homework or self-efficacy (adj-R^2 .35, .58, .61) [40, 43, 88]). In pre-score in Figure 4.b, PLTutor also has more dark high post-scorers coming from lower scores vs. CC. This improved equity in outcomes may help scale learning in diverse populations. Future work should confirm this pattern and see if normalizing has the downside of reducing outlier high outcomes (compare far right of 4.e & 4.f).

We also saw learning gains comparable to full quarter or semester long courses with both tutorials in ~4 hours (see Figure 4.a), similar to prior work [42], yet unexplained by prior CS knowledge or traits we measured. Some gains varied from losing to gaining 2-3 points on the post-test, perhaps guessing noise. However, our participants' post-test distribution looked similar to those near the end of CS1 in [64]; this was either genuine learning, recruiting bias that skewed our sample towards more motivated or at-risk students, or test-retest carry-over score inflation. Even extreme learning was not uncommon; in ~4 hours, in PLTutor 4 learners (22%) moved from a below average pre-score to nearly above a SD of [64]'s mean (3 (16%) above 13.18), and one from a score of 8 to 20, the maximum from 189 students in [64] (in CC, one 8 to 14 and an 11 to 20 also). In PLT these outcomes continue in the midterm (see dark at 4.e).

What skills or knowledge explains such fast learning without prior domain knowledge? Can we teach it and dramatically improve CS1 and even other CS education? Most learning theories frame learning as hard and time consuming, and transfer as fragile; they poorly explain these results. In contrast, causal inference theory says learning is facile and transfer instantaneous with the right conditions. We applied this theory in our pedagogy design and saw large gains, making it a promising direction. Future work may search for factors that lead to rapid learning by measuring learners' prior knowledge or traits then analyzing learning outcomes only, or jointly change the design of pedagogy or tools used, in an attempt to either increase or reduce extreme learning gains.

Decades of studies have attempted to improve outcomes for learning programming; we found something one can measure in only 8 hours (learning gain from PLTutor) which is highly predictive of long-term outcomes. We might be able to use this (or other good predictors) to improve the rate of experimentation and discovery, going from 3-4 studies per year using course outcomes to one per day using a proxy (if larger studies confirm their predictive ability).

Future work should investigate tools and curricula based on comprehension-oriented strategies, especially given the comparative lack of exploration and positive early results (ours and others like [30]). PLTutor had as good or better overall performance compared to a mature writing-oriented tutorial created with millions in funding. It seems unlikely that our team of three people, with almost no curriculum experimentation, has found the ceiling for comprehension tutorials or pedagogy.

ACKNOWLEDGMENTS

This material is based upon work supported by Microsoft, Google, Adobe, and the National Science Foundation (Grant No. 12566082, 1539179, 1314399, 1240786, and 1153625). Any opinions, findings, and conclusions or recommendations expressed in this material are those of the author(s) and do not necessarily reflect funder views.

REFERENCES

[1] Mary J. Allen and Wendy M. Yen. 2001. *Introduction to Measurement Theory.* Waveland Press.

[2] John R. Anderson, Frederick G. Conrad, and Albert T. Corbett. 1989. Skill acquisition and the LISP tutor. *Cognitive Science* 13, 4 (1989), 467–505. DOI: http://dx.doi.org/10.1016/0364-0213(89)90021-9

[3] Ian Arawjo, Cheng-yao Wang, Andrew C Myers, Erik Andersen, and François Guimbretière. 2017. Teaching Programming with Gamified Semantics. In *Proceedings of the SIGCHI conference on Human factors in computing systems Reaching through technology - CHI '17.* ACM Press, New York, New York, USA.

[4] Sally Bailes, Eva Libman, Marc Baltzan, Rhonda Amsel, Ron Schondorf, and Catherine S. Fichten. 2006. Brief and distinct empirical sleepiness and fatigue scales. *Journal of Psychosomatic Research* 60, 6 (2006), 605–613. DOI: http://dx.doi.org/10.1016/j.jpsychores.2005.08.015

[5] Piraye Bayman and Richard E. Mayer. 1988. Using conceptual models to teach BASIC computer programming. *Journal of Educational Psychology* 80, 3 (1988), 291–298. DOI: http://dx.doi.org/10.1037/0022-0663.80.3.291

[6] Mordechai Ben-Ari. 2001. Constructivism in computer science education. *Journal of Computers in Mathematics and Science Teaching* 20, 1 (2001), 45–73.

[7] Dave Berry. 1991. *Generating Program Animators from Programming Language Semantics.* Ph.D. Dissertation. University of Edinburgh. DOI: http://dx.doi.org/10.1016/0377-0427(93)90083-N

[8] Lisa S Blackwell, Kali H Trzesniewski, and Carol Sorich Dweck. 2007. Implicit theories of intelligence predict achievement across an adolescent transition: a longitudinal study and an intervention. *Child development* 78, 1 (jan 2007), 246–63. DOI: http://dx.doi.org/10.1111/j.1467-8624.2007.00995.x

[9] Peter L. Bonate. 2000. *Analysis of Pretest-Posttest Designs.* CRC Press.

[10] J. D. Bransford, A. L. Brown, and R. R. Cocking. 2000. *How People Learn: Brain, Mind, Experience, and School: Expanded Edition.* National Academies Press. 1–27 pages. DOI: http://dx.doi.org/10.1016/0885-2014(91)90049-J

[11] Ruven Brooks. 1983. Towards a theory of the comprehension of computer programs. *International Journal of Man-Machine Studies* 18, 6 (jun 1983), 543–554. DOI: http://dx.doi.org/10.1016/S0020-7373(83)80031-5

[12] L.D. Brown, T.T. Cai, and A. DasGupta. 2001. Interval Estimation for a Binomial Proportion. *Statist. Sci.* 16, 2 (2001), 101–133. https://www.scopus.com/inward/record.uri?eid=2-s2.0-0000460102&partnerID=40&md5=0997011d7da77720486e29c728a95d34 cited By 988.

[13] Teresa Busjahn and Carsten Schulte. 2013. The use of code reading in teaching programming. *Proceedings of the 13th Koli Calling International Conference on Computing Education Research* (2013), 3–11. DOI: http://dx.doi.org/10.1145/2526968.2526969

[14] William Campbell and Ethan Bolker. 2002. Teaching programming by immersion, reading and writing. In *32nd Annual Frontiers in Education*, Vol. 1. IEEE, T4G–23–T4G–28. DOI: http://dx.doi.org/10.1109/FIE.2002.1158015

[15] David Clark, Cara MacNish, and Gordon F Royle. 1998. Java as a teaching languagefi?opportunities, pitfalls and solutions. *Proceedings of the 3rd Australasian conference on Computer science education* (1998), 173–179. DOI: http://dx.doi.org/10.1145/289393.289418

[16] Codecademy. 2016. https://www.codecademy.com. (2016). Accessed: 2016-12-12.

[17] CodingBat. 2016. https://www.codingbat.com. (2016). Accessed: 2016-12-12.

[18] Giuseppe Curcio, Michele Ferrara, and Luigi De Gennaro. 2006. Sleep loss, learning capacity and academic performance. *Sleep Medicine Reviews* 10, 5 (2006), 323–337. DOI: http://dx.doi.org/10.1016/j.smrv.2005.11.001

[19] J Dalbey and Marcia C Linn. 1985. The demands and requirements of computer programming: A review of the literature. *Journal of Educational Computing Research* 1, 3 (1985), 253–274. DOI: http://dx.doi.org/10.2190/BC76-8479-YM0X-7FUA

[20] M. De Raadt, M. Toleman, and R Watson. 2002. Language Trends in Introductory Programming Courses On the internet. *Informing Science* (2002), 329–337. http://proceedings.informingscience.org/IS2002Proceedings/papers/deRaa136Langu.pdf

[21] Lionel Deimel and David Moffat. 1982. A More Analytical Approach to Teaching the Introductory Programming Course. In *Proceedings of the National Educational Computing Conference.* 114–118.

[22] Julia F. Dewald, Anne M. Meijer, Frans J. Oort, Gerard A. Kerkhof, and Susan M. Bögels. 2010. The influence of sleep quality, sleep duration and sleepiness on school performance in children and adolescents: A meta-analytic review. *Sleep Medicine Reviews* 14, 3 (2010), 179–189. DOI: http://dx.doi.org/10.1016/j.smrv.2009.10.004

[23] Allen Downey and Lynn Stein. 2006. Designing a small-footprint curriculum in computer science. In *Proceedings. Frontiers in Education. 36th Annual Conference.* IEEE, 21–26. DOI: http://dx.doi.org/10.1109/FIE.2006.322660

[24] Benedict du Boulay, Tim O'Shea, and John Monk. 1981. The black box inside the glass box: presenting computing concepts to novices. *International Journal of Man-Machine Studies* 14, 3 (apr 1981), 237–249. DOI: http://dx.doi.org/10.1016/S0020-7373(81)80056-9

[25] Jennifer L. Dyck and Richard E. Mayer. 1989. Teaching for Transfer of Computer Program Comprehension Skill. *Journal of Educational Psychology* 81, 1 (1989), 16–24. DOI: http://dx.doi.org/10.1037//0022-0663.81.1.16

[26] Allison Elliott Tew. 2010. Assessing fundamental introductory computing concept knowledge in a language independent manner. December 2010 (2010), 147. http://search.proquest.com/docview/873212789

[27] Matthias Felleisen, Robert Bruce Findler, Matthew Flatt, and Shriram Krishnamurthi. 2001. How to Design Programs. *MIT Press* (2001), 720. DOI: http://dx.doi.org/10.1136/bjsm.27.1.58

[28] Thomas L. Griffiths and Joshua B. Tenenbaum. 2009. Theory-based causal induction. *Psychological Review* 116, 4 (2009), 661–716. DOI: http://dx.doi.org/10.1037/a0017201

[29] Philip J. Guo. 2013. Online python tutor. In *Proceeding of the 44th ACM technical symposium on Computer science education - SIGCSE '13.* ACM Press, New York, New York, USA, 579. DOI: http://dx.doi.org/10.1145/2445196.2445368

[30] Matthew Hertz and Maria Jump. 2013. Trace-Based Teaching in Early Programming Courses. *Proceedings of the 44th ACM Technical Symposium on Computer Science Education* (2013), 561–566. DOI: http://dx.doi.org/10.1145/2445196.2445364

[31] Klaus Hinkelmann and Oscar Kempthorne. 2008. *Design and Analysis of Experiments, Volume I: Introduction to Experimental Design.* Wiley.

[32] Jean-Michel Hoc and Anh Nguyen-Xuan. 1990. Chapter 2.3 - Language Semantics, Mental Models and Analogy. In *Psychology of Programming*, J.-M. Hoc, T.R.G. Green, R. Samuray, and D.J. Gilmore (Eds.). Academic Press, London, 139 – 156. DOI: http://dx.doi.org/10.1016/B978-0-12-350772-3.50014-8

[33] Aaron Hochanadel and D. Finamore. 2015. Fixed And Growth Mindset In Education And How Grit Helps Students Persist In The Face Of Adversity. *Journal of International Education Research fi First Quarter* 11, 1 (2015), 47–51. DOI: http://dx.doi.org/10.19030/jier.v11i1.9099

[34] Ville Karavirta, Riku Haavisto, Erkki Kaila, Mikko-Jussi Laakso, Teemu Rajala, and Tapio Salakoski. 2015. Interactive Learning Content for Introductory Computer Science Course Using the ViLLE Exercise Framework. *2015 International Conference on Learning and Teaching in Computing and Engineering* (2015), 9–16. DOI: http://dx.doi.org/10.1109/LaTiCE.2015.24

[35] Ken Kelley. 2007. Confidence Intervals for Standardized Effect Sizes :. *Journal of Statistical Software* 20, 8 (2007), 1–24. DOI: http://dx.doi.org/10.18637/jss.v020.i08 arXiv:arXiv:0908.3817v2

[36] Ken Kelley. 2007. Methods for the Behavioral, Educational, and Social Sciences: An R package. *Behavior Research Methods* 39, 4 (nov 2007), 979–984. DOI: http://dx.doi.org/10.3758/BF03192993

[37] John G Kemeny, Thomas E Kurtz, and David S Cochran. 1968. *Basic: a manual for BASIC, the elementary algebraic language designed for use with the Dartmouth Time Sharing System.* Dartmouth Publications.

[38] Takayuki Kimura. 1979. Reading before composition. In *Proceedings of the tenth SIGCSE technical symposium on Computer science education - SIGCSE '79.* ACM Press, New York, New York, USA, 162–166. DOI: http://dx.doi.org/10.1145/800126.809575

[39] Michael Kölling, Bruce Quig, Andrew Patterson, and John Rosenberg. 2003. The BlueJ System and its Pedagogy. *Computer Science Education* 13, 4 (2003), 249–268. DOI: http://dx.doi.org/10.1076/csed.13.4.249.17496

[40] A. Krapp, S. Hidi, and K.A. Renninger. 1992. Factors Affecting Performance in First-year Computing. *The Role of interest in learning and development* 32, 2 (1992), 368.

[41] Olivier Lecarme. 1974. Structured programming, programming teaching and the language Pascal. *ACM SIGPLAN Notices* 9, 7 (jul 1974), 15–21. DOI: http://dx.doi.org/10.1145/953224.953226

[42] Michael J. Lee and Andrew J. Ko. 2015. Comparing the Effectiveness of Online Learning Approaches on CS1 Learning Outcomes. *Proceedings of the eleventh annual International Conference on International Computing Education Research - ICER '15* (2015), 237–246. DOI: http://dx.doi.org/10.1145/2787622.2787709

[43] Alex Lishinski, Aman Yadav, Jon Good, and Richard Enbody. 2016. Introductory Programming : Gender Differences and Interactive Effects of Students ' Motivation , Goals and Self-Efficacy on Performance. *Proceedings of the 12th International Computing Education Research Conference* (2016), 211–220. DOI: http://dx.doi.org/10.1145/2960310.2960329

[44] Raymond Lister, Colin Fidge, and Donna Teague. 2009. Further evidence of a relationship between explaining, tracing and writing skills in introductory programming. *ACM SIGCSE Bulletin* 41, 3 (2009), 161. DOI: http://dx.doi.org/10.1145/1595496.1562930

[45] Raymond Lister, Otto Seppälä, Beth Simon, Lynda Thomas, Elizabeth S. Adams, Sue Fitzgerald, William Fone, John Hamer, Morten Lindholm, Robert McCartney, Jan Erik Moström, and Kate Sanders. 2004. A multi-national study of reading and tracing skills in novice programmers. *ACM SIGCSE Bulletin* 36, 4 (dec 2004), 119. DOI: http://dx.doi.org/10.1145/1041624.1041673

[46] J Littlefield, V Delclos, S Lever, K Clayton, J Bransford, and J Franks. 1988. Learning Logo: Methods of teaching, transfer of general skills, and attitudes toward school and computers. In *Learning computer programming: Multiple research perspectives*, Richard E. Mayer (Ed.). Erlbaum, Hillsdale, NJ, 111–135.

[47] Dastyni Loksa and Andrew J. Ko. 2016. The Role of Self-Regulation in Programming Problem Solving Process and Success. In *Proceedings of the 2016 ACM Conference on International Computing Education Research (ICER '16).* ACM, New

York, NY, USA, 83–91. DOI: http://dx.doi.org/10.1145/2960310.2960334

[48] Dastyni Loksa, Andrew J. Ko, Will Jernigan, Alannah Oleson, Christopher J. Mendez, and Margaret M. Burnett. 2016. Programming, Problem Solving, and Self-Awareness: Effects of Explicit Guidance. In *Proceedings of the 2016 CHI Conference on Human Factors in Computing Systems (CHI '16)*. ACM, New York, NY, USA, 1449–1461. DOI: http://dx.doi.org/10.1145/2858036.2858252

[49] Mike Lopez, Jacqueline Whalley, Phil Robbins, and Raymond Lister. 2008. Relationships between reading, tracing and writing skills in introductory programming. *Proceeding of the fourth international workshop on Computing education research - ICER '08* (2008), 101–112. DOI: http://dx.doi.org/10.1145/1404520.1404531

[50] Andrew Luxton-Reilly. 2016. Learning to program is easy. *Proceedings of the 2016 ACM Conference on Innovation and Technology in Computer Science Education* (2016), 284–289. DOI: http://dx.doi.org/10.1145/2899415.2899432

[51] John Maloney, Mitchel Resnick, and Natalie Rusk. 2010. The Scratch programming language and environment. *ACM Transactions on Computing Education* 10, 4 (2010), 1–15. DOI: http://dx.doi.org/10.1145/1868358.1868363.http arXiv:-

[52] Richard E. Mayer. 1979. *Analysis of a Simple Computer Programming Language: Transactions, Prestatements and Chunks*. Technical Report. Series in Learning and Cognition, Tech. Rep. No. 79-2, U. of California, Santa Barbara, California. 1–34 pages. https://eric.ed.gov/?id=ED207549

[53] Richard E. Mayer. 1981. The Psychology of How Novices Learn Computer Programming. *Comput. Surveys* 13, 1 (1981), 121–141. DOI: http://dx.doi.org/10.1145/356835.356841

[54] Richard E. Mayer. 1985. *Learning In Complex Domains: A Cognitive Analysis of Computer Programming*. Vol. 19. Academic Press. 89–130 pages. DOI: http://dx.doi.org/10.1016/S0079-7421(08)60525-3

[55] Anneliese Von Mayrhauser and a Marie Vans. 1995. Program Comprehension During Software Maintenence and Evolution. *Computer* 28, 8 (1995), 44–55. DOI: http://dx.doi.org/10.1109/2.402076

[56] Michael McCracken, Tadeusz Wilusz, Vicki Almstrum, Danny Diaz, Mark Guzdial, Dianne Hagan, Yifat Ben-David Kolikant, Cary Laxer, Lynda Thomas, and Ian Utting. 2001. A multi-national, multi-institutional study of assessment of programming skills of first-year CS students. *ACM SIGCSE Bulletin* 33, 4 (dec 2001), 125. DOI: http://dx.doi.org/10.1145/572139.572181

[57] Andrés Moreno, Niko Myller, Erkki Sutinen, and Mordechai Ben-Ari. 2004. Visualizing programs with Jeliot 3. *Proceedings of the working conference on Advanced visual interfaces - AVI '04* (2004), 373. DOI: http://dx.doi.org/10.1145/989863.989928

[58] Briana Morrison, Lauren Margulieux, and Mark Guzdial. 2015. Subgoals, Context, and Worked Examples in Learning Computing Problem Solving. In *Proceedings of the eleventh annual International Conference on International Computing Education Research - ICER '15*. ACM Press, New York, New York, USA, 267–268. DOI: http://dx.doi.org/10.1145/2787622.2787744

[59] Laurie Murphy and Lynda Thomas. 2008. Dangers of a fixed mindset: implications of self-theories research for computer science education. *ACM SIGCSE Bulletin* 40, 3 (2008), 271–275. DOI: http://dx.doi.org/10.1145/1597849.1384344

[60] Michael O'Brien. 2003. *Software Comprehension - A review and research direction*. Technical Report UL-CSIS-03-3. University of Limerick. 1–29 pages.

[61] D. B. Palumbo. 1990. Programming Language/Problem-Solving Research: A Review of Relevant Issues. *Review of Educational Research* 60, 1 (jan 1990), 65–89. DOI: http://dx.doi.org/10.3102/00346543060001065

[62] John F Pane. 2002. *A programming system for children that is designed for usability*. Ph.D. Dissertation. Carnegie Mellon University.

[63] Seymour Papert. 1971. *A Computer laboratory for elementary schools*. Technical Report. Massachusetts Institute of Technology. Artificial Intelligence Laboratory. 19 pages.

[64] Miranda C Parker and Mark Guzdial. 2016. Replication, validation, and use of a language independent CS1 knowledge assessment. *Proceedings of the 12th International Computing Education Research Conference* (2016), 93–101. DOI: http://dx.doi.org/10.1145/2960310.2960316

[65] Randy Pausch, Wanda Dann, and Stephen Cooper. 2000. Alice : a 3-D Tool for Introductory Programming Concepts. *Journal of Computing Sciences in Colleges* 15, 5 (2000), 107–116.

[66] Roy D Pea. 1986. Language-independent conceptual" bugs" in novice programming. *Journal of Educational Computing Research* 2, 1 (1986), 25–36. DOI: http://dx.doi.org/10.2190/689T-1R2A-X4W4-29J2

[67] Arnold Pears, Stephen Seidman, Lauri Malmi, Linda Mannila, Elizabeth Adams, Jens Bennedsen, Marie Devlin, and James Paterson. 2007. A Survey of Literature on the Teaching of Introductory Programming. In *Working Group Reports on ITiCSE on Innovation and Technology in Computer Science Education (ITiCSE-WGR '07)*. ACM, New York, NY, USA, 204–223. DOI: http://dx.doi.org/10.1145/1345443.1345441

[68] PracticeIt. 2016. http://practiceit.cs.washington.edu. (2016). Accessed: 2016-12-12.

[69] Anthony Ralston. 1971. Fortran and the First Course in Computer Science. *Acm Sigcse* 3, 4 (1971), 24–29. DOI: http://dx.doi.org/10.1145/382214.382499

[70] Vennila Ramalingam, Deborah LaBelle, and Susan Wiedenbeck. 2004. Self-Efficacy and Mental Models in Learning to Program. *Proceedings of the 9th annual SIGCSE conference on Innovation and technology in computer science education - ITiCSE '04* 36, 3 (2004), 171–175. DOI: http://dx.doi.org/10.1145/1007996.1008042

[71] Vennila Ramalingam and Susan Wiedenbeck. 1999. Development and validation of scores on a computer programming self-efficacy scale and group analyses of novice programmer self-efficacy. *Journal of Educational Computing Research* 19, 4 (1999), 367–381. DOI: http://dx.doi.org/10.2190/C670-Y3C8-LTJ1-CT3P

[72] Stuart Reges. 2006. Back to basics in CS1 and CS2. *ACM SIGCSE Bulletin* 38, 1 (2006), 293. DOI: http://dx.doi.org/10.1145/1124706.1121432

[73] Eric Roberts. 2004. The dream of a common language. *Proceedings of the 35th SIGCSE technical symposium on Computer science education - SIGCSE '04* 36, 1 (2004), 115. DOI: http://dx.doi.org/10.1145/971300.971343

[74] Anthony Robins, Janet Rountree, and Nathan Rountree. 2003. Learning and Teaching Programming: A Review and Discussion. *Computer Science Education* 13, 2 (jun 2003), 137–172. DOI: http://dx.doi.org/10.1076/csed.13.2.137.14200

[75] Carsten Schulte, Tony Clear, Ahmad Taherkhani, Teresa Busjahn, and James H. Paterson. 2010. An introduction to program comprehension for computer science educators. *Proceedings of the 2010 ITiCSE working group reports on Working group reports - ITiCSE-WGR '10* (2010), 65. DOI: http://dx.doi.org/10.1145/1971681.1971687

[76] Ben Shneiderman. 1977. Teaching programming: A spiral approach to syntax and semantics. *Computers & Education* 1, 4 (jan 1977), 193–197. DOI: http://dx.doi.org/10.1016/0360-1315(77)90008-2

[77] Ben Shneiderman and Richard Mayer. 1979. Syntactic/semantic interactions in programmer behavior: A model and experimental results. *International Journal of Computer & Information Sciences* 8, 3 (jun 1979), 219–238. DOI: http://dx.doi.org/10.1007/BF00977789

[78] D. Sleeman, Ralph T. Putnam, Juliet Baxter, and Laiani Kuspa. 1986. Pascal and high school students: A study of errors. *Journal of Educational Computing Research* 2, 1 (1986), 5–23. DOI: http://dx.doi.org/10.2190/2XPP-LTYH-98NQ-BU77

[79] Juha Sorva. 2013. Notional machines and introductory programming education. *ACM Transactions on Computing Education* 13, 2 (2013), 1–31. DOI: http://dx.doi.org/10.1145/2483710.2483713

[80] Juha Sorva and Otto Seppälä. 2014. Research-based design of the first weeks of CS1. *Proceedings of the 14th Koli Calling International Conference on Computing Education Research (Koli Calling '14)* November 2014 (2014), 71–80. DOI: http://dx.doi.org/10.1145/2674683.2674690

[81] Juha Sorva and Teemu Sirkia. 2010. UUhistle: a software tool for visual program simulation. *Proceedings of the 10th Koli Calling International Conference on Computing Education Research Koli Calling 10* (2010), 49–54. DOI: http://dx.doi.org/10.1145/1930464.1930471

[82] Juha Sorva and Teemu Sirkiä. 2011. Context-sensitive guidance in the UUhistle program visualization system. *Proceedings of the Sixth Program Visualization Workshop (PVW 2011)* (2011), 77–85.

[83] C. Taylor, D. Zingaro, L. Porter, K.C. Webb, C.B. Lee, and M. Clancy. 2014. Computer science concept inventories: past and future. *Computer Science Education* 24, 4 (2014), 253–276. DOI: http://dx.doi.org/10.1080/08993408.2014.970779

[84] Franklyn Turbak, Constance Royden, Jennifer Stephan, and Jean Herbst. 1999. Teaching recursion before loops in CS1. *Journal of Computing in Small Colleges* 14, May (1999), 86–101. http://cs.wellesley.edu/

[85] Jeroen J. G. Van Merrienboer and Hein P. M. Krammer. 1987. Instructional strategies and tactics for the design of introductory computer programming courses in high school. *Instructional Science* 16, 3 (sep 1987), 251–285. DOI: http://dx.doi.org/10.1007/BF00120253

[86] Anne Venables, Grace Tan, and Raymond Lister. 2009. A Closer Look at Tracing, Explaining and Code Writing Skills in the Novice Programmer. *Proceedings of the Fifth International Workshop on Computing Education Research Workshop - ICER '09* 2009 (2009), 117–128. DOI: http://dx.doi.org/10.1145/1584322.1584336

[87] Antti Virtanen, Essi Lahtinen, and Hannu-Matti Jarvinen. 2005. VIP, a Visual Interpreter for Learning Introductory Programming with C++. *Koli Calling 2005 Conference on Computer Science Education* November (2005), 125–130. http://citeseerx.ist.psu.edu/viewdoc/download?doi=10.1.1.101.9111

[88] Christopher Watson, Frederick W B Li, and Jamie L Godwin. 2014. No tests required: comparing traditional and dynamic predictors of programming success. *Proceedings of the 45th ACM technical symposium on Computer science education - SIGCSE '14* (2014), 469–474. DOI: http://dx.doi.org/10.1145/2538862.2538930

[89] Brenda Cantwell Wilson and Sharon Shrock. 2001. Contributing to success in an introductory computer science course: a study of twelve factors. *ACM SIGCSE Bulletin* 33, 1 (2001), 184–188. DOI: http://dx.doi.org/10.1145/366413.364581

[90] Leon E. Winslow. 1996. Programming Pedagogy - A Psychological Overview. *ACM SIGCSE Bulletin* 28, 3 (1996), 17–22. DOI: http://dx.doi.org/10.1145/234867.234872

[91] Cecile Yehezkel. 2003. Making program execution comprehensible one level above the machine language. *ITiCSE '03 Proceedings of the 8th annual conference on Innovation and technology in computer science education* (2003), 124. DOI: http://dx.doi.org/10.1145/961290.961547

Sometimes, Rainfall Accumulates:
Talk-Alouds with Novice Functional Programmers

Kathi Fisler
Brown University
Providence, RI
kfisler@cs.brown.edu

Francisco Enrique Vicente Castro
WPI
Worcester, MA
fgcastro@cs.wpi.edu

ABSTRACT

When functional programming is used in studies of the Rainfall problem in CS1, most students seem to perform fairly well. A handful of students, however, still struggle, though with different surface-level errors than those reported for students programming imperatively. Prior research suggests that novice programmers tackle problems by refining a high-level program schema that they have seen for a similar problem. Functional-programming students, however, have often seen multiple schemas that would apply to Rainfall. How do novices navigate these choices? This paper presents results from a talk-aloud study in which novice functional programmers worked on Rainfall. We describe the criteria that drove students to select, and sometimes switch, their high-level program schema, as well as points where students realized that their chosen schema was not working. Our main contribution lies in our observations of how novice programmers approach a multi-task planning problem in the face of multiple viable schemas.

KEYWORDS

Rainfall; program schemas; functional programming

1 INTRODUCTION

Soloway's Rainfall problem [17] has become a benchmark in computing education. This problem (which essentially asks students to compute the average of a sequence of numbers that appear before a sentinel value) is interesting because it appears straightforward while having non-trivial underlying complexity. Over the years, several authors have noted some of the challenges with Rainfall (see section 2), leading some to question whether the community is making progress on "beating" the Rainfall problem [8].

Most existing work on the challenges of Rainfall was conducted in the context of imperative programming [15–17, 20]. Some researchers have begun to publish studies of Rainfall with students who used functional programming [7], but those studies have not reported particular challenges that arise when students attempt Rainfall in this context. Given that different programming languages have different idioms and affordances, a better understanding of

how students solve—and struggle with—Rainfall in different pedagogic contexts and programming languages will enhance our understanding of this deceptively interesting programming problem.

The functional perspective is particularly interesting because students who learn functional programming are typically exposed to *multiple viable solution structures* for Rainfall. Studying how students approach Rainfall with functional programming thus provides an opportunity to explore how novice students navigate multiple applicable schemas, each of which they may only partly understand from CS1. Formally, the research question explored in this paper is:

When novice programmers have seen multiple schemas that might apply to a problem, how does their solution emerge and evolve?

We explore this question qualitatively, through narratives of four students' attempts at Rainfall in a talk-aloud session at the end of a CS1 course. These studies exposed factors in how novice students select, switch, and apply program schemas to problems requiring plan composition.

2 RELATED WORK

Most published studies of Rainfall involved students who were programming imperatively, in languages such as Pascal [17], Java [15], Python (also [15]), or C++ [16]. Ebrahimi had groups of students working in various languages, one of them Lisp [5]: however, his students had learned imperative constructs within Lisp.

Fisler published the first study of Rainfall with functional programming [7]. Her data was from multiple schools that were using the *How to Design Programs* (henceforth HTDP) curriculum, but with a variety of languages (Racket, OCaml, and Pyret). In her sample of 218 students, 186 had a (mostly) correct solution to Rainfall. Furthermore, her participants produced at least three different high-level structures of solutions (two appear in section 5). In contrast, imperative studies have typically produced a common high-level structure, taking only a single pass over the input sequence (whether with for or while loops), maintaining the running sum and item count in variables [15–17] (also seen in our own imperative studies). The study participants in this paper were also learning HTDP, but they are from a school that did not participate in Fisler's original study.

Castro and Fisler [1] captured the computer screens of HTDP students working on a different plan-composition problem called *Adding Machine*. That problem asks for a list of sums of sublists of input as separated by zeros, stopping when two consecutive zeros are discovered. Castro and Fisler's students performed quite poorly on the problem, with many of them following the HTDP design processes into an initial program structure that was not suitable to solve the problem. One participant in this study shared

ICER '17, August 18-20, 2017, Tacoma, WA, USA
© 2017 Copyright held by the owner/author(s). Publication rights licensed to Association for Computing Machinery.
ACM ISBN 978-1-4503-4968-0/17/08. . . $15.00
https://doi.org/10.1145/3105726.3106183

this problem; others avoided it, but could have gone down this path. Section 7 discusses our students' design processes in detail.

Pirolli et al.'s studies of learning recursive programming observed that novices modify already-learned solutions to fit the context of a new problem [11, 12]. Spohrer and Soloway's studies of the end-product programs of students and their talk-aloud protocols (verbal reports of planning, implementation, and debugging steps taken in programming a solution) echo this [19]: they suggest that students either (1) use previously learned programming knowledge (programming plans) to write the code, or (2) translate relevant non-programming knowledge (non-programming plans) into code. Students repair coding decisions after testing uncovered unexpected code behavior. Rist [13, 14] refined these models, describing two paths programmers take when writing code. When a programmer knows a viable schema, she takes a *plan retrieval* path, implementing code in *top-down* fashion, with smaller-scale modifications to address problem subtleties. When the programmer has no schema in her memory, she takes a *plan creation* path. She identifies a core computation called a *focus* (usually, a major computation required in the problem such as adding in an averaging problem) writes code to implement the focus, and then builds around that code *bottom-up* until a working solution is achieved. None of these theories of novice program construction addresses what happens when programmers have weaker knowledge of multiple viable schemas, or how novice programmers switch schemas mid-stream. This is the main question explored in our study.

de Raadt et al. used Rainfall to study impacts of explicitly teaching planning strategies [3]; they do not discuss change in strategy.

3 BACKGROUND: THE RAINFALL PROBLEM

Soloway proposed the Rainfall problem in the 1980s in the context of studying student difficulties with plan composition [17]. The original wording asked students to compute the average of a sequence of numbers, which were input through keyboard I/O, that occurred before a sentinel value had been entered. Soloway identified four sub-tasks that needed to be composed: taking in input, summing the inputs, computing the average (which involves counting the inputs), and outputting the average. Over the years, other researchers studied variations of Rainfall: some added noisy data in the form of negative numbers, some added additional reporting requirements (such as printing the maximum daily rainfall as well as the average). All variations have shared common core goals of summing, counting, averaging, input, and output.

Our formulation of Rainfall includes noisy data, but only asks for the average as output. We provide the inputs in a data structure, as our host course does not teach I/O. Our version reads:

> Design a program called rainfall that consumes a list of numbers representing daily rainfall readings. The list may contain the number -999 indicating the end of the data of interest. Produce the average of the non-negative values in the list up to the first -999 (if it shows up). There may be negative numbers other than -999 in the list representing faulty readings. If you cannot compute the average for whatever reason, return -1.

This version requires six tasks:

- Sentinel: Ignore inputs after the sentinel value

```
|| ; A list-of-number is
|| ; - empty, or
|| ; - (cons number list-of-number)
||
|| ;; TEMPLATE for list-of-number (generic name lon-func)
|| #|
|| (define (lon-func alon)
||   (cond [(empty? alon) ...]
||         [(cons? alon) ... (first alon)
||                       ... (lon-func (rest alon)) ...]))
|| |#
```

Figure 1: The HTDP input-type description and template for a program to process a list of numbers. The input-type description is a comment (semicolon is the comment character in Racket, the stick/hash create a block comment). cons creates a new list from an element and an existing list (it does not modify the existing list). The template has one conditional branch for each variant in the datatype (here, empty list and non-empty list). In the non-empty case (marked by cons?), the template recurs on the rest of the list to guarantee traversal of all elements. The ellipses get filled when the template is used to solve a specific problem.

- Negative: Ignore negative inputs
- Sum: Total the non-negative inputs
- Count: Count the non-negative inputs
- DivZero: Guard against division by zero
- Average: Average the non-negative inputs

4 BACKGROUND: THE *HOW TO DESIGN PROGRAMS* CURRICULUM

HTDP [6] is an introductory computing curriculum that teaches students how to leverage the structure of input data and multiple representations of functions to design programs. Students are taught a multi-step process called the *design recipe* for approaching a new programming problem. Roughly, the steps include identifying the type of input and output data for a problem, writing concrete examples of the input data, writing a type signature (though in comments rather than a formal type language) for a function that solves the problem, writing several illustrative examples or test cases for the function, writing a skeleton of code (called the *template*) that fully traverses the input type but ignores details of the desired output, and filling in the template with details of the given problem. Figure 1 shows the type description and template for a list of numbers, the datatype used in Rainfall.

The template is the most relevant aspect of the design recipe for this study. Templates provide schemas for programs. Unlike some schemas, which are contextualized to a style of problem, templates mirror the structure of a particular data type. In the early part of an HTDP course, students are taught to always start with the template that matches the type of their input data. Later in the course, as programming problems get more complex, students learn other schemas and the contexts in which to use them (thus relaxing, or at least broadening, the template step of the design recipe). Students in our study course had been exposed to two other schemas that could apply to Rainfall; we discuss these in section 5.

Week	Topics	Assignment
1	Arithmetic expressions and functions	Composing images
2	Conditionals and structures	Functions over structs (movie theater data), conditionals, test cases
3	Lists of atomic data, the design recipe	Functions over structs (capturing weather events), functions over lists of strings
4	Lists of structs	Lists of structs (political ads)
5	Trees	Binary search trees
6	Locals and higher-order functions	N-ary trees (system of rivers and tributaries)
7	Accumulators	map and filter (revisit political ads), accumulators (variant on numeric max)
8	Variables, mutation	None (end of course)

Figure 2: The topic sequence in the host course for this study. Our Rainfall talk-alouds occurred at the end of week 7.

In HTDP, functions and data types are the building blocks for programs, not variables and loops as in curricula based on imperative programming. Courses start with writing non-parameterized expressions to compute with numbers and images (e.g., composing images to create flags), then teach abstraction over concrete similar expressions to create functions in roughly the third lecture. Students then cover a series of data structures—structs/records, lists of atomic data, lists of structures, binary trees, n-ary trees—each following the same design recipe to scaffold program design based on the shape of the input data structures. All of this material precedes mutable variables (covered much later in the course).

The HTDP Instance for this Study

The course in which we conducted the study was a CS1 course for students with limited or no prior programming experience (those with prior experience take a different course). The course uses Racket (a variant of Scheme) as its programming language. Figure 2 outlines the sequence of topics and assignments in the course. The course ran over 8 weeks, with 4 hours of lecture per week and one hour of lab per week. The Rainfall study occurred during week 7.

The course did not explicitly cover plan composition or decomposing problems into sub-tasks. The course did emphasize creating *helper functions* to break down larger computations, with appropriate use of helpers counting significantly in homework grading. Prior to the Rainfall session, every problem covered in lecture or assigned for homework had either been a structural traversal of a recursively-defined data structure (a list, a binary tree, or an n-ary tree), or a function that used a single additional parameter to accumulate one running value (such as the sum of elements so far in a list). In particular, students had not yet seen a problem that wasn't a direct instantiation of an HTDP template.

5 RAINFALL UNDER HTDP

At first glance, Rainfall seems a natural fit with HTDP: the problem involves straightforward functions over lists of numbers (counting and summing, both canonical recursive functions that students see in lecture when lists of numbers are introduced). The fit is less clear, however, in the context of the template. If a student followed the basic recipe blindly, applying the list-of-numbers template, they would start with the following code:

```
;; rainfall : list-of-number -> number
;; compute average of non-neg nums before -999
(define (rainfall alon)
  (cond [(empty? alon) ...]
        [(cons? alon) ... (first alon)
                      ... (rainfall (rest alon)) ...]))
```

This code is hard to modify into a working Rainfall solution: because rainfall is called recursively on the rest of the list, filling in the ellipses in the cons? case requires computing the average of a list from the average of the rest of the list. This is more complicated than the usual algorithm of dividing the sum of the list by its length. Each of sum and count are straightforward applications of the HTDP template, but the rainfall function itself needs to decompose its computation into these two sub-tasks.

HTDP exposes students to multiple viable Rainfall solutions (which is what makes this study interesting in the first place). Figure 3 shows a solution that reduces the input data to the list of numbers to average (truncating at -999 and removing the negatives), then calls a function to average the clean list. Observe that the sum and actual-rain functions follow the list-of-numbers template, but the overall rainfallc function does not (it decomposes the average task into the sum and count tasks instead). This structure was the most common in Fisler's earlier Rainfall study with functional programming [7].

Figure 4 shows a solution structure based on what HTDP terms *accumulators*. This program includes a nested function with parameters for each of the running count and sum of data to average. Once the end of the data or -999 is reached, another local function is called to produce the average. This structure traverses the data only once, and is closer in style to what an imperative programmer would produce with a loop and variables for the sum and count.

6 STUDY LOGISTICS

Our data were collected as part of a course-long study of how CS1 students (at a selective US university) approach program design. In one session of this study, 13 students talked aloud as they spent 30 minutes trying to solve Rainfall (as defined in section 3). After 30 minutes, we archived the student's code and interviewed them about how they approached the problem: what they found difficult, what information they drew on, and what inspired their design decisions. Both the talk-aloud and the interview were audio-recorded, then transcribed verbatim for analysis. Students worked on a computer, in the course's standard programming environment.

Participants: This paper presents data from four students from the overall study (additional narratives did not fit in the page limits). Of the four, two are female and two are male. We selected these four to reflect variety in course performance, prior experience, and the structure of students' final solutions. Figure 5 summarizes each student's grades and programming experience prior to CS1.

```
;; sum : list-of-number -> number
;; produces the sum of the given list of numbers
(define (sum alon)
  (cond [(empty? alon) 0]
        [(cons? alon) (+ (first alon) (sum (rest alon)))]))

;; actual-rain : list-of-number -> list-of-number
;; produces list of non-negative values that occur before -999
(define (actual-rain alon)
  (cond [(empty? alon) empty]
        [(cons? alon) (cond [(= (first alon) -999) empty]
                            [(negative? (first alon)) (actual-rain (rest alon))]
                            [else (cons (first alon) (actual-rain (rest alon)))])]))

;; rainfallC : list-of-number -> number
;; produces average of non-negative nums in list before -999, or -1 if no such nums exist
(define (rainfallC alon)
  (local [(define good-data (actual-rain alon))]
    (if (> (length good-data) 0)
        (/ (sum good-data) (length good-data))
        -1)))
```

Figure 3: Rainfall solution in Racket, clean-first style. The overall function (rainfallC) calls a helper function (actual-rain) to truncate and clear negative numbers from the input data. It then computes the sum and length to compute the average. length is a built-in operator that returns the length of a list. Semicolon is the Racket comment character. This solution could be adapted to use higher-order functions: fold can compress the sum to a single expression, and filter could be used to remove the negatives if a separate function had been used to truncate data after -999. [18] humorously presents a Scala version.

```
;; rainfallA : list-of-number -> number
;; produces average of non-negative nums in list before -999, or -1 if no such nums exist
(define (rainfallA alon)
  (local [;; produce-average: number number -> number
          ;; computes average given count and sum, producing -1 if count is 0
          (define (produce-average count sum)
            (if (> count 0) (/ sum count) -1))

          ;; rainfall-accum: list-of-number number number -> number
          (define (rainfall-accum data count sum)
            (cond [(empty? data) (produce-average count sum)]
                  [(cons? data)
                   (cond [(= (first data) -999) (produce-average count sum)]
                         [(negative? (first data)) (rainfall-accum (rest data) count sum)]
                         [else (rainfall-accum (rest data) (+ 1 count) (+ (first data) sum))])]))]
    (rainfall-accum alon 0 0)))
```

Figure 4: Rainfall solution in Racket, accumulator style. The overall function (rainfallA) contains two local (nested) function definitions: one for computing the average and one that recurs through the input list, accumulating the sum and count of non-negative values until -999 is reached. Semicolon is the Racket comment character.

ID (Gender)	Experience	Exam	Course
STUDA (F)	C++, Online courses	71 (C)	76.47
STUDB (M)	Java, Python, Ruby, Self-study	87 (B)	94.36
STUDC (M)	Python, JavaScript, Java, HTML5, CSS, PHP, Self-study, AP class, High school class, Online courses	89 (B)	81.08
STUDD (F)	None	93 (A)	87.14

Figure 5: Participant overview. Experience was self-reported via checkboxes on a survey. The exam was in course week 3.

Data Analysis: The first author developed the narratives in section 7 from the typed talk-aloud and interview transcripts. She is an experienced HTDP instructor, but did not teach this instance of the course. The second author conducted the talk-alouds and interviews. He reviewed the first author's narratives for accuracy. We divided work this way so that the narratives would reflect the pedagogy and learning of HTDP more than personalities of the students. The first author does not know the identities of the students.

The narrative methodology here is influenced in part by the narrative analysis method used by Whalley and Kasto in their investigation of novices' code writing strategies [21]. They developed descriptive accounts of how students used existing schema to write

15

code from think-aloud and interview data. We also draw on ideas from grounded theory [9], in terms of the narrative reconstructions that describe how students varied in how they chose constructs, patterns, or techniques to build their Rainfall solutions.

In the analysis, we marked comments pertaining to choice of schemas, choice of language constructs, discussion of design choices, mentions of problem tasks (whether or not they were reflected in code), and rationale for editing previously-written code. We also marked comments on how students perceived the Rainfall problem.

7 NARRATIVES

This section presents narratives of each participants' design process[1]. We also summarize both the correctness and the structure of each final solution. Possible correctness values are *poor* (far from working), *fair* (in the right direction, but with many errors), and *almost correct* (very close and could have been fixed easily after some straightforward testing to show the bugs). We show final code for some students, but space precludes including it for all.

7.1 StudA

Correctness: poor
Overall Structure: Accumulator, but role of parameter unclear

StudA begins by writing the function name and input type. She proceeds to write the list-of-numbers template (as in fig. 1). Inside the non-empty list case, she inserts a conditional to check whether the first element of the list is positive.

She thinks of using an accumulator in order to track the running sum of positive numbers. She goes back to her notes to check on how to write an accumulator function, then adds a local definition for a function with an accumulator parameter. She recalls that accumulator functions return the accumulator parameter in the base case; accordingly, she replaces the -1 she was originally returning in the base case with the accumulator parameter.

She notes that *"I can do the division at the end"*, then goes back to working on the running sum. If the first list element is negative, she calls the function recursively with the same parameter value. She returns to thinking about where to handle the division: *"I feel like the division should happen inside the function. So I don't want to be adding here ... I want to divide the rainfall - actually no wait I want to add the rainfall"* (at this point, she is wrestling with how to integrate the sum and average tasks within the same area of code).

StudA notices that her current code never returns -1 (by inspection, not by running it): *"So now my issue is nothing will turn up -1 if the average can't be produced or if the list is just empty. So somehow I have to work that in there."* She decides to try running the code. She tries an input of all positive numbers, but gets back a negative average. She realizes this can't be right. She correctly articulates that an average is computed by dividing the sum by the count.

After this point, StudA starts to thrash. She articulates a variety of possible edits involving -1 and the accumulator parameter. Her comments include statements like *"somehow I have to store the divided value into the accumulator or to make that produce at the end."*. She continues to try to reason out how her code works. She realizes that there are multiple subtasks: *"somehow I have to get*

the three of these things together without adding all three together". She seems to keep switching the task (addition, division, counting, or returning -1) to do around the recursive call on the rest of the list—her final code (below) reflects this confusion. Just before time is up, she thinks of using a separate helper function: *"So maybe I need to make a helper function where I just add them all up and then divide out later."*. Time runs out before she can try it in code.

```
(define (rainfall alon)
  (local
    [(define (rainfall alon acc)
      (cond [(empty? alon) acc]
            [(cons? alon)
             (if (> (first alon) 0)
                 (/ (rainfall (rest alon) (first alon))
                    (+ 1 acc))
                 (rainfall (rest alon) acc))]))]
    (rainfall alon 0)))
```

During the interview after the coding session, StudA remarks *"I thought accumulator would be useful because every time it finds another positive value [...] the average changes because the bottom number would keep getting bigger. So the accumulator would keep adjusting to that."* The student has associated some behavior with accumulators, but does not understand the pattern well enough to get close to a working solution.

7.2 StudB

Correctness: fair (count of data inaccurate)
Overall Structure: Accumulator with parameter for running sum

StudB begins by writing the function name, input type, and output type as he reads the problem. The student starts to follow the template by creating a conditional, articulating that the function should return 0 if the list is empty (this appears to be a pattern of habit, as the correct answer on empty input would have been -1). As the student is thinking out what to do when the list is non-empty, he articulates the algorithm for computing the average, and says *"we want to divide something by the length of [the input list]"*, observing that only the non-negative values should be considered.

The student realizes he needs a helper function that sums the values in a list. The student articulates the type signature and writes a sum function following the HTDP template for lists of numbers. This function does not account for negative numbers or the -999 sentinel. The student then goes back to the original function and starts to handle the negatives, introducing a conditional that checks the sign and value of the first number on the list. When -999 is encountered, the student notes that the program should return the average (but doesn't completely fill in the needed code). As the student continues filling in the conditional, he starts to question whether the helper could be handled by built-in primitives.

The student finishes filling in the conditional and tries running the program, but discovers it goes into an infinite loop. At this point, the buggy program follows the pattern to recursively sum the positive numbers, returning the average when the -999 is encountered: one branch of the conditional within the recursion is implementing the sum task while another implements the average task (which can't work since this leaves no base case for the sum task). The student realizes that the code isn't *"storing the value"* of

---

[1]We follow Dziallas and Fincher [4] in calling these narratives, not case studies.

the running sum, and switches to an accumulator-based design, with a parameter to hold the running sum.

The student then begins a cycle of editing the code, testing it, having the tests fail, then editing again. As the student talks through the cycle, he begins looking for fragments of code to delete or modify: for example, he tries removing various branches of conditionals, including the one that terminates the recursion if the list becomes empty before reaching -999 (this branch never gets restored before time is called).

Next the student tries to figure out where to return -1: *"So this is still working but this is not working. So it's not producing -1. And so if the element's negative it's running the recursion on the rest of the list. Maybe - no. Maybe the [accumulator] could be set to something else other than just [the current accumulator value] or but I can't think of what it needs to be set to."* The student hits on the idea of a different helper function to handle the case in which all numbers in the original input list are negative. He proceeds to write a straight-up (correct) recursive function to check whether all numbers in a list are negative, then uses this to guard computation of the average once -999 is detected. That said, the student never got the tasks and their code mapping straight in his head. He kept modifying the in-progress code with Rist-like focals, rather than thinking about how to decompose the problem.

The final code contains two major errors: it does not handle input lists that lack the -999, and the average computation uses the wrong denominator (the length of the suffix that follows the -999, not the count of non-negative numbers before the -999).

7.3 StudC

Correctness: fair (conflates sum and average tasks)
Overall Structure: Accumulator with filter (latter not integrated)

StudC starts by writing the function signature and purpose. He begins to write the list template, filling in -1 as the answer in the empty-list case based on the problem statement. He wonders whether he should be using local, which is part of the standard pattern for writing functions with accumulators in the course. The student starts to write the inner accumulator function, again following the template. But this time, the student returns the accumulator value in the empty-list/base case. That is the standard usage pattern students have seen with accumulator functions to this point in the course. To this point, StudC has not articulated what the accumulator variable represents; his work seems entirely syntactic.

The student talks about checking whether the first number in the list is negative, then about creating a helper function to compute the average; this comes up more as a side comment than as part of the flow of where this helper might get called from the overall Rainfall computation. The student realizes that the average computation will need both the running sum and the count of items, and thinks about how to obtain both values: *"it almost seems like I would use an accumulator to show how many times I've actually gotten through that. [...] so I guess we'll use another local"* (whether the student is suggesting another locally-defined accumulator function or another parameter within the existing accumulator is not clear at this point).

The student notes the requirement to stop at the first -999 and to ignore negatives. The student recognizes that filter could ignore the negative numbers, and would eliminate the need to check the

sign of individual list elements during the accumulator function. The student writes a helper function that uses filter to remove all non-positive numbers from an input list. (The student does not, however, call this helper function from the accumulator function. The helper remains uncalled in the final code).

Next, the student adds a conditional to check for a value *less than* -999 (incorrect logic, changed in final). For the "then" branch, the student articulates calling the function recursively to process the rest of the list, while adding the new value to the accumulator. As shown in the final code below, the student adds another parameter (times) to track the count of values. He tries to compute the average and use it as a new parameter value (he never articulates a clear role for this parameter). The else case of the conditional gets a recursive call to the function that takes the rest of the list and leaves the two accumulator parameters unchanged.

```
(define (rainfall alon acc times)
  (cond [(empty? alon) acc]
        [(cons? alon)
         (if (> (first alon) -999)
             (rainfall (rest alon)
                       (/ (+ (first alon) acc) times)
                       (+ 1 times))
             (rainfall (rest alon) acc times))]))
```

The student then enters a testing phase, running his code on a single test case. The test fails. The student correctly diagnoses that the execution never satisfies the -999 check and reverses the less-than computation in his conditional check. The student adjusts initial values for his accumulator parameters, but does not correctly trace the execution to isolate the actual errors in his code.

7.4 StudD

Correctness: Almost correct (sans two cond cases reversed)
Overall Structure: Clean-first with accumulator (for cleaning)

StudD begins by writing the function name, input type, and output type as she reads the problem statement. She proceeds to start writing the template, inserting -1 as the answer in the base case based on the problem statement. She instinctively questions whether the base case answer should instead be 0, but decides to follow the problem statement and see where it goes. She does not appear to write the non-empty case of the template blindly, but instead talks through what might need to happen in this case.

She fairly quickly ponders whether she will need an accumulator, but she isn't entirely sure why this would be necessary. She thinks she should have a function that *"goes through each number in the list just to make sure it's not -999"*. She goes on to say that *"with every number that it passes that is not -999, it's gonna add those all up"*. So at this point, StudD has decided to write a function that traverses the list and adds up all the relevant data.

StudD begins to change course once she thinks about what to do upon finding the -999: *"so then I would need another helper function. Once it hit the -999, it would divide it by the [...] number of terms it went through but I don't know how I would do that yet"*. As she tries to write the base case of her accumulator function, she realizes that summing and the overall rainfall problem require different base-case answers: *"if it's empty, that would return either–it would return -1 for the rainfall purposes, but for this one I don't know if it would return 0 [or] -1"*. This prompts her to change her accumulator to instead build a list of the relevant (clean) data, with separate functions to compute the average of this list. Her final solution is a clean-first style, but with an accumulator in the function that cleans the data. During the reflection interview, she remarks how accomplished she feels for solving the problem.

8 ANALYSIS AND DISCUSSION

This paper opened with a specific research question: *when novice programmers have seen multiple schemas that might apply to a problem, how does their solution emerge and evolve?* All four students started saying they would use the list template and ended up using accumulators in some fashion. Whether the students perceived these as different patterns, or whether they view accumulators as a variation on the list template, is not evident in our transcripts. However, all four students commented on the typical base cases of these patterns, suggesting that they had internalized them separately.

The trigger to use accumulators differed across the students: STUDA and STUDB initially associated the accumulator with tracking the sum (though STUDA lost this association once she started to thrash); STUDC switched without a clear justification and never stated a purpose for the accumulator (following the schema purely syntactically). STUDD explicitly ruled out an accumulator at first, then found it useful for tracking clean data. Use of accumulators was likely influenced by the timing of our Rainfall session. The course had just covered accumulators: the pattern was fresh and students may have assumed they *should* be using them. The lectures had shown the use of accumulators for summing a list of numbers.

As discussed in section 2, we have not found existing theories about how novices navigate or switch between multiple schemas. Observations from our data suggest possible elements of such theories, each raising open questions that would inform a theory.

OBSERVATION 1. *Students who copy-and-paste the template (as HTDP recommends for beginners) get more stuck than those who recall the template and write it down "as they go".*

STUDA mechanically wrote down the list-of-number template before thinking about the details of Rainfall. The course teaches this practice, though once students have mastered the template, they tend to interleave writing the template with filling in the holes (particular in easy spots, such as the base case). STUDB, STUDC, and STUDD all stated that they were going to use the list-of-number template, but they proceeded to work in "write as you go" fashion, which meant they started thinking about how they would fill in the holes around the recursive call to Rainfall before they committed to calling their function on the rest of the list. These students generally introduced an accumulator at this point, effectively switching their program schema mid-session. STUDA, in contrast, struggled more with the schema change and ended up farthest away from a working Rainfall solution.

OPEN QUESTION 1. *When students know multiple schemas for a problem, do those who write out most of one (incorrect) schema have a harder time adapting their approach than those who reproduce schemas on the fly?*

OPEN QUESTION 2. *Is there a systematic method for helping students realize when they might need to switch schemas? Or how to recognize apriori when a problem needs more than the basic schemas that they know?*

OBSERVATION 2. *Students who articulated only the syntactic schema of accumulators, but not the underlying concept, struggled to adapt them to the needs of Rainfall.*

As instructors, it is easy to assume that once students have seen the *idea* of a parameter that accumulates a running value, then they will add as many such parameters as a problem requires. This assumes that students understood the underlying idea, however, rather than simply absorbing the syntactic pattern. Students in our course had only seen examples with a single accumulator parameter, and in each of those programs, the value in that parameter was returned in the base case of the recursion. An accumulator-based Rainfall solution either needs two parameters (one for the running sum and one for the running count) or one parameter for the running list of clean data. Students had only seen examples that accumulated numbers up to this point in the course. Unless students understood the point of the accumulator, adapting to multiple parameters could be a significant challenge.

Interpreting this in an imperative context, it would be as if students had only ever seen programs with a single numeric variable, and did not immediately realize that they could have two variables. This is not a confusion that we have seen reported in other Rainfall studies. In functional programming, additional "variables" become additional parameters—perhaps that seems more complex to novices than additional standalone variables (which could be ignored while still allowing the program to run, whereas additional parameters need values or a syntax error results). Perhaps students in the imperative studies of Rainfall made different errors depending on whether they had seen programs with multiple variables. The point here is simply that different linguistic constructs have different affordances and pitfalls, and different courses prepare students for problems in subtle ways that we have likely overlooked in reporting studies. We need to understand our benchmark problems in multiple contexts to know what makes them challenging.

> STUDA: *I guess [the hardest part] was trying to figure out how to work in the -1 with the accumulator there because I didn't know where to put it [...] all the examples we put the accumulator after empty [...] but in this one the answer wasn't stored in the accumulator.*

OBSERVATION 3. *Students who connected accumulator parameters or parts of their code to specific tasks, and maintained those connections through the schema switch, produced more correct code.*

The two students with clear roles for the accumulator were also the ones who more generally connected specific problem tasks to parts of their code. One of these was the only student who mentioned using `filter` to help deal with the negative numbers (though he never got that part integrated with his accumulator-based program for computing the average). These observations reinforce the idea that failure to decompose problems into tasks—not just failure to compose code—underlies student challenges with multi-task problems (others' work showing that students can handle similar problems when explicitly taught strategies or patterns supports this [3, 10]). Had someone suggested decomposing the problem into separate sum and count functions, we suspect the two weakest students might well have done better, since their transcripts showed they did have basic facility with the list template.

OBSERVATION 4. *Students had not understood that each sub-task that traverses a list needs its own function or accumulator parameter.*

Both HTDP and the host course explain that a single recursive function can perform only one traversal-based operation (this initially comes up when discussing insertion sort, to explain why separate functions are needed for insertion and the overall sort). Our host course did not, however, reinforce this via assignments. Accumulator parameters enable a single function to track outputs of multiple tasks in a single traversal, but the course does not currently teach the explicit link between traversal-tasks and parameters. Our narratives show students struggling to integrate multiple traversal tasks (e.g., summing and counting) in a single function, even once they introduce accumulators. The connections between tasks, parameters, templates, and traversals are not (or have not been made) clear enough to these students, yet they seem critical to producing a correct Rainfall solution in any programming language.

Students similarly struggled to handle the sentinel. All prior problems in the course terminated a list recursion at the end of the list, not at a particular value. Most students recognized the sentinel as another base case for recursion, but they struggled to reconcile the return values in the empty-list and sentinel cases, especially in light of the -1. This is again a failure to separate tasks in their code.

OPEN QUESTION 3. *Would more emphasis on the "one task per function or parameter" rule enable students to solve Rainfall, even if they hadn't seen sentinels or multiple accumulator parameters?*

The first author has begun teaching students how to identify tasks and map them to each of functions or parameters/variables as part of program design. We are in the early stages of studying the impact on students' abilities to solve plan-composition problems.

OBSERVATION 5. *Students thought the problem was complex just from the problem statement.*

Our version of Rainfall has more constraints and detail than Soloway's original phrasing, which read:

> *Write a program that will read in integers and output their average. Stop reading when the value 99999 is input.*

Later versions of the problem have included negative numbers, but even compared to those, our problem description has additional details such as: (a) -999 may never appear, (b) -999 may appear more than once, (c) an explicit instruction to return -1 if the average cannot be computed, and (d) use of the term "faulty readings" to contextualize the other negative numbers.

Prior versions of the problem typically omitted instructions on what to return if there is no data to average (detail (c)). We agree with Seppälä et al. [15] that this omission makes it hard to interpret students' mistakes. While throwing an error would be better than returning -1, our students had not yet learned error handling.

Details (a) and (b) regarding the sentinel are necessary because the input comes as a list rather than being entered interactively. Requiring the list to contain -999 actually complicates the problem for one who follows HTDP (or any datatype-based discipline) strictly. A list with a guaranteed sentinel would have a different data type (in which the base case is a list with the sentinel as the first element,

not the empty list); this would lead to a different template. The current wording retains the schema that students already know. Taken together, however, all of these details have a price in terms of how students perceive the problem complexity:

> STUDC: *From what we've learned in class we generally use just simpler problems, and we rarely [...] put them all together. So when you are approached with a problem such as this, you almost struggle to figure out how to put it together 'cause you've never done it before. [...] [usually] it would be more in a Part A, Part B, Part C, Part D style.*

Future research should explore relationships between the level of detail in the problem statement, whether examples are provided [15], and when students perceive sub-tasks in more complex problems:

OPEN QUESTION 4. *Does a more detailed Rainfall description help students recognize more sub-tasks before they start coding?*

OPEN QUESTION 5. *Does providing examples or test cases with the Rainfall description lead students to recognize more sub-tasks before they start coding?*

9 CONCLUSIONS

Our study data allowed us to ask a unique question in the context of Rainfall: how do novice students manage having seen multiple viable schemas for a programming problem? Students do not yet know the limitations of these schemas well (unlike experts). We would expect, then, to see students switching schemas or perhaps trying to merge them. We are not aware of theories of how novices switch schemas. We need to understand this, however, so we can teach students how to handle such situations more effectively.

Our data drive home the power—and hold—of previously-seen patterns for novice programmers. Instructors may think they are teaching a general approach (such as using an accumulator), but if students have only seen examples that use that approach in a single way (such as a single parameter that is returned as the final answer), they may struggle to adapt patterns to new situations. Approaches such as subgoal labeling [2] might help counter the syntactic power of a pattern. In the context of this paper, the key takeaway is that the class examples instructors choose may inadvertently complicate problems like Rainfall for students. If we want to know what makes Rainfall hard or easy, we need to consider the course context at a finer granularity than has been reported in previous studies.

Our students did not seem to perform as well as those in Fisler's study [7]. Our participants had only just started working with higher-order functions, which many students used in Fisler's study. Perhaps curricular differences addressed our observations for Fisler's study courses. It would be interesting to run similar talk-alouds with students at the schools from the original study.

As a community, we can't claim to have "beaten the Rainfall problem" [8] until we have findings that we can explain and reproduce across courses. This needs studies that report on finer-grained curricular details and how students draw on them when selecting designs. While we continue to work on those, programming instructors should continue to carry an umbrella.

ACKNOWLEDGMENTS

Work supported by US-NSF Grant No.s 1116539 and 1500039.

REFERENCES

[1] Francisco Enrique Vicente Castro and Kathi Fisler. 2016. On the Interplay Between Bottom-Up and Datatype-Driven Program Design. In *Proceedings of the 47th ACM Technical Symposium on Computing Science Education (SIGCSE '16)*. ACM, New York, NY, USA, 205–210. DOI: https://doi.org/10.1145/2839509.2844574

[2] Richard Catrambone. 1998. The subgoal learning model: Creating better examples so that students can solve novel problems. *Journal of Experimental Psychology: General* 127 (1998), 355–376. DOI: https://doi.org/10.1037/0096-3445.127.4.355

[3] Michael de Raadt, Richard Watson, and Mark Toleman. 2009. Teaching and Assessing Programming Strategies Explicitly. In *Proceedings of the Eleventh Australasian Conference on Computing Education - Volume 95 (ACE '09)*. Australian Computer Society, Inc., Darlinghurst, Australia, Australia, 45–54. http://dl.acm.org/citation.cfm?id=1862712.1862723

[4] Sebastian Dziallas and Sally Fincher. 2016. Aspects of Graduateness in Computing Students' Narratives. In *Proceedings of the 2016 ACM Conference on International Computing Education Research (ICER '16)*. ACM, New York, NY, USA, 181–190. DOI: https://doi.org/10.1145/2960310.2960317

[5] Alireza Ebrahimi. 1994. Novice programmer errors: language constructs and plan composition. *International Journal of Human-Computer Studies* 41 (1994), 457–480.

[6] Matthias Felleisen, Robert Bruce Findler, Matthew Flatt, and Shriram Krishnamurthi. 2001. *How to Design Programs*. MIT Press. http://www.htdp.org/

[7] Kathi Fisler. 2014. The Recurring Rainfall Problem. In *Proceedings of the Tenth Annual Conference on International Computing Education Research (ICER '14)*. ACM, New York, NY, USA, 35–42. DOI: https://doi.org/10.1145/2632320.2632346

[8] Mark Guzdial. 2010. A Challenge to Computing Education Research: Make Measurable Progress. https://computinged.wordpress.com/2010/08/16/a-challenge-to-computing-education-research-make-measurable-progress/. (Aug. 2010). Accessed April 14, 2017.

[9] Päivi Kinnunen and Beth Simon. 2012. Phenomenography and grounded theory as research methods in computing education research field. *Computer Science Education* 22, 2 (June 2012), 199–218. DOI: https://doi.org/10.1080/08993408.2012.692928

[10] O. Muller, B. Haberman, and D. Ginat. 2007. Pattern-oriented instruction and its influence on problem decomposition and solution construction. In *Proceedings of ITiCSE*.

[11] Peter L. Pirolli and John R. Anderson. 1985. The Role of Learning from Examples in the Acquisition of Recursive Programming Skills. *Canadian Journal of Psychology/Revue canadienne de psychologie* 39, 2 (1985), 240–272.

[12] Peter L. Pirolli, John R. Anderson, and Robert G. Farrell. 1984. *Learning to program recursion*. 277–280.

[13] Robert S. Rist. 1989. Schema Creation in Programming. *Cognitive Science* (1989), 389–414.

[14] Robert S. Rist. 1991. Knowledge Creation and Retrieval in Program Design: A Comparison of Novice and Intermediate Student Programmers. *Hum.-Comput. Interact.* 6, 1 (Mar 1991), 1–46.

[15] Otto Seppälä, Petri Ihantola, Essi Isohanni, Juha Sorva, and Arto Vihavainen. 2015. Do We Know How Difficult the Rainfall Problem is?. In *Proceedings of the 15th Koli Calling Conference on Computing Education Research (Koli Calling '15)*. ACM, New York, NY, USA, 87–96. DOI: https://doi.org/10.1145/2828959.2828963

[16] Simon. 2013. Soloway's Rainfall Problem Has Become Harder. *Learning and Teaching in Computing and Enginering* (2013), 130–135. DOI: https://doi.org/10.1109/LaTiCE.2013.44

[17] Elliot Soloway. 1986. Learning to Program = Learning to Construct Mechanisms and Explanations. *Commun. ACM* 29, 9 (Sept. 1986), 850–858.

[18] Juha Sorva and Arto Vihavainen. 2016. Break Statement Considered. *ACM Inroads* 7, 3 (Aug. 2016), 36–41. DOI: https://doi.org/10.1145/2950065

[19] James C. Spohrer and Elliot Soloway. 1989. *Simulating Student Programmers*. Morgan Kaufmann Publishers Inc., 543–549.

[20] Anne Venables, Grace Tan, and Raymond Lister. 2009. A Closer Look at Tracing, Explaining and Code Writing Skills in the Novice Programmer. In *Computing Education Research Workshop (ICER)*. 117–128.

[21] Jacqueline Whalley and Nadia Kasto. 2014. A Qualitative Think-aloud Study of Novice Programmers' Code Writing Strategies. In *Proceedings of the 2014 Conference on Innovation & Technology in Computer Science Education (ITiCSE '14)*. ACM, New York, NY, USA, 279–284. DOI: https://doi.org/10.1145/2591708.2591762

Using Learners' Self-Explanations of Subgoals to Guide Initial Problem Solving in App Inventor

Lauren Margulieux
Georgia State University
Learning Technologies Division
Atlanta, GA 30302-3978
lmargulieux@gsu.edu

Richard Catrambone
Georgia Institute of Technology
School of Psychology
Atlanta, GA 30332-0170
richard.catrambone@psych.gatech.edu

ABSTRACT

Our goal for the present research was to improve upon the subgoal learning framework and further enhance problem solving performance for novice programmers learning to use a block-based programming language. In particular, we are expanding upon recent work done by Margulieux and Morrison that prompts learners to self-explain the subgoals, or functional pieces, of a problem solving process to create their own instructional explanations of the process. We added to this work by exploring whether learners' self-explained instructions could be used to effectively scaffold initial problem solving attempts (i.e., practice problems) to further improve performance. In this experiment, learners self-explained subgoals using the most successful conditions from Margulieux and Catrambone's [1] prior work and then were given practice problems that were either unscaffolded (control condition), scaffolded with their own subgoal explanations, or scaffolded with explanations constructed by an instructional designer and computer scientist. Learners who were scaffolded with their own explanations performed better on later problem solving (i.e., an assessment test) than those scaffolded with the experts' explanations or those with no scaffolding. The results show that scaffolding initial problem solving with learners' explanations of the problem solving process can lead to better problem solving performance than scaffolding from experts if the learners construct explanations with adequate support.

KEYWORDS

problem solving, constructive learning, subgoal learning, self-explanation, block-based programming

1 INTRODUCTION

Subgoals learning is a framework from educational psychology that is being adapted for computing education to improve students' problem solving performance [2, 3, 4, 5].

ICER'17, August 18-20, 2017, Tacoma, WA, USA
© 2017 ACM. ISBN 978-1-4503-4968-0/17/08...$15.00.
http://dx.doi.org/10.1145/3105726.3106168

Subgoal learning addresses the expert-novice gap in problem solving by breaking down procedures into subgoals, functional pieces of a problem solving procedure, that are easier for novices to grasp but are hard for experts to articulate because they have been automated [6, 7]. Identifying the subgoals of a problem solving procedure, however, is a time-intensive process, often taking 1-2 hours to create 30-45 minutes of instruction, which requires both a domain expert and an instructional design expert [8]. To make subgoal learning more pervasive in computing, researchers have recently tried crowdsourcing subgoal identification [9, 10] and prompting learners to self-explain the subgoals of procedures [2, 3, 4, 5]. Self-explanation is another framework from educational psychology that encourages deeper processing of information by asking students to explain the problem solving process to themselves and thus connect the principles that they are learning to the problems that they are solving [11, 12]. By asking students to self-explain subgoals, the process of identifying subgoals becomes shorter because the instructional designer needs to only parse one subgoal from the next, not come up with a context-independent description of the subgoal that would explain its function to a novice [1]. Most importantly, self-explaining subgoals can improve learners' novel problem solving in some situations [1, 4, 5, 13, 14]. The current research builds upon this research and further improves learner' novel problem solving by using learners' self-explanation to scaffold initial problem solving.

1.1 Prior Work in Subgoals and Self-Explanation

The original subgoal learning framework taught subgoals by decomposing a worked example (or several) into the subgoals and labeling those subgoals with the function that they serve. For example, in Figure 1 the subgoal labels "Handle event" and "Set output" describe the function served by the steps of the worked example. This work found that statistics students who learn the subgoals of a procedure are better at retaining and transferring their knowledge to solve novel problems [6].

Similar to subgoal learning, self-explanation also improves retention and transfer. Self-explanation helps learners use reasoning and prior knowledge to make sense of new information.

Subgoal Labeled Worked Example	Worked Example with Placeholders for Learner-Constructed Subgoal Labels
Problem: Create an app that plays a drum sound when the image of a drum is touched.	Problem: Create an app that plays a drum sound when the image of a drum is touched.
<u>Handle Event</u>	Label 1: _____
Click on "My Blocks" to see the blocks for components created	Click on "My Blocks" to see the blocks for components created
Click on "clap"	Click on "clap"
Drag out a *when clap.Touched* block	Drag out a *when clap.Touched* block
<u>Set Output</u>	Label 2: _____
Click on "clapSound"	Click on "clapSound"
Drag out *call clapSound.Play*	Drag out *call clapSound.Play*
Connect it after *when clap.Touched*	Connect it after *when clap.Touched*

Figure 1: Worked example formatted with subgoals labels (included for demonstration only, this type of example was not included in the present study) or placeholders for learners to construct labels.

Therefore, self-explaining learners construct new knowledge within mental organizations that already exist, making it easier to access later [12]. To blend these two effective learning strategies, Margulieux and Catrambone [1] examined multiple methods of guiding learners to create their own subgoal labels.

In their study using a block-based programming procedure, Margulieux and Catrambone [1] compared five types of support for learners creating their own subgoal labels. Only the two best performing types are relevant and will be discussed here. Both types looked like the right side of Figure 1. The worked example was decomposed into subgoals and a space was provided for the learner to write their own label. The learner was given some guidance on creating subgoal labels because the worked example was already subdivided into subgoals. In addition, the worked example indicated which subgoals achieved which functions. For instance, all four instances of handling an event (one instance shown in Figure 1), were prefaced with "Label 1," to indicate that they achieved the same subgoal even though the contexts were different. The difference between the two groups from Margulieux and Catrambone was that one group received hints about the function of the subgoal and the other did not. A hint pointed out the similarities among the different instances of the same subgoal. For instance, the hint for Label 1 was, "Subgoals marked with Label 1 all have to do with inputs from the user."

The other aspect of instruction that Margulieux and Catrambone [1] varied was whether learners received feedback on the labels that they had constructed. For participants who received feedback, after they had constructed their own labels, they were given another copy of the worked example that included subgoal labels constructed by the experts (left side of Figure 1). This group of participants was told that the subgoal labels were constructed by experts. They were then asked to compare their labels to those constructed by the expert to prompt them to reflect on the similarities or differences between the two. This type of feedback is different from many types of feedback that tell learners whether their answers were right or wrong, but it is similar to the typical feedback given for self-explanations [12]. Participants who did not receive feedback were asked to re-read the example after they had constructed

their own labels to make time on task more similar to that of participants who received feedback, as is common in the self-explanation literature [11]. The two groups in Margulieux and Catrambone [1] who performed best were the group that received either hints while constructing labels or feedback on their constructed labels. The groups that received both hints and feedback or received neither hints nor feedback did not perform as well. Margulieux and Catrambone [1] found that learners who received hints constructed high quality labels for themselves, as supported by qualitative data analysis of the labels collected. They argued that when learners who received hints also received feedback (an expert's explanation of the subgoals) the learners discounted the value of the labels that they had constructed and tried to learn the expert's labels - diminishing the benefits of creating their own labels. For the group that did not receive hints, the labels that they constructed were not as high in quality, making the feedback more beneficial and corrective in their construction of knowledge. This work demonstrated that guiding learners to create their own explanations of subgoals can improve their problem solving performance, but that learners performed best with just enough support and that too much or too little support hurt performance.

1.2 Instructional Intervention in the Present Study

The present research expands upon this junction of subgoal learning and self-explanation by exploring the benefits of using learner-constructed subgoal labels to scaffold initial problem solving attempts. The problem completion effect states that learners perform better on later problem solving when they receive more guidance during initial problem solving [15]. Most of the problem completion work by Sweller, Ayres, and Kalyuga used partially worked examples in which learners fill in the gaps of partially solved problems. Partially worked example are similar to a common computing education tool, practice problems that strongly resemble worked examples. The solution to the practice problem can be mostly completed by copying the steps of a worked example, but some near transfer is required to complete the solution. This experiment tested whether learner-constructed (middle column Figure 2) or expert-constructed labels (right column Figure 2) could effectively scaffold practice problems to improve later problem solving performance (i.e., assessment problems) over unscaffolded practice problems (left column Figure 2). Because Margulieux and Catrambone [1] argued that the expert-constructed labels impacted learners differently depending on whether they received hints, the current study added another manipulation: type of support received while constructing subgoal labels. For this manipulation, groups either constructed labels with hints but without feedback or they constructed labels without hints but with feedback. These two groups are the same as the best performing groups from Margulieux and Catrambone [1] discussed previously (see Table 1).

Table 1. Summary of six experimental groups

	Received Hints	Received Feedback
Unscaffolded Practice Problems	Condition 1	Condition 2
Learner-Constructed Label Scaffold	Condition 3	Condition 4
Expert-Constructed Label Scaffold	Condition 5	Condition 6

Participant performance was measured through a problem solving assessment that took place after the practice problems. This means that different groups saw different practice problem formats (though the problems were the same) and that the final test that they took was exactly the same for all participants. We expected that, if learner-constructed labels represent well-organized knowledge about the procedure, participants who received practice problems that were scaffolded with their own labels would perform better on later problem solving than those who did not receive scaffolding or those who received problems scaffolded with an expert's subgoal labels. Therefore, we hypothesized that participants who received hints while constructing labels would perform best on later problem solving when their practice problems were scaffolded with their own subgoal labels. We also expected, however, that if participants struggled to make their own labels or did not trust that their explanations were correct, then learner-constructed labels would not provide guidance during practice problems. Therefore, we hypothesized that participants who did not receive hints and

instead received feedback on their constructed labels would perform best on later problem solving when they received practice problems that were scaffolded with expert-constructed labels than practice problems scaffolded with their own labels or unscaffolded problems. Based on these hypotheses, the results of the study would provide evidence for whether scaffolding practice problems with subgoal labels improves problem solving performance *and* provide information about the quality of the labels that participants constructed.

The problem solving domain for the present study was programming. Programming instruction typically includes worked examples and practice problems in instruction. The acquisition of programming skill has been facilitated by self-explanation of goals and procedural structure [16, 17] and subgoal learning [1, 3, 4, 5, 7, 13]. Participants in the study were novice programmers to control for effects of prior knowledge. To help the novices focus on programming concepts instead of syntax, the present study used a drag-and-drop programming language. Drag-and-drop languages are more easily understood by novice learners because they can select and drag pieces of code from a menu, which does not require learning the syntax and semantics of a programming language [18, 19]. The programming language used was Android App Inventor, which is used to create applications (apps) for Android devices (see Figure 3). In the study, participants used App Inventor to create an app that has buttons that play sounds when pressed. Because the worked example was long (taking about 30-35 minutes to read through and reconstruct in the App Inventor interface), participants received only one worked example. Within the example participants saw multiple instances of each subgoal. Seeing multiple instances of subgoals is critical to constructing context-independent subgoal labels because it allows the learner to compare subgoals that achieve the same function but comprise different steps in different contexts [7].

2 METHOD

2.1 Participants

Each of the six conditions (see Table 1) had 20 participants ($N = 120$). Participants were students at a technological institute in the southeastern United States and compensated with course credit. They came from a range of academic majors and were mostly in STEM fields.

Unscaffolded Practice Problems	Learner Labeled Practice Problem	Expert Labeled Practice Problem
Problem: Create an app that plays a cymbal sound when the image of a cymbal is touched.	Problem: Create an app that plays a cymbal sound when the image of a cymbal is touched. Subgoal 1: Subgoal 2:	Problem: Create an app that plays a cymbal sound when the image of a cymbal is touched. Handle Event: Set Output:

Figure 2: Practice problems that are either unguided or guided with learner-constructed or expert-constructed labels.

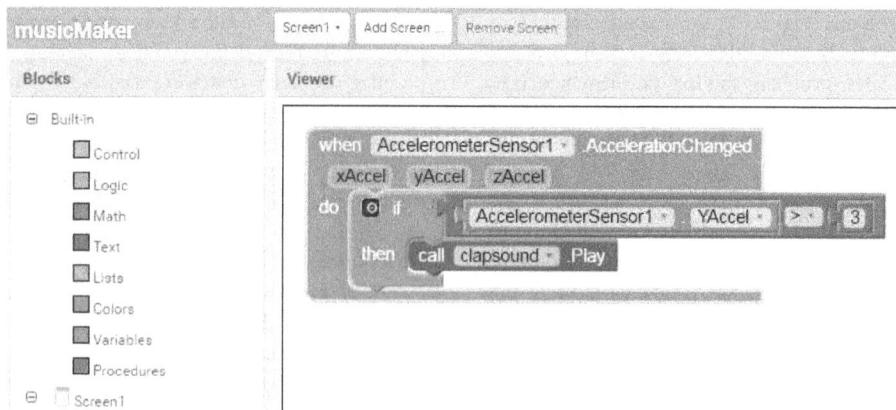

Figure 3: Screenshot of App Inventor interface with blocks pieced together from menu on the left.

Participants did not have prior experience with App Inventor. They also had not taken more than one high school or college-level course in computer science or programming. Because we collected data within the first five weeks of the semester, any current computer science courses that they were taking did not count towards this requirement. These limitations were necessary because instructional materials were designed for novices.

Demographic information was collected for participants' age, gender, academic major, high school GPA, college GPA, year in school, computer science experience, comfort with computers, and expected difficulty of learning App Inventor because they are possible predictors of performance [20]. These demographic characteristics were not found to correlate with performance (see Table 2), meaning that the interventions had an equivalent impact on all students, regardless of these personal characteristics.

2.2 Pre-instruction procedure and materials

Sessions took between 80 and 110 minutes, depending on how quickly participants completed each of the tasks. First, participants completed the demographic questionnaire, working memory measure, and pre-test, which took 10 to 15 minutes. Participants' working memory capacity was measured with the Shapebuilder task [21] because previous research has found that working memory capacity predicted success at self-explanation [12]. We used the Shapebuilder task because it closely resembles the mechanics of using a block-based programming language (i.e., dragging and dropping certain shapes that have certain colors) and, therefore, was well-suited to measuring working memory for this task. Performance on the Shapebuilder task matched the population mean and standard deviation reported in Atkins et al. [21] and was not correlated with problem solving performance (see Table 2).

In addition to the working memory measure, participants completed a multiple-choice pre-test to ensure that they did not have prior knowledge of the procedure. The five pre-test questions asked about the most basic App Inventor features to capture any rudimentary knowledge that participants had. For each question in the pre-test, one of the answer choices was "I

don't know" to avoid forcing participants to guess and introducing unnecessary error. The majority of participants (84%) scored a zero on the pre-test, and no participants scored higher than one point out of five.

2.3 Instructional procedure and materials

After the pre-instruction period, participants started the instructional period, which took 40 to 55 minutes. All manipulations occurred within the instructional period. The instructional period started with an overview video of the App Inventor interface that was the same across all participants. The purpose of this video was to introduce participants to the App Inventor interface and the types of tasks that can be completed within it. Palmiter, Elkerton, and Baggett [22] suggested that videos are a medium that help participants intuitively learn direct manipulation interfaces, like App Inventor.

After the introductory video, participants received subgoal label training. The training explained the rationale behind subgoals and then gave participants an example of subgoal labeling and an activity to help them actively learn to construct labels. In the activity, participants constructed subgoal labels for a mathematic order of operations problem and received feedback on the labels that they constructed.

Next, participants received the worked example. The worked example listed the steps taken to create a Music Maker app that plays musical sounds when images of instruments are pressed or the device is shaken. For instance, a drum sound would play when a drum image is pressed, or a tambourine sound would play when the phone is shaken. The format of the worked example depended on which group participants were randomly assigned to. The two options, based on the most effective conditions from Margulieux and Catrambone [1], were with or without hints. Both looked like the right side of Figure 1. When participants who did not receive hints finished the first pass through the worked example, they were then given the same worked example with the expert-constructed subgoal labels (feedback). Participants who received hints did not receive feedback and were instead prompted to re-read the example to maintain similar time on task between groups, as is common in the self-explanation literature [12].

Table 2: Demographic averages for participants and their correlation with problem solving performance.

	Averages		Correlations	
	M	SD	r or ρ*	p
Gender	58% male	-	.11*	.32
Age	19.6	2.2	.03	.74
Academic Major	62% engineering	-	.10*	.36
High School GPA	3.65	.26	.05	.64
Year in College	2.08	1.3	-.09	.41
College GPA	3.32	.45	.12	.27
Comfort with Computers (out of 7)	4.15	1.6	-.06	.56
Expected Difficulty (out of 7)	4.13	1.3	.04	.69
Score on Working Memory Task	1747 (normative mean = 1581)	411 (normative SD = 472)	.07	.51
Previous CS Courses	44% taken 1 course	-	.06*	.55

To give participants practice completing tasks in App Inventor before the assessments, they were asked to complete practice problems. Participants received practice problems that were unguided, guided with the subgoal labels that they had constructed, or guided with expert-constructed labels (see Figure 2), depending on which group they were randomly assigned to. Of the four practice tasks that participants completed, two required isomorphic transfer from the worked example, meaning that they used the same context and procedural steps as the worked example and differed only in surface features. For instance, the worked example showed the steps to create a drum image that plays a drum sound when pressed. An isomorphic transfer practice problem asked participants to create a cymbal image that plays a cymbal sound when pressed. The other two practice problems required contextual transfer, meaning that they used the same procedural steps as the worked example and differed in surface and contextual features. Based on the drum example, a contextual transfer practice problem asked participants to create a button that changes color when pressed. Both use an event and an outcome, but the individual steps taken to achieve the solution are different. With few exceptions, all participants were able to solve the four practice problems correctly within 8-12 minutes total. Participants were allowed to use the instructions while working on the practice problems.

2.4 Assessment procedure and materials

To measure cognitive load experienced during the instructional period, participants completed a questionnaire for measuring cognitive load induced during programming instruction that was adapted for programming and validated by Morrison, Dorn, and Guzdial [23]. This 10-item questionnaire was given directly after the instructional period, including both worked example and practice problems, to measure load during instruction. Following the cognitive load questionnaire, participants took a post-test that contained the exact same items as the pre-test. The post-test served as a learning check because the questions were about the most basic features of App Inventor. The majority of participants

(88%) scored the full five points on this post-test, and no participants scored lower than four points. Therefore, no participants were excluded from the analyses based on post-test score. Participants were also asked to rate how well they understood the instructions and how comfortable they would be solving novel problems.

After these checks, participants completed assessment tasks that measured learning. During this assessment period, participant did not have access to the instructional materials. They were told of this restriction at the beginning of the session. The first assessment was problem solving tasks that asked participants to modify or add components to their Music Maker app. Of the five tasks, two required contextual transfer from the worked example, meaning that the superficial features of the app components were different but the procedural steps used to create them were the same. The remaining three tasks required procedural transfer from the worked example, meaning that the individual steps used to create the app components were different but the procedure used to create them was structurally the same. For instance, the worked example showed steps to make a sound play when an image is clicked, and a problem solving task asked participants to make a label display text when an image is clicked. Participants had up to 25 minutes to complete all of the problem solving tasks. Similar to a test, participants did not have unlimited time to work on problems, though most participants completed the tasks on time.

2.5 Design

This study was two-by-three factorial, between-subjects design. That means that participants were assigned to one of six groups that varied on subgoal learning method (with-hints-without-feedback or without-hints-with-feedback) and scaffolding of practice problems (unguided, guided by learner-constructed subgoal labels, or guided by expert-constructed subgoal labels). Performance measurements were performance on the problem solving tasks and time on task for the assessments and for the instructional period. Demographic characteristics, working memory capacity, pre-test and post-test score, subjective cognitive load, and perception of understanding were also collected as possible predictors of performance (see Table 2 and section 3.3). The subgoal labels that participants construct were collected and analyzed for content, and quality of label was analyzed as a predictor of performance.

3 RESULTS AND DISCUSSION

The data set was analyzed to determine whether it matched a normal distribution. Both skewness (whether the bell curve is symmetrical) and kurtosis (whether the data is too concentrated around the mean or too dispersed) for all measurements were within the acceptable +/- 2 range [24, 25], meaning that they meet the normal distribution assumption for inferential statistics.

3.1 Scaffolding with learner-constructed labels improved problem solving performance

For the problem solving assessment, participants received a score for number of correct steps taken towards problem solutions. Because the tasks involved multiple steps, scoring based on steps rather than whole answers provided more sensitivity for measuring performance. The maximum possible score was 25. We report effect size in both partial η^2 (i.e., proportion of variance accounted for by treatment) and f (i.e., the difference between means using the standard deviation as the unit of measurement). For example, a partial η^2 of 0.15 means that 15% of the variance in scores is accounted for by the manipulation. A medium effect size is 0.1-0.2 with smaller numbers representing a smaller effect and larger numbers representing a larger effect. For f, a value of 0.5 means that the difference between means is half of a standard deviation. A medium effect size is 0.25-0.4 with smaller numbers representing a smaller effect and larger numbers representing a larger effect.

Practice problem scaffolding affected performance, $F(2, 114) = 9.81$, MSE = 21.5, $p < .001$, partial $\eta^2 = .15$, $f = .40$ (see Figure 4). A Bonferroni post hoc analysis was used analyze effect across the three groups. Participants who received scaffolding with their own constructed labels ($M = 21.6$, $SD = 3.86$) performed statistically better than those who received scaffolding with expert-constructed labels ($M = 17.1$, $SD = 4.95$; Mean Difference = 4.55, $p < .001$) or no scaffolding ($M = 18.8$, $SD = 3.90$; Mean Difference = 2.80, $p = .024$). Participants who received scaffolding with expert-constructed labels did not perform statistically differently from those with no scaffolding, Mean Difference = 1.75, $p = .28$. Subgoal learning method did not affect performance, $F(2, 114) = 0.19$, MSE = 21.5, $p = .67$, partial $\eta^2 = .002$, nor was there an interaction, $F(2, 114) = 1.04$, MSE = 21.5, $p = .35$, partial $\eta^2 = .02$.

These findings suggest that when learner-constructed labels are used to scaffold initial problem solving, later problem solving improves. This improvement had a relatively large effect size, meaning that the scaffolding accounts for a large portion of the differences among groups. Contrary to hypotheses, there was no difference between groups who received hints-but-not-feedback or feedback-but-not-hints. In addition, receiving expert-constructed labels as scaffolds did not improve performance. We had expected expert-constructed labels to improve performance because they provide short instructional explanations of the solution, similar to how an instructor would scaffold problems. We especially expected participants who had received expert labels as feedback to perform well because they had already seen the expert labels and thought about them in the context of the procedure. This group, however, did not perform differently from the no-feedback group, and neither of these groups performed better than the unscaffolded groups.

The conclusion that we would like to draw from these results is that expert labels, at least static ones, do not provide helpful support to learners during practice problems. Because this situation includes novice learners, who need more support than more advanced learners, it is not likely that expert labels would provide helpful support to more advanced learners either. We must temper this conclusion, however, with a limitation. The expert labels given to learners in this experiment were short, only three to five words long each. It is possible that these labels were too terse to adequately convey their meaning to learners and instead of providing instructional support, provided only ambiguous words.

We do not believe that this possibility is likely, however, because the expert labels served as effective feedback in previous research [1]; therefore, we know that learners can make sense of them and use them to improve their performance. We believe that it is more likely that connecting the practice problems to the learners' labels caused the learners to connect the practice problems to the knowledge that they had constructed while creating the labels, which was more valuable than static expert guidance. Regardless of why expert guidance was not effective, we can conclude that for learners who constructed subgoal labels with the support of hints or with the support of feedback, the two best performing conditions from previous research [1], problem solving performance can be improved by scaffolding initial problem solving with learner-constructed labels.

3.2 Quality of learner-constructed labels does not predict performance

Another surprising finding was that participants who constructed better labels did not perform better than those who constructed worse labels. The labels that participants constructed were scored as one of three types of labels: *correct and context independent*, meaning that they did not include any contextual details from the example, *correct and context dependent*, meaning that they did include contextual details, or *incorrect*, meaning that they were not based on the functions achieved in the solution (see Table 3). These categorizations are based on the qualitative analysis that Margulieux and Catrambone [1] conducted. Two raters scored labels from 20% of the participants to determine rater reliability. Interrater reliability was measured with intra-class correlation coefficient of agreement because the type of measurement was nominal and absolute agreement was necessary. Reliability was high, ICC(A) = .96, and the remaining 80% of participants were scored by one rater.

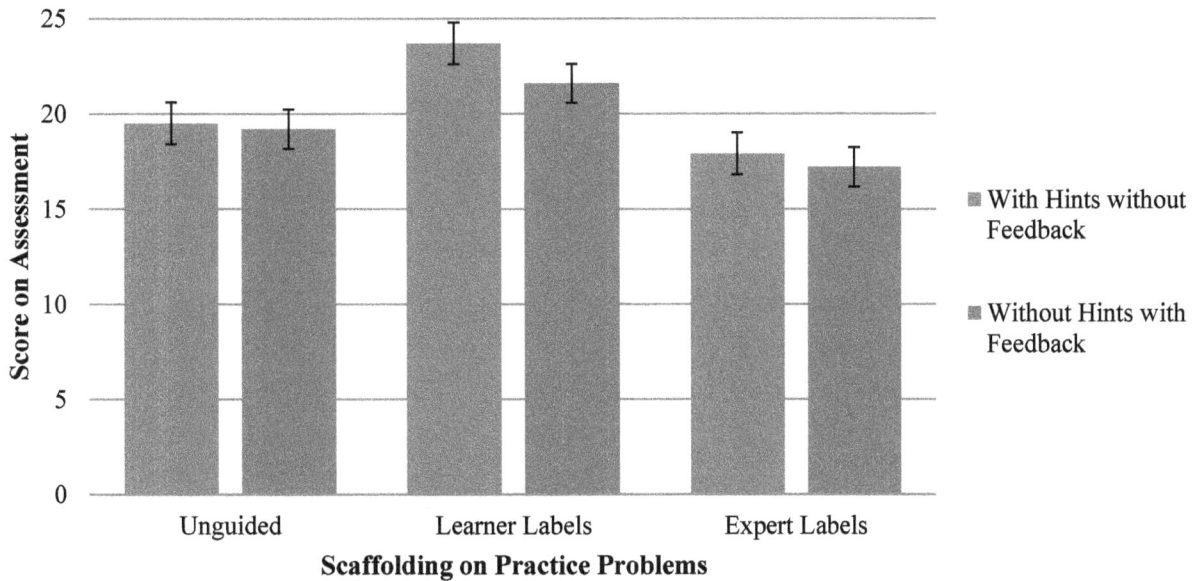

Figure 4: Problem solving performance among groups. Error bars show standard error.

Table 3: Examples of subgoal labels constructed by participants for each of the coding classifications.

Expert-Constructed Label	Context-Dependent	Context-Independent	Incorrect
Create component	Create image sprite	Add component to app	Define variable
Set properties	Name and add picture to image sprite	Edit component	Select/drag
Handle input	Add condition for when clap is touched	Add interface command	Program functions
Set output	Make clapsound play when clap is touched	Set command result	Specify function
Set conditions	Make something happen if the user moves the phone	Add command conditions	New function

Context-independent labels were considered better than context-dependent labels because they could be applied to any problem. Both types of correct labels were considered better than the non-function-based labels.

Similar to previous research [1], 75% of participants who constructed labels with hints made context-independent labels compared to 35% of participants who constructed labels without hints and made context-independent labels. Both groups made between 4% and 7% incorrect labels; therefore, most labels were correct and the main difference between groups was quality. Despite the differences in quality of subgoal labels constructed, there was not a concomitant difference in performance for those scaffolded with the labels that they had constructed, $F(2, 114) = 0.19$, MSE = 21.5, $p = .67$, partial $\eta^2 = .002$. For the learners who constructed context-dependent labels but also received feedback (i.e., context-independent expert labels), perhaps that feedback helped them to decontextualize their labels. Participants did not externally update their labels after receiving feedback, however, so we do not know how feedback changed their understanding.

Future work should explore how participants' understanding changes over time. From the cognitive psychology literature, we know that novices understand concepts differently than experts. They tend to store information about problem solving procedures with contextual details, and then latter prune that contextual information away once it has been determined to be irrelevant [26, 27, 28]. These extra steps, though inefficient from a learning perspective, are not detrimental to knowledge construction unless the learner is unable to make analogies between the contexts of an old problem and a new problem, failing to recognize that the same problem solving procedure is used to solve both [28]. In future work, participants could be asked to write notes before creating subgoal labels, create subgoal labels, and edit their labels after practice problems. We would expect that the pre-label notes, or perhaps even the first set of labels, would include contextual information that would then be removed to create an abstract label. In fact, this process of decontextualizing labels might be what our data captured but does not have the granularity to disentangle. From this perspective, it make sense that connecting practice problems to learners' constructed knowledge, whether their written labels included context or not, resulted in better learning than connecting practice problems to expert labels.

3.3 No differences in other metrics

The time that participants spent completing each part of the procedure was recorded. Participants spent an average of 34.1 minutes (SD = 5.99) completing the subgoal training and using the worked example to construct subgoal labels. This time was not problems, $F(2, 114)$ = 1.12, MSE = 10.4, p = .33, subgoal learning method, $F(2, 114)$ = 0.37, MSE = 10.4, p = .54, nor an interaction, $F(2, 114)$ = 0.65, MSE = 10.4, p = .52, meaning that the different conditions under which participants solved practice problems did not affect the amount of time it took them to complete the practice problems. During the problem solving assessment, participants took an average of 23.2 minutes (SD = 2.58). This time was not affected by scaffolding on practice problems, $F(2, 114)$ = 0.51, MSE = 6.79, p = .61, subgoal learning method, $F(2, 114)$ = 0.34, MSE = 6.79, p = .56, nor an interaction, $F(2, 114)$ = 0.87, MSE = 6.79, p = .42. Therefore, the participants who had practice problems scaffolded with their own labels performed better on the problem solving assessment than participants in other conditions but did not take longer to complete the practice problems or the assessment.

After the instructional period, participants rated how well they understood the instructions from "1 – Not well at all" to "7 – Very well." Participants rated that they understood the instructions well (M = 6.00, SD = 0.98). These ratings were not affected by the scaffolding of practice problems, $F(2, 114)$ = 1.99, MSE = 0.96, p = .14, subgoal learning method, $F(2, 114)$ = 0.54, MSE = 0.96, p = .47, nor the interaction of both, $F(2, 114)$ = 0.61, MSE = 0.96, p = .55. Participants also rated how comfortable they were solving novel problems using the procedure from "1 – Not comfortable at all" to "7 – Very comfortable." Participants rated that they were comfortable solving new problems (M = 5.75, SD = 1.0). These ratings were not affected by the scaffolding of practice problems, $F(2, 114)$ = 2.44, MSE = 1.08, p = .09, subgoal learning method, $F(2, 114)$ = 0.21, MSE = 1.08, p = .65, nor the interaction of both, $F(2, 114)$ = 0.07, MSE = 1.08, p = .93. These results indicate that, on average, participants in different conditions felt equally prepared to solve novel problems regardless of the scaffolding that they received when solving the practice problems or the method by which they learned subgoals.

No differences were found among the groups for participants' self-reported cognitive load, which was measured after the instructional period and before the problem solving assessment. Out of a possible rating of 100, the mean score was 39.7 (SD = 12.1). This rating was not affect by scaffolding on practice problems, $F(2, 114)$ = 0.85, MSE = 155.4, p = .43, subgoal learning method, $F(2, 114)$ = 0.37, MSE = 155.4, p = .54, nor an interaction, $F(2, 114)$ = 0.20, MSE = 155.4, p = .82. These results suggest that participants did not perceive differences in cognitive load among the conditions.

4   CONCLUSIONS

The superior performance by participants who received their own subgoal labels as scaffolds provides evidence that participants can construct their own high-quality subgoal labels. Furthermore, those subgoal labels represent an effective mental organization of information that can be applied as effective scaffolds to practice problems. Effective scaffolds help students to apply procedural knowledge to novel problems [29], and if learner-constructed labels can serve this purpose, then they must have been high quality. In addition, when learners constructed their own subgoal labels, scaffolding practice problems with expert-constructed labels did not improve performance over unguided practice problems, suggesting that the expert-constructed labels did not help guide participant problem solving. Imposing expert-constructed labels on participants who had developed their own effective organization of the procedure did not seem to help the participants in any way.

This finding is similar to findings from the memory literature on subjective organization. In the subjective organization research, people are better able to recall words when they use their own method of organizing the words than when given a prescribed organization (e.g., told to recall the words in alphabetical order; 30). In the subjective organization literature, the words being memorized are unrelated, meaning that there is not a correct way to organize them. In the present study, however, there was a correct conceptual understanding of the procedure, making the similarity in results interesting because it suggests that the learner's organization can guide the learner better than an expert's organization, even when there are incorrect ways of organizing information. This finding implies that learners' organizations of knowledge are as effective as the organization provided by the instructional designer or that learners' organizations are better for guiding problem solving even if they are different from the instructional designer's organization. The finding is especially valuable for people who have prior knowledge, views of knowledge, or strategies for learning that are different than the instructional designers'.

In summary, scaffolding learners' first attempts at problem solving with subgoal labels that they constructed while studying worked examples can improve later problem solving performance compared to unguided or expert-guided initial problem solving attempts. The quality of the subgoal labels constructed by learners were not a significant predictor of problem solving success. Therefore, it might be the case that learners can create labels that are beneficial to them but that an instructional designer would not recognize as a good label. This disconnect between labels that are beneficial to learners and those that a designer would consider beneficial might be due to prior knowledge of the learner or differences in mental organization. In this case, it is possible that prompting and supporting students to create their own labels can better support a more diverse group of learners than designing instructions from the perspective of one (or even several) instructional designer(s). This support of a wider range of students might also explain Margulieux and Catrambone's [1] results that learners who received support while creating their own labels performed better than learners who did not construct their own labels or those who made their own labels but without support.

5 ACKNOWLEDGMENTS

Our thanks to the reviewers who helped to improve this paper. We also thank Mark Guzdial and Briana Morrison for their help in guiding this research.

6 REFERENCES

[1] Margulieux, L. E., & Catrambone, R. (2016). Using subgoal learning and self-explanation to improve programming education. In, Proceedings of the 38th Annual Conference of the Cognitive Science Society (pp. 2009-2014). Austin, TX: Cognitive Science Society.

[2] Margulieux, L. E., & Catrambone, R. (2016b). Improving problem solving with subgoal labels in expository text and worked examples. Learning and Instruction, 42, 58-71. doi: 10.1016/j.learninstruc.2015.12.002

[3] Margulieux, L. E., Guzdial, M., & Catrambone, R. (2012). Subgoal-labeled instructional material improves performance and transfer in learning to develop mobile applications. Proceedings of the Ninth Annual International Conference on International Computing Education Research (pp. 71-78). New York, NY: Association for Computing Machinery. doi: 10.1145/2361276.2361291

[4] Morrison, B. B., Margulieux, L. E., & Guzdial, M. (2015, July). Subgoals, context, and worked examples in learning computing problem solving. In Proceedings of the Eleventh Annual International Conference on International Computing Education Research (pp. 21-29). ACM.

[5] Morrison, B. B., Margulieux, L. E., Ericson, B., & Guzdial, M. (2016, February). Subgoals help students solve Parsons problems. In Proceedings of the 47th ACM Technical Symposium on Computing Science Education (pp. 42-47). ACM.

[6] Catrambone, R. (1998). The subgoal learning model: Creating better examples so that students can solve novel problems. Journal of Experimental Psychology: General, 127(4), 355-376. doi: 10.1037/0096-3445.127.4.355

[7] Margulieux, L. E., Catrambone, R., & Guzdial, M. (2016). Employing subgoals in computer programming education. Computer Science Education, 26(1), 44-67. doi: 10.1080/08993408.2016.1144429

[8] Catrambone, R. (2011). Task analysis by problem solving (TAPS): Uncovering expert knowledge to develop high-quality instructional materials and training. Paper presented at the 2011 Learning and Technology Symposium (Columbus, GA, June).

[9] Kim, J., Miller, R. C., & Gajos, K. Z. (2013, April). Learnersourcing subgoal labeling to support learning from how-to videos. In CHI'13 Extended Abstracts on Human Factors in Computing Systems (pp. 685-690). ACM.

[10] Weir, S., Kim, J., Gajos, K. Z., & Miller, R. C. (2015, February). Learnersourcing subgoal labels for how-to videos. In Proceedings of the 18th ACM Conference on Computer Supported Cooperative Work & Social Computing (pp. 405-416). ACM.

[11] Chi, M. T. H., de Leeuw, N., Chiu, M., & LaVancher, C. (1994). Eliciting self-explanations improves understanding. Cognitive Science, 18(3), 439-477.

[12] Wylie, R., & Chi, M. T. H. (2014). The self-explanation principle in multimedia learning. In R. Mayer (Ed.) The Cambridge Handbook of Multimedia Learning, 2nd Edition (pp.413-432). Cambridge University Press.

[13] Morrison, B. B., Decker, A., & Margulieux, L. E. (2016b). Learning loops: A replication study illuminates impact of HS courses. In Proceedings of the Twelfth Annual International Conference on International Computing Education Research (pp. 221-230). New York, NY: Association for Computing Machinery. doi: 10.1145/2960310.2960330

[14] Margulieux, L. E., Morrison, B. B., Guzdial, M., & Catrambone, R. (2016b). Training learners to self-explain: Designing instructions and examples to improve problem solving. In Proceedings of Transforming Learning, Empowering Learners: The International Conference of the Learning Sciences (ICLS) 2016. International Society of the Learning Sciences [online].

[15] Sweller, J. (2010). Element interactivity and intrinsic, extraneous, and germane cognitive load. Educational Psychology Review, 22(2), 123-138.

[16] Soloway, E. (1986). Learning to program = learning to construct mechanisms and explanations. Communications of the ACM, 29(9), 850-858.

[17] Pirolli, P., & Recker, M. (1994). Learning strategies and transfer in the domain of programming. Cognition and Instruction, 12(3), 235-275.

[18] Grover, S., & Pea, R. (2013). Computational Thinking in K-12: A Review of the State of the Field. Educational Researcher, 42(1), 38–43. https://doi.org/10.3102/0013189X12463051

[19] Hundhausen, C. D., Farley, S. F., & Brown, J. L. (2009). Can direct manipulation lower the barriers to computer programming and promote transfer of training?: An experimental study. ACM Transactions in CHI, 16(3). doi:10.1145/1592440.1592442

[20] Rountree, N., Rountree, J., Robins, A., & Hannah, R. (2004). Interacting factors that predict success and failure in a CSI course. SIGCSE Bulletin, 33(4), pp 101-104.

[21] Atkins, S. M., Sprenger, A. M., Colflesh, G. J. H., Briner, T. L., Buchanan, J. B., Chavis, S. E., ... Dougherty, M. R. (2014). Measuring working memory is all fun and games: A four-dimensional spatial game predicts cognitive task performance. Experimental Psychologist, 61(6), 417-438.

[22] Palmiter, S., Elkerton, J., & Baggett, P. (1991). Animated demonstrations versus written instructions for learning procedural tasks: A preliminary investigation. Int. Journal of Man-Machine Studies, 34, 687-701.

[23] Morrison, B. B., Dorn, B., & Guzdial, M. (2014). Measuring cognitive load in introductory CS: adaptation of an instrument. In Proceedings of the 10th Annual Conference on ICER, 131–138.

[24] Gravetter, F., & Wallnau, L. (2014). Essentials of statistics for the behavioral sciences (8th ed.). Belmont, CA: Wadsworth.

[25] Trochim, W. M., & Donnelly, J. P. (2006). The research methods knowledge base (3rd ed.). Cincinnati, OH:Atomic Dog.

[26] Bransford, J. D., Brown, A. L., & Cocking, R. R. (2000). How people learn.

[27] Anderson, J. R., Bothell, D., Byrne, M. D., Douglass, S., Lebiere, C., & Qin, Y. (2004). An integrated theory of the mind. Psychological review, 111(4), 1036.

[28] Chi, M. T., Feltovich, P. J., & Glaser, R. (1981). Categorization and representation of physics problems by experts and novices. Cognitive science, 5(2), 121-152.

[29] Pea, R. D. (2004). The social and technological dimensions of scaffolding and related theoretical concepts for learning, education, and human activity. The journal of the learning sciences, 13(3), 423-451.

[30] Tulving, E. (1962). Subjective organization in free recall of "unrelated" words. Psych. Review, 69(4), 344-354.

Students' Emotional Reactions to Programming Projects in Introduction to Programming: Measurement Approach and Influence on Learning Outcomes

Alex Lishinski
Michigan State University
East Lansing, Michigan
lishinsk@msu.edu

Aman Yadav
Michigan State University
East Lansing, Michigan
ayadav@msu.edu

Richard Enbody
Michigan State University
East Lansing, Michigan
enbody@cse.msu.edu

ABSTRACT

Previous research has found that programming assignments can produce strong emotional reactions in introductory programming students. These emotional reactions often have to do with the frustration of dealing with difficulties and how hard it can be to overcome problems. Not only are these emotional reactions powerful in and of themselves, they have also been shown to induce students to make self-efficacy judgments, which can in turn cause adaptive or maladaptive behaviors, depending on the valence of the judgment. These results have been found in previous qualitative research in programming, however, to date no one has done a larger scale quantitative examination of emotional reactions in introductory programming students. Furthermore, no one has tried to connect these emotional reactions systematically to student learning outcomes. Therefore, this study reports on the pilot use of a basic emotional reactions survey with a large class of undergraduate introductory programming students. Preliminary results are presented on how these emotional reactions affect students' course outcomes over the short and longer term.

KEYWORDS
CS1, Emotions

1 INTRODUCTION

Educational psychology provides many theoretical constructs for understanding how students learn, which can deepen our understanding of how students learn to program, but CS education research has largely neglected to draw upon them [1][23]. One example of this neglect is in the domain of students' affective experiences, which are an important part of the learning process in any subject. Emotional reactions are one such affective construct with a basis in educational psychology research, but which has not been examined much in the context of learning to program. Some qualitative research in CS education has investigated the role of emotional reactions and found some significant commonalities in the ways that

students experience learning to program emotionally [11][12][13]. However, a broader quantitative examination of these constructs is still non-existent.

Students' emotions while doing academic tasks have been studied in a variety of settings, and have been shown to be connected to other affective characteristics (such as self-efficacy) as well as academic outcomes [14]. One study found that emotions experienced while doing homework assignments were different from emotions experienced in the classroom, and that homework emotions were linked to academic self-concept and achievement outcomes [9]. Another study found that unpleasant emotions during homework sessions was negatively related to both effort and achievement, and that unpleasant emotions were related to the perceived quality of the homework assignment [7]. Previous research related to non-routine problem solving found a significant influence of emotions on students' self-regulation during problem solving tasks [10]. Given the salience of emotional episodes particular to programming, as documented by Kinnunen and Simon, as well as the significant impact of emotions on academic outcomes generally, the topic of students' emotional reactions to programming projects merits further investigation.

1.1 Emotional Reactions and the CS Gender Participation Gap

Prior research on gender participation gap in CS has indicated that part of the explanation for the gap may have to do students' affective experiences, because male and female students have been found to differ in their affective experiences, both in CS and across academic settings. For example, girls have been found to have lower self-efficacy than boys in math and science, despite no prior differences on aptitude or performance [17]. Likewise, female students in computer science have lower self-efficacy and comfort levels than their male peers [3][5]. Research has also suggested that there are differences in attributions of success between genders, with female students being more likely than male students to attribute success in CS to luck rather than ability [30][6].

Previous research has also indicated that the affective factors that influence success may differ between male and female students. For example, women's performance in CS courses is significantly related to comfort level and perceptions of gender equity, which is not the case for male students [3][2]. Likewise, differences in emotional reactions between genders have been found in other settings, with previous studies finding that female students felt less pride and greater shame in response to their work in a math class than their male peers [26]. Given these indications of the importance of affective experiences and the importance of the gender gap in CS education research, gender differences in emotional reactions also merit further investigation.

1.2 Research Questions

- RQ1: What are the connections between students' emotional reactions to programming projects and their performance on those projects?
- RQ2: Which emotional reactions are most significantly related to programming project outcomes?
- RQ3: Are there any gender differences in students' emotional reactions to programming projects?
- RQ4: Do students' emotional reactions to programming projects indirectly affect later programming performance?

2 LITERATURE REVIEW

2.1 Emotional Reactions in CS Education Research

The emotional experiences students have while learning to program and their influence on students' learning are the major focus of this study. In a series of studies, Kinnunen and Simon offered a detailed qualitative account of students' emotional experiences while working on programming assignments using data from open-ended interviews [11][12][13]. Their study was informed by earlier work of Eckerdal et al. which examined CS threshold concepts, which are core disciplinary concepts around which curriculum should be organized [16], but are often troublesome to learn [8]. One of the questions investigated by Eckerdal et al. [8] was: what emotional reactions do students express when learning threshold concepts? Through interviews they learned that students often felt frustrated, depressed, and humbled, but also eventually became confident, when they had succeeded in grasping the concept. The goal of Kinnunen and Simon's study was to further investigate the common emotional experiences of programming students [11]. Kinnunen and Simon's initial interviews elicited high level reflections from students at the end of the first year of starting a programming course [11]. It is important to note that Kinnunen and Simon did not have access to students' immediate emotional reactions to the programming projects, because they interviewed students at the end of the term. The authors narrowed the emotions of interest down to five categories: Proud/Accomplished, Frustrated/Annoyed, Inadequate/Disappointed, Relaxed/Relief, and Apprehensive/Reluctant. They also identified an overall emotional trajectory that was a prototype of what students generally experienced, highlighting the most emotionally salient events. The authors found that students often felt unsure when beginning an assignment, which often caused them to make negative self-efficacy judgments of themselves. Next, after working for a while, students inevitably encountered difficulties, which often caused a unique sort of emotional reaction. Kinnunen and Simon described this as the "struck by lightning" experience, which is characterized by difficulties that were very surprising to students. The authors found that this rapid change of emotion when experiencing a difficulty often led to negative self-efficacy assessments.

2.1.1 Emotional Reactions and Self-efficacy. Kinnunen and Simon's initial study found general patterns of students' emotional reactions to programming assignments, but there was one important commonality to all students' experiences [11]. Students made self-efficacy assessments as a result of their emotional reactions when working on programming assignments. Based on this observation, Kinnunen and Simon followed up with a study that examined how students' emotional reactions influenced their self-efficacy assessments [12]. The results suggested that both positive and negative programming experiences could result in either positive or negative self-efficacy assessments. The combination of positive experiences and positive self-efficacy judgment and negative experiences with negative self-efficacy judgments were unsurprising. However, students also made counterintuitive self-efficacy assessments in some situations. For example, the authors found that some students who had a negative programming experience could maintain a positive self-efficacy judgment, being confident that they would eventually get it, despite current difficulties. By contrast, students who had a positive programming experience, such as finishing the project, may have also received other cues that led them to maintain a negative self-efficacy assessment. Based on their observations in this study, Kinnunen and Simon made a number of recommendations to help students avoid difficulties due to negative self-efficacy judgments. For example, they recommended that programming instructors avoid inducing repeated failures early on in the learning experience [12].

The connection between emotional reactions and self-efficacy is important because of the known influence of self-efficacy on students' academic success, which has been well documented in many subject areas, such as mathematics [18], science [4], and language arts [19]. Self-efficacy has also been shown to be related to resiliency in response to complex and difficult tasks [25].

Self-efficacy has also been found to significantly influence success in CS [28][31][22]. Furthermore, previous work in CS education has suggested that self-efficacy beliefs function as a reciprocal feedback loop [15]. This suggests that emotional reactions, by influencing self-efficacy judgments, could have longer term impacts on students' learning outcomes. Given the documented importance of self-efficacy, emotional reactions merit further investigation as possible precursors to self-efficacy that can help us better understand the process by which self-efficacy beliefs are formed.

3 PURPOSE AND GOALS OF STUDY

The purpose of this study is to provide a quantitative exploration of students' emotional reactions when doing programming assignments in CS1. The previous qualitative work by Kinnunen and Simon provided an informative picture of typical emotional reactions that students have when doing programming assignments, but it remains unclear what impact these emotional reactions have on students' learning outcomes, and what patterns emerge when examining these emotional reactions with a larger set of students. Given the previously observed influence of affective experiences in explaining student outcomes as well as the under-explored but promising usefulness of affective experiences for explaining the gender participation gap, emotional reactions merit further study.

The goal of this study is to pilot an emotional reactions survey administered concurrently with students' programming project experiences. The questions seek to measure the most important categories of emotional reactions identified by Kinnunen and Simon, but to do so in the most valid way possible by measuring students' emotions as part of their programming project experiences. This study then seeks to connect students' emotional reactions with their learning outcomes, and to investigate their relative importance in influencing these outcomes. The overall goal for these analyses is to provide a clearer picture of the impact of these emotional experiences.

4 METHODS

4.1 Participants and Setting

This study investigated students' emotional reactions to programming assignments with a sample of 388 students enrolled in an introductory programming course (CS1) at a large research university. The sample included 302 (77.8%) male students, and 86 (22.2%) female students. The course was taught in a flipped format where students watched video lectures and attended lab sessions with a TA to complete lab exercises.

4.2 Measurement Approach

The data for this study was collected using a set of 4 self-report Likert items. Three of these four items were devised specifically for this study to measure students' emotional reactions to working on programming assignments. The three items were written based on Kinnunen and Simon's qualitative research, which identified five main categories of emotions that students used to describe their emotions while doing programming assignments [11]. These categories included: happy/proud, frustrated/annoyed, inadequate/disappointed, relaxed/relief, and tired/apprehensive. Of these five categories of student emotions, the first three were used as the basis for the emotional response survey. This was done to keep the survey very brief, and also because the final two categories seemed somewhat redundant. Students were asked to respond to these questions on a 7-point Likert scale indicating the degree to which their experiences working on the project made them feel proud, frustrated, and inadequate. The fourth item was taken from the self-efficacy sub-scale of the Motivated Strategies for Learning Questionnaire (MSLQ) [20]. The self-efficacy item was included due to the intertwined nature of emotional reactions and self-efficacy [12], and in order to provide a known basis for comparison for the emotion question data. The self-efficacy item used the prompt *"Considering the difficulty of the course, the teacher, and my skills, I think I will do well in this class."* This item was chosen because it had a high correlations with the MSLQ self-efficacy scale as a whole (Pintrich et al. 1993), and it was administered on a 7 point likert scale. The 4 questions are included in appendix A.

4.3 Programming Learning Outcomes

The course grade consisted of 3 multiple choice examinations (2 midterm and 1 final), which made up 45% of the course grade, 11 programming projects, which made up 45% of the course grade, and homework exercises, which made up 10% of the course grade. The analysis for this study focused on the project grades because

the study examined students' emotional reactions to programming assignments specifically, which also provide a deeper look at students' understanding of programming. The projects were graded according to a rubric that varied from project to project, but included some common themes such as correct coding format, and correct implementation of subcomponents of the program.

5 DATA COLLECTION AND ANALYSIS

The four questions were administered to all students nine times over the semester by instructing students to insert their responses as a comment at the bottom of their project source code file for projects 3-11. This was done in order to gauge emotional reactions as close to the actual experience as possible.

To answer the research questions of this study, several statistical analyses were done. All analyses were performed in R version 3.2.3 [21], with plots produced by the ggplot2 package [29] and the DiagrammeR package [27], and structural equation models done using the lavaan package [24].

To determine the connections between the emotional reactions and students' project scores, Pearson correlation coefficients are reported for each of the nine repeated measures of the four emotional reaction questions with their corresponding project scores.

To determine whether gender differences exist on emotional reactions, the mean differences between male and female students across the nine repeated measures are reported for each of the four emotional reaction questions, along with the statistical significance of these differences drawn from t-tests.

To determine which of the emotional reaction questions had the largest influence on student learning outcomes, a multiple regression analysis was conducted. Mean emotional reactions were combined from across the nine repeated measures, and the influence of these four average emotional reactions on total programming project scores was assessed with the regression model; regression coefficients and variance explained are reported.

Finally, to determine whether students' emotional reactions had a significant impact on their later project performance, mediation analysis was conducted for each of the four emotional reactions. Each of the emotional reaction questions were analyzed for their short and long term impact on students' programming outcomes using path analysis models, taking account of both direct and indirect effects of emotional reactions while controlling for previous project performance.

6 RESULTS

6.1 Descriptive Statistics

To determine the connection between emotional reactions and project scores, Pearson correlations were calculated. The correlations between emotional response questions and their corresponding project are shown in table 1.

The correlations between the emotional reaction questions and the project scores supported the face validity of the questions, with the correlations for the proud and self-efficacy (will do well) questions being consistently positive, and the correlations for the frustrated and inadequate questions being consistently negative. Furthermore, the correlations were statistically significant in almost

Table 1: Correlations Between Project Scores and Emotional Response Questions

	Frustrated	Proud	Inadequate	Self-Eff.
P3	-0.31 ***	0.09	-0.25 ***	0.29 ***
P4	-0.19 *	0.23 **	-0.21 **	0.22 **
P5	-0.09	0.4 ***	-0.12 .	0.29 ***
P6	-0.18 **	0.18 **	-0.24 ***	0.22 ***
P7	-0.2 **	0.38 ***	-0.16 *	0.4 ***
P8	-0.16 *	0.03	-0.13 .	0.14 *
P9	-0.3 ***	0.47 ***	-0.34 ***	0.37 ***
P10	-0.24 **	0.43 ***	-0.27 ***	0.41 ***
P11	0.07	0.1	-0.01	0.13

Will Do Well Means by Gender

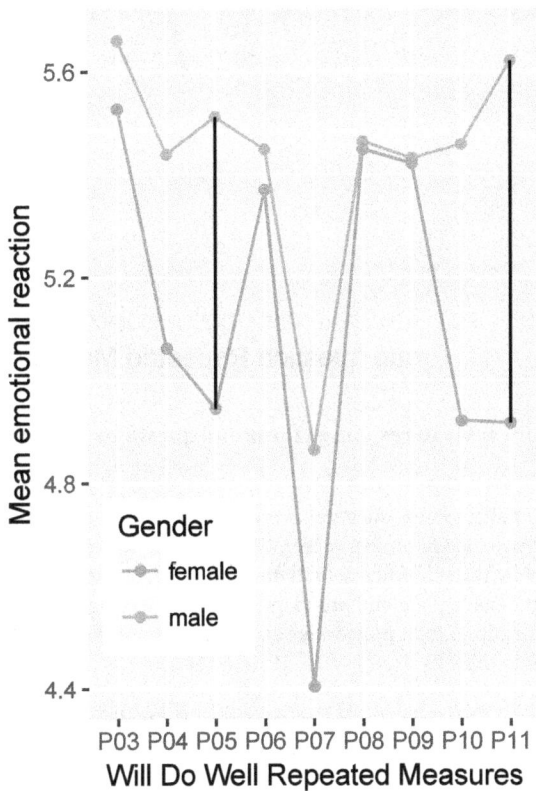

Figure 1: Mean responses for self-efficacy (will do well) questions by gender. Black bars indicate significant mean differences (p<.05)

every instance, which is evidence supporting the robustness of these relationships.

6.1.1 Gender Differences in Emotional Reactions. The levels of the emotional reactions were examined for differences between male and female students. The mean differences for each of the repeated measures of the questions are shown in figures 1-4. Figure 1 shows the gender mean differences for the self-efficacy (will do

Frustrated Means by Gender

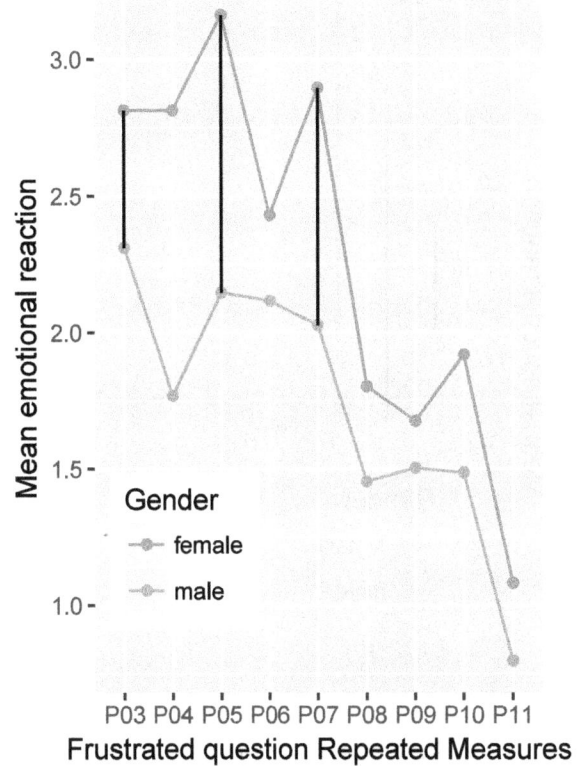

Figure 2: Mean responses for frustrated questions by gender. Black bars indicate significant mean differences (p<.05)

well) question. In every instance of the self-efficacy question, male students rated themselves on average more likely to do well than did female students, but only 2 of these differences were statistically significant.

Figure 2 shows the gender mean differences for the frustrated questions. In every instance of the frustrated questions, male students rated themselves as feeling less frustrated than female students on average. These differences were statistically significant in three instances, all in the first half of the course, after which male and female reported frustration levels converged while both decreased substantially over time.

Figure 3 shows the gender mean differences for the inadequate questions. In every instance of the inadequate questions, female students rated themselves as feeling more inadequate than male students on average. These differences were statistically significant in the first three instances of the question, after which male and female reported inadequacy levels converged as both decreased substantially over time.

Figure 4 shows the gender mean difference for the proud questions. The proud questions showed no significant differences by gender.

Inadequate Means by Gender

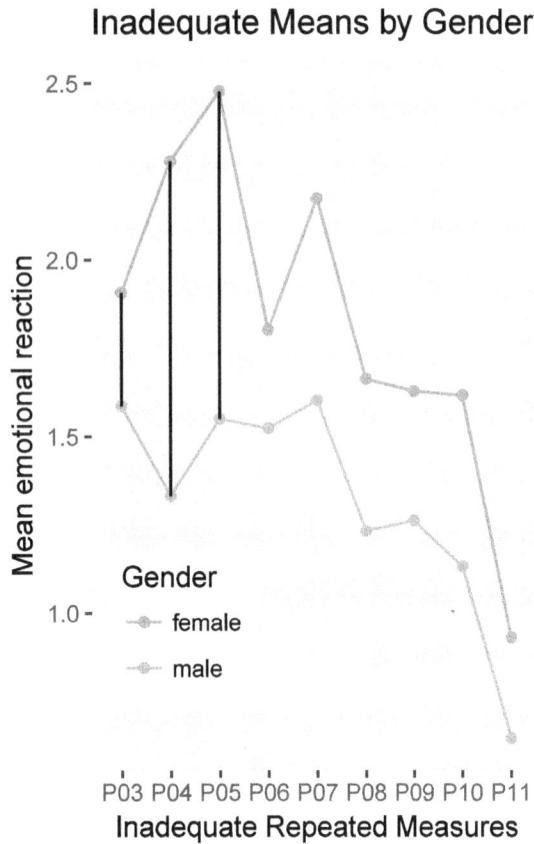

Proud Means by Gender

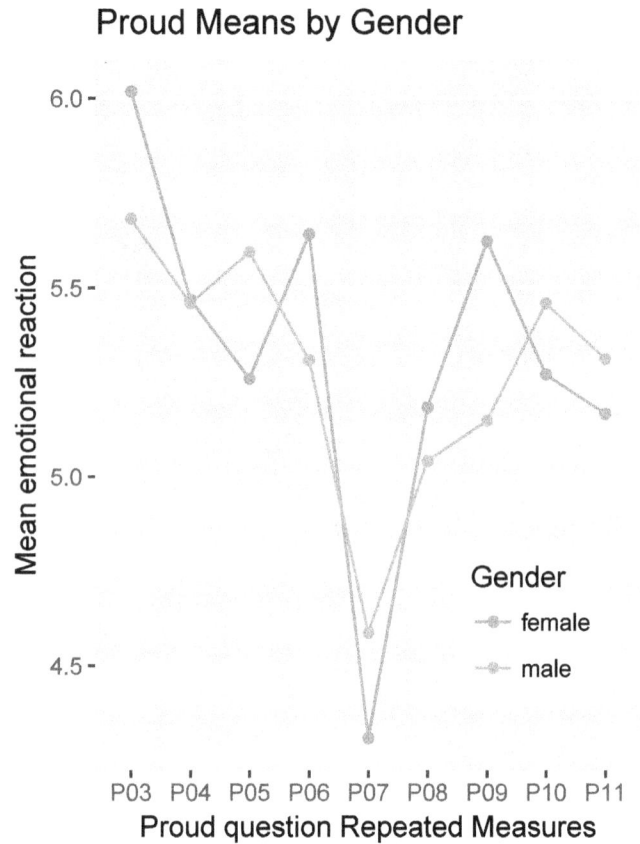

Figure 3: Mean responses for inadequate questions by gender. Black bars indicate significant mean differences (p<.05)

Figure 4: Mean responses for proud questions by gender.

Overall these results do not warrant any strong general conclusions about gender differences in emotional reactions, but the significant takeaway is that for three of the four questions, male and female students showed consistently different levels of emotional reactions, even though most of these differences were not significant. Also of note is the fact that for the two negative emotions (frustration and inadequacy), the largest differences between male and female students came at the beginning of the course. This pattern fits with findings from previous research showing that the affective component of the experience of learning to program has a greater influence at the beginning of the course [12], particularly for female students [15]. At the very least, these results suggest that further investigation of the differences between male and female students' affective experiences while learning to program is warranted.

6.2 Regression Analysis

Multiple regression analysis was conducted to determine how much variance in overall project scores was explained by the emotional reaction questions. The outcome was total project scores, and the independent variables were the average over all the repeated measures of the emotional reaction questions for each student. The four

emotional response question averages explained a total of 16.5% of the variance in project scores. This variance was explained primarily by the self-efficacy (will do well) and frustrated questions, with the inadequate and proud questions not having a significant relationship to total project scores. The regression coefficients are shown in table 2.

Table 2: Multiple Regression: Overall Project Scores Regressed on Aggregate Emotional Reaction Scores

	Coef.	Std. Coef.	Std. Err	p-value	sig.
(Intercept)	305.87	0.00	37.19	0.0000	***
Self-efficacy	17.79	0.26	4.83	0.0003	***
Frustrated	-14.62	-0.22	4.92	0.0032	**
Inadequate	2.76	0.04	4.99	0.5800	
Proud	4.51	0.06	4.48	0.3151	

Overall, these results show that certain aspects of students' emotional reactions to programming assignments are more important than others. Students' confidence that they will do well had a positive impact on outcomes, which corresponds to what prior research says about the importance of self-efficacy. Results also suggested that students' frustration with the assignment has a strong negative

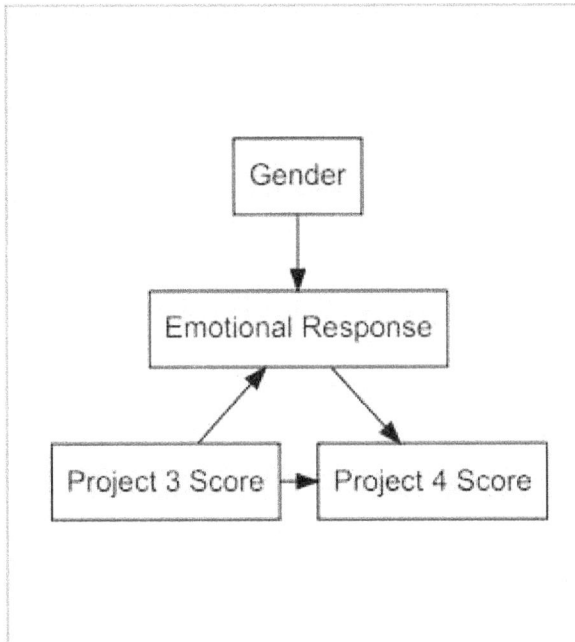

Figure 5: Path Model for Short Term Effects of Emotional Responses on Project Scores

influence on outcomes. The data does not warrant any conclusions about why frustration had more of an influence than feelings of inadequacy or pride, but perhaps frustration is a feeling that is more immediate to the experience of programming, so when students were asked at the end of the experience to assess this feeling, they were more able to do so, whereas the feeling of inadequacy and pride were more removed from the experience which became more distinct with reflection.

6.3 Path Analysis Models

Path analysis models were used to perform mediation analysis to determine whether or not emotional reactions mediated the relationship between past performance and future performance. The hypothesis was that performance on a project would have a direct and indirect effect on future performance. A direct effect corresponds to the influence of the programming competency that the student has gleaned from the earlier assignment. Indirect effects, on the other hand, would indicate that performance on the earlier assignment caused an emotional reaction, which then in turn affected future performance

The direct and indirect effects of each of the four emotional reactions were investigated both in the short and long term. To test these two possible relationships, two mediation model specifications were used for each emotional reaction. First, to investigate short term effects, the emotional reactions from project 3 (the first time that the emotional reaction questions were asked) were tested for direct and indirect effects on project 4 scores. The model specification included direct effects of both project 3 and the emotional reaction question on project 4, as well as the indirect effect of project 3 on project 4, mediated by the emotional reaction. The model is

shown in figure 5. The impact of gender on the emotional reaction question was also included to control for any gender differences. The direct and indirect effects for each of the 4 emotional reactions are shown in tables 3-6. All coefficients shown are standardized.

Table 3 shows the short term effects of the self-efficacy (will do well) question. The direct effect of the will do well question was significant, and about 25% the size of the effect of project 3. The indirect effect of the will do well question was not significant.

Table 3: Short term direct and indirect effects of self-efficacy (will do well question): standardized path coefficients

Dep. Var.	Indep. Var.	Coef.	SE	Z	p-value
Proj 4	Proj 3 (direct)	0.33	0.06	5.30	0.00
Self-Eff_3	Proj 3	0.28	0.06	4.66	0.00
Self-Eff_3	Gender	-0.04	0.06	-0.59	0.55
Proj 4	Self-Efficacy_3	0.08	0.06	1.35	0.18
Proj 4	Proj 3 (indirect)	0.02	0.02	1.30	0.19
Proj 4	Proj 3 (total)	0.35	0.06	5.91	0.00

Table 4 shows the short term effects of the frustrated question. The direct effect of the frustrated question was significant, and about 60% of the size of the effect of project 3. The indirect effect of the frustrated question was also significant, indicating that students' frustration with project 3 negatively impacted their outcomes on project 4.

Table 4: Short term direct and indirect effects of feelings of frustration: standardized path coefficients

Dep. Var.	Indep. Var.	Coef.	SE	Z	p-value
Proj 4	Proj 3 (direct)	0.29	0.06	4.56	0.00
frust_3	Proj 3	-0.30	0.06	-5.08	0.00
frust_3	Gender	0.18	0.06	2.95	0.00
Proj 4	frust_3	-0.14	0.06	-2.25	0.02
Proj 4	Proj 3 (indirect)	-0.04	0.02	-2.06	0.04
Proj 4	Proj 3 (total)	0.24	0.07	3.40	0.00

Table 5 shows the short term effects of the inadequate question. Neither the direct or indirect effects of the inadequate question were significant, indicating that students sense of inadequacy after project 3 had no impact on their performance on project 4.

Table 5: Short term direct and indirect effects of feelings of inadequacy: standardized path coefficients

Dep. Var.	Indep. Var.	Coef.	SE	Z	p-value
Proj 4	Proj 3 (direct)	0.30	0.06	4.77	0.00
inadeq_3	Proj 3	-0.25	0.06	-4.07	0.00
inadeq_3	Gender	0.12	0.06	1.90	0.06
Proj 4	inadeq_3	-0.10	0.06	-1.62	0.11
Proj 4	Proj 3 (indirect)	-0.02	0.02	-1.50	0.13
Proj 4	Proj 3 (total)	0.27	0.07	3.99	0.00

Table 6 shows the short term effects of the proud question. Neither the direct or indirect effects of the proud question were significant, indicating that students sense of pride after project 3 had no impact on their performance on project 4.

Table 6: Short term direct and indirect effects of feelings of pride: standardized path coefficients

Dep. Var.	Indep. Var.	Coef.	SE	Z	p-value
Proj 4	Proj 3 (direct)	0.29	0.06	4.73	0.00
proud_3	Proj 3	0.09	0.06	1.37	0.17
proud_3	Gender	0.10	0.06	1.64	0.10
Proj 4	proud_3	0.03	0.06	0.43	0.66
Proj 4	Proj 3 (indirect)	0.00	0.01	0.41	0.68
Proj 4	Proj 3 (total)	0.29	0.06	4.78	0.00

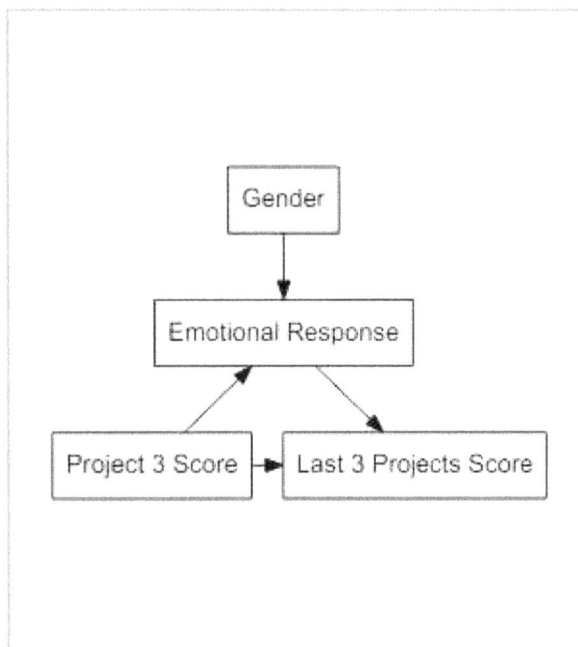

Figure 6: Path Model for Long Term Effects of Emotional Responses on Project Scores

Overall these results were consistent with the previous regression model, with significant effects only coming from the frustrated and self-efficacy (will do well) questions. The significant effects of these two questions show that students' general sense of frustration and self-efficacy impacted their short term future performance. The indirect effect of frustration indicated that frustration on one project has a negative impact on future performance, which suggested that doing worse on project 3 not only caused students to do worse on project 4 due to the effects of not gaining the competency from project 3, but also because of the frustration caused by doing poorly. This pattern is an indication of an emotional feedback loop for frustration.

The second mediation model specification tested the long term direct and indirect effects of early emotional reactions. These models included the direct effects of project 3 and the emotional reaction question on the aggregate of the last three projects completed in the course (projects 9,10,11). The aggregate was taken to make the investigation of longer term effects more robust. The model also included the indirect effect of project 3 on the last three project,

mediated by the emotional reaction question. The model is shown in figure 6. The impact of gender on the emotional reaction question was also included to control for any gender differences. The direct and indirect effects for each of the four emotional reactions are shown in tables 7-10.

Table 7 shows the long term effects of the self-efficacy (will do well) question. The direct effect of self-efficacy on the last three project scores was significant, and about 45% of the size of the impact of project 3 scores. The indirect effect was also significant, indicating that students' later project scores were not just impacted by the programming ability evinced by their scores on project 3 but also by how the project affected their confidence that they will do well.

Table 7: Long term direct and mediation effects of self-efficacy (will do well question): standardized path coefficients

Dep. Var.	Indep. Var.	Coef.	SE	Z	p-value
Last 3 Proj	Proj 3 (direct)	0.40	0.06	6.86	0.00
Self-Eff_3	Proj 3	0.28	0.06	4.66	0.00
Self-Eff_3	Gender	-0.04	0.06	-0.59	0.55
Last 3 Proj	Self-Eff_3	0.18	0.06	3.07	0.00
Last 3 Proj	Proj 3 (indirect)	0.05	0.02	2.56	0.01
Last 3 Proj	proj 3 (total)	0.45	0.06	7.92	0.00

Table 8 shows the long term effects of the frustrated question. The direct effect of the frustrated question on the last three project scores was significant, and about 45% of the size of the impact of project 3 scores. The indirect effect was also significant, indicating that students' later project scores were not just impacted by the programming ability evinced by their scores on project 3 but also by how the project made them frustrated with programming.

Table 8: Long term direct and indirect effects of frustration question: standardized path coefficients

Dep. Var.	Indep. Var.	Coef.	SE	Z	p-value
Last 3 Proj	Proj 3 (direct)	0.39	0.06	6.78	0.00
frust_3	Proj 3	-0.30	0.06	-5.08	0.00
frust_3	Gender	0.18	0.06	2.95	0.00
Last 3 Proj	frust_3	-0.21	0.06	-3.65	0.00
Last 3 Proj	Proj 3 (indirect)	-0.06	0.02	-2.96	0.00
Last 3 Proj	Proj 3 (total)	0.33	0.07	4.92	0.00

Table 9 shows the long term effects of the inadequate question. The direct effect of the inadequate question on the last three project scores was significant, and about 30% of the size of the impact of project 3 scores. The indirect effect was also significant, indicating that students' later project scores were not just impacted by the programming ability evinced by their scores on project 3 but also by how the project made them feel inadequate with programming.

Table 10 shows the long term effects of the proud question. Neither the direct nor the indirect effects of the pride question were significant, indicating that students' sense of pride had little to no impact on their later performance in programming.

Table 9: Long term direct and indirect effects of inadequate question: standardized path coefficients

Dep. Var.	Indep. Var.	Coef.	SE	Z	p-value
Last 3 Proj	Proj 3 (direct)	0.39	0.06	6.82	0.00
inadeq_3	Proj 3	-0.25	0.06	-4.07	0.00
inadeq_3	Gender	0.12	0.06	1.90	0.06
Last 3 Proj	inadequate_3	-0.21	0.06	-3.63	0.00
Last 3 Proj	Proj 3 (indirect)	-0.05	0.02	-2.71	0.01
Last 3 Proj	Proj 3 (total)	0.34	0.06	5.32	0.00

Table 10: Long term direct and indirect effects of inadequate question: standardized path coefficients

Dep. Var.	Indep. Var.	Coef.	SE	Z	p-value
Last 3 Proj	Proj 3 (direct)	0.42	0.06	7.14	0.00
proud_3	Proj 3	0.09	0.06	1.37	0.17
proud_3	Gender	0.10	0.06	1.64	0.10
Last 3 Proj	proud_3	0.02	0.06	0.28	0.78
Last 3 Proj	Proj 3 (indirect)	0.00	0.01	0.27	0.79
Last 3 Proj	Proj 3 (total	0.42	0.06	7.19	0.00

Overall the results on the longer term effects of the emotional reaction questions bolster the results found in the shorter term effects. The significant direct effects demonstrated that students' self-efficacy, as well their feelings of frustration and inadequacy caused by their early experiences have a lasting impact on their later performance over the length of the course. The significant indirect effects provided evidence for a feedback loop process for these emotional reactions as well, although in the case of students self-efficacy and feelings of inadequacy, these indicators only showed up over the long term. Nevertheless, the path models indicated that with the exception of feelings of pride, students' emotional reactions to programming projects had significant effects on future programming project outcomes.

7 DISCUSSION AND CONCLUSIONS

The results of this study both confirm and clarify the importance of students' emotional reactions to programming assignments. Students' emotional reactions correlate with their performance on programming projects, with the valence of the emotion dictating the direction of the correlation. There were some systematic differences in emotional reactions for male and female students, although future research is needed to further investigate the robustness and implications of these differences. The most important emotional reaction was frustration, and self-efficacy was also important as previous research would suggest. Finally, three of the four emotional reactions exhibited significant long or short term effects on future programming performance, indicating that they significantly influenced future performance, and that these effects on future performance can be long lasting. The observed indirect effects of emotional reactions provided evidence that emotional reactions contribute to a feedback loop process in learning to program, and that previous performance impacts future performance both by virtue of the effect that past experiences have on learning, but also

via the effect that past experiences have on emotions. Overall, the results of this study illustrate that students' emotional reactions while learning to program are significant and need to be examined further.

The results of this study are limited in a couple of main ways. First, students' emotional reactions were measured with single indicators that have not been previously validated. Given the exploratory nature of this study we believe this was a reasonable approach, but future investigations might aim to make use of previously developed instruments that may offer more reliable and robust indicators of students' emotional reactions. Second, using a more robust and established theoretical framework for understanding students emotions would potentially make the results more reliable and generalizable. The study was designed to extend the previous research by Kinnunen and Simon, but there are other formal frameworks for modeling emotions that could potentially enable more robust follow up research.

A EMOTIONAL RESPONSE QUESTIONS

The 4 survey questions used for this study were presented as follows:

For each of the following statements, please respond with how much they apply to your experience completing the programming project, on a 7-point scale where 1 = Not true of me at all and 7 = Extremely true of me:

- Upon completing the project, I felt proud/accomplished
- While working on the project, I often felt frustrated/annoyed
- While working on the project, I felt inadequate/stupid
- Considering the difficulty of this course, the teacher, and my skills, I think I will do well in this course.

REFERENCES

[1] Vicki L Almstrum, Orit Hazzan, Marian Petre, and Mark Guzdial. 2005. Challenges to Computer Science Education Research. *Computer Science Education* (2005), 191–192. https://doi.org/10.1145/1047344.1047415
[2] Danielle R. Bernstein. 1991. Comfort and Experience with Computing: Are They the Same for Women and Men? *SIGCSE Bull.* 23, 3 (1991), 57–61.
[3] Sylvia Beyer. 2008. Predictors of Female and Male Computer Science Students' Grades. *Journal of Women and Minorities in Science and Engineering* 14, 4 (2008), 377–409. https://doi.org/10.1615/JWomenMinorScienEng.v14.i4.30
[4] Shari L. Britner and Frank Pajares. 2006. Sources of science self-efficacy beliefs of middle school students. *Journal of Research in Science Teaching* 43, 5 (2006), 485–499. https://doi.org/10.1002/tea.20131
[5] Tor Busch. 1995. Gender Differences in Self-Efficacy and Attitudes Toward Computers. *Journal of Educational Computing Research* 12, 2 (1995), 147–158. https://doi.org/10.2190/H7E1-XMM7-GU9B-3HWR
[6] J.M. Cohoon. 2003. Must there be so few? Including women in CS. *25th International Conference on Software Engineering, 2003. Proceedings.* (2003), 668–674. https://doi.org/10.1109/ICSE.2003.1201253
[7] Swantje Dettmers, Ulrich Trautwein, Oliver Lüdtke, Thomas Goetz, Anne C Frenzel, and Reinhard Pekrun. 2011. Students' emotions during homework in mathematics : Testing a theoretical model of antecedents and achievement outcomes. *Contemporary Educational Psychology* 36, 1 (2011), 25–35. https://doi.org/10.1016/j.cedpsych.2010.10.001
[8] Anna Eckerdal, Robert Mccartney, Jan Erik Moström, Kate Sanders, Lynda Thomas, and Carol Zander. 2007. From Limen to Lumen : Computing students in liminal spaces. *Proceedings of the third international workshop on Computing education research* (2007).
[9] Thomas Goetz, Ulrike E Nett, Sarah E Martiny, Nathan C Hall, Reinhard Pekrun, Swantje Dettmers, and Ulrich Trautwein. 2012. Students' emotions during homework: Structures, self-concept antecedents, and achievement outcomes. *Learning and Individual Differences* 22, 2 (2012), 225–234. https://doi.org/10.1016/j.lindif.2011.04.006
[10] Markku S Hannula. 2015. Emotions in Problem Solving. In *Selected Regular Lectures from the 12th International Congress on Mathematical Education.* 269–288.

https://doi.org/10.1007/978-3-319-17187-6

[11] Päivi Kinnunen and Beth Simon. 2010. Experiencing Programming Assignments in CS1 : The Emotional Toll. *Proceedings of the Sixth international workshop on Computing education research (ICER '10)* (2010), 77–85. https://doi.org/10.1145/1839594.1839609

[12] Päivi Kinnunen and Beth Simon. 2011. CS Majors' Self-Efficacy Perceptions in CS1: Results in Light of Social Cognitive Theory. *Proceedings of the seventh international workshop on Computing education research - ICER '11* (2011), 19–26. https://doi.org/10.1145/2016911.2016917

[13] Päivi Kinnunen and Beth Simon. 2012. My program is ok âĂŞ am I? Computing freshmen's experiences of doing programming assignments. *Computer Science Education* 22, 1 (mar 2012), 1–28. https://doi.org/10.1080/08993408.2012.655091

[14] Lisa Linnenbrink-garcia and Reinhard Pekrun. 2011. Students ' emotions and academic engagement : Introduction to the special issue. *Contemporary Educational Psychology* 36, 1 (2011), 1–3. https://doi.org/10.1016/j.cedpsych.2010.11.004

[15] Alex Lishinski, Aman Yadav, Jon Good, and Richard Enbody. 2016. Learning to Program: Gender Differences and Interactive Effects of Students' Motivation, Goals and Self-Efficacy on Performance. *Proceedings of the 12th Annual International ACM Conference on International Computing Education Research (ICER '16)* (2016).

[16] Jerry Mead, Simon Gray, John Hamer, Richard James, Juha Sorva, Caroline St. Clair, and Lynda Thomas. 2006. A cognitive approach to identifying measurable milestones for programming skill acquisition. *ACM SIGCSE Bulletin* 38, 4 (2006), 182. https://doi.org/10.1145/1189136.1189185

[17] Judith L. Meece, Beverly Bower Glienke, and Samantha Burg. 2006. Gender and motivation. *Journal of School Psychology* 44, 5 (oct 2006), 351–373. https://doi.org/10.1016/j.jsp.2006.04.004

[18] Frank Pajares and M. David Miller. 1994. Role of self-efficacy and self-concept beliefs in mathematical problem solving: A path analysis. *Journal of educational psychology* 86, 2 (1994), 193. http://psycnet.apa.org/journals/edu/86/2/193/

[19] Frank Pajares and Gio Valiante. 1997. Influence of Self-Efficacy on Elementary Students' Writing. *Journal of Educational Research* 90, 6 (1997), 353–360. https://doi.org/10.1080/00220671.1997.10544593

[20] Paul Pintrich, David A.F. Smith, Teresa Garcia, and Wilbert J. McKeachie. 1991. *A Manual for the Use of the Motivated Strategies for Learning Questionnaire (MSLQ)*. Technical Report The Regents of The University of Michigan.

[21] R Core Team. 2015. R: A Language and Environment for Statistical Computing. (2015). http://www.r-project.org/

[22] Vennila Ramalingam, Deborah LaBelle, and Susan Wiedenbeck. 2004. Self-efficacy and mental models in learning to program. *Proceedings of the 9th annual SIGCSE conference on Innovation and technology in computer science education - ITiCSE '04* (2004), 171. https://doi.org/10.1145/1007996.1008042

[23] Anthony Robins. 2015. The ongoing challenges of computer science education research. *Computer Science Education* 25, 2 (2015), 115–119. https://doi.org/10.1080/08993408.2015.1034350

[24] Yves Rosseel. 2012. lavaan: An R package for structural equation modeling. *Journal of Statistical Software* 48, 2 (2012), 1–36. arXiv:arXiv:1501.0228 http://www.jstatsoft.org/v48/i02/paper

[25] Dale H. Schunk. 1995. Self-Efficacy and Education and Instruction. In *Self-Efficacy, Adaptation, and Adjustment: Theory Research and Application*. 281–303.

[26] Deborah J Stipek and J Heidi Gralinski. 1991. Gender Differences in Children ' s Achievement-Related Beliefs and Emotional Responses to Success and Failure in Mathematics. *Journal of Educational Psy* 83, 3 (1991), 361–371.

[27] Knut Sveidqvist, Mike Bostock, Chris Pettitt, Mike Daines, Andrei Kashcha, and Richard Iannone. 2016. DiagrammeR: Create Graph Diagrams and Flowcharts Using R. (2016). http://cran.r-project.org/package=DiagrammeR

[28] Christopher Watson, Frederick W B Li, and Jamie L Godwin. 2014. No Tests Required: Comparing Traditional and Dynamic Predictors of Programming Success. *Proceedings of the 45th ACM Technical Symposium on Computer Science Education (SIGCSE '14)* (2014).

[29] Hadley Wickham. 2009. *ggplot2: elegant graphics for data analysis*. Springer New York. http://had.co.nz/ggplot2/book

[30] Brenda Cantwell Wilson. 2010. A Study of Factors Promoting Success in Computer Science Including Gender Differences. *Computer Science Education* 12, 1-2 (2010), 141–164. https://doi.org/10.1076/csed.12.1.141.8211

[31] Brenda Cantwell Wilson and Sharon Shrock. 2001. Contributing to success in an introductory computer science course: a study of twelve factors. *ACM SIGCSE Bulletin* 33, 1 (2001), 184–188. https://doi.org/10.1145/366413.364581

The 'Art' of Programming: Exploring Student Conceptions of Programming through the Use of Drawing Methodology

Adon Christian Michael Moskal
Otago Polytechnic
Dunedin
New Zealand
adon.moskal@op.ac.nz

Joy Gasson
Otago Polytechnic
Dunedin
New Zealand
joy.gasson@op.ac.nz

Dale Parsons
Otago Polytechnic
Dunedin
New Zealand
dale.parsons@op.ac.nz

ABSTRACT

In this exploratory study, we analysed 396 drawings by first-year programming students in response to the question "what does programming mean to you". We were surprised by the level of care that students gave to their drawings, and we were confronted by the degree of emotion contained within the drawings. To date, few studies have focused specifically on programming students' emotional reactions to their learning experiences. Here, we analysed our student drawings as 'group data', taking note of recurring artefacts, actors, activities, aspirations and affect across the entire dataset. The observed patterns noted in the drawings raised questions around how students conceptualise programming, both as a subject and potential future profession. As contributions to the field, we: (1) discuss the potential of drawing as a research methodology for computer science; (2) present our findings and observations; and (3) suggest how this type of data could be used to better inform teaching practice in novice programming courses.

CCS CONCEPTS

• **Social and professional topics~Computer science education** • **Social and professional topics~CS1**

KEYWORDS

Programming education; drawing methodology; student affect

ACM Reference format:

A. C. M. Moskal, J. Gasson, and D. Parsons. 2017. The 'art' of programming: exploring student conceptions of programming through the use of drawing methodology. In *Proceedings of ICER '17, Tacoma, WA, USA, August 2017*, 9 pages.
DOI: 10 http://dx.doi.org/10.1145/3105726.3106170

1 INTRODUCTION

In 1974, accepting his Turing Award for contributions to the field of computing, Donald Knuth delivered a lecture questioning the classification of programming as an art or a science. "Programming," he said, "can give us both intellectual and emotional satisfaction, because it is a real achievement to master complexity and to establish a system of consistent rules." [1:670] We believe it is exactly this juxtaposition of science and art, logic and emotion, that comes to bear when novices learn programming.

In this exploratory study, we used a novel approach to investigate the learning experiences of first-year programming students—drawing methodology. We begin with an overview of the challenges of teaching novice programmers, explain our rationale for using drawing as our research methodology, and finally discuss our findings and wider implications. The aims of this paper are twofold: (1) to explore generally the potential of using drawing data in computer education research; and (2) to specifically use drawing methodology to investigate the programming experiences of our first-year students, to see if we can gain insights for improving our teaching practices.

2 TEACHING NOVICE PROGRAMMERS

The challenges inherent in teaching novices programming are well-documented [2, 3]. Students find it hard to grasp fundamental concepts, and get frustrated when programs do not work as planned or at all. As educators, we are constantly seeking new ways to improve our teaching methods, curriculum design, and ultimately the learning experiences of our students.

Any investigation into the teaching and learning of programming should consider the interplay between three entities: (1) the course content, (2) the teacher, and (3) the student, each of which can impact on the success of the novice to grasp introductory programming concepts [4].

First, thinking of the content of introductory programming courses, it is difficult for many students to learn the abstract concepts of programming (such as conditionals and loops), wrestle with the syntactic constraints of different languages, and constantly apply their emerging knowledge to new and unfamiliar problems, making rote learning a challenging task [5]. As well as the difficulties in learning explicit coding skills, introductory programming courses can also address peripheral subjects, such as logic thinking and problem-solving, 'soft skill' development (such as communication and teamwork, typically in the form of pair programming exercises), mathematics, and business/client considerations.

Second, there is considerable variation in how teachers teach introductory programming. For example, Pears, et al. [6] present a comprehensive review of the factors that can vary from teaching context to teaching context, including choice of teaching strategy, programming language, or support tools (such as an Integrated Development Environment, or IDE).

Third, the personal qualities of the student can dramatically affect their performance in an introductory programming course. Many studies have explored students' personal attributes to determine predictors of student success in introductory programming courses [7]. As well as being cognitively challenging, introductory programming has also been shown to carry a high emotional load; for example, Kinnunen and Simon [8] explore the effect that student experiences of programming (positive and negative) can have on their self-efficacy. Gasson, Parsons, Wood and Haden [9] have also shown a clear link between student affect and performance in first-year programming papers.

Student conceptions and misconceptions of programming can also contribute to their overall success [10], and it can often be difficult for computer science educators to comprehend where these conceptions come from [11]. Student conceptions of computer science have been examined from a number of perspectives: for example, Liang, Su and Tsai [12] present an assessment of Taiwanese college students' conception of and approaches to learning computer science; Stamouli and Huggard [13] explore undergraduate computing students' perceptions of program 'correctness'; Krpan, Mladenović and Rosić [14] look at the relationship between novice programmers' perceptions and success in introductory programming courses; and Eckerdal, Thuné and Berglund [15] report on first year computing students' understandings of what it means to 'learn to program'.

3 DRAWING AS A RESEARCH METHODOLOGY

"If I could say it in words, there would be no reason to paint."
— Edward Hopper

Answering Fincher, Tenenberg and Robins' [16] call that computer science education needs to augment its traditional research methods, we utilised drawing as our research approach to investigate novice programmers' conceptions of programming. Similar visualisation techniques have been employed in computer science education research, for instance Hübscher-Younger and Narayanan's [17] novel approach to teaching algorithms; however, we could not find any studies in computer education specifically employing drawing as their research approach.

Drawing as a research method(ology) has been used extensively in the social sciences, particularly in the areas of psychology, and then particularly with children [18, 19]. Primarily, the benefits include being able to express one's self without having to rely on words—e.g. for children with an underdeveloped vocabulary, or for comparisons between international contexts—or to represent things which are difficult to convey in words (for instance, motion). For our purposes, while our students are not children, as novices they are likely to have a similarly underdeveloped disciplinary and academic vocabulary [20, 21]. And, as Guillemin [22:275] notes, "Drawings … are about how people see the world in both its simplicities and its complexities. Drawings are intricately bound up with power relations, social experiences, and technological interactions".

Within primary and secondary school education, drawing has been utilised as a research methodology to explore students' conceptions of various subjects. For example, Selwyn, Boraschi and Özkula [23] asked primary school students to express their conceptions of information and communications technologies in schools through drawings. More recently, drawing has also been used to explore secondary student conceptions of 'learning' [24, 25]. In both examples, the authors espouse the benefits of using drawings to allow their participants to express themselves in new and different ways than traditional text-based approaches (such as interviews or questionnaires).

Drawing as a research methodology has also been used in higher education. For example, Sim [26] used 'participatory drawing' for research into PhD students' conceptions of their doctoral research process—students were invited to depict their research process in diagrammatic form, with the diagrams being used later as stimulus for further discussion. Similar to the primary and secondary school examples above, the use of drawing (in this case, coupled with participant discussions) "offered the opportunity for participants to convey deeper and more varied internal representations or meanings." Köse [27] also used drawing with students at a Turkish university to uncover their misconceptions about science.

4 METHOD

This study took place at Otago Polytechnic, in Dunedin, New Zealand, within the Bachelor of Information Technology (BIT) degree. We analysed 396 first-year student drawings in response to the question "Draw, sketch, illustrate, paint, depict or otherwise portray what programming means to you." 206 drawings were from Programming 1, and 190 drawings were from Programming 2 (henceforth, P1 and P2 respectively). P1 focuses on programming fundamentals (e.g. variable manipulation, and flow of control) and patterns, while P2 introduces students to Object Oriented (OO) concepts, such as classes, objects, inheritance and polymorphism. The drawings were produced at the end of the final exam for each class, the last question on the exam paper inviting the students to draw their representations of programming. The drawing data represents 6 years' worth of data, collected since 2010.

Our method for analysing the drawings was largely informed by Selwyn, Boraschi and Özkula [23], who used drawing as a research methodology to investigate primary students' conceptions of ICT in schools. Following their lead, we analysed our drawings as group data, looking for patterns across the entire dataset, rather than trying to unpack what individual drawings might be saying about specific students. We analysed the drawings and applied codes where the content or items were 'meaningful' to the concept of 'programming'; drawings could have multiple codes, but individual codes were only attributed once to each drawing. Student responses that were purely text-based with no pictorial component were excluded from the analysis.

The entire dataset of drawings was analysed and coded collaboratively by the three researchers. Researchers B and C are lecturers in the first year of the BIT degree, and have each taught on the degree programme for over 20 years; researcher A is a lecturer in the second and third year of the degree, and has been with the department for less than a year. As such, researchers B and C offered 'inside' or emic perspectives on the drawings, while researcher A offered an 'outside' or etic perspective.

We chose to collaborate on the coding process to capitalise on these different perspectives [28], discussing the codes, negotiating meanings, and socially constructing our interpretations. As Nielsen [29:2] argues:

Collaboration in qualitative data analysis runs the risk of being reduced to comparing their individual analyses and thus eliminating the opportunities in collaborative analysis. Collaborative analysis performed by a (small) group of researchers may well create the advantage to the researchers informing, influencing, and justifying through a dialogue with each other on how they can arrive at a joint analysis. Differences in perceiving the data can then be viewed as an opportunity for learning rather than merely a source of reduced reliability.

We used the four themes determined by Selwyn, Boraschi and Özkula [23] to guide our coding:

1. *artefacts*: programming objects or 'concepts' represented in the drawings;
2. *actors*: people represented in the drawings;
3. *activities*: what the people appear to be doing/their actions in relation to programming;
4. and *aspirations*: the aims/goals that the drawings seemed to be suggesting (with regard to programming).

Through our coding process, we also came up with a fifth category, *affect*, or the emotions about programming that the drawings appeared to be conveying. Each theme was further divided into subthemes as necessary. The findings of our coding process are described in the next section.

5 FINDINGS

We will now outline the primary findings of the coding process, according to theme. Example student drawings from each category are shown below, and further examples can be viewed at http://bit.ly/2u1ZB3D.

5.1 Artefacts

Out of the 396 drawings analysed, 47% (n=185) contained programming artefacts, such as depictions of computers or snippets of pseudocode. Personal computer components were the most frequently depicted, such as monitors (24%, n=96),

peripherals (e.g. mice and keyboards; 20%, n=81), and CPU units (9%, n=35); laptop or tablet devices were depicted least frequently (3%, n=13). Other programming artefacts such as snippets of code (7%, n=29), blocks of logical pseudocode (6%, n=25), and logic/flow diagrams (3%, n=13) also featured throughout the dataset. Examples of drawings containing programming artefacts are shown in Figure 1.

5.2 Actors

Students most frequently depicted no actors in their drawings (52%, n=207), followed by one actor only being shown (44%, n=173). Drawings showing more than one actor were far less frequent (4%, n=16). Figure 2 shows an example of each of these categorisations—no actor depicted, one actor depicted, and more than one actor depicted.

5.3 Activities

Only two activities pertaining to 'programming' were identified in the student drawings: 10% (n=41) contained depictions of actors programming or writing code (as discerned by representations of 'hands on keyboard'), and 3% (n=11) showed some representation of problem solving (e.g., puzzles being solved). Figure 3 shows examples of these activities.

5.4 Aspirations

Some of the drawings (19%, n=77) depicted future-thinking imagery, such as goals, hopes or ambitions, or motivations for learning programming. Ambitions or motivations included: wanting to 'create something' (8%, n=32); money or fame (7%, n=26); job or career (3%, n=13); being able to contribute to the world or future society (3%, n=10); and a degree or grades/marks (2%, n=7). Examples of aspirations are shown in Figure 4.

5.5 Affect

As well as objects and actors, the majority of student drawings were also interpreted as having an emotional or affective component (67%, n=265). This was typically exhibited through symbols such as smiling or frowning faces, or through scenarios such as harm or misfortune befalling an actor; we did not code images where no clear emotions were indicated, or where the emotional 'reading' of the image was disputed by the three coders. Some drawings were coded with multiple emotions, particularly ones divided into different sections (i.e. in a 'comic strip' style), or where textual hints had been added, thus clearly explaining the different emotional states represented.

Positive emotions (such as 'happy/generally positive', 'enjoyable/fun' or 'success/achievement') were found in 38% (n=149) of student drawings. However, there was a noticeable difference between the P1 and P2 datasets—46% (n=95) of P1 drawings showed positive affect, compared with only 28% (n=54) of P2 drawings. We theorise possible explanations of this discrepancy in the Discussion section.

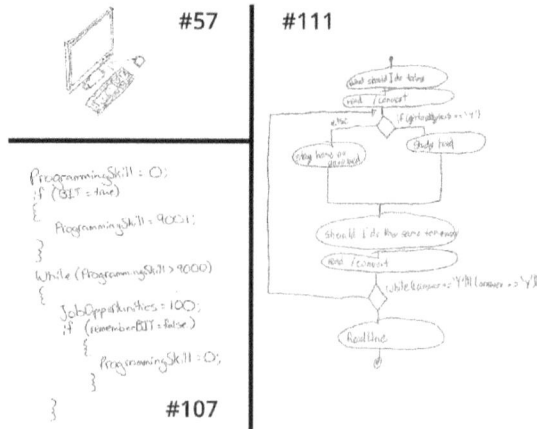

Figure 1. Examples of student drawings depicting programming artefacts. Drawing #57 shows a monitor with peripherals (mouse and keyboard); #107 shows a block of pseudocode; and #111 shows a logic/flow diagram.

Figure 2. Examples of student drawings depicting different actor configurations. Drawing #30 shows no actor present; #173 shows one actor present; and #210 shows more than one actor present.

Figure 3. Examples of student drawings showing activities related to programming. Drawings #70 and #258 depict programming as an activity (hands on keyboard); #127 shows a drawing interpreted as 'problem solving'.

Figure 4. Examples of student drawings showing programming aspirations. Drawing #51 depicts being motivated by 'money or fame'; #164 shows being motivated by the ability to 'create something'.

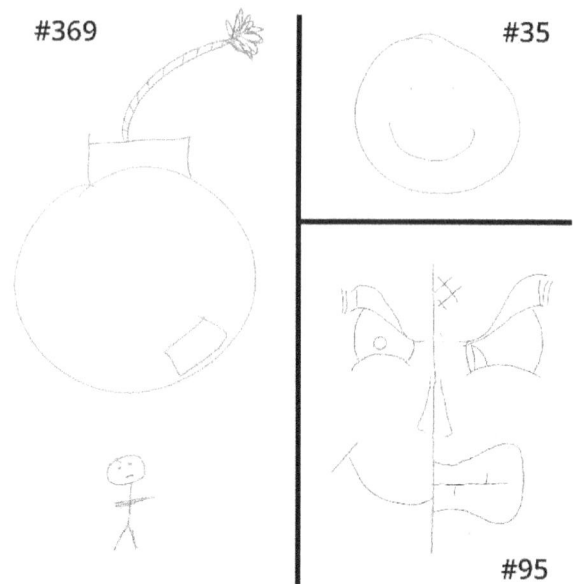

Figure 5. Examples of student drawings showing affect/emotion. Drawing #369 is coded as 'despair'; #35 is coded as 'happy/generally positive'; and #95 is coded as 'mixed emotion'.

Negative emotions (such as 'frustration', 'confusion', 'anger/rage' or 'despair') were found in 28% (n=109) of student drawings. Again, there was a difference between P1 and P2 data, although not as severe as the positive emotion data—23% (n=48) of P1 drawings showed negative affect, compared with 32% (n=61) of P2 drawings.

A comparatively small proportion of drawings (15%, n=60) were coded as 'mixed emotions'—these drawings tended to show conflicting emotions within a single image (i.e. positive and negative emotions in one symbol, such as a halved face with both a smile and frown). Drawings that exhibited some sort of progression over time (either linear or cyclic) between positive and negative emotions were also marked as 'mixed'. Examples of drawings showing affect/emotion are exhibited in Figure 5.

6 DISCUSSION

> "Good art is not what it looks like, but what it does to us."
> — Roy Adzak

Asking students to describe what programming means to them provides some insight into how students visualise both the act of programming and their role in relation to programming. The use of drawing methodology certainly elicited emotional responses from many students. While it is difficult to draw any definitive conclusions from our interpretations of the student drawings, the data do provide some insights into the student 'way of thinking', and raise some interesting questions for further discussion. In this section, we present observations that we found particularly interesting or surprising, and reflect on how these insights relate to our teaching practice.

Overall, the student drawings depicted programming from a very narrow perspective. Notably, programming as an activity was almost always depicted in conjunction with classroom imagery or references to working on specific in-class assignments; drawings of programming outside of the confines of the classroom were rare. While it may not be surprising that novice programmers' conceptions of programming are primarily tied to their classroom experiences, it does raise questions about student professional identity formation—that is, developing from 'programming students' to 'programmers'. Specifically, when do novice programmers develop a sense of professional identity, and how can introductory programming courses better encourage this development?

A number of studies identify the central role of higher education institutions to foster and facilitate students' emerging professional identities (for a comprehensive review of the literature, see [30]). Reid, Dahlgren, Petocz and Dahlgren [31:738-739] note the key role that strong professional identity formation plays in student learning, stating "professional expectations and values influence the ways that students engage with their learning" and "students find relevance for learning through the obvious applicability of their knowledge".

One specific example from the drawings that suggests student professional identity might not be developing in these introductory courses was a distinct lack of multiple actors across all drawings (Figure 6).

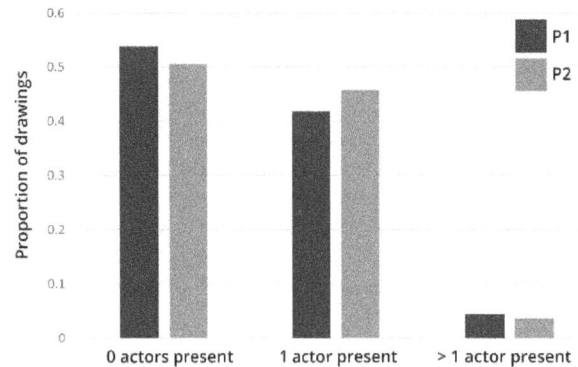

Figure 6. The distribution of drawings with no actors present, one actor present and more than one actor present between P1 and P2.

Collaboration and teamwork are core components of successful software development teams [32]; fostering these attributes as part of a novice programmer's emerging professional identity is an important goal for higher education institutions. Collaborative strategies such as 'pair programming' are widely acknowledged as effective for introductory computing courses [33] In our specific context, researchers B and C both explicitly teach pair programming as a core component of P1 and P2, and have found it to be a particularly beneficial practice for their first-year programmers [34].

The lack of multiple actors in the student drawings, however, suggests that despite continuous exposure to pair programming, social aspects of programming may not be regarded as particularly important by novice programmers. Observations by all three researchers of students in their second year support the idea that pair or social programming is not yet embedded in everyday student practice at this novice stage. As students progress through the later stages of the degree programme (i.e. third year), these collaborative traits tend to be better developed, and this is likely due to the students' involvement in larger-scale, group software engineering projects.

A possible explanation is that pair programming in first year—while demonstrating academic benefit and being viewed positively by students—is being perceived by novices as a teaching and learning strategy, not as a professional skill or part of everyday programming practice. As students experience more 'real-life' programming situations in later years, and begin to develop their identities as 'programmers' rather than 'students', these collaborative practices transition from the academic realm to the professional realm.

Tied to this notion of professional identity formation, relatively few drawings depicted programming as a part of the students' future (i.e. career). When 'future-thinking' imagery was seen, drawings tended to show *unrealistic* conceptions of programming careers, such as programmers surrounded by big bags of money. Jenkins [35:56] found that a 'lucrative career' was a powerful motivator for programming students to undertake computing degrees, but that they may also "[approach] programming from an ill-informed position" regarding the actual skills necessary to get programming jobs.

This misinformed/unrealistic career conception is to be expected in novice programmers—as Leventhal and Chilson [36] found, prolonged exposure to computer science can influence student career expectations, and, particularly, decrease the priority of extrinsic job features, such as monetary compensation. However, the question remains as to how we as computer science educators can better help students visualise themselves in programming careers, and develop healthy expectations of what those careers are likely to be.

The other principal observation we made about the student drawings was the high level of affect present—two-thirds of all student drawings showed clear emotional reaction to programming. As discussed previously, learning to program can be an emotional experience, and this can impact on student performance [8, 9].

There are a number of questions here around how much emotional load is healthy for students to experience in introductory programming, and how can we, as educators, tap into that emotional data to make decisions about our courses?

We highlight an example from the student data related to these questions. There was a noticeable difference between the proportion of positive and negative emotions depicted in the P1 and P2 drawings—overall, the P1 drawings exhibited more positive affect imagery and less negative affect imagery (Figure 7).

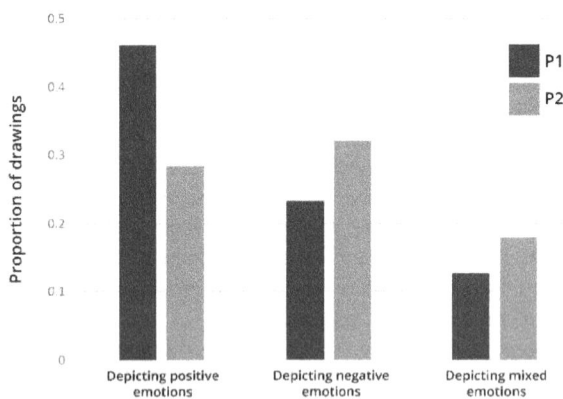

Figure 7. The distribution of drawings showing positive, negative and mixed emotions between P1 and P2.

However, this data is at odds with other measures of student experience in these classes, such as the results of student satisfaction surveys. For instance, the results of the 2016 student satisfaction surveys show the same levels of positive feedback between P1 to P2 (80% and 81% overall satisfaction respectively). Our drawing data, though, would suggest that the student experience of these classes is more nuanced than the relatively blunt satisfaction metric indicates.

Recent research into student 'happiness' supports this conjecture—Dean and Gibbs [37:16] found that indicators of student 'happiness' and student 'satisfaction' tend to be different. They found that 'satisfied' students "seemed to be more concerned with external loci, that is, on how things done to and for them were delivered, rather than in their engagement with the process."

Researchers B and C theorise that this perceived decrease in positive affect as students move from P1 to P2 is likely due to the conceptual shift required between the two subjects; specifically, from:

- programming fundamentals to abstract OO concepts;
- console-based development to using an IDE and GUI (Graphical User Interface); and
- discrete tasks aimed at skill development, to more open-ended applications of skills.

For example, the difficulties in getting novice programmers to grasp OO concepts is a well-documented challenge for CS educators [38, 39]; anecdotally, researchers B and C share this view that students find programming in P2 more confusing than P1.

However, a level of challenge (i.e. confusion of frustration) can be beneficial to the learning process. This concept is widely espoused in educational literature: Wass and Golding [40] suggest pitching teaching at the extreme limits of a student's zone of proximal development (ZPD, or tasks too hard to do independently, but achievable with assistance); Bjork and Bjork [41] talk about 'desirable difficulties' or challenges that can help trigger cognitive process and enhance learning; and D'Mello and Graesser [42] argue that the 'cognitive disequilibrium' experienced during difficult tasks leads to deeper learning.

However, as with many theories of learning, transforming these concepts into practical advice for teachers is less straightforward. For example, Wass and Golding [40] acknowledge that determining the actual boundaries of a student's ZPD is difficult; similarly, D'Mello and Graesser [42] caution that too much disequilibrium can have the opposite effect, causing students to give up or become disengaged, and tasks should be tailored to individual learners.

We suggest that drawing methodology might offer a useful approach for teachers to tease out student affective states, and hence infer the level of challenge currently experienced by students. When viewed as group data, our drawings give an overall 'emotional snapshot' of the course—we would expect to see a balance of positive and negative emotions across the entire cohort of students. Too much positive emotion could indicate the course is not challenging enough (and thus not conducive to deep learning), while too much negative emotion could indicate the course is too challenging (and thus lead to student disengagement).

Obviously, this type of exploratory and interpretive data is problematic: the analysis process is time-consuming; the process is heavily dependent on context, and therefore not easily transferrable to other teaching scenarios; and it is difficult to draw definitive conclusions from the data. However, all three researchers found the student drawing data offered a far richer picture of student in-class experiences than other traditional measures, and this in turn sparked extensive discussions and reflection around the content and delivery of our introductory programming courses. This sort of deeply personal data gave us a window into our students' experiences, and helped us remember that our students are more than pass-rates and enrolment dollars—they are complex and emotional people.

7 FUTURE RESEARCH

Throughout our research, we noted several potential directions for future research.

First, we are curious to know whether repeating this exercise with second and third-year students would reveal any different patterns than the first-year cohorts. Specifically, we are interested in seeing whether more indicators of student professional identity formation are present in drawings from students further along in the degree.

Second, similar to above, we would be interested in getting graduates and industry professionals to complete the drawing activity to see if this cohort produces any significantly different drawings. Comparing student drawings to an industry 'exemplar' set of drawings could reveal further insights into student experiences.

Third, in this study we did not explicitly correlate student drawings with performance; this was for two main reasons: (1) as reported, we were more interested in looking at patterns across the data as a group; and (2) a preliminary look at a sampling of the drawings did not show any obvious correlations to student performance (i.e., the drawings were attached to their final exam papers, and there did not seem to be any obvious patterns relating to the exam marks). However, a more thorough exploration of the five themes (artefacts, actors, activities, aspirations and affect) in conjunction with student performance measures should be carried out in future.

Fourth, to augment our methodology, we could repeat the activity with students and incorporate a discussion element to assist with our analysis. This might involve sitting down with students and letting them explain their drawings in a semi-structured interview fashion, or providing students with our analyses and comparing and contrasting our interpretations with those from a student perspective.

Fifth, we acknowledge that the timing of the exercise—that is, at the end of a final exam—may be confounding the data, particularly around our interpretations of student emotions. We came up with two possible issues that warrant further investigation to substantiate: (1) the drawings may be a cathartic outlet for students following a stressful event (e.g. the exam), and emotions such as frustration, rage, relief, or joy may pertain specifically to the exam, rather than the overall course itself; and (2) particularly positive emotions about the course could simply be placatory toward the lecturer about to mark the exam paper. This brings up questions around the possible teacher-student power relations embedded in the drawings [22].

Finally, there are several demographic comparisons that we could focus on with future studies: for example, traditionally computer science has a challenge with attracting and retaining female students, and it could be worthwhile seeing if male and female student drawings produce different conceptions of programming (of course, with so few female students, getting enough drawings to constitute a viable dataset could be a challenge). Other demographics that would be of interest to our context would be whether we see differences with Māori and Pacific Island students, or between school-leavers and adult students.

8 CONCLUSIONS

As with any good art, our student drawings have provoked questions and reflection. As a window into the student experience of learning programming, the student drawings reveal a rich dataset of conceptions, perspectives, aspirations and emotions. The observed patterns noted in the drawings raised questions particularly around the formation of students' professional programming identities, and the role of affect in learning to program. As educators, we are constantly looking for new ways to improve our teaching practice and the learning experiences of our students. In this study, drawing methodology proved to be a useful means of tapping into the affective states of our first-year students and gaining insight into their learning experiences.

ACKNOWLEDGMENTS

Thanks to all the students that took the time to produce a drawing.

REFERENCES

[1] D. Knuth. 1974. Computer programming as an art. *Communications of the ACM, v.17 n.12*, pp.667-673, Dec 1974.

[2] E. Lahtinen, K. Ala-Mutka, and H-M. Järvinen. 2005. A study of the difficulties of novice programmers. *Acm Sigcse Bulletin, vol. 37, no. 3*, pp.14-18. ACM, 2005.

[3] A. Robins, J. Rountree, and N. Rountree. 2003. Learning and teaching programming: a review. *Computer Science Education. 13, 2*, pp.137-172.

[4] A. Berglund, and R. Lister. 2010. Introductory programming and the didactic triangle. In *Proceedings of the Twelfth Australasian Conference on Computing Education-Volume 103* (pp. 35-44). Australian Computer Society, Inc.

[5] M. Butler, and M. Morgan. 2007. Learning challenges faced by novice programming students studying high level and low feedback concepts. In *Proceedings of the 24th ascilite Conference* (pp. 2-5).

[6] A. Pears, S. Seidman, L. Malmi, L. Mannila, E. Adams, J. Bennedsen, M. Devlin, and J. Paterson. 2007. A survey of literature on the teaching of introductory programming. *ACM SIGCSE Bulletin, 39*(4), pp.204-223.

[7] S. Fincher, A. Robins, B. Baker, I. Box, Q. Cutts, M. de Raadt, P. Haden, J. Hamer, M. Hamilton, R. Lister, and M. Petre. 2006. Predictors of success in a first programming course. In *Proceedings of the 8th Australasian Conference on Computing Education-Volume 52* (pp. 189-196). Australian Computer Society, Inc., Jan 2006.

[8] P. Kinnunen, and B. Simon. 2012. My program is ok–am I? Computing freshmen's experiences of doing programming assignments. *Computer Science Education, 22*(1), pp.1-28.

[9] J. Gasson, D. Parsons, K. Wood, and P. Haden. In review. Student affect in CS1: Insights from an easy data collection tool. *Koli Calling*, November 16–19, 2017, Koli, Finland.

[10] C. Edmondson. 2008. Teaching tales: some student perceptions of computing education. *ACM SIGCSE Bulletin, 40*(4), pp.103-106.

[11] L.C. Kaczmarczyk, E.R. Petrick, J.P. East, and G.L. Herman. 2010. Identifying student misconceptions of programming. In *Proceedings of the 41st ACM technical symposium on Computer science education* (pp. 107-111). ACM. Mar 2010.

[12] J.C. Liang, Y.C. Su, and C.C. Tsai. 2015. The assessment of Taiwanese college students' conceptions of and approaches to learning computer

science and their relationships. *The Asia-Pacific Education Researcher, 24*(4), pp.557-567.

[13]   I. Stamouli, and M. Huggard. 2006. Object oriented programming and program correctness: the students' perspective. In *Proceedings of the second international workshop on Computing education research* (pp. 109-118). ACM. Sep 2006.

[14]   D. Krpan, M. Rosić, and S. Mladenović. 2014. Teaching basic programming skills to undergraduate students. In *Contemporary issues in economy and technology.* Jan 2014.

[15]   A. Eckerdal, M. Thuné, and A. Berglund. 2005. What does it take to learn 'programming thinking'?. In *Proceedings of the first international workshop on Computing education research* (pp. 135-142). ACM. Oct 2005.

[16]   S. Fincher, J. Tenenberg, and A. Robins. 2011. Research design: necessary bricolage. In *Proceedings of the seventh international workshop on Computing education research* (pp. 27-32). ACM. Aug 2011.

       T. Hübscher-Younger, and N.H. Narayanan. 2003. Dancing hamsters and

[17]   marble statues: characterizing student visualizations of algorithms. In *Proceedings of the 2003 ACM symposium on Software visualization* (pp. 95-104). ACM. Jun 2003.

[18]   C. Golomb. 2003. *The child's creation of a pictorial world.* Psychology Press.

[19]   R.P. Jolley. 2010. *Children and pictures: Drawing and understanding.* John Wiley & Sons.

[20]   M.R. Lea, and B.V. Street. 1998. Student writing in higher education: an academic literacies approach. *Studies in higher education 23*(2), pp. 157-172.

[21]   K. Hyland. 2008. As can be seen: lexical bundles and disciplinary variation. *English for specific purposes, 27*(1), pp. 4-21.

[22]   M. Guillemin. 2004. Understanding illness: Using drawings as a research method. *Qualitative health research, 14*(2), pp.272-289.

[23]   N. Selwyn, S. Boraschi, and S.M. Özkula. 2009. Drawing digital pictures: An investigation of primary pupils' representations of ICT and schools. *British Educational Research Journal, 35*(6), pp.909-928.

[24]   W.M. Hsieh, and C.C. Tsai. 2016. Learning illustrated: An exploratory cross-sectional drawing analysis of students' conceptions of learning. *The Journal of Educational Research,* pp.1-12.

[25]   W.M. Hsieh, and C.C. Tsai. 2017. Exploring students' conceptions of science learning via drawing: a cross-sectional analysis. *International Journal of Science Education,* pp.1-25.

[26]   K.N. Sim. 2016. *An investigation into the way PhD students utilise ICT to support their doctoral research process* (Doctoral dissertation, University of Otago).

[27]   S. Köse. 2008. Diagnosing student misconceptions: Using drawings as a research method. *World Applied Sciences Journal, 3*(2), pp.283-293.

[28]   F. Cornish, A. Gillespie, and T. Zittoun. 2013. *Collaborative analysis of qualitative data.* Sage Publications Limited.

[29]   P.A. Nielsen. 2016. Towards a Design Theory for Collaborative Qualitative Data Analysis. *Practice-based Design and Innovation of Digital Artifacts.*

[30]   F. Trede, R. Macklin, and D. Bridges. 2012. Professional identity development: a review of the higher education literature. *Studies in Higher Education, 37*(3), pp.365-384.

[31]   A. Reid, L.O. Dahlgren, P. Petocz, and M.A. Dahlgren. 2008. Identity and engagement for professional formation. *Studies in Higher Education, 33*(6), pp.729-742.

[32]   Y. Lindsjørn, D.I. Sjøberg, T. Dingsøyr, G.R. Bergersen, and T. Dybå. 2016. Teamwork quality and project success in software development: A survey of agile development teams. *Journal of Systems and Software, 122,* pp.274-286.

[33]   C. McDowell, L. Werner, H. Bullock, and J. Fernald. 2002. The effects of pair-programming on performance in an introductory programming course. *ACM SIGCSE Bulletin, 34*(1), pp.38-42.

[34]   K. Wood, D. Parsons, J. Gasson, and P. Haden. 2013. It's never too early: pair programming in CS1. In *Proceedings of the Fifteenth Australasian Computing Education Conference-Volume 136* (pp. 13-21). Australian Computer Society, Inc. Jan 2013.

[35]   T. Jenkins. 2001. The motivation of students of programming. In *ACM SIGCSE Bulletin* (Vol. 33, No. 3, pp. 53-56). ACM. Jun 2001.

[36]   L.M. Leventhal, and D.W. Chilson. 1989. Beyond Just a Job: Expectations of Computer Science Students. *Computer Science Education, 1*(2), pp.129-143.

[37]   A. Dean, and P. Gibbs. 2015. Student satisfaction or happiness? A preliminary rethink of what is important in the student experience. *Quality Assurance in Education, 23*(1), pp.5-19.

[38]   M. Kölling. 1999. The problem of teaching object-oriented programming. *Journal of Object Oriented Programming, 11*(8), pp.8-15.

[39]   K. Sanders, J. Boustedt, A. Eckerdal, R. McCartney, J.E. Moström, L. Thomas, and C. Zander. 2008. Student understanding of object-oriented programming as expressed in concept maps. *ACM SIGCSE Bulletin, 40*(1), pp.332-336.

[40]   R. Wass, and C. Golding. 2014. Sharpening a tool for teaching: the zone of proximal development. *Teaching in Higher Education, 19*(6), pp.671-684.

[41]   E.L. Bjork, and R.A. Bjork. 2011. Making things hard on yourself, but in a good way: Creating desirable difficulties to enhance learning. *Psychology and the real world: Essays illustrating fundamental contributions to society,* pp.56-64.

[42]   S. D'Mello, and A. Graesser. 2012. Dynamics of affective states during complex learning. *Learning and Instruction, 22*(2), pp.145-157.

Social Perceptions in Computer Science and Implications for Diverse Students*

Jennifer Wang
Google, Inc.
1600 Amphitheatre Pkwy.
Mountain View, CA 94043 USA
jtw@google.com

Sepehr Hejazi Moghadam
Google, Inc.
1600 Amphitheatre Pkwy.
Mountain View, CA 94043 USA
shmoghadam@google.com

Juliet Tiffany-Morales
Google, Inc.
1600 Amphitheatre Pkwy.
Mountain View, CA 94043 USA
jtmorales@google.com

ABSTRACT

The barriers to diversity in computer science (CS) are complex, consisting of both structural and social barriers. In this paper, we focus on social perceptions for students in grades 7–12 in the U.S. using surveys of nationally representative samples of 1,672 students, 1,677 parents, 1,008 teachers, 9,805 principals, and 2,307 superintendents. Building on qualitative work by Lewis, Anderson, and Yasuhara [1,2], we sought to understand social beliefs regarding students' fit and ability as well the external context. We examined these factors' relationships to students' interest. The results are consistent with the current body of research on gender differences in social perceptions in CS. They also identify new findings for race/ethnicity, specifically Black and Hispanic students. As K–12 CS expands, these findings could inform differentiation strategies in equitably engaging students.

KEYWORDS

Race; ethnicity; gender; Black; African American; Hispanic; Latinx; females; girls; women; K-12; pre-university; middle school; high school; perceptions; ability; mindset; confidence; fit; identity; media; encouragement; parents; teachers; interest

1 INTRODUCTION

Efforts to broaden access to K–12/pre-university computer science (CS) have gained tremendous traction and momentum in recent years. Despite these efforts, underrepresentation of certain demographics persists at this level.

Our previous study found that between 2014–15 and 2015–16, the percentage of U.S. K–12 principals who said they offered CS classes with programming increased from 25% to 40% [3]. This increase in overall access, however, does not guarantee a similar improvement in equity of access. As demonstrated in the extensive qualitative study by Margolis et al. [4], even when advanced CS courses are available in school, students of color may not be participating in them.

Through our national surveys, we probe the social factors that may be influencing students to not participate in CS, providing quantitative and representative data on U.S. students. In particular, we aim to explore factors that could be holding back students who may have access to CS opportunities. Moving beyond structural access, we dive into social perceptions around fit and ability [1,2], and investigate differences by race/ethnicity and gender from both the intervening perspectives through students and the external context through parents' and educators' perspectives. Our primary research goal is to determine how pervading social perceptions play out for students of various demographics, specifically females compared to males, and between Black, Hispanic, and White students, and these factors' relationships with students' interest in learning CS.

We hope that our findings can help move us beyond just offering CS as the ultimate solution and towards truly ensuring that all students are enabled to learn CS. As we see, however, social perceptions play out differently for each demographic, which are further complicated by variations within each group.

2 LITERATURE

We build on a large body of work in CS education research, particularly those investigating issues related to underrepresentation for Black and Hispanic students and for girls. Our work contributes new findings to the research on race/ethnicity and confirms much of the research on gender in CS education. In particular, we contribute new knowledge on pre-university students and related social perceptions.

Little prior research has explored identity in CS with specific focus on race/ethnicity. However, previous research has shown that Black and Hispanic students have been found to be less likely to know an adult in the tech industry, compared to White or Asian students [5]. We contribute to research exploring identity in CS.

Previous studies have also identified interest in technology among Black/African American and Hispanic/Latinx youth and parents. For instance, Colby et al. [5] found that Black and Hispanic students have a more positive perception of the CS field, compared to White and Asian students. Rideout, Scott, and Clark [6] also found that there is high interest among Black youth to learn how to do new activities on the computer, and their parents think that "being good at computers" is important to their children's career and education. Interest in CS among

ICER '17, August 18-20, 2017, Tacoma, WA, USA
© 2017 Copyright is held by the owner/author(s).
ACM ISBN 978-1-4503-4968-0/17/08.
http://dx.doi.org/10.1145/3105726.3106175

students and parents, however, has not been broadly explored for differences by race/ethnicity, which we investigate in this paper.

Prior research has found that lack of CS exposure is possibly a large reason for the dearth of knowledge and encouragement [7] and prior experience is one of the most important predictors of computer attitudes [8] while other studies have found that students without prior experience identified CS as more broadly meaningful [e.g., 9].

For confidence, differences by race/ethnicity may not be as consistent with representation in CS. For instance, Blacks and Hispanics have been found to be more likely than Whites or Asians to say that they would be good at working with computers [5]. On the other hand, Margolis et al. found that Hispanic students have low confidence [4]. Exposure to computers may also be important, as experience with computers has been found to positively affect confidence and attitudes [8,10]. This is especially relevant as Black and Hispanic students are less likely to have exposure to computers at home and school [3].

There is conflicting research on whether identifying with people who engage in CS, in particular stereotypes, promotes interest in CS [1]. While only a small segment of the research focusing on gender is directly related to identity, Cheryan et al. propose that masculinity in CS is a large deterrent for girls [11]. Another study finds that females are 2.5 times as likely as males to say that people in tech are "boring" and "not like me" [5]. Other studies [1,12-14] further found that girls are more likely to see CS as asocial, competitive, and individualistic. Girls are also less likely to be aware and have knowledge of CS [7].

Given these factors, it is not surprising that many studies have found that interest in computers is lower among girls than boys [15]. In particular, boys are more likely to have chosen to learn CS, through playing with computers and participating in computing activities [15-20]. Females have generally less favorable attitudes towards CS and STEM [20,21]. Our paper contributes a broad quantitative exploration of interest in CS with nationally representative students.

Prior studies have also found that girls have lower confidence than boys, particularly in STEM and CS. For example, even when teachers rated boys and girls equally competent or test scores were similar among boys and girls, boys were more likely than girls to indicate self-efficacy and confidence [21,22]. Other studies in after-school contexts with different ages consistently demonstrate lower confidence among girls [15,16,23,24].

The following sections provide the details of our large-scale national study, describe the extent to which our results confirm the existing literature, and attempt to contribute new insights on differences between races/ethnicities.

3 THEORETICAL FRAMEWORK

In late 2015–early 2016, we conducted national surveys of U.S. students, parents, teachers, principals and superintendents as part of a study on the status of CS education in the U.S. Details on the methodology are in the next section. Here, we describe the theoretical framework for the analyses in this paper.

Our resulting descriptive statistics are intended to fill a critical need for national data on the diversity gaps in CS in the U.S. With such a rich source of national data, we investigated how these data might be analyzed to add to the field's understanding of the status of CS education in the U.S., particularly for the underrepresented populations of Black students, Hispanic students, and girls.

We build on a framework from Lewis, Yasuhara, and Anderson, who interviewed college students in introductory CS courses about their decision-making process for choosing to major or not major in CS [1,2]. The authors identified five "interrelated factors" students consider in their process including: ability, enjoyment, fit, utility, and opportunity costs. They explore two of the five factors—ability and fit—and offer theoretical frameworks for understanding how students go about assessing their CS ability and fit [1,2].

Lewis et al. [2] posit that college students go through a two-stage process of self-assessment when determining whether or not they have the ability to major in CS. In the first stage, students measure their own ability (*central phenomenon*) based on "uninterpreted measurements of ability" (e.g., grades in CS courses) and consider the culture and environment in which they will be learning CS (referred to as *external context*). Lewis et al. also suggest that in this first stage, students' "mindsets" impact their assessment of their CS ability (referred to as *intervening conditions*). For example, students with a "fixed mindset" believe that intelligence or ability is fixed or innate whereas students with a "growth mindset" believe that intelligence or ability is something that can be built on or increased with effort. In the second stage of the self-assessment process, students evaluated their ability by interpreting the meaning of measurements (e.g., relevance of their CS experience to the CS major, benchmarking grades with peers at similar CS experience levels – rather than comparing grades against the entire class).

Lewis et al.'s theoretical framework surfaced the question of whether our national survey data measured components of this two-stage process of self-assessment at the middle and high school level. An analysis of our national survey questions found several questions mapped to the first stage of assessing CS ability. These include questions on confidence and self-assessment, which represent intervening conditions influenced by their "mindsets," as measured by our survey question on the perception of the need to be "smart." We also found several survey items that measure identity aligned to CS, a component of fit outlined in Lewis et al. [2]. These include questions on students' perceptions of their skills in various subjects as well as their agreement with positive statements of CS careers. We also include a question on how students identify with representations of CS in the media. The third input we explored was the external social context, which include questions on exposure and encouragement, as well as parent survey questions on factors that may influence their encouragement of their children. See Table 1 for a crosswalk of the theoretical framework components and national survey items.

Table 1: Crosswalk of Theoretical Framework with Our Study's National Survey Items

	Theoretical Framework Components	National Survey Items
Inputs	Ability	**Student Survey** • Confidence in learning CS • Self-rated skills in math and science • Perception that you have to be "smart" to pursue computer science
	Fit (alignment of identity with CS)	**Student Survey** • Self-rated skills in various subjects • See computer science as an opportunity to work on fun and exciting projects • Agree that people who do computer science make things that help improve people's lives • Believe that computer science can be used in a lot of different types of jobs. • Likelihood to have a job that uses computer science • Frequency of seeing people "like you" in the media doing computer science
	External context	**Student Survey** • Teacher and parent messages to student that they would be good at computer science • Whether student knows an adult who works in the tech field **Parent Survey** • Perception of student interest in CS • Parent desire for students to learn CS • Parent rating of their child's skills • Perceived reasons for underrepresentation of certain groups • Perception that you have to be "smart" to pursue computer science
Outputs	Interest	**Student Survey** • Interest in learning CS in the future

Lewis et al.'s theoretical frameworks [1,2] provide a foundation to investigate the extent to which middle and high school students in our study reported positive self-assessments of CS ability and fit, along with external context. We use the frameworks to explore the relationship between these factors and interest in pursuing CS.

4 METHODS

This two-year study surveyed about 16,000 students, parents, teachers, principals, and superintendents each year across the United States. Table 2 shows the mode and respondents for the study. These populations were selected to understand social perceptions from students and the external context through parents and educators (influencers in the students' education). This paper focuses on findings from the second year of the study.

Gallup Inc. conducted telephone surveys with students, parents, and teachers currently living in all 50 states and the District of Columbia using a combination of the Gallup Panel and the Gallup Daily tracking survey. The Gallup Panel is a probability-based panel of U.S. adults selected using random-digit-dial (RDD) and address-based sampling methods. The Gallup Panel is not an opt-in panel. The Gallup Daily tracking survey sample includes national adults with a quota of 50% cellphone and 50% landline respondents, with additional minimum quotas by time zone within region. Landline and cellphone numbers are selected using RDD methods. Landline respondents are chosen at random within each household based

on which member had the most recent birthday. Eligible Gallup Daily tracking respondents who previously agreed to future contact were contacted to participate in this study.

Student and parent samples included targeted, detailed data on underrepresented populations (Blacks and Hispanics, including Spanish-speaking only). All Hispanic students are categorized as Hispanic in this study. Non-Hispanic Black students and non-Hispanic White students are categorized as Black and White, respectively. Participating students were from grades 7–12 (typically ages 12–18). Participating parents had one or more children in these grades. Teachers in the sample taught 1st–12th grade, with approximately 21% teaching or have taught computer science. The population for principals was sampled from a list of 99% of U.S. public schools and approximately 30% of U.S. private schools. The population for superintendents was from a panel including more than 20% of all U.S. K–12 superintendents.

Table 2: Methodology overview for the five populations.

Population	Mode	Grades	Sample Year 2
Students	Phone	7–12	1,672, including • 228 Black • 310 Hispanic
Parents	Phone	7–12	1,677, including • 197 Black • 264 Hispanic
Teachers	Phone	1–12	1,008
Principals	Web	K–12	9,805
Superintendents	Web	K–12	2,307

Student and parent samples were weighted to correct for unequal selection probability and nonresponse. Student data were weighted to match national demographics of age, gender, race, ethnicity and region. Parent data were weighted to match national demographics of age, gender, education, race, ethnicity and region. Demographic weighting targets were based on the most recent Current Population Survey [25].

Teacher samples were weighted to correct for unequal selection probability and nonresponse. The data were weighted to match demographics of age, gender, education, race, ethnicity and region. Demographic weighting targets were based on Gallup Inc.'s tracking information.

Principal and superintendent samples were weighted to match national demographics of school ZIP code, school enrollment size, and census region. The margin of sampling error for each population is between ±1.0 and ±3.9 percentage points at the 95% confidence level [26].

The inclusion of K–12 students as well as influencers in their education (i.e., parents and educators at various levels) provides us with a wider lens to understand the social factors for students from both the intervening perspective (from the students themselves) and the external context. We oversampled Black and Hispanic students and parents, which, along with representative samples of the U.S., allowed for comparisons among Black, Hispanic, and White populations. Other races were included in the representative sample, but their sample sizes were too small for comparisons. The representative samples also allowed us to analyze differences by gender for the students and parents.

The surveys for students, parents, teachers, and principals each lasted about 10 minutes, with 30-40 questions. Superintendents were surveyed as part of another regular online survey, with 10 closed-ended questions for this study.

To ensure that respondents were considering CS properly, we provided them with a definition of CS at the beginning, and gave reminders with the definition multiple times throughout the survey. The definition we provided is as follows:

Computer science involves using programming/coding to create more advanced artifacts, such as software, apps, games, websites and electronics, and computer science is not equivalent to general computer use.

Surveys for all five groups covered topics on perceptions of CS, interest in and desire for CS, in- and out-of-school opportunities for CS, participation in CS, and obstacles to providing and accessing CS opportunities. Survey items were closed-ended, with agreement for yes/no questions and Likert scales for agreement with statements (1-3 Likert for students and parents and 1-5 Likert for teachers, principals, and superintendents). Surveys were not completely the same from the first year to second year, as new questions were introduced based on findings from the first year. Many questions were retained so that trends could be tracked over the entire research study.

After data were collected, a rigorous quality assurance process was used to clean the data. The data were then coded and reviewed by response. Factors were analyzed using regression to understand trends across and within the surveyed populations and Pearson's correlation to identify relationships between variables. When analyzing differences by race or gender, income was controlled. Factors were categorized to include ability, fit, and external context as well as interest in CS.

5 FINDINGS

We explore our findings through the lens of our theoretical framework and delineate how they confirm some of the literature on racial/ethnic differences at a larger scale with respect to CS education while further contributing new findings, particularly on social factors at the K–12 level, and how they confirm much of the prior research on gender differences, focusing on the K–12 level. With the framework, we focus on ability, fit, and external context as factors that influence pursuit of CS, which we investigate through students' reported interest in CS.

5.1 Ability

We build on Lewis et al.'s framework of ability [2] by exploring it within the K–12 context, rather than at the postsecondary level. Therefore, rather than understanding ability within the context of a CS learning experience, we examined ability through intervening conditions: students' confidence to learn CS, their ratings of skills related to CS, and their perception of the need to be smart to do CS since most have not learned CS.

For confidence, we found that Black students were more likely to indicate that they were "very confident"' they could learn CS, with 68% saying so compared to 51% of Hispanic and 56% of White students. This is surprising given the underrepresentation of both Black and Hispanic students, yet the former have high confidence while the latter have low confidence in CS. By gender, our results confirm much of the research on confidence [e.g., 16,20-24]. We found 65% of boys said that they were "very confident" they could learn CS compared to just 48% of girls.

When looking at students' self-rated skills in math and science, results are similar to confidence in CS. While differences were negligible in math by race/ethnicity, Hispanic students were less likely to say that they were "very skilled" in science, with 36% indicating so compared to 50% of Black students and 41% of White students. We did find that students' self-rated skills in math and science were correlated with their confidence to learn CS (math PC = 0.199, $p < 0.001$; science PC = 0.243, $p < 0.001$). Girls were less likely than boys to say they were "very skilled" in math or science, with 48% of boys saying this for each, compared with 37% of girls for math and 33% for science.

Finally, we looked at students' perception of the need to be smart as an indicator of their mindset about CS [27], as it affects students' perspectives of their ability. Over half of all students agreed that "people who do CS need to be very smart," indicating that there is a strong perception of innate or fixed ability. By race/ethnicity, we found patterns similar to confidence, with Black students least likely to agree and most likely to disagree that "people who do CS need to be very smart" while Hispanic students were most likely to agree and least likely to disagree (see Figure 1). However, by gender, we found no difference with 53% of both females and males agreeing with the need to be smart.

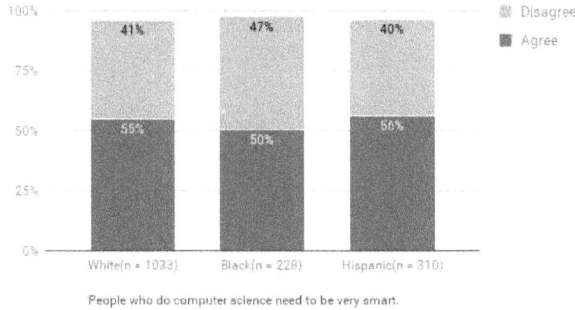

Figure 1: Student agreement with "People who do computer science need to be very smart," by race/ethnicity.

In sum, our findings indicate that Black students have greater self-perceived ability in CS. On the other hand, our results indicate that Hispanic students may not be as well supported for ability, as indicated by their weak self-assessments of the three ability items (Table 1). By gender, we found that boys had greater self-perceived ability, though we found no difference by gender in their mindset about the need to be smart.

5.2 Fit

Building off of the grounded theory of fit from Lewis et al.' [1], we expand to K–12 students. In particular, we use students' self-rated skills in various subjects to determine if they identify with the singularly focused aspect of CS, in which perceptions of people in CS are that they do not have other interests. We also consider perceptions of CS and whether they fit the stereotypes of being asocial, competitive, and male. Finally, we look at how students envision their fit in CS through their indication of whether their future jobs would involve CS and whether they identify with those they see represented as practicing CS.

To understand if students who identified as skilled in math and science and not other subjects were more likely to be interested in pursuing CS, we asked students how skilled they considered themselves in math, science, English (reading and writing), music, sports, searching the Internet, and working with other people. Interestingly, by race/ethnicity, we found the Black students tended to rate their skills higher than White or Hispanic students across most areas while Hispanic students were less likely to rate their skills high (see Figure 2). Hispanic students were less likely to rate their skills in academic subjects high, and as noted above, particularly in math and science. By gender (Figure 2), also discussed above, girls are less likely than boys to say that they are "very skilled" in math or science. On the other hand, girls are more likely than boys to say that they are very skilled in English or music, with 46% of boys versus 60% of girls indicating they are "very skilled" in English and 36% of

boys versus 48% of girls indicating they are "very skilled" in music. Thus, while no pattern is apparent by race/ethnicity, there are clearer indicators by gender of the singular focus of CS playing out in terms of representation in CS.

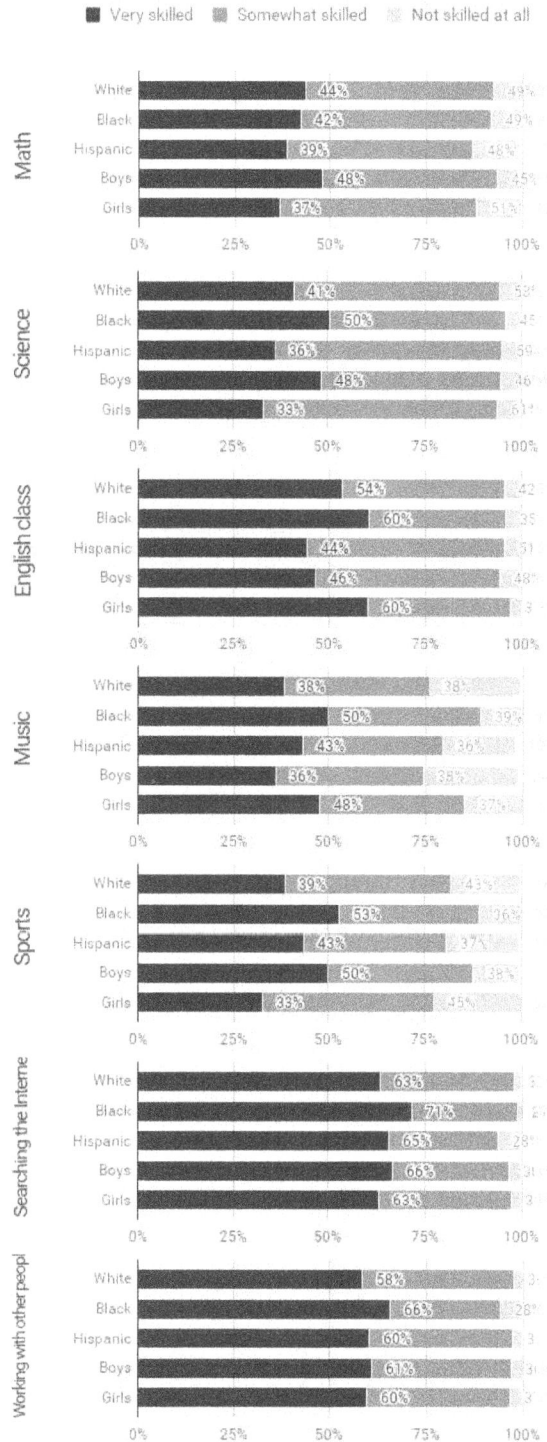

Figure 2: Students' self-rated skills in various areas, by race/ethnicity (White n = 1033, Black n = 228, Hispanic n = 310) and by gender (boys n = 901, girls n = 771).

Table 3: Students' views of people engaged in computer science in the media.

How often do you see or read about people doing computer science in each of the following places? How about _____?		White (n = 1033)	Black (n = 228)	Hispanic (n = 310)	Male (n = 901)	Female (n = 771)
In TV shows	Often	20%	34%	23%	25%	21%
	Sometimes	62%	44%	54%	55%	61%
	Never	18%	22%	22%	20%	19%
In movies	Often	24%	36%	23%	28%	23%
	Sometimes	62%	47%	60%	59%	61%
	Never	13%	16%	17%	13%	16%
Online through social media, articles	Often	34%	32%	36%	39%	26%
or videos	Sometimes	47%	51%	50%	43%	55%
	Never	19%	17%	14 %	17%	18%
If often or sometimes see people "doing computer science" in TV, movies, or online:		(n = 998)	(n = 217)	(n = 299)	(n = 870)	(n = 744)
Thinking about all of the people you see or read about doing computer science in TV shows, in movies or online, how often do you see people like you doing computer science?	Often	16%	26%	13%	21%	11%
	Sometimes	59%	54%	65%	61%	57%
	Never	25%	20%	22%	18%	31%

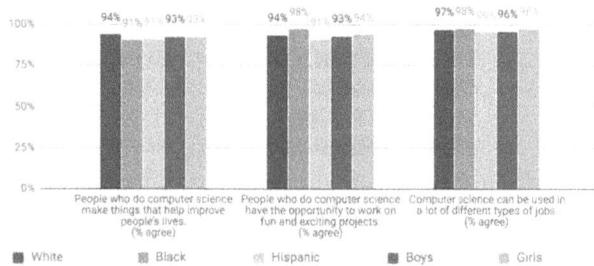

Figure 3: Students' agreement with perceptions about CS, by race/ethnicity (White n = 1033, Black n = 228, Hispanic n = 310) and by gender (boys n = 901, girls n = 771).

Common perceptions of CS are that the field is boring, asocial, competitive, individualistic, and male. We asked students about their agreement with various statements about CS. Surprisingly, we found very positive perceptions about the field of CS across races/ethnicities and genders, with no significant difference, with over 92% of students agreeing that CS helps improve people's lives, involves fun and exciting projects, and can be used in many different types of jobs (see Figure 3).

Finally, we examined how students envisioned their fit through their anticipated careers as well as through representations in the media. We found that by race/ethnicity, Hispanic students were more likely than White students to say that it is "very likely" that they will have a job where they will need to know CS (38% of Hispanic students versus 26% of White students and 30% of Black students). By gender, boys were more likely to indicate that it is "very likely" they will have a job needing CS, with 35% indicating so compared to 22% of girls.

Regarding representations in the media, Black students were more likely to see people engaged in CS in TV shows and movies (Table 3). Of students who see people engaged in CS in the media, Black students were also more likely than White or Hispanic students to often see someone "like [themselves]" while

Hispanic students were least likely to often see someone "like [themselves]." By gender, girls were not only less likely than boys to see representations of CS in the media overall, of students who do see people engaged in CS in the media, girls were also less likely to often see someone "like [themselves]" (11% of girls versus 21% of boys) while they were more likely to never see someone "like [themselves]" (31% of girls versus 18% of boys).

Interestingly, we found that negative perceptions of CS were low, with a large majority of all students noting very positive perceptions about CS, yet fit, as examined through alignment of identity with CS, varied by group. Overall, we found that fit for Black students was strong. For Hispanic students, it was mixed. Hispanic students indicated high likelihood to have a job needing CS but also rated their CS and related skills low and were less likely to see someone "like [themselves]" in CS in the media. By gender, boys' fit was extremely strong across all aspects we examined whereas girls' fit was weak.

5.3 External context

The final influencing factor we examined was external social context from the perspectives of parents and educators. We explore encouragement, parents' perceived skills of their children, perceived interest by demographic, knowing a role model in the field, and parents' and educators' mindsets.

For encouragement, we explored whether students have been told by a teacher or parent that they would be good at CS, finding no significant difference by race/ethnicity. However, we found that boys were more likely than girls to say that they have been told by a teacher or parent that they would be good at CS. In fact, 39% and 46% of boys said they have been told this by a teacher or parent, respectively, compared to 26% and 27% of girls. Not surprisingly, we found that while there is no difference in parents' rating of their child's skills in math or science by the children's genders, parents were more likely to say that girls are more skilled in English (reading and writing), music, and working with others, with 70% of parents of girls versus 49% of parents of boys indicating their child is "very skilled" in English, 46% of parents of girls versus 34% of parents of boys indicating their child is "very skilled" in music, and 69% of parents of girls versus 59% of parents of boys indicating their child is "very skilled" in working with other people.

When looking at perceived interest, parents of Black and Hispanic children were actually more likely than parents of White children to think that their children are "very interested" in learning CS (26% of parents of White children, 32% of parents Black children, and 42% of parents of Hispanic children; see Figure 4) while parents of boys were more likely than parents of girls to say so (37% versus 25%, respectively). This follows from students' reported encouragement. Adults may be more likely to support students who they believe are interested. In fact, parents of boys were more likely to want their children to learn CS than parents of girls (91% versus 83%). Similarly, Black and Hispanic parents were more likely to say that they want their children to learn CS, with 92% indicating so compared 84% of White parents.

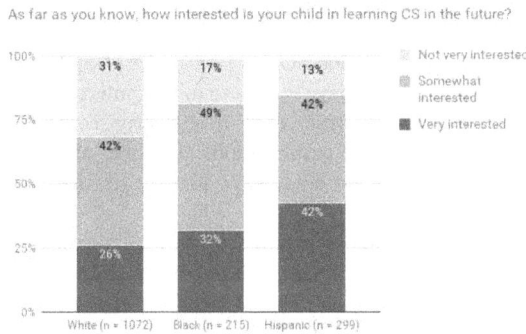

Figure 4: Parents' perceptions of their children's interest in learning CS, by race/ethnicity of child.

Furthermore, when asked about why certain groups (women, Blacks, and Hispanics) are underrepresented in CS, parents were slightly more likely to cite lack of interest and motivation compared to educators while teachers were more likely to cite lack of opportunity and exposure. This implies that parents may be more likely to believe that underrepresented students are opting out of engaging in CS rather than facing external barriers.

Another piece of the external context is whether students know adults who work in the field. When asked about if they know someone "who works with computers or other types of technology," Hispanic students were least likely to say they do, with 49% saying so compared to 68% of White students and 65% of Black students. By gender, there was no difference with 63% of boys and girls saying that they know an adult in the field.

Finally, the adults' mindsets along with how they perceive students may determine how they support students. Among parents, we found similar trends to students by demographic in their agreement with "people who do computer science need to be very smart," with 47% of parents of Black children, 56% of

parents of Hispanic children, and 51% of parents of White children agreeing. We also found that females were more likely to disagree, with 47% of female parents versus 43% of male parents disagreeing and 19% of female teachers versus 12% of male teachers disagreeing (Figure 5).

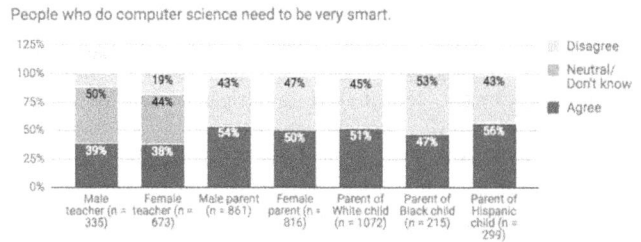

Figure 5: Adults' perceptions of the need to be smart to do computer science, by teacher and parent gender and by parent race/ethnicity.

In summary, the external social context is mixed for Black and Hispanic students in that while they and their parents are more likely to value and be interested in CS, Hispanic students are less likely to know someone in the field and they and their parents are more likely to believe people doing CS need to be very smart. On the other hand, boys are well supported in the external social context, with greater encouragement as well as greater perceived CS and relevant skills and interest.

5.4 Interest

Based on the theoretical framework [1,2], ability, fit, and external context have been found to be key indicators for students' interest in pursuing CS among college students. We expand this to K–12 students, specifically in middle and high schools, to understand indicators of which groups are, or are not, socially supported in CS. By race/ethnicity, we found mixed indicators with Black students having greater self-perceived ability, stronger fit via identity with CS, and more supportive external social contexts while Hispanic students had low self-perceived ability, mixed fit, and mixed support in their external social contexts. These social factors point to complex barriers, as both of these groups continue to be underrepresented in the CS field. In contrast, by gender, the indicators were much more straightforward in that girls had low self-perceived ability, weak fit, and less supportive external contexts, and correspondingly are underrepresented in CS.

To explore possible outcomes from these indicators, we asked students about their interest in learning CS. We found that students' interest was correlated with confidence (PC = 0.397, p < 0.001) and encouragement from teachers and parents (teachers PC = 0.313, p < 0.001; parents PC = 0.360, p < 0.001), components of ability and external context. We also found that interest was correlated with students' reported likelihood to have a job needing CS (PC = 0.422, p < 0.001), a component of fit. Therefore, components of each of the input categories from the theoretical framework [1,2], ability, fit, and external context, are confirmed by our study to be correlated with interest in learning CS.

We found that Black students and Hispanic students were more likely than White students to say that they are "very interested" in learning CS, with 31% of Black students, 35% of Hispanic students, and 21% of White students saying so. This follows from our exploration of social indicators of ability, fit, and external context for Black students, while the mixed social indicators for Hispanic students may have certain components that are stronger, contributing to Hispanic students' greater interest.

Given the strong social indicators by gender, it is not surprising that we found that boys were over twice as likely as girls to say that they were "very interested" in learning CS (34% of boys versus 16% of girls) and that girls were almost twice as likely as boys to say that they were "not at all interested" (13% of boys versus 24% of girls).

6 LIMITATIONS

While we categorize students into male or female and Black, Hispanic, or White, it is important to understand that the differences are based on the distributions of the entire groups. Therefore, there are always individuals who are outliers or deviate from the mean and we must therefore be careful not to overgeneralize the findings. When working with students, it is key to view them as individuals and with empathy towards their unique backgrounds [28-31].

Furthermore, we only examined differences between males and females and between Black, Hispanic, and White students and did not look at groups outside of these categories due to small sample sizes. Additionally, while the intersections between gender and race/ethnicity are important and involve unique social perceptions, their small sample sizes would have yielded results with high margins of error, and we wanted to be careful to not draw conclusions from these types of results.

Finally, as a quantitative survey study, we were limited to what we asked and were not able to collect information beyond our questions. There are many factors that we were not able to consider that may have large contributions to students' interest to pursue CS. Additionally, while we defined CS at the beginning and reminded respondents multiple times throughout our survey, there is still the possibility that their understanding of CS differed from the definition we provided.

7 SIGNIFICANCE

The theoretical framework from Lewis et al. [1,2] provided a lens to explore why students choose to pursue or not pursue CS. We built on their work with an exploration of what is happening quantitatively by demographic, at a national scale, for the factors of ability, fit, and external context. We confirmed that components of these factors correlate with interest in learning CS. We built on and confirmed much of the previous research on factors influencing gender gaps. We also fill in gaps in the literature with new analyses of social factors by race/ethnicity.

The implication of our work is the need to consider both structural and social factors. Our findings indicate that different supports are needed for each group. While we found that Black students have greater self-perceived ability, stronger fit, and more supportive external social contexts, and are more likely to be very interested in CS, they continue to be underrepresented. Their high confidence as well as lower agreement with the mindset that one needs to be smart to do CS also point towards what should be greater representation. Other research [e.g., 3] found that Black students have lower access to CS learning opportunities. Thus, structural barriers may be greater. We hypothesize that the high confidence and ratings may be the result of minimal access to more advanced CS activities [26], and students may not know their actual abilities and overestimate their abilities. Along with increasing access, efforts should focus on supporting these social factors and ensuring new exposure does not discourage students.

Furthermore, we found that the factors are mixed for Hispanic students, who, along with their parents, appear to value CS and envision its importance to their future careers, yet they are less likely to know a role model in tech or identify with those represented as engaging in CS in the media and are less confident in their CS and related skills. Confidence has been found to be correlated with persistence [32], so Hispanic students' low confidence should be of major concern to efforts that support this population. Other research [e.g., 3] found that Hispanic students have lower exposure to computers. Similar to Black students, these structural barriers may contribute to Hispanic students' lower participation. Teachers of Black and Hispanic students should find ways to support their greater interest.

Finally, girls' underrepresentation aligns with our findings on ability, fit, and external context, which confirm bodies of work in this area. The challenge here is that girls have lower interest in learning CS, which may cause their influencers to view that as an independent choice. However, our research highlights that this interest is correlated with confidence, encouragement, and perceived likelihood to need CS for their careers. Therefore, encouragement could change a girl's interest. Efforts should focus on supporting influencers around girls and changing perceptions about who does and does not belong in CS.

To ensure that all students are enabled to learn CS, it is not enough to focus solely on providing access nor is it enough to focus solely on positive campaigns around CS. Our paper indicates that factors are much more complex and a holistic approach towards equity should be taken, in which all factors are considered and engagement is catered to each individual's circumstances. We believe that the research detailed in this paper builds upon and contributes to the body of knowledge regarding how social factors play out for different demographics before college and can therefore help to inform efforts to broaden access to CS at the K–12 level.

ACKNOWLEDGMENTS

The authors would like to acknowledge the contributions of many of our colleagues at Google and Gallup.

REFERENCES

[1] Lewis, Colleen M., Ruth E. Anderson, and Ken Yasuhara. 2016. I Don't Code All Day: Fitting in Computer Science When the Stereotypes Don't Fit. In *Proceedings of the 2016 ACM Conference on International Computing Education Research*, 23-32. ACM, 2016.

[2] Lewis, Colleen M., Ken Yasuhara, and Ruth E. Anderson. 2011. Deciding to major in computer science: a grounded theory of students' self-assessment of ability. In *Proceedings of the seventh international workshop on Computing education research*, 3-10. ACM, 2011.

[3] Google Inc. & Gallup. 2016. Trends in the State of Computer Science in U.S. K-12 Schools. Retrieved from http://goo.gl/j291E0.

[4] Margolis, Jane, Rachel Estrella, Joanna Goode, Jennifer Jellison Holme, and Kim Nao. 2010. *Stuck in the shallow end: Education, race, and computing*. MIT Press, 2010.

[5] Susan Colby, Helen Ma, Kelsey Robinson, and Lareina Yee. 2016. What It Will Take to Make the Tech Industry More Diverse. *Harvard Business Review*.

[6] Victoria J. Rideout, Kimberly A. Scott, and Kevin A. Clark. 2016. *The Digital Lives of African American Tweens, Teens, and Parents: Innovating and Learning with Technology*. (Fall 2016). Retrieved April 1, 2017 from https://cgest.asu.edu/sites/default/files/digital_lives_report_0.pdf.

[7] Lori Carter. 2006. Why students with an apparent aptitude for computer science don't choose to major in computer science. *ACM SIGCSE Bulletin* 38, 1 (2006), 27-31.

[8] Tor Busch. 1995. Gender differences in self-efficacy and attitudes toward computers. *Journal of educational computing research* 12, 2 (1995), 147-158.

[9] Anne-Kathrin Peters and Arnold Pears. 2013. Engagement in Computer Science and IT--What! A Matter of Identity?. In *Learning and Teaching in Computing and Engineering (LaTiCE), 2013*, 114-121. IEEE, 2013.

[10] Tamar Levine and Smadar Donitsa-Schmidt. 1998. Computer use, confidence, attitudes, and knowledge: A causal analysis. *Computers in human behavior* 14, 1 (1998), 125-146.

[11] Allison Master, Sapna Cheryan, and Andrew N. Meltzoff. 2016. Computing whether she belongs: Stereotypes undermine girls' interest and sense of belonging in computer science. *Journal of Educational Psychology* 108, 3 (2016), 424.

[12] Linda J. Sax, Kathleen J. Lehman, Jerry A. Jacobs, M. Allison Kanny, Gloria Lim, Laura Monje-Paulson, and Hilary B. Zimmerman. 2017. Anatomy of an enduring gender gap: The evolution of women's participation in computer science. *The Journal of Higher Education* 88, no. 2 (2017), 258-293.

[13] Amanda B. Diekman, Elizabeth R. Brown, Amanda M. Johnston, and Emily K. Clark. 2010. Seeking congruity between goals and roles: A new look at why women opt out of science, technology, engineering, and mathematics careers. *Psychological Science* 21, 8 (2010), 1051-1057. doi:10.1177/0956797610377342.

[14] Jacquelynne S. Eccles. 2007. *Where Are All the Women? Gender Differences in Participation in Physical Science and Engineering*. In S. Ceci (Ed); Williams, Wendy M. (Ed). (2007). Why aren't more women in science?: Top researchers debate the evidence, (pp. 199-210). Washington, DC, US: American Psychological Association, xx, 254 pp

[15] David C. Webb and Susan B. Miller. 2015. Gender analysis of a large scale survey of middle grades students' conceptions of computer science education. In *Proceedings of the Third Conference on GenderIT*, 1-8. ACM, 2015.

[16] Jill Denner, Linda Werner, Lisa O'Connor, and Jill Glassman. 2014. Community college men and women: A test of three widely held beliefs about who pursues computer science. *Community College Review* 42, 4 (2014), 342-362.

[17] Monica M. McGill, Adrienne Decker, and Amber Settle. 2016. Undergraduate Students' Perceptions of the Impact of Pre-College Computing Activities on Choices of Major. *ACM Transactions on Computing Education (TOCE)* 16, no. 4 (2016), 15.

[18] Mark Guzdial, Barbara J. Ericson, Tom McKlin, and Shelly Engelman. 2012. A statewide survey on computing education pathways and influences: Factors in broadening participation in computing. In *Proceedings of the 9th Annual International Conference on International Computing Education Research (ICER'12)*. ACM, New York, NY, 143–150. http://doi.acm.org/10.1145/2361276.2361304.

[19] Joanna Goode, Rachel Estrella, and Jane Margolis. 2006. *Lost in translation: Gender and high school computer science*. na, 2006.

[20] Joanne M. Badagliacco. 1990. Gender and race differences in computing attitudes and experience. *Social Science Computer Review* 8, 1 (1990), 42-63.

[21] Thomas J. Smith, Spencer L. Pasero, and Cornelius M. McKenna. 2014. Gender effects on student attitude toward science. *Bulletin of Science, Technology & Society* 34, 1-2 (2014), 7-12.

[22] Yuk Fai Cheong, Frank Pajares, and Paul S. Oberman. 2004. Motivation and academic help-seeking in high school computer science. *Computer Science Education* 14, 1 (2004), 3-19.

[23] Heather Dryburgh. 2000. Underrepresentation of girls and women in computer science: Classification of 1990s research. *Journal of educational computing research* 23, 2 (2000), 181-202.

[24] Allan Fisher, Jane Margolis, and Faye Miller. 1997. Undergraduate women in computer science: experience, motivation and culture. In *ACM SIGCSE Bulletin*, vol. 29, 1, pp. 106-110. ACM, 1997.

[25] United States Census Bureau. 2016. Current Population Survey. Retrieved from https://www.census.gov/programs-surveys/cps.html. Google Inc. & Gallup. 2016. Diversity Gaps in Computer Science: Exploring the Underrepresentation of Girls, Blacks and Hispanics. Retrieved from http://goo.gl/PG34aH.

[26] Google Inc. & Gallup. 2016. Diversity Gaps in Computer Science: Exploring the Underrepresentation of Girls, Blacks and Hispanics. Retrieved from http://goo.gl/PG34aH.

[27] Carol S. Dweck. 2008. *Mindset: The new psychology of success*. Random House Digital, Inc., 2008.

[28] Irene V. Blair. 2002. The malleability of automatic stereotypes and prejudice. *Personality and Social Psychology Review* 6, 3 (2002), 242-261.

[29] Molly Carnes, Patricia G. Devine, Linda Baier Manwell, Angela Byars-Winston, Eve Fine, Cecilia E. Ford, Patrick Forscher, Carol Isaac, Anna Kaatz, Wairimu Magua, Mari Palta, and Jennifer Sheridan. 2015. Effect of an intervention to break the gender bias habit for faculty at one institution: a cluster randomized, controlled trial. *Academic medicine: journal of the Association of American Medical Colleges* 90, 2 (2015), 221.

[30] Sarah M. Jackson, Amy L. Hillard, and Tamera R. Schneider. 2014. Using implicit bias training to improve attitudes toward women in STEM. *Social Psychology of Education* 17, 3 (2014), 419-438.

[31] Jason A. Okonofua, David Paunesku, and Gregory M. Walton. 2016. Brief intervention to encourage empathic discipline cuts suspension rates in half among adolescents." *Proceedings of the National Academy of Sciences* (2016). doi: 10.1073/pnas.1523698113.

[32] Robert W. Lent, Steven D. Brown, and Kevin C. Larkin. 1984. Relation of self-efficacy expectations to academic achievement and persistence. *Journal of counseling psychology* 31, 3 (1984), 356.

Taking Advantage of Scale by Analyzing Frequent Constructed-Response, Code Tracing Wrong Answers

Kristin Stephens-Martinez
UC Berkeley
Berkeley, CA 94720
ksteph@cs.berkeley.edu

An Ju
UC Berkeley
Berkeley, CA 94720
an_ju@berkeley.edu

Krishna Parashar
UC Berkeley
Berkeley, CA 94720
kcparashar@berkeley.edu

Regina Ongowarsito
UC Berkeley
Berkeley, CA 94720
regina.ongowarsito@gmail.com

Nikunj Jain
UC Berkeley
Berkeley, CA 94720
nikunj.jain@berkeley.edu

Sreesha Venkat
UC Berkeley
Berkeley, CA 94720
sreeshavenkat@berkeley.edu

Armando Fox
UC Berkeley
Berkeley, CA 94720
fox@cs.berkeley.edu

ABSTRACT

Constructed-response, code-tracing questions ("What would Python print?") are good formative assessments. Unlike selected-response questions simply marked correct or incorrect, a constructed wrong answer can provide information on a student's particular difficulty. However, constructed-response questions are resource-intensive to grade manually, and machine grading yields only correct/incorrect information. We analyzed incorrect constructed responses from code-tracing questions in an introductory computer science course to investigate whether a small subsample of such responses could provide enough information to make inspecting the subsample worth the effort, and if so, how best to choose this subsample. In addition, we sought to understand what insights into student difficulties could be gained from such an analysis.

We found that ≈5% of the most frequently given wrong answers cover ≈60% of the wrong constructed responses. Inspecting these wrong answers, we found similar misconceptions as those in prior work, additional difficulties not identified in prior work regarding language-specific constructs and data structures, and non-misconception "slips" that cause students to get questions wrong, such as syntax errors, sloppy reading/writing.

Our methodology is much less time-consuming than full manual inspection, yet yields new and durable insight into student difficulties that can be used for several purposes, including expanding a concept inventory, creating summative assessments, and creating effective distractors for selected-response assessments.

ICER'17, August 18–20, 2017, Tacoma, WA, USA.
© 2017 Copyright held by the owner/author(s). Publication rights licensed to ACM.
ISBN 978-1-4503-4968-0/17/08...$15.00
DOI: http://dx.doi.org/10.1145/3105726.3106188

KEYWORDS

constructed-response questions; introductory computer science; education; massive courses; formative assessments; student errors; code-tracing questions

1 INTRODUCTION

The goals of formative assessment are to provide feedback to the student to improve their attainment in cases of error and to inform the teacher as to how to modify or improve pedagogy to address weaknesses in student attainment [1]. In large-enrollment courses, selected-response questions (e.g. multiple choice) are often used as both formative and summative assessment instruments because they can be mechanically graded. However, it is difficult to write selected-response questions whose distractors effectively target common student misunderstandings [13]. Writing constructed-response questions (CRQs), such as filling in blanks, is easier because the teacher does not need to create specific distractors. Additionally, requiring the student to construct a response may also provide richer insight into their level of understanding compared to asking them to identify a correct choice from a list.

However, manually analyzing constructed responses to determine student errors can be prohibitively time-consuming in large-enrollment courses. We considered the wrong constructed responses from code-tracing questions and set about to answer the following research questions:

- **R1**: Can analyzing a small subsample of wrong constructed responses yield information about student difficulties that makes it worth the time investment?
  - **R1.A**: If so, assuming the same questions are used in subsequent course offerings, can the information so gained be applied to future course offerings, further amortizing the time investment?
  - **R1.B**: If so, how should that subsample be chosen and how large must it be?

- **R2:** What insights about student difficulties can be gained from analyzing the subsample?

We address these questions by examining a corpus of 332,829 responses to 92 code-tracing, univalent (having a single correct answer) CRQs. The data comes from responses by 4,068 students in 3 offerings of a large-enrollment introductory computer science (CS) course. We found that a ≈5% subsample of the most frequent wrong answers covers ≈60% of the wrong constructed responses. The frequent wrong answers are consistent in how much they overlap for a given question set and semester pair, but the level of overlap varies between question sets and semester pairs. Therefore frequency should be taken into account when choosing a sample to inspect.

In addition to discovering student difficulties similar to those found in prior work, we also identify new difficulties not reported in prior work such as language-specific constructs and data structures.

After defining terminology and surveying related work, we describe our data set and the emergent coding process we used to analyze it. We then report on how our analysis informs the answers to our research questions. We conclude with a discussion on known and potential uses for our findings.

2 TERMINOLOGY

- *Machine-marked-wrong answer (MMWA)* - A (question, string) pair the automated system marks as incorrect.
- *Wrong answer* - A MMWA that is actually incorrect, as opposed to a false positive marked incorrect by the automated system.
- *Response* - A (student, MMWA) pair; many students may give the same MMWA.
- *Tag* - Human experts' interpretation of a specific student difficulty that could lead to an observed student error.
- *Taggable* - A wrong answer is taggable if at least one tag can be applied to it.

3 RELATED WORK

Misconceptions leading to student programming errors have been intensively studied. Clancy [5] reviews potential causes of programming misconceptions and inappropriate attitudes that interfere with learning programming. Sorva [17] provides an extensive catalog of novice misconceptions about introductory programming content. We find similar misconceptions, but also new misconceptions about data structures and language-specific constructs, which are less studied in prior work. In addition, because we focused on *how* students got wrong answers, we also found student difficulties with syntax and sloppy reading or writing.

While machine-gradable selected-response exercises with carefully-constructed distractors can reveal common student errors, effective distractors are hard to create [13]. This is true especially in introductory programming courses, where instructors' beliefs about student errors have only a weak correlation with the errors students actually make [3]. Others have therefore attempted to extract information about CS students' misunderstandings from various types of CRQs, such as code explanations [10, 15] or code submissions [7, 9, 12, 14], programming process byproducts such as error logs [4, 6], and univalent CRQs as in our work. Univalent CRQs

are particularly appealing: like other CRQs, they can reveal useful information about student difficulties without requiring creation of distractors in advance, but unlike other CRQs, they can be easily machine-graded.

The closest work to ours is Sirkiä and Sorva's work analyzing students' missteps when using a visual simulation tool for program tracing [16]. Students use the tool to indicate at each execution step what they expect the code to do, and the tool records every student mistake. The authors identified 200 mistakes each made by at least 10 students, and they analyzed the 26 most popular mistakes to find them to be either a usability-related issue, previously-known conceptual difficulty, or previously-unreported conceptual difficulty. In contrast, our code-tracing questions elicit only a single answer from the student, namely the overall result of running the code. In addition, our *tags*, which code the way(s) students could arrive at a wrong answer, are the equivalent of student mistakes but we allow multiple tags that in combination or separately could cause the wrong answer. Some questions include intermediate `print` statements so we can gain more fine-grained information as the student traces the code. In this regard, both systems encourage students to fix earlier errors before continuing their code-tracing, so we view them as complementary.

Finally, others outside CS have also used the content of wrong answers to understand a student's current knowledge. For basic arithmetic problems, Tatusoka categorized student errors using a two-dimensional Rule Space, with regions of this space representing erroneous rules students use to solve the problems [19, 20]. We instead assign as many tags as necessary to capture the individual or combined student errors that would lead a student to arrive at a wrong answer.

Another way to understand student difficulties is to construct a student model; this is the approach of Repair Theory [2] and systems such as PROUST [8] and MARCEL [18]. Building such models requires enumerating both the student's knowledge and a "bug" list representing ways to mutate that knowledge. While our technique does not result in an explicit student model, it provides insight into common student difficulties without this up-front cost.

4 DATA COLLECTION AND ANALYSIS

Our data comes from three recent offerings of a large-enrollment introductory CS course that teaches programming and the basics of programming abstraction using Python and Scheme. One formative-assessment activity consists of univalent CRQs involving code-tracing: a typical question (Figure 1, left) presents $1 - 20$ lines of code and asks the student what the interpreter's state will be at various points during execution. A *question set* groups questions about a similar topic, for example, lambda-expressions.

4.1 Data Collection and Preprocessing

The questions are administered through an automatic system running in a terminal window that poses each question and prevents the student from proceeding to the next question until the current one has been answered correctly; unlimited attempts are allowed. Grading is based on completion of the question sets. We record and timestamp every student response; this corpus forms the basis of our dataset.

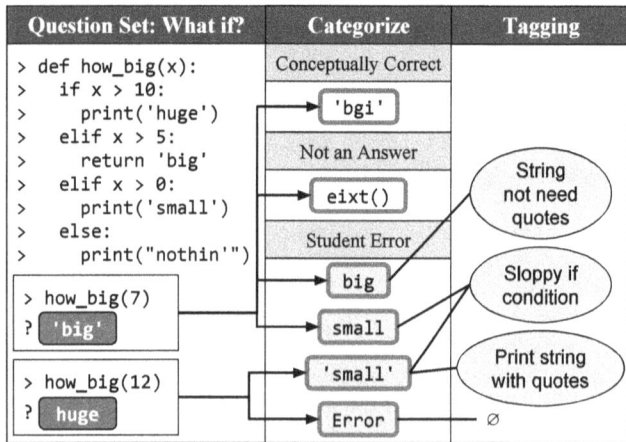

Figure 1: The flow of assigning categories and tags to MMWAs. Left: question set example with two questions on control flow with the correct answers in dark green round-corner rectangles. MMWAs for these questions are in the middle, all with a red bold border. These MMWAs are categorized as: "conceptually correct", "not an answer", or "student error"; the top two categories are false positives. Wrong answers with yellow/non-transparent rounded-corner rectangles are either taggable (top three answers have tags, shown in blue circles) or not taggable (bottom answer).

We cleaned the data by removing all blank answers and any duplicate responses made by the same student. Since the questions are answer-until-correct, every student will have the same set of correct responses, so we examine only their machine-marked wrong responses. Therefore, all future discussion of responses is only about the MMWAs. We did not do any merging of answers, as we found that fixing common typos such as 'TRue' for 'True' barely changed our results.

We collected data from the Fall 2015, Spring 2016, and Fall 2016 offerings of the course. Different instructors taught the Fall versus Spring offerings. We report our findings on 11 question sets.

As shown in Figure 1, one weakness of the automatic question administration system is its inflexibility in grading answers, resulting in two kinds of false positives. A *typo* might be the student entering 'bgi' rather than the correct answer 'big'; a human instructor would likely recognize that the student was trying to provide the correct answer. A *mode error* might be a student typing 'eixt()' rather than 'exit()' when intending to exit a session; these responses are also marked as wrong, even though the student was not attempting to answer the question at all. In the next section, we explain how we deal with such responses in our analysis process.

Figure 2 and Figure 3 summarize information about the question sets we used, ordered chronologically with some order swapping between semesters. Although some question sets showed significant variation in the total number of unique MMWAs across semesters (Figure 2) or percentage of students making at least one mistake when tackling that question set (Figure 3), we find that the properties of the frequent wrong answers remain relatively consistent,

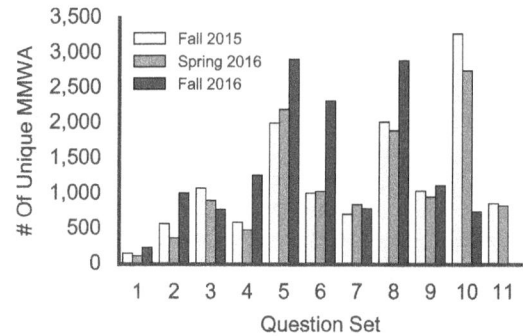

Figure 2: Distribution of the number of unique MMWAs for each semester and each question set. Ex: Question Set 6 had ≈1,000 unique MMWAs for Fall 2015 and Spring 2016 but ≈2,250 for Fall 2016.

as we describe in the next section. A noteworthy outlier is Question Set 1, which has outlier behavior in almost all of our analyses because it tests simple Boolean logic and is therefore easier than the other question sets. In addition, in Fall 2016 that question set was optional, and stronger students (who would be more likely to get all the questions correct on the first attempt) may have simply skipped it.

4.2 Tagging Process

Three content experts inspected the MMWAs. Two were experts who did well in the course and continued on to higher-level courses; the third expert was a former teaching assistant (TA) for the course. For each question set, we first chose a subset of MMWAs. For this set of MMWAs, we completed two phases with multiple steps each.

Our process uses emergent coding to create and assign the tags [11]. Section 5.4 includes details of how much time each phase took, what MMWAs we inspected, inter-rater-reliability, and results of the tagging process.

Phase 1: Tag Creation

(1) Propose Tags: One expert inspects the MMWA set to generate a set of proposed tags with a name, description, and example. (Time here recouped during Phase 2, Step 1 & 2)
(2) Finalize Tags: All three experts discuss the proposed list until deciding on a revised list of final tags.

Phase 2: Tagging Answer Set

(1) Categorize: Two experts separately inspect the MMWA set and assigned each MMWA a category (middle of Figure 1).
   - **conceptually correct:** marked wrong due to a typo
   - **not an answer:** marked wrong but was not intended as an answer because of a mode error or misunderstanding what text contains the question.
   - **student error:** conceptual errors and carelessness, further discussed in a later section.
(2) Assign Tags: Those answers categorized as "student error" are assigned zero or more tags (right of Figure 1).
(3) Consolidate/Discuss: The two experts consolidate their assignments into a single set of category and tag(s), discussing until they reach agreement.

Question Set	Question Count	Fall 2015			Spring 2016			Fall 2016		
		Students	Responses	% Students Wrong	Students	Responses	% Students Wrong	Students	Responses	% Students Wrong
1 Booleans	3	1,271	1,337	54	848	1,046	61	1,093	3,135	83
2 Short Circuit	10	1,283	9,570	95	847	5,234	94	1,692	19,032	99
3 if...else	11	1,293	8,145	97	840	5,843	97	1,022	6,901	99
4 Loops	4	1,278	4,744	81	830	3,766	87	1,675	13,103	96
5 Lambdas	12	1,239	23,124	99	827	19,316	99	1,614	37,666	99
6 HOF	6	1,203	9,698	93	783	8,624	96	1,581	27,121	99
7 OOP	5	907	4,146	92	767	4,147	94	1,516	5,431	90
8 OOP	19	1,042	12,344	99	767	10,760	99	1,510	28,199	99
9 Link Lists	9	1,010	5,543	91	753	4,525	92	1,479	6,478	87
10 Scheme Lists	11	1,040	17,050	99	739	12,791	99	359	3,614	100
11 Iterators	2	870	5,834	92	722	4,562	94	-	-	-

Figure 3: Statistics on the question sets used for this analysis for all course offerings. "HOF" stands for Higher Order Functions and "OOP" for object-oriented programming. "Students" is the number of students attempting that question set; low values are often due to the question sets being optional in certain semesters. "% Students Wrong" is the percentage of students who made at least one error on any question in the question set.

(4) Review/Confirm: During initial training of experts, a third expert inspects consolidated assignments and confirms them. If this expert disagrees, there is a discussion among all three experts until they reach agreement.

5 RESULTS

5.1 R1: Useful to Examine Small Subset of MMWAs?

Our main findings are that frequent MMWAs appear *much more* frequently than infrequent ones, and that for most students, most of their wrong answers are in the frequent set. Therefore, inspecting a small subset of these most frequent MMWAs results in good coverage of cumulative responses covered, rapidly decreasing response coverage, and good coverage of a student's individual MMWAs. This section provides details to support the above findings, which affirmatively answer R1. The results presented refer to the Spring 2016 offering, as there was little difference among the three course offerings. We will note differences as appropriate.

Frequent wrong answers are very frequent. Figure 4 shows the behavior of the 1,000 most frequent MMWAs. Even though Figure 2 shows a wide range in the number of unique MMWAs per question set and per course offering, the cumulative percent of responses covered quickly reaches 50% using no more than the top-100 MMWAs for each question set. In other words, to cover the majority of responses from students, less than 100 MMWAs will need to be inspected per question set, with most question sets needing less than 50. This behavior is confirmed by noticing that the percent of students that submit a given unique MMWA quickly drops to below ≈5% by 100 MMWAs, even though almost all question sets have over 500 unique MMWAs.

For most students, most of their MMWAs are frequent. If we, therefore, use the top-100 unique MMWAs as a simple definition of "frequent MMWAs," we can ask how many students have a given percentage of their MMWAs within that top-100 frequent set. As

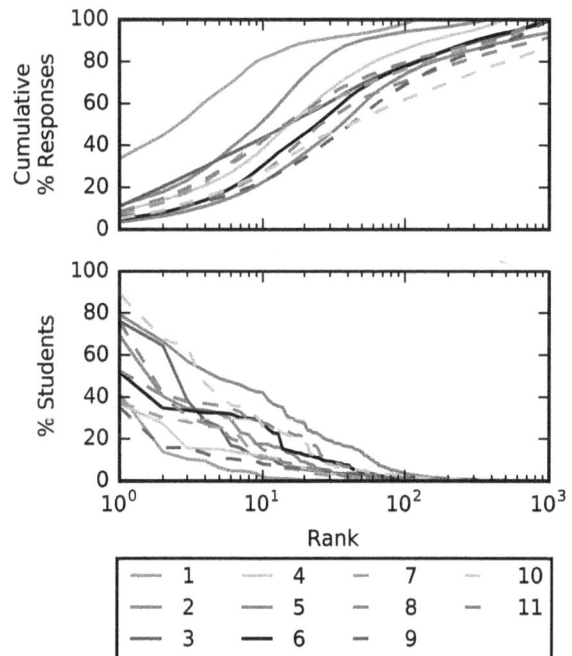

— 1	— 4	— 7	— 10
— 2	— 5	— 8	— 11
— 3	— 6	— 9	

Figure 4: Frequency of the unique MMWAs in Spring 2016. Each line represents a question set. The x-axis (log scale) is the 1,000 most frequently occurring MMWAs ordered by frequency. Upper: Cumulative percent of responses covered by up to the Xth most frequent answer, e.g. Question Set 1's top 10 MMWA covered ≈80% of wrong responses. Lower: Percent of students that submitted the Xth most frequent MMWA, e.g. Question Set 11's 10th most frequent MMWA was submitted by ≈42% of the students that submitted a wrong response to this question set.

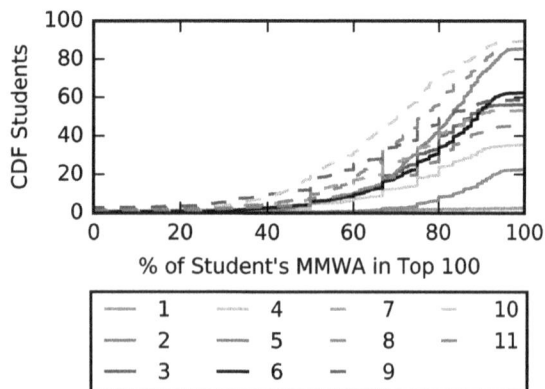

Figure 5: CDF showing the percent of students that have at least the x-axis percentage of their MMWAs in the top 100. Ex: For Question Set 10, ≈75% of students have at least ≈80% of their MMWA in this question set's top 100.

the CDF in Figure 5 shows, for any given question set, 80% or more of the students have the majority of their MMWAs in the top 100. Therefore, most of a student's MMWAs are in the top 100 and the infrequent wrong answers are coming from many students as opposed to a concentrated subset of students. This gives us greater confidence that by inspecting only the most frequent MMWAs, we are examining at least some, if not the majority of, MMWAs from every student.

5.2 R1.A: Are frequent MMWAs stable across course offerings?

Figure 6 shows the overlap of the most frequent MMWAs between a pair of course offerings. (When ordering MMWAs, we broke ties arbitrarily by sorting the answer text alphabetically.) The beginning of the graph is noisy due to a small denominator (the x-axis value). The amount of non-overlapping frequent MMWAs is an estimate of how many MMWAs would need to be inspected in a new offering of the course.

For some question sets there is a high level of overlap between course offerings. Almost all question sets for all pairs of semesters stabilize starting at ≈50 MMWAs and stay stable until ≈150 MMWAs or beyond. 150 is well past the number of MMWAs we need to inspect to cover the majority of responses. Therefore, there will always be some tagging that can be reused, but the amount depends on the question set and other factors that are currently unclear.

The differences between the pairs of semesters is unclear, especially since the Fall 2015 and 2016 offerings were taught by the same instructor, yet have lower MMWA overlap than Fall 2015 with Spring 2016 (since the course material did not change, we would expect that a change of instructor would result in lower overlap than the same instructor teaching the same material twice.). Our best guess as to why this is happening is that the TA staff between the Fall 2015 and Spring 2016 overlapped much more than with the Fall 2016 TA staff. Each course offering had 50 to 87 TAs versus a single lecturer, so it is possible that a teaching effect happening at the TA level is causing the differences in the MMWAs overlap.

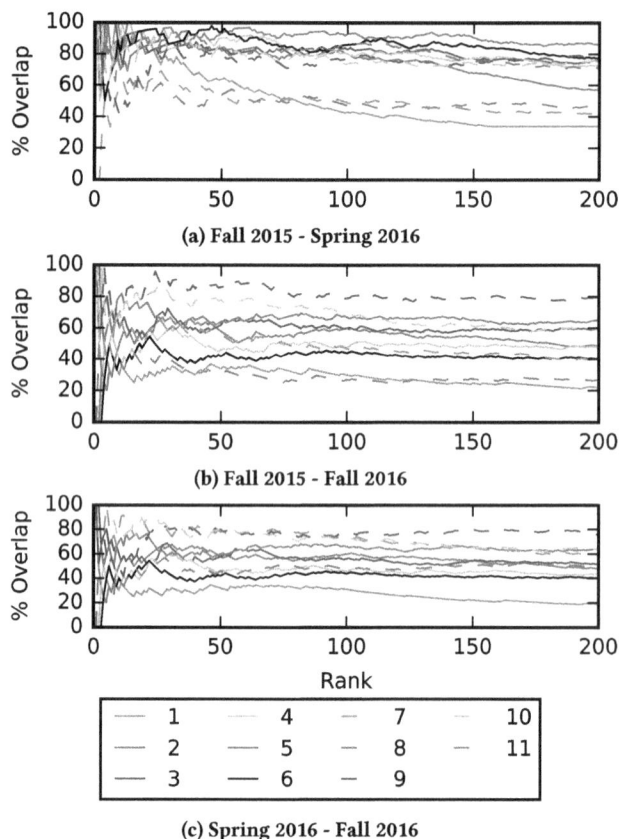

(a) Fall 2015 - Spring 2016

(b) Fall 2015 - Fall 2016

(c) Spring 2016 - Fall 2016

Figure 6: Percent of MMWAs that appear in a pair of semester's X most frequent MMWAs, e.g.: comparing Fall 2015 and Spring 2016, ≈85% of Question Set 6's top-100 MMWAs overlapped between the semesters. Note: Fall 2016 did not have Question Set 11 to compare with.

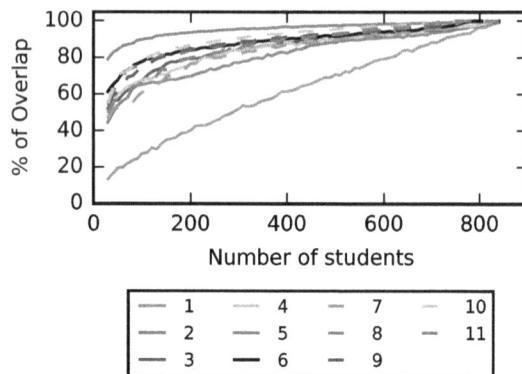

Figure 7: Empirical Monte Carlo analysis results when sampling x-axis students 50 times and plotting the mean overlap across the samples with the entire course offering's top-100 most frequent wrong answers for each question set. Ex: For Question Set 5, when we sampled 100 students 50 times, the mean overlap of the top-100 MMWA with the entire cohort's top-100 MMWA was ≈90%.

Tagging Step	Human effort required
Finalize Tags	≈ 10 mins./tag
Assign Tags	≈ 1.5 mins./answer
Consolidate/Discuss	≈ 0.5 mins./answer
Review/Confirm	≈ 0.1 mins./answer

Figure 8: Human-expert time required for each tagging step. Total time was ≈87 tagger-hours to create tags and ≈36 expert-hours to tag the FrequentSet. We also spent ≈127 expert-hours to tag the StudentSet, required only for our own validation and not integral to the technique.

Figure 7 shows the result of an empirical Monte Carlo simulation on the Spring 2016's data using the following steps and the simple definition of the top-100 unique MMWAs as "frequent": (1) Sample successive values of N students (x-axis value), 50 times, (2) For each sample compute the overlap of the top-100 most frequent MMWAs between the sample and the entire offering, and (3) Plot the mean overlap across the samples.

Figure 7 shows high overlap is achieved between 150 and 250 students, with marginal returns afterward. (Question Set 1 once again is an outlier, most likely due to how few unique MMWAs it had.) Therefore, given our data, frequent MMWAs are stable for a much smaller course than the size we had available (enrollments between 800 and 1,700).

5.3 R1.B: How to choose subsample, and how large?

Using taggability (whether or not a wrong answer has a tag) as a proxy for information about student difficulties, our main finding is that *frequently-occurring wrong answers are more likely to yield information about student difficulties than rarely-occurring ones*, suggesting that the subsample should be created by choosing the most "popular" wrong answers.

We arrived at this conclusion by applying our tagging process to two different MMWA sets. One focused on only the *frequent* MMWAs per question set, hereafter the *FrequentSet*, and the other was *all* MMWAs submitted by a subsample of 50 randomly chosen *students* for each question set, hereafter the *StudentSet*. The main deciding factor for choosing each MMWA set was how much human-expert resources we had to tag these MMWAs. For the FrequentSet, we chose ≈500 MMWAs to tag; for the StudentSet, after getting a better sense of the resources required, we chose ≈2,000. Figure 8 summarizes the person-hours required.

For each question set, we ranked the MMWAs by frequency and then used thresholds on two metrics: (1) total coverage—include the most "popular" MMWAs that cover 60% of all responses, and (2) marginal coverage—then add further MMWAs (still ranked by frequency) as long as each additional MMWA covers at least 0.4% more responses. The interaction between these metrics (Figure 4) led us to explore their value ranges jointly; our parameter values resulted in 508 MMWAs to tag.

Our inter-rater agreement when categorizing wrong answers in the FrequentSet and StudentSet were 96.2% and 86.7% respectively. The fraction of tags given by both experts was 33.2% for the FrequentSet and 46.3% for the StudentSet. The tag overlap is lower than

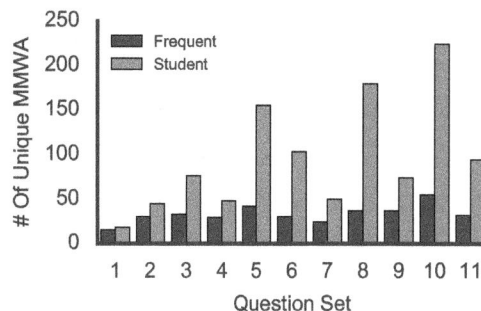

Figure 9: Number of MMWAs in each MMWA set per question set. All MMWAs in the FrequentSet also appeared in the StudentSet and therefore are counted in both bars. Ex: For Question Set 6, the FrequentSet had ≈50 MMWA and the StudentSet had ≈250.

we would like, which could be for three possible reasons that we will address in future work. First, since a question set tested a main topic, a misapplied tag was usually misapplied for multiple answers. Second, in some cases, one expert used a more specific tag than the other, for example, "sloppily evaluating a variable" versus "sloppily evaluating an *attribute* of a variable" (an important distinction in Python). During consolidation, the more specific tag was always used. The inter-rater-reliability scores were not compensated for either of these situations. Third, taggers might need more training. The FrequentSet was the first time tagging for our experts, so training occurred while tagging. The increase in agreement between the FrequentSet and StudentSet, despite there being more wrong answers to tag in the latter, supports this reasoning.

Despite the low agreement on tags, however, the agreement on categories is high, supporting the assertion that frequent wrong answers are more likely to be taggable. In addition, the main focus of this work is on whether the wrong answer was tagged (and therefore whether insights can be gained from it), as opposed to which tag(s) it was given.

By design, there are many more MMWAs in the StudentSet than the FrequentSet (Figure 9). However, the number of MMWAs per question set is much more varied, making this method of choosing MMWAs more likely to result in higher variability in which MMWAs are chosen. In addition, we found the StudentSet included all the MMWAs in the FrequentSet because (in accord with intuition) we were more likely to randomly choose a student that gave a particular frequent MMWA than a particular rare one. Therefore, the graph represents the Frequent MMWAs twice, once in the FrequentSet and once in the StudentSet. This is further evidence that the frequent MMWAs would be sufficient to yield information on student difficulties that is representative of all MMWAs.

Figure 10 also shows that across question sets, there are more MMWAs categorized as "conceptually correct" or "not an answer" for the StudentSet than the FrequentSet. Since our interests are mainly in MMWAs categorized as "student error" and the FrequentSet yields relatively more of these, we have further support that frequency is a good way to choose which MMWAs to inspect.

	Frequent			Student		
	NA	C	SE	NA	C	SE
Mean	1.0%	5.8%	93.1%	4.4%	8.1%	87.5%
Median	0%	4.5%	94.6%	3.2%	4.9%	90.8%
Variance	0.1	0.3	0.4	0.2	0.4	0.4

Figure 10: Statistics on the % of MMWA per category for the FrequentSet and StudentSet. NA - "Not an Answer," C - "Conceptually Correct," and SE - "Student Error."

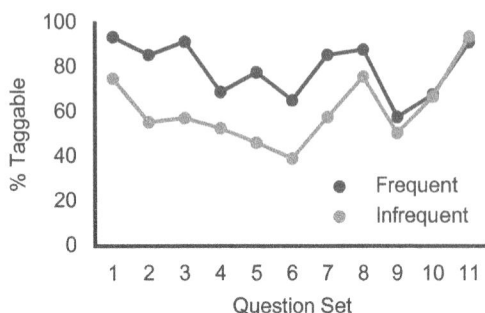

Figure 11: Percent of taggable wrong answers between the frequent and infrequent wrong answers in the StudentSet. Ex: For Question Set 6, ≈67% of the frequent wrong answers in the StudentSet were taggable and 40% of the infrequent wrong answers were taggable. Note: All MMWA in the FrequentSet are the frequent wrong answers in the StudentSet.

Finally, Figure 11 shows that the percentage of taggable MMWAs is higher for the frequent wrong answers than the infrequent ones for all but one question set. While the question sets are ordered chronologically, it is unclear why the percentages are converging but not stabilizing. However, since almost all question sets have a higher percentage of taggable wrong answers for the frequent wrong answers than infrequent wrong answers in the StudentSet, we count this as further evidence that frequent MMWAs are more informative than rare ones.

5.4 R2: What insights can be gained from subsample?

We created a total of 173 tags, which is more than the catalog of novice misconceptions provided by Sorva [17]. In addition, 63% of our tags did not fit the topics in the catalog. This is because our tags focus on what the student did to create the wrong answer, as opposed to the conceptual idea the student misunderstood. In Figure 12 we list the topics from the catalog and ones we created, the number of tags for that topic, and an exemplar tag. Only an exemplar tag is included due to space. A full discussion of the insights we gained will be left to future work.

"Language-Specific Constructs" are tags about student difficulties specific to the language, such as idioms, constructs, and implementations. "Syntax" tags focused on ways students were wrong due to syntax errors or misunderstandings. "Sloppy" tags focused on ways students either read the code they were tracing poorly or submitted their answer without proofreading. Finally, we created the topic

"Data Structures" because, even though it is not as well studied in prior work, we found student difficulties with data structures using our analysis. We were able to do this because our data set included questions testing concepts with linked lists, regular lists, dictionaries, sets, and trees.

These insights were gained from question sets created by teaching staff prior to this work and without a rigorous, data-driven design process. We believe more insights could be gained through an iterative process where current insights inform the design of new questions, who's wrong answers are then analyzed, and hopefully more insights are gained. This we, also, leave to future work.

5.5 Research Question Summary

R1: Can analyzing a small subsample of wrong constructed responses yield information about student difficulties that makes it worth the time investment?

Yes, the frequent MMWAs constitute only a ≈5% subsample of the MMWAs in the data set, yet the wrong answers in the FrequentSet are more likely to be taggable.

R1.A: If so, assuming the same questions are used in subsequent course offerings, can the information so gained be applied to future course offerings, further amortizing the time investment?

How much can be applied to another course offering is currently inconclusive. The amount of overlap for a given question set and pair of semesters is consistent between the most frequent ≈50-150 wrong answers. However, how much it overlaps between a question set and pair of semesters is highly dependent on the question set and factors that are currently unclear, such as teaching effects.

R1.B: If so, how should that sample be chosen and how large must it be?

We believe the best way to choose MMWAs is by first ordering them by their frequency and then choosing the most frequent, thresholding based on both the cumulative percent of responses covered and the marginal additional coverage of each additional MMWA. The parameter values can be chosen together based on the number of human-expert hours available for tagging, with the understanding that a lower threshold will affect the results of the set's representativeness and stability.

R2: What insights about student difficulties can be gained from analyzing the subsample?

Using MMWAs from univalent-constructed-response, code-tracing questions with our tagging process, we found both misconceptions similar to those identified in prior work and new misconceptions based on topics appearing in our assessments but not used in prior work, such as difficulties with language-specific constructs and data structures.

6 APPLICATIONS

When we shared our tags with the course's teaching staff, they used the tags to create univalent CRQs for the exams. The wrong answer taggings could also be used to discover common student errors in the class to then create targeted distractors for selected-response assessments and to change the teaching materials to proactively target those errors. In addition, analyzing the MMWAs categorized

Topic	# of Tags	Exemplar Tag		
		Name	Description	Example Code (in Python)

General, Control, OOP, References, Misc	27	Sequential `if` statements are `if...else`	This WA demonstrates that the student believes two if's next to each other are actually an if..else clause	`>>> x = 5`
				`>>> if x <= 5: a = 1`
				`>>> if x > 3: a = 2`
				`>>> print(a)`
				`1`

Variable Assignment	22	Expression not evaluated	This WA demonstrates that the student does not recognize the need to evaluate an expression and instead a code snippet is "passed around."	`>>> a = 1 + 2`
				`>>> a`
				`1 + 2`

Calls	15	Evaluating a function name is a function call	This WA demonstrates that the student believes when the name of a function is in a line of code (but not called) the function is being called.	`>>> f = lambda x: 1`
				`>>> f`
				`1`

Language Specific Constructs*	39	List comprehension does not return a list	This WA demonstrates that the student believes a list comprehension does not return a list, but just a value.	`>>> [x for x in range(3)]` `0`
Syntax*	34	List does not need commas	This WA demonstrates that the student believes a list does not need commas.	`>>> [x for x in range(3)]` `[0 1 2]`
Sloppy*	15	Sloppy sorting	This WA is wrong because the student is being sloppy in how they are sorting the values	`>>> sorted(['b','a','c'])` `['a','c','b']`

Data Structures*	21	Link lists cannot cycle	This WA demonstrates that the student believes that linked lists cannot link back to itself, so if a line of code does that, it is as if did not happen.	`>>> l = Link(1, Link(2, Link(3)))`
				`>>> l.rest = l`
				`>>> l.rest.rest.first`
				`2`

Figure 12: The number of our tags per topic in Sorva's catalog [17] with exemplars. Those with * are topics we created.

as "conceptually correct" can reveal how the system is poor at marking answers correctly. This can lead to either improvements in the automated system or in the questions to reduce such errors. For the MMWAs categorized as "not an answer," they can also be used to understand ways to improve the question or the system. This category led us to discover a confusing question where students thought they were answering the comment that was written as a question next to the code rather than predicting the output of the code. Finally, wrong answer taggings can be used to develop a model to detect student difficulties as they work through the automatically graded assessments. When the model detects a stable difficulty in the student, formative feedback could be delivered immediately in situ.

If the wrong answers tagged in a prior offering of a course do not cover the current offering, more wrong answers need to be collected and tagged. However, the stability we found across cohorts leads us to believe that the desired level of tagged frequent wrong answers will eventually be achieved and/or the number of wrong answers will never be so great as the initial effort of tagging. There is, however, a caveat when using this technique between offerings. If the teacher is using the formative assessments to inform changes in teaching strategies, they are now tracking a moving target since the cohorts are likely changing in their common errors based on the instruction they receive.

7 CONCLUSION

We set out to investigate if the information gained from analyzing responses from univalent-constructed-response, code-tracing questions is worth the effort expended. We analyzed a corpus of 332,829

responses to 92 questions by 4,068 students across 3 offerings of a large-enrollment introductory CS course. We found inspecting the frequent wrong answers are worth the opportunity cost because they are a small sample compared to all the unique wrong answers and cover a majority of the wrong responses. When comparing the overlap of the frequent wrong answers between two course offerings, our results show that the level of overlap is almost always consistent for the frequent wrong answers, but that level varies between question sets and course offering pairs.

In addition, we report on the insights we gained from inspecting these frequent wrong answers. We found similar misconceptions discussed in prior work. Our inspecting process focused on identifying ways students arrive at wrong answers, so we also identified student difficulties with syntax and how students can be sloppy when they read the code or answer questions. Finally, we readily found student difficulties with language-specific constructs (Python and Scheme for this class) and data structures, areas with less prior work on student misconceptions.

REFERENCES

[1] John D Bransford, Ann L Brown, and Rodney R Cocking. 1999. *How people learn: Brain, mind, experience, and school.* National Academy Press.

[2] John Seely Brown and Kurt VanLehn. 1980. Repair theory: A generative theory of bugs in procedural skills. *Cognitive science* 4, 4 (1980), 379–426.

[3] Neil C.C. Brown and Amjad Altadmri. 2014. Investigating Novice Programming Mistakes: Educator Beliefs vs. Student Data. In *Proceedings of the Tenth Annual Conference on International Computing Education Research (ICER '14).* ACM, New York, NY, USA, 43–50. DOI:https://doi.org/10.1145/2632320.2632343

[4] Adam S. Carter, Christopher D. Hundhausen, and Olusola Adesope. 2015. The Normalized Programming State Model: Predicting Student Performance in Computing Courses Based on Programming Behavior. In *Proceedings of the Eleventh Annual International Conference on International Computing Education Research (ICER '15).* ACM, New York, NY, USA, 141–150. DOI:https://doi.org/10.1145/2787622.2787710

[5] Michael Clancy. 2004. Misconceptions and attitudes that interfere with learning to program. *Computer science education research* (2004), 85–100.

[6] Matthew C. Jadud and Brian Dorn. 2015. Aggregate Compilation Behavior: Findings and Implications from 27,698 Users. In *Proceedings of the Eleventh Annual International Conference on International Computing Education Research (ICER '15).* ACM, New York, NY, USA, 131–139. DOI:https://doi.org/10.1145/2787622.2787718

[7] W Lewis Johnson, Stephen Draper, and Elliot Soloway. 1983. *Classifying Bugs is a Tricky Business.* Technical Report. DTIC Document.

[8] W. L. Johnson and E. Soloway. 1985. PROUST: Knowledge-Based Program Understanding. *IEEE Transactions on Software Engineering* SE-11, 3 (March 1985), 267–275. DOI:https://doi.org/10.1109/TSE.1985.232210

[9] Antti-Jussi Lakanen, Vesa Lappalainen, and Ville Isomöttönen. 2015. Revisiting Rainfall to Explore Exam Questions and Performance on CS1. In *Proceedings of the 15th Koli Calling Conference on Computing Education Research (Koli Calling '15).* ACM, New York, NY, USA, 40–49. DOI:https://doi.org/10.1145/2828959.2828970

[10] Raymond Lister, Beth Simon, Errol Thompson, Jacqueline L. Whalley, and Christine Prasad. 2006. Not Seeing the Forest for the Trees: Novice Programmers and the SOLO Taxonomy. In *Proceedings of the 11th Annual SIGCSE Conference on Innovation and Technology in Computer Science Education (ITICSE '06).* ACM, New York, NY, USA, 118–122. DOI:https://doi.org/10.1145/1140124.1140157

[11] Matthew B Miles, A Michael Huberman, and Johnny Saldana. 2013. *Qualitative data analysis: A methods sourcebook.* SAGE Publications, Incorporated.

[12] Craig S. Miller and Amber Settle. 2016. Some Trouble with Transparency: An Analysis of Student Errors with Object-oriented Python. In *Proceedings of the 2016 ACM Conference on International Computing Education Research (ICER '16).* ACM, New York, NY, USA, 133–141. DOI:https://doi.org/10.1145/2960310.2960327

[13] Michael C Rodriguez. 2005. Three options are optimal for multiple-choice items: A meta-analysis of 80 years of research. *Educational Measurement: Issues and Practice* 24, 2 (2005), 3–13.

[14] Otto Seppälä, Petri Ihantola, Essi Isohanni, Juha Sorva, and Arto Vihavainen. 2015. Do We Know How Difficult the Rainfall Problem is?. In *Proceedings of the 15th Koli Calling Conference on Computing Education Research (Koli Calling '15).* ACM, New York, NY, USA, 87–96. DOI:https://doi.org/10.1145/2828959.2828963

[15] Simon and Susan Snowdon. 2014. Multiple-choice vs Free-text Code-explaining Examination Questions. In *Proceedings of the 14th Koli Calling International Conference on Computing Education Research (Koli Calling '14).* ACM, New York, NY, USA, 91–97. DOI:https://doi.org/10.1145/2674683.2674701

[16] Teemu Sirkiä and Juha Sorva. 2012. Exploring Programming Misconceptions: An Analysis of Student Mistakes in Visual Program Simulation Exercises. In *Proceedings of the 12th Koli Calling International Conference on Computing Education Research (Koli Calling '12).* ACM, New York, NY, USA, 19–28. DOI:https://doi.org/10.1145/2401796.2401799

[17] Juha Sorva and others. 2012. *Visual program simulation in introductory programming education.* Aalto University.

[18] James C. Spohrer and Elliot Soloway. 1989. Simulating Student Programmers. In *Proceedings of the 11th International Joint Conference on Artificial Intelligence - Volume 1 (IJCAI'89).* Morgan Kaufmann Publishers Inc., San Francisco, CA, USA, 543–549. http://dl.acm.org/citation.cfm?id=1623755.1623841

[19] Kikumi K Tatsuoka. 1983. Rule space: An approach for dealing with misconceptions based on item response theory. *Journal of educational measurement* 20, 4 (1983), 345–354.

[20] Kikumi K Tatsuoka. 1985. A probabilistic model for diagnosing misconceptions by the pattern classification approach. *Journal of Educational and Behavioral Statistics* 10, 1 (1985), 55–73.

Investigating Static Analysis Errors in Student Java Programs

Stephen H. Edwards, Nischel Kandru, and Mukund B. M. Rajagopal
Virginia Tech, Department of Computer Science
2202 Kraft Drive
Blacksburg, VA 24060, USA
{s.edwards, nischelk, mrmukund}@vt.edu

ABSTRACT

Research on students learning to program has produced studies on both compile-time errors (syntax errors) and run-time errors (exceptions). Both of these types of errors are natural targets, since detection is built into the programming language. In this paper, we present an empirical investigation of static analysis errors present in syntactically correct code. Static analysis errors can be revealed by tools that examine a program's source code, but this error detection is typically not built into common programming languages and instead requires separate tools. Static analysis can be used to check formatting or commenting expectations, but it also can be used to identify problematic code or to find some kinds of conceptual or logic errors. We study nearly 10 million static analysis errors found in over 500 thousand program submissions made by students over a five-semester period. The study includes data from four separate courses, including a non-majors introductory course as well as the CS1/CS2/CS3 sequence for CS majors. We examine the differences between the error rates of CS major and non-major beginners, and also examine how these patterns change over time as students progress through the CS major course sequence. Our investigation shows that while formatting and Javadoc issues are the most common, static checks that identify coding flaws that are likely to be errors are strongly correlated with producing correct programs, even when students eventually fix the problems. With experience, students produce fewer errors, but the errors that are most frequent are consistent between both computer science majors and non majors, and across experience levels. These results can highlight student struggles or misunderstandings that have escaped past analyses focused on syntax or run-time errors.

Keywords

Java; Web-CAT; static analysis; Checkstyle; PMD; coding style; formatting; documentation; coding standard

ACM Reference format:

S.H. Edwards, N. Kandru, and M.B.M. Rajagopal. 2017. Investigating Static Analysis Errors in Student Java Programs. In *Proceedings of International Computing Education Research, Tacoma, WA USA, August 2017 (ICER'17)*, 9 pages.
DOI: http://dx.doi.org/10.1145/3105726.3106182

1. INTRODUCTION

Programming is a complex task that is a core skill for computer science students. It is common for students to encounter many errors before coming up with a successful program. Other researchers have investigated syntax errors (compile-time errors) and exceptions (run-time errors) that beginners experience as they learn to program. This paper focuses on a separate category of errors that has received little research attention: static analysis errors.

Static analysis errors can be detected by programs that examine the source code only, without running it. At the same time, they are distinct from syntax errors. Syntax errors are driven by the programming language's definition, and indicate when a series of tokens is malformed—meaningless in the programming language under consideration. In compiled languages, one function of the compiler is to detect and report syntax errors, since syntactically invalid programs are by definition meaningless. Static analysis errors, on the other hand, occur in syntactically valid programs that can be successfully compiled—they represent problems or issues that can occur in a program, even though its syntactic structure follows the rules of the programming language. These errors are called *static analysis* errors because they are identified by *static analysis tools*—software tools that analyze a program just by examining its source code, without running it (without dynamic analysis). Lint is an example of a static analysis checker for C programs. Static analysis checkers have been written for many other programming languages as well, with the aim of spotting problems earlier so they can be fixed earlier, even if the problems are not syntax errors. Checkstyle and PMD are two common static analysis checkers for Java.

In this paper, we analyze static analysis errors occurring in student-written Java programs, and detected using Checkstyle or PMD. We collected 9,913,817 errors occurring in 1,172,157 source files written by 3,691 students over two and a half years from Fall 2014-Fall 2016. These source files were included in 502,159 submission attempts made by these students on programming assignments. This data set includes work from all of the students in four courses at Virginia Tech, the introductory Java service course for non-CS majors, together with the CS1, CS2, and advanced data structures courses for CS majors. By including results from both majors and non-majors, and from beginners as well as more experienced students, a deeper understanding of changing error patterns is possible.

Our goal in analyzing this data set is to gain a better understanding of static analysis error behaviors and how they relate to student populations. We aim to answer the following research questions:

1. What are the most frequent static analysis errors?
2. Do the most frequent errors vary by course and experience level?
3. Which errors appear in students' very first attempt at an assignment?
4. Which errors persist in students' final work?
5. Are static analysis errors related to program grade (marks)?
6. Which errors take the least (or most) time to fix?

Section 2 begins by discussing related work. The static analysis tools used in this study, and the errors they detect, are discussed in Section 3. Section 4 describes the study data set, and Section 5 presents the analysis and results. Future work is discussed in Section 6.

2. RELATED WORK

There have been many studies involving errors students experience while learning to program. We will restrict ourselves to such studies specifically focused on Java programs. Most of these studies analyze compile-time errors. Altadmri et al. [2] used a large dataset comprising of over a years' worth of compilation events of 250,000 students. This dataset of compilation errors provides a robust analysis about the frequencies of errors, error commonality, and time for fixing various errors. Denny et al. [4] also studied the frequency of various syntax errors and the time spent in resolving them.

Ahmadzadeh et al. [1] collected data on debugging of errors by providing specific assignments to students. They then captured the compiler-generated syntax errors, semantic errors and lexical errors that students made and analyzed the frequency of these errors. They also analyzed the debugging capability of students and compared it with their proficiency in programming.

McCall et al. [3] found all the logical errors in the students' code rather than the diagnostic error messages that the compiler provides. This data was used to study various categories of errors and the frequencies of such errors.

There also have been studies focused on characterizing students by analyzing their ability to program. Jadud et al. [5] used the error quotient algorithm (EQ) to score and characterize student programming behavior in terms of their ability to address syntax errors reported by a compiler. Tabanao, Rodrigo et al. [6] tried identify academically at-risk students using indicators from their progress in the task of writing programs. They collected novice compilations and explored the errors novices encountered, the locations of these errors, and the frequency with which novices compiled their programs and

developed linear regression models that allowed prediction of students' scores on a midterm exam. Rodrigo et al. [7] also have analyzed a sample of novice programmer compilation log data to see how low-achieving, average, and high-achieving students vary in their grasp of introductory programming concepts. They observed that all groups of students had difficulties finding small errors.

Unlike prior work on syntax errors or runtime errors, our work is focused on the analysis of static analysis errors detected in Java code. We used Checkstyle and PMD to detect errors on submissions made to the Web-CAT automated grading system, as discussed in Section 3. In comparison, Truong, Roe and Bancroft [9] have introduced a static analysis framework which can be used to give beginning students feedback to their programs, practice in writing better quality Java programs and to assist teaching staff in the marking process. Artho and Biere [10] have also worked on static analysis for Java, building on Jlint, a Java checking tool inspired in part by the successful Lint tool for C. They extended Jlint to perform static analysis on large-scale multi-threaded java programs. They included checks on synchronization practices on arbitrary objects in order to detect incorrect or error-prone use of Java's concurrency constructs.

There has also been prior research evaluating the usefulness of static analysis of code. Ayewah et al. [14] discuss the use of the static analysis tool FindBugs to identify bugs that were not previously identified. They classified the newly detected bugs into false positives, trivial bugs, and serious bugs. Using the tool helped them identify bugs that had an impact on the behavior of the code and to fix them. Nagappan and Ball [15] built a model to use the data from static error analysis to predict a system's reliability or error-proneness. This helped to make informed decisions on testing, code inspections, design rework and budget planning.

3. STATIC ANALYSIS OF STUDENT PROGRAMS

Static analysis is a method of code checking that is performed by examining the code without actually executing it. This process provides an understanding of the code structure and ensures that the code adheres to specific standards. Static analysis enables programmers to identify and diagnose various types of bugs or errors such as style issues, potential overflows, memory and pointer errors like possible null pointer dereferences, and other issues.

Automated tools assist programmers by carrying out static analyses. These tools evaluate the program only based on its form, structure, content or documentation. Based on the errors recorded in this study, we have grouped static analysis errors into the following categories:

Braces: When optional braces are omitted from control constructs, which increases the potential for mistakes, particularly during code editing.

Coding Flaws: Constructs that are almost certainly bugs (such as checking for null after a pointer is used instead of before), or at least will change the behavior of the program.

Documentation: Missing or incorrect Javadoc elements.

Excessive Coding: Size issues, such as methods, classes, or parameter lists that exceed expected limits and may indicate readability problems.

Formatting: Incorrect indentation, or missing whitespace (reduces readability).

Naming: Names that violate capitalization conventions, are too short, or are not meaningful.

Readability: Issues other than formatting that reduce the readability of the code.

Style: Code that can be simplified or that does not follow common idioms.

Testing: Errors in the structure of student-written unit tests, such as tests that do not assert any behavioral expectations, or behavioral assertions that are trivially true at compile time.

Some of these categories indicate cosmetic issues with a program that do not affect its behavior. Formatting issues, documentation issues, and naming issues cover a variety of cosmetic concerns. Other categories, such as style, readability, braces, or excessive coding, indicate issues where code might need to be refactored or rewritten to be easier to understand. However, the *coding flaws* category stands out as one were issues typically represent defects (bugs) that almost certainly need to be fixed. The testing category is similar, indicating problems with software tests that are not checking program behaviors.

3.1 Checkstyle

Checkstyle is an open-source static analysis tool for Java. While Checkstyle excels at identifying styling issues where Java code does not conform to specified coding conventions or has layout or formatting issues, it also supports detection of a number of potential coding problems that indicate possible program bugs, suspicious coding that is likely to be hard to read, or coding patterns that make it easier to introduce bugs as code is maintained and evolved. Checkstyle is used in industry for automatically checking conformance to published coding standards.

Checkstyle's options are controlled using an XML configuration file that indicates which checks to apply, and specifies any parameters that tailor each rule's behavior. Checkstyle can be run either as an Ant task or as a command line tool. Checkstyle can be extended by writing new checks implemented in Java. Examples of some of the checks Checkstyle can perform include:

Coding Flaws:

- **CovariantEquals:** When the `equals()` method is defined with the wrong argument type, instead of `Object`.

- **StringLiteralEquality**: When string objects are compared using == instead of `equals()`.

Documentation:

- **JavadocMethod**: Checks the Javadoc of a method or constructor, including its embedded tags.

Formatting:

- **Indentation**: Checks for correct indentation of Java code.

- **WhitespaceAround**: Checks that operators and other elements are separated from neighboring tokens by whitespace to improve readability.

- **LineLength**: Checks for long lines, which reduce readability and speed of visually scanning code.

Naming:

- **MemberName**: Validates that identifiers for non-static fields and methods follow established conventions.

3.2 PMD

PMD is also an open-source static analysis tool for Java, although it is evolving to support a wide variety of other programming languages as well. Although the issues that PMD can detect overlaps significantly with Checkstyle, PMD has less of a focus on formatting conventions and more emphasis on programming guidelines, design recommendations, and recommended programming practices. Like Checkstyle, PMD can be extended by adding new checks. However, in adition to adding checks by writing Java code, PMD also allows checks to be written as XPath expressions matched against the abstract syntax tree (AST) of the program being analyzed. While not all checks can be implemented as structural AST patterns, the ability to define new checks in this way is both powerful and convenient.

Examples of some of the checks performed by PMD include:

Coding Flaws:

- **MisplacedNullCheck**: In a compound condition, the null check is placed after the corresponding variable is used instead of before, leading to a bug.

- **JumbledIncrementer**: In a nested loop, when the inner loop increments the index variable belonging to the enclosing loop.

Coding Style:

- **UnusedImports**: Checks if there are packages imported which are not used.

- **SingularField**: A field that is only used inside one method, where a local variable may be more appropriate.

Naming:

- **FormalParametersNeedMeaningfulNames**: Checks if method parameters have been left with IDE-auto-generated names instead of being given real names.

- **AvoidFieldNameMatchingTypeName**: A field with the same name as the enclosing type is confusing.

Testing:

- **JUnit3TestsHaveAssertions**: Checks if the unit tests contain assertions (there is a similar check for JUnit 4 tests).

- **UseAssertSameInsteadOfAssertTrue**: This rule detects JUnit assertions that check object reference equality. Using more specific methods produces more meaningful diagnostic messages.

3.3 Collecting Student Programs Using Web-CAT

At Virginia Tech, we use an automated grading system to collect student submissions to programming assignments and to provide immediate feedback so students can correct problems and resubmit before the deadline. We use Web-CAT for this purpose. Web-CAT is a free, open-source tool for automatically grading programs. Its plug-in-based structure allows it to support virtually any programming language, but its most mature plug-in provides support for assessing Java programs. It is most famous for allowing instructors to grade students on how well the student tests their own work, rather than only on correctness.

Among the features of the Java grading plug-in for Web-CAT is support for static analysis using both Checkstyle and PMD. We use this feature to grade student work for conformance to coding style expectations and proper formatting. As a side-effect, these analysis tools are applied on every student submission for all of our Java programming courses.

4. METHOD

This study is based on data compiled from all student work submitted across four courses at Virginia Tech over a 5-semester period from Fall 2014 through Fall 2016. The four courses included in this study are: CS 1054, a CS1 service course for non-CS majors; CS 1114, the CS1 course taken by CS majors; CS 2114, a traditional CS 2 course; and CS 3114, a junior-level data structures and algorithms course taken by more advanced students. Students in all four courses submitted their programs to Web-CAT for automated and manual grading. Students were allowed to submit their work multiple times, and received immediate feedback on the automated portion of their grade so that they could correct mistakes and rework their solutions to

achieve the score desired. In cases where instructors configured assignments to turn off all static analysis, the corresponding program submissions were excluded from data analysis. As outlined in Section 1, nearly 10 million errors in over a million source files were analyzed.

5. RESULTS & DISCUSSION

5.1 Most Frequent Errors

Figure 1 shows the top ten most common errors, after tabulating occurrences of all errors in the data set and normalizing by program length (lines of code). Missing Javadoc was the most common, accounting for 23% of all errors, occurring at a rate of 5.7 times per thousand lines of code (per KLOC). This likely is a result of students waiting to add Javadoc to their assignments until they have completed their solution, leading to repeated errors on every submission attempt they make while refining their work. Surprisingly, indentation errors were the second most common problem. Given that the development environments used in these course all support automatic indentation, the source of this frequency may be worth investigation.

Rates are used here instead of raw counts, since longer source files have greater opportunities for containing errors and will exhibit higher counts. Instead, we follow the model used in software engineering when reporting bugs, where rates normalized by program size promote comparability across situations. Here, we use the same technique, calculating error rates as the mean number of occurrences per thousand lines of source code. For reference, CS 1054 programs (non-majors CS1) had a mean size of 121 lines, with CS majors averaging 537 lines per program in CS1, 761 lines per program in CS2, and 2,435 lines in CS3.

The majority of the errors in Figure 1 are formatting and

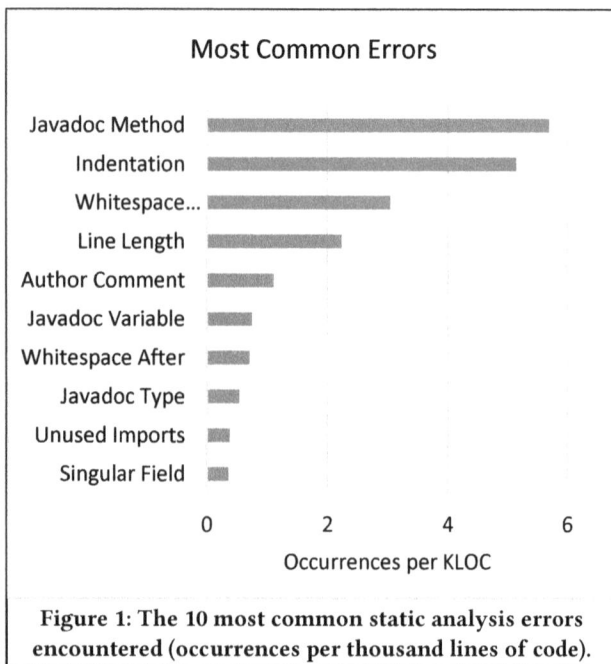

Figure 1: The 10 most common static analysis errors encountered (occurrences per thousand lines of code).

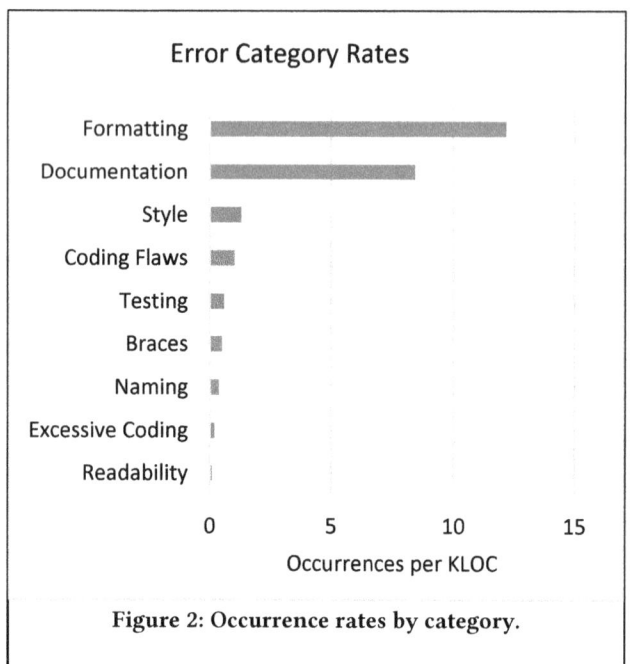

Figure 2: Occurrence rates by category.

documentation errors. However, the last two are examples of style issues, with SingularField often representing a design flaw or misunderstanding in CS1 programs.

5.2 Most Frequent Error Categories

A total of 114 distinct static analysis errors were observed across both analysis tools in this study. To summarize all of the errors, Figure 2 shows the occurrence rates for each category of errors, using the categories introduced in Section 3

Among all the categories chosen for grouping errors, formatting errors occur most often (including four of the ten most common errors) at 12 errors per KLOC, followed by documentation (Javadoc errors, also including four of the ten most common errors) at 8.4 errors per KLOC. Together, these two categories account for 83% of static analysis errors reported in this study (49% formatting, 34% documentation).

Notably, coding flaws were the fourth most common category, with an average of 1 error per KLOC. For example, when students are writing 500-line programs, this error rate would translate to identifying a coding flaw bug in approximately half of a student's attempts at an assignment. In later courses as assignments grow in complexity and length increases, the number of coding flaws revealed would also increase. In other words, even though this error rate seems low in an absolute sense, it translates into a noticeable number of notifications when developing even moderately sized programs. Anecdotally, many students pay little attention to static analysis errors because they are dominated by formatting and documentation issues, which means they miss the situations where these tools report problems that should be addressed—and that aren't reported by compiler messages.

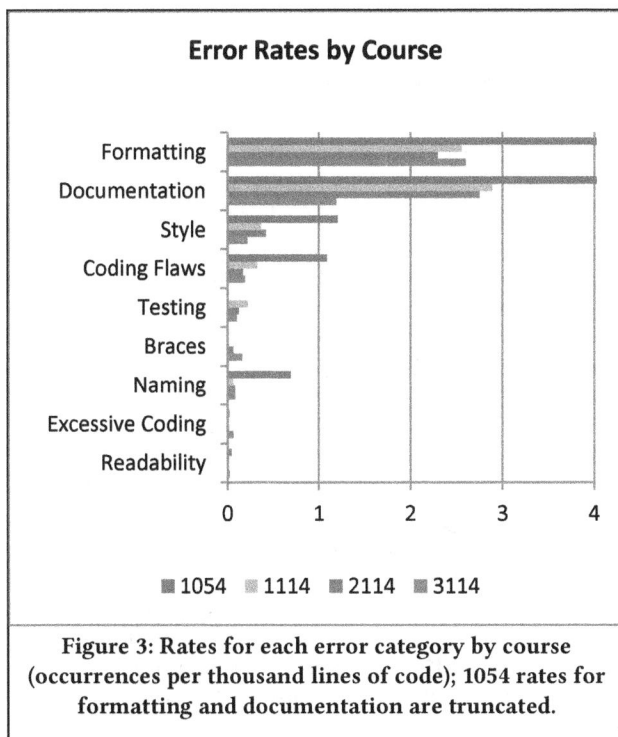

Figure 3: Rates for each error category by course (occurrences per thousand lines of code); 1054 rates for formatting and documentation are truncated.

5.3 Evolution of Errors across Courses

While Figures 1 and 2 give insight into the most common errors experienced overall, the question of whether students in different courses see different errors is also of interest. Figure 3 shows the rates for each error category in each course. In Figure 3, the rate bars for 1054 formatting (22.4/KLOC) and documentation (13.7/KLOC) were so much higher than other courses that they were truncated to keep the chart readable. The rate of formatting errors was an order of magnitude greater for the CS1 non-majors course than for the in-majors course. The non-majors course also earned the highest rate of style errors, coding flaws, and naming errors as well.

A one-way analysis of variance shows that the overall error rates do differ significantly by course (F = 526, p < 0.0001). Tukey's HSD indicates that each course is different from the three others, with its own distinct overall error rate. Taking all possible errors into account, 1054 students saw a mean error rate of 70/KLOC, 1114 students saw 30/KLOC, 2114 students saw 19/KLOC, and 3114 students saw 43/KLOC.

Among CS majors, the difference between courses indicated by the ANOVA appears in Figure 3 as a general decrease in error rates as students progress from CS1 to CS2 to CS3. Formatting errors are a notable exception, showing little difference across the three in-majors courses. This suggests that formatting errors at the rate of approximately 2.5 per thousand lines of code, are accidents of typing, rather than an indicator of learned skill. Overall, the comparisons discussed here give a feel for how error behaviors change as beginners gain more experience, and how non-major beginners compare to CS majors.

5.4 Initial Submissions Compared to Final Work

We are also interested in determining which errors appear in student's very first attempt at an assignment, and which errors persist in students' final work. This is of interest because some errors might seem more difficult to fix or more likely to remain in a student's final answer than others, and also we expect students to develop skills at avoiding or removing errors over time, and thus might expect initial submissions to become relatively error-free after some time.

Figure 4 compares the rates of each category of error, calculated separately for initial submissions to each assignment, and for final submissions to each assignment. The "mean" columns represent the overall means across all submissions, as shown in Figure 2. A one-way ANOVA indicates that initial submissions, means, and final submissions are significantly different, and Tukey's HSD shows that each is different from the other two. As shown in Figure 4, initial submissions have the highest error rates, with rates dropping when all submissions are averaged together, and dropping to their lowest when only final submissions are considered. This trend holds across all four classes—although error rates on initial submissions appear to decrease with experience, error rates on initial submissions are always significantly higher than mean rates for the same course.

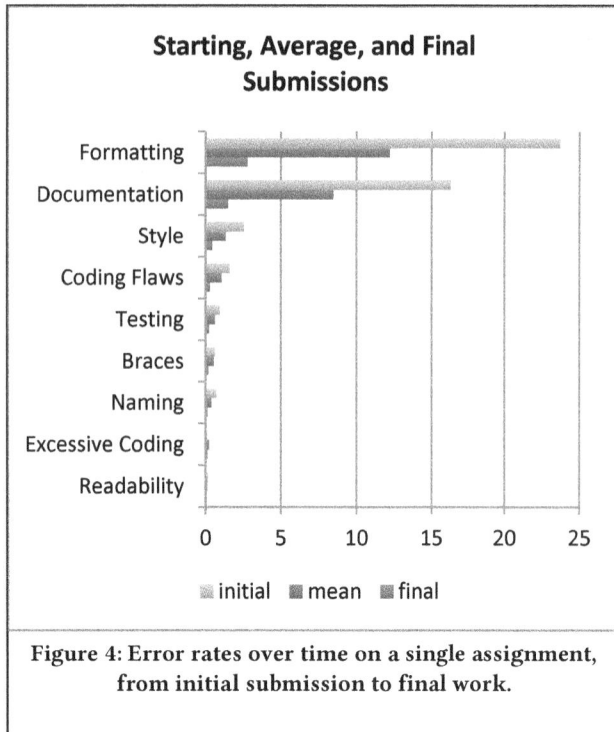

Figure 4: Error rates over time on a single assignment, from initial submission to final work.

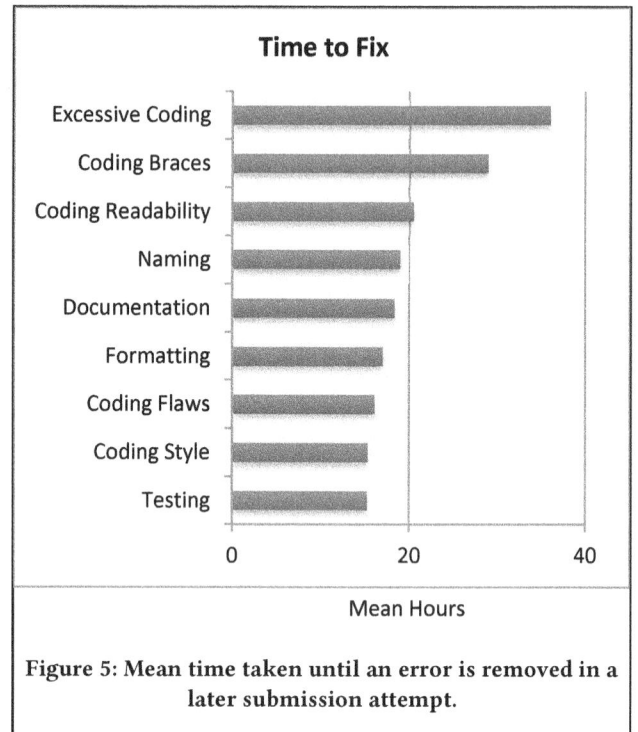

Mean Hours

Figure 5: Mean time taken until an error is removed in a later submission attempt.

Interestingly, however, the categories with the highest rates remain the same, whether considered across courses, or considered from initial submissions, through intermediate submissions, to final submissions. The only exception is errors flagging excessive coding, which are slightly more frequent in final submissions (0.09/KLOC) than in initial submissions (0.07/KLOC). Problems with excessive coding make up only 0.8% of all errors overall, however.

5.5 Relationship with Grades

Are static analysis errors related to student achievement, in terms of earning grades? While an ANCOVA suggests a relationship between individual error rate on an assignment and the corresponding score (F = 5211, pp < 0.0001), examining a scatterplot of the two variables does not reveal a clear visible trend (correlation R = -0.27). However, a narrower focus yields a striking relationship.

The coding flaws category, ranked fourth most frequent in Figure 2, includes static analysis errors that are usually associated with bugs. One might expect these errors to be an indicator of programs that have other quality issues. We classified student final programs based on whether or not they contained any coding flaw errors, and also whether or not the student exhibited any coding flaw errors during any submissions leading up to finishing the assignment. An analysis of variance including course, the presence of coding errors in the final product, and the presence of coding errors at any point during development of the solution indicated that coding flaws are significantly related to program grades earned (F = 2755, p < 0.0001). Presence of coding flaws at any point when developing a solution resulted in significantly lower scores on the assignment

(mean without flaws detected = 91.8%, mean with flaws detected = 84.5%, F = 46.5, p < 0.0001). The overall standard deviation for project scores was 22.2%, resulting in an effect size of 0.33. Further, presence of coding flaws in the final submission itself was associated with dramatically lower scores (mean without flaws in final work = 91.4%, mean with flaws in final work = 48.2%, F = 7710, p < 0.0001), with an effect size of 1.97—almost two standard deviations separating the means of the two groups.

5.6 Which Errors Take Longest to Fix?

We also examined which errors take the most time to resolve. In some cases, errors that are more difficult may take more time. In other cases, students may simply postpone fixing errors because they are concentrating on a different aspect.

To determine the time taken to address an error, we considered the number of specific errors in each source file of a student's work. On a subsequent submission by the student, if the same file contained a higher count for the same specific error, this was treated as the introduction of new errors. However, if the file had a lower count for the same specific error, this was treated as the resolution or removal of existing errors. We processed the entire series of submission attempts by each student, individually tracking the errors counts for each distinct error in order to gauge the times at which individual errors were introduced and removed.

Aggregating this information results in Figure 5, which shows the mean time (in hours) between the submission where an error was introduced, and the later submission where the error was resolved, arranged by error category. From this, although documentation and formatting errors are by far the most common, they do not take the most time to fix. Instead, students remove these errors in under a day on average.

The errors that stay around the longest are those identifying excessive coding. One might expect that resolving issues with methods that are too long would require some amount of code refactoring, and that this would take more time than fixing indentation mistakes. However, the error category that took the second longest average amount of time to remove are missing (optional) braces around the bodies of control statements—a situation that can be addressed very quickly. Overall, the spread of times across error categories is not that great, and appears to be dominated more by the times between program submissions than the amount of time actually used to address the error.

6 CONCLUSION

Static analysis offers a useful way to check conformance to coding standards, while also offering additional kinds of error checking that may find errors compilers do not report and that may go undetected at run-time without careful testing. While syntax errors have been widely studied, no one has systematically examined patterns in static analysis errors.

In this study, we examined nearly 10 million static analysis errors produced by 3,691 students over five semesters. Data was drawn from multiple courses, including a non-majors service course, traditional CS1 and CS2 courses, and an advanced CS3 course on data structures and algorithms. This breadth of data allowed us to answer our research questions.

We found that the most common static analysis errors are formatting and documentation (Javadoc commenting) errors. Which errors are most common remains remarkably consistent across courses as students gain experience, and is also the same between CS majors and non-majors in our service course. Although the errors (and categories) that are most common remain the same, the rate at which students experience errors do change, generally decreasing with experience. However, informal discussions with students indicate that formatting and documentation errors are *too* common, leading them to believe that *all* static analysis errors are "cosmetic".

We also see that the static analysis issues students are most likely to experience on the initial versions of their work are the same as the issues that are most frequent overall. Students clearly experience more errors on initial submissions than average, and have significantly fewer static analysis errors in their final work.

While there is not strong evidence for a direct relationship between the number of static analysis errors in general and final grade, we examined the coding flaws category more closely. Presence of coding flaws at any point during a student's work is associated with lower scores. Presence of any coding flaws in the final submission is associated with a significant drop in assignment score, with an effect size of 1.97 standard deviations. Presence of coding flaws may be a good indicator that a student is struggling, and calling attention to these types of errors may by useful as an aid to students.

More importantly, the prevalence of formatting and documentation issues may make it more likely that students will overlook non-cosmetic issues that are reported, including coding flaws. Educators should take this into account when employing static analysis tools in the classroom if they wish for such tools to be useful to students in identifying bugs.

Finally, if time to fix an issue is measured between the submission attempt where an error was introduced and the the submission where it was resolved, excessive code and missing optional braces are the categories that persist the longest.

The analysis presented here is the first attempt to explore the meaningful properties of static analysis errors. At the same time, there are many limitations to the analysis that affect the validity and generalizability of the results. First, any such investigation is limited by the checks supported by the tools used. A different static analysis tool might provide better (or worse) checks with greater (or lesser) utility. Similarly, different target programming languages provide different opportunities for static analysis, and often a different partitioning between compile-time or run-time errors. Whether an instructor uses static analysis errors for scoring some of the marks on an assignment, or differentially weights different types of errors, is also likely to have an effect on results reported here. Finally, even the user interface used to present reported errors to students is a significant factor worth considering. Just presenting a simple list of errors makes it easier for frequent (cosmetic) errors to "drown out" coding flaws, which may encourage students to become "blind" to the value of static analysis errors. All of these issues should be taken into account in further studies of this useful diagnostic approach.

ACKNOWLEDGEMENTS

This work is supported in part by the National Science Foundation under grants DUE-1625425. Any opinions, findings, conclusions, or recommendations expressed in this material are those of the authors and do not necessarily reflect the views of the National Science Foundation.

APPENDIX: ERROR CATEGORIES

Braces	
pmd	ForLoopsMustUseBraces
pmd	IfElseStmtsMustUseBraces
pmd	IfStmtsMustUseBraces
pmd	WhileLoopsMustUseBraces
Coding Flaws	
checkstyle	CovariantEquals
checkstyle	EmptyStatement
checkstyle	FallThrough
checkstyle	HiddenField
checkstyle	InnerAssignment
checkstyle	StringLiteralEquality
pmd	AvoidBranchingStatementAsLastInLoop
pmd	AvoidMultipleUnaryOperators
pmd	BrokenNullCheck
pmd	ClassCastExceptionWithToArray
pmd	IdempotentOperations
pmd	JumbledIncrementer
pmd	MisplacedNullCheck

pmd	MissingStaticMethodInNonInstantiatableClass
pmd	NonCaseLabelInSwitchStatement
pmd	ProhibitedGreenfootImport
pmd	SwitchStmtsShouldHaveDefault
pmd	UnusedLocalVariable
pmd	UnusedPrivateField
pmd	UnusedPrivateMethod
pmd	UselessOperationOnImmutable
Readability	
checkstyle	NeedBraces
checkstyle	UpperEll
pmd	AvoidUsingOctalValues
pmd	MethodWithSameNameAsEnclosingClass
checkstyle	DefaultComesLast
checkstyle	EmptyBlock
pmd	EmptyCatchBlock
pmd	EmptyFinallyBlock
pmd	EmptyIfStmt
pmd	EmptyInitializer
pmd	EmptyStatementBlock
pmd	EmptyTryBlock
pmd	EmptyWhileStmt
Style	
checkstyle	RedundantThrows
checkstyle	RegexpMultiline
checkstyle	SimplifyBooleanReturn
pmd	AvoidRethrowingException
pmd	AvoidThrowingNewInstanceOfSameException
pmd	AvoidThrowingNullPointerException
pmd	BooleanInstantiation
pmd	CollapsibleIfStatements
pmd	DontImportJavaLang
pmd	DuplicateImports
pmd	EqualsNull
pmd	ExtendsObject
pmd	ForLoopShouldBeWhileLoop
pmd	ImportFromSamePackage
pmd	InstantiationToGetClass
pmd	LogicInversion
pmd	ReturnFromFinallyBlock
pmd	SimplifyBooleanAssertion
pmd	SimplifyBooleanExpressions
pmd	SimplifyBooleanReturns
pmd	SimplifyConditional
pmd	SingularField
pmd	StringInstantiation
pmd	TooFewBranchesForASwitchStatement
pmd	UnconditionalIfStatement
pmd	UnnecessaryCaseChange
pmd	UnnecessaryConversionTemporary
pmd	UnnecessaryFinalModifier
pmd	UnnecessaryReturn
pmd	UnusedImports

Documentation	
checkstyle	JavadocMethod
checkstyle	JavadocType
checkstyle	JavadocVariable
checkstyle	RegexpSingleline
checkstyle	TodoComment
pmd	UncommentedEmptyConstructor
pmd	UncommentedEmptyMethod
pmd	UncommentedEmptyMethodBody
Excessive Coding	
pmd	ExcessiveClassLength
pmd	ExcessiveMethodLength
pmd	ExcessiveParameterList
pmd	TooManyFields
Formatting	
checkstyle	ArrayTypeStyle
checkstyle	FileTabCharacter
checkstyle	GenericWhitespace
checkstyle	Indentation
checkstyle	LineLength
checkstyle	MethodParamPad
checkstyle	MultipleVariableDeclarations
checkstyle	NoWhitespaceAfter
checkstyle	NoWhitespaceBefore
checkstyle	OneStatementPerLine
checkstyle	RightCurly
checkstyle	WhitespaceAfter
checkstyle	WhitespaceAround
Naming	
checkstyle	ClassTypeParameterName
checkstyle	ConstantName
checkstyle	LocalFinalVariableName
checkstyle	LocalVariableName
checkstyle	MemberName
checkstyle	MethodName
checkstyle	ParameterName
checkstyle	StaticVariableName
checkstyle	TypeName
pmd	AvoidFieldNameMatchingTypeName
pmd	FormalParametersNeedMeaningfulNames
Testing	
pmd	JUnit3ConstantAssertion
pmd	JUnit3TestsHaveAssertions
pmd	JUnit4ConstantAssertion
pmd	JUnit4TestsHaveAssertions
pmd	JUnitSpelling
pmd	JUnitTestClassNeedsTestCase
pmd	UseAssertNullInsteadOfAssertTrue
pmd	UseAssertSameInsteadOfAssertTrue

REFERENCES

[1] M. Ahmadzadeh, D. Elliman, and C. Higgins. An analysis of patterns of debugging among novice computer science students. In Proceedings of the 10th Annual SIGCSE Conference on Innovation and Technology in Computer Science Education, ITiCSE '05, pages 84{88, New York, NY, USA, 2005. ACM.

[2] A. Altadmri and N. C. C. Brown. 37 Million Compilations: Investigating Novice Programming Mistakes in Large-Scale Student Data. SIGCSE '15 Proceedings of the 46th ACM Technical Symposium on Computer Science Education. Pages 522-527

[3] D. McCall and M. Kolling. Meaningful categorisation of novice programmer errors. In Frontiers In Education Conference, pages 2589-2596, 2014.

[4] P. Denny, A. Luxton-Reilly, and E. Tempero. All syntax errors are not equal. In Proceedings of the 17th ACM Annual Conference on Innovation and Technology in Computer Science Education, ITiCSE '12, pages 75-80, New York, NY, USA, 2012. ACM.

[5] M. C. Jadud and B. Dorn. Aggregate Compilation Behavior: Findings and Implications from 27,698 Users. ICER '15 Proceedings of the eleventh annual International Conference on International Computing Education Research. Pages 131-139

[6] E. S. Tabanao, M. M. T. Rodrigo, and M. C. Jadud. Predicting at-risk novice Java programmers through the analysis of online protocols. In Proceedings of the Seventh International Workshop on Computing Education Research, ICER '11, pages 85-92, NewYork, NY, USA, 2011. ACM.

[7] M. M. T. Rodrigo, T. C. S. Andallaza, F. E. V. G. Castro, M. L. V. Armenta, T. T. Dy, and M. C. Jadud. An analysis of java programming behaviors, affect, perceptions, and syntax errors among low-achieving, average, and highachieving novice programmers. Journal of Educational Computing Research, 49(3):293–325, 2013.

[8] S. H. Edwards and M. A. Perez-Quinones. Web-cat: automatically grading programming assignments. In ACM SIGCSE Bulletin, volume 40, pages 328– 328. ACM, 2008.

[9] N. Truong, P. Roe and P. Bancroft. Static analysis of students' Java programs. ACE '04 Proceedings of the Sixth Australasian Conference on Computing Education - Volume 30 Pages 317-325.

[10] C. Artho and A. Biere. Applying Static Analysis to Large-Scale, Multi-Threaded Java Programs. ASWEC '01 Proceedings of the 13th Australian Conference on Software Engineering. Page 68

[11] Fenwick, J.B.Jr., Norris, C., Barry, F.E., Rountree,J., Spicer,C.J. and Cheek, S.D. 2009. Another look at the behaviors of novice programmers. SIGCSE Bull. 41, 1 (March 2009), 296-300. DOI=10.1145/1539024.1508973

[12] A. Stefik and S. Siebert. An empirical investigation into programming language syntax. Trans. Comput. Educ., 13(4):19:1{19:40, Nov. 2013.

[13] Mengel, S. and Yerramilli, V. (1999): A Case Study Of The Static Analysis Of the Quality Of Novice Student Programs. Proc. Thirtieth SIGCSE technical symposium on Computer science education, New Orleans, Louisiana, United States, 13:78-82.

[14] N. Ayewah, W. Pugh, J. David Morgenthaler, J. Penix and Y. Zhou. Evaluating Static Analysis Defect Warnings On Production Software. PASTE '07 Proceedings of the 7th ACM SIGPLAN-SIGSOFT workshop on Program analysis for software tools and engineering, San Diego, California, United States. Pages 1-8. June 2007

[15] N. Nagappan and T. Ball. Static Analysis Tools as Early Indicators of Pre-Release Defect Density. ICSE '05 Proceedings of the 27th international conference on Software engineering. Pages 580-586. St. Louis, MO, USA — May 15 - 21, 2005.

On Novices' Interaction with Compiler Error Messages: A Human Factors Approach

James Prather, Raymond Pettit,
Kayla Holcomb McMurry, Alani Peters,
John Homer, Nevan Simone
Abilene Christian University
ACU Box 28036
Abilene, TX 79601
jrp09a,rsp05a,kmh12c,alp13d,jdh08a,nfs13a@acu.edu

Maxine Cohen
Nova Southeastern University
3301 College Avenue
Fort Lauderdale, FL 33314
cohenm@nova.edu

ABSTRACT

The difficulty in understanding compiler error messages can be a major impediment to novice student learning. To alleviate this issue, multiple researchers have run experiments enhancing compiler error messages in automated assessment tools for programming assignments. The conclusions reached by these published experiments appear to be conflicting. We examine these experiments and propose five potential reasons for the inconsistent conclusions concerning enhanced compiler error messages: (1) students do not read them, (2) researchers are measuring the wrong thing, (3) the effects are hard to measure, (4) the messages are not properly designed, (5) the messages are properly designed, but students do not understand them in context due to increased cognitive load. We constructed mixed-methods experiments designed to address reasons 1 and 5 with a specific automated assessment tool, Athene, that previously reported inconclusive results. Testing student comprehension of the enhanced compiler error messages outside the context of an automated assessment tool demonstrated their effectiveness over standard compiler error messages. Quantitative results from a 60 minute one-on-one think-aloud study with 31 students did not show substantial increase in student learning outcomes over the control. However, qualitative results from the one-on-one think-aloud study indicated that most students are reading the enhanced compiler error messages and generally make effective changes after encountering them.

CCS CONCEPTS

• **Human-centered computing** → **Empirical studies in HCI**; *User studies*; *Usability testing*; • **Social and professional topics** → **CS1**; *Student assessment*; • **Applied computing** → **Computer-assisted instruction**; *Interactive learning environments*;

Table 1: Definition of Frequently Used Terms

Term	Meaning
CEM	Compiler Error Message
ECEM	Enhanced Compiler Error Message
Athene	Automated assessment tool used in this experiment

KEYWORDS

HCI, human factors, usability, automated assessment tools, education, CS1, ethnography

ACM Reference format:
James Prather, Raymond Pettit, Kayla Holcomb McMurry, Alani Peters, John Homer, Nevan Simone and Maxine Cohen. 2017. On Novices' Interaction with Compiler Error Messages: A Human Factors Approach. In *Proceedings of ICER '17, Tacoma, WA, USA, August 18-20, 2017,* 9 pages.
https://doi.org/10.1145/3105726.3106169

1 INTRODUCTION

It is well-documented that novice programmers often struggle in understanding compiler error messages (CEMs) caused by incorrect syntax [3, 7, 32, 42]. This is a motivating factor in the development of automated assessment tools [36]. In one very popular tool, BlueJ, students placed their difficulty in interpreting CEMs high amongst their other concerns [16]. Bennedsen has suggested that this is a contributing factor in the high failure rates in CS1 courses [5]. Specifically called out in 1976 [44] as an impediment to learning syntax, CEMs are still just as cryptic and hard to understand as they were forty years ago [4]. In an attempt to alleviate novice frustration, several papers have recently attempted to improve upon the design of standard CEMs in automated assessment tools from an HCI perspective [2, 31, 33, 42], which we will call enhanced compiler error messages (ECEMs).

Several recent studies have enhanced default CEMs and performed empirical experiments to determine if ECEMs have a positive impact on student learning in CS1 [4, 9, 37]. These studies all provide quantitative data and analysis of student performance, but stated conflicting conclusions. Denny et al. [9] and Pettit et al. [37] could not find conclusive evidence that enhancing error messages was helpful to students. Becker [4], however, was able to show that ECEMs were more helpful for those in his study.

We postulate five possible explanations for these conflicting results:

(1) students do not read ECEMs,
(2) researchers are measuring the wrong thing,
(3) the effects are hard to measure,
(4) the ECEMs are not properly designed, therefore students do not understand them,
(5) the ECEMs are properly designed but students do not understand ECEMs in context due to increased cognitive load.

For this study, we constructed experiments to test the possibilities that (1) students do not read ECEMs or (5) the ECEMs already implemented are properly designed but cognitive load in students reduces the positive effects. Our research questions are therefore:

- **RQ1:** Do novice students read ECEMs?
- **RQ2:** Are ECEMs helpful for novice students in a setting with low cognitive load?
- **RQ3:** Are the ECEMs helpful for novice students in a setting with high cognitive load?

We begin by reviewing related work on automated assessment tools, ECEMs in automated assessment tools, and the design of these ECEMs. We next describe the methodology by which we attempt to answer the research questions above. In section 4, we describe both quantitative and qualitative results from our mixed-methods study. In section 5 we summarize our conclusions.

2 RELATED WORK

Automated assessment tools for programming assignments have been around since at least 1960, when Hollingworth built a way to automatically assess the programs that students submitted in his course via punch cards [19]. Today, many different automated assessment tools exist, some focused more on assessment and some focused more on helping students learn to program. Still others are focused on test-driven development, such as the popular automated assessment tool Web-CAT [12]. For a general review of automated assessment tools see Ala-Mutka [1], Douce [10], and Ihantola [21].

2.1 Error messages in automated assessment tools

Many creators of automated assessment tools have attempted to enhance the standard syntax/compiler error messages that students receive. One of the earliest examples is CAP developed by Schorsh in 1995 [39]. The intent of CAP was to provide students in an introductory programming course with user-friendly feedback pertaining to syntax, logic, and style errors. In 2012, Watson discussed the tool BlueFix, which applied his principle of adapting the compiler messages to the level of the students [43]. Upon the first encounter of a compiler error, students saw the standard error. If the student generated the same error a second time in a row, they received an enhanced version of the error message. After a third consecutive generation of the same compiler error, the student received a suggested fix to their code. This adaptive process involved an extensive analysis of the student's existing code and prediction of the student's intent. Students were then able to vote on whether or not the suggested fix worked. In this way, Watson was able to introduce crowdsourcing techniques into automated assessment

tools. Other examples of enhancing compiler error messages for novice students include Thetis [15], HiC [18], Expresso [20], Gauntlet [14], a tool by Dy [11], LearnCS! [27], an IDE by Barik [3], and ITS-Debug [6].

2.2 Students have trouble with CEMs

Syntax and compiler error messages have long been documented to be a great source of confusion and frustration to students. Traver addresses problems with compiler error messages, highlighting some of the challenges in improving messages and showing many actual examples of the misleading messages that compilers produce [42]. He offers suggestions on improving these messages based on HCI research and sound pedagogy. Murphy et al. were part of a large multi-institution group analyzing debugging strategies of novice programmers [32]. Observations from class sessions and one-on-one interviews make apparent the frustrations student have related to misunderstanding errors in programming code. Finally, Marceau et al. discuss how poor error messages lead to student frustrations, one issue researchers sought to address in creating and improving DrRacket [30]. Furthermore, Marceau observes that some languages used to teach introductory programming, such as Alice [23] and Scratch [29] were created with a goal of protecting students from any possibility of creating syntax errors in their early programs.

2.3 Empirical evidence of helpfulness of ECEM (Denny, Becker, Pettit)

In 2014, Denny et al. reported on the tool CodeWrite and the enhanced error messages the compiler generates [9]. Researchers used the CodeWrite tool for Java programmers, intercepting the compiler error messages that the tool returned. The researchers replaced existing compiler error messages with much more descriptive error messages geared to the novice programmer. The conclusion of the experiment was that there was no statistically significant difference in the students' behavior: students submitted as often as others had before to get past the same compile errors. These results were unexpected and seemed non-intuitive. In contrast, Becker [4] similarly enhanced error messages in the automated assessment tool, Decaf, also used for Java programming. His findings showed that these enhanced messages actually did change student behavior. After viewing an enhanced error message, students were less likely to generate the same error in the future. Finally, Pettit et al. enhanced CEMs in an automated assessment tool, Athene, used for C++ programming [37]. They could not find conclusive results that the ECEMs were more helpful than standard CEMs.

2.4 Design of ECEMs in automated assessment tools

Hartmann et al. [17] created their own automated assessment tool, HelpMeOut, which provides students with feedback similar to Denny et al. [9]. HelpMeOut queries a database of similar errors and presents users with examples and how to fix them. Previous approaches, such as those discussed above, have implemented enhanced feedback through a selection of top errors provided by instructors. These lists of potential errors are driven by experts and not user observation. A weakness to this approach is evidenced by one such implementation discussed above, Gauntlet [14], that was later found by Jackson et al. [22] to not contain the most commonly encountered errors by novices. HelpMeOut overcomes this weakness through a dynamic list of real student bugs that can better reflect actual user experience. Furthermore, the suggestion that appears at the top of the list is accomplished through crowdsourced voting by students. In other words, the dominating metric of which examples of similar bugs that students will see is based heavily on user experience. While the solution is quite novel, Hartmann, et al., do not attempt to measure whether their automated assessment tool helped novice programmers create a better mental model of the errors they received or whether it increased learnability for novice programmers. Furthermore, as Traver et al. note, this requires a large database of student suggestions and crowd-sourced data [42].

Marceau et al. [31] questioned the computer science education research community for investigating whether or not feedback messages helped users learn without approaching it from the perspective of users. They provide both a quantitative and qualitative human factors approach via a statistical analysis of user errors after introducing enhanced feedback and follow-up interviews with four of those same students. They discovered that students were grossly misinterpreting the feedback messages and were confused at the highly specialized vocabulary of their automated assessment tool, DrRacket. They postulate that perhaps students do not take the time to read the messages, but rather use it only as an "oracle" that somehow knows how to fix their code or that students prefer to read only the code highlights that indicate the necessary change. In following work, Marceau et al. [30] provide a rubric for evaluating the effectiveness of error messages based on student behavior after encountering them. They recommend changes to error messages: simplify vocabulary, be more explicit in pointing to the problem, help students match terms in the error message to parts of their code (e.g. using color coded highlighting), design the programming course with error messages in mind (rather than an afterthought), and teach students how to read and understand error messages during class time.

Several other recent studies utilize aspects of a human factors approach to an automated assessment tool. Traver et al. discuss the theory behind error message design and propose eight specific principles for the design of ECEMs [42]. Lee and Ko discuss personifying feedback in a game that teaches programming [25]. Their tool, Gidget, personifies feedback by accepting blame when a program works incorrectly. Participants in the experimental group where personification was increased completed more levels of the game in a similar amount of time compared to the control group. Barik et al. performed an experiment with eye tracking software to determine if students read error messages [2]. These students were a mix of undergraduate and graduate students who had an average of 1.4 years of professional software engineering experience within a company. While the study by Barik et al. is closely related to the present study, we examine the problem from the perspective of novice programmers in their very first programming course. Barik et al. found that intermediate students do indeed read CEMs. They also found that, as error messages become more difficult and cryptic, programmers cycled between the error message and the offending

code more times, negatively correlating with success. Their findings provide empirical justification for the necessity of enhancing CEMs. Loksa et al. performed a study on a code camp where the control group was taught to program and the experimental group was additionally trained in the cognitive aspects of coding [28]. They suggest training students in metacognitive awareness, upon the assumption that "programming is not merely about language syntax and semantics, but more fundamentally about the iterative process of refining mental representations of computational problems and solutions and expressing those representations as code," and report that students with this training were significantly better able to understand error feedback. Loksa's work suggests an entirely different direction for this research, one that is beyond the scope of this study.

2.5 Think-aloud studies in CS1

One research tool often employed in evaluating changes made to CS1 classes is the think-aloud protocol where students are observed writing code and asked to verbalize their thoughts while doing so. Yuen performed a think-aloud study on his CS1 class to understand the differences in how novices construct knowledge compared to experts [46]. He collected data from four sources: an initial survey, participants' work on paper, transcripts of the interviews, and the researcher's field notes. Their results show three kinds of student behavior in response to various levels of knowledge construction. The least desirable response, "need to code," is when the student does not seek to first understand and determine a solution, but instead turns directly to the code. A better response is the second, "generalizing the problem," where the novice is able to take what they have previously learned and try to generalize it to the present scenario, sometimes leading to a valid solution. The third and most desirable behavior, "designing effective solutions," is when the student is able to properly take their knowledge construction and apply it to create a working solution. These three categories will be useful in this study's data analysis.

Teague et al. perform a think-aloud study watching novices trace code and then attempt to explain in a single sentence what it does [40]. They follow the classic think-aloud protocols by Ericsson and Simon [13]. Teague's results suggest that students who cannot trace code cannot build appropriate abstractions to understand complex programming tasks. One important contribution they make is in noting that think-aloud studies are difficult for novices. The task of programming is already cognitively overloading novices and therefore asking them to also think-aloud during a study could threaten the ability to replicate the same silent attempt. To offset this, they began their study with a short think-aloud practice session so the participant could become familiar with the think-aloud protocol and the interviewer. We follow Ericsson and Simon for think-aloud protocol and follow Teague in adding a short practice session at the beginning to hopefully offset cognitive load on novices.

Whalley and Kasto perform a think-aloud study watching novices solve three programming challenges [45]. Researchers narrated the problem-solving process and showed how some students who might otherwise get stuck were able to solve the challenges with some redirection and scaffolding. They also note that think-aloud studies are difficult with novice programmers because the cognitive load is already very high and so they have a difficult time concentrating on solving the problem and can't continually verbalize their thoughts. In order to offset this, they also used a short practice session so participants could get used to the think-aloud protocol.

Qualitative research methods complement our quantitative methods in this study. These qualitative methods will give us access to information that submission data and quiz results do not, such as the students motivations for behaving in a certain way, their beliefs about what they are doing, and the feelings that they are having when performing certain actions. All of these serve to give us a better explanation of why students make certain choices. For a thorough review of qualitative research approaches, see Lincoln and Guba [26] or Patton [34]. For more information specifically on mixed method approaches, see Creswell [8].

3 METHODOLOGY

3.1 Pilot Studies

Two usability pilot studies were conducted in fall 2016, each with six participants in ten minute sessions that used a simple Fibonacci problem requiring a while-loop to solve. The automated assessment tool used in this study was Athene due to its adoption and use at the university where the study was conducted [35, 37, 41]. Participants were provided with a code file that contained six bugs and asked to submit the code, fixing errors as they found them, until Athene accepted the program as complete. The program used a method that takes n as a parameter and returns the nth Fibonacci number, computed using a while loop. After the first pilot study, the ECEMs in Athene were redesigned using the guidelines from the literature [17, 31, 42]. The second pilot study performed the same experiment with the redesigned ECEMs which led to a further refining of their design. This included changing wording to better match user expectations, streamlining the design, and removing pieces that confused users. Perhaps the most interesting change was to the text in the title of the enhanced portion of the message from "Need More Help?" to "More Information." Most participants in the second pilot study indicated that they did not want more help - even the ones that struggled. The design of the button used the words "Need More Help?" and most participants balked at that phrasing as a threat to their ego. Follow-up questions about why they felt this way revealed they thought that looking at something titled "Need More Help?" was almost like cheating or like giving up and they wanted to do it themselves without looking at the answer. The phrasing was picked to be a neutral and clear label about the button's function, but it clearly was not perceived this way by participants. Thus, it was changed to "More Information" as in Figure 1 and Figure 2. The attitude among the participants led to the creation of question #3 in the follow-up questions in the think-aloud study.

3.2 Error Message Quizzes

Participants that were enrolled in CS1 for Spring 2017 at Abilene Christian University were given six quizzes in class to determine if the newly refined ECEMs were more helpful than the standard compiler messages. This was done in an attempt to answer RQ2: are ECEMs helpful for novice students in a setting with low cognitive

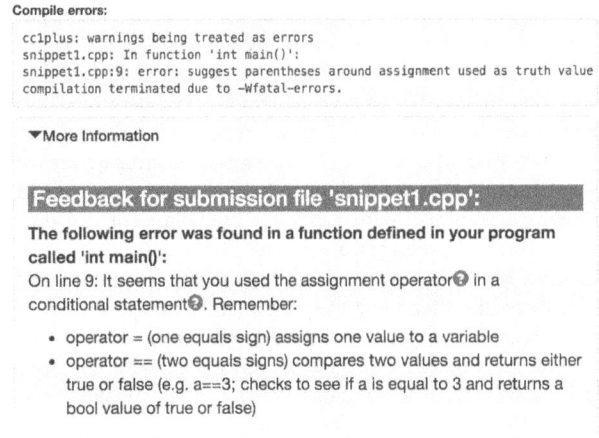

```
Compile errors:

cc1plus: warnings being treated as errors
snippet1.cpp: In function 'int main()':
snippet1.cpp:9: error: suggest parentheses around assignment used as truth value
compilation terminated due to -Wfatal-errors.
```

▼More Information

Feedback for submission file 'snippet1.cpp':

The following error was found in a function defined in your program called 'int main()':
On line 9: It seems that you used the assignment operator❓ in a conditional statement❓. Remember:

- operator = (one equals sign) assigns one value to a variable
- operator == (two equals signs) compares two values and returns either true or false (e.g. a==3; checks to see if a is equal to 3 and returns a bool value of true or false)

Figure 1: The error message from error message quiz 1B (enhanced) with the enhanced message expanded

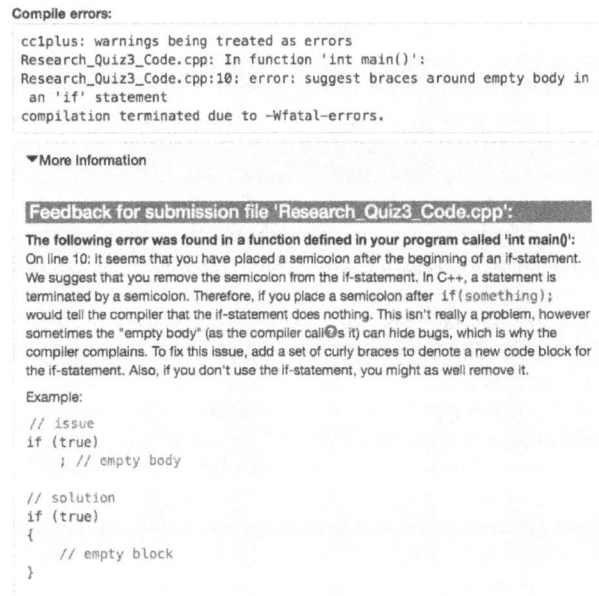

```
Compile errors:

cc1plus: warnings being treated as errors
Research_Quiz3_Code.cpp: In function 'int main()':
Research_Quiz3_Code.cpp:10: error: suggest braces around empty body in
an 'if' statement
compilation terminated due to -Wfatal-errors.
```

▼More Information

Feedback for submission file 'Research_Quiz3_Code.cpp':

The following error was found in a function defined in your program called 'int main()':
On line 10: It seems that you have placed a semicolon after the beginning of an if-statement. We suggest that you remove the semicolon from the if-statement. In C++, a statement is terminated by a semicolon. Therefore, if you place a semicolon after if(something); would tell the compiler that the if-statement does nothing. This isn't really a problem, however sometimes the "empty body" (as the compiler calls it) can hide bugs, which is why the compiler complains. To fix this issue, add a set of curly braces to denote a new code block for the if-statement. Also, if you don't use the if-statement, you might as well remove it.

Example:

```
// issue
if (true)
    ; // empty body

// solution
if (true)
{
    // empty block
}
```

Figure 2: The error message from error message quiz 4A (enhanced) with the enhanced message expanded

load. These quizzes all took place outside of the context of Athene as part of a replacement for a daily quiz where cognitive load would be much lower. In order to provide a control group and an experimental group, the class of 31 was divided in to two groups of similar demographics: A and B. Each quiz contained a code snippet with a bug that would lead to a specific compile error, a feedback message produced by Athene when that code is submitted, and a short-answer question asking students to determine where the error is, what the error is, and how they would fix it. In every case students had seven minutes to solve the quiz. In odd-numbered quizzes, the students in group A saw only the standard compiler error message as feedback from Athene, while the students in group B saw the standard compiler error message as well as the enhanced error message from Athene. For the even-numbered quizzes, group A saw the standard and enhanced messages while group B saw only the standard messages. This was repeated for all six quizzes. Thus, each student saw a standard message for three quizzes and the enhanced message for three quizzes. Each quiz contained a different code snippet with a different compile error and thus a different feedback message from Athene. The compile errors chosen for the six quizzes were the six errors students encountered most frequently while attempting the programming assignment used in the think-aloud study below. The difficulty of the code snippets that students were asked to analyze scaled along with the content of the semester in an effort to make them consistently challenging.

3.3 Think-Alouds

As a classroom enhancement, the researcher canceled class and instead held hour-long one-on-one sessions in CS1 during week 6 of classes for Spring 2017 at Abilene Christian University. All 31 students participated. Each student met one-on-one with a researcher where the student was observed completing a "practical quiz" and received feedback on their process. A practical quiz is similar to a homework assignment - students receive a programming problem in Athene, but must solve it in a proctored 35 minute time window. Students were asked to verbalize their thoughts while they solved the problem, especially when they encountered the enhanced feedback messages. The primary researcher supervised two researchers conducting these one-on-one studies. Occasionally a second supervisor also observed these sessions. This was done to ensure standardization of practices between observers. In an effort to control for differing development environments and the help students might or might not receive from certain ones, students were only allowed to type their code in the default Windows notepad application.

The general format of the think-aloud study follows the usability testing guidelines found in Rubin and Chisnell [38] and Krug [24], including pre- and post-testing checklists and scripts. At the beginning of each session, the evaluator read from a script outlining the reason for the session, the goal of the session, and what was expected of the student. Students were then given a very simple task and asked to think-aloud so they can get used to verbalizing their thoughts, the observer, and the process, as suggested by Teague et al. [40] and Whalley and Kasto [45]. This simple task was to write a program that would output "Hello, world." This particular task was chosen because it was cognitively the easiest code to write for any level of student at that point in the semester, so practicing the think-aloud protocol would be easier during this time.

Students were then asked to complete a practical quiz, similar to a simple homework assignment, with a time limit of 35 minutes. The task was this: given n numbers, compute whether there were more positive or negative integer numbers provided as input. Students would need to understand the following concepts: console input, console output, conditionals, and loops. This particular problem, rather than the Fibonacci problem used for the pilot studies, was chosen because it has been used as an in-class assessment in

previous semesters and a majority of students from those previous semesters completed the problem within the same 35 minute time limit. While solving the problem, a researcher took extensive notes on what the student did and said. This study follows the recommendations made by Ericsson and Simon [13] for carrying out think-aloud studies, specifically minimizing social interaction with participants and trying to gently keep them focused on the task at hand. For instance, if the student stopped talking, then the researcher would say, "Keep speaking," and not "Tell me what you're thinking." This encouraged speaking, but the participant was not asked to formulate responses or socially interactive dialogue.

After the students successfully completed the problem or the time limit expired, they were asked up to five interview questions and their responses were recorded. They were asked up to five because some questions may not have pertained to that particular student, depending on their experience solving the quiz. For instance, students could not be asked about their perception of the ECEMs if they did not encounter any of them. Below are the questions that the students were (potentially) asked:

(1) When you encountered the enhanced feedback messages (with the "More information" drop-down), were they helpful? Why or why not?

(2) When you see a feedback message from Athene, how does it make you feel?

(3) Would you rather read the enhanced message under "More information" first, or would you rather wait until you can't figure it out yourself? Why?

(4) (If they saw an enhanced message and did not click it) When you saw the enhanced message, why did you choose not to click on it?

(5) In this class, how often before the deadline do you usually make your first attempt (uploading your program to Athene) on your homework?

These questions were designed to get the student talking about their experience with the ECEMs that they potentially encountered. Getting at perception can be difficult, so the first three questions were all designed to hit around the same issue. The fourth question was for those students that we knew would see them and not use them. The final question was added in an attempt to try and correlate perceived work ethic with use of the ECEMs.

The think-aloud study with post-assessment interview was designed to answer research questions (1) Do Students read ECEMs? and (3) Are the ECEMs helpful for novice students in a setting with high cognitive load?

3.4 Think-Aloud Analysis

The ethnographic portion of the study consisted of participant observation and post-assessment interview questions. This allowed us to record the participants' actions, thought process, problem solving process, reactions to error messages, and their answers to the end-of-session interview questions. Because the participants were asked to use the think-aloud protocol, we were better able to record their thought-process as they solved the assessment. Participant-specific data were separately recorded and then phenomena were coded and grouped into categories. In this way, larger trends began to emerge from the natural groupings of the qualitative data.

We put all of the data into ATLAS.ti and used it for the coding process. We began the coding process by combing through each document and creating quotations and adding codes for participants receiving error messages. For each error message, we coded if it was or was not an enhanced error message. The ECEMs were then broken down into a numbering system so that we could see how many times students received each ECEM. The error messages that were not enhanced were coded as "unenhanced," but were not given a specific error message number. If the error message was enhanced, we then coded if the participant expanded the "more information" section (see Figure 1 and Figure 2 and note the collapsible "more information" section). If the "more information" section was expanded, we then coded whether it proved to be helpful or unhelpful based on their next code edit and submission. However, if the "more information" section remained collapsed, we did not code for that ECEM's helpfulness. Next, we coded for completion time. Completion time was divided into five groups: less than 10 minutes, 10-20 minutes, 20-30 minutes, 30-35 minutes, and incomplete. Each participant document received one of the completion time codes, which allowed us to analyze the progress of each student. At the conclusion of each one-on-one session, the evaluator asked several questions and then gave feedback on the participant's performance in the quiz. We therefore coded each participant's response to these follow-up questions in order to receive an overall perception for the error messages. There were 28 unique codes and these codes were used a total of 370 times.

3.5 Program Logs Analysis

The particular programming assignment that was given in our one-on-one think-aloud sessions was given as an in-class assessment in three other semesters of the same Programming 1 course. For each submission, Athene logged the student's information, a snapshot of the code submitted, the test results or error message produced by Athene, time submitted and current grade on the assessment. The logs of these semesters were pulled and analyzed as a control to compare against our one-on-one session results. For each semester, we measured the number of students who completed the programming assignment with a correct solution, average score, and average time until completion in both the control and experimental groups.

4 RESULTS

4.1 Error Message Quizzes

The error message quizzes were given to students outside of the context of an assessment in Athene to determine if the redesigned ECEMs, on their own, were more helpful than the standard CEMs. Twenty-seven students from the Spring 2017 CS1 class were present for all six quizzes. The results of these quizzes (see Figure 3) show that the experimental case (ECEMs) was more helpful than the control (standard CEMs). The mean percent of incorrect answers among participants in the control group was 17.28% while the mean percent of incorrect answers in the experimental condition was 6.17%. Therefore, the experimental condition displayed a statistically significant improvement over the control ($p < 0.035$, n = 27, paired two sample for means).

Out of the 27 participants present for all six quizzes, 13 students gave an incorrect answer on at least one quiz. As shown in Figure

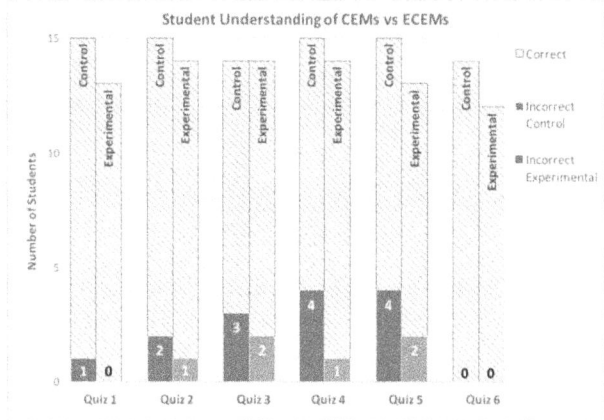

Figure 3: Number of incorrect responses for each condition by quiz

Control (CEM)	Experimental (ECEM)	# of Students
0	1	1
0	2	1
1	0	7
1	1	2
2	0	1
3	0	1

Figure 4: Incorrect Understanding of CEM vs. ECEM

4 (rows 3, 5 and 6), 9 of the 13 students were helped more by the ECEMs. One particularly interesting case is the student who incorrectly answered all three control quizzes, but correctly answered all three in the experimental condition (row 6). Another outlier in the opposite direction was the student who incorrectly answered two experimental quizzes, but correctly answered all in the control condition (row 2).

4.2 Program Logs

Data that can be pulled from Athene's database on assessment submissions has been previously reported by Pettit et al. [35, 37]. However, in previous studies, students were allowed to compile offline and only submitted their code to Athene when making an attempt at correctness. While other tools discussed above capture all student compilations, the automated assessment tool used in the present study, Athene, has previously not been able to report that data. The one-on-one think-aloud study allowed this data to be gathered using Athene for the first time. The difference in student behavior when they can only use Athene to compile versus when they can compile offline is an interesting subject for a future report, but cannot be discussed fully here due to space limitations. We do expect student behavior to change when the compiling constraints change, such as an increase in the number of submissions and therefore the number of errors encountered.

For those students in the experimental section that completed the assessment during the 35 minute time limit, the average time

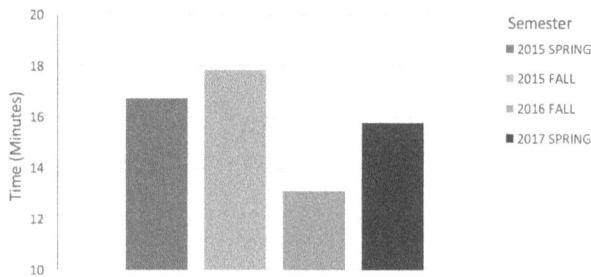

Figure 5: Average time to complete the problem by semester

to completion was 15:46 with a standard deviation of 7:03. In the control, the previous three semesters when this assessment was given the average completion times were: 16:44, 17:50, and 13:05 (Figure 5). This data indicates that the experiment did not adversely affect student outcomes.

The average score for all students in the experimental section was 67%. The average score for the previous three control semesters was 90%, 88.2%, and 84.2%. This seems to indicate that students in the experimental section may have been adversely affected. However, this may have been an artifact of the way the procedure was performed. As mentioned above, students have previously been able to compile offline and many students will use previous programs they have written as a bootstrap for any new program they attempt. In the case of the experimental group, 10 students did not complete the quiz at all, 6 of which suffered from problems with the basic structure of their code. All of these 6 students could not remember include statements and how to write their main function. If this assessment had been carried out in a previous semester, these students would have had access to previous programs and may have solved the problem. Instead, they could not move past the structural compiler errors. Furthermore, none of the structural compiler errors had been enhanced because we based our choices about which messages to enhance on the frequency with which a CEM was encountered in previous semesters. Since students in previous semesters had access to their prior programs before starting the quiz, none of these errors had been encountered in any of the control semesters. Therefore, it is interesting to note that removing these 6 students from the group brings the average score up to 84.8%, which is in range of the control semesters.

The error message quiz results above indicate that the ECEMs are more helpful than standard CEMs. However, the quantitative data from the program logs seems to contract this conclusion, or is inconclusive at best. This is where the qualitative data illuminates a possible explanation.

4.3 Think-Alouds

With regard to the errors that participants received, observational data - both spoken thought and behavior - allowed for the evaluator to be certain when ECEMs were expanded and read. An ECEM was marked as "helpful" in the observational data if the student solved that specific error or made steps towards solving it after reading the ECEM. Conversely, an ECEM was marked as "unhelpful" if the student made changes after viewing the ECEM that were not on the

path to solving the error or the student read the message and didn't know how to proceed. Post-assessment ethnographic interviews and reflection revealed participants' feelings towards the ECEMs in greater depth, from gratefulness to frustration.

4.3.1 Observational. Although there were 21 students who completed the quiz and 10 students who did not complete the quiz, the total number of errors received was roughly equal at 56 for those who completed the quiz and 60 errors for those who did not, making 116 total errors tagged by evaluators. The group of participants that did not complete the quiz had a higher number of errors without enhanced messages (31) and a lower number of enhanced error messages (29), though this was dominated by a single participant who encountered the most (15). The incomplete quiz participants had under half of the number of read enhanced messages (9) when compared to the participants that completed the quiz (23). From this data it seems that encountering these messages really did prove helpful for the completion of the quiz.

The incomplete quiz participants also had over double the amount of unread enhanced messages (20) when compared to the completed quiz participants (8). For the participants that completed the quiz, there were 19 instances where the "more information" section of the ECEM proved helpful. This is over six times the amount of instances for those who did not complete the quiz (3). The incomplete quiz participants also contained more instances of unhelpful enhanced messages (6) when compared to the completed quiz participants (4).

The data presented in Figure 6 summarizes these observations and appears to indicate that the ECEMs helped students better understand the errors they were encountering, fix those errors, and ultimately complete the quiz.

4.3.2 Ethnographic: Perception of overall helpfulness comparing complete and incomplete. Of the ten students that did not solve the assessment in the 35 minute time limit, only two read the ECEMs and believed they were unhelpful. Another two students that did not complete the quiz read the ECEMs and believed them to helpful. The other six students did not receive an enhanced error message and were therefore unable to confirm whether or not the enhanced messages were helpful. See Figure 7.

4.3.3 Ethnographic: Perception of helpfulness of students with repeated error messages. There were four participants that received a repeated ECEM at least once and did not finish the quiz. One of them received three repeated ECEMs and thought that they were unhelpful. However, another one received the same ECEM ten times in succession, neglected to read the first nine, finally read it the tenth time, and subsequently corrected the error. Even though this participant did not finish the quiz, he still believed the ECEMs to be helpful. The other two participants that received repeated error messages and did not finish the quiz only received one repeated message and they both found the enhanced messages helpful.

4.4 Discussion

The results of the error message quizzes compared with the quantitative program log results from the assessment seem contradictory. The observational and ethnographic data presented above tells a different story. The students who struggled, but ultimately succeeded

Participants	# Students	# Errors	# Errors w/o Enhanced	# Errors w/ Enhanced	# Enhanced Read	# Unread	# Helpful	# Unhelpful	# Repeated
Total Complete	21	56	25	31	23	8	19	4	6
Total Incomplete	10	60	31	29	9	20	3	6	15

Figure 6: Student Perception of ECEMs in Complete vs. Incomplete Quizzes

Quiz Result	Interaction with Enhanced Messages	# of Students
Solved	Unread or Unreceived	10
Solved	Read and Helpful	9
Solved	Read and Unhelpful	2
Not Solved	Unread or Unreceived	6
Not Solved	Read and Helpful	2
Not Solved	Read and Unhelpful	2

Figure 7: Unique student groups based on quantitative and qualitative data

in completing the problem, brought down the average score and increased the average time to completion. However, these same students were helped the most by the ECEMs and expounded on this in great detail during the post-assessment interview. Although they struggled with the assessment, observational and ethnographic data shows that it was ultimately the ECEMs that helped them across the finish line. This is precisely what we want. Furthermore, a very small group of students who did not complete the quiz, and therefore brought down the average score, were not helped by the ECEMs and were frustrated by them in the post-assessment interviews. These two students were so unfamiliar with the material and so fundamentally lost that the additional information provided by the ECEMs only added insult to injury. We conjecture that the increased cognitive load of the assessment may have tipped the scales from helpful ECEMs to unhelpful.

From all of the data above, the students can be broken up into six distinct groups as seen in Figure 7.

5 CONCLUSIONS

This study has made several important contributions. First, do novice students read ECEMs? Observational and ethnographic data seem to indicate that novices in CS1 do, in fact, read ECEMs. Students also generally find the ECEMs more helpful than the standard CEMs. The corroborating evidence by Barik et al. [2] on eye tracking with intermediate students lends more weight to our finding. This helps to answer RQ1 and warrants further investigation.

Second, are ECEMs helpful for novice students in a setting with low cognitive load? The results of the error message quizzes shows a statistically significant decrease in incorrect understanding of ECEMs when compared to standard CEMs in an independent environment. This data answers RQ2.

Finally, are the ECEMs helpful for novice students in a setting with high cognitive load? Even though the quantitative program log data from the think-aloud study seems inconclusive, the qualitative data seems to indicate that ECEMs are also effective in an environment with a higher cognitive load. Students that struggled to complete the quiz successfully used the ECEMs to arrive at a correct solution. Here the qualitative think-aloud data provided a window into student behavior that the quantitative program log

data could not provide. This helps to answer RQ3 and warrants further investigation.

There are several threats to validity of these findings. First, the control groups for the think-aloud study took place over multiple semesters and had two different professors. We attempted to minimize this threat by keeping the curriculum (assignments, schedule, the use of Athene, etc.) roughly the same from semester to semester. Second, control groups for the think-aloud study took the practical quiz in class, were not asked to think-aloud, and had access to previous code files to bootstrap their code. By contrast, students in the think-aloud study were in a one-on-one setting, were asked to think-aloud, and did not have access to previous code. It is possible that all of these factors increased student cognitive load in the think-aloud study and therefore skewed the results. We attempted to offset this by adding in the warm-up exercise as suggested by Teague et al. [40].

6 FUTURE WORK

This study should be replicated to further strengthen the findings presented here. Having more than one experimental group would add weight to these findings. It should also be replicated by those previous studies that found no evidence or inconclusive evidence for the helpfulness of ECEMs.

As mentioned above, Barik et al. [2] use eye tracking software to examine whether intermediate students read error messages. It would be helpful to replicate their work with novices in CS1.

Finally, even though this study followed the design guidelines by Marceau et al. [31] it would also be useful to use their rubric [30] to evaluate the helpfulness of the EECMs used in this study.

7 ACKNOWLEDGMENTS

The authors would like to thank Abilene Christian University (ACU) for providing necessary funding for this study. We would also like to thank the reviewers for their careful and thorough feedback.

REFERENCES

[1] Kirsti M Ala-Mutka. 2005. A survey of automated assessment approaches for programming assignments. *Computer science education* 15, 2 (2005), 83–102.
[2] Titus Barik, Justin Smith, Kevin Lubick, Elisabeth Holmes, Jing Feng, Emerson Murphy-Hill, and Chris Parnin. 2017. Do Developers Read Compiler Error Messages?. In *Proceedings of the International Conference of Software Engineering*. ACM.
[3] Titus Barik, Jim Witschey, Brittany Johnson, and Emerson Murphy-Hill. 2014. Compiler error notifications revisited: an interaction-first approach for helping developers more effectively comprehend and resolve error notifications. In *Companion Proceedings of the 36th International Conference on Software Engineering (ICSE Companion 2014)*. ACM, 536–539.
[4] Brett A Becker. 2016. An effective approach to enhancing compiler error messages. In *Proceedings of the 47th ACM Technical Symposium on Computing Science Education*. ACM, 126–131.
[5] Jens Bennedsen and Michael E. Caspersen. 2007. Failure rates in introductory programming. *ACM SIGCSE Bulletin* 39, 2 (2007), 32–36.
[6] Elizabeth Carter. 2015. Its debug: practical results. *Journal of Computing Sciences in Colleges* 30, 3 (2015), 9–15.

[7] Maria Christakis and Christian Bird. 2016. What developers want and need from program analysis: An empirical study. In *Proceedings of the 31st IEEE/ACM International Conference on Automated Software Engineering*. ACM, 332–343.

[8] John W Creswell. 2013. *Research design: Qualitative, quantitative, and mixed methods approaches*. Sage publications.

[9] Paul Denny, Andrew Luxton-Reilly, and Dave Carpenter. 2014. Enhancing syntax error messages appears ineffectual. In *Proceedings of the 2014 conference on Innovation & technology in computer science education*. ACM, 273–278.

[10] Christopher Douce, David Livingstone, and James Orwell. 2005. Automatic test-based assessment of programming: A review. *Journal on Educational Resources in Computing (JERIC)* 5, 3 (2005), 4.

[11] Thomas Dy and Ma Mercedes Rodrigo. 2010. A detector for non-literal Java errors. In *Proceedings of the 10th Koli Calling International Conference on Computing Education Research*. ACM, 118–122.

[12] Stephen H Edwards and Manuel A Perez-Quinones. 2008. Web-CAT: automatically grading programming assignments. In *ACM SIGCSE Bulletin*, Vol. 40. ACM, 328–328.

[13] Karl Anders Ericsson and Herbert Alexander Simon. 1993. *Protocol analysis*. MIT press Cambridge, MA.

[14] Thomas Flowers, Curtis A Carver, and James Jackson. 2004. Empowering students and building confidence in novice programmers through Gauntlet. In *Frontiers in Education, 2004. FIE 2004. 34th Annual*. IEEE, T3H–10.

[15] Stephen N Freund and Eric S Roberts. 1996. Thetis: an ANSI C programming environment designed for introductory use. In *SIGCSE*, Vol. 96. 300–304.

[16] Dianne Hagan and Selby Markham. 2000. Teaching Java with the BlueJ environment. In *Proceedings of Australasian Society for Computers in Learning in Tertiary Education Conference ASCILITE 2000*. Citeseer.

[17] Björn Hartmann, Daniel MacDougall, Joel Brandt, and Scott R Klemmer. 2010. What would other programmers do: suggesting solutions to error messages. In *Proceedings of the SIGCHI Conference on Human Factors in Computing Systems*. ACM, 1019–1028.

[18] Robert W Hasker. 2002. HiC: a C++ compiler for CS1. *Journal of Computing Sciences in Colleges* 18, 1 (2002), 56–64.

[19] Jack Hollingsworth. 1960. Automatic graders for programming classes. *Commun. ACM* 3, 10 (1960), 528–529.

[20] Maria Hristova, Ananya Misra, Megan Rutter, and Rebecca Mercuri. 2003. Identifying and correcting Java programming errors for introductory computer science students. In *ACM SIGCSE Bulletin*, Vol. 35. ACM, 153–156.

[21] Petri Ihantola, Tuukka Ahoniemi, Ville Karavirta, and Otto Seppälä. 2010. Review of recent systems for automatic assessment of programming assignments. In *Proceedings of the 10th Koli Calling International Conference on Computing Education Research*. ACM, 86–93.

[22] James Jackson, Michael Cobb, and Curtis Carver. 2005. Identifying top Java errors for novice programmers. In *Frontiers in Education, 2005. FIE'05. Proceedings 35th Annual Conference*. IEEE, T4C–T4C.

[23] Caitlin Kelleher, Randy Pausch, and Sara Kiesler. 2007. Storytelling alice motivates middle school girls to learn computer programming. In *Proceedings of the SIGCHI conference on Human factors in computing systems*. ACM, 1455–1464.

[24] Steve Krug. 2014. Don't make me think revisited: A common sense approach to web and mobile usability. (2014).

[25] Michael J Lee and Andrew J Ko. 2011. Personifying programming tool feedback improves novice programmers' learning. In *Proceedings of the seventh international workshop on Computing education research*. ACM, 109–116.

[26] Yvonna S Lincoln and Egon G Guba. 1985. *Naturalistic inquiry*. Vol. 75. Sage.

[27] Derrell Lipman. 2014. LearnCS!: a new, browser-based C programming environment for CS1. *Journal of Computing Sciences in Colleges* 29, 6 (2014), 144–150.

[28] Dastyni Loksa, Andrew J Ko, Will Jernigan, Alannah Oleson, Christopher J Mendez, and Margaret M Burnett. 2016. Programming, Problem Solving, and Self-Awareness: Effects of Explicit Guidance. In *Proceedings of the 2016 CHI Conference on Human Factors in Computing Systems*. ACM, 1449–1461.

[29] John Maloney, Mitchel Resnick, Natalie Rusk, Brian Silverman, and Evelyn Eastmond. 2010. The scratch programming language and environment. *ACM Transactions on Computing Education (TOCE)* 10, 4 (2010), 16.

[30] Guillaume Marceau, Kathi Fisler, and Shriram Krishnamurthi. 2011. Measuring the effectiveness of error messages designed for novice programmers. In *Proceedings of the 42nd ACM technical symposium on Computer science education*. ACM, 499–504.

[31] Guillaume Marceau, Kathi Fisler, and Shriram Krishnamurthi. 2011. Mind your language: on novices' interactions with error messages. In *Proceedings of the 10th SIGPLAN symposium on New ideas, new paradigms, and reflections on programming and software*. ACM, 3–18.

[32] Laurie Murphy, Gary Lewandowski, Renée McCauley, Beth Simon, Lynda Thomas, and Carol Zander. 2008. Debugging: the good, the bad, and the quirky–a qualitative analysis of novices' strategies. In *ACM SIGCSE Bulletin*, Vol. 40. ACM, 163–167.

[33] Marie-Hélène Nienaltowski, Michela Pedroni, and Bertrand Meyer. 2008. Compiler error messages: What can help novices?. In *ACM SIGCSE Bulletin*, Vol. 40. ACM, 168–172.

[34] Michael Quinn Patton. 2014. *Qualitative research & evaluation methods: Integrating theory and practice*. Sage.

[35] Raymond Pettit, John Homer, Roger Gee, Susan Mengel, and Adam Starbuck. 2015. An empirical study of iterative improvement in programming assignments. In *Proceedings of the 46th ACM Technical Symposium on Computer Science Education*. ACM, 410–415.

[36] Raymond Pettit and James Prather. 2017. Automated Assessment Tools: Too Many Cooks, Not Enough Collaboration. *J. Comput. Sci. Coll.* 32, 4 (April 2017), 113–121. http://dl.acm.org/citation.cfm?id=3055338.3079060

[37] Raymond S Pettit, John Homer, and Roger Gee. 2017. Do Enhanced Compiler Error Messages Help Students?: Results Inconclusive.. In *Proceedings of the 2017 ACM SIGCSE Technical Symposium on Computer Science Education*. ACM, 465–470.

[38] Jeffrey Rubin and Dana Chisnell. 2008. *Handbook of usability testing: how to plan, design and conduct effective tests* (2 ed.). John Wiley & Sons.

[39] Tom Schorsch. 1995. CAP: an automated self-assessment tool to check Pascal programs for syntax, logic and style errors. In *ACM SIGCSE Bulletin*, Vol. 27. ACM, 168–172.

[40] Donna Teague, Malcolm Corney, Alireza Ahadi, and Raymond Lister. 2013. A qualitative think aloud study of the early neo-piagetian stages of reasoning in novice programmers. In *Proceedings of the Fifteenth Australasian Computing Education Conference-Volume 136*. Australian Computer Society, Inc., 87–95.

[41] Dwayne Towell and Brent Reeves. 2009. From Walls to Steps: Using online automatic homework checking tools to improve learning in introductory programming courses. (2009).

[42] V Javier Traver. 2010. On compiler error messages: what they say and what they mean. *Advances in Human-Computer Interaction* 2010 (2010).

[43] Christopher Watson, Frederick WB Li, and Jamie L Godwin. 2012. Bluefix: Using crowd-sourced feedback to support programming students in error diagnosis and repair. In *International Conference on Web-Based Learning*. Springer, 228–239.

[44] Richard L Wexelblat. 1976. Maxims for malfeasant designers, or how to design languages to make programming as difficult as possible. In *Proceedings of the 2nd international conference on Software engineering*. IEEE Computer Society Press, 331–336.

[45] Jacqueline Whalley and Nadia Kasto. 2014. A qualitative think-aloud study of novice programmers' code writing strategies. In *Proceedings of the 2014 conference on Innovation & technology in computer science education*. ACM, 279–284.

[46] Timothy T Yuen. 2007. Novices' knowledge construction of difficult concepts in CS1. *ACM SIGCSE Bulletin* 39, 4 (2007), 49–53.

Theorem Provers as a Learning Tool in Theory of Computation

Maria Knobelsdorf, Christiane Frede
Universität Hamburg
Fachbereich Informatik (Department of Informatics)
Vogt-Kölln-Straße 30
22527 Hamburg, Germany
{knobelsdorf, frede}@informatik.uni-hamburg.de

Sebastian Böhne, Christoph Kreitz
Universität Potsdam
Fachbereich Informatik (Department of Informatics)
August-Bebel-Straße 89
14882 Potsdam, Germany
{boehne, kreitz}@uni-potsdam.de

ABSTRACT

This paper presents first results of an evaluation study investigating whether an interactive theorem prover like Coq can be used to help undergraduate computer science (CS) students learn mathematical proving within the field of theory of computation. Set within an educational design research approach and building on cognitive apprenticeship and socio cultures cognition theories, we have collected empirical, mainly qualitative observational data focusing on students' activities with Coq in an introductory course specifically created for that matter. Our results strengthen the assumption that a theorem prover like Coq, indeed, can be beneficial in mediating undergraduate students' activities in learning formal proving. In comparison to pen & paper proofs, students were profiting strongly from the system's immediate feedback and scaffolding. These results encourage the idea to extend the scientifically dominated use of theorem provers like Coq to pedagogical use cases in undergraduate CS education.

CS CONCEPTS

• **Social and professional topics~Computer science education** • **Applied computing~Interactive learning environments** • Applied computing

KEYWORDS

Computer science education; theorem prover; students; theory of computation; distributed cognition theory; qualitative research; observational study; proofs; logic; data structures.

1 INTRODUCTION

The theory of computation is an important field of undergraduate computer science (CS) education ([30], p. 55-60) and in consequence, CS majors are required to take introductory courses covering topics like automata theory, computability, or complexity [55]. The corresponding concepts, theories, and algorithms are strongly mathematical in nature, both because of the formalized descriptions used for the discourse and because of a strong focus on mathematical proofs for the presented theories and approaches. By introducing idealized mathematical models of the computer and discussing methods for designing and analyzing them, students are supposed to develop the ability of thinking abstractly about computational processes and models. Introductory courses to theory of computation traditionally are organized around weekly lectures that present the course topics using blackboard or slides. The lectures are accompanied by weekly homework assignments based on the current lecture topics, which students are expected to solve individually or in small groups and submit in writing for reviewing and grading by tutors. Tutorial and supervised exercise sessions usually round off this approach, which is also very common in introductory undergraduate courses to mathematics or physics, see also [41]. [36]. There are obviously computing departments and teachers that work with other pedagogies, but in many universities all over the world, especially in Germany, this is the predominant approach.

Many undergraduate CS students have difficulties in theory courses with considerable dropout and poor performance in final exams, see for example [11][25][47]. So far suggested alternative pedagogical approaches and tools in this field address mainly a lack of interest and engagement as well as inabilities to understand theoretical concepts, both potential reasons assumed causing students failure in theory of computation [12][23][54][48][20][27]. Empirical insights on student difficulties with theory of computation are rare. But recent studies including our own investigations, indicate that students rather seem to have specific difficulties with mastering mathematical language and creating formal proofs in corresponding assignments of theory of computation [35][43][47][33]. Also in mathematics education, students' difficulties with formal proofs and reasoning have been investigated outlining the complexity this domain-specific proficiency has in mathematics education [1][4][60]. We argue that within the domain of theory of computation, educational designs and pedagogical approaches are required that focus specifically on guiding and supporting students how to create formal proofs as well as formally reason within a proof. For that reason, we have started investigating whether and how an

ICER '17, August 18-20, 2017, Tacoma, WA, USA
© 2017 Association for Computing Machinery.
ACM ISBN 978-1-4503-4968-0/17/08...$15.00
http://dx.doi.org/10.1145/3105726.3106184

interactive theorem prover like Coq [7] might be a suitable learning tool for that purpose. Theorem provers support creating and checking formal proofs while operating on an explicit and high level of formalization. We belief that this makes them suitable to scaffold students' learning and investigate relevant questions related to formal proving practices and how students develop domain-specific competencies [49] within theory of computation.

Set within an educational design research [38] approach, we have collected empirical, mainly qualitative observational data focusing on students' activities with Coq in an introductory course to logic and data structures specifically created for that matter. Educational design research (which also goes by the name design-based research) has its roots in design research, which focuses on designing and investigating instructional interventions and learning environments in the settings for which they are intended, with the dual purpose of developing and refining theories of learning as well as testing and revising the design itself. A central feature of design research is a reliance on iterations of intervention, analysis, and redesign in four interrelated phases to allow researchers to test, revise, and refine conjectures. This paper, then, is neither representing just an empirical evaluation study, nor just an experience report. It is explicitly an educational design research paper, with the purpose of presenting a first iteration of theoretical considerations combined with empirical insights most relevant to the development of a student-oriented pedagogy in the field of theory of computation.

The remainder of this paper is structured as follows: In the next section, we will start with a brief overview of the theoretical background our pedagogical considerations and research focus are based on. In section 3, we will then introduce the theorem prover Coq and discuss its potential for being turned into a learning tool while comparing it with related work. In section 4, we will present research questions that framed this first iteration of educational design research and continue with describing the course design and methods used for its evaluation. The results of this evaluation in section 5 contain a category system capturing students' activities with Coq observed during the course, additional analysis and observations, and a discussion with further interpretations. The paper concludes in section 5.

2 THEORETICAL BACKGROUND

We build on an understanding of teaching and learning shaped by socio-cultural cognition theories [58] focusing mainly on cognitive apprenticeship [13][14] and distributed cognition theory [28][44][32]. These approaches strongly relate to Vygotskian developmental psychology [59] understanding learning activities of students to be embedded within a socio-cultural environment and mediated by material and representational systems (e.g., symbols, inscriptions, visuals), which are often metaphorically referred to as tools or mediational means [61]. Cognitive processes are regarded to be, not just individual and mental, but also situated within and constituted through a specific community of practice [13][58] and a related cognitive system as the interplay between one or several human beings, their activities, and tools used in these activities [28][29].

For educational research this has the important implication that we have to consider that the unit that we are studying just as the pedagogy that we are creating is considering "people in action using tools of some kind" ([51], p. 147) embedded within a community of practice.

Speaking of theory of computation as a domain-specific community of academic research practice [34], its culture and tools have strong roots in mathematics [57]. Here, tools used specifically by members of this community involve mathematical formal inscriptions, i.e., symbols, visuals and notations created with pen & paper and on black-/whiteboard, designed to conceive theoretical objects and to mediate mental and collaborative processes of human agents in writing and in speech that lead to these objects. In studying theory of computation, undergraduate CS students have to master using these tools when working on their weekly assignments. This tool mastering can be regarded as an enculturation process within the community of practice of theory of computation and it is strongly shaped by the educational and pedagogical design used in theory of computation courses (see also section 1). For that matter, students can observe the teacher using the tools during lecture (model-based learning) and also learn from textbooks and by interacting through verbal speech and writing with their peer students and tutors. As has been investigated and outlined before, it is extremely challenging for novice students to uncover domain-specific competencies on their own when the pedagogical approach of a course is solely focusing on presenting factual knowledge [14][53] and without sufficient distinction between knowledge as the item of inquiry and competencies that are needed to handle it ([6],p. 295ff).

Speaking of educational and pedagogical approaches that address students' domain-specific competency development, *cognitive apprenticeship* has been suggested with concepts called *modelling, coaching, scaffolding,* or *fading* [13][14]. These techniques in many ways are based on the concept of *zone of proximal development (ZPD)* referring to a student's potential of mastering new tasks (i.e. developing a new competency) with assistance and guidance or in collaboration with external agents [59][62][45]. Based on the insights we have about students difficulties with theory of computation assignments [35][43], we hypothesize that pen & paper as a mediational mean and learning tool embodies not enough knowledge to scaffold students' ZPD and will always require additional scaffolding from tutors, textbooks, or other sources. Theorem prover on the other hand embody knowledge of formal proofs. For that matter, we have started investigating whether and how an interactive theorem prover like Coq [7] might be turned into a suitable tool that is scaffolding students learning within the discussed context and in the next section, we will introduce Coq and extend on this argument.

3 THEOREM PROVERS IN EDUCATION

Theorem provers have been developed since the late 1960's, when Nicolas de Bruijn pioneered the field with his Automath proof checker. Automath's modern descendants – systems such as Coq, Nuprl, Isabelle, HOL, or Agda [7][2][15][42][9]– have evolved to a state that they are increasingly used for formalization and verification tasks in frontier applications in mathematics and computer science, see for example [24][21]. Most existing typical proofs created for machine verification not only require users to have a deep understanding of the underlying logic and of the system that was used for the formalization but also have little resemblance to proofs presented in textbooks and university lectures. Therefore, when introduced in education, theorem provers are generally used in advanced coursework in mathematics and theory of computation for the same purpose addressing graduate students with a profound background in mathematics and functional programming [3][15][26]. Only a few, though promising examples of using theorem proving in introductory courses can be found in the literature. One line of this related work focuses on teaching students how to use proof automation and the relevant programming, but is not teaching formal proving as such [50][46]. The other line of work is using theorem provers as underlying system for providing (intelligent) tutoring systems that support the development of less detailed proofs [5][22][52]. Systems like the EPGY Theorem Proving Environment [56] allows step-wise proof development similar to pen and paper proofs. But, the approach is not based on a theorem prover with an expressive formal language and is thus difficult to extend to more complex fields in theory of computation like automata theory. In [22], the theorem prover Coq has been extended by a visualization tool in order to teach high-school students geometry. While this approach is based on the same theorem prover as ours, it focuses on a bottom-up construction of proofs, which is better for the presentation of proofs but makes it more difficult to find them. Also here, an extension to more complex fields of theory of computation seems not possible.

In the next subsections, we will discuss how the theorem prover Coq can be used as a learning tool, starting with a short introduction of Coq.

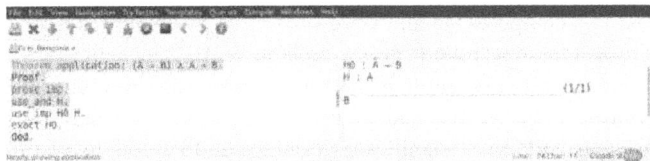

Figure 1: The Coq IDE, showing in the left-hand window a proof as sequence of applied proof steps. Steps already evaluated are marked green. The current result of executing a step can be seen in the right-hand window, while error-messages are displayed in the lower right-hand window.

3.1 The theorem prover Coq

The theorem prover Coq has been developed in the 1980's by researchers at the French "Institut national de recherche en informatique et en automatique (INRIA)" [7]. The system allows formalizing mathematical assertions and developing related formal proofs that are evaluated by the system. Like many theorem provers, Coq implements a higher-order type theory and thus theorems in Coq are understood as types and the proofs for theorems as elements of the respective type. Almost all theorems include implications and/or universal quantifiers. Underlying proofs of such theorems are functions (typed λ-calculus) so that

such proof assistants are closely interwoven to functional programming.

Coq offers an IDE comparable to a typical IDE for programming (see Figure 1). In the main left-hand window, a user can generate a proof step-by-step, applying so-called *tactics* similar to invoking commands. A tactic is comparable to a procedure or subroutine in a program written in a functional programming language. Being called in a proof, a tactic splits an assertion into sub-assertions following "backward reasoning" (from conclusion to premises). In the evaluation, every step of the proof is evaluated for its formal correctness comparable to compiling and running a program code. In the Coq IDE, the user can manually step through the proof and see every sub-goal of the proof displayed in the right-hand window, indicating the next step in the proof. This way, Coq provides direct feedback through the entire process of creating a proof, especially which steps the user still has to perform before completing and whether a proof step is successfully applicable. Thus, creating proofs with Coq has many similarities to write and debug computer programs.

3.2 Turning Coq into a learning tool

Coq has been developed with the purpose to support experts in formalization and verification tasks. Using the full capabilities of Coq requires proficiency in type theory and functional programming. Also in terms of usability, the Coq IDE was not designed for novice students' needs. We will give three examples that emphasize potential issues for novice students: 1) While the proof is built through backward reasoning (see previous section), writing the proof down happens from top to bottom of the left-hand window which intuitively might be understood by students as forward reasoning and confuse them. 2) The right-hand window shows only the subgoals created last but not previously accomplished steps, which might cause students to get lost. 3) Predefined tactics for a proof are not displayed anywhere in the IDE (comparable to block elements in Scratch) and students have to remember that they exist.

Nevertheless, Coq has several advantages that make it a potential learning tool. Because of its interactive nature it provides immediate, individual feedback especially if a step is correct and whether a proof is finished or requires additional steps and can therefore be regarded as formative assessment monitoring students learning. This advantage strongly contrasts the common practice, where students create proofs with pen & paper and receive feedback from their tutors usually one week later, which is summative assessment. In addition, working with Coq and creating proofs in a programming-debugging sort of manner certainly represents activities for CS students that are more close to the computing culture and therefore could be additionally motivating and engaging.

Another advantage of Coq is its explicit and high level of formalization, which suits particularly well to scaffold students' learning. This sounds paradoxical at first, since students already struggle with the formalisms in pen and paper proofs. Developing a proof is creating arguments in a logical sequence of steps using deductive reasoning. However, there are different degrees of formalization and precision and we believe that this is not made explicit and clear enough for students. Building on this argument, we hypothesize that students' problems are not so much related with the formalistic elements themselves but the mixture between formal and informal aspects. Coq, by contrast, explicitly defines one level of formalization providing orientation within the chain of formal reasoning.

In order to be used by students without any prerequisites in functional programming and type theory, we suggest using an *information hiding* principle. Within this pedagogically motivated approach, students are provided with a proof assignment to be created in Coq and corresponding predefined tactics that function as building blocks of the proof (the idea roughly corresponds to BlueJ and Scratch where specific elements of programming languages are hidden and visual representations of them are used instead). As an example, consider the proof of the following statement from logic: (A → B) ∧ A → B in Coq. For proving the implication in Coq (see also Figure 1 above), (A → B) ∧ A has to be assumed and it has to be shown that B follows. This is realized by a backward reasoning tactic that we call *prove_imp*. The conjunction is then decomposed by another predefined tactic called *use_and*. An implication like A → B can be used if we know its premise, too. Since this is the case here we can apply *use_imp* to both hypotheses to obtain B, with which we can conclude the proof.'. With these predefined tactics, students can focus on the reasoning without having to understand type theory, implementation of tactics, or other internals of Coq.

In the long run, we intend to create assignments with corresponding tactics that cover what is regarded to be the basic topics from theory of computation (e.g. automata theory, Turing machines). The latter is obviously not trivial as it requires formalizing the corresponding domain and developing tactics that can serve as adequate building blocks for novices to be used in their proofs. Hence, this is a long-term objective, which we start investigating by creating and evaluating a first educational design, which will be presented in more detail in the next section.

4 COURSE SETUP AND EVALUATION

In the previous section, we have outlined a potential approach how Coq could be modified in order to act as a learning tool to help novice students learning to create formal proofs within theory of computation. In a first step, we were interested whether undergraduate students with no prerequisites in functional programming and type theory are able to master creating formal proofs with Coq if being provided with assignments and predefined tactics as building blocks as suggested in Sec. 3.2. In particular, we focused on the following **research questions**:

1. What kind of problems and issues do students run into when working with Coq, especially usability issues?

2. Do students enjoy working with Coq leading to more satisfaction in creating formal proofs than using pen & paper?

3. Is Coq significantly better supporting students in creating formal proofs due to its scaffolding quality in comparison to pen & paper proof assignments?

In order to start investigating these research questions, we have created a two weeks, full time, elective course, which took place in early October 2016 at Universität Hamburg, Germany, addressing CS undergraduate students in their second or higher year as a major. As course content, we chose propositional logic for the first three days and predicate logic for the next two days of the course, as well as data structures (i.e., lists, natural numbers, and binary trees), which covered the last five days of the course. Also, by focusing on logic and rather simple data structures, creating predefined tactics that serve as building blocks for student proofs required far less time than, e.g., formalizing automata theory. In the next subsections, we introduce the course setup and its implementation in more detail and describe what kind of data we collected during the course and how we analyzed it afterwards.

4.1 Course Design and Participants

Following our theoretical considerations, the pedagogy of our course was implementing the cognitive apprenticeship approach [14] focusing on scaffolding and fading [45]. However, we decided to keep also the traditional framework of lecture & assignments because we intend our approach to be used in future within this traditional teaching setting. Here, we relied on experiences of previously implementing cognitive apprenticeship within the traditional framework of an introductory course to theory of computation [36].

We used lecture elements in order to introduce the course content and demonstrate relevant competencies. Co-author Böhne of this paper gave all lectures during the entire course using slides and a blackboard. Aligned with the lecture content, students received assignments, which they were supposed to work on individually or in small groups. These sessions took place in a seminar room and in a computer lab and were supervised by co-author Böhne and an additional tutor (a graduate CS student). They both walked around constantly through the room, answering questions and offering help. At the end of each exercise session, they also presented the most significant questions and key points of the assignments that had occurred before in individual discussions with students. Each day started with a one-hour lecture and was followed by a two-hour exercise session with assignments to be worked on. After a lunch break, afternoon started with another one-hour lecture and was again followed by a two-hour session. As students required more time than expected to work on their assignments, we replaced three lecture sessions by additional exercise time. The fifth and tenth day were the last days for the appropriate topic and not introducing any new content but providing additional time for unsolved assignments from the days before.

For every day, an assignment sheet was offered with approx. 15-20 assignments requiring between 5-20 minutes each. In sum, we offered 221 assignments (70 covering propositional logic, 48 predicate logic and 103 data structures). Among these 221 assignments, 51 assignments were not about proving but about understanding logic (24) and data structures (10), getting familiar with Coq without creating proofs (4) and defining functions in

Coq without proving (13). The remaining 170 assignments covered proofs that were supposed to be created by using:

- only pen and paper (39 first week, 1 second week)
- first pen and paper than the same assignment with Coq (18 first and 1 second week)
- only Coq (23 first week, 45 second week)
- first Coq directly and then using Coq's text editor for "pen & paper"-alike proofs with natural language and math symbols (18 first week, 25 second week).

This mixture of proof assignments (going back and forth between pen & paper and Coq) was supposed to provide us with insights relevant for our research questions, especially how students perform in working on the same assignment while using different tools. In addition, during the first week students were also asked to comment most of their Coq proofs within their "proof code" just like they are used to do with programming. This step was inserted because of the problems appearing while the students should go back from Coq to pen and paper. Two weeks after the end of the course, we offered a final exam that students could attend in order to get credit points for the course.

Regarding drop out, 21 undergraduate CS majors registered for the course and on average, 16 (11 male and 5 female students) attended all morning and afternoon sessions of the course. Most of these students just finished their first or second year as CS major. Almost all students had attended an introductory course of mathematics and theory of computation (including propositional and predicate logic) in their first year and passed it with grades between B and C. In addition, all students attended introductory programming courses in Java in their first year. Being asked in a survey at the beginning of the course, students reported to have taken our course because they were interested to use Coq and wanted to improve their ability of creating formal proofs and be better prepared for further courses in theory of computation.

4.2 Data Collection and Analysis

Within the entire course, we conducted three surveys during lecture time using pre-defined measuring instruments as well as self-defined items. The first survey focused on students' prior knowledge and motivation (gathered on first day), students' self-perceived first impressions of Coq usability and working with Coq (third day), as well as a final feedback on working with Coq, the course concept, and self-perceived knowledge gain (last day). For space reasons, we will not report on these data further but wanted to mention its existence for conclusive reasons.

Because we were interested in how students worked with Coq in a regular classroom environment and what kind of problems and challenges they faced, we approached the research field following the *Natural Inquiry* paradigm ([37], p. 36ff) collecting observational data during all assignment sessions, which took place in the computer lab. Here, we focused on collecting students' questions and problems they faced during their individual working sessions with the assignments. Because most of the students were working in groups of two or three (13 out of 16), we had natural think-aloud sessions that could easily be observed without interfering with students' activities. Especially, we focused on observing students discussing intensively a problem or asking for help and capturing these observations by taking notes. Within this first iteration, we wanted to get a general broad picture of the working progress of all students instead of explicitly observing one group intensively, e.g. using videos. Because of the group size and the majority of students working in groups, it was possible to capture most discussions and create first insights into how students manage to work with Coq. Obviously, our data is not representing exactly 100% of all problems that students ran into and only those that were discussed aloud.

Creating notes, we started with writing down students' discussions while observing them. After capturing several such discussions, it was possible to create summarizing first codes to capture a situation comparable to open coding. Here, we distinguished between problems students had solved on their own and problems where the tutor had to help. In addition, we noticed that students were discussing different problems that we organized around first forms of categories. Moreover, at the end of every day, everyone present during these sessions exchanged their individual observations they had made during the day. All these written notes and the first codes capturing student problems were further coded with qualitative content analysis [39] and the coding software MaxQDA using a summarizing technique. Because the notes were already summarized during the exercise sessions, a student discussion of a problem was defined as the smallest data unit. While using MaxQDA, new categories appeared or were changed, resulting in a category system, which is presented next.

5 RESULTS

As described in the previous subsection, our qualitative data consists of directly observed situations in which students were dealing with problems. In the data collection process, we distinguished each observed situation in which students were discussing a problem: there were problems students were able to solve alone or with the help of other students, (we will call these problems *S-problems*) and problems that students were not able to solve alone or with the help of other students. In that case, the teacher and tutor were called for help (we will call this *T-problems*). Because this definition is built on the way a problem was solved in the end, situations where students had a long discussion about a current problem but asked for help in the end will be considered as a T-problem instead of S-problem. We make this particular distinction between S- and T-problems because it provides insight to which extent Coq reduced T-problems due to its scaffolding qualities.

5.1 Category System

Coding and interpreting all observed student activities, we derived a category system that will be presented next. Each category describes a specific kind of problem students ran into when working on their assignments and each problem of a category was distinguished as S- or T-problem. However, the presented categories only covers problems that were related to the course content and pedagogy and especially to the research

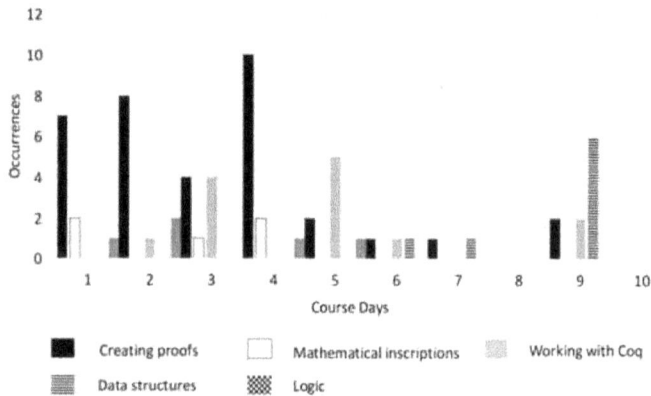

Figure 3: Occurrences of T-problems

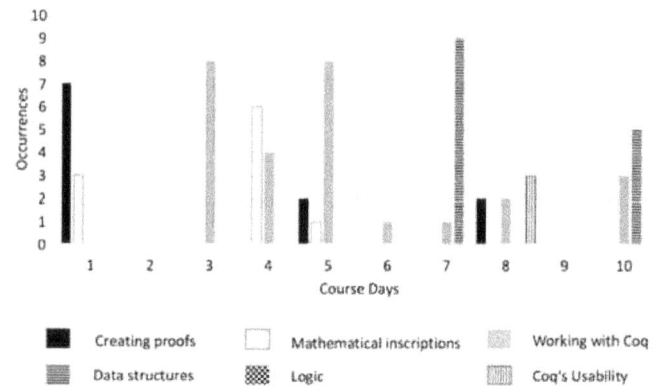

Figure 2: Occurrences of S-problems

questions. We also observed and coded technical issues regarding hardware infrastructure, e.g. login problems, or system failures with Coq that were caused by the predefined tactics or the Coq version used. As these problems were not relevant for our research questions, we will not consider them further here

Coding and interpreting all observed student activities, we derived a category system that will be presented next. Each category describes a specific kind of problem students ran into when working on their assignments and each problem of a category was distinguished as S- or T-problem. However, the presented categories only covers problems that were related to the course content and pedagogy and especially to the research questions. We also observed and coded technical issues regarding hardware infrastructure, e.g. login problems, or system failures with Coq that were caused by the predefined tactics or the Coq version used. As these problems were not relevant for our research questions, we will not consider them further here.

Creating proofs
Problems students had with creating a proof. These included recognizing and understanding assumptions as well as how to start a proof and decide whether it is complete and correct.

Mathematical inscriptions
Problems students faced with mathematical inscriptions especially how to write a step or argument down in a formal way.

Coq's Usability
Problems students had with the Coq IDE (e.g. using menu functions, understanding meaning of displayed elements).

Working with Coq
Problems students faced with Coq (e.g. choosing the correct tactic or variables) including typing errors while copy-pasting an assignment from the sheet into the IDE.

Data Structures
Problems occurring about data structures like understanding the concept of a list or a tree.

Logic
Problems students faced with the aspects of logic like syntax and semantics of definitions or using quantifiers.

In the following closer examination of these categories, we will provide quantitative information about these categories'

occurrences over the days with further specification of the single problems. As mentioned in section 4, the course content covered during lectures and assignments was organized as follows:

- Day 1-3: propositional logic
- Day 3-5: predicate logic
- Day 6-10: data structures

5.2 T-Problems

In total, we observed 66 situations in which students were asking the teacher or tutor for help (51 in the first week and 15 in the second week). Relating these numbers to the categories (see also Figure 3), the T-problems occurred as follows:

- Creating proofs (35 times)
- Mathematical inscriptions (5 times)
- Coq's usability (0 times)
- Working with Coq (13 times)
- Data structures (8 times)
- Logic (5 times)

Creating proofs: During the first two days, when working with pen and paper, the students had problems recognizing the assumption and whether a proof was complete or whether there were any missing steps (e.g. "How many steps do I need?", "How do I proceed next?", "Have I shown everything?"). Another frequent problem students had was to decide if their proof was complete. In addition, they were confusing premises with conclusions and frequently asked what was given and what they were supposed to prove. After starting to work with Coq in the afternoon of day two, these problems stayed mostly the same, but their number was decreasing. In the afternoon of day three, the course topic changed from propositional logic to predicate logic and the students were ought to create pen & paper proofs again. The occurring high number of problems were mostly the same as during the first two days during pen & paper proofs from propositional logics. After returning to Coq in the afternoon of day four, T-problems decreased.

Mathematical inscriptions: T-problems regarding mathematical inscriptions occurred in just few cases during week one and were related to proof assignments with pen and paper and focusing on questions about formal correctness and the meaning of symbols and definitions.

Working with Coq: After introducing Coq on day two and three, the T-problems of working with Coq during the first week were about using variables and universal quantifiers in the correct way or loading data into Coq as well as whether they had to write every single step down. Students also made typing errors frequently and transferred the assignment incorrectly from the assignment sheet to Coq. In the second week, the only T-problems that occurred while working with Coq were few cases on day nine about using specific tactics.

Coq's usability: There were no T-problems regarding Coq's usability.

Data structures: About 50% of all T-problems occurring in the second week were problems with the content-related parts of the course, i.e. data structures. More precisely, the students had problems with understanding and working with binary-trees and recursion.

Logic: The T-problems regarding logic were about quantifiers and syntax but mostly about basic comprehension regarding predicate logic.

Further remarks: On day eight and ten no T-problems of the regarding categories occurred. A reason could be that the lecturer reminded the students on day eight to use what they had already covered in the lecture before. Another reason could be that the students were using day ten to finish the assignments they had started the days before. But, this was also the case on day 5.

5.3 S-Problems

In total, we observed 65 situations in which students were discussing problems and solving them on their own (39 in the first week and 26 in the second week). Relating these numbers to the categories (see also Figure 2), the S-problems occurred as follows:

- Creating proofs (11 times)
- Mathematical inscriptions (10 times)
- Coq's usability (3 times)
- Working with Coq (27 times)
- Data structures (14 times)
- Logic (0 times)

Creating proofs: On the first day, the S-problems were similar to the T-problems and students talked about the given assumption and how they were not able to get an idea for the solution while solving a proof with paper & pen. From day two to four, there were no problems with creating proofs that students could be able to solve by their own. On day five, there occurred S-problems with obtaining the correct assumption again and how to use previously created proofs. On the eighth day, two student groups discussed problems about how a proof should be formulated in natural language.

Mathematical inscriptions: S-problems of this category occurred on day four, when the students discussed how to write down a proof in natural language and in the correct way.

Working with Coq: The S-problems of this category from the third day on featured problems about working with Coq after using

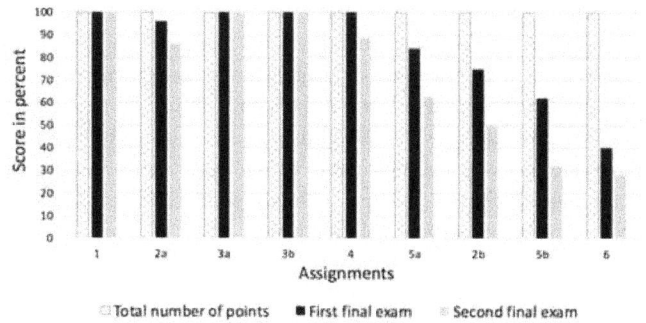

Figure 4: Achieved points in final exam

it for the first time and were similar to T-problems. Students also had problems with typing errors while transferring the assignment sheet to Coq. But in this case instead of the occurrences of T-problems, the students recognized the mistakes without help from the teacher or tutor. Furthermore, there were discussions about choosing the correct tactics.

Coq's usability: On day eight, the students were confused that Coq removes the brackets if a subgoal is executed. This was the only situation in which students had usability difficulties.

Data structures: In the second week, most S-problems of this category involved problems again about understanding the covered data structures. Most observed problems were regarding lists, which were introduced on day seven. Almost all problems with binary-trees on day nine resulted in T-problems and we could not observe situations in which the students solved problems about this topic on their own.

5.4 Students' Results of Final Exam

Fourteen students participated in the final exam and all of them passed it (the exam was offered twice for those who could not attend the first one). The grades obtained resembles a typical bell curve with the peak between B and C indicating that the exam assignments had an appropriate level of difficulty. The final exam had the four following assignment types: 1) Working with and in Coq (1, 2a, 3a, 3b, 4, 5a); 2) giving line-by-line comments for a proof in Coq (2b); 3) solving a proof with pen & paper that was solved in Coq before (5b); and 4) solving a proof with pen & paper that was not solved in Coq before (6) (see Figure 4 that is sorted by assignment types). The first and second assignment covered proofs about propositional and predicate logic, the third assignment was defining a data type while assignment four to six were about proofs about data structures.

Students scored best with proofs to be created with Coq. The scores were slightly worse for assignment types 2 and 3 if the students were suggested to write line-by-line comments for their code or had to write a proof in natural language that they had already solved in Coq. In detail, the students had problems being precise in their choice of words especially in assignment type 2 and problems with proof structuring in assignments type 3. The worst scores appeared with assignments of type 4, when students had to write the proof down without solving it in Coq first. Here, just like during exercise sessions, students' results indicated problems with identifying the assumption of a proof and using it correctly in the chain of reasoning. Also, they were using wrong mathematical notations and seemed to be uncertain or confused about what information they already had and what they had to prove. In several cases, they only delivered an idea of what they were supposed to prove. However, this was mainly related to the assignment about data structures, which was the topic with which the students struggled most during the two-weeks block course.

5.5 Discussion

In this section, we will discuss our research questions stated in the beginning of section 4 while relying on the results presented in the previous subsections.

Research Question (RQ) 1: When starting with Coq, students required surprisingly little training to get used to work with the theorem prover. We were expecting students to be challenged by the way Coq displays the backward reasoning of a tactic in the right-hand upper window of the IDE (see also section 3.2). But, students seemed quickly understand this part. Except for one problem with the usage of brackets, we did not observe any serious usability issues with Coq. This indicates that provided presentations and explanations of how Coq works during lecture seemed to be sufficient. Also, we hypothesize that students were probably able to transfer their familiarity with programming IDEs (from previous programming courses attended at our department they are familiar at least with BlueJ and Eclipse) to the usage of Coq's IDE.

RQ 2: While the students were solving their first assignments with pen & paper on day one, it became obvious that they only had limited understanding of propositional and predicate logic and how to develop a formal proof within these topics (e.g. repeatedly, they tried using truth tables for developing a proof). This was the case although they all had attended an introductory course in theory of computation that covered propositional and predicate logic and most of our students had attended this course just three months earlier. The fact that creating proofs problems appeared with assignments about propositional logic and then again with predicate logic showed that the students could not easily transfer their understanding. With the pen & paper proofs it became quite obvious how difficult it was for the students to start a proof and decide when they had accomplished it. Instead, working with Coq seemed to lead to more satisfaction: The low attrition rate and overall positive feedback in the surveys regarding their interaction with Coq, indicates that students were very motivated to work with the tool and within the created setting.

RQ 3: Comparing T- and S-problems in both diagrams (see Figure 3 and Figure 2) we have reason to believe that working with Coq indeed seemed to help scaffolding students' activities in developing a formal proof. We conclude this from the strong decreasing amount of T-problems of category *creating proofs* during first week once Coq was introduced as well as remaining S-problems indicating that students were strongly working on their assignments but not relying anymore on the teacher or tutor. The more the course advanced, the less students ran into problems that were related to *creating proofs* or *working with Coq*. Also, the more skilled students became with using Coq, the less it was necessary or requested by the students to discuss all solutions in plenary by the

end of each exercise session. Instead, students were able to discuss most questions and problems with each other. While Coq's scaffolding qualities seemed to support students strongly, the tool's strictness did not seem to limit students' activities. On the contrary, comparing their proof activities on the first day when using only pen & paper with days three and four while using Coq, the limitation of potential approaches enabled students to master at least one way of proof development instead of getting lost by to many options. Supporting our hypothesis of Coq's scaffolding ability, another observation is that through the entire course as well as during final exam students constantly performed better when using Coq in comparison to using pen & paper first or after using Coq (see corresponding assignment 5b and 6 in the final exam in Figure 4). This also corresponds to observations during exercise sessions where students displayed a dislike to start proofs with pen & paper as well as to switch back from Coq to pen & paper alike proofs.

One possible interpretation of students performing well in Coq but still struggling with pen & paper could be that they did not really master Coq proofs but got a solution by trial and error only. Although this strategy would have been possible for provided logic assignments, it would not have worked with data structures. Also, as we observed students working with Coq and in their questions they asked, this explanation seems to be rather unlikely. Instead, we rather believe that within our course design we did not pay enough attention to how Coq as a scaffolding element is dismantled carefully. This is also supported by situated cognition theory: Activities learned and practiced with a specific tool are not easily transferable to activities with another tool, especially when the tools embody different knowledge ([58], p. 10). In the next iteration of improving and testing our course design, we will pay particular attention to this aspect investigating further how Coq is mediating students understanding of formal proofs and what needs to be provided in order to create better transfer between tools.

6 CONCLUSION

The presented educational design research approach suggests the theorem prover Coq as a new learning tool for introductory courses to theory of computation. Theorem provers are designed and used for scientific and industrial purposes. Through creating specific assignments with predefined tactics, it was possible to transfer Coq into a learning tool and make it available to students in an introductory course on logic and data structures. Our evaluation shows that, contrary to prevailing assumptions, the students managed well to work with Coq. Our results strengthen the assumption that with our approach, indeed, Coq can be beneficial in scaffolding undergraduate students' activities of formal proofs. Especially the ability of creating a formal proof step-by-step and distinguishing between single elements of a proof, students were profiting strongly from the program's immediate feedback and scaffolding quality in comparison to pen and paper alike proofs. Open questions for future investigations will concern the nature of student understanding of formal proofs as it is mediated by Coq in comparison to pen and paper.

REFERENCES

[1] P. Anapa and S. Hatice. 2010. Investigation of undergraduate students' perceptions of mathematical proof. Procedia-Social and Behavioral Sciences 2.2: 2700-2706. S.

[2] S. Allen, M. Bickford., R. Constable, R. Eaton, C. Kreitz,, L. Lorigo, and E. Moran. 2006. Innovations in Computational Type Theory using Nuprl. Journal of Applied Logic, 4, 4, 428-469.

[3] P. Andrews, C. Brown, F. Pfenning, M. Bishop, S. Issar and H. Xi. 2004. Etps: A system to help students write formal proofs. Journal of Automated Reasoning, 75-92.

[4] D. Almeida. 2000. A survey of mathematics undergraduates' interaction with proof: some implications for mathematics education. International Journal of Mathematical Education in Science and Technology 31.6: 869-890.

[5] S. Autexier, D. Dietrich and M. Schiller. 2012. Towards an Intelligent Tutor for Mathematical Proofs. In Proceedings THedu'11: 1-28.

[6] C. Bereiter. 1997. Situated cognition and how to overcome it. In Situated cognition: Social, semiotic, and psychological perspectives, Kirshner, D. and Whitson, J. A., Eds. NJ: Erlbaum, Hillsdale, 281-300.

[7] Y. Bertot and P. Casteran. 2004. Interactive Theorem Proving and Program Development Coq'Art: The Calculus of Inductive Constructions, Springer.

[8] W. Billingsley and P. Robinson 2007. Student Proof Exercises Using MathsTiles and Isabelle/HOL in an Intelligent Book. Journal of Automated Reasoning, Volume 39(2): 181-281.

[9] Bove, P. Dybjer and U. Norell. 2009. A Brief Overview of Agda - A Functional Language with Dependent Types. In TPHOLs 2009, LNCS 5674, Springer, 73-78.

[10] E. Brady. 2013. Idris, a General Purpose Dependently Typed Programming Language: Design and Implementation. Journal of Functional Programming, 23(5):552-593.

[11] W. Brookes, W. (2004, January). Computing theory with relevance. In Proceedings of the Sixth Australasian Conference on Computing Education-Volume 30. Australian Computer Society, Inc., 9-13.

[12] C. Chesñevar, M. González and A. Maguitman. 2004. Didactic strategies for promoting significant learning in formal languages and automata theory. In Proceedings of the 9th annual SIGCSE conference on Innovation and technology in computer science education. ITiCSE '04. ACM, 7-11.

[13] J.S. Brown, A. Collins and P. Duguid. 1989. Situated cognition and the culture of learning. Educational Researcher, 18, 32–42.

[14] A. Collins, J. S. Brown and A. Holum. 1991. Cognitive apprenticeship: Making thinking visible. American Educator, 6(11):38-46.

[15] R. Constable et.al. 1986. Implementing Mathematics with the Nuprl Development System, Prentice-Hall.

[16] Q. Cutts, S. Esper, M. Fecho, S. Foster and B. Simon. 2012. The Abstraction Transition Taxonomy: Developing Desired Learning Outcomes through the Lens of Situated Cognition. In Proceedings of the ninth annual International Conference on International Computing Education Research. ICER'12. ACM, 63-70.

[17] E. Deitrick, B. Shapiro, M. Ahrens, R. Fiebrink, P. Lehrman and S. Farooq. 2015. Using Distributed Cognition Theory to Analyze Collaborative Computer Science Learning. In Proceedings of the eleventh annual International Conference on Computing Education Research. ICER'15. ACM, 51-60.

[18] D. Delahaye, M. Jaume and V. Prevosto. 2005. Coq, un outil pour l'enseignement. Technique et Science Informatiques, 24, 9, 1139-1160.

[19] V. Durand-Guerrier, P. Boero, N. Douek, S. S. Epp, and D. Tanguay. 2012. Examining the Role of Logic in Teaching Proof. In Proof and Proving in Mathematics Education, Volume 15 of the series New ICMI Study Series, 369-389.

[20] C. García-Osorio, I. Mediavilla-Sáiz, J. Jimeno-Visitación and N. García-Pedrajas. 2008. Teaching push-down automata and turing machines. ACM SIGCSE Bulletin, 40, 3.

[21] G. Gonthier, A. Asperti, J. Avigad, Y. Bertot, C. Cohen, F. Garillot and I. Pasca. 2013. A machine-checked proof of the odd order theorem. In International Conference on Interactive Theorem Proving. Springer Berlin Heidelberg. 163-179..

[22] F. Guilhot. 2005. Formalisation en Coq et visualisation d'un cours de géométrie pour le lycée. TSI, 24, 1113-1138

[23] H. Habiballa and T. Kmet. 2004. Theoretical branches in teaching computer science. International Journal of Mathematical Education in Science and Technology. 35, 6, 829-841.

[24] T. Hales, M. Adams, G. Bauer, D.T. Dang, J. Harrison, L.T. Hoang and T. Q. Nguyen. 2015. A formal proof of the Kepler conjecture. arXiv preprint arXiv:1501.02155.

[25] M. Hamilton, J. Harland and L. Padgham. 2003Experiences in teaching computing theory via aspects of problem-based learning. In Proceedings of the fifth Australasian conference on Computing education, Volume 20, Australian Computer Society, 207-211.

[26] M. Henz and A. Hobor. 2011. Teaching Experience: Logic and Formal Methods with Coq. In Certified Programs and Proofs, Lecture Notes in Computer Science, Vol. 7086, Springer, 199-215.

[27] M- Hielscher and C. Wagenknecht. 2006. AtoCC: learning environment for teaching theory of automata and formal languages. In Proceedings of the 11th annual SIGCSE conference on Innovation and technology in computer science education. ITICSE '06. ACM, 306-306.

[28] J. Hollan, E. Hutchins and D Kirsh. 2000. Distributed cognition: toward a new foundation for human-computer interaction research. ACM Transactions on Computer-Human Interaction (TOCHI), 7(2), 174-196.

[29] E. Hutchins. 1995. Cognition in the Wild. Bradford: MIT Press.

[30] IEEE Computer Society and ACM. 2013. Computer Science Curricula. DOI: 10.1145/2534860

[31] INRIA. The Coq Webpage with a collection of teaching practices: https://coq.inria.fr/cocorico/CoqInTheClassroom

[32] I. Karasavvidis. 2002. Distributed Cognition and Educational Practice, In Journal of Interactive Learning Research, 13 (1/2), 11-29.

[33] F. Kiehn, C. Frede and M. Knobelsdorf. 2017. Was macht Unentscheidbarkeit und Turinmaschinen so schwierig? Ergebnisse einer qualitativen Einzelfallstudie. HDI 2017. 7,5. HDI-Workshop des GI-Fachbereichs Informatik und Ausbildung / Didaktik der Informatik

[34] M. Knobelsdorf. 2015. The Theory Behind Theory - Computer Science Education Research Through the Lenses of Situated Learning. In Proceedings of the 8th International Conference on Informatics in Schools: Situation, Evolution, and Perspectives (ISSEP), Lecture Notes in Computer Science, Volume 9378, Springer, 21-21.

[35] M. Knobelsdorf and C. Frede. 2016. Analyzing Student Practices in Theory of Computation in Light of Distributed Cognition Theory. In Proceedings of the 12th ICER Conference, ACM, 73-81.

[36] M. Knobelsdorf, C. Kreitz, C., and S. Böhne. 2014. Teaching theoretical computer science using a cognitive apprenticeship approach. In Proceedings of the 45th ACM technical symposium on Computer science education. SIGCSE '45. ACM, New York, 67-72.

[37] Y. Lincoln, and E. Guba. 1985. Naturalistic Inquiry. Sage Publications. Newbury Park, California.

[38] S. McKenney and C. Reeves. 2012. Conducting educational design research. New York, Routledge.

[39] P. Mayring. 2000. Qualitative Content Analysis. Forum: Qualitative Social Research [Online Journal], 1, 2, Art. 20.

[40] R. Nederpelt and H. Geuvers. 2014. Type Theory and Formal Proof: An Introduction, Cambridge University Press.

[41] J. Nespor. 1994. Knowledge in Motion. Taylor & Francis ISBN 978-0-7507-0270-6.

[42] T. Nipkow, L. Paulson and M. Wenzel. 2002. Isabelle/HOL A Proof Assistant for Higher-Order Logic, Lecture Notes in Computer Science, Vol. 2283, Springer.

[43] M. Parker and C. Lewis. 2014. What makes big-O analysis difficult: understanding how students understand runtime analysis. Journal of Computing Science in Colleges, 29, 4, 164-174.

[44] R. Pea. 1993. Practices of distributed intelligence and designs for education. In Distributed cognitions: Psychological and educational considerations. G. Salomon, Ed. Cambridge: Cambridge University Press, 47-87.

[45] R. Pea. 2004. The Social and Technological Dimensions of Scaffolding and Related Theoretical Concepts for Learning, Education, and Human Activity. Journal of the Learning Sciences, 13(3), 423-451.

[46] B. Pierce et al. 2017. Software Foundations. https://softwarefoundations.cis.upenn.edu/current/index.html

[47] N. Pillay. 2009. Learning Difficulties Experienced by Students in a Course on Formal Languages and Automata Theory. SIGCSE Bulletin. 41, 4, 48-52.

[48] S. H. Rodger, B. Bressler, T. Finley, S. and Reading, S. 2006. Turning automata theory into a hands-on course. In Proceedings of the 37th SIGCSE technical symposium on Computer science education. SIGCSE '06. ACM, 379-383.

[49] S. Rychen, L. H. Salganik. 2003. A holistic model of competence. In Key Competencies for a Successful Life and a Well-Functioning Society Rychen, S., Salganik, L. H. Ed, Hogrefe & Huber, Seatlle, 41-62.

[50] J. Sakowicz and J. Chrząszcz. 2007. Papuq, a Coq assistant. In Proceedings of PATE'07 conference, Elsevier, 79-96.

[51] R. Säljö. 1998. Learning as the use of tools: a sociocultural perspective on the human-technology link. *In Learning with computers*. Littleton, K. and Light, P., Ed. Routledge, New York, 144-161.

[52] M. Schiller, D. Dietrich and C. Benzmüller. 2008. Proof step analysis for proof tutoring – a learning approach to granularity. Teaching Mathematics and Computer Science 6.2: 325-343.

[53] A. H. Schoenfeld. 1994. Reflections on doing and teaching mathematics. In *Mathematical thinking and problem solving*, Schoenfeld, A. H., Ed. Routledge, 53-70.

[54] S. Sigman. 2007. Engaging students in formal language theory and theory of computation. SIGSCE Bulletin. 39, 1, 450-453

[55] M. Sipser. 2012. Introduction to the Theory of Computation Cengage Learning, Boston, USA.

[56] R. Sommer and G. Nuckols. 2004. A Proof Environment for Teaching Mathematics. Journal of Automated Reasoning, Volume 32(3): 227-258.

[57] M. Tedre and E. Sutinen. 2008. Three traditions of computing: what educators should know. Computer Science Education, 18, 3, 153-170.

[58] J. Tenenberg and M. Knobelsdorf. 2013. Out of our minds: a review of sociocultural cognition theory. Computer Science Education, 24, 1, 1-24.

[59] L. S. Vygotsky. 1978. Mind in Society: The Development of Higher Psychological Processes: Harvard University Press.

[60] K. Weber. 2001. Student difficulty in constructing proofs: The need for strategic knowledge. Educational studies in mathematics 48.1: 101-119.

[61] J.W. Wertsch. 1993. Voices of the Mind: Sociocultural Approach to Mediated Action. Harvard University Press.

[62] D. Wood, J. Bruner and G. Ross. 1976. The role of tutoring in problem solving. Journal of Child Psychology and Child Psychiatry, 17, 89–100

RoboBUG: A Serious Game for Learning Debugging Techniques

Michael A. Miljanovic
University of Ontario Institute of Technology
2000 Simcoe Street North
Oshawa, Ontario, Canada
michael.miljanovic@uoit.ca

Jeremy S. Bradbury
University of Ontario Institute of Technology
2000 Simcoe Street North
Oshawa, Ontario, Canada
jeremy.bradbury@uoit.ca

ABSTRACT

Debugging is an essential but challenging task that can present a great deal of confusion and frustration to novice programmers. It can be argued that Computer Science education does not sufficiently address the challenges that students face when identifying bugs in their programs. To help students learn effective debugging techniques and to provide students a more enjoyable and motivating experience, we have designed the RoboBUG game. RoboBUG is a serious game that can be customized with respect to different programming languages and game levels.

CCS CONCEPTS

• **Social and professional topics** → **Computer science education**; • **Software and its engineering** → *Software testing and debugging*; • **Applied computing** → Computer games;

KEYWORDS

debugging, programming, software engineering, computer science, education, serious games, game-based learning

1 INTRODUCTION

Research related to programming and software development often focuses on advancing the state-of-the-art in software developer practices, techniques and tools. Research into programming and software development learning tools is equally important as software developers must first learn best practices before they can effectively perform them.

It is essential that programmers who seek to write reliable, high quality source code be able to efficiently identify and repair bugs in program code [24]. The process of fixing these bugs, *debugging*, has been shown to consume up to 50% of a programmer time in large software projects [5]. Furthermore, the ability to debug code is not easily acquired, and experts have a significant advantage over novices [3]. In addition to experience, experts have knowledge of a variety of debugging techniques including code tracing, instrumentation and the use of breakpoints in debuggers.

Game-based learning has already been implemented and proven effective for computer programming education [10, 16] which suggests that it may also prove useful in debugging education. Serious games should not only help players achieve learning outcomes but should also provide a fun and positive experience. Previous studies have shown that motivated and engaged learners will perform more effectively [8, 18]. Finally, the benefits of serious games suggest they may be an effective way to counter the frustration typically associated with debugging.

First year courses often do not teach debugging explicitly, and expect students to learn it for themselves. This lack of preparedness is compounded by the fact that there is no established set of best practices for teaching debugging [7]. This is compounded by a lack of online resources dedicated to helping novices learn to debug [3]. Even students with a good understanding of how to write programs still struggle with debugging [1]. These students may have the ability to fix bugs in their programs, but only after accomplishing the difficult task of finding the bugs first.

In general, the lack of accessibility to debugging techniques leads students to have a primarily negative experience, even when given the opportunity to learn debugging [20]. This fact is particularly problematic when students conclude that debugging skills are based on aptitude and are unable to be learned [4]. We hope to address the problem of accessibility and frustration with debugging education by creating RoboBUG, a puzzle-based serious game, that is designed to help students achieve debugging learning outcomes in an enjoyable rather than tedious way.

The creation of RoboBUG required us to address a number of challenges, including:

(1) **Game design:** How can debugging activities be represented as game tasks/actions? How can these tasks be connected to produce enjoyable and cohesive gameplay?
(2) **Game learning data:** What debugging topics and learning materials should be used in the game to achieve the desired learning outcomes while minimizing frustration?
(3) **Game evaluation:** How do we design our study to effectively assess debugging learning and level of enjoyment?

In addition, we needed to consider if the combination of game design and learning data challenges will allow a player to retain debugging technique knowledge after the game's completion.

In the remaining sections of our paper we present background on debugging and game-based learning (Section 2), an overview of our RoboBUG serious game (Section 3), the results of a pilot study (Section 4.1) as well as the results of two full studies (Section 4.2 and Section 4.3). Our studies were conducted with undergraduates at the University of Ontario Institute of Technology (UOIT).

ICER '17, August 18-20, 2017, Tacoma, WA, USA.
© 2017 ACM. 978-1-4503-4968-0/17/08...$15.00
DOI: http://dx.doi.org/10.1145/3105726.3106173

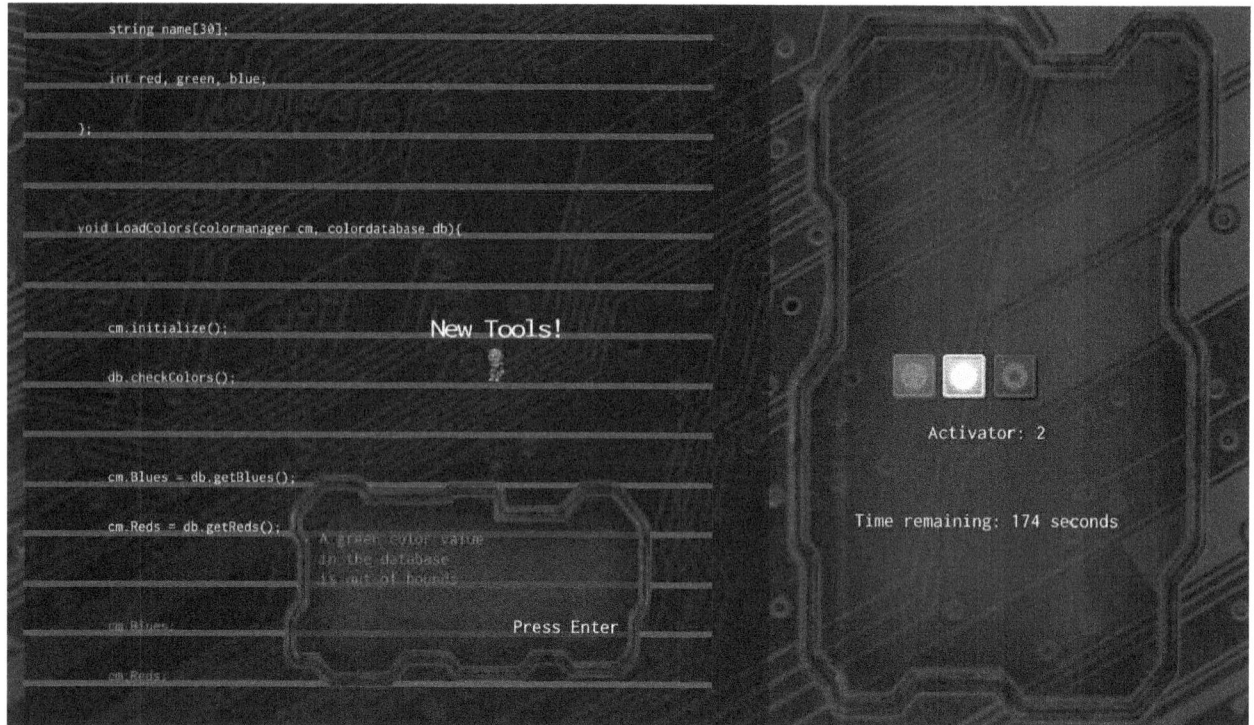

Figure 1: A screenshot of the RoboBUG game

The RoboBUG game interface is divided into two regions: (1) The code region (left) in which the user controls an avatar to navigate the source code while using different debugging tools to eventually find bugs, (2) The sidebar region (right) in which the user can view information about available debugging tools, the currently active tool and the time remaining in the level. In addition to these two regions, the RoboBUG game also utilizes dialogs (bottom) to provide contextual information to the user including feedback from debugging activities.

2 BACKGROUND

2.1 Debugging

As mentioned in the previous section, debugging is the processing of finding and fixing problems (bugs) in a program. Debugging can involve the use of dedicated debugger tools and can use a combination of both static static and dynamic debugging techniques. Static techniques are those that do not require execution of the program while dynamic techniques rely on run-time information. Common debugging techniques include code tracing, print statements, divide-and-conquer and breakpoints. **Code tracing** is a static technique in which the programmer reads through code to make sure it is behaving properly. **Print statements** are a code injection approach to inserting output statements into the program that display internal program status information as output. **Divide-and-conquer** is a debugging strategy that allows a programmer to systematically separate source code into sections in an effort to isolate a bug. **Breakpoints** are a common feature in modern debuggers that allows the execution of a program to be paused in order to allow the programmer to view the internal value of variables at specific execution points.

After conducting a review of debugging techniques we decided to select the above four techniques for inclusion in the RoboBUG game. Other debugging techniques, such as black-box testing, were excluded in order to constrain the duration of the game. Although the chosen techniques are only applied in specific levels of the game, there is an overarching theme of program comprehension. Experts are faster and more effective debuggers than novices due to superior program comprehension strategies [14], which is why we chose to emphasize the importance of comprehension by having players debug code they did not write themselves.

In addition, we selected types of bugs that are common in student-written code. As syntax errors are often identified by compilers, they tend to be less problematic for students than logic or data errors [9]. Thus, we chose to include only logic and data errors in our tool, and because we believe the techniques we selected are best explained through their abilities to find these types of errors.

2.2 Game-based Learning

Serious games for Computer Science is an active research area [17, 23], especially with respect to learning how to write computer programs. Games such as Code Hunt [21] help learners develop their skills through puzzle tasks that require players to write programs in order to solve a specific problem. Serious programming games usually focus on the act of creating programs by writing source code, or alternatively by writing a drag-and-drop interface, as seen with Program Your Robot [11]. A nonstandard example of a puzzle-based programming game is Robot ON! [15], that does not require

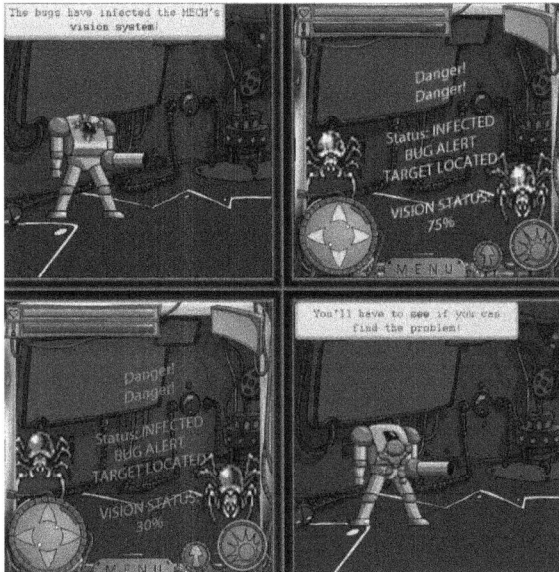

Figure 2: A RoboBUG comic storyboard used to advance the game plot and setup a new game level

The RoboBUG game utilizes a plot to engage the user in the debugging learning tasks. Each level begins with a four panel comic that provides plot details and connects each level with an overall story. For example, in the above comic, alien bugs have infected the player's mech suit and caused the vision system to malfunction. In the corresponding level the user is tasked with detecting bugs in the mech suit's vision system source code.

players to write any programs. Instead, Robot ON! focuses on program understanding and comprehension by requiring players to read source code written by someone else.

Some games such as Gidget [13] have been designed with an emphasis on helping players learn about debugging. However, Gidget is meant to introduce general debugging, and uses unique pseudocode instead of a common language such as C++ or Java. In addition, we did not find any serious games in the literature that specifically focus on learning debugging techniques.

3 THE ROBOBUG GAME

RoboBUG[1] (see Figure 1) is a serious game intended to be played by first-year computer science students who are learning to debug for the first time. We chose to design RoboBUG as a puzzle-type game, as puzzles have been shown to be effective for both helping to learn material as well as demonstrating higher level concepts such as critical thinking and problem-solving [19].

RoboBUG was implemented in C# using the Unity game engine[2] and open source media elements. Although the standard version of RoboBUG is based on debugging in C++, it also includes a framework that allows instructors to create their own levels using other programming languages. New levels are specified using XML and

---

[1]https://github.com/sqrlab/robobug
[2]https://unity3d.com/

can be customized with respect to different aspects of a level, including time limit, available tools, output text, and source code. These new levels can be inserted into the game with minimal effort.

In the RoboBUG game a player takes the role of a scientist whose world is under attack from an alien bug world. The alien world has sent an advanced army of tiny bugs that infect technology in the scientist's world – including the scientist's 'Mech Suit' (a robotic suit of armour). In order to help save the world from the alien bugs, the scientist must first purge bugs from the infected 'Mech Suit'. Bugs are purged by the scientist by virtually entering the infected source code to find all of the alien bugs. In each level the player (taking the role of the scientist) must fix a particular part of the Mech Suit (e.g. the vision system) by figuring out where the bug is hiding (see Figure 2). the game is finished once the player has completed all levels, found all of the bugs, and has a working Mech Suit. The actions required by different debugging techniques are represented as tools that the player can aim at lines of code. For example, a Breakpointer tool can be aimed at a line of code to insert a break point and a Warper tool can be aimed at a function call to jump to another part of the code (the function definition).

The default version of RoboBUG includes four levels that teach different debugging techniques in C++ (see Table 1). Each of these levels includes: a tutorial that introduces new debugging tools, 2-3 subproblems that contain small debugging tasks and partial source code and a final challenge that combines the tools introduced in the tutorials and the knowledge gained from the subproblems. The final challenge will typically involve detecting a bug in the full program.

A player's progress through the game is recorded in a set of log files that allow gameplay to stopped and resumed. Prototype testing has shown that the game with the default levels takes approximately 30 minutes to complete. RoboBUG has been used with the four default levels during an introductory programming course at UOIT.

3.1 Game Levels

In developing the default version of RoboBUG, we thought about the order and content that should be included in the game levels. We chose to first introduce code tracing as it can be used in combination with other techniques and it is not too time-consuming due to the short length of the example programs. Next, we selected the use of print statements in order to help novices learn to identify program behavior at run-time. This was followed by the strategy of divide-and-conquer, where novices can reduce the search space for bugs by commenting out code that is guaranteed to contain no bugs. Finally, we adapted some features of a debugger so that novices can learn the concepts of breakpoints and the value of observing a program's execution state during run-time.

The following subsections provide a brief walkthrough of the game levels in RoboBUG. Each level includes several parts that build upon each other with the final part requiring the player to debugging a subsystem of the 'Mech Suit'.

3.1.1 Level 1: Code Tracing.

- *Subproblem A:* A mathematical function definition is provided to the player that includes input, output, and behavior. The function is intended to return an average of a set of values (a floating point number), and the player's goal is to trace through the code and identify that the 'avgf'

Table 1: An overview of the levels and tools in RoboBUG

Level	Tools	Description
Level 1	Bugcatcher	The Mech Suit is unable to stand because it cannot correctly calculate the physical forces acting upon it. The player must practice **code tracing** by identifying bugs while reading through source code that calculates the average value of a set of physical forces.
Level 2	Bugcatcher, Activator	The Mech Suit is failing to correctly identify the most dangerous creatures that appear in its viewing area. The player needs to use **print statements** to identify program bugs in an algorithm that sorts the externally viewable bugs from most to least dangerous (threat assessment).
Level 3	Bugcatcher, Activator, Commenter, Warper	The Mech Suit vision system has been infected and no longer functions at all. To fix it, the player must search for a bug in the robot's visual color database. Since the database is large, the player will need to employ a **divide-and-conquer** strategy and comment out different blocks of source code.
Level 4	Bugcatcher, Activator, Breakpointer, Warper	The Mech Suit is not able to correctly calculate which creatures are closest in proximity. This is the most challenging level, requiring the player to use several debugging tools to locate bugs across multiple functions. This includes the use of **breakpoints** to display variable values and program state at run-time while locating the bug in a distance calculation function.

variable (responsible for storing the average) has a type (boolean) that doesn't match its intended use.

- *Subproblem B:* The source code from Subproblem A is expanded to calculate the average of a list of numbers using a loop; however, the player needs to identify that the loop adds the 'avgf' variable to a running total sum rather than properly averaging the numbers.
- *Subproblem C:* The source code is expanded again and now contains the full function for calculating the average of physical forces acting upon the 'Mech Suit'. However, an extraneous line of source code is present that increments the average after it has been calculated correctly.

3.1.2 Level 2: Print Statements.

- *Subproblem A:* The player is presented with a function that should swap two numbers; however, the final line of code performs the operation in reverse, and assigns the values incorrectly. This behavior can be identified when the player enables the appropriate print statements which show that the final result only includes one correctly swapped value.
- *Subproblem B:* The swap function from the Subproblem A has been incorporated into a function that sort a list of numbers that unfortunately includes an out-of-bounds indexing error. Using print statements the player can discover this area and identify that the bug is in the loop condition (a '>=' sign is used instead of a '>').
- *Subproblem C:* The final expanded source code is part of the threat assessment component in the 'Mech Suit' and contains a function that sorts a list of threat rankings. The print statements in this level show the state of the list at different stages of sorting. Observing each print statement should help the player realize that the first element of the list is accidentally not sorted and leads to an incorrect list.

3.1.3 Level 3: Divide and Conquer.

- *Subproblem A:* The player is presented with a large list of integer red-green-blue (RGB) color tuples, which each range between 0 and 255; these represent different colors in the 'Mech Suit' vision subsystem. A print statement at the beginning of the function indicates that one of the green values is out of bounds. By using a divide-and-conquer approach to commenting out the different code sections for different colors, the player can identify that one of the colors has an out of range green value.

- *Subproblem B:* The code in this level consists of multiple large lists of RGB colors, and a print statement at the beginning of the code indicates that there is an invalid blue color value. The player must use the commenter tool to comment out each list of colors until the error is located.
- *Subproblem C:* This level is similar to Subproblem B, except the source code color lists are divided across multiple files that must be checked separately. The player uses the commenting tool to comment out each file until they discover which file contains the error. Using their 'warper' tool, they can then warp to that file and isolate the invalid value.

3.1.4 Level 4: Breakpoints.

- *Subproblem A:* The source code in this part takes two pairs of numbers representing a location (x and y coordinates), and indicates which pair has a lower magnitude. The player uses code tracing to discover that there is a '=' instead of a '==' in a comparison statement. While this part of the level does not use breakpoints it is included to show the benefits of breakpoints in the subsequent parts of the level.
- *Subproblem B:* This part of the level requires the player to use breakpoints to check the values of coordinates used in each function, and identify a small logic error.
- *Subproblem C:* This part is similar to Subproblem B, but contains an error where a variable is unintentionally reassigned instead of used in a calculation.
- *Subproblem D:* The source code in the final subproblem of this level contains a small logic error in a purposefully obfuscated calculation. The error is obfuscated to enhance the benefits of breakpoints in finding the bug. This source code is from the 'Mech Suit' subsystem that calculates locations to target.

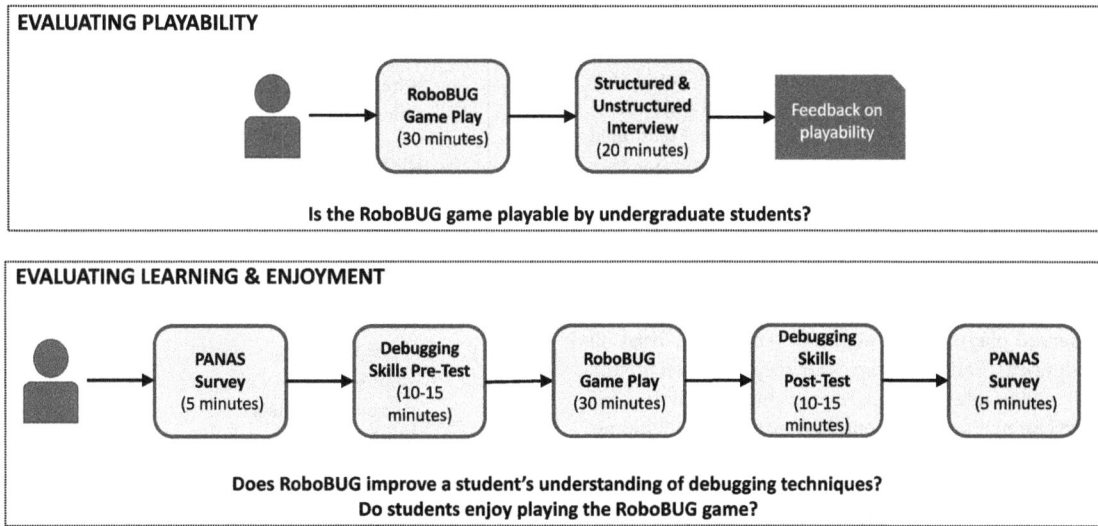

Figure 3: The RoboBUG evaluation methodology

3.2 Game Mechanics

In order to complete a level, the player must navigate the avatar in the code region of the game interface (see Figure 1) using the arrow keys. Once a bug has been found, the player uses the *bugcatcher* tool to "capture" the bug at a specific line of code. If the location is incorrect, the player fails the level and must start it again. The player can also fail if he or she expends all of the available tools, or does not complete the level within the time allotted. As the game progresses, the player is given access to additional kinds of tools that can activate print statements (*activator* tool), comment out source code (*commenter* tool), set and trigger breakpoints (*breakpointer* tool) and jump to different regions of the program (*warper* tool). Completion of each level requires the player to use the tools available before using the 'bugcatcher' tool to complete the level.

4 ROBOBUG EVALUATION

Serious games, including those in the Computer Science education literature, tend to be published without a proper evaluation [12] making it difficult to assess their impact on learning. The most effective type of evaluation to determine the efficacy of a game for learning is a user study [6]. In our evaluation of RoboBUG we have conducted three separate user studies with 23, 5 and 14 participants respectfully. Our first study (Section 4.1) was a pilot study of a first prototype of RoboBUG, our second study (Section 4.2) assessed the playability of the refined version of RoboBUG and our third study (Section 4.3) assessed the enjoyability and the achievement of learning outcomes in the refined version of RoboBUG.

4.1 Pilot Study

A pilot study of an early RoboBUG prototype assessed the value of the game in comparison with traditional assignment-based learning. All participants were undergraduate students at UOIT with knowledge of the C++ programming language. Participants were split into two random groups: a control group of 12 participants who

1	2	3	4	5
Very Slightly / Not at all	A Little	Moderately	Quite a bit	Extremely

1. Interested _____
2. Distressed _____
3. Excited _____
4. Upset _____

5. Strong _____
6. Guilty _____
7. Scared _____
8. Enthusiastic _____

Figure 4: Positive-Negative Affect Scale (PANAS) [22]

The Positive-Negative Affect Scale is a self-evaluation assessment of affect based on words that associate with positive or negative emotions. Total affect is calculated by adding all of the positive or negative item ratings, with higher scores representing higher affect levels.

completed a short assignment, and an experimental group of 11 participants who played the RoboBUG game. Both the assignment and the game were based on the same debugging techniques (see Section 2.1) and included similar source code – each level in the RoboBUG game had a corresponding assignment question.

The evaluation found no significant difference with regards to achieving learning outcomes between the assignment-based learning activity and the RoboBUG prototype. We believe this result was impacted by the fact that study participants who played the RoboBUG prototype found it complicated, and some participants were not able to complete the game without hints. Despite this, participants who played RoboBUG tended to find it to be more 'fun'. After the results of the pilot study RoboBUG was updated to address these issues, by subdividing levels, reducing complexity, and providing opportunities for players to fail and replay the levels.

4.2 Evaluating Playability

To evaluate the current version of RoboBUG, we first conducted a user study to address the following research question:

• *Is the RoboBUG game playable by undergraduate students?*
This was an important research question to answer first because not identifying and addressing issues with playability could serious impact our ability to assess the learnability and enjoyment of RoboBUG. In other words, we don't want design and technical issues to confound our evaluation of RoboBUG's potential as a learning tool for debugging.

Our evaluation involved the participation 5 first year Computer Science students at UOIT who were familiar with C++. Participants were between the ages of 18 and 25, with mixed demographics. Participants individually took part in a 1 hour session during which they were observed playing the RoboBUG game for at least 30 minutes (see Figure 3). Following the game play, the participants completed a 20 minute interview where they answered both structured and unstructured questions about their experience, including:

• What did you learn about debugging that you didn't know before?
• What aspect/part of the game was most enjoyable?
• What aspect/part of the game was the most frustrating?
• What aspect/part of the game was most innovative?
• What aspect/part of the game would you like to see improved?

During the interview, participants provided feedback about parts of the game where they became stuck or frustrated. The goal was for RoboBUG to be playable before measuring its efficacy as a game.

Overall, the game was viewed positively by the participants, who particularly enjoyed the game elements that differentiated RoboBUG gameplay from real debugging tasks. During the interviews, the participants gave the following opinions:

• *"[I enjoyed] trying to test my skills with how good I am with debugging."*
• *"It's a great tool, that's what I can say."*
• *"The way that the divide and conquer was set up was pretty cool."*
• *"The inclusion of breakpoints was kind of innovative."*
• *"[The warper tool] was interesting because I thought all of the code would be in one class."*
• *"I think that the warper/commenting, being able to zip between different segments of code was really good."*

While participants enjoyed playing RoboBUG, our study did identify some important playability issues with the game, including control problems and concerns with some of the game's levels. In particular, participants in all our evaluations had significant challenges trying to debug a level containing an off-by-one index bug. This bug was cited by participants to be especially frustrating, due to players having trouble identifying print statements that would help them find the bug. There was also some confusion with the way that the game handled commenting out source code, as players did not realize that a persisting error meant the bug was **not** commented out. A frequently requested change to the game was the idea of a 'hint' system that would provide better feedback to players who become frustrated or fail to complete levels.

RECALL – WHAT?

What can **print statements** be used for in debugging?

a. **Outputting the value of a particular variable**
b. Indicating the code that is not run during execution
c. Printing a fixed version of buggy code
d. Separating buggy code from bug-free code using text

UNDERSTANDING – WHEN?

Suppose you are debugging code where you need to know the values of variables during run-time. Which methods are appropriate?

e. **Print statements or breakpoints**
f. Breakpoints or divide-and-conquer
g. Divide-and-conquer or print statements
h. Print statements, breakpoints or divide-and-conquer

APPLICATION – HOW?

In the code below, where is the best place for a breakpoint if you want to find out the array values during each iteration of the sort?

i. Line 5
j. Line 7
k. Line 9
1. **Line 11**

```
1.          //Sorts a list of numbers
2.   //Input : List of numbers
3.   //Output : Sorted list
4.
5.   void BubbleSort (int array[],int
     size)
6.   {
7.       int i = 0;
8.       int temp;
9.       bool swapped = true;
10.      while(swapped){
11.          swapped = false;
12.          while(i<size-1){
13.              if(array[i]<array[i+1]){
14.                  temp = array[i];
15.                  array[i] = array[i+1];
16.                  array[i+1] = temp;
17.                  swapped = true;
18.              }
19.              i++;
20.          }
21.      }
22. }
```

Figure 5: Sample Skill-Testing Questions

*Listed in this figure are three of the ten questions included in the skill test given to participants before and after gameplay. The test was divided into three categories of questions: **recall** about **what** the techniques were, **understanding when** to use each technique, and **application** of **how** to use debugging techniques.*

Positive Keyword	Average Change	Negative Keyword	Average Change
Interested	-0.64	Anxious	-0.21
Enthusiastic	-0.64	Nervous	-0.14
Alert	-0.50	Guilty	-0.07
Excited	-0.36	Stressed	-0.07
Determined	-0.36	Depressed	-0.07
Attentive	-0.36	Scared	0.00
Proud	-0.14	Distressed	0.07
Inspired	-0.14	Hostile	0.07
Happy	-0.07	Jittery	0.29
Confident	0.00	Afraid	0.29
Active	0.07	Irritable	0.36
Strong	0.14	Upset	0.43
		Ashamed	0.43

Figure 6: Positive-Negative Affect Scores

*This graph shows the average change of affect for all participants based on each question on the PANAS. Positive scores indicate that participants associated **more** with that emotion after playing RoboBUG, and negative scores indicate that players associate **less** with that emotion after playing RoboBUG.*

4.3 Evaluating Learning and Enjoyment

To further evaluate the current version of RoboBUG, we conducted a second user study to address the following research questions:

- *Does RoboBUG improve a student's understanding of debugging techniques (i.e., achieve learning outcomes)?*
- *Do students enjoy playing the RoboBUG game?*

Our evaluation again involved the participation of first year Computer Science students at UOIT between the ages of 18 and 25, with mixed demographics, gender, and race.

In this study we evaluated the game's ability to help students achieve learning outcomes as well as the user experience. This study involved a larger sample size than the accessibility study (14 students) and took approximately 1 hour to complete. Participants in this study first completed the Positive and Negative Affect Scale (PANAS) [22], which assesses the user's feelings (see Figure 4). The PANAS scale in our study contained 12 positive words and 13 negative words. After completing PANAS, participants completed a debugging skills pre-test. This pre-test included ten multiple choice questions about the four debugging techniques used in the game (see Section 2.1). These questions tested participant abilities to recall, understand, and apply the debugging techniques. The first four questions tested knowledge about the usage of each debugging technique. The next four questions tested understand of when the techniques should be used. Finally, the last two questions involved the application of the techniques themselves. Examples of these questions can be observed in Figure 5. Once the pre-test was complete, participants played the RoboBUG game for approximately 30 minutes. After the game, participants completed the debugging skills test and the PANAS questionnaire again.

The results of both the pre- and post-game PANAS data and skill test data were analyzed to identify any changes in positive and

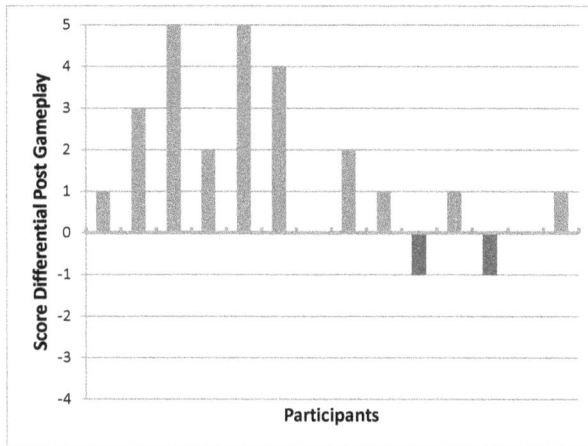

Figure 7: Change in Skill Test Scores by Participant after playing RoboBUG

Each bar represents a single participant's score differential on the Skill Test after playing RoboBUG. The participants are ordered from left to right based on increasing initial Skill Test scores (before playing RoboBUG). An interesting observation is that the largest positive score differentials were achieved by students with the lowest initial Skill Test scores.

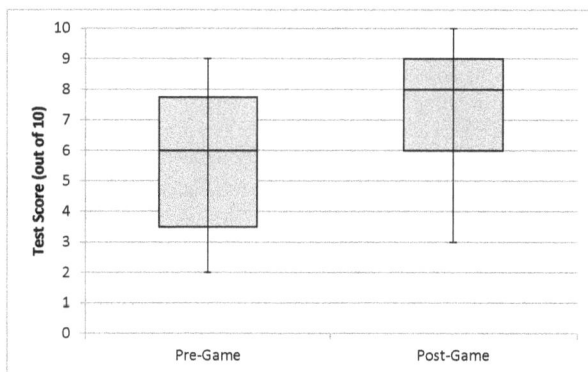

Figure 8: Box plot of the Skill Test Scores before and after playing RoboBUG

negative effect as well as debugging skills. The analysis was conducted using a paired t-test (see Figure 9). Our results indicate that RoboBUG helps students to achieve the debugging learning outcomes (see Figure 7 and Figure 8). Players became familiar with the nature of the debugging techniques, and were able to practice debugging and solve problems in a satisfying manner. In addition, the largest improvements in test scores were observed for participants with low initial test scores, suggesting that the game is most helpful for participants who are in the greatest need of assistance. Unfortunately, there was a non-statistically significant decrease in positive affect and a non-statistically significant increase in negative affect, indicating that the game still led to some user frustrations. It is possible that the game remains less frustrating than real debugging tasks, but our observations of participants suggest that the lack of

Paired-samples t-test				
	Mean	Std. Dev.	t(13)	p value
Test Scores			3.0970	0.0085
Pre-Game	5.71	2.46		
Post-Game	7.36	2.10		
Positive Affect			2.1272	0.0531
Pre-Game	45.93	5.40		
Post-Game	42.93	8.92		
Negative Affect			0.7555	0.4634
Pre-Game	18.86	5.67		
Post-Game	20.21	10.64		

Figure 9: Paired-samples t-test

There was a significant increase in debugging test scores after the game was played. No significant changes in positive or negative affect scores were observed.

a hint system and the difficulty of the tasks were major challenges. Ultimately, our game still requires participants to debug code and completely removing frustration related to debugging remains an open problem.

5 SUMMARY & CONCLUSIONS

We have presented the RoboBUG game as a serious game solution to the challenge of learning debugging in first year Computer Science courses. RoboBUG was evaluated for playability, learning benefits and enjoyment. Our evaluation of RoboBUG showed that the game helps students to achieve learning outcomes, but has a non-statistically significant impact on enjoyment (positive and negative affect). In addition, the game seemed to be most effective at aiding students who were not initially skilled at debugging. The RoboBUG game and source code are available online at https://github.com/sqrlab/robobug.

The short length of the game, chosen to fit within the experiment time frame, meant that we had to limit the amount of content we could include. It is possible that different effects on learning benefits and enjoyment might be observed with an extended play session, or with added new content. RoboBUG is designed to make the addition of levels accessible for instructors, but introducing new game mechanics requires further work from the game developers.

Since the completion of our study, we have continued to improve RoboBUG by updating the interface design elements, implementing a hint system to reduce frustration and enhancing the ability to extend RoboBUG with new levels. In addition, we have also developed a prequel game that will allow RoboBUG to be played by users who have limited programming experience [15]. Future areas of work include the addition of a points system for competitive play, adding a cooperative multi-player mode, and improving the replay-ability by using program mutation [2] to generate random bugs each time a level is played.

In addition to enhancing the RoboBUG game we are also focusing on additional evaluation. Specifically, we are in the process of conducting a longitudinal study of RoboBUG in a first year programming course at UOIT and believe this larger in-class study will complement the information from our controlled experiments.

6 ACKNOWLEDGMENTS

This research was partially funded by the Natural Sciences and Engineering Research Council of Canada (NSERC). We thank the reviewers for their thoughtful comments and suggestions.

REFERENCES

[1] Marzieh Ahmadzadeh, Dave Elliman, and Colin Higgins. 2005. An analysis of patterns of debugging among novice computer science students. In *Proc. of 10th SIGCSE Conf. on Innovation and Technology in Comp. Sci. Education (ITICSE '05)*. 84–88.
[2] James H Andrews, Lionel C Briand, and Yvan Labiche. 2005. Is mutation an appropriate tool for testing experiments?. In *Proc. of International Conference on Software Engineering 2005 (ICSE '05)*. 402–411.
[3] Elizabeth Carter and G.D. Blank. 2014. Debugging Tutor: preliminary evaluation. *J. of Computing Sciences in Colleges* (2014), 58–64.
[4] Mei-Wen Chen, Cheng-Chih Wu, and Yu-Tzu Lin. 2013. Novices' debugging behaviors in VB programming. In *Proc. of Learning and Teaching in Comp. and Eng. (LaTiCE 2013)*. 25–30.
[5] Du Chuntao. 2009. Empirical study on college students' debugging abilities in computer programming. In *Proc. of 1st Int. Conf. on Info. Sci. and Eng. (ICISE 2009)*. 3319–3322.
[6] Heather Desurvire, Martin Caplan, and Jozsef A. Toth. 2004. Using heuristics to evaluate the playability of games. In *Proc. of 2004 Conference on Human Factors in Computing Systems (CHI '04) - Extended Abstracts*. 1509–1512.
[7] Sue Fitzgerald, Renée McCauley, Brian Hanks, Laurie Murphy, Beth Simon, and Carol Zander. 2010. Debugging from the student perspective. *IEEE Trans. on Education* 53, 3 (2010), 390–396.
[8] R. Garris, R. Ahlers, and J. E. Driskell. 2002. Games, motivation, and learning: a research and practice model. *Simulation & Gaming* 33, 4 (2002), 441–467.
[9] Morgan Hall, Keri Laughter, and Jessica Brown. 2012. An empirical study of programming bugs in CS1, CS2, and CS3 homework submissions. *J. of Comp. Sci. in Colleges* 28, 2 (2012), 87–94.
[10] Roslina Ibrahim, Rasimah CM Yusoff, Hasiah M Omar, and Azizah. Jaafar. 2010. Students perceptions of using educational games to learn introductory programming. *Comp. and Info. Sci.* 4, 1 (2010), 205–216.
[11] Cagin Kazimoglu, Mary Kiernan, Liz Bacon, and Lachlan Mackinnon. 2012. A serious game for developing computational thinking and learning introductory computer programming. *Procedia - Social and Behavioral Sciences* 47 (2012), 1991–1999.
[12] Fengfeng Ke. 2009. A qualitative meta-analysis of computer games as learning tools. *Handbook of Research on Effective Electronic Gaming in Education* (2009).
[13] Michael J Lee and Andrew J Ko. 2014. A demonstration of gidget, a debugging game for computing education. In *Visual Languages and Human-Centric Computing (VL/HCC), 2014 IEEE Symposium on*. IEEE, 211–212.
[14] Renee McCauley, Sue Fitzgerald, Gary Lewandowski, Laurie Murphy, Beth Simon, Lynda Thomas, and Carol Zander. 2008. Debugging: a review of the literature from an educational perspective. *Computer Science Education* 18, 2 (2008), 67–92.
[15] Michael A Miljanovic and Jeremy S Bradbury. 2016. Robot ON!: a serious game for improving programming comprehension. In *Proc. of the 5th International Workshop on Games and Software Engineering*. ACM, 33–36.
[16] Mathieu Muratet, Patrice Torguet, Jean-Pierre Jessel, and Fabienne Viallet. 2009. Towards a serious game to help students learn computer programming. *Int. J. of Comp. Games Tech.*, 1–12.
[17] Jackie O'Kelly and J. Paul Gibson. 2006. RoboCode & problem-based learning : A non-prescriptive approach to teaching programming. In *Proc. of 11th SIGCSE Conf. on Innovation and Technology in Comp. Sci. Education (ITICSE '06)*. 217–221.
[18] Valerie J Shute. 2011. Stealth assessment in computer-based games to support learning. In *Computer Games and Instruction*, Vol. 55. 503–524.
[19] A.C. Siang. 2003. Theories of learning: a computer game perspective. In *Proc. of 5th Int. Symp. on Multimedia Soft. Eng. (ISMSE 2003)*. 239–245.
[20] Beth Simon, Sue Fitzgerald, Renée McCauley, Susan Haller, John Hamer, Brian Hanks, Michael T Helmick, Jan Erik Moström, Judy Sheard, and Lynda Thomas. 2007. Debugging assistance for novices. In *Working Group Reports on Innovation and Tech. in Comp. Sci. Education (ITiCSE-WGR '07)*. 137–151.
[21] Nikolai Tillmann and Judith Bishop. 2014. Code Hunt: searching for secret code for fun. In *Proc. of 7th Int. Work. on Search-Based Soft. Testing (SBST 2014)*. 23–26.
[22] David Watson, Lee a. Clark, and Auke Tellegen. 1988. Development and validation of brief measures of positive and negative affect: The PANAS scales. *J. of Personality and Social Psychology* 54, 6 (1988), 1063–1070.
[23] Wai-Tak Wong and Yu-Min Chou. 2007. An interactive Bomberman game-based teaching/learning tool for introductory C programming. In *Proc. of 2nd Int. Conf. on Edutainment*. 433–444.
[24] Andreas Zeller. 2009. *Why programs fail: a guide to systematic debugging*. Elsevier.

Students and Teachers Use An Online AP CS Principles EBook Differently

Teacher Behavior Consistent with Expert Learners

Miranda C. Parker
Georgia Institute of Technology
85 5th St NW
Atlanta, Georgia 30332
miranda.parker@gatech.edu

Kantwon Rogers
Georgia Institute of Technology
85 5th St NW
Atlanta, Georgia 30332
KantwonRogers@gatech.edu

Barbara J. Ericson
Georgia Institute of Technology
801 Atlantic Drive
Atlanta, Georgia 30332
ericson@cc.gatech.edu

Mark Guzdial
Georgia Institute of Technology
85 5th St NW
Atlanta, Georgia 30332
guzdial@cc.gatech.edu

ABSTRACT

Online education is an important tool for supporting the growing number of teachers and students in computer science. We created two eBooks containing interactive content for Advanced Placement Computer Science Principles, one targeted at teachers and one at students. By comparing the eBook usage patterns of these populations, including activity usage counts, transitions between activities, and pathways through the eBook, we develop a characterization of how student use of the eBook differs from teacher use. We offer design recommendations for how eBooks might be developed to target each of our populations. We ground our recommendations in a theory of teachers as expert learners who possess a greater ability to regulate their own learning process.

CCS CONCEPTS

•**Applied computing** → **E-learning;** *Interactive learning environments;*

KEYWORDS

eBook; CS Principles; log file analysis; expert learner

1 INTRODUCTION

Efforts to give every child an opportunity to learn computer science (CS) can not succeed without trained teachers. In response to this need, initiatives such as CS10K and Computing at School or communities like CS for All Teachers work to increase the number of teachers committed and equipped to teach CS. Additionally, greater understanding of how teachers learn CS is critical for growing the number of CS teachers, as this improved understanding may lead to developing learning opportunities that are catered to teacher learning styles. Through all of this, we recognize that there are time limitations for teacher availability. If we are going to provide professional development opportunities to all teachers, our primary challenge is to provide learning opportunities to in-service teachers so they can learn CS in their available time [1]. One strategy is to provide ebooks to teachers. Books are familiar to teachers and teachers can pace their way through books. EBooks can use interactive content to enhance learning and make it more efficient. As part of this strategy, we built an in-browser eBook for teachers learning how to teach the new Advanced Placement course: Computer Science Principles (AP CSP, or CS Principles) [9].

Our eBook for teachers learning AP CSP was designed using educational psychology principles and design-based research [9, 10]. Our approach is focused on providing worked examples interleaved with practice problems. Interactive elements in the eBook include multiple choice problems, fill in the blank questions, audio, videos, editable and executable code widgets, step-by-step code visualizations, and Parsons problems. It is different from a MOOC and strives to promote more learning and engagement than most MOOCS which are usually centered on video lectures and passive learning [9]. Our eBook is designed for teachers. It contains sections describing pedagogical content knowledge, which is how to teach computer science concepts and misconceptions, near relevant sections of content. We aim to provide the knowledge that CS teachers need, in an efficient and effective manner. We previously reported on a pilot study of teachers using the eBook and a larger study, including insights as to how the teachers were using this resource [7, 8, 10].

As part of building the number of teachers in K-12 CS, we wanted to ensure teachers had companion material to their eBook for their students to use. Several teachers from previous studies used their teacher eBook with their high school students during the pilot AP CSP class and intended to use it again the following year. In response to these needs, we developed and released a student version of the eBook that parallels the teacher version. The two eBooks have the same content, but the student version removes end-of-chapter exam answers and pedagogical content knowledge notes.

Figure 1: Qualities of a expert learner from Ertmer & Newby

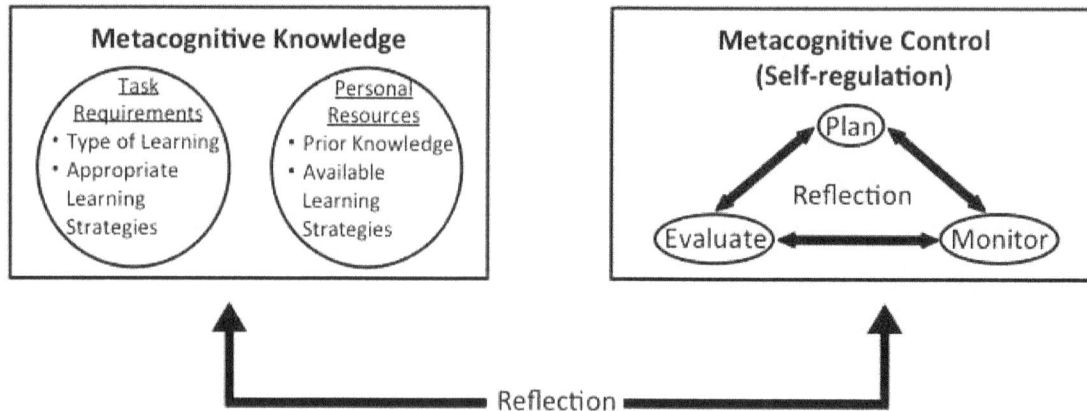

This process is similar to how teacher-student companion textbooks or study books are made. We hypothesized that the students and teachers would use the eBooks differently based on their goals and motivations to learn. We proposed a set of research questions to compare teachers and students using similar eBooks: *How does teacher use of the eBooks differ from student use? In what ways do they learn from the eBook differently?*

We answer these questions quantitatively with log file data from use of the student and teacher eBooks. This usage data focuses on use per activity type, attempts per problem, and progression through the book (both in terms of pages and time). Our data analysis is contextualized by interviews with teachers who use the eBooks. We use a theory of expert learners to frame our analysis and describe CS teachers' behavior using the eBook. This lens leads us to present design guidelines for teacher-student companion eBooks.

In the rest of this paper, we discuss background research on expert learners, detail our data collection and analysis, and present and discuss our findings and their implications for teacher and student eBook design in a computing context.

2 EXPERT LEARNERS

We viewed the teacher usage data through an expert learner lens [2–4, 6, 11, 18]. Expert learners are learners metacognitively aware of their process of learning. As Ertmer and Newby describes, they are strategic, self-regulated, and reflective [11]. We refer to less-expert learners (learners who are less strategic, self-regulated, and/or reflective) as novice learners in this paper. It is important to note that the difference between expert and novice learners is not just a quantitative difference in the content knowledge each has, but also a qualitative difference in strategies and approaches [11]. As Figure 1 describes, expert learners are defined by metacognitive knowledge and control. Metacognitive knowledge refers to not merely the learner's prior content knowledge, but their knowledge of learning strategies and how and when to apply them. Metacognitive control refers to the learner's ability to self-regulate through a cycle of planning, monitoring, and evaluating, all guided by the use of reflection throughout the process.

Within metacognitive knowledge, expert and novice learners apply a wide range of learning strategies. Zimmerman and Pons outline 15 strategies, including organizing, keeping records, environment setting, memorizing, and reviewing records [19]. In the context of the eBooks, learning strategies refer to the different activity types and the pattern in which they are used. The activities fall into categories of expository, worked examples, and practice problems. Patterns of activity use includes what activities are used the most, transition between activity types, and jumps between different parts of the eBook.

Metacognitive control includes reflection on plans, monitor, and evaluation of learning. Schraw presents a regulatory checklist within these three categories, which we summarize here [16]. Planning is when the learner cognates on the nature of the task at hand and their goal in learning the task. An expert learner also exhibits planning when they consider the time and resources they need to reach their goal. Expert learners monitor their learning by reflecting on their understanding of what they are doing and how it does or does not agree with their plan. Monitoring can also include asking if changes should be made to their plan or to their current actions. Finally, evaluating learning involves checking if the learner has reached their goal. An expert learner may ask themselves what worked, didn't work, and what they would do differently if they did it again.

When looking for explanations for the differences between teacher and student behavior, we found it productive to *explain teacher behavior in terms of expert learner behavior, and explain student behavior in terms of novice learner behavior.* We found that teachers usage behaviors mapped well to expert learning strategies described in research literature. Characterizing teacher and students in this way leads to design recommendations for intentional eBook designs that target each audience.

It is important to make a distinction between expert learner and expert teacher [17]. In our case, the teachers are learners and so we are discussing their expertise on learning, not their expertise on teaching.

3 METHODOLOGY

We performed a log file analysis on unique user profiles from 445 teachers and 516 students in the teacher and student eBooks respectively. Teachers and students were recruited to use the eBook through word-of-mouth. We advertised the eBook through email lists, blogs, workshops, and at conferences. When we released the student version, we encouraged the teachers to use the student version in their classes. According to IP addresses recorded in our system, the participants primarily came from the United States, but other countries from across the globe were also present in our user set.

We first looked at measures of use, like time spent on activities and number of times an activity was used. The differences in use led us to explore theoretical explanations. We came upon the expert learner hypothesis, defined hypotheses about strategies that experts might use in the ebook, and then did more log file analyses in order to test our hypotheses.

We ran Wilcoxon-Mann-Whitney tests on activity usage data to determine statistically significant difference in activity use among students and teachers. We grouped activities by the interaction types we included in the design of the eBooks: expository, worked examples, and practice. The activities were sorted accordingly:

- Expository
  - Text
  - Video
- Worked Examples
  - Code visualization
  - Audio
  - Code editing and running
- Practice
  - Multiple choice
  - Fill in the blank
  - Parsons Problem

This grouping based on interactivity allowed for clearer perception of differences in use of interactive elements.

We used Markov chain analysis on the log files to help illuminate patterns in students and teachers use of the eBooks [12]. Markov analysis refers to transition between states. In our analysis, we calculate the probability of a user transitioning from one activity to another. This probability analysis allowed for comparison in behavior in using the eBook features between students and teachers. These lead to further analysis based on perceived differences among the probabilities of transitions. For example, the difference in probabilities of a teacher transitioning from running active code to editing active code, and vice versa, compared to a student's transitioning between those activities leads to a deeper analysis in use of the active code function.

To further characterize the user behaviors, we generated progression charts based on each users activities. For each user, we created a graphic to represent each activity they did in each chapter, what kind of activity, and at what time relative to when they started to use the eBook. These charts helped us identify and categorize user use of the eBook on an individual- and large-scale. After generating progression charts for all students and teachers, we eliminated progression charts that had fewer than three days of activity and less than five chapters with activities. Two researchers

rated users in categories based on patterns of use visible in the charts. There were five categories for students and teachers, totaling ten categories. These categories included whether a user repeated whole sections of the book, went back and reviewed sections, skipped chapters, completed chapters in large amounts in short times (binged), and if they skimmed chapters by doing some but not all activities within. We computed inter-rater reliability on our ratings in each category using a quadratic weighted Cohen's kappa. The kappa value was greater than 0.8 for eight out of ten of the categories, and the remaining two were in the 0.61 to 0.8 range. After confirming reliability of our ratings, we calculated the average of each category for students and teachers and compared them between the two groups. We selected two progression charts from each group (students and teachers) seen in Figure 2 to provide specific cases of what the differences looked like on an individual level. We acknowledge these charts are not representative samples of each group, but rather serve as a case study of use.

We contextualize our findings through interviews we did with two teachers who use the eBook. These two teachers were interviewed because they were using the student eBook in their classes, not because they learned from the teacher eBook. Thus, their comments help us understand student eBook behavior, e.g., we have greater insight into what the students were being required to do with the eBook. They are not representative of teachers learning computer science with the eBook. We identified teachers to interview based on their students' eBook activities and emailed those teachers with requests for interviews. Both of the teachers we interviewed had prior experience teaching computer science (10+ years).

It is important to note that in this analysis we are not controlling to prior exposure to computer science or computing experience. The differences that we describe between the teachers and students may be due to a difference in their knowledge of the subject area. Since our analysis based on log files, we cannot presume intentionality. However, we expect that teachers or students with significant prior content knowledge would be unlikely to interact with the eBook to the extent that we see in our analyses. Teachers or students with significant prior content knowledge may be using our eBook less, or not at all. In any case, we do not have data on prior computing experience and cannot control for it in these analyses.

4 FINDINGS

We first establish that teachers and students do use the eBooks differently by statisically analyzing their interactions with the eBooks. We then present hypotheses of what an expert learner using the eBook would do, and what their use would look like in our data. We tested these hypotheses and present support for our teacher as expert learner hypothesis.

4.1 Differences in Usage Patterns

We gathered data from the log file analysis and processed it by counting the number of interactions within each activity type. For example, if a user ran the same code segment five times, that would count as five interactions with a code segment. We ran a Wilcoxon rank sum test to determine if there were differences in activity

Table 1: Wilcoxon Rank Sum Test on Activities by Interaction Type

Type	W	Sig.	Mean S	Mean T
Expository	254,934	0.000*	87.83	22.83
Worked Examples	249,124	0.000*	188.90	44.10
Practice	260,664	0.000*	153.87	20.30

levels, grouped by interaction types, between the students and teachers, as seen in Table 1.

For all interaction types, activity level was significantly higher for students rather than teachers. That is to say, students did more expository, worked example, and practice activities, on average. This supports the general claim that the students and teachers used their eBooks differently. This finding initiated our further analysis into *how* the students and teachers used the eBooks differently.

In addition to this, our initial analysis of the Markov chain data indicated distinct difference in behaviors. The transition probabilities are shown in part in Tables 2 and 3. From the tables, we know that teachers are more likely to run and then edit a code segment, or sequentially edit it, than students were. We also know that students are more likely to run a code segment and then immediately run it again. This is discussed in more detail in Section 4.3.

Progression charts (which are described in detail in Section 3) support our argument that teachers and students use the eBooks differently. We rigorously defined this difference by rating each valid chart in five categories: review, repeat, skim, skip, and binge. We performed inter-rater reliability using Cohen's kappa on each of the five categories for students and teachers. We found that on average, teachers binged their use of the eBook more than students, which is to say they completed more activities in one sitting on average. Additionally, students skimmed more than teachers, implying teachers did more activities in each chapter where students would only do some activities.

These points were in agreement with what we found during our interviews with teachers. Teachers noted they would look at the teacher eBook to see what was in it and how it might fit with their curriculum. They described "spot checking" the eBook and doing some activities throughout the chapters to see what was there. Meanwhile, the teachers would assign sections or problems from the student eBook for their students to complete. These teachers would use their eBook in one manner, and ask the students to use their eBook a different way.

4.2 Expert Learner Hypothesis

When thinking of teachers using this book as expert learners and students as novice learners, we developed hypotheses of what an expert learner would do with our eBook. We then compared with our findings, discussed in Section 4.3. As discussed in Section 2, we expect expert learners to demonstrate aspects of metacognitive control and knowledge.

4.2.1 Metacognitive knowledge: Available and appropriate learning strategies. Within metacognitive knowledge, we hypothesize

expert learners using the eBook would recognize the different learning strategies (i.e., the ebook activities) available to them, as well as how to best make use of those strategies. For example, we would expect an expert learner to try every activity type. Additionally, we would expect expert learner users to use the different activity types at different times to best make use of them.

4.2.2 Metacognitive control: Plan, monitor, and evaluate. Metacognitive control is the learner making choices about how they learn and what they do to learn. We would expect to see expert learners planning their learning, monitoring their understanding, and evaluating their learning.

An expert learner plans learning activities so that she learns. For example, an expert learner spaces learning activities rather than crams. Planning also involves setting their goal (learning AP CS Principles), taking sequential steps towards their goal (reading/doing one chapter at a time), and identifying any obstacles to achieving their goal (not understanding portions of the curriculum). They recognize the task demands, their personal resources (namely, time), and use their resources efficiently to meet demands. Given the nature of quantitative data as opposed to the internal nature of planning, we are only able to make shallow claims on whether the teachers are planning, and no claims on how they might be planning. This can only be rigorously addressed through detailed interviews with teachers and students that include questions specifically asking about their planning process.

Additionally, expert learners monitor their learning, which involves looking at their plan and decided how to take the next step. In the context of the eBook, this would involve going back to review a concept when the user reads a chapter that builds on that chapter.

Evaluating learning involves assessing the way the expert learner is learning and whether or not they are meeting their goals. We hypothesize an expert learner using the eBook would go back periodically to test their understanding and making changes to their learning strategies if their previous plan had not met their goals.

4.3 Hypothesis Testing

We tested our expert learner hypothesis and present our findings here. We break our findings down into metacognitive knowledge and metacognitive control, with further distinctions as previously discussed in Section 2. Expert learners are characterized by metacognitive knowledge, which is their knowledge of what learning strategies are available to them and how to apply those strategies. They can also be characterized by their metacognitive control, or their ability to cyclically monitor, plan, and evaluate their learning through constant reflection. We present supports for each of these parts in turn.

4.3.1 Available Learning Strategies. We know that students did significantly more activities from Table 1, but that only shows counts of each individual activity. After reviewing the progression charts, we noted that students may be doing *more* in the eBook in terms of activity use, but teachers were spreading their activity across different activity types. We provide charts to illustrate these claims.

Figure 2 shows two teachers' progression charts on the top row, and two student progression charts on the bottom row. The charts

Table 2: Probabilities of transition between and among activities in the student eBook

	Code Edit	Code Run
Code Edit	0.171	0.755
Code Run	0.222	0.475

Table 3: Probabilities of transition between and among activities in the teacher eBook

	Code Edit	Code Run
Code Edit	0.249	0.707
Code Run	0.322	0.407

contain colored dots in reference to the activities each user completed on an individualized time line. The X-axis is divided by chapters, and contains all activities across all chapters. The Y-axis is the time, in days, since the user started using the eBook to their last activity. Through these charts we can see how a user navigated through the eBook, what activities they focused on, and what their pacing through the eBook was.

The teacher progression charts have four distinct colors, identifying four distinct activity types that teachers primarily participated in (code runs and edits, Parsons, and multiple choice). For students, the bottom of Figure 2 paints a different picture. These charts are dominated by two colors, and thus indicate two different activity types that students focused on (code run and multiple choice). We can see the difference in usage between students and teachers, as teachers made use of more activities while learning CSP in the eBook. This observation is consistent with a claim of greater metacognitive knowledge as more use of different activity types indicates awareness of the different learning strategies available to the user.

4.3.2 Appropriate Learning Strategies. Teachers used the learning activities differently than the students (see Tables 2 and 3). Specifically analyzing the code edits and code runs, we can see in Table 2 that students are more likely to run a code segment and then immediately run it again (0.475 compared to 0.407). However, Table 3 shows that teachers are more likely to run and then edit a code segment, or edit and then edit it again (0.322 compared to 0.222, or 0.249 compared to 0.171). This pattern suggests teachers are exploring code, using the code editing and running area as a learning activity. Simply repeatedly running the code is unlikely to lead to any learning insights for the students. They are simply re-running the same, unedited code. We do not see evidence that the students are developing hypotheses about their code, then editing the code and re-running to test the hypotheses.

4.3.3 Plan: Not evident in quantitative data. We do not have evidence to make a claim that teachers, as expert learners, were planning their use of the eBook. We can begin to make an argument for teachers using spaced practice, an expert learner approach. A progression chart in Figure 2 supports a claim that teachers space

their use of the eBook. This user sequentially uses the eBook, jumping back occasionally to re-visit previously completed activities. The user also spends three days (Day 18-20) repeating the same set of activities before continuing to the next chapter. These two aspects of the user's behavior in the eBook demonstrate a spaced practice approach to their learning. We do not know if that is a planned, intentional process, or simply when the teacher had time to use the eBook.

However, spaced practice is not unique to the teacher progression charts. The student progression charts also show a nice pacing of the eBook–one chapter at a time and spaced in time. However, we hypothesize this is more due to the course structure and teacher directions than the student's choice, considering this general pattern is seen across nearly all student users. This is in agreement with our interviews, where we found that teachers were assigning problems and chapters to their students on a weekly basis.

We need significant qualitative data before we can claim that teachers plan their learning when using the eBook. Interview or survey data could reveal whether or not teachers are goal-setting, identifying obstacles, recognizing task demands, or considering personal resources.

4.3.4 Monitor: Retrieval practices in progression charts. In comparing the student and teacher progression charts in Figure 2, we can construct an understanding of the way teachers monitor their learning. We found in our analysis of the progression charts that students repeated more than teachers. Students would more often repeat nearly all problems in a given chapter previously completed on another day. Teachers did this some, but on average less than the students. The progression charts discussed here display these characteristics. In both teacher progression charts, there are jumps back to previously visited sections of the eBook. These jumps are typically followed by a few activities, and then the users go back to where they were in the book before. The student progression charts also include jump-backs, but student jump-backs precede heavy activity use. Students are completely repeating all activities in a certain section, where teachers will choose a handful of activities. These actions demonstrate a difference in how the users are monitoring learning. Teachers may recognize when they do not understand or remember something, re-visit a problem to retrieve their prior knowledge on the topic, and then return to their place in the book. However, students may recognize when they do not understand a previously covered topic, but they fully repeat the entire chapter that contains the topic, thereby completing a less-effective method of reviewing through repeated activity use. An alternative explanation for the usage data is that teachers may be assigning students to review chapters so the students' behavior may not be indicative of their self-regulation.

4.3.5 Evaluate: Knowing when to quit on Parsons problems. Teachers evaluate their learning, which is shown through their behaviors with Parsons problems. Figures 3 and 4 show the number of times students and teachers attempted Parsons problems before getting it correct or giving up, i.e. they never submit the correct solution. The graphs can be read as the number of users that gave X number of attempts on Parsons problems, and then either answered correctly or gave up. It is clear from these graphs that teachers make less attempts before getting it correct and before giving up. Students,

Figure 2: Progression charts through the eBook for teachers (top row) and students (bottom row)

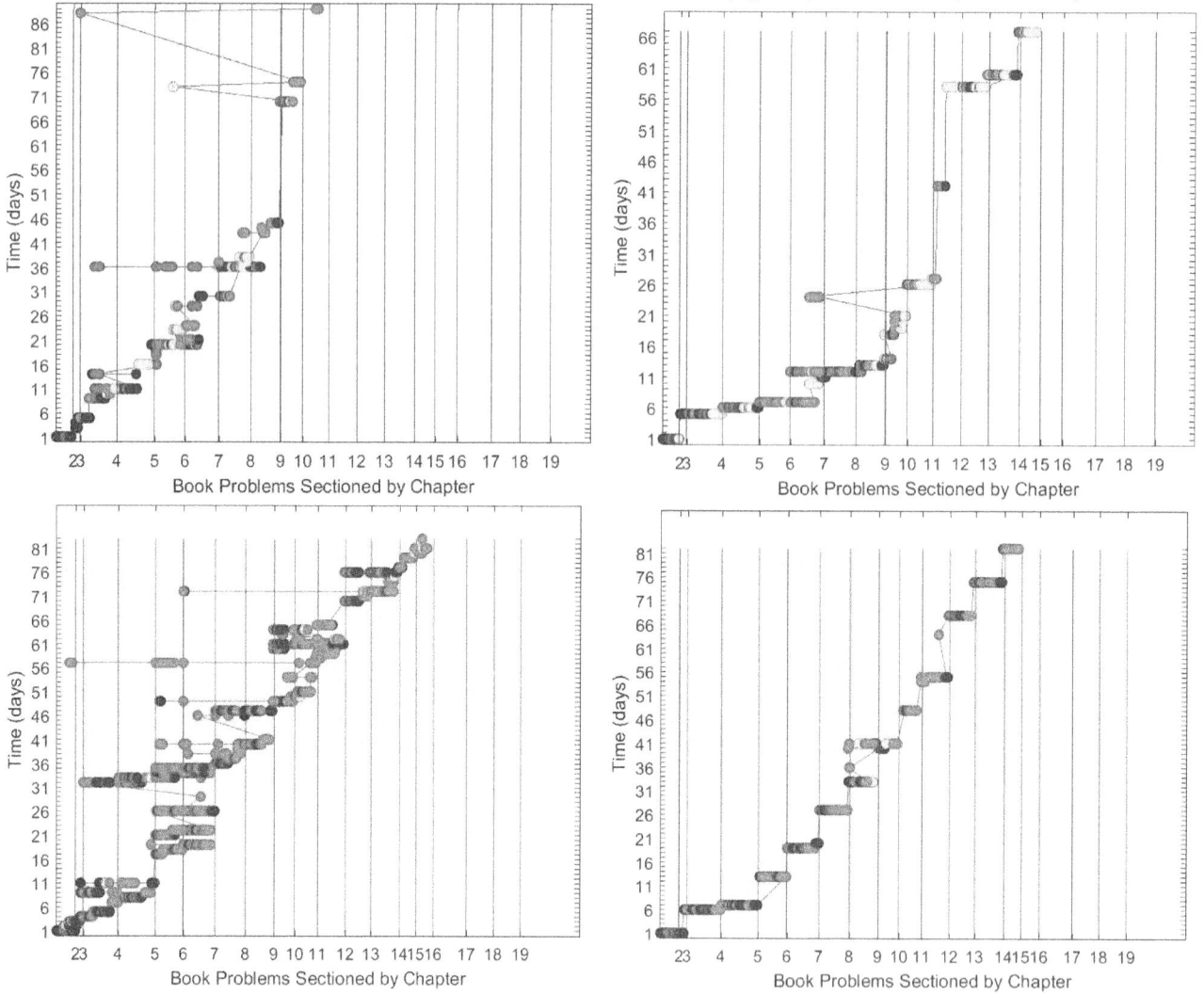

Figure 3: Teacher (left) vs. Student (right) On Number of Users Per Number of Attempts on All Parsons Problems Eventually Answered Correctly

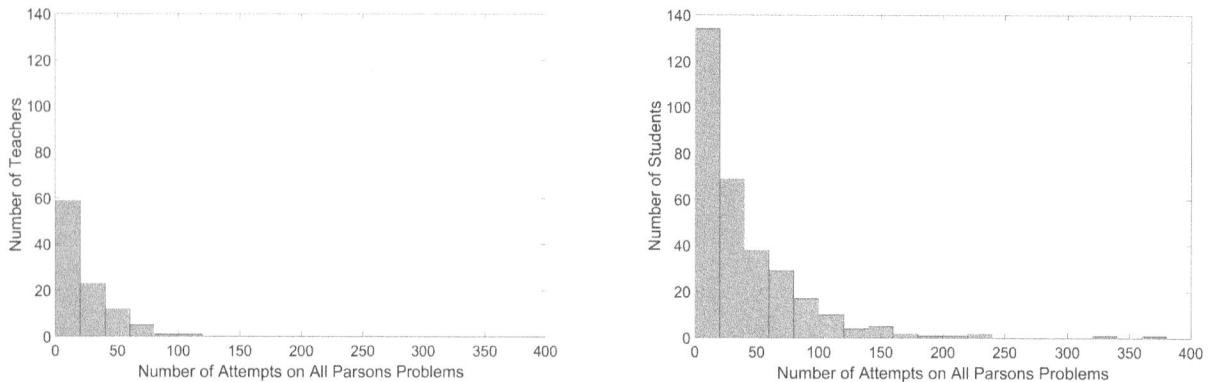

Figure 4: Teacher (left) vs. Student (right) On Number of Users Per Number of Attempts on All Parsons Problems Quit On

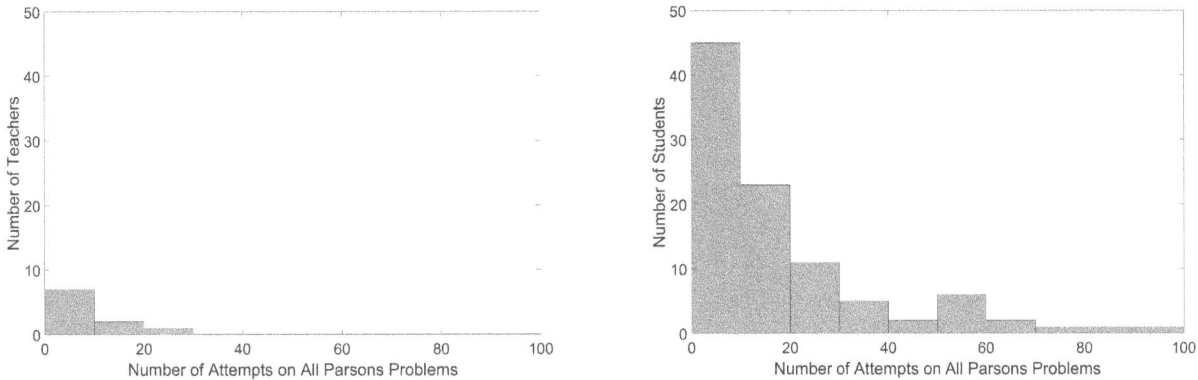

however, tend to try more times before reaching a correct answer or giving up. After further analysis, we discovered that students would even attempt a Parsons problem more times than there were permutations of answers. That is to say, students repeated distinct attempts multiple times, and occasionally still did not get the problem correct. This agrees with existing research on students getting stuck on Parsons problems and repeating the same incorrect permutation [13]. We hypothesize this pattern demonstrates that teachers were able to be cognizant of their attempts on the problem, and recognize when they were stuck. On the other hand, students tended to "flail" and try more attempts than possible, without evaluating their learning strategy.

5   DESIGN RECOMMENDATIONS

As demonstrated, students and teachers are different and need differentiated designs for eBooks. We know that having a design that is more beneficial for novices can be ineffective for expert learners through expertise reversal effect [14]. We present here design recommendations that are derived from explaining teachers' use as expert learners and students' use as novice learners.

We cannot design simply based on usage data. From this data, we can't know if users were frustrated and needed more support, or did exactly what they wanted to do. However, we can design based on our hypotheses about teachers attempting to use expert learner strategies and students using novice learner strategies. Our design recommendations aim to make the teachers more efficient as expert learners, and to help students develop better learning strategies.

5.1   Teacher eBook Recommendations

Our design recommendations for the teacher version of the eBook are presented in Table 4.2. Based on the aspects of expert learning presented previously, we developed recommendations on how to promote or enhance the presence of expert learner behaviors.

Teachers used multiple activity types. However, not all activity types that were available were used much, and some were rarely used. In case the issue is lack of awareness of the different features of the eBook, we could introduce all types of activities before the content of the book or in the context of the book, e.g. with tutorials throughout the introductory chapters.

We believe teachers monitor their learning through retrieval practices. Teachers tended to jump back to skim previously covered content. This practice could be aided by adding links to allow for quicker navigation between main topics.

Teachers' use of Parsons problems suggests that they might have been evaluating their learning and deciding what might be useful (and what might not be). Design recommendations regarding evaluation involve creating more assessments to gauge understanding. Alternatively, an adaptive assessment could be made that the user could navigate to at any time and would test their understanding of all topics the user had already covered.

We could not make a claim as to how teachers plan their learning. Further detailed interviews would better inform our understanding of this aspect of the teachers' expert learning. Until then, we refrain from making design recommendations based on this aspect of the expert learner hypothesis.

5.2   Student eBook Recommendations

We hypothesize that students are novice learners. As such, our design recommendations for the student eBook are different from the recommendations for the teacher eBook.

Students could be prompted to monitor their learning through guided or adaptive problems. Adaptive Parsons or code problems would prompt the students if an ineffective method was used, such as runs without any edits, or if there was a repeated run from a prior attempt. A guided problem would identify when a student tried more than half the possible solutions or submissions to a problem and prompt the student to move along or ask for help.

Evaluation of understanding and learning could take the form of unlocking chapters. Chapters could be presented as objects that are locked. The locked chapters could only be unlocked when the user demonstrates knowledge and understanding of the topics covered prior to that chapter.

Students could be encouraged to plan their learning through promoting spaced practice. This could take the form of incentivizing students to log in everyday to keep their "streak" of activity. Alternatively, we could schedule the system to send email or text reminders to students to log in to learn and practice their skills.

Table 4: Current Expert Learner Behavior and Teacher eBook Design Recommendations

Expert Learner Behavior	Current eBook Use	Evidence	Design Recommendation
Available Learning Strategies	Multiple activity types used	Figure 2	Make all learning strategies that are available clear
Appropriate Learning Strategies	Run and edit code rather than run and then run again	Tables 2, 3	None; "appropriate" may differ based on learning goals
Monitor	Retrieval practices	Figure 2	Quicker navigation between main topics and keywords through hyperlinks at each mention to its initial description
Evaluate	Know when to quit on Parsons problems	Figures 3, 4	Create more benchmarks for assessing understanding, or an adaptive benchmark that can be visited at any point in the book
Plan	Not present	Not present	None available

We are making recommendations that our hypotheses and evidence support, and as such do not have a recommendation as to whether to promote expert learning techniques within the student version of the eBook. Alternatively, there could be more added to the teacher book on how to teach expert learning skills [5]. There is a careful balancing act of how much scaffolding to put in the student eBook. If too much scaffolding is put in, it could get in the students' way or interfere with learning [15]. However, if too little scaffolding is added then you are presuming the user is an expert learner with metacognitive skills to guide them through the eBook.

6 CONCLUSIONS

Students interacted more with the eBook than teachers, on average. However, more interaction does not mean more learning. Rather, it might indicate more flailing, and less effective and efficient learning. We believe the interactions students had with the eBook are characteristic of a novice learner, unaware of how to best learn. This can be seen by their flailing tactics, massed practice, and erratic progression through the book. On the other hand, teachers interacted with the activities in the eBook statistically significantly less. We argue that the interactions they did have promote greater learning. They tended to space their practice, know when to quit, and go through the eBook in a reasonable manner.

We set out to discover how teachers use the eBooks differently than students, and in what ways they might learn differently. We used an expert learner lens to help understand those differences, which is how we frame this discussion. In establishing that students and teachers use the eBook differently, we used statistically significant results on activity use which showed students did more activities across expository, worked examples, and practice activities. It would be easy to look at those numbers and claim that students learned more, were more motivated to learn, or more engaged in their learning, because they did more. However, we hypothesize that students did more activities in ways that did not apply appropriate learning strategies. While teachers did fewer activities, they seemed to do activities using learning strategies and monitored those strategies to check on what was best for them.

Because we are using log files, we do not know the users' contexts of use. We cannot distinguish between different uses of the ebook, such as a teacher preparing lesson content versus learning concepts for herself, or a student studying for a test versus completing a homework assignment. Different contexts would likely lead to different patterns of use, e.g., a teacher would be expected to do fewer practice exercises when preparing a lesson, but more when learning for herself. We cannot make claims about how contexts drive use. However, we can claim that the patterns we see do cross contexts. We look at the behavior of each subgroup in the aggregate, regardless of any individual's goals in any particular situation of use. Future research should explore how teachers and students use ebooks differently in different contexts. What we offer here is an initial description, to provide guidance for developers aiming to support computing teachers or computing students. Our finding is that students and teachers use ebooks differently, whatever their contexts, and that should inform design. We believe these findings contribute to the emerging understanding and design of computing education through eBooks.

The difference in learner profiles between students and teachers suggest a need for eBook designs that cater to each learner. With teachers as expert learners, more activities could be provided that provide more benchmarks, connection between topics, and activity tutorials. Students as novice learners need more scaffolding in activities such as through guided or adaptive Parsons problems. The design could also encourage some form of spaced practice with review problems that connect to previous topics learned, perhaps at the beginning of a chapter.

ACKNOWLEDGMENTS

The work is supported by the National Science Foundation under Grant No.: 1432300 and the National Science Foundation Graduate Research Fellowshipnder Grant No. DGC-1148903. Any opinions, findings, and conclusions or recommendations expressed in this material are those of the authors and do not necessarily reflect the views of the National Science Foundation.

REFERENCES

[1] Klara Benda, Amy Bruckman, and Mark Guzdial. 2012. When Life and Learning Do Not Fit: Challenges of Workload and Communication in Introductory Computer Science Online. *Trans. Comput. Educ.* 12, 4, Article 15 (Nov. 2012), 38 pages. DOI : https://doi.org/10.1145/2382564.2382567

[2] David C Berliner. 1994. Expertise: The wonder of exemplary performances. *Creating powerful thinking in teachers and students* (1994), 161–186.

[3] Barry K Beyer. 1987. *Practical strategies for the teaching of thinking.* ERIC.

[4] Ann L Brown and Judy S DeLoache. 1978. Skills, plans, and self-regulation. *Children's thinking: What develops* (1978), 3–35.

[5] Deborah L Butler and Philip H Winne. 1995. Feedback and self-regulated learning: A theoretical synthesis. *Review of educational research* 65, 3 (1995), 245–281.

[6] Michelene TH Chi, Robert Glaser, and Marshall J Farr. 2014. *The nature of expertise.* Psychology Press.

[7] Barbara Ericson, Mark Guzdial, Briana Morrison, Miranda Parker, Matthew Moldavan, and Lekha Surasani. 2015. An eBook for teachers learning CS principles. *ACM Inroads* 6, 4 (2015), 84–86.

[8] Barbara Ericson, Steven Moore, Briana Morrison, and Mark Guzdial. 2015. Usability and usage of interactive features in an online ebook for CS teachers. In *Proceedings of the Workshop in Primary and Secondary Computing Education.* ACM, 111–120.

[9] Barbara J Ericson, Mark J Guzdial, and Briana B Morrison. 2015. Analysis of interactive features designed to enhance learning in an ebook. In *Proceedings of the eleventh annual International Conference on International Computing Education Research.* ACM, 169–178.

[10] Barbara J Ericson, Kantwon Rogers, Miranda Parker, Briana Morrison, and Mark Guzdial. 2016. Identifying Design Principles for CS Teacher Ebooks through Design-Based Research. In *Proceedings of the 2016 ACM Conference on International Computing Education Research.* ACM, 191–200.

[11] Peggy A Ertmer and Timothy J Newby. 1996. The expert learner: Strategic, self-regulated, and reflective. *Instructional science* 24, 1 (1996), 1–24.

[12] Mark Guzdial. 1993. *Deriving software usage patterns from log files.* Technical Report. Georgia Institute of Technology.

[13] Juha Helminen, Petri Ihantola, Ville Karavirta, and Lauri Malmi. 2012. How do students solve parsons programming problems?: an analysis of interaction traces. In *Proceedings of the ninth annual international conference on International computing education research.* ACM, 119–126.

[14] Slava Kalyuga, Paul Ayres, Paul Chandler, and John Sweller. 2003. The expertise reversal effect. *Educational psychologist* 38, 1 (2003), 23–31.

[15] Lauren Elizabeth Margulieux. 2016. *Using subgoal learning and self-explanation to improve programming education.* Ph.D. Dissertation. Georgia Institute of Technology.

[16] Gregory Schraw. 1998. Promoting general metacognitive awareness. *Instructional science* 26, 1 (1998), 113–125.

[17] H Lee Swanson, James E OfiConnor, and John B Cooney. 1990. An information processing analysis of expert and novice teachersfi problem solving. *American Educational Research Journal* 27, 3 (1990), 533–556.

[18] Claire E Weinstein and Gretchen van Mater Stone. 1993. Broadening our conception of general education: The self-regulated learner. *New directions for community colleges* 1993, 81 (1993), 31–39.

[19] Barry J Zimmerman and Manuel Martinez Pons. 1986. Development of a structured interview for assessing student use of self-regulated learning strategies. *American educational research journal* 23, 4 (1986), 614–628.

Describing Elementary Students' Interactions in K-5 Puzzle-based Computer Science Environments using the Collaborative Computing Observation Instrument (C-COI)

Maya Israel
University of Illinois-Urbana
Champaign
misrael@illinois.edu

Quentin M. Wherfel
University of Illinois-Urbana
Champaign
wherfel2@illinois.edu

Saadeddine Shehab
University of Illinois-Urbana
Champaign
shehab2@illinois.edu

Oliver Melvin
University of Illinois-Urbana
Champaign
omelvin2@illinois.edu

Todd Lash
University of Illinois-Urbana
Champaign
toddlash@illinois.edu

ABSTRACT

Despite efforts to integrate computer science (CS) into K-12 education, there are numerous unanswered questions about how students learn CS, how to provide positive computing experiences, and how students interact with each other during CS instruction. To begin to deconstruct these complexities for a diverse range of students, it is important to not only study the outcomes and products of students' computational experiences, but also the processes they take in creating those products. In recognizing the necessity for targeted, narrow research questions, this paper focused on how elementary students interacted with each other during puzzle-based CS instruction. Future work will focus on comparing these findings to students' collaborative interactions in more open-ended computing situations. Data analysis made use of the Collaborative Computing Observation Instrument (C-COI) [6] to analyze video screen captures of nine students as they engaged in CS activities within Code.org's Code Studio. Findings confirmed three predominant types of collaborative interactions: Collaborative problem solving, excitement and accomplishment related to CS activities, and general socialization.

CCS CONCEPTS

• **Social and professional topics** → **K-12 education**; • **Applied computing** → **Collaborative learning**;

KEYWORDS

K-12 Computer science education; collaborative computing; assessing computational behaviors; Collaborative Computing Observation Instrument (C-COI)

ICER'17, August 18-20 2017, Tacoma, WA, USA
© 2017 Association for Computing Machinery.
ACM ISBN 978-1-4503-4968-0/17/08...$15.00
https://doi.org/10.1145/3105726.3106167

1 INTRODUCTION

There is a growing body of literature regarding the importance and benefits of teaching computer science (CS) and computational thinking (CT) in K-12 settings to a broad range of learners. In fact, the newly reauthorized Every Student Succeeds Act, in its definition of a well-rounded education, includes CS alongside other subjects such as writing, mathematics, and science. This legislative mandate occurred at the same time as school districts such as Chicago Public Schools, New York City Schools, and San Francisco Unified School District are rapidly increasing the CS opportunities offered to students from early elementary school through high school.

Although computing at the elementary grades is not a new concept [e.g. 19], there is an increased focus on providing early CS experiences to both provide unique instructional opportunities and increase the diversity of the CS field [1, 16], students with disabilities, students from lower socioeconomic households, and students from culturally and linguistically diverse backgrounds in CS [17]. Leveraging research in science education that points to the importance of early and sustained exposure [2], the focus of this study is on CS instruction in elementary school.

Several options for computing software exist that can be used to teach CS to young learners at the elementary and middle school grades. These typically utilize visually intuitive block-based programming languages and fall into one of two broad categories: (a) Sequential, linear tutorial-focused experiences, and (b) open exploration experiences. Within the sequential experiences, examples include Code.org's Code Studio (https://studio.code.org/). These offer increasingly complex coding challenges, games, and maze completions [11]. Open-ended platforms such as Scratch (https://scratch.mit.edu/) provide a virtual playground where students explore computing concepts and practices in a more open-ended fashion [21].

1.1 Uncertainty in Ill-Defined CS Tasks

When evaluating students' interactions within computing environments, it is helpful to consider them along a continuum of experiences including scenarios where the students are familiar with the task and have the necessary strategies to successfully address the task as well as situations where the students are uncertain about how to address a computing challenge or problem. Within computing instruction, students often experience uncertainty, wherein they do not know how to solve a problem that they face. Jordan and McDaniel (2014) defined uncertainty as an "individual's subjective experience of doubting, being unsure, or wondering about how the future will unfold, what the present means, or how to interpret the past" (p. 492) and stated that these times of uncertainty can facilitate social interactions among the students as they attempt to unpack or solve the problem [7].

When observing students during computing experiences, it quickly becomes apparent that students often experience uncertainty. It is, therefore, important to consider how students navigate uncertainty, how they interact with each other, and the outcomes that occur as a result of the students' problem solving.

1.2 Collaborative Computing

Several models of collaborative computing exist from student-driven to teacher-facilitated. Student-driven collaborations often occur because programming environments for novices typically encourage young learners to create computational artifacts that they and their peers will value [4]. These environments rely on social processes in which students are encouraged to share their work with peers both during the creation process and once they have products that they have completed. More generally and within CS education, collaboration, in fact, has been studied in the context of helping students increase persistence and engage in productive struggle [3, 18, 24]. Because students often naturally share successes and seek each other during problem solving, these types of collaborations occur without facilitation by teachers. There are also models of teacher-facilitated collaborations including peer tutoring [5] and pair programming [13].

Despite the social aspects of these programming environments, we have yet to fully understand the types of collaboration that exist between learners and the benefits that students gain through these collaborative computing experiences [4]. In fact, Good (2011) stated that the current computing environments are ideal "playgrounds for studying collaboration in the wild" (p. 21). We should, thus, begin to examine how to leverage collaboration to support student learning within K-12 CS activities.

1.3 Theoretical underpinnings of dialogicality

The focus of this study is on naturally-occurring conversations that students engage in while working on computing activities. The emphasis on naturally-occurring discourse has theoretical underpinnings within dialogicality, which posits that conversations between partners result in joint problem solving spaces that contribute to group cognition; thus, learning often occurs through social interactions [9], this perspective is important when considering technology-mediated discourse that occurs as students discuss their computing experiences. Stahl and colleagues (2014) explained that collaborative discourse in computer supported collaborative learning (CSCL) contexts constitutes new forms of discussion and provides innovative ways of exploring that discourse [22].

1.4 Purpose of this Study

To understand the computing interactions that students engage in during CS instruction, it is important to examine both puzzle-based and open inquiry CS approaches. It is also important to examine both naturally-occurring and teacher-facilitated interactions. However, it is imperative to not confound these different approaches. Therefore, this study focuses on naturally-occurring student collaborations within puzzle-based environments with the intent of examining the various interactive behaviors students exhibit while engaged in such activities. Future studies will focus on examining other environments as well. In this way, we can have a focused research question that will lead to increased understanding in future studies. Our research question was: What kinds of collaborative interactions occur during puzzle-based computing environments?

2 METHOD

This qualitative study made use of the Collaborative Computing Observation Instrument (C-COI) [6], a validated observation instrument for evaluating students' individual and collaborative interactions within computer-mediated learning, to code data from nine students in third and fourth grades across multiple observations within Code Studio Play Lab.

2.1 Participants

This study took place in one Midwestern elementary school that included computing and computational thinking as part of its K-5 curriculum. The classrooms of two teachers (3rd and 4th grades) were purposefully selected to participate in this study based on the level of academic and demographic diversity in those classes as well as the integration of computing into their classes. Both teachers were in their 3rd year of implementing computing instruction in their classrooms and during the current study, they scheduled 45-minute computing sessions at least once per week. During these computing times, students typically worked through computing activities in Code.org Code Studio or on unplugged activities that taught computational concepts in hands-on non-computing activities.

The research team created a matrix that included the following information for each student whose parents provided informed consent: Gender, socioeconomic status, disability status, students' level of computing expertise, and students' level of collaboration during classroom instruction. Based on this matrix, nine students were purposefully selected to attain a diverse sample (see Table 1). The research team classified socioeconomic status based on whether the students received free or reduced lunch. Disability status was coded based on whether the students received special education services and had an individualized education program (IEP). Lastly, the teachers provided information about students' level of computing ability as well as whether they generally collaborated with their peers. Because these variables were based on teachers' perceptions, they were not used as variables for analysis. Rather, they provided another means of ensuring diversity within our sample. The rationale for purposeful selection of a small sample of students is consistent with video data analysis methodology. Video data analysis examines interactions of students with their peers, teachers, and the computing software and, therefore, is more conducive to small

Table 1: Student Demographic Information

Pseudonym	Grade	Gender	Free/Reduced Lunch	Special Education
Adam	3	M	No	No
Jacob	3	M	Yes	No
Denny	3	M	Yes	No
Liza	4	F	No	No
Tonya	4	F	No	No
Kevin	4	M	No	No
Diana	4	F	Yes	No
Allison	4	F	No	Yes
Jason	4	M	Yes	No

sample size studies due to the qualitative nature of the analysis. The nine students in this study were observed multiple times over the course of the study to ascertain whether observed interactions remained consistent across observations or differed from one observation to another. For example, students may work independently during one computing session, but then display more collaborative behaviors during other times. It was important, therefore, to observe students at least three times in order to understand trends in the data more fully.

2.2 Video Screen Capture Collection

Students each had access to a laptop computer and could either work independently or collaboratively with peers. Teachers encouraged students to collaborate and seek help from their peers before asking the teacher whenever they encountered a problem. Student data was gathered using video screen capture through Screencastify, an open-source, Google Chrome application (https://www.screencastify.com/). This software recorded students' computer screens as well as their voices as they engaged in computing tasks. It was necessary to have access to both the computer screens and voices as it helped to fully capture the collaborative interactions around computing tasks. At the start of data collection sessions, the research team started the screen recording for the purposefully selected students. At the end of each computing session, the recordings were given a label based on predetermined student ID number and the date of the recording. To gain a sufficient control for data analysis, three or four observations were collected for each student in this study. In total, 29 individual student video sessions were collected across the nine students with an approximate total of 13.4 hours of coded videos.

2.3 Data Analysis

The primary data analysis tool in this study was the Collaborative Computing Observation Instrument (C-COI), a validated instrument developed to analyze video screen capture data of students as they engaged in computing activities [6]. It was developed and validated through a two-year process that involved multiple student observations as well as content and construct validity checks with experts in the fields of computer science education, collaborative learning, instrument development, and assessment of student behaviors.

The C-COI was used to analyze the on-screen behaviors of the students as well as the conversations that they had while they completed their computing tasks. The C-COI measures (1) time on task/persistence, (2) help seeking behaviors, and (3) individual and collaborative problem-solving behaviors. This instrument includes codes specifically related to how students engaged in computing activities as independent and collaborative behaviors by choosing among 16 nodes and the associated sub-nodes that describe those behaviors. These nodes indicate (a) the student's actions, (b) if the student encounters a problem during the computing activity, (c) if and to what extent the student is socializing with their peers or adults, and (d) how peers or adults respond to the student [6]. Additionally, field notes and transcriptions of student conversations were taken to add context to the accompanying codes.

Once the videos were analyzed with the C-COI codes, the data was used to generate directed graphs that visually displayed the data [23]. In these directed graphs, the nodes are states represented as questions (e.g. How did the adult or student begin the interaction?) and the edges (referred to as subnodes in the CCOI) are the actions taken by a student, peer, or instructor. These directed graphs allow for visual understanding of the students' interaction patterns.

2.3.1 Interrater Agreement. As with any study that analyzes student behaviors, it was important to achieve a high rate of internal consistency between researchers who coded the video data. Given the number of subnodes within each node in the C-COI, the research team made use of a rigorous procedure for establishing percent agreement [14]. This procedure was established because there would be too many subnode calculations per video to efficiently calculate Cohen's kappa (a measure of interrater reliability) per subnode. The following interrater agreement procedure was validated with the support of two research methodologists who were not connected to this research study. A matrix was developed in which the columns represented different researchers and the rows represented the nodes and subnodes within the C-COI. Each cell in the matrix was populated with the codes each researcher noted from the video analysis. Each time the researchers did not note the same code, a zero was placed in the matrix and each time the researchers noted the same code, a one was placed in the matrix. This matrix allowed the researchers to establish the percent agreement for each subnode and then calculate overall agreement for each video.

Across the twenty-nine videos analyzed, six (approximately 20%) were coded to establish interrater agreement by four members of the research team. Agreement procedures involved two phases. Phase 1 consisted of agreement on initial path: Collaborative or independent path. This is denoted with Nodes 0-A (collaboration path) or 0-B (independent path) in the C-COI as well as a time stamp of when the path began. To move onto Phase 2 of the interrater agreement procedure, 100% agreement in Phase 1 was needed to be established. In Phase 2, agreement was established within each subnode. The research team reached 100% agreement in Phase 1 across all six videos. For Phase 2, interrater agreement ranged between 80% and 89% across the 6 videos. These percentages of interrater agreement are within the acceptable range for "strong agreement" [12].

2.3.2 Limitations. This analysis was not intended to be the only way to evaluate students' collaborative computing processes. Rather, it provided one lens to further explain how students engaged in computing instruction. Consequently, the C-COI should ideally be used alongside other methodological processes such as the use of qualitative observations with field notes. In this study, therefore, the C-COI was used along with extensive field notes gathered from the transcripts of students' conversations as well as descriptions of what occurred on students' computer screens. Despite efforts to triangulate findings between codes and field notes, we acknowledge that the C-COI analyzes complex constructs that are still not fully understood in the CS education research community. Additionally, there were situations wherein the students' conversations were inaudible. For example, it can be difficult to track student conversations as they move around the classroom. In these cases, the C-COI includes codes for when the rater cannot decipher the conversations. Future work is underway to address this limitation through the use of more powerful mics and voice detection procedures.

3 RESULTS

Across the nine students in this study, 29 observations were collected and analyzed for collaborative interactions. When observing the video screen recordings, the research team began coding interactions each time a student transitioned from working independently to interacting with a peer or teacher. If, for example, a student was working independently, and he or she asked a peer a question, the team would begin coding that interaction. There were instances, however, in which a student appeared to talk with a peer, but this talk served as "self talk." For example, when a student was excited, she might state, "Oh, awesome!" or she might engage in a think-aloud such as, "Ok, I need to go left" while problem solving. These verbalizations, however, were not directed specifically towards another student or teacher. In these cases, the researchers coded those verbalizations as independent work with self talk.

Data analysis confirmed three recurring and distinct types of collaborative interactions: (1) computing-specific collaborative problem solving, (2) conversations that express excitement/curiosity/accomplishment related to the computing activities, and (3) general, off-topic socialization. Interestingly, although the C-COI includes numerous student behaviors including independent computing and various interactions, these three types of interactions proved to be most prevalent. Additionally, although these interactions are described as distinct types of interactions, it is important to note that the students in this study engaged in all three types of interactions and transitioned between these interaction types fluidly as they interacted with each other and with their teachers. Lastly, it is important to note that the students in this study also worked independently. However, our research question related to the kinds of collaborative interactions that students had while computing so the independent behaviors were outside the scope of this study. The C-COI, however, does allow researchers to analyze independent time on task as well as capture field notes of that independent work.

When examining the conversations initiated by students, 38% (n=78) of the interactions were related to solving computational problems or difficulties that the students encountered, 31% (n=63) of the interactions were socializations wherein students were engaged in non-computing discussions, and 16% (n=33) of the interactions involved conversations related to computing, but not for the purpose of problem solving, such as students describing an accomplishment related to their computing activity or excitement over a peer's computational work. There was an additional 15% (n=30) of the instances that either did not result in a full interaction (e.g., the student addressed a peer and the peer did not respond) or the coder was unable to hear the peer's voice. Each collaborative category is described below with illustrative case examples from the data.

3.1 Collaborative Problem Solving

When examining the C-COI data, the majority of interactions (n=78; 38%) that occurred were related to attempting to solve a computational problem. This was true for both student-initiated and teacher-initiated conversations. Most of these problems related to issues such as lack of understanding about the different blocks that the students encountered and ways of debugging code that was not working as intended. The students that exhibited collaborative problem solving varied greatly and included both students who sought help from peers due to a challenge they faced with the computing activity, or they were giving support to their peers.

For example, during the four observations of Diana, a 4th grade student from a low socioeconomic household, she usually entered collaborative conversations to problem solve computing difficulties that she encountered. The C-COI revealed that Diana interacted with a peer or adult 32 times, and most of her interactions revolved around problem solving (n=21; 65%). Of these 32 interactions, 23 were initiated by Diana wherein she sought help related to a computing task (n=14), socialized with peers (n=2), and expressed excitement about her work or the work of others (n=3). The data also included three instances wherein she addressed a peer and the peer did not respond.

The most prevalent C-COI path in Diana's data was:
0-A to node 1: Beginning of collaborative interaction
1-A to node 2: Student verbally addressed a peer
2-B to node 5: Student expressed a need for help, but not explicit to the problem
5-A to node 6: The problem related to computing/programming
6-A to node 7: Peer and student interacted
7-A to node 9: Peer and student discussed the problem/difficulty
9-A/9-B to node 15: Problem solved/problem not solved

Figure 1 provides a representation of Diana's typical C-COI codes. It is not a directed graph; instead, it is a simplified representation of Diana's progression from beginning a collaborative interaction through the end of that interaction.

For Diana, after only few seconds of attempting to work independently to solve a problem, which typically involved moving a single block, she immediately sought help from a peer (code 1-A) or adult (code 1-B). For example, one interaction began when Diana expressed, "Someone wanna help me? Anyone? I need help. Hey, one of you guys, help me." In these instances, a peer either solved the computational problem for Diana or ignored her request.

Additionally, when examining how Diana asked for help, the C-COI analysis indicated that she frequently sought help without

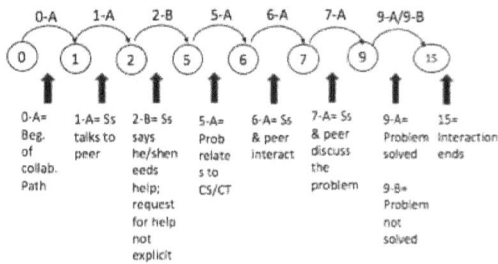

Figure 1: Diana's Most Common Interaction Type

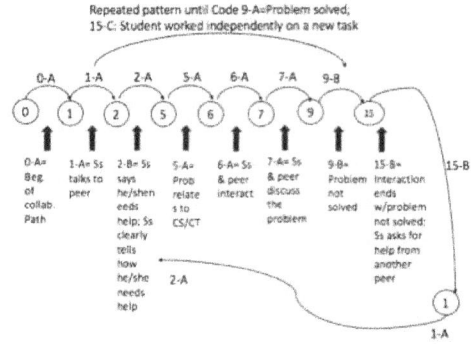

Figure 2: Tonya's Most Common Interaction Type

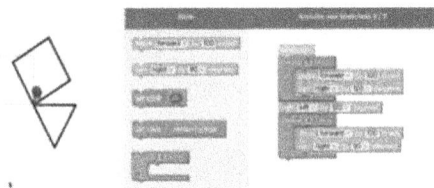

Figure 3: Tonya's Code Studio Problem Solving Example

verbalizing what challenges she faced (code 2-B). Rather than stating what she attempted to do or what did not work in her program, she simply stated that she needed help.

3.1.1 Help Seeking. As provided in Diana's example, many collaborative interactions occurred when a student expressed the need for help. Although students often did not explicitly describe the types of problems they faced with their peers initially (code 2-B=Student says he or she needs help, but the request does not provide explicit information about the problem), many interactions involved the peer and student engaging in a rich problem-solving discussion about the computational problem. An example of this type of interaction occurred between Tonya and two peers. Tonya worked on manipulating her code and iterated twice before leaving her computer to bring a friend over to help her.

Tonya brought Maria to her computer and asked for help by explicitly stating what she tried to do:

Tonya: See, I did it. I had forty [degrees]
Jacob: I had this. I will try to help you. Did you try this in here?
Tonya: I think it should be right there and this should be twenty [Tonya adds a turn right by 90 degrees block and
changes the 40 times in the repeat block to 20; then she clicks the reset and run button, the problem is not solved].
Jacob: Get rid of the right [Tonya removes the turn right by 90 degrees block]
Tonya: Okay, I got it [Tonya tries another combination of codes, clicks the reset + run button, the problem is still not solved.]

This problem remained unsolved, so Tonya asked another peer for help and began another conversation.

Allison: So again, what are you trying to do?
Tonya: I am trying to do that square (see Figure 2)
Allison: What could you do ifâĂę
Tonya: Now I am doing 150 [Tonya changes the 120 degrees to 150 degrees in the turn left by 120 degrees block, clicks the Reset + Run button, the problem is not solved; then the student changes the 150 degrees to 180 degrees, clicks the Reset + Run button, the problem is solved].

The codes for Tonya and her two peers is presented in Figure 2. Like Figure 1, this figure provides a simplified representation of Tonya's progression from encountering a problem to solving that problem.

Students often received help from their teachers rather than peers. In these situations, unsurprisingly, the conversations were much more focused on problem solving steps and isolating where the students were stuck. The teachers often explicitly problem solved with the students to help them understand the difficulty they were facing and why their codes were not working. An example interaction between Jason, a 4th grader, and his teacher showcased this type of interaction:

Jason: I put the blocks there but they would not run.
Teacher: Ok, so let's look and see what you got. So you said, when run, repeat until you get to the flower, do this. Turn right. Move forward. Turn right. Move forward. Turn right. Okay. So the first thing you are asking it to do is turn right and move forward.
Jason: You said turn right move forward. Turn right. Move forward.
Teacher: I was just reading what you had.
Jason: Ohhh!
Teacher: That's all I was doing. I was just decomposing the code you had written.
Jason: I have no idea how to do it.
Teacher: Okay, soâĂę.Look at your zombie and think about what you want him to do first.
Jason: Right. Turn right. Move forward.
Teacher: Ok, so he has to turn right and move forward. Then, what is he going to do?
Jason: Turn left.
Teacher: Turn left and move forward. Okay. Try that. You took it a part and decomposed it.

In this way, the teacher made the problem-solving steps explicit of first reading the code and then reflecting on what Jason wanted to do. Interestingly, she did not provide Jason with the "correct" answer. Rather, she read his code out loud as a way of helping him think through his steps. She also used the term decompose, a computational thinking vocabulary that she had previously introduced. By using the term decomposition within the context of problem solving, she was both modeling the thinking process and providing an explicit connection with previous instruction on computational thinking practices.

3.2 Excitement, Curiosity, and Accomplishment

Approximately 16% of all conversations (n=33) students engaged in during computing instruction involved students discussing their computing experiences outside the context of problem solving. These conversations typically involved expressing excitement about their computing activities, curiosity about the work of their peers, or accomplishment for completing a computational task. If, for example, a student found something peculiar or surprising in their program, the student would often express curiosity, which would generate a conversation with a peer or adult. If a student persisted through a difficult problem that resulted in success, the student would often express a sense of accomplishment to their peers or teachers.

A typical excitement/accomplishment conversation can be seen with another student, Kevin, a 4th grade student and his peers:

Kevin: Mr. Connor, check this out. Woah, its darkly shaded. It's a black hole. I made a black hole. See? [Mr. Connor did not respond because he was working with other students]
Liza: Try to make it bigger.
Kevin: Oh look at that. Doesn't that look like space in the middle?
Liza: Oh yeah! It does. That is so cool!
Kevin: Doesn't that look like you're going into space?
Liza: Yeah. It's so cool, man.
Denny: It's like the end in Minecraft.
Kevin: It looks like Star Trek. [Sings: de-de-da-deeeeeee]

As compared with the collaborative problem-solving conversations, these conversations did not involve any degree of frustration or a request for help. Rather, these conversations occurred while students either worked independently on their own computing projects or were watching other students work.

Although explaining an entire directed graph with all the C-COI nodes and subnodes is outside the scope of this study, figure 4 illustrates how Adam, a 3rd grader who was observed three times during computing instruction, had both independent work and collaborative interactions. The collaborative interactions involved general talk about his project in which he showed excitement about his work or the work of his peers.

Adam's C-COI analysis revealed 25 observed collaborative instances. When examining these collaborative interactions in more detail, it was noted that there was a fairly even split between the interactions that he initiated (n=14) and those that a peer initiated (n=11). Out of 14 instances wherein Adam addressed a peer, 9 of those instances (82%) were related to expressing curiosity or excitement.

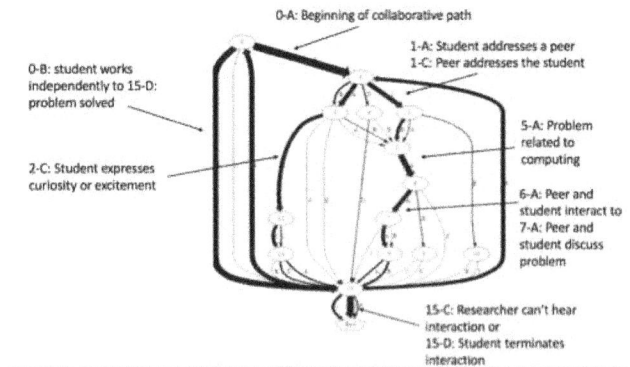

Figure 4: Adam's directed graph of excitement/socialization/accomplishment

Adam both worked independently (0-B: Student works independently to 15-D: Student worked independently on the same problem or topic until solved), and interacted with others (0-A: Beginning of a collaborative path). Most of Adam's interactions were with peers (1-A: Student verbally addresses a peer; 1-C: Student is initiated by a peer). In fact, Adam only had three interactions with an adult (1-D: Student is initiated by an adult) during the computing times. In examining the peer interactions, most of these involved Adam talking with a peer to express curiosity and excitement (2-C: Student expresses curiosity, excitement, or accomplishment). This excitement or sharing of an accomplishment was typically related to his own work rather than to the work of his peers (11-C: Student is excited about something associated with his/her own work; 11-E: Student is showing or expressing accomplishment on his/her own work).

3.3 Socialization

A final type of interaction occurred when students interacted with peers or adults on topics unrelated to computing. This type of interaction accounted for approximately 31% (n=63) of all student-initiated conversations. The typical path within the CCOI that captures these socialization instances was:

1-A to node 2: Student verbally addresses peer
2-D: Student socializes
13-A: Student socializes around an off-task topic
14-A: Peer verbally responds to the student's socialization or
14-B: Adult verbally responds to the student's socialization

As anticipated, these conversations varied greatly based on student interests, classroom activities, and social dynamics between the students. Socialization conversations could be related to what the students would do after school, their families, discussions of popular music or videos, etc. Interestingly, even though the students knew they were being recorded, it did not appear to stop them from talking freely with each other. For example, during the three sessions in which Kevin was observed, he had 28 interactions. He initiated 17 of these interactions and of those 17 interactions, 10 were related to socialization, 6 were conversations wherein he was expressing excitement/curiosity/ accomplishment, and 1 interaction was related to problem solving.

One of Kevin's socialization conversations occurred after viewing a video hint from Mark Zuckerberg within Code.org Code Studio. The conversation was as follows:

Kevin: Mr. Connor. Mark made Facebook. He made Facebook.
Mr. Connor: That's why he is the richest man in America.
Kevin: Wait, he's rich?
Devin: Yes.
Macy: Every person who buys it, it like costs money to make it. There is probably over a million people that have it.
Kevin: Yeah, even in China. Da zing!

4 DISCUSSION

This is the first of a series of K-12 studies examining students' independent and collaborative experiences during computational activities. The purpose of this study was to describe elementary students' collaborative behaviors that occurred within a computing context. We began to attend to what it looks like from students' perspectives to be "stuck" on a computing problem, and how they maneuver around being stuck. Do they give up? Do they persist by thinking outside-the-box and using strategies to find the solution? Do they interact and ask a friend? Does the extent to which using CS/CT language relate to their computational knowledge?

4.1 Answering our research question: What kinds of collaborative interactions occur during puzzle-based computing environments?

As mentioned above, this is the first of several studies that will use the C-COI as a validated instrument to capture the "process" of students' individual and collaborative behaviors when presented with a computing task. This study revealed that there were three prevalent types of collaborative interactions and all students engaged in all three types of interactions: (a) Collaborative problem solving, (b) conversations about the computing activities that typically expressed curiosity, accomplishment, and excitement, and (c) conversations in which students socialized with each other. Additionally, the students tended to interact more with their peers than with the teachers. Instead, the teachers offered support, monitored learning, and encouraged the students to interact and collaborate with each other.

Although, this is a small sample and generalizations cannot be made to larger samples, we have begun to see trends that are encouraging for the K-5 computing education community. First, given the opportunity to collaborate, students are interacting around computational themes and helping each other solve problems. In the case examples of Diana and Tonya, she would purposely seek out peers and ask for their help. These types of collaborations produced rich conversations as students negotiated ideas, tried different strategies, and worked together to solve the problem. Secondly, in many instances, even when students encountered challenging computing activities, they would persist. For example, Tonya worked through

her problem independently and engaged with two of her peers to understand the computing challenge she faced.

We do not, however, have answers yet regarding why some students persisted and others did not. Interestingly, although outside the scope of our research question, in analyzing the video screen captures of students as they struggled with their computing tasks, it appeared that many students struggled because they were working in puzzle levels that were too difficult. Several students, for example, skipped to harder levels because they wanted to be at the same level as their peers. Consequently, as the level of complexity increased in these levels, students became frustrated and required additional support.

4.2 Implications for Future Research

To begin to build instructional practices that support students' persistence, collaborative problem solving, and computational thinking, it is important to methodically study the processes that students undertake as they engage in computing activities. This study showcased how the C-COI could be used to obtain such deep-level data to begin to examine the processes students undertake when involved in computing tasks. Additionally, this study highlighted three types of collaborative conversations that were observed across the nine students in this study. Given the paucity of research into how students interact during computing instruction, this study left many unanswered questions. Future research should extend into the following areas:

(1) Examination of students' computational processes during open-ended computing tasks: This study made use of Code.org Code Studio wherein students worked through increasingly sophisticated computing puzzles. The types of interactions that were observed during this study where, therefore, mediated by the curricular organization of these computing tasks. One would anticipate that students' interactions may be different when they are engaged in more ill-defined and open-ended computing activities. For example, although Jordan and McDaniel (2014) described uncertainty as an individual's experience of doubting and being unsure [7], that experience may be different in more ill-defined and open ended computing experiences as compared to the ones within this study. Future research should, therefore, investigate differences and similarities of students' collaborative interactions within these different computing environments.

(2) Examination of students over time after introduction of pedagogical strategies: This study highlighted the need to more explicitly teach students strategies such as how to debug their projects when stuck, how to ask for help in more adaptive ways, and how to actively participate with peers during collaborative problem solving. For example, when observing Diana's data, it appeared that she demonstrated help seeking behaviors in a manner that may be consistent with learned helplessness theory, which posits that students exhibit passive behaviors if they have experienced failure or believe that they cannot succeed in a task [15, 20]. She did not attempt to individually problem solve before requesting assistance. Rather, she asked for help in a non-explicit manner as a request, rather than articulating her difficulty. Some studies have highlighted that help seeking, on its own, is not a negative trait. Instead, how students

ask for help can either promote learning or impede it [8]. Additionally, learned helplessness may be considered domain specific rather than general [10], so the way students behave in computing environments may not be representative of their behavior in other content areas. Research questions that should be studied include: (a) When students ask for help by fully articulating the issue rather than by saying things such as "I don't get it" or "help", are they more likely to develop stronger connections with the CS content? (2) What is the relationship between learned helplessness and help seeking behaviors within computing instruction as compared to other content areas? and (3) Do instructional practices that encourage collaboration lead students to seek help rather than attempt to individually problem solve? Addressing these questions requires research methodologies beyond the C-COI such as use of student interviews to obtain their perceptions of challenges as well as strategies to overcome those challenges.

This study began to describe the interactive behaviors that students engage in during computing activities. The C-COI provided a new lens for gaining perspective on how students problem solved and the kinds of conversations they had around computing tasks. The methodology presented can be used by CS education researchers to examine multiple research questions about computing instruction including to what extent students are engaging in collaborative problem solving and whether they are persisting through difficult, ill-defined computing tasks. Our hope is that the C-COI and findings from similar studies will help teachers create lessons that are accessible, engaging, and appropriately challenging to a broader range of learners.

ACKNOWLEDGMENTS

This work was partially supported by the National Science Foundation STEM+C Program (Award No. 1639837)

REFERENCES

[1] S. Cooper, S. Grover, M. Guzdial, and B Simon. 2014. A future for computing education research. *Commun. ACM* 57, 11 (2014), 34–36.

[2] N. DeJarnette. 2012. America's children: Providing early exposure to STEM (science, technology, engineering and math) initiatives. *Education* 133, 1 (2012), 77–84.

[3] J. Denner, L. Werner, S. Campe, and E. Ortiz. 2014. Pair programming: Under what conditions is it advantageous for middle school students? *Journal of Research on Technology in Education* 46, 3 (2014), 277–296.

[4] J. Good. 2011. Learners at the wheel: Novice programming environments come of age. *International Journal of People-Oriented Programming (IJPOP)* 1, 1 (2011), 1–24.

[5] M. Israel, J. Pearson, T. Tapia, Q. M. Wherfel, and G. Reese. 2015. Supporting all learners in school-wide computational thinking: A cross case analysis. *Computers & Education* 82 (2015), 263–279.

[6] M. Israel, Q. Wherfel, S. Shehab, E. Ramos, A. Metzger, and G. Reese. 2016. Assessing collaborative computing: Development of the Collaborative-Computing Observation Instrument (C-COI). *Computer Science Education* 26, 2-3 (2016), 208–233.

[7] M. E. Jordan and R. R. McDaniel Jr. 2014. Managing uncertainty during collaborative problem solving in elementary school teams: The role of peer influence in robotics engineering activity. *Journal of the Learning Sciences* 23, 4 (2014), 490–536.

[8] S. A. Karabenick and R. S. Newman. 2009. Seeking help: Generalizable self-regulatory process and social-cultural barometer. *Contemporary motivation research: From global to local perspectives* (2009), 25–48.

[9] Timothy Koschmann. 1999. Toward a dialogic theory of learning: Bakhtin's contribution to understanding learning in settings of collaboration. In *Proceedings of the 1999 conference on Computer support for collaborative learning.* International Society of the Learning Sciences, 308–313.

[10] I. Krejtz and J. B. Nezlek. 2016. It's Greek to me: Domain specific relationships between intellectual helplessness and academic performance. *The Journal of social psychology* 156, 6 (2016), 664–668.

[11] D. Kumar. 2014. Digital playgrounds for early computing education. *ACM Inroads* 5, 1 (2014), 20–21.

[12] James M. LeBreton and Jenell L. Senter. 2008. Answers to 20 questions about interrater reliability and interrater agreement. *Organizational research methods* 11, 4 (2008), 815–852.

[13] C. M. Lewis. 2011. Is pair programming more effective than other forms of collaboration for young students? *Computer Science Education* 21, 2 (2011), 105–134.

[14] M. L. McHugh. 2012. Interrater reliability: the kappa statistic. *Biochemia medica* 22, 3 (2012), 276–282.

[15] K. J. McKean. 1994. Academic helplessness: Applying learned helplessness theory to undergraduates who give up when faced with academic setbacks. *College Student Journal* 28, 4 (1994), 456–462.

[16] Jesús Moreno-León and Gregorio Robles. 2016. Code to learn with Scratch? A systematic literature review. In *Global Engineering Education Conference (EDUCON).* IEEE.

[17] National Center for Science National Science Foundation and Engineering Statistics. 2017. *Women, Minorities, and Persons with Disabilities in Science and Engineering: 2017.* Technical Report. Special Report NSF 17-310. www.nsf.gov/statistics/wmpd/

[18] R. S. Newman. 1994. Adaptive help-seeking: A strategy of self-regulated learning. In *Self-regulation of learning and performance: Issues and educational applications,* D. H. Schunk and B. T. Zimmerman (Eds.). Erlbaum, Hillsdale, NJ, 283–301.

[19] S. Papert. 1980. *Mindstorms: Children, computers, and powerful ideas.* Basic Books, Inc.

[20] C. Peterson, S. F. Maier, and M. E. P. Seligman. 1993. *Learned helplessness: A theory for the age of personal control.* Oxford University Press, New York.

[21] M. Resnick and D Siegel. 2015. A different approach to coding: How kids are making and remaking themselves from Scratch. (2015). https://brightreads.com/a-different-approach-to-coding-d679b06d83a

[22] G. Stahl, N. Law, U. Cress, and S. Ludvigsen. 2014. Analyzing roles of individuals in small-group collaboration processes. *International Journal of Computer-Supported Collaborative Learning* 9, 4 (2014), 365–370.

[23] M. M. Tatsuoka. 1986. Graph theory and its applications in educational research: A review and integration. *Review of Educational Research* 56, 3 (1986), 291–329.

[24] J. D. Wilson, N. Hosking, and J. T. Nosek. 1993. The benefits of collaboration for student programmers. *ACM SIGCSE Bulletin* 25, 1 (1993), 160–164.

117

Understanding Student Collaboration in Interdisciplinary Computing Activities

Elise Deitrick
Tufts University
Paige Hall
Medford, Massachusetts 02155
elise.deitrick@tufts.edu

Michelle Hoda Wilkerson
University of California, Berkeley
Tolman Hall
Berkeley, California 94720
mwilkers@berkeley.edu

Eric Simoneau
Boston Public Schools
2300 Washington St
Roxbury, MA 02119
eric@stats4stem.org

ABSTRACT

Many students are introduced to computing through its infusion into other school subjects. Advocates argue this approach can deepen learning and broaden who is exposed to computing. In many cases, such interdisciplinary activities are student-driven and collaborative. This requires students to balance multiple learning goals and leverage knowledge across subjects. When working in groups, students must also negotiate this balance with peers based on their collective expertise.

Balance and negotiation, however, are not always easy. This paper presents data from a project to infuse computing into high school statistics using the R programming language. We analyze multiple episodes of video data from two pairs of students as they negotiated (1) the statistics and computing goals of an activity, (2) the knowledge needed to meet those goals, and (3) whose expertise can help achieve those goals. One pair consistently reached agreement along these dimensions, and engaged productively with both subject matter and computing. The other pair did not reach agreement, and struggled to accomplish their tasks. This work provides examples of productive and unproductive interdisciplinary computing collaborations, and contributes tools to study them.

CCS CONCEPTS

•**Human-centered computing** →**Collaborative and social computing design and evaluation methods; Empirical studies in collaborative and social computing;** •**Social and professional topics** →*K-12 education; Computer science education;*

KEYWORDS

Collaborative Learning; Research Methods; Interdisciplinary Curriculum; Computing Education; Computational Thinking

1 INTRODUCTION

In the precollegiate curriculum, students are often exposed to computing through its infusion into other school subjects [3, 12, 18, 24]. A biology class may engage students in building computational models of ecological systems. Or, a statistics class may make use of analysis and visualization libraries in R or Python. There is ongoing debate about whether Computer Science should be introduced as a standalone subject or though an integrative approach [24]. Regardless, interdisciplinary computing has taken root in the precollegiate curriculum, supported by large national initiatives including the National Science Foundation's STEM + Computing Partnerships (STEM+C) program. Given the growth and popularity of infusing computing into other disciplines, it is important to understand whether and how learning unfolds in these contexts.

Advocates of the interdisciplinary approach argue that it can expose a larger diversity of students to computing, since science and mathematics courses are core curricular subjects [31] whereas elective Computer Science courses typically serve students that disproportionately identify as White and male [16]. Additionally, mathematics, the sciences, and nearly every other subject is increasingly computationally-driven [2, 6]. Including computing in these subjects, it is argued, reflects professional practice and presents computing as applicable and relevant to learners' interests [22].

Interdisciplinary computing activities are often done collaboratively in pairs or small groups. This makes sense: as problems increase in scope, and as computation offers new tools to deal with scale and complexity, computing has become a team challenge. Having students work together to solve problems also aligns well with sociocultural perspectives that highlight the criticality of discourse and participation in communities for learning [5, 17]. Collaboration has also been shown to provide career preparation and to facilitate retention [20]. Of particular relevance to Computer Science Education is the spread of paired programming—demonstrating benefits ranging from better learning outcomes to better products [7, 33].

Despite these expected benefits, there is evidence that difficulties and inequities can also emerge from collaborative work [8, 27]. Complex social and ideological factors contribute to these difficulties, including friendship, race, gender, access to educational artifacts, and how students' identities are co-constructed over time within a given educational context [11]. One important factor that affects the success of collaborations is what students interpret to be the goal of a given activity. Collaboration requires students to agree upon and work together toward a shared goal [4], and is strengthened when that goal involves mutual understanding of the content to be learnt. Within the domain of computing, Lewis and Shah found that inequitable dynamics emerged during paired programming activities when students' goals were to complete tasks quickly, rather than to make sense of code [19]. How students negotiated shared goals in the moment are in turn affected by systemic

ICER'17, August 18-20, 2017, Tacoma, WA, USA.
© 2017 Copyright held by the owner/author(s). Publication rights licensed to ACM.
978-1-4503-4968-0/17/08...$15.00
DOI: http://dx.doi.org/10.1145/3105726.3106193

and local dynamics involving gender, race/ethnicity, perceptions student competence, discourse norms, and more [1].

The complexity of negotiating activity goals can be further exacerbated students are expected to collaborate on interdisciplinary activities. Students with different levels of computing and subject matter expertise may feel more or less prepared to engage in particular aspects of the activity. Or, they may take a 'divide and conquer' approach that creates boundaries between computing and subject matter content, and limits who has access to computing experiences. Additionally, what students are expected to learn about computing versus what they are expected to learn about the subject matter may be unrelated, or even in tension. For example, a course that brought applied mathematicians and biologists together to create models of ecological systems revealed tensions in goals related to domain - mathematicians sought efficient and computationally viable models, biologists sought ecologically faithful ones [28]. In prior work we have found that students who prioritize creating a working program in R over creating a valid statistical model may engage in shallow computation, without learning benefits [32].

What students understand the goals of an interdisciplinary collaborative activity to be, then, is important. It can affect what students learn, and how they interact with one another. This yields the questions: *How do students understand, and come to agreement about, the goals of interdisciplinary collaborative computing activities? And, how do they work to achieve those goals?*

2 THEORETICAL FRAMEWORK

There have been calls to underpin computing education research with rigorous theoretical frameworks in order to facilitate comparison, generalization, and reproduction of studies [13, 21]. Theory-based analytical tools can also help us answer questions useful for software designers (How do students understand their learning environment?), for educational experience designers (How do students take up computing as authentic or inauthentic?), and for learning scientists (How does having a partner change what kind of cognitive work students are doing during computing activities?). Here, we begin by reviewing theoretical literature on *framing, perspectival framing*, and *framing alignment*. These constructs provide tools to understand how different people perceive tasks, how those perceptions affect their knowledge and sense of competence, and they come to agreement about those perceptions.

2.1 Framing

Framing explores how people answer the question 'What is going on here?' as they participate in a social activity. Frames are constructed based upon situational cues, and shape what a person pays attention to and how they make sense of things. If a student is told to "think of variables" in a mathematics class, they may think of a letter used to represent a set of numbers that satisfy certain constraints ($x > 3$). If they are in a computing class, they may think about a way to label and store data (myData = []). Frames are context dependent, and small changes to a situation may change what students perceive or expect. For example, if a student in a computing class is told to "think of variables" while struggling with a programming task, they may interpret this to mean that there is an error in how they are declaring and setting variables in their program. But if they are

told to "think of variables" at the beginning of a new unit, they may expect to be introduced to a new data type. In this way, frames are "structured expectations formed from previous experiences...active and responsive, perpetually evolving as they are informed, shaped and tuned with new experiences" [23, p.47].

Frames are not correct or incorrect, nor are they correctly or incorrectly applied. Different frames foreground different aspects of a situation, and may be more or less useful. Typically, when people find a frame is not useful, they will replace it. For example, one might initially sit down at a restaurant, expecting to have their order taken. If a server does not appear, that person may start looking for a cashier or counter instead [29]. Framing affects what knowledge (e.g., pieces of knowledge and connected knowledge structures; [10]) people believe will be relevant in a given situation [14]. It also affects how notions of competence are constructed in learning environments and beyond, with implications for equity and access to learning opportunity [15].

2.2 Perspectival Framing

Van de Sande and Greeno's notion of *perspectival framing* emphasizes that frames are likely to differ across people as a result of the different sets of knowledge and schemata they hold, based on their individual experiences and perspectives [30]. It contributes analytic tools to highlight how an individual's framing of a situation influences what knowledge they bring to bear, and how they perceive themselves and others. The authors identify three dimensions of perspectival framing: epistemological, conceptual, and positional.

Epistemological framing is "participants' understanding of kinds of knowledge that are relevant for use in their activity and the kinds of knowledge, understanding, and information they need to construct to succeed in their activity" [30, p.2] (see also [14]). A student's epistemological framing answers the question 'What is my goal for this activity?' In interdisciplinary computing activities, it is assumed that students will recognize subject-specific, computing, and even other related knowledge as relevant.

Conceptual framing is "the way or ways in which participants organize information in the situation they are discussing and the problem they are working on" [30, p.2]. Given how they frame a situation, a person will have a set of expectations about a situation that will cause them to foreground and background different knowledge resources. A student's conceptual framing answers the question 'What do I already know that can help me accomplish my goal?' In interdisciplinary activities, it is taken for granted that students will both have (or build) and leverage their subject-specific and computing knowledge.

Positional framing refers to the way participants understand everyone's role in a situation. Positional framing "includes a human participant who is inquiring, which we call a listener, and a source, which may be another human participant or a non-human system" [30, p.1]. The role of listener is fluid; the listener can be a simple recipient, a director of "the interaction, actively questioning the source," or a role taken up "actively and jointly by more than one participant acting collaboratively" [30, p.40]. In interdisciplinary computing activities, it is assumed that learners will share the roles of source and active listener, each contributing to conversation and asking for elaboration as needed.

All three of these types of framing are interrelated. The knowledge a student leverages for an activity (conceptual framing) depends on what knowledge that student thinks is relevant to accomplish their goals (epistemological framing). Knowledge changes for a listener as they receive information and restructure their understanding accordingly, and may change for a source as they adapt the information they are communicating to the listener's needs. And, the position of listener and source (positional framing), or the information that each seeks and provides, may change as participants recognize different goals or knowledge to be at play.

2.3 Framing Alignment

Van de Sande and Greeno emphasize that perspectival framing is rooted in individual perspectives. People may have different expectations for what is going on, different sets of knowledge that they may or may not leverage, and different understandings about who should be the source or listener during an activity. Thus it is unlikely groups will automatically agree in their framing of a collaborative interdisciplinary task.

Framing alignment is defined as a way for participants to co-construct framings of a situation. If two students are employing contradicting frames, they will reach a moment of conflict that they will then try to resolve. For example, if one student frames an assignment as an occasion to demonstrate knowledge and another student frames the task as a chance to check for understanding of previously learned concepts, one student might want to work quickly while the other may wish to take time and review why they got a particular answer. In order for this group to make progress, one or both of the students will need to shift their frame to align with the other student. When their frames align, the conflict resolves, signaling mutual understanding.

Framing alignment has been explored in other work. Scherr and Hammer [26] explored framing in a collaborative educational setting through analysis of student behaviors including vocal register, gestures, and body language. They identified four clusters of behavior they argued indicated different shared framings of educational activities: (1) completing worksheets, (2) discussion, (3) responding to the Teaching Assistant, and (4) joking. For example, completing worksheets was characterized by students with their heads down, writing. Discussion was characterized by students' heads up, shifting gaze to one another and activity materials.

The analysis revealed that individual students would often make bids to move the group from one frame to another through body position. For example, when a student was done working on a worksheet problem, they might sit up, ready to discuss. If after a few moments no member joined them in the new proposed frame, the student would typically revert back to completing worksheets. This demonstrates that students often work to negotiate shared frames during collaborative activities, and that such negotiation is not always straightforward.

Van de Sande and Greeno tracked framing over time to explore how students in a group reached alignment through talk [30]. They presented three ways that participants' conceptual framings can be aligned: (1) participants possess and activate knowledge structures that are well-aligned, (2) the listener lacks pre-existing knowledge consistent with the source and therefore uses information from

the source to construct a new knowledge structure, or (3) both participants lack pre-existing schemata, and switch roles as listener and the source to jointly construct new knowledge structures. These processes have different levels of complexity in terms of the work that is required, and the learning that is achieved. An activity that requires students to activate the same pre-existing schema, like something previously learned in class, is likely to be less complex and produce less new knowledge than one where students need to jointly construct a new conceptual frame.

Positional framing alignment is likely negotiated in interaction. For example, a student might take up the role of source by stating an answer. Their peer may respond in a way that accepts role of listener (for instance, by asking for clarification about the answer provided), or by making a bid for the source position (by critiquing the answer provided). The latter represents a misalignment of positional framings; this misalignment would be renegotiated or resolved by future interactions between the students and other materials or people involved in the activity. For example, students may achieve realignment of positional framing by agreeing to consult a textbook, positioning both of themselves as listeners relative to a material informational source.

3 METHODS

Our goal in this paper is to understand students' perspectival framings of interdisciplinary collaborative activities, and how those framings come into alignment. We are interested in what students understand (1) the activity to be, (2) what knowledge they need or have for the activity, and (3) how to acquire or share that knowledge.

3.1 CodeR4STATS and Computing in Statistics

We explore this process in the context of an NSF-funded research project called CodeR4STATS (IIS-1418163), which seeks to transform high school statistics through activities that employ the R statistical programming language to work with large and authentic datasets. Rather than just replacing the graphing calculators typically employed in Statistics classes, R is used to infuse concepts that have been identified as central to computing such as automation, abstraction, modeling, data and analysis, and social dimensions of computing [3, 9] into statistical exploration. For example, one activity involves measuring and documenting the lengths and widths of leaves from two different trees, and then constructing fit models to examine patterns within and across samples. Another involves investigating university admissions reports, and developing an algorithm to help make college admissions decisions for a large, hypothetical set of applicant records.

3.2 Study Context and Case Selection

Our data are drawn from a non-AP statistics class participating in the CodeR4STATS project at a selective public high school in New England. The teacher of this class is a designer of the CodeR4STATS materials, and was accustomed to teaching with R. Over the course of the school year, we captured classroom data daily during periods of time when students were working intensively with R. Two authors of this paper were present during data collection. We captured video and audio of consented students using small video cameras mounted on computer monitors, as well as synchronized video recordings of those student's on-screen activity.

We focus on two pairs of students in this class during a month-long unit about linear and nonlinear regression toward the beginning of the academic year. For these activities students were expected to submit their assignments individually, but encouraged to work collaboratively (including collecting and analyzing shared data). Over the course of the data collection period, these four students often worked together. However, the two pairs were strong sub-units with very different collaborative dynamics. Each focal pair included one student that identified as male, and one that identified as female. These students were not representative of the class as a whole in terms of their collaborative dynamics, class performance, or demographics. Our selection of these cases thus reflected an information-seeking rather than representative sampling method. That is, we selected these two groups because of the dramatic contrast in their interactions, which influenced the ways in which each pair worked to understand one another and their success on group projects.

3.3 Analysis

After the school year was over, video was organized and tagged by one of the researchers present during classroom activities. The data for these two groups, identified in field notes as interesting because of their contrasting collaboration dynamics, were selected for further analysis. A summary of these groups' dynamics over the course of the year was constructed, and several specific video cases representing critical or representative events were extracted and transcribed. This method is particularly well-suited for dense video data collected over long periods of time to study the development of ideas and norms in classroom contexts [25]. These summary analyses and video cases were then shared with a third researcher who was not present during data collection, for triangulation. Analyses were further elaborated through repeated watching and shared viewing, to enhance the validity and clarity of findings.

4 RESULTS

We present episodes from two activities the pairs completed during the curricular unit. In the first set of episodes, the intended emphasis of the activity was a statistical content goal, correlation. In the second set of episodes, the intended emphasis was a computational goal, learning to build plots in R. Transcript excerpts are presented chronologically, and within each set, each group's transcript is from the same day and is using the same activity materials.

4.1 Statistics

As students learned R, the teacher had them engage with familiar statistics concepts. Both groups in the following transcripts discussed the concept of correlation. But while one group engages in a productive debate, the other group's dynamics shut down discussion after one student asks the other to clarify what he is doing.

4.1.1 Group 1: Dan and Mary. The first episode we present demonstrates what we identify as productive pair dynamics, in which students co-construct understandings through discussion during the activity. This pair's excerpt begins with a researcher/facilitator (R) prompting Dan to reflect on the meaning of a correlation he

has calculated on the computer. When Dan makes a claim about correlation, Mary quickly begins to challenge him.

1 **R** So what did you learn now that you've plotted it?
2 **Dan** That increase in manatee death is correlated to power-boat registrations?
3 **R** Is that surprising in any way shape or form?
4 **Dan** I mean I could see- I could see the amount of [inflation?] contributing to the amount of like cows being born but that didn't mean anything. Like, it's two variables that correlate but there is no evidence besides numbers. I could throw numbers at you and I could prove anything.

The researcher asked questions they did not know the answer to, in an effort to position themselves as a listener and counteract their intrinsic authority. Dan raises the difference between correlation and causation, emphatically illustrating that they are not equivalent by saying if they were he could "prove anything". With this idea on the conversational floor, Mary moves to engage with the conceptual content of Dan's claim.

5 **Mary** Well if they're wrong numbers, yeah. But right numbers I mean typically -
6 **Dan** I'm saying they're right numbers but they could be two unrelated things
7 **Mary** So it's unrelated that the boats that kill all the manatees and if they're more boats there are more manatees dying?
8 **Dan** No, it's not that -
9 **Mary** It's unrelated?
10 **Dan** It's registration.

Mary challenges Dan's claim, using other information she has about the situation under investigation to assert that the correlation in this case does imply causation. Both Mary and Dan interrupt one another (lines 6,9) during the conversational back and forth. Throughout the exchange, they are listening to and engaging in one another's ideas, rather than attacking or talking past one another.

11 **Mary** And if its registered it's like a car, if it's registered it's there
12 **Dan** yeah
13 **Mary** If you are using your boat-
14 **Dan** You're not listening to me. I am saying that you can have increase in manatee deaths. You could also have an increase in power boat registrations. That doesn't mean that every single power boat going out there is mowing them down
15 **Mary** I'm not saying every single one but this is specifically killed by boats in Florida
16 **Dan** oh
17 **Mary** It literally says in the paragraph. Killed by boats, so you're wrong
18 **Dan** Leave me alone. God.

Although Dan claims at one point that Mary is not listening (line 14), there is evidence that both students are listening to one another and adjusting their own conceptual understandings accordingly. Mary works to make clear to Dan what evidence in the text supports her argument. Once this is presented, Dan finds it convincing, accepts it, and tries to end the conversation. In this way, both students switch back and forth as they negotiating for the position as knowledgeable. At this point, the researcher intervenes, asking a clarifying question about Mary's evidence.

> 19 **R** Specifically powerboats?
> 20 **Dan** Yeah!
> 21 **R** Maybe they are sitting there in a row boat just like clubbing manatees with an oar
> 22 **Dan** Yeah. How do you like them apples?
> 23 **R** It would be interesting to know like maybe one boat is sitting there doing donuts where there is a lot of them. And maybe that is killing them?

The researcher's effort to present an unlikely edge case disrupts the apparent stability between Dan and Mary. It positions Mary as less knowledgeable, and introduces a new argument in support of Dan's conceptual claim. Dan agrees with the researcher socially, affirming the claim.

> 24 **Mary** See if that's the case then that doesn't explain how or why like the increase in power boat registrations-
> 25 **Dan** It could really be that one guy who's always killing manatees but goes to where the manatees are and just doing donuts trying to run them over

Mary engages conceptually with Dan and the Researchers' newly presented line of argument, but gets interrupted as Dan takes up and engages conceptually with the edge case. In response to this, Cameron, another member of the group of four focal students who is sitting on the other side of Dan, joins the conversation.

> 26 **Cameron** Anywhere where there are actually known manatees there is like a no wake zone. So it's like literally [inaudible]
> 27 **Mary** Yeah, they're endangered so they try to preserve them

Cameron's contribution reorients the focus of the discussion away from unlikely edge cases back to real world knowledge. Mary supports Cameron's line of argument, and Dan yields the floor, ending the debate and implicitly accepting Mary's argument.

Employing the notion of perspectival framing allows us to understand the complex dynamics at play during this exchange. The conversation illustrates a negotiation between Dan, Mary, and other interlocutors around the *epistemological framing* of the activity. Dan starts the conversation by making a general proposition about statistics – that correlation does not represent causation (lines 4, 6). Mary re-orients the conversation to focus on the specific textbook problem they are working on (lines 15, 17), which provides additional contextual information that supports a causal interpretation. There are moments, however, where real world knowledge is also included as relevant in the discussion - including unlikely edge cases and known laws (lines 23, 26, 27). Thus throughout the conversation, both students understand the goal of the activity to be reasoning about statistical correlation; and co-construct an understand of what evidence can be used to inform such reasoning.

Between Dan and Mary we see two distinct *conceptual framings*. Dan maintains through the discussion that correlation does not imply causation - on multiple occasions expressing that the two variables are not necessarily related (lines 4, 6, 14, 25). In this way, Dan is leveraging general notions of statistical correlation as his conceptual focus. Mary's conceptual focus, on the other hand, is

tied to the specific context of the problem: the negative impact of powerboats on the manatee population. Thus Mary is not appealing to change Dan's general idea that correlation means causation, but rather an effort to re-negotiate the epistemological framing of the activity to recognize that *in this case* it does. These different conceptual framings, Dan's application of general statistical concepts and Mary's application of knowledge about the problem at hand, remain opposed throughout the discussion.

Finally, throughout the discussion, both Dan and Mary adopt the position of both 'source' and 'active listener'. There is evidence throughout the conversation that both Dan and Mary are substantively engaging with one another's ideas, and adjusting their own arguments and interpretations of the situation in response. In this way, we posit that the two students share a relatively balanced *positional framing*.

4.1.2 Group 2: Ann and Cameron. The second episode demonstrates what we identify as unproductive pair dynamics. The excerpt below begins shortly after Cameron had physically taken over Ann's keyboard, after she asked for help identifying errors in her R code.

> 1 **Cameron** Let's make some magic happen. I'm going to eventually do this too so.
> 2 **Cameron** Model
> 3 **Ann** What's abline do?
> 4 **Cameron** It means your mom. That's what that means. You don't have like commas anywhere. You don't even have parenthesis around the fucking word. That's not where the parenthesis is.

Here, Cameron begins as the source of knowledge, since he was allowed to take Ann's keyboard. Ann reinforces this position by asking a question about abline (a function in R that adds a trendline to a scatterplot, from which students could extract a calculated correlation coefficient). However, Cameron does not conceptually engage with Ann's question, instead replying "your mom" before chastising her for lack of syntax. While Cameron does address some of Ann's mistakes in the code, the issues he brings up are syntactic and do not relate to Ann's question or the statistics content that is the focus of the lesson.

> 5 **Cameron** I can't - why is your shift bar messed up?
> 6 **Cameron** You can't use the shift bar? That's stupid
> 7 **Ann** It's not working
> 8 **Cameron** Okay, that's not-no-you need parentheses
> 9 **Ann** That is a parentheses
> 10 **Cameron** I mean you need quotation marks
> 11 **Ann** Oh
> 12 **Cameron** Like that. Alright, umm... comma, okay it's going to assume [inaudible]
> 13 **Cameron** I don't know why you put that there

Even when Ann corrects Cameron, he asserts his position as source and treats Ann as listener. Despite these dynamics, Ann is an 'active listener' and tries to direct the conversation toward parts of the code that are related to the statistical content of the lesson.

> 14 **Ann** What's lty mean?
> 15 **Cameron** It's like the line thingy ma do

16 **Cameron** Yeah, that shit. Um... is your thing good? Is that all you have? so far?

17 **Cameron** I'm going to use more hashtag signs. Hashtag correlation. I misspelled correlation for you.

18 **Cameron** Correlation. Marine corps parenthesis, next we have y.

This time, Ann asked about lty, a way of setting the type of line that will appear on the plot (visually illustrating the correlation between variables plotted on the axes). Cameron again does not take up her question, instead stating aloud the characters her is typing without evident explanation.

19 **Cameron** And then we do it again.

20 **Ann** Why?

21 **Cameron** Because you gotta do it again

22 **Ann** Why, is there like a-?

23 **Cameron** I don't know you gotta tell it to run multiple times. For accuracy. It's like we have to tell it to run [inaudible]

24 **Cameron** But that is all now cuz this is cheese.

Finally, Cameron states that the correlation has to be calculated a second time (line 19). Ann, who has been positioned as listener throughout the exchange and whose questions about statistically relevant parts of the code had not been answered, asks why the calculation needs to be repeated (lines 20, 22). Ann's question is especially important - there is no reason that the correlation needs to be recalculated, and Cameron's repetition suggests a misunderstanding of either correlation as a statistical concept, or the way in which correlation is calculated in R. Cameron offers a noncommittal response and then explicitly ends the conversation (line 24).

Throughout this episode, we see evidence that Ann and Cameron hold very different *epistemological framings* of the activity. Cameron's comments suggest he is most concerned with getting the R code to work quickly. He comments on to syntactical errors in the code, and when prompted to explain the purpose of different functions he either ignores them or responds noncommitally in ways that suggest he does not think such explanations are important (lines 4, 10, 15, 26). Although Ann does not speak much, when she does she is asking questions about the R code Cameron is writing that is most related to the statistical content that is the focus of the lesson (lines 3, 14, 20, 22). This suggests that Ann is framing the activity as an opportunity to learn about connections between correlation as a statistical concept and the R language.

These epistemological framings lead each student to a different *conceptual framing*. Cameron, who is concerned with getting a working program, talks mostly about syntax and does not leverage statistical knowledge or conceptual code-based knowledge in his explanations. Ann, who is concerned about understanding the code in relation to the statistics concepts, seeks such knowledge. She also demonstrates her own conceptual understanding of correlation in questioning an error in Cameron's approach (lines 20, 22).

The *positional framing* of the two students stays constant throughout the transcript. Cameron is positioned as the source, and Ann is positioned as the listener. While Ann plays an active listener, reading over Cameron's shoulder and asking questions, her bids for information are not taken up seriously.

4.2 Computing

The first set of exchanges we presented occurred during an activity that focused on correlation as a statistical learning goal. Similar dynamics were observed when students worked on activities focused on computing learning goals, as well. In the following two episodes, we present data from both groups working on an activity involving creating visualizations in R.

4.2.1 Group 1: Dan and Mary. This excerpt begins as Dan trying to move the plot he created in R to a googleDoc he will submit for a grade. He asks Mary for help, and she points out that his plot is lacking axis labels.

1 **Dan** Wait, how do you do it? Can I just drag the photo?

2 **Mary** What?

3 **Dan** What is it doing?

4 **Mary** What are you doing? Let go

5 **Dan** That's cool

6 **Mary** What are you trying to do? Label it?

7 **Dan** No, I'm -

8 **Mary** No, you have to label it first anyways. You have to put the main title, and the ylab and xlab. The teacher literally just said that.

Mary re-negotiates Dan's goal in this moment by pointing out he missed a step. She tells Dan the commands without other support.

9 **Dan** How?

10 **Cameron** It doesn't do it when you-

11 **Mary** Yeah it does. You put it under plot x y. Right here. Plot x y Your main is your title, xlab is the name for your x, ylab is the label for your y, then the color of the points, and then you do the abline.

12 **Dan** Calm down

13 **Mary** It's the exact same way if you were going to plot anything and then you just tell it all the stuff that you want

14 **Dan** It never worked but okay

Dan asks how to add the labels (line 4), while Cameron claims the method they have been taught does not work (line 5). Mary provides an explanation by describing the optional parameters available for the plotting method they are using, which take strings for the x and y axis (xlab, ylab). When Dan is reluctant (line 7; hesitation to type into his workspace), Mary adjusts her explanation to a level of abstraction that better connects with Dan's existing conceptual understanding (line 8). She notes that it is "the same way if you were going to plot anything", relating to Dan's construction of graphs in past assignments. Dan takes this up and adds the labels to the method call, which then generates a labeled graph.

15 **Dan** Mary can't tell time

16 **Mary** That's fine you can do that

As soon as Dan's graph appears, he teases Mary, whose reaction times on a physical test comprised the dataset.

At the beginning of this episode, we see explicit efforts on Mary's part to understand and align herself to Dan's *epistemological framing*; that is, what his goal is in that moment. She repeatedly prompts him (lines 2, 4, 6) to tell her what problem he is trying to solve. Once she figures out that he is trying to export his plot, she then works to re-orient what he is doing (line 8). We do not see this kind of explicit alignment work in their first episode, where Dan and Mary had a shared epistemological frame (sensemaking). We also do not see this kind of work done by Ann and Cameron, even though there is considerable evidence that their epistemological framings are not aligned.

Having established the mutual goal of adding labels to the plot, Mary explains in greater and greater detail how to do so (lines 8, 11, 13). It is clear that in her *conceptual framing* she understands the idea of method parameters. However, she adjusts these explanations to Dan's needs, first elaborating how labels should be added (line 11) and then connecting the process to what she knows to be Dan's prior experiences (line 13). While there was not as much explicit engagement in each other's conceptual ideas as in the first episode, the episode illustrates that both students have productive computing resources that can be leveraged to help them accomplish what is now their shared goal. We also see Mary not only provide computational code, but also explain that code and connect it to other instances to help Dan situate his knowledge.

Throughout this episode, it is evident that the pair have a shared *positional framing* where Mary is the source and Dan is the listener. Dan is an active listener, asking questions. Mary performs secondary listening and does explicit work to make sure the group aligns both their epistemological and conceptual framings over the course of the exchange.

4.2.2 Group 2: Ann and Cameron. The other group starts a similar way, with one student asking the other for help.

1 **Ann** How do you get the x and y?
2 **Cameron** xlab. x
3 **Ann** xlab equals?
4 **Cameron** Whatever you want your thing to be then ylab. Think of it as abbreviations for things. X label. Y label. Main title. Scatter plot.

It is unclear at the beginning of this episode what each student's epistemological framing is, and they do not explicitly work to understand or align with one another. It may be that the goals of one or both of the pair are to get these specific labels to show up in the plot, or to understand in more detail how the method works. It is also unclear what Ann is asking of Cameron in line 3. Cameron engages conceptually with Ann's question in a way that may or may not be aligned with her goals, noting that method parameters such as xlab and ylab can be thought of as abbreviations for English language descriptions such as "X label".

5 **Ann** x lab equals... y lab equals....
6 **Ann** What is the y again?
7 **Cameron** Hold on
8 **Ann** What was the y?
9 **Cameron** Hold on. You don't have to do the same thing as me. It's an individual project. It's the cheese. So do I get rid of the stupid box now?
10 **Ann** It said unexpected - it's saying it doesn't work. It's not working

Ann asks what the y label should be, indicating a possible gap in her knowledge about this plot or what it is meant to represent. Cameron begins to reject his position of source, by reminding Ann

that they do not have to do the same thing despite using a shared data set. In another bid for help, Ann reads aloud the error that her code is producing.

11 **Cameron** Oh my god, you have to put commas at the end of things.
12 **Ann** Where? This? This?
13 **Cameron** No.
14 **Ann** Where?
15 **Cameron** Ask one of the teachers. It's beyond my control now

Cameron identifies a syntactical error in Ann's code unrelated to her earlier conceptual questions. He does not provide enough information for her to fix the error he identified easily, and Ann asks where he is seeing the syntactical error. Cameron again rejects the position of source, redirecting Ann to seek help from others.

Looking at this entire episode, it appears as though Ann and Cameron seem to share an *epistemological framing*. Both are trying to get code to work (lines 1, 10, 11).

In terms of *conceptual framing*, Cameron seems to be leveraging more knowledge related to the shared goal of getting the code to work. At the beginning of the excerpt, he even engages conceptually with Ann's question, providing a way to make sense of the connection between parameters and their meanings (line 4). However, there is little explicit negotiation of conceptual framing between the two students, and the explanation that Cameron provides proves insufficient for helping Ann make progress.

Ann and Cameron's *positional framing* begins as shared, with Cameron as source and Ann as listener. However, Cameron ultimately rejects the position of source (lines 9, 15).

5 DISCUSSION

We present a brief summary of our analysis in Table 1. Together, the episodes illustrate the utility of perspectival framing for providing multidimensional insight into collaborative dynamics. Examining one dimension alone would not have been sufficient for describing these groups and their work outcomes. For example, Episodes 4.1.2 and 4.2.1 both present cases in which group members did not initially hold a shared epistemological frame. Dan and Mary, however, negotiated and ultimately aligned their framing while Ann and Cameron did not, instead "talking past" one another. Episodes 4.1.1 and 4.2.2 demonstrate instances in which each pair held aligned epistemological frames, but only one of these episodes featured productive exchange. Similarly, the productivity of a group was not predicted only by alignment of positional framing.

The episodes also demonstrate that productive group work is not necessarily predicted by full alignment across *all* frames, but rather the acknowledgement and negotiation thereof. In both of Dan and Mary's cases, the initial misalignment of conceptual and (in the second case) epistemological frames provoked productive discussion. Misalignment of more than one frame, however, especially without acknowledgement is a good predictor of unproductive collaborations. When Ann and Cameron lacked a common epistemological frame, they spoke past one another; Ann's conceptual questions were not answered and Cameron did not take up the opportunity to interrogate his statistical understandings. Even when they shared

Table 1: Summary of Framing Dimensions Over Four Cases

Episode	Epistemological	Conceptual	Positional
4.1.1 (Statistics) Dan and Mary	ALIGNED Reason about statistical correlation found in data	CONFLICT M: Correlation provide evidence of a causal relationship D: Statistical correlation does not imply causation	ALIGNED Alternating source and listener
4.2.1 (Computing) Dan and Mary	NEGOTIATED Learn plotting methods in R.	NEGOTIATED M: Knowledgeable about R plotting methods D: Constructing knowledge about R plotting methods	ALIGNED D: Listener M: Source
4.1.2 (Statistics) Ann and Cameron	CONFLICT A: Learn relationship b/t R methods and correlation C: Produce workable code	CONFLICT A: Knowledgeable about statistical correlation C: Knowledgeable about R Syntax	ALIGNED A: Listener C: Source
4.2.2 (Computing) Ann and Cameron	ALIGNED Produce workable code	CONFLICT A: Needs knowledge about R Syntax C: Knowledgeable about R Syntax	CONFLICT A: Listener C: Rejects role as Source

and epistemological frame, their lack of alignment along other dimensions – conceptually, without an effort to understand one another's knowledge, and positionally, as Cameron refused to help Ann, led to a lack of progress.

We are careful to note that of the episodes presented in this paper, only one includes clear evidence of new learning and improved work outcomes, Episode 4.2.1. This is the episode in which Mary helped Dan label his plot, connecting the method to Dan's prior successes constructing plots with other R methods. However, we still understand Episode 4.1.1 as productive insofar as students engaged in reasoned argumentation. We also tentatively highlight an apparent crystalization of perspectival framings over time. Whereas Dan and Mary seem to develop facility in negotiating and aligning frames from one activity to the next, Ann and Cameron's framings (producing working code, Ann as passive listener) continue.

Our findings suggest additional detail is needed about positional framings, beyond mere alignment. Across the episodes, students navigated position in different and consequential ways. In Episode 4.2.1, Mary and Dan's positions as source and listener paralleled those of Cameron and Ann in Episode 4.1.2. However, Mary and Dan treated one another as sources of knowledge, and substantively engaged with conceptual content of one another's talk (even when their conceptual framings were different). Indeed, in Episode 4.1.1, they maintained their relative positionality even as the Researcher, an adult in a position of authority, offered further evidence in support of Dan's claim. In contrast, Cameron actively maintained the role of source but mostly rejected Ann's contributions.

Secondary listening, where a source also takes up a temporary listener role to understand the primary listener's conceptual framing, can help here. This distinction plays out when the sources attempt to help their listeners with computing (Section 4.2). Mary adjusts her explanation of x and y labels to a more conceptual level after realizing that she needed to better situate her advice to Dan. In contrast, Cameron did not react to Ann's bids for more conceptually rich computing help. In this way, attending to secondary listening can reveal mechanisms by which students recognize one another's frames, and thus have opportunities to negotiate and align them.

5.1 Limitations and Future Work

This paper reflects a preliminary effort to analyze collaborative interdisciplinary computing in an educational setting, and is limited in some important ways. Our analysis relies on video of student interactions during R-intensive activities. The collaborative group dynamics observed here may have been consequentially shaped by events not included in our data. Findings would be strengthened by first-hand reports or interviews with students. The analysis reported here is part of a larger effort to explore how collaborative unfold across different groups during interdisciplinary computing activities over the course of a school year. We may find evidence to challenge the findings presented as work continues.

6 CONCLUSION

To understand how students learn computing in interdisciplinary projects, it important to consider what they perceive their goals to be for a given activity. Given that most such activities are collaborative, it is also important to consider whether and how students align their understandings to make joint progress. Interdisciplinary computing curricula often take for granted the strength of conceptual connections between computing and disciplinary learning goals, but those connections may not always be evident to students.

This paper demonstrates the utility of perspectival framing analysis to explore how student groups navigate what they expect to do, learn, and contribute during such activities. It also contributes detailed, concrete examples of how such dynamics unfold across time and task. Understanding student positioning during collaborative work is especially critical for understanding equity and access in computing education as it unfolds alongside other contextual factors (e.g. [15, 19]). Such an approach is especially useful given the interdisciplinary expectations of computing-infused curricula.

ACKNOWLEDGMENTS

Thanks Kristen Wendell, Jessica Swenson and Karen Miel for feedback on analysis and early drafts of this work, and to the student participants in this study. CodeR4STATS is funded by NSF grant IIS-1418163; conclusions do not necessarily reflect views of the NSF.

REFERENCES

[1] Kate T. Anderson. 2009. Applying positioning theory to the analysis of classroom interactions: Mediating micro-identities, macro-kinds, and ideologies of knowing. *Linguistics and Education* 20, 4 (2009), 291–310. DOI : https://doi.org/10.1016/j.linged.2009.08.001

[2] David H Bailey and Jonathan M Borwein. 2011. Exploratory experimentation and computation. *Notices othe AMS* 58, 10 (2011), 1410–1419.

[3] Valerie Barr and Chris Stephenson. 2011. Bringing computational thinking to K-12. *ACM Inroads* 2, 1 (2011), 48. DOI : https://doi.org/10.1145/1929887.1929905

[4] Brigid Barron. 2003. When Smart Groups Fail. *Journal of the Learning Sciences* 12, 3 (July 2003), 307–359.

[5] Ann L Brown and JC Campione. 1994. Guided discovery in a community of learners. In *Classroom lessons: integrating cognitive theory and classroom practice.* 229–270. DOI : https://doi.org/10.1037/000276

[6] Sanjay Chandrasekharan and Nancy J. Nersessian. 2015. Building cognition: The construction of computational representations for scientific discovery. *Cognitive Science* 39, 8 (2015), 1727–1763. DOI : https://doi.org/10.1111/cogs.12203

[7] Alistair Cockburn and Laurie Williams. 2000. The costs and benefits of pair programming. *Extreme programming examined* (2000), 223–247.

[8] Karen A. Cole. 1995. Equity Issues in Computer-based Collaboration: Looking Beyond Surface Indicators. In *The First International Conference on Computer Support for Collaborative Learning (CSCL '95).* L. Erlbaum Associates Inc., Hillsdale, NJ, USA, 67–74. DOI : https://doi.org/10.3115/222020.222068

[9] CSTA Standards Task Force. 2016. *[Interim] CSTA K-12 Computer Science Standards.* Technical Report. http://c.ymcdn.com/sites/www.csteachers.org/resource/resmgr/Docs/Standards/2016StandardsRevision/INTERIM_StandardsFINAL_07222.pdf

[10] Andrea A DiSessa. 1993. Toward an epistemology of physics. *Cognition and instruction* 10, 2-3 (1993), 105–225.

[11] Lesley Dookie. 2014. A Case Study Examining the Microdynamics of Social Positioning within the Context of Collaborative Group Work. In *International Conference of the Learning Sciences (ICLS) Conference.* 402–409.

[12] Shuchi Grover and Roy Pea. 2013. Computational thinking in K-12: A review of the state of the field. *Educational Researcher* 42, 1 (2013), 38–43. DOI : https://doi.org/10.3102/0013189X12463051

[13] Mark Guzdial. 2013. Exploring hypotheses about media computation. In *Proceedings of the ninth annual international ACM conference on International computing education research.* ACM, 19–26.

[14] David Hammer, Andrew Elby, Rachel E Scherr, and Edward F Redish. 2005. Resources, framing, and transfer. In *Transfer of learning from a modern multidisciplinary perspective.* 89–120. DOI : https://doi.org/10.1002/car.1158

[15] Victoria Hand, William R. Penuel, and Kris D. Gutiérrez. 2013. (Re)Framing educational possibility: Attending to power and equity in shaping access to and within learning opportunities. *Human Development* 55, 5-6 (2013), 250–268. DOI : https://doi.org/10.1159/000345313

[16] Marva Hinton. 2016. Eight states have fewer than 10 girls take AP computer science exam. *Education Week* (nov 2016). http://blogs.edweek.org/edweek/curriculum/2016/11/eight

[17] Jean Lave. 1991. Situating learning in communities of practice. In *Perspectives on socially shared cognition.* 63–82. DOI : https://doi.org/10.1037/10096-003

[18] Irene Lee, Fred Martin, Jill Denner, Bob Coulter, Walter Allan, Jeri Erickson, Joyce Malyn-Smith, and Linda Werner. 2011. Computational thinking for youth in practice. *Acm Inroads* 2, 1 (2011), 32–37. DOI : https://doi.org/10.1145/1929887.1929902

[19] Colleen M Lewis and Niral Shah. 2015. How Equity and Inequity Can Emerge in Pair Programming. In *Proceedings of the eleventh annual International Conference on International Computing Education Research.* ACM, 41–50.

[20] Colleen M Lewis, Nathaniel Titterton, and Michael Clancy. 2012. Using collaboration to overcome disparities in Java experience. In *Proceedings of the ninth annual international conference on International computing education research.* ACM, 79–86.

[21] Lauri Malmi, Judy Sheard, Roman Bednarik, Juha Helminen, Päivi Kinnunen, Ari Korhonen, Niko Myller, Juha Sorva, Ahmad Taherkhani, and others. 2014. Theoretical underpinnings of computing education research: what is the evidence?. In *Proceedings of the tenth annual conference on International computing education research.* ACM, 27–34.

[22] Jane Margolis, Joanna Goode, and Jean J Ryoo. 2015. Democratizing computer science. *Educational Leadership* 72, 4 (2015), 48–53.

[23] Mary E McCormick and David Hammer. 2016. Stable Beginnings in Engineering Design. *Journal of Pre-College Engineering Education Research (J-PEER)* 6, 1 (2016), 4.

[24] National Research Council. 2011. *Committee for the workshops on computational thinking: Report of a workshop of pedagogical aspects of computational thinking.* National Academies Press, Washington, DC. DOI : https://doi.org/10.17226/12840

[25] Arthur B. Powell, John M. Francisco, and Carolyn A. Maher. 2003. An analytical model for studying the development of learners' mathematical ideas and reasoning using videotape data. *Journal of Mathematical Behavior* 22, 4 (2003), 405–435. DOI : https://doi.org/10.1016/j.jmathb.2003.09.002

[26] Rachel E Scherr and David Hammer. 2009. Student behavior and epistemological framing: Examples from collaborative active-learning activities in physics. *Cognition and Instruction* 27, 2 (2009), 147–174.

[27] Niral Shah, Coleen Lewis, and Roxane Caires. 2014. Analyzing equity in collaborative learning situations: A comparative case study in elementary computer science. In *International Conference of the Learning Sciences (ICLS) Conference.* 495–502.

[28] Shawn; Confrey Jere Smith, Erick; Haarer. 1997. Seeking diversity in mathematics education: mathematical modeling in the practice of biologists and mathematicians. *Science & Education* 6 (1997), 441–472.

[29] Deborah Tannen. 1993. Whatfis in a frame? Surface evidence for underlying expectations. *Framing in discourse* 14 (1993), 56.

[30] Carla C van de Sande and James G Greeno. 2012. Achieving alignment of perspectival framings in problem-solving discourse. *Journal of the Learning Sciences* 21, 1 (2012), 1–44.

[31] Uri Wilensky, Corey E. Brady, and Michael S. Horn. 2014. Fostering computational literacy in science classrooms. *Commun. ACM* 57, 8 (2014), 24–28. DOI : https://doi.org/10.1145/2633031

[32] Michelle Wilkerson, Elise Deitrick, and Eric Simoneau. 2017. Integrating computational thinking in high school statistics through data modeling with R. (2017).

[33] Laurie Williams and Richard L Upchurch. 2001. In support of student pair-programming. In *ACM SIGCSE Bulletin,* Vol. 33. ACM, 327–331.

Factors Influencing Students' Help-Seeking Behavior while Programming with Human and Computer Tutors

Thomas W. Price
North Carolina State University
Raleigh, NC 27606
twprice@ncsu.edu

Zhongxiu Liu
North Carolina State University
Raleigh, NC 27606
zliu24@ncsu.edu

Veronica Cateté
North Carolina State University
Raleigh, NC 27606
vmcatete@ncsu.edu

Tiffany Barnes
North Carolina State University
Raleigh, NC 27606
tmbarnes@ncsu.edu

ABSTRACT

When novice students encounter difficulty when learning to program, some can seek help from instructors or teaching assistants. This one-on-one tutoring is highly effective at fostering learning, but busy instructors and large class sizes can make expert help a scarce resource. Increasingly, programming environments attempt to imitate this human support by providing students with hints and feedback. In order to design effective, computer-based help, it is important to understand how and why students seek and avoid help when programming, and how this process differs when the help is provided by a human or a computer. We explore these questions through a qualitative analysis of 15 students' interviews, in which they reflect on solving two programming problems with human and computer help. We discuss implications for help design and present hypotheses on students' help-seeking behavior.

1 INTRODUCTION AND BACKGROUND

Programming is a challenging skill to learn, particularly for novices. Getting "stuck" on an assignment can place an emotional toll on students [19] and may result in the student giving up. Ideally in these situations, a student will be able to seek help from a professor or teaching assistant and receive one-on-one, expert tutoring, arguably the most effective form of instruction [6]. However, experts – or even knowledgeable peers – are not always available or accessible, especially in overcrowded classrooms, and they may be absent altogether in informal learning settings. To address this, researchers and educators are increasingly augmenting programming environments with help features to aid students who are stuck when no human is available.

There are many forms of embedded help found in programming environments, including enhanced error messages [13], program visualization tools [38] and debugging aides [22]. Particularly promising are Intelligent Tutoring Systems (ITSs), which attempt to play the role of the human tutor [42]. In the domain of computing, ITSs can offer intelligent, contextual help through hints (e.g. [32, 34]), feedback (e.g. [16]) and curated examples (e.g. [43]). Working with an ITS can improve computing students' performance and decrease their programming time on problems, both when help is available and afterwards, outside of the tutor [10], leading to claims that ITSs can match the learning gains of human tutors [11].

However, researchers have noted that students' use of help features in ITSs is far from ideal, with students avoiding help when they need it, or abusing help to expediently solve the problem [1, 4], behaviors negatively correlated with learning [35]. ITSs for learning programming are not immune to these problems, with studies showing evidence of help avoidance and abuse [32, 33]. This leads us to ask, *what do we know about how and why students seek programming help from computer tutors – or from human tutors?* With a few exceptions [21, 40], little work has investigated help-seeking in the domain of computing. Existing models of help-seeking focus on general classroom learning [29, 30] or on *desired* help-seeking behavior in an ITS [2]. However, educational psychology results from other domains do not always apply to computing [27, 28], and we are interested in how and why students *actually* seek help, not just how they *should*. In this work, we investigate factors that influence novice programmers' help-seeking behavior and how this differs with human and computer tutors. We present a qualitative analysis of 15 students' interviews, in which they reflect on solving two programming problems: one with a human tutor and one with intelligent, computer-based help. We discuss design implications and hypotheses that arise from these results.

1.1 Help-Seeking in the Classroom

Help-seeking can be defined as "the ability to solicit help when needed from a teacher, peer, textbook" or other information source [2]. Most models of how students seek help are rooted in original work by Nelson-Le Gall [29], who proposed a cognitive and behavioral model of help-seeking in school-aged children, consisting of five components: 1) Awareness of the need for help, 2) Decision to seek help, 3) Identification of potential helpers, 4) Employment of strategies to elicit help, 5) Reactions to help-seeking attempt(s). The

ICER'17, August 18-20, 2017, Tacoma, WA, USA.
© 2017 Copyright held by the owner/author(s). Publication rights licensed to ACM.
978-1-4503-4968-0/17/08...$15.00
DOI: http://dx.doi.org/10.1145/3105726.3106179

model was intended as a heuristic aid, rather than a formal theory, and focuses on *instrumental* help-seeking, in which the child is seeking only enough help to allow them to complete the problem on their own. Newman [30] expanded this model, in part by presenting step (2) as a comparison between a learner's self-efficacy level (SEL), a dynamic self-assessment of confidence and ability for a given problem or step, and their confidence tolerance level (CTL), the threshold of challenge and risk the student is willing to accept, inherent in the student's beliefs. Both authors stress that *dependence* (evidenced by requests for help) and *independence* are not mutually exclusive ends of a spectrum, but rather that students can use instrumental, adaptive help-seeking as a self-regulatory skill that maintains independent work [29, 30].

Researchers have also identified key factors that influence students' decision to seek or avoid help in the classroom. Students may avoid help for practical reasons: help may be inaccessible or inconvenient, and the use of help may be prohibited or go against social norms of the classroom [37]. Students may avoid help because of concerns about the help-giver's competence (e.g. if it is a peer), a desire for independence [41], or because of a perceived threat to competence [7]. Lower-performing students and students with lower self-esteem are more likely to feel a threat to competence by seeking help, and this threat can manifest in help avoidance or seeking expedient help (with the goal of finishing the problem), rather than instrumental help to foster learning [17]. Students with a *performance* achievement-goal orientation, focused on others' perception of their relative competence, are less likely to seek help than those with a textitmastery orientation, focused on learning and self-improvement. Help-seeking in the classroom is also a social experience, and students with a social status-goal orientation, focused on social visibility and prestige, may feel increased social costs of help-seeking and therefore avoid help [36, 37].

1.2 Help-Seeking with Computer-Based Help

While most research has focused on how students seek help in the classroom, a more recent effort has been made to understand how this work translates to the context of intelligent, computer-based help. Aleven and Koedinger [1] noted that help-usage in their PACT Geometry Tutor ITS was far from ideal. Students in the tutor requested help on only 22-29% of steps, and when they did request help, students skipped through all the levels of help to get to a "bottom-out" hint that explained the answer on 82-89% of steps. The authors addressed this by formulating their own model of ideal help-seeking behavior in a Cognitive Tutor [2]. This model drew on the previous models of Nelson-Le Gall and Newman, but situated itself in the context of step-by-step problem solving with on-demand computer help. Additionally, theirs was a model of *ideal* help-seeking, which noted where students might deviate from this model as "help-seeking errors." They used this model as the basis for the Help Tutor, a cognitive tutor which teaches the metacognitive skill of help-seeking as students solve problems in the Geometry Tutor. In an empirical evaluation, the authors found that help-seeking errors negatively correlated with domain learning, that the Help Tutor reduced the incidence of some of these errors, but that it had no impact on domain learning [35]. Mercier and Frederiksen [26] attempted to generalized the model put forward by Aleven et al.

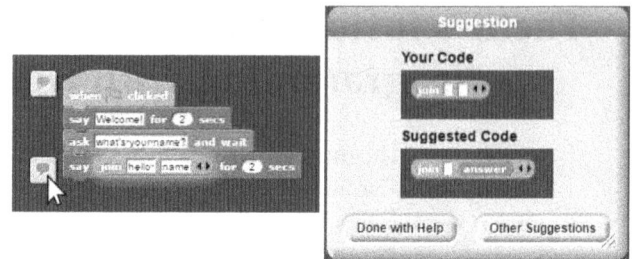

Figure 1: iSnap annotates code with hint buttons (left). When clicked, they suggest a change to the code (right).

to create a cognitive model of help-seeking in interactive learning environments, which added steps for diagnosing the problem and comprehending help.

Others have explored student factors that impact help-seeking with computer-based help [4]. Wood and Wood [45] found that students with lower prior knowledge were more likely to seek on-demand help and benefit from it in the QUADRATIC math learning environment. This contrasts with classroom research on help-seeking, which shows that lower-achievers (or those who perceive themselves to be) seek less help [37]. In a later study, Wood used a pretest to select challenging problems for each student [44]. In this case, prior knowledge did not predict help-seeking, suggesting that the original effect was due to subjective problem difficulty, rather than prior knowledge alone. Bartholomé et al. [5] studied pairs of students working in a "plant identification" learning environment with on-demand help and found that pairs with mixed (high and low) prior knowledge were more likely to seek help and less likely to produce errors, but they found no effect of pairs' "motivational orientation" or interest. Vaessen et al. [40] studied help-seeking in the context of a *computing* learning environment for Haskell with on-demand help. They clustered students' attempts at short programming problems based on log data to identify help-seeking strategies. They identified 5 strategies, and noted that students' achievement-goal orientations were predictive of 3 of the strategies. Research into help-seeking in ITSs appears to agree with some, but not all, results on classroom help-seeking, leaving open research questions and prompting calls for further research [3, 40].

2 ISNAP

This study investigates students' help-seeking behavior with human and computer tutors. For our computer tutor, we selected iSnap [32], an extension of Snap! [15], a block-based programming environment for novices. iSnap adds on-demand hints, which offer next-step suggestions to students on how to progress their code towards a solution. Unlike compiler messages, the hints are semantic, not syntactic (Snap! does not have syntax errors); they concern the structure of code and how closely it matches a correct solution. Hints are contextual, generated based on the student's current code and how it compares to previous students' solutions [31].

A student requests help in iSnap by clicking a button, which annotates their code with one or more hint buttons (see Figure 1). Hovering over a button highlights the code to which the hint applies. When a hint button is clicked, all buttons disappear and the student is shown a next-step hint window. The hint generally suggests a single edit to the student's code, such as inserting, deleting or reordering a code element. The hints are presented visually, demonstrating the edit to make. These are similar to "bottom-out" hints, in that they tell the student exactly what to do, but they do omit some details, such as variable names and literal values. Students can continue to work with the hint window visible, or they can dismiss it to search for another hint that suits their needs.

3 METHOD

This work was motivated by two primary research questions:

RQ1 Why do novices seek and avoid help when programming?
RQ2 How is the process of help-seeking different when novices are working with human help and computer-based help?

We focus on novice programmers because that is the target population for many programming ITSs [16, 34], including iSnap. The analysis presented in this paper is part of a larger study to investigate help-seeking and help use in computing, the procedures of which are explained below. This analysis represents an initial attempt at understanding our data and formulating hypotheses that lay the groundwork to answer these research questions.

3.1 Population

We recruited 15 undergraduate students at a large U.S. research university to participate in our study. We recruited students who had completed or enrolled in an introductory programming course (AP CS, Java, Matlab or Python), but not a more advanced course. We made short, in-class announcements about the study, and we accepted the first 15 participants to volunteer. To encourage less eager programmers to participate, we compensated participants with a $20 gift card. Our participants included 4 females and 11 males, with most students identifying as White (11) or Asian (2), one as Hispanic/Latino and one as Other. Participants' majors were primarily CS (5) or other engineering fields (8), and 9 had taken or were enrolled in the introductory Java course for CS majors. None reported having used Snap! or Scratch more than a few times.

3.2 Procedure

Each participant completed the study[1] individually in a single session. Participants completed two programming assignments, one with a human tutor available and one with iSnap help available, and then participated in a semi-structured interview, which is the focus of our analysis. Participants each attended an individual research session with two researchers: an experimenter and a tutor. In this study, both tutors were female. The participant began by completing a short logic puzzle for 5 minutes to practice thinking aloud, with the tutor available for help if needed. The tutor then led the participant through a short tutorial on the core Snap! programming concepts the participant would need for approximately 20 minutes. To reduce bias, no indication was given whether the research team was involved with the development of Snap!, and the whole system, including the iSnap help features, was simply referred to as Snap!. The participants then worked on two programming tasks, each for up to 30 minutes. Students were prompted to think aloud while

[1]Full study materials available at: http://go.ncsu.edu/icer2017-materials

working on these tasks. Before starting, the participant was asked to read the assignment instructions out loud and to ask the tutor any questions they had *just on the instructions.*

For the first task, the participant was encouraged to ask the tutor for help if they needed it, or to work independently if not. For the second task, the tutor left the room, and the participant was similarly encouraged to ask iSnap for help if they needed it. Before starting, participants were shown a 3 minute video on the help features of iSnap. In both cases, if the student appeared to be struggling with the same issue for at least 45 seconds, the tutor (in the first task) or experimenter (in the second task) intervened by saying, "remember, you can ask me/snap for help." Assignments were selected from the first two units of the Beauty and Joy of Computing curriculum (bjc.edc.org) [15] to be appropriate for novice Snap! programmers. In the Guessing Game, the program should greet the player by name and then repeatedly ask them to guess a stored random number, telling them if it is too high, too low or correct. In the Brick Wall, students create custom blocks (procedures) to draw a brick wall with an arbitrary number of alternating rows. The order of the assignments was randomized, with 10 receiving the Guessing Game first with human tutor help. Because iSnap was not designed to answer questions about the Snap! programming interface itself, we ordered human tutor help first for all participants so that they had an opportunity to ask the tutor any additional interface questions during their first assignment.

After completing both assignments, the experimenter conducted an interview for 10-15 minutes, and the tutor remained out of the room. The experimenter used a semi-structured interview protocol to investigate the student's perceptions of the tutor's help, iSnap's help, comparisons between the two and any suggestions the participant had for iSnap. The questions explored why the student did or did not seek help, the quality of the help and whether the student trusted the help for both assignments. The experimenter also followed up on interesting points and inquired about specific behaviors observed during the programming exercises using notes. While future work will explore the various types of data collected (think aloud protocols, survey responses, finished programs), we focus in this work on the interview data, as it provides a good starting point for understanding participants' experiences.

3.3 Qualitative Analysis

We investigated our research questions using a qualitative analysis, based in Grounded Theory (GT). GT is a set of techniques for building theory that is "discovered, developed and provisionally verified through systematic data collection and analysis" [39, pp. 23]. These techniques, discussed in the next section, were appropriate because of the qualitative nature of our data, the open-endedness of our research questions and the lack of existing, satisfying theory addressing help-seeking in programming. GT has also been applied in CS Education research in a number of contexts [14, 19, 20, 23, 24]. We focused on the variants of GT detailed by Strauss and Corbin [12, 39] and Charmaz [8, 9], and drew on the detailed work of Kinnunen and Simon [18] to apply GT to CS Education.

GT is more than just a set of analysis techniques; it is an iterative approach to "gathering, synthesizing, analyzing and conceptualizing qualitative data" [8, pp. 82]. As in previous work [18], we primarily applied these techniques to data that had already been collected, so we recognize that our work borrows from GT but does not embody it. The analysis we present is an initial attempt to understand our data and research questions. Due to the limitations of our sample size and methods, our goal is not to definitively answer these questions, but rather to describe and interpret the phenomena we observed, discuss how our results relate to existing theory, and generate hypotheses. This is an expected first step in qualitative research, which can take many iterations to generate a full theory.

3.3.1 Coding. We began by performing line-by-line, open coding [8] on transcriptions of the interviews we collected. We started with two intentionally selected interviews, from P12 and P15, which the experimenters identified as containing rich content that directly addressed our research questions. The four researchers that conducted the study served as coders. They coded the interviews independently, with two coding each of the two chosen examples, generating a total of 191 independent codes. The researchers met to discuss these codes and collectively sorted them (written on cards) into conceptual groups. Each group of similar codes was refined and named to produce an initial set of 36 *focused codes*. Examples include "trust" (a participant's trust, or lack of trust, in the tutor or provided help) and "independence" (a participant's beliefs about independence and actions taken based on these beliefs).

One researcher compiled these focused codes into a codebook and wrote brief descriptions for the other researchers to reference. The codes were not tutor-specific (e.g. "trust in *human*" vs "trust in *iSnap*") and could be applied in reference to either the human or computer tutor. The referent ("human" or "iSnap") was noted when the code was applied to a segment. Three of the original researchers then performed open coding on the full set of 15 interviews, during which the codes were further refined for a final set of 43 focused codes. They coded a total of 713 segments (over 30,000 words), with an average 1.8 codes per segment. Since the primary purpose of coding was to help us organize and understand our data, not to quantify and reduce it, each interview had one primary coder, and we therefore did not calculate inter-rater reliability. Instead, as in previous qualitative studies, we worked to establish rigor by discussing and refining codes throughout the analysis [18, 24].

Near the end of coding, the researchers again physically sorted the codes, this time into broader conceptual *categories*. Drawing on the paradigm model of GT [39], we identified a central phenomenon of interest, "Help-seeking Behavior," and related other categories to that phenomenon as causal conditions, context, and consequences. For this paper, we narrowed our focus to factors *influencing* help-seeking behavior (rather than the help-seeking itself or its outcomes), which included 3 of the 8 categories we identified. We compiled, summarized and discussed the interview segments coded with each code in these categories, which we present in the next section. We applied constant comparison [39] throughout the process, writing extensive memos that contrasted segments and explored relationships among the codes and the categories.

4 RESULTS

Our results focus on three categories of codes and their relationship to students' help-seeking behavior. We briefly explain these categories and then discuss the most prominent codes from each:

Inputs are static factors that exist outside of the problem solving session, such as a student's previous experiences, the student's existing knowledge and beliefs, and attributes of the programming assignment. The tutor (or ITS designer) has no direct control over these factors, and they are unlikely to change in the course of problem solving. While they may not influence help-seeking behavior directly, Inputs set a baseline for the Student Mindset.

The **Student Mindset** is how a student interprets their relationship to the programming problem, the tutor and the help the tutor offers. Examples include perceptions of the tutor's trustworthiness, the accessibility of help and how stuck the student is. Unlike Inputs, the mindset is dynamic and can change throughout problem solving, especially but not exclusively when the student seeks help. A student's help-seeking behavior is a response to this mindset.

Attributes of Help are qualities of a tutor's help which determine its effectiveness and perceived value, such as specificity, interpretability and utility. Unlike codes in the Student Mindset category, these attributes can only be experienced by the student after seeking help from the tutor. They affect the outcome of receiving help, possibly leading to changes in the Student Mindset.

4.1 Inputs

4.1.1 Previous Experiences. Previous Experiences encompass students' past encounters with human or computer help and how these experiences shape their behavior during problem solving. Participants related the human tutor to past experiences with TAs and professors. When asked what it was like working with the human tutor, one participant said it was *"just like office hour[s]... I don't know how to do my homework, and I ask the TA for help"* [P2]. Another participant expressed how their previous experiences in the classroom made help-seeking unfamiliar: *"I'm also just not used to asking for help in [programming] classes"* [P15]. Participants discussed avoiding human help during the study due to negative past experiences receiving programming help: *"I've definitely experienced before where I had my- the design of my program in mind for a project... and then someone would be like, "oh no do it this way"... And I'm not saying [the tutor] did this. I'm just saying this is my experience that made me quick to dismiss her at first."* [P11]. P11 rarely asked for help from the human tutor, even after explicit reminders. These previous experiences, appear to strongly influence students' later help-seeking behaviors.

Participants attempted to relate iSnap to previous experiences with computer help, compilers and IDEs. One participant noted how iSnap defied those expectations for the better: *"in Python or in Matlab you don't have little help buttons like that... I was expecting syntactic help... but [iSnap] gives you pretty exact advice... that was pretty cool "* [P15]. Another wished iSnap had behaved more aggressively like a compiler: *"in eclipse or any other IDE [if] you enter a... statement where you... have an argument that isn't compatible it will immediately flag that as red"* [P5]. Other participants explicitly linked previous experiences with computer help to their help-seeking behaviors. One participant's confidence rejecting one of iSnap's suggestions was *"not based on... my experience in this [study] but rather what I felt in my experience prior"* [P5]. Another participant never used iSnap's help, and also noted *"I don't like using Java help"* [P7]. We hypothesize that prior experiences played an important role in shaping participants' expectations of the computer tutor, as discussed in Section 4.1.2.

4.1.2 Expectations of the Tutor. Expectations of the Tutor refers to a student's preconceptions of how a human or computer will provide help and how these expectations are confirmed or defied. Students had generally high expectations of the human tutor's knowledge and experience, assuming *"she's an expert"* [P1] and *"she understands it"* [P13]. These expectations were largely met during the study: *"she had the answer right away"* [P10].

In contrast, participants' expectations for iSnap were quite low. Many noted the fact that the help came from a computer as a specific source of low expectation, saying *"it's just a computer"* [P12], *"listening to a computer... is hard"* [P3], and more exact, perceptive help is *"not really something you should expect from little computer help buttons"* [P15]. For many participants, these low expectations produced a satisfactory experience, even for some who rarely used the help or described it as being generally unhelpful. iSnap was *"good enough"* [P1], and it *"does everything well enough"* [P4]. For others, however, these low expectations meant never using the help in the first place, as was the case for one who saw iSnap as helping with the *"basics of programming"* [P7]. As noted in Section 4.1.1, iSnap defied these low expectations in some cases.

4.1.3 Independence. Independence refers to students' beliefs and preferences about working without help. When asked what discouraged them from asking for help, nearly all participants expressed some form of the sentiment that they wanted to *"figure it out myself"* [P12], often using very similar language. They cited the belief that independent work leads to self-improvement or learning: *"it's more beneficial for me to just figure it out on my own"* [P11], or that asking for help lowers self-efficacy: *"if they ask for help, they feel like they can't do it themselves"* [P13]. One was willing to *"keep trying myself until I'm too frustrated to keep trying"* [P10], and another expressed an unwillingness to ask for help on math errors, *"something I should be responsible for"* [P5]. Two students mentioned that programming *in particular* may lend itself to independent work because *"you can just kinda puzzle your way through it and figure it out on your own"* [P15]. Some of these responses may reflect a selection bias in our participants, who willingly participated in a programming study and may be more motivated learners.

While participants also cited a desire to *"figure this out myself"* [P13] as a reason not to use computer-based help, it may not trigger the same threat to independence that human help does: *"I'd probably click on the little computer help things quicker than going to an actual tutor just because I'm not asking someone else for help [laughs] per say"* [P6]. Another participant got deep into debugging a problem without the human tutor's help, but said *"maybe if help indicators had been turned on for that program I would have gone back"* [P5]. However, independence may also lead students to invest less effort in understanding hints: *"I don't think I really gave it a good enough chance... I didn't actually over-analyze the structure [of the hint]... because I wanted to figure it out myself"* [P10].

4.2 Student Mindset

4.2.1 Trust. Trust refers to a student's confidence in the tutor's ability and the quality of their help. Participants clearly trusted the human tutor in our study, citing assumptions about the tutor's experience (see Section 4.1.2), the fact that the tutor was *"encouraging... friendly and approachable"* [P11] and provided affective support, the perceived quality of the advice itself, which *"made sense"* [P10], and the perceptiveness of the tutor (see Section 4.2.4). Trust did not always lead to help-seeking: *"I... trust that she has the answer, but I felt it did not really motivate me to ask [for help]"* [P1], indicating that it may be a necessary but not sufficient condition for help-seeking. Two participants' negative previous experiences with human tutors did lead to initial mistrust and few help requests (see Section 4.1.1), but when asked directly the same students still described the study's tutor as *"definitely"* [P11] trustworthy, again indicating that trust alone does not lead to help-seeking.

Participants generally expressed Trust in iSnap, though not as unanimously. When asked whether they trusted iSnap's help, one participant expressed wariness because a computer could not adapt to the *"many different ways that you can go about [solving the problem]... [iSnap] can't know everything that I've done"* [P12]. One trusted iSnap, but *"a little less than an actual tutor"* [P6]. Others expressed confidence that iSnap had more experience than they did with Snap! programming *"because its... Snap itself that gives me advice"* [P8]. Another found the directness of the advice trustworthy: *"of course I trust it because... it just tells you... what needs to be done"* [P7]. Trust may be less important if students feel confident evaluating help quality: *"if you're a programmer you should probably know... what advice is good and what advice is bad"* [P15].

There was a small breach of procedure for P1, in which the tutor remained in the room during the second programming exercise. After being prompted to use iSnap's help, P1 asked the tutor how the help was generated, and she explained. This changed P1's trust of iSnap: *"I only trusted... it after I asked [the tutor]... where is it getting this information and she said it's based on previous students"* [P1]. This may suggest that the human tutor "lent" iSnap some of her trustworthiness by explaining it, or that simply understanding the help mechanism makes it more trustworthy.

4.2.2 Stuck. A student is Stuck when they are no longer making progress on the problem. Many students noted this as a primary motivator for seeking help. This was true for both human help: *"whenever I got stuck and like literally didn't know what the next step was... then I was like, okay I need to ask for help"* [P15], as well as computer-based help: *"I was motivated to click on the hint bubbles when I couldn't figure it out on my own"* [P11]. For iSnap in particular, participants noted that the presence of the help was reassuring when stuck: *"it was kind of a good feeling that you knew you had that little bit that could help you if you were stuck"* [P12]. Some participants also expressed reluctance to ask for help, even when stuck, and in retrospect recognized this as a harmful behavior that *"comes back and bites me because... I really needed to ask a question, but I didn't"* [P13]. Participants described Stuck as a state one enters for a duration with degrees of intensity, rather than a single incident: *"sitting there thinking too long"* [P13] or *"just sitting there stuck"* [P15]. When this reaches a threshold, it can prompt help-seeking: *"then I was like okay, I need to ask for help"* [P15].

While participants were generally positive about the human tutor's role in getting them unstuck, they had mixed opinions on iSnap's ability to do so. Some mentioned its ability to nudge them in the right direction, "*if you're stuck, kinda getting me on the right path*" [P12], or to help them solve the problem without wasting time: "*this kind of help is better on... programming efficiency*" [P15]. Two mentioned that iSnap should intervene in these situations: "*if you're having issues too many times, then maybe it can provide some suggestions*" [P13], while others thought this could be disruptive. Some participants noted that iSnap was useful even when they weren't stuck, as a means of "*confirming that I was doing the right thing*" [P15]. Others found that iSnap "*wasn't really helping*" [P3] them get unstuck, due to difficulty interpreting the hints or iSnap's lack of perceptiveness.

4.2.3 Accessibility and Salience. Accessibility refers to the perceived availability of the tutor and their help, and how convenient it is to access help[2]. Salience is often intertwined with Accessibility and refers to how noticeable the help is, or how present it is in the minds of students. Participants spoke of Accessibility and Salience almost exclusively in regards to iSnap, which had a "*convenient feature to ask for help*" [P14]. The help buttons were considered a "*low risk, high reward*" [P4] option because they "*were there, and it's really quick and easy just to click on one and see what it says*" [P12]. Many noted that iSnap's help buttons "*were kind of there*" [P4], subtly pervasive "*from the very start*" [P15], though one did recall forgetting about iSnap until prompted by the experimenter. While salient, the buttons were also appreciated for their subtlety; they were "*non-intrusive and non-intrusive; I think is a very good way of having it*" [P4]. iSnap's Accessibility and Salience were important factors in enabling help-seeking for some, especially when stakes were otherwise low: "*I figured I might as well at least see what it's trying to suggest*" [P4]. Participants noted for both tutors that they sometimes asked for help because the experimenter or tutor prompted them to (as described in Section 3.2), indicating that the help was not salient: "*I was motivated to click on the hint bubbles... when you reminded me I could have help if I wanted*" [P11].

Our human tutor's help was not described as *inaccessible*; however, when asked about useful aspects of the human tutor, participants rarely mentioned Accessibility or Salience. One participant did say that "*it wasn't really an issue having to ask [the tutor]*" [P9]. However, another participant did describe *previous experiences* with professors' inaccessibility, having "*to wait on... the professor to come help you*" [P15], and others mentioned that iSnap would be useful when humans were unavailable: "*the little automated stuff is helpful... especially if I'm doing something in my room*" [P6]. One noted that the inaccessibility of human help can be an intentional aspect of coursework: "*I wouldn't be allowed to access [help] because it's a project for school*" [P10].

4.2.4 Perceptiveness. Perceptiveness refers to the student's belief that a tutor is aware of the student's code, current objectives and possible mistakes, and can provide help based on this knowledge. There was consensus that the human tutor was highly perceptive. The human tutor knows "*what you're trying to do*" [P14], "*what your goal is*" [P7] and "*where I'm going wrong*" [P1]. The human was also perceived to understand the context of the programming assignment. Participants did not directly link the human tutor's

perceptiveness to help-seeking, but it was cited as a reason to trust the tutor: "*[her help] was very reliable, since she's right here can see exactly what I have and what I've done*" [P12].

There was a general sentiment that iSnap was not perceptive. iSnap "*only can respond to what I'm putting on [the screen]*" [P11], and so it misses important visual and audio queues that the human would pick up, especially since the participant is thinking out loud. It was perceived as being unresponsive to changes in student code: "*It doesn't know when you make an error*" [P7] and it "*couldn't anticipate what I wanted so it couldn't really help*" [P14]. When asked what discouraged them from using iSnap, one participant explained, "*it doesn't know what I want to do so it can't tell me what to... do*" [P14]. Another responded that in the instructional video for iSnap, the speaker advised students to use their best judgement when receiving help, noting that one suggestion in the demo was not useful in this situation. This possibility for error made the participant "*feel like the computer doesn't understand*" [P1]. It is clear that a lack of perceptiveness directly dissuaded students from using iSnap. One student did describe iSnap as perceptive, "*I realize it knows what what I'm trying to get at*" [P3], but thought iSnap was unable to translate this knowledge into an interpretable hint. Another, who had a more positive experience with iSnap, experienced some perceptiveness: "*it looks at your code and then it tells what you should probably do*" [P15].

4.3 Attributes of Help

4.3.1 Specificity. Specificity refers to how precise a tutor's help was, whether it consisted of directly actionable suggestions or a higher-level outline. Participants appreciated the human tutor's ability to provide *both* exact advice: "*it was more precise... she would be able to say exactly what I needed*" [P12], and high-level advice: "*tutors have always been helpful... they don't just give you the answers... they actually try to walk you through how to find the answer*" [P6]. The former was appreciated for its efficiency and helpfulness, while the latter was appreciated because it allowed participants to retain a sense of independence and agency (see Section 4.1.3). As one participant noted, "*instead of straight-up just telling me where the commands were, she provided a path for me to think... I think that was helpful*" [P8]. While participants did not directly link Specificity to help-seeking or avoidance, it was tied to the perceived "helpfulness" of the tutor's advice.

Participants also perceived iSnap as providing a variety of types of help. Participants noted appreciating high-level advice: "*it was really good to get the outline of like 'oh this is what needs to be done, not what I have'*" [P12], as well as "*pretty exact advice*" [P15]. Others perceived the help to be so low-level that it was too basic, "*more syntactic than anything else*" [P11]. Participants who never used iSnap's help had mixed expectations of how specific it would be, inferring either that it helps with low-level things "*like the formatting*" [P7] or high-level things like the "*skeleton of the program*" [P9]. Since all participants viewed the same instructional video on iSnap's help, these diverse opinions may have been reflections of expectations based on previous experiences with computer help.

4.3.2 Interpretability. Interpretability refers to how easily the help provided by the tutor can be understood and applied by the student. Participants rarely discussed the interpretability of the human

---

[2]We are not referring here to accessibility as a system's ability to support users regardless of physical or mental ability

tutor, but when they did their comments were positive and terse. The tutor's help simply *"made sense"* [P10], and this influenced participants' trust of the tutor: *"I would trust in her opinion... whenever I followed what she did it made sense"* [P15]. Participants were much more critical of iSnap's interpretability: *"half the things you would click on didn't make sense for the program"* [P10]. A common reason was that iSnap offered no explanation for its suggestions: *"I found it unhelpful, mostly because I wasn't quite sure why it was offering the help that it was offering. It was just like, here's a suggestion- but why?"* [P4]. One participant followed the advice but found the results difficult to interpret: *"I did that and nothing different happened"* [P1]. Others chose not to follow the advice because of difficulty interpreting: *"I saw it, I just wasn't quite sure how to go about implementing it"* [P12].

While some students found the hints too difficult to interpret, others found the need for active interpretation to be worth the time it took: *"I would kind of have to interpret and figure out what it meant... If I was completely lost it would be a really good idea to figure out what it was"* [P12]. Participants recalled that hints that did not make sense at first could become more clear in retrospect after progressing further in the program: *"[it] gave me a hint as to where I need to go later, even though I didn't think it was applicable when I first saw it"* [P15]. One participant even realized, in the middle of explaining why a hint did not make sense, that its suggestion was in fact applicable but hard to understand in the moment: *"they wanted me to change it to an equals sign... um come to think of it I should have set that equal to something... it just wasn't like saying things clearly"* [P14]. Sometimes this interpretation can lead to a student making an unintended discovery. One participant added a custom length parameter to their "draw brick" block, a more advanced feature, based off of a misinterpreted, unrelated hint.

5 DISCUSSION

We now return to our research questions. To address RQ1, we identified key factors which influenced participants' willingness to seek help. Many of these correspond to factors identified in previous research, such the importance of Trust in a tutor's ability [41] or the Accessibility of help [37]. Independence, and the threat that help can present to it, are also well established reasons for help avoidance [7, 17]. Students' experiences of being Stuck leading to help-seeking fit nicely into Newman's dynamic self-efficacy level (SEL), which can prompt help-seeking if it falls below a threshold [30]. However, our results place more emphasis than existing work on students' Previous Experiences and Expectations, as well as their beliefs about the tutor's qualities, such as Perceptiveness. Our results show these factors have direct and indirect influence on help-seeking behavior. Additionally, while previous work mentions "evaluating help" as an important step in help-seeking [26, 29, 30], our results explore specific attributes of help, such as Specificity and Interpretability, that may be particularly relevant when evaluating the quality of computer-based help.

Our results also speak to how the domain of programming specifically impacts students' help-seeking behavior. Programming students are more likely to have had Previous Experiences with computer-based help (e.g. compilers and documentation) that shape

their Expectations. Programming problems have many valid solutions and require students to make design choices, which may make it difficult to Trust help that contradicts those choices: *"that way would work but my way will also work too"* [P11]. That same open-endedness makes clear explanations particularly important when offering help, and participants noted that iSnap's lack of explanation hindered its Interpretability. Some participants believed that one can *"puzzle your way through"* [P15] programming problems with enough time and effort, which justified their decision to continue working Independently. Each of these attributes of programming present specific obstacles that should be addressed to provide effective, computer-based help in this domain.

5.1 Differences and Design Implications

In this section, we address RQ2, which deals with differences in how students experience help-seeking factors with human and computer tutors. We focus on how these differences have design implications for programming ITSs. While not every student needs help, many students do avoid help when they need it [4, 33], so it is important that ITSs are designed to facilitate help-seeking. Our methods and analysis were not intended as an evaluation of iSnap; rather, we use students' experiences with iSnap to highlight the challenges and opportunities that arise when providing computer-based, on-demand help to novice programmers.

Our study highlights some key challenges faced specifically by computer-based help. Unlike with human help, few students have experienced intelligent computer tutoring, which can lead to very low expectations for computer tutors. These expectations will shape how students interact with help, whether or not their preconceptions are accurate. Designers may be able to address this by explaining how their help system works, how it can be used effectively and how it differs from other help technologies (e.g. compilers, documentation). iSnap, for example, could explicitly state that its hints contain advice on achieving a correct solution based on previous students' work, which P1 noted as important in changing their perceptions and trust. Compared to human tutors, participants described trusting a computer as difficult, in part because of preconceptions about its inherent limitations. This was closely tied to a feeling that the computer was not, or could not be, perceptive or adaptive in the way that a human could. For help systems that rely on intelligent algorithms, it may be possible to mitigate this by subtly displaying what the help system *does* perceive and believe about the student's current state. iSnap could accomplish this by displaying the assignment objective it believes the student is currently pursuing, along with hints for this objective. In short, transparency and explanations of the computer's behavior may help to avoid confusion and unfounded mistrust.

Participants also noted some key advantages of computer-based help, describing it as efficient, salient and accessible. iSnap achieved efficiency in part by keeping help light-weight and visual, avoiding the need for *"3 paragraphs for each [hint]"* [P4], which one participant cautioned against. However, the simplicity of the helpfis presentation may have also led students to believe that the help was not very sophisticated (i.e. perceptive/intelligent). iSnap's accessibility and salience were enhanced by embedding the help buttons directly into the code, with help constantly visible and available.

iSnap also seemed to enable some students to seek help but still feel independent. This may be because computer-based help is private and does not risk impacting how others perceive one's competence or social status, as human help does [37]. Just as students may be more willing to seek help from peers than teachers [41], they may be even more willing to seek help from computers. Designers should craft help which minimizes the threat to students' independence and avoids unnecessary intervention, e.g. like *"Microsoft Word and Clippy... popping up"* [P4]. iSnap addressed this in part with the subtlety of its hints, but it could go further by adapting the quantity and specificity of hints to a student's ability level as other ITSs do [25, 45]. Overall, our results suggest that computer tutors are not simply a "worse" version of human tutors; rather, they offer distinct advantages and disadvantages, and may fill an important niche for students unable or unwilling to seek human help.

5.2 Hypotheses

In addition to to addressing our research questions, our results also prompted us to propose new hypotheses about how and why students seek programming help from humans and computers:

H1: The same factors shape students' help-seeking process with both human and computer tutors. We found that few of our initial line-by-line codes directly referenced the human or computer, and when they did, they were often pairs (e.g "human sees what I'm doing"; "iSnap doesn't know what I'm doing"). We therefore selected focused codes that were independent of the tutor itself (e.g. "Perceptiveness"). Our results suggest that the same factors (e.g., Independence, Trust, Accessibility) were relevant with human and computer tutors, but they may matter more for one type of tutor. Our presentation of results reflects this, as the description of each factor includes references to both human and computer tutors. For some factors, one type of tutor was referenced more frequently, perhaps indicating increased importance.

H2: Help-seeking is not simply a triggered response to difficulty; it can be a problem solving strategy. It is clear from our results that being Stuck, on its own, did not always lead to help-seeking, in part due to the participants' desire for Independence. However, participants also reported asking for help for reasons besides perceived difficulty, such as the Salience of help (*"buttons were kind of there"* [P4]), a desire to check one's work (*"confirming that I was doing the right thing"* [P15]), or expediency (*"I just want to get it right quickly"* [P7]). For these students, help was not simply a means of overcoming difficulty, but rather a tool to use in problem solving. We hypothesize that the extent to which students view help-seeking as a viable strategy is the product of a constant negotiation of many factors, which we call the Student Mindset. This contrasts with existing models of help-seeking, in which a help request always arises from a student's recognition of difficulty [26, 29, 30]. We believe that difficulty is a key factor in prompting a student to seek help, but it is neither necessary nor sufficient.

5.3 Limitations

This qualitative analysis of a small dataset has inherent limitations, and our results therefore lend themselves to recommendations and hypotheses rather than definite conclusions. This work is a necessary and expected first step in a larger research effort to understand help-seeking in computing. Our analysis required thoughtfulness and creativity on the part of the researchers, which means it is also a reflection of the researchers and their biases [39]. We attempted to minimize this by recognizing our biases, discussing results among the coders, and consistently supporting our claims with quotations.

The assignments we selected, especially the Guessing Game, were designed for novice programmers and may have been too easy to produce a genuine need for help in some of our more advanced participants, a few of whom reported having done a similar assignment in class. Participants were also new to Snap!, and some help requests centered on its interface, rather than programming generally, which may confound our results. Lastly, we have intentionally avoided a discussion of gender in this paper, as we felt that our dataset included too few females (4) to produce a meaningful comparison, but we acknowledge that it is also a major factor in help-seeking [4, 7].

6 CONCLUSION AND FUTURE WORK

In this work we have presented a qualitative analysis of 15 students' interviews after solving programming problems with both human and computer-based help. We identified 3 categories of factors that directly and indirectly impact students' help-seeking behavior: Inputs, Student Mindset, and Attributes of Help. Our results suggest that students have very different expectations of human and computer tutors, rooted in previous experiences. These Inputs set a baseline for how the student perceives the tutor and the role of help (the Student Mindset), which impacts their help-seeking behavior. If and when students experience help, the Attributes of Help may alter their perceptions of the tutor. We contrasted students' experiences of these factors to understand the differences in how human and computer tutors are perceived. For our participants, a human tutor seemed more trustworthy, perceptive and interpretable, while a computer tutor seemed more accessible and less threatening to a studentfis sense of independence. These initial results have important implications for how we provide help to students, especially through the design of ITSs for computing, as discussed in Section 5.1.

Future work will address aspects of the help-seeking process that we identified but did not discuss here: the ways students seek and avoid help, the types of help the tutor provides, the interface through which help is mediated, outcomes of receiving help and how the students' perceptions are updated after seeking or avoiding help. Our goal is to construct a preliminary model of help-seeking for both human and computer tutoring in the domain of programming, which can serve as a theoretical basis for designing more effective help systems. We plan to use the think-aloud and log data we collected while students programmed to help construct this model and address the hypotheses raised earlier.

7 ACKNOWLEDGEMENTS

The authors thank Jen Tsan for her invaluable help, which made this work possible. This material is based upon work supported by the National Science Foundation under grant 1623470.

REFERENCES

[1] Vincent Aleven and Kenneth R. Koedinger. 2000. Limitations of Student Control: Do Students Know When They Need Help?. In *Intelligent tutoring systems*. 292–303. DOI:http://dx.doi.org/10.1007/3-540-45108-0_33

[2] Vincent Aleven, Bruce M. McLaren, Ido Roll, and Kenneth R. Koedinger. 2006. Toward Meta-cognitive Tutoring: A Model of Help Seeking with a Cognitive Tutor. *International Journal of Artificial Intelligence in Education* 16, 2 (2006), 101–128. DOI:http://dx.doi.org/10.1.1.121.9138

[3] Vincent Aleven, Ido Roll, Bruce M. McLaren, and Kenneth R. Koedinger. 2016. Help Helps, But Only So Much: Research on Help Seeking with Intelligent Tutoring Systems. *International Journal of Artificial Intelligence in Education* 26, 1 (2016), 1–19. DOI:http://dx.doi.org/10.1007/s40593-015-0089-1

[4] Vincent Aleven, Elmar Stahl, Silke Schworm, Frank Fischer, and Raven Wallace. 2003. Help Seeking and Help Design in Interactive Learning Environments Vincent. *Review of Educational Research* 73, 3 (2003), 277–320.

[5] Tobias Bartholomé, Elmar Stahl, and Rainer Bromme. 2004. Help-Seeking in Interactive Learning Environments: Effectiveness of Help and Learner-Related Factors in a Dyadic Setting. In *Proceedings of the 6th international conference on Learning sciences*. 81–88.

[6] Benjamin S. Bloom. 1984. The 2 sigma problem: The search for methods of group instruction as effective as one-to-one tutoring. *Educational Researcher* 13, 6 (1984), 4–16. DOI:http://dx.doi.org/10.3102/0013189X013006004

[7] Ruth Butler. 1998. Determinants of Help Seeking: Relations Between Perceived Reasons for Classroom Help-Avoidance and Help-Seeking Behaviors in an Experimental Context. *Journal of Educational Psychology* 90, 4 (1998), 630–643. DOI:http://dx.doi.org/10.1037/0022-0663.90.4.630

[8] Kathy Charmaz. 2008. Grounded Theory. In *Qualitative Psychology* (2 ed.), Johnathan A Smith (Ed.). SAGE Publications, Inc., 81–110.

[9] Kathy Charmaz and Linda Liska Belgrave. 2012. *Qualitative Interviewing and Grounded Theory Analysis*. SAGE Publications, Inc. 347–366 pages. DOI:http://dx.doi.org/10.4135/9781452218403

[10] Albert Corbett and John R. Anderson. 2001. Locus of Feedback Control in Computer-Based Tutoring: Impact on Learning Rate, Achievement and Attitudes. In *Proceedings of the SIGCHI Conference on Human Computer Interaction*. 245–252.

[11] Albert T. Corbett. 2001. Cognitive Computer Tutors: Solving the Two-Sigma Problem. In *Proceedings of the 8th International Conference on User Modeling*. 137–147. http://link.springer.com/chapter/10.1007/3-540-44566-8

[12] Juliet Corbin and Anselm Strauss. 2008. *Basics of Qualitative Research* (3 ed.). 379 pages. DOI:http://dx.doi.org/10.4135/9781452230153

[13] Paul Denny, Andrew Luxton-Reilly, and Dave Carpenter. 2014. Enhancing Syntax Error Messages Appears Ineffectual. In *Proceedings of the 19th ACM Conference on Innovation & Technology in Computer Science Education*. 273–278. DOI:http://dx.doi.org/10.1145/2591708.2591748

[14] Sue Fitzgerald, Beth Simon, and Lynda Thomas. 2005. Strategies that Students Use to Trace Code. *Proceedings of the 2005 International Workshop on Computing Education Research* (2005), 69–80. DOI:http://dx.doi.org/10.1145/1089786.1089793

[15] Dan Garcia, Brian Harvey, and Tiffany Barnes. 2015. The Beauty and Joy of Computing. *ACM Inroads* 6, 4 (2015), 71–79.

[16] Alex Gerdes, Bastiaan Heeren, Johan Jeuring, and L. Thomas van Binsbergen. 2016. Ask-Elle: an Adaptable Programming Tutor for Haskell Giving Automated Feedback. *International Journal of Artificial Intelligence in Education* 27, 1 (2016), 1–36.

[17] Stuart A. Karabenick. 2004. Perceived Achievement Goal Structure and College Student Help Seeking. *Journal of Educational Psychology* 96, 3 (2004), 569–581. DOI:http://dx.doi.org/10.1037/0022-0663.96.3.569

[18] Päivi Kinnunen and Beth Simon. 2010. Building Theory about Computing Education Phenomena: A Discussion of Grounded Theory. *Proceedings of the 10th Koli Calling International Conference on Computing Education Research* (2010), 37–42. DOI:http://dx.doi.org/10.1145/1930464.1930469

[19] Päivi Kinnunen and Beth Simon. 2010. Experiencing Programming Assignments in CS1: The Emotional Toll. *Icer'10* (2010), 77–85. DOI:http://dx.doi.org/10.1145/1839594.1839609

[20] Päivi Kinnunen and Beth Simon. 2011. CS Majors' Self-Efficacy Perceptions in CS1: Results in Light of Social Cognitive Theory. *Icer'11* (2011), 19–26. DOI:http://dx.doi.org/10.1145/2016911.2016917

[21] Daniel Knox and Sally Fincher. 2013. Where Students Go for Knowledge and What They Find There. *Proceedings of the ninth annual international ACM conference on International computing education research - ICER '13* (2013), 35. DOI:http://dx.doi.org/10.1145/2493394.2493399

[22] Andrew J. Ko and Brad A. Myers. 2004. Designing the Whyline: A Debugging Interface for Asking Questions about Program Behavior. *Focus* 6, 1 (2004), 151–158. DOI:http://dx.doi.org/10.1145/985692.985712

[23] Colleen M. Lewis, Ruth E. Anderson, and Ken Yasuhara. 2016. "I Don't Code All Day": Fitting in Computer Science When the Stereotypes Don't Fit. *Proceedings of the 2016 ACM Conference on International Computing Education Research - ICER '16* (2016), 23–32. DOI:http://dx.doi.org/10.1145/2960310.2960332

[24] Colleen M. Lewis, Ken Yasuhara, and Ruth E. Anderson. 2011. Deciding to major in Computer Science: A grounded Theory of Sudents' Self-Assessment of Ability. In *Proceedings of the Seventh International Workshop on Computing Education Research*. 3–10. DOI:http://dx.doi.org/10.1145/2016911.2016915

[25] Rosemary Luckin and Benedict Du Boulay. 1999. Ecolab: The Development and Evaluation of a Vygotskian Design Framework. *International Journal of Artificial Intelligence in Education* 10 (1999), 198–220.

[26] Julien Mercier and Carl Frederiksen. 2008. The Structure of the Help-Seeking Process in Collaboratively Using a Computer Coach in Problem-Based Learning. *Computers and Education* 51, 1 (2008), 17–33. DOI:http://dx.doi.org/10.1016/j.compedu.2007.03.004

[27] Briana B. Morrison. 2015. Computer Science Is Different! Educational Psychology Experiments Do Not Reliably Replicate in Programming Domain. In *Proceedings of the International Computing Education Research (ICER) Conference*. 267–268.

[28] Briana B Morrison, Lauren E Margulieux, and Cherry Street. 2015. Subgoals, Context, and Worked Examples in Learning Computing Problem Solving. In *International Computing Education Research Conference (ICER)*. 21–29. DOI:http://dx.doi.org/10.1145/2787622.2787733

[29] Sharon Nelson-Le Gall. 1981. Help-seeking: An Understudied Problem-Solving Skill in Children. *Developmental Review* 1, 3 (1981), 224–246. DOI:http://dx.doi.org/10.1016/0273-2297(81)90019-8

[30] Richard S. Newman. 1994. Adaptive Help Seeking: A Strategy of Self-Regulated Learning. In *Self-regulation of learning and performance: Issues and educational applications*. 283–301.

[31] Thomas W Price, Yihuan Dong, and Tiffany Barnes. 2016. Generating Data-driven Hints for Open-ended Programming. In *Proceedings of the International Conference on Educational Data Mining*.

[32] Thomas W. Price, Yihuan Dong, and Dragan Lipovac. 2017. iSnap: Towards Intelligent Tutoring in Novice Programming Environments. In *Proceedings of the ACM Technical Symposium on Computer Science Education*.

[33] Thomas W Price, Rui Zhi, and Tiffany Barnes. 2017. Hint Generation Under Uncertainty: The Effect of Hint Quality on Help-Seeking Behavior. In *Proceedings of the International Conference on Artificial Intelligence in Education*.

[34] Kelly Rivers and Kenneth R. Koedinger. 2015. Data-Driven Hint Generation in Vast Solution Spaces: a Self-Improving Python Programming Tutor. *International Journal of Artificial Intelligence in Education* 16, 1 (2015).

[35] Ido Roll, Vincent Aleven, Bruce M. McLaren, Eunjeong Ryu, Ryan SJD Baker, and Kenneth R. Koedinger. 2006. The Help Tutor: Does Metacognitive Feedback Improve Students' Help-Seeking Actions, Skills and Learning?. In *International Conference on Intelligent Tutoring Systems*. 360–369. DOI:http://dx.doi.org/10.1007/11774303_36

[36] Allison M. Ryan and Paul R. Pintrich. 1997. "Should I ask for help?" The role of motivation and attitudes in adolescents' help seeking in math class. *Journal of Educational Psychology* 89, 2 (1997), 329–341. DOI:http://dx.doi.org/10.1037/0022-0663.89.2.329

[37] Allison M. Ryan, Paul R. Pintrich, and Carol Midgley. 2001. Avoiding Seeking Help in the Classroom: Who and Why? *Educational Psychology Review* 13, 2 (2001), 93–114. DOI:http://dx.doi.org/10.1023/A:1009034420053

[38] Juha Sorva, Ville Karavirta, and Lauri Malmi. 2013. A Review of Generic Program Visualization Systems for Introductory Programming Education. *ACM Transactions on Computing Education* 13, 4 (2013), 15.1 – 15.64. DOI:http://dx.doi.org/10.1145/2490822

[39] Anselm Strauss and Juliet Corbin. 1990. Basics of Qualitative Research: Grounded Theory Procedure and Techniques. *Qualitative Sociology* 13, 1 (1990), 3–21.

[40] Bram E. Vaessen, Frans J. Prins, and Johan Jeuring. 2014. University Students' Achievement Goals and Help-Seeking Strategies in an Intelligent Tutoring System. *Computers and Education* 72 (2014), 196–208.

[41] Hans Van der Meij. 1988. Constraints on Question Asking in Classrooms. *Journal of Educational Psychology* 80, 3 (1988), 401–405. DOI:http://dx.doi.org/10.1037/0022-0663.80.3.401

[42] Kurt Vanlehn. 2006. The Behavior of Tutoring Systems. *International Journal of Artificial Intelligence in Education* 16, 3 (2006), 227–265.

[43] Gerhard Weber and Peter Brusilovsky. 2001. ELM-ART: An Adaptive Versatile System for Web-based Instruction. *International Journal of Artificial Intelligence in Education* 12, 4 (2001), 351–384. DOI:http://dx.doi.org/10.1.1.66.6245

[44] David Wood. 2001. Scaffolding, contingent tutoring and computer-supported learning. *International Journal of Artificial Intelligence in Education* 12 (2001), 280–292.

[45] H. Wood and D. Wood. 1999. Help seeking, learning and contingent tutoring. *Computers & Education* 33, 2-3 (1999), 153–169. DOI:http://dx.doi.org/10.1016/S0360-1315(99)00030-5

Conceptions and Misconceptions about Computational Thinking among Italian Primary School Teachers

Isabella Corradini
Themis Research Centre
Rome, Italy
isabellacorradini@themiscrime.com

Michael Lodi
University of Bologna
Dep. of Comp. Science and Eng.
Bologna, Italy
michael.lodi2@unibo.it

Enrico Nardelli
University of Roma "Tor Vergata"
Department of Mathematics
Rome, Italy
nardelli@mat.uniroma2.it

ABSTRACT

Many advanced countries are recognizing more and more the importance of teaching computing, in some cases even as early as in primary school. "Computational thinking" is the term often used to denote the conceptual core of computer science or "the way a computer scientist thinks", as Wing put it. Such term - given also the lack of a widely accepted definition - has become a "buzzword" meaning different things to different people. We investigated the Italian primary school teachers' conceptions about computational thinking by analyzing the results of a survey (N=972) conducted in the context of "Programma il Futuro" project. Teachers have been asked to provide a definition of computational thinking and to answer three additional related closed-ended questions. The analysis shows that, while almost half of teachers (43.4%) have included in their definitions some fundamental elements of computational thinking, very few (10.8%) have been able to provide an acceptably complete definition. On a more positive note, the majority is aware that computational thinking is not characterized by coding or by the use of information technology.

KEYWORDS

Computational thinking definition; Informatics education; Conceptions and misconceptions; Primary school teachers

ACM Reference format:
Isabella Corradini, Michael Lodi, and Enrico Nardelli. 2017. Conceptions and Misconceptions about Computational Thinking among Italian Primary School Teachers. In *Proceedings of ICER '17, Tacoma, WA, USA, August 18-20, 2017,* 9 pages.
https://doi.org/10.1145/3105726.3106194

1 INTRODUCTION

1.1 Context

The wide popularity gained by the expression "computational thinking" (CT, from now on) after the Wing's paper [20] risks to spoil the original aim. More and more people are now considering CT a new subject, somehow different or distinct from computer science ("computing" in UK, "informatics" in Europe).

We are convinced this approach is wrong and misleading: in the long run it will do more harm than benefit to informatics. After all, in schools they do not teach "linguistic thinking" or "mathematical thinking", with specific "body of knowledge" or "assessment methods". Others, e.g. [7], [2], and [9], share our concerns for the dangers of such an approach.

On the other side, the concept of computational thinking, interpreted as "being able to think like a computer scientist and being able to apply this competence to every field of human endeavor" is sorely needed. In fact, it supports the goal of teaching scientific and cultural aspects of computing in schools, focusing on principles and methods more than on systems and tools. This is required since informatics is the science underlying the digital technology pervading all aspects of contemporary society.

Teachers' conceptions regarding a subject are essential for a proper teaching of the subject itself. We therefore investigated the Italian primary school teachers' conceptions about computational thinking and information technology (IT) and how they relate to computer science concepts and principles.

We conducted our investigation in the context of "Programma il Futuro" project[1] [15], whose goal is to increase awareness of informatics as the scientific basis of digital technologies among teachers in Italian primary and secondary schools. The project has adapted Code.org learning material and has introduced it to Italian schools with the support of a dedicated web site, featuring also an introduction to CT. Response has been enthusiastic in terms of participation: in the first two school-years (2014-15 and 2015-16) more than one million students have been engaged and have completed a total of 10 million hours of informatics in schools [6].

1.2 Purpose of the study

Our research has investigated the knowledge level of CT among Italian primary school teachers. More specifically, we addressed the following research questions:

RQ1 which level of understanding do they have with respect to the concept of computational thinking?
RQ2 how do they perceive the relation between technology and computational thinking?
RQ3 how much do they feel prepared to teach computational thinking?

---

[1]https://programmailfuturo.it

In this paper we use the term *misconception*. In general, the term indicates an incorrect view based on faulty thinking or understanding[2]. In Computer Science Education research literature, the term is often used in the specific context of learning to program, and refers to an inadequate understanding of fundamental programming concepts (for a review see [19]). In this paper we are not referring to such difficulties, but rather to incorrect ideas about what CT is; so we are using the term in its general sense (like, e.g., in [8]).

2 LITERATURE OVERVIEW

2.1 Definition of CT

2.1.1 Five (of many) definitions. The term "computational thinking" was firstly used by Seymour Papert in his book *Mindstorms* [16] and in a work on Mathematics education [17]. After this expression was revived in 2006 by Jeannette Wing [20], many definitions emerged, mainly to support the introduction of CT in K-12 education. In this paper we discuss five important definitions:

- the "Cuny Snyder Wing" definition of CT [22] (that builds on the informal definition in [20] and the philosophical discussion in [21]);
- the 2011 Operational Definition from International Society for Technology in Education (ISTE) and the Computer Science Teachers Association (CSTA) [14];
- the definition proposed by Google in its collection of CT resources [11];
- the definition by Brennan and Resnick [4] about CT in Scratch;
- the definition from UK project Barefoot CAS [5].

Wing informally defines CT as "thinking like computer scientists" [20] and then more formally as "*the thought processes involved in formulating problems and their solutions so that the solutions are represented in a form that can be effectively carried out by an information-processing agent*" [22][3]. In her papers she also identifies characteristic elements of CT. In particular she states the most important elements are *abstraction* (the "mental" tool of computing) and *automation* (using computer, the "metal" tool of computer scientists) - she states that "computing is the automation of our abstractions" [21]. In [22] she recognizes important overlapping or inclusions between CT and other types of thinking: logical thinking, algorithmic thinking, parallel thinking, compositional reasoning, pattern matching, procedural thinking, and recursive thinking.

ISTE and CSTA propose an operational definition, targeting specifically K-12 educators. They define CT as "*a problem-solving process that includes (but is not limited to) the following characteristics: Formulating problems in a way that enables us to use a computer and other tools to help solve them; Logically organizing and analyzing data; Representing data through abstractions such as models and simulations; Automating solutions through algorithmic thinking (a series of ordered steps); Identifying, analyzing, and implementing possible solutions with the goal of achieving the most efficient and effective combination of steps and resources; Generalizing and transferring this*

problem-solving process to a wide variety of problems." Moreover they state that CT is "*supported and enhanced by a number of dispositions or attitudes*" that includes "*Confidence in dealing with complexity; Persistence in working with difficult problems; Tolerance for ambiguity; The ability to deal with open ended problems; The ability to communicate and work with others to achieve a common goal or solution*" [14]. Finally they propose a CT vocabulary [13], listing a set of CT terms with a brief definition/explanation: *Data Collection; Data Analysis; Data Representation; Problem Decomposition; Abstraction; Algorithms and Procedures; Automation; Simulation; Parallelization.*

Google assumes the same ISTE/CSTA definition but - instead of a vocabulary - lists and (re)defines a series of CT concepts [11], pointing out that they are *mental processes* or *tangible outcomes*: *Abstraction; Algorithm Design; Automation; Data Analysis; Data Collection; Data Representation; Decomposition; Parallelization; Pattern Generalization; Pattern Recognition; Simulation.*

Brennan and Resnick [4] present a *computational thinking framework*, to describe learning and development that take place when designing and programming interactive media with Scratch platform. They state CT involves three dimensions: *computational concepts* designers employ as they program: sequences, loops, parallelism, events, conditionals, operators, and data; *computational practices* designers develop as they program: being incremental and iterative, testing and debugging, reusing and remixing, and abstracting and modularizing; *computational perspectives* designers form about the world around them and about themselves: expressing, connecting, and questioning.

CAS [5] assumes a Wing-like definition: CT is "*learning to think in ways which allow us, as humans, to solve problems more effectively and, when appropriate, use computers to help us do so*" and then states it involves six concepts (*Logic; Algorithms; Decomposition; Patterns; Abstraction; Evaluation*) and five approaches (*Tinkering; Creating; Debugging; Persevering; Collaborating*).

2.1.2 Common aspects. We compared CT elements found in the analyzed definitions, in analogy with what was done in [9].

Those who give a precise definition agree on the fact that CT is a **way of thinking** (thought process) for **problem solving**. They all somehow specify that it is not just problem solving: the formulation and the solution of the problem must be expressed in a way that allows a **processing agent** (a human or a machine) to carry it out.

Apart from the general statement, all definitions list some constitutive elements of CT. These elements are of very different kinds (from thinking habits to specific programming concepts) and many authors group them in categories, but there is no common agreement on the classification.

We classified all the elements in four categories. For each category we list the elements, trying to summarize all aspects stated in the analyzed definitions. Note that many elements are shared between informatics and other scientific disciplines, but computing features a unique combination of them.

- **Mental processes**: mental strategies useful to solve problems.
  - *Algorithmic thinking*: use algorithmic thinking [14, 21, 22] to design a sequence of ordered step (instructions) to solve a problem, achieve a goal or perform a task [4, 5, 11, 13].

---

[2]Oxford Dictionary, https://en.oxforddictionaries.com/definition/misconception
[3]This definition is attributed to Jan Cuny, Larry Snyder and Jeannette M. Wing, in an unpublished work ("Demystifying Computational Thinking for Non-Computer Scientists", 2010). Moreover, Wing says it was originated by a discussion with Alfred Aho, who provided a very similar (but with a more "algorithmic thinking" flavor) definition [1]

- *Logical thinking*: use logical thinking [22] and reasoning to make sense of things, establish and check facts [5].
- *Problem Decomposition*: split a complex problem in simpler subproblems to solve it more easily [5, 11, 13]; modularize [4]; use compositional reasoning [21].
- *Abstraction*: get rid of useless details to focus on relevant information/ideas [4, 5, 11, 13, 22].
- *Pattern recognition*: discover and use regularities in data, problems [5, 11, 22].
- *Generalization*: use discovered similarities to make predictions or to solve more general problems [5, 11].
- **Methods**: operational approaches widely used by computer scientists.
  - *Automation*: automate the solutions [14, 21]; use a computer or a machine to do repetitive tasks [11, 13].
  - *Data Collection, Analysis and Representation*: gather information/data, make sense of them by finding patterns, represent them properly [11, 13]; store, retrieve and update values [4].
  - *Parallelization*: carry out tasks simultaneously to reach a common goal [4, 11, 13], use parallel thinking [22].
  - *Simulation*: represent data and (real world) processes through models [11, 14], run experiments on models [13].
  - *Evaluation*: implement and analyze solutions [14] to judge them [5], in particular for what concerns effectiveness, efficiency in terms of time and resources [14].
  - *Programming*: use some common concepts in programming (eg. loops, events, conditionals, mathematical and logical operators [4]).
- **Practices**: typical practices used in the implementation of computing machinery based solutions.
  - *Experimenting, iterating, tinkering*: in iterative and incremental software development, one develops a project with repeated iterations of a design-build-test cycle, incrementally building the final result [4]; tinkering means trying things out using a trial and error process, learning by playing, exploring, and experimenting [5].
  - *Test and debug*: verify that solutions work by trying them out [4]; find and solve problems (bugs) in a solution/ program [5].
  - *Reuse and remix*: build your solution on existing code, projects, ideas [4].
- **Transversal skills**: general ways of seeing and operating in the world; useful life skills enhanced by thinking like a computer scientist.
  - *Create*: design and build things [5], use computation to be creative and express yourself [4].
  - *Communicate and collaborate*: connect with others and work together to create something with a common goal and to ensure a better solution [4, 5, 14].
  - *Reflect, learn, meta-reflect*: use computation to reflect and understand computational aspects of the world [4].
  - *Be tolerant for ambiguity*: deal with non-well specified and open-ended real-world problems [14].

- *Be persistent when dealing with complex problems*: be confident in working with difficult or complex problems [14], persevering, being determined, resilient and tenacious [5].

2.2 Related work

A few works investigated teachers' conceptions about CT, computing and their relation with IT.

Yadav and colleagues conducted two experiments [23, 24] to asses pre-service teachers' "attitudes towards and understanding of computational thinking" and how they changed after attending a CT module in a course of an Education major. Both a pre and a post questionnaire were used in these studies. The first one (N=100) did not have a control group, that was introduced in the second study (N = 294, 141 in the treatment group and 153 in the control group). In both experiments, results showed such module was effective to influence teachers' understanding of CT and to improve their positive attitudes toward CT and its integration into the classroom.

Bower and Falkner [3] conducted a pilot survey on 44 pre-service teachers, investigating their awareness of CT, conceptions regarding the term, use of IT and pedagogical strategies for CT development, and confidence in teaching CT.

Duncan and colleagues [9] report the post-lesson feedbacks from 13 primary school teachers (with no previous experience in teaching computer science) participating in an ongoing study on teaching CT in New Zealand. They report about teacher confidence, level of difficulty of the lessons, common themes emerged in the answers, and teachers' misconceptions.

3 METHODS

3.1 Instrument

Periodical surveys are conducted in "Programma il Futuro" project by means of on-line questionnaires collecting quantitative and qualitative data.

We investigated our research questions in this context. A questionnaire, with some additional questions relevant to the current research, was sent in December 2016, after the CS Educational Week, to all 24,939 teachers enrolled into the project. They filled it out anonymously and we received 3,593 answers up to the end of January 2017.

Teachers belong to all level of schools, from kindergarten to higher secondary schools. Some of them participated this school-year to the project for the first time, others for the second or third time.

For our research, we asked teachers to complete - if they wished - the sentence

Q1 *"In my view computational thinking is..."*

that is we asked them to provide their definition of CT.

We also asked teachers to choose their level of agreement, on a 4-point Likert scale, with the following statements:

Q2 *Being able to use technological devices means having developed computational thinking competences*

Q3 *Computational thinking competences can be adequately developed in primary schools without using technological devices*

We finally asked teachers to grade (4-point Likert scale)

Q4 *How much do you feel prepared to develop computational thinking in your students?*

and to indicate the

Q5 *Most important initiatives to improve your preparation*

by choosing up to 3 answers among:

- training
- availability of technology
- organizational support
- methodological guidelines
- learning objectives and teaching content

In the current study we focus only on answers from primary schools teachers who participated this school-year for the first time (N=972).

3.2 Sample description

We provide here a description of the sample, 93,7% of which are women, apparently not far from the national value (96,4%) for primary school teachers. But this implies 6,3% are men, which is almost the double of the national value (3,6%): this appears to be a confirmation of the current situation where men are more attracted to computing than women.

Figure 1 shows the distribution of teaching seniority in our sample, while figure 2 shows age distribution.

Teaching seniority (years)

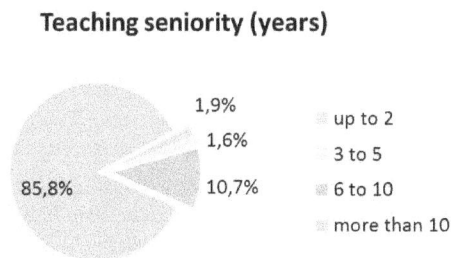

Figure 1: Teacher seniority in years.

Both of them show our sample is made, to a very large extent (>80%), by mature and experienced teachers. This grounds our findings on a reliable base of subjects, but on the other side indicates most probably they have not received any formal or structured training in informatics.

3.3 Procedures

3.3.1 Quantitative analysis. We used standard descriptive statistical methods to analyze closed-ended answers (Q2 to Q5). More specifically, we computed the frequency distribution of these answers.

3.3.2 Qualitative analysis. Among the 972 answers, we filtered out those (116) that did not provide a definition and also those (77) that were completely out of scope (e.g.: they answered "interesting" or "useful").

Age (years)

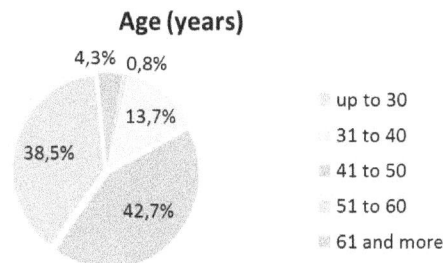

Figure 2: Age of teachers in years.

We then proceeded to identify, by reading and discussing, the conceptual categories present in the remaining 779 definitions.

In a first phase each of us independently analyzed the definitions and proposed a set of conceptual categories to classify them. We used a mixed approach: some categories were defined "a priori", on the basis of literature overview and related work described in section 2, others were grounded on the definitions themselves. We then met to examine the proposed sets of categories and through discussion we agreed to a preliminary set.

We then manually assigned each answer to one or more category, if the statement either declared CT was of the same nature as the category or stated CT had relations to or was useful for the category.

For this process the set of answers was split in three, and each of us assigned answers in his/her set to one or more category. During this process proposals for modifications to categories emerged. Then we met again and jointly examined both these proposed modifications and assignments. Through discussion, we came to agree on the final set of 17 categories (described in subsection 5.1) and the final assignment of each definition to one or more category.

3.3.3 Measuring CT knowledge. To be able to measure the *level* of teachers' knowledge about CT we used the following procedure. We assigned a weight (see discussion in subsection 5.1) to each category according to its relevance (in our view) for CT definition, in the light of the main definitions known in the literature (see subsection 2.1). Finally, the *level* of an answer was computed as the sum of weights of categories it is assigned to.

4 QUANTITATIVE RESULTS

4.1 Technology and computational thinking

The distribution of agreement with the two statements (Q2, Q3) investigating relations between computational thinking and technological devices are respectively shown in figures 3 and 4.

It is positive that almost half of the teachers *disagree* with Q2, and just 17.1% *agrees* or *strongly agrees* with the statement. This shows Italian primary schools teachers have a sufficiently clear understanding that computing is not the same thing as using IT devices. This is supported by the qualitative analysis results discussed in section 5. We observe the results discussed in [3, 23, 24] appear to show a much higher level of misconceptions regarding CT in teachers but we note that those analysis were conducted on

Q2. Being able to use technological devices means having developed CT

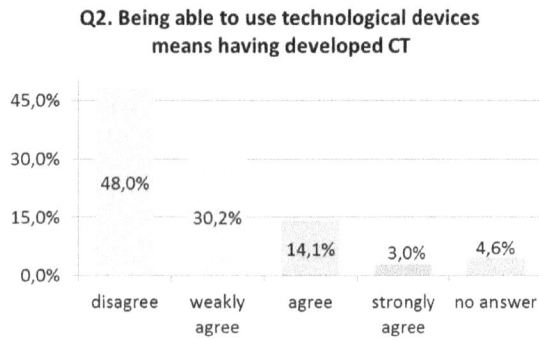

Figure 3: Technological devices and CT.

Q3. CT can be adequately developed in primary schools without using technological devices

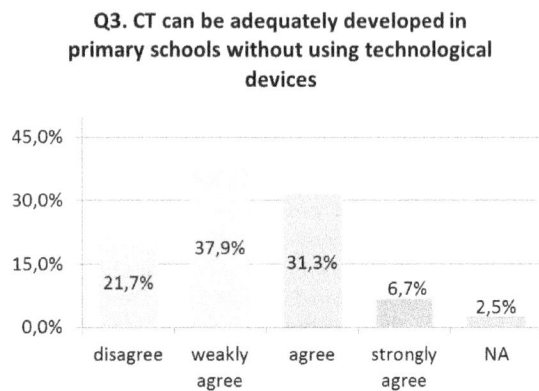

Figure 4: CT without technological devices.

Q4. How much do you feel prepared to develop CT in your students?

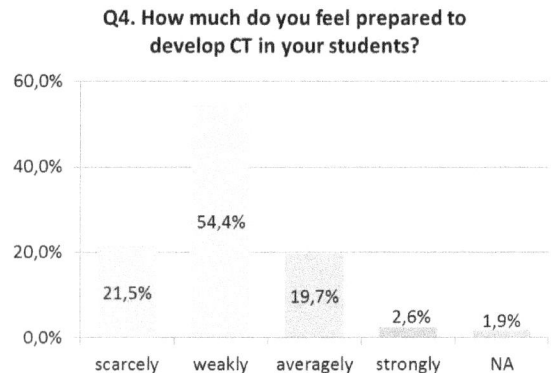

Figure 5: Teachers self-perception of their preparation.

Q5. Most important initiatives to improve your preparation

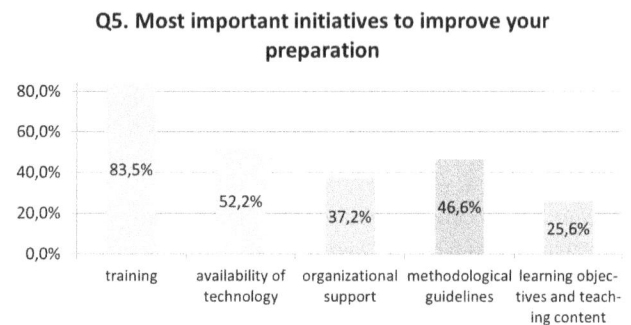

Figure 6: Most important initiative to improve teachers' preparation.

a different (smaller) sample (pre-service teachers) operating in a different culture (USA or Australia).

A positive insight is also given by answers to Q3. In fact, only less than a quarter (21.7%) of teachers thinks an adequate development of CT requires the use of technological devices, while 38.0% *agrees* or *strongly agrees* with Q3. It has also to be noted that spontaneous skill transfer among domain is an unsupported claim [12, 18].

4.2 Teachers' preparation

Self-perception of teachers with respect to their level of preparation to develop CT competences in their students (Q4, Q5) is shown in figure 5.

It is apparent that a large majority does not feel adequately prepared. This is coherent with the following facts regarding Italian schools:

- preparation of primary school teachers is not focused on specific disciplines but has a broad scope
- there is not a specific training program in computing for school teachers of primary and lower secondary levels

Figure 6 shows which initiatives teachers consider most important to improve their preparation (they could choose up to 3 items). Training is by far the most chosen one, which we feel is depending on the nature of our sample. This choice has also a rational support

in the positive training effects noted in [23, 24]. A bit more worrying, in our view, is that slightly more than half of the teachers does not feel the need for *methodological guidelines* and just one quarter considers *learning objectives and teaching content* important to improve their preparation.

5 QUALITATIVE RESULTS

5.1 Categories

We now describe the 17 categories emerged from our analysis. We present them in four classes and indicate between parentheses the weight assigned to each category in a class for the purpose of the procedure described in 3.3.2.

- **Fundamental** (+2) - these categories express elements absolutely necessary in any definition of CT.

  PSOL Problem solving: action(s) or process(es) leading to solve a problem, to reach a goal, to face a complex situation.

  MENT Mental process or tool: a cognitive ability, a mental competence.

  ALGO Algorithmic thinking: devising an algorithm to solve a problem; defining an effective method or strategy or plan; solving a problem by means of a sequence of elementary steps.

AUTO Giving instructions/automation: instructing some agent to solve a problem; providing a procedure to an information processing agent.

METH Using/learning informatics methods: the ability of using informatics concepts and methods; learning informatics.

- **Important** (+1) - these categories express elements that are important for a definition of CT but are not fundamental.

  DECO Problem decomposition: splitting a complex problem in simpler subproblems to solve it more easily.

  LOGI Logical thinking: logical or reasoning or analytical skills.

  ABST Abstraction: focusing on common characteristic of general value; reusing a solution in other situations; devising a solution for a more general situation.

  CODE Write programs: writing programs; coding.

- **Part-of** (0) - these categories express elements that are somehow present in definitions of CT reported in the literature; in some sense they are not necessary for a well-formed definition of CT.

  MCOG Meta-cognition: reflecting about thinking or learning; learning to learn.

  TRAN Transversal competence: e.g. fourth skill, transversal skill, life skill, useful in other fields, of general use, useful for teaching and learning.

  CREA Creative thinking: being able to find creative or original solutions to problems; creativity.

  UNIT Understanding information technology: understanding how information technology devices work; understanding science behind IT.

  LANG Programming language: a language to communicate with IT devices.

  ITER Iterative development: operating by means of successive refinements, possibly based on trial and error or testing and debugging.

- **Misleading** (-1) - these categories express elements whose presence in the definition of CT takes away from a correct understanding.

  THPC "Think" like a computer: act mechanically like a machine, not behaving like a human.

  UDEV Using IT: being able to use information technology devices and programs as an end-user.

5.2 Analysis of category distribution

The distribution of assignments of definitions to categories is shown in figure 7, where different colors code different classes (remember each definition was classified under one or more category).

To better understand the distribution and its analysis, note that "Programma il Futuro" website provides some introductory information[4], with a discussion on the role of computer science in the digital society and the importance of informatics as an autonomous scientific discipline, based on [10]. It also informally describes what CT is ("*Computational thinking is a mental process for problem-solving with distinctive techniques and general intellectual practices*")[5].

---

[4] https://programmailfuturo.it/progetto/perche-partecipare
[5] https://programmailfuturo.it/progetto/cose-il-pensiero-computazionale

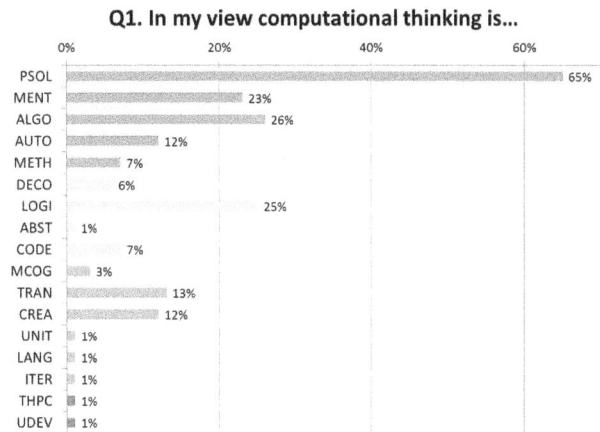

Figure 7: Frequency of each category in Q1.

This may explain why two thirds of the answers identified *problem solving* as an element of the definition of CT.

We note that some categories have a surprisingly high frequency relatively to their importance (in our view) for the definition of CT: *logical thinking*, *transversal competence*, and *creative thinking*. A possible motivation is that a Google query in Italian about computational thinking returns these terms in the first few results.

Also, it is somewhat surprising the low frequency of use of *abstraction* to characterize CT, given the very strong stance taken by Wing in respect to it. We think the conceptual difficulty inherent with the role of abstraction in informatics may explain this outcome.

It is worth noting that *writing programs* has a relatively low frequency: this shows that not so many teachers make the mistake of equating coding and CT.

5.3 Analysis of answer values distribution

5.3.1 Approach. Since all definitions (with their constitutive elements) of CT considered in subsection 2.1, if classified and evaluated with our procedure in 3.3.3, have a value of at least 8, we decided to use this as the threshold to identify the class of "good definitions". We also set the "acceptable definition" threshold at 6. In fact, to reach 6, an answer must have been labeled with categories defined in subsection 5.1 so that it falls within one of the following cases:

- (c1) at least 3 fundamental
- (c2) 2 fundamental and at least 2 important
- (c3) 1 fundamental and 4 important

In other words, there is no way for an answer to be evaluated as an "acceptable definition" if it does not have at least 1 fundamental. But 1 or 2 fundamental alone are not enough, if they are not accompanied by a large enough number of important.

We consider all definitions whose value is 5 or less as misconceptions.

5.3.2 Outcome. Our procedure evaluates just 8 of the 779 answers as "good definitions". The number of those being acceptable

Answer values distribution

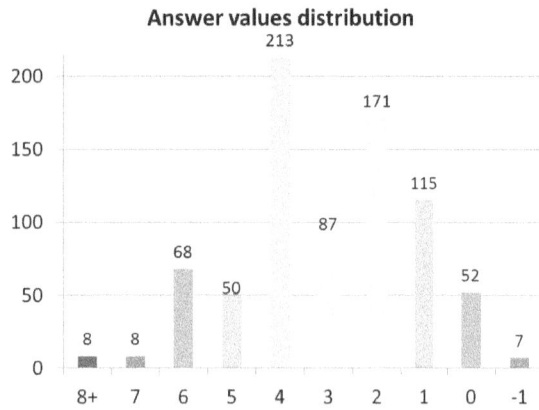

Figure 8: Answer values distribution.

but not good are 76, resulting in a total of just about 10.8% of all answers being at least acceptable. This result appears to be correlated with the feeling of a weak preparation reported in figure 5.

Also, all of not acceptable answers with a value of 5 and 96% of those with a value of 4 have at least 2 fundamental. This leads to a comforting 43.4% of answers that features the presence of at least two fundamental components for a CT definition.

The 695 not acceptable answers (i.e., the misconceptions) are roughly evenly split among those with a value at least 3, and those with a value less than 3: see in figure 8 the overall distribution.

Moreover, we investigated the frequency with which each couple of categories appeared in the definition. We report in table 1 the 27 most frequent couples with at least 2% frequency. This table

Table 1: Most frequent (%) couples of categories.

	MENT	ALGO	AUTO	METH	DECO	LOGI	CODE	TRAN	CREA
PSOL	17	22	8	5	5	10	2	6	8
ALGO	4				2	4		2	
AUTO	2	2				2	2		
METH	4							2	
LOGI	2				2			2	
TRAN	5								
CREA	2	3				4			2

therefore shows the frequency with which (at least) both categories have labeled answers, that is their frequency of co-occurrence. Row and column headings appear in the same order as in subsection 5.1 and, to make the table more compact, not all categories are listed.

Note that PSOL plays a leading role, which is understandable given two thirds of definitions have received its label. A positive element is the relatively high frequency of co-occurrence of PSOL with ALGO (22%): this can be interpreted as an evidence that that about 11% of answers (22%-10.8%), even if not acceptable, are characterized by a sound (even if incomplete) description of computing.

5.4 Conceptions and misconceptions regarding CT

Examining all the answers that are at least acceptable we observe just 29 distinct sets. Table 3 on next page shows the count, the value according to our procedure in 3.3.3, and the constituent categories of each set.

Table 2: Distinct sets and counts of not acceptable answers

Value	Count	Labels
...		
4	88	PSOL, ALGO
4	51	PSOL, MENT
4	28	PSOL, AUTO
...		
3	24	PSOL, LOGI
3	11	PSOL, DECO
...		
2	80	PSOL
2	19	PSOL, CREA
2	11	MENT
...		
1	67	LOGI
1	13	CODE
1	11	LOGI, CREA
...		
0	26	TRAN
...		

There is no example of a set belonging to case (c3), see 5.3.1, and just 4 lines of the table show sets belonging to case (c2), explicitly indicated in the table, meaning the overwhelming majority of acceptable answers belongs to case (c1).

Moreover, three different sets have a high count (marked with a * in the "Case" column): {PSOL, MENT, METH}, {PSOL, MENT, ALGO}, and {PSOL, MENT, METH TRAN}. We think this is a positive result since these answers are all instances of case (c1), even if many examples in these sets are clearly molded after the information provided in "Programma il Futuro" website.

The most frequent not acceptable answers are shown in table 2.

A large number of misconceptions is characterized either by PSOL alone or by its coupling with exactly one of these categories: MENT, LOGI, DECO, CREA (first 7 lines of the table). In all these cases a very partial view of informatics emerges, given the absence of categories describing the *information-processing agent*. A similar situation happens for MENT and LOGI (next 2 lines). This reinforces our concerns that considering CT as a subject somewhat distinct from computing may give raise to misconceptions about IT.

Another misconception is shown by the relatively high count of TRAN alone (last line), which shows the evidence of a view of CT as an instrumental discipline, not important in itself. This is possibly deriving from attempts to convince teacher of the importance of CT by focusing mainly on its value for other disciplines and as a general learning tool.

Table 3: Distinct sets and counts of acceptable answers

Value	Count	Case	Labels										
12	1		PSOL	MENT	ALGO	AUTO	METH	DECO	LOGI				
11	1		PSOL	MENT	ALGO		METH	DECO	LOGI	ABST		CREA	
9	1		PSOL	MENT	ALGO		METH			ABST			
8	3		PSOL	MENT	ALGO	AUTO							
8	1		PSOL	MENT	ALGO		METH				TRAN	CREA	
8	1		PSOL	MENT	ALGO		METH						
7	2		PSOL	MENT	ALGO			DECO					
7	2		PSOL		ALGO	AUTO			LOGI				
7	1		PSOL	MENT			METH		LOGI		TRAN	CREA	
7	1		PSOL	MENT	ALGO					ABST	TRAN		
7	1		PSOL		ALGO		METH		LOGI				
7	1		PSOL		ALGO	AUTO				ABST			
6	17	*	PSOL	MENT			METH						
6	11	*	PSOL	MENT	ALGO								
6	10	*	PSOL	MENT			METH				TRAN		
6	7		PSOL		ALGO	AUTO							
6	6		PSOL	MENT		AUTO							
6	2	c2	PSOL		ALGO			DECO	LOGI			CREA	
6	2	c2	PSOL		ALGO			DECO	LOGI				
6	2		PSOL	MENT	ALGO						TRAN	CREA	
6	2		PSOL	MENT	ALGO						TRAN		
6	2		PSOL	MENT	ALGO							CREA	
6	1	c2	PSOL			AUTO		DECO	LOGI				
6	1		PSOL	MENT		AUTO					TRAN		
6	1		PSOL	MENT		AUTO							ITER
6	1		PSOL		ALGO	AUTO					TRAN		ITER
6	1	c2	PSOL		ALGO				LOGI	ABST			
6	1		PSOL		ALGO		METH						
6	1		PSOL			AUTO	METH						

6 CONCLUSIONS AND FURTHER WORK

Outcome of our work shows the vast majority of Italian primary school teachers has not a sound and complete conception about CT (RQ1).

This negative finding is somewhat balanced by the evidence regarding teachers in relation to information technology (IT). In fact, it is sufficiently clear to them that (1) computer science and the use of IT are two distinct fields, and (2) IT devices are not absolutely needed to develop CT competences in students (RQ2).

Finally, teachers feel themselves not enough prepared to develop CT competences in their students and identify in specific training the most important initiative (RQ3).

What we reported in this paper is only a first analysis of the situation in Italy regarding CT in schools in relation to "Programma il Futuro". We plan to complete the analysis by considering also answers from teachers at all school levels, and by investigating possible differences between teachers newly came to the project and those involved since the beginning.

ACKNOWLEDGMENTS

We greatly thank teachers and students involved in Programma il Futuro project (coordinated by EN and Giorgio Ventre) and Code.org for its cooperation.

We acknowledge the financial support of TIM; Engineering; CA Technologies, Cisco, De Agostini Scuola; SeeWeb. Other companies have financially supported the project during the first two school-years only: Samsung Italia; Microsoft Italia; Hewlett-Packard; Oracle; Facebook.

Rai Cultura, the culture department of Italian national public broadcasting company, is a media partner of the project since February 2017.

ML greatly thanks University of Bologna for funding his research and his Ph.D. advisor, Simone Martini, for fruitful discussions and support.

We greatly thank anonymous referees for insightful comments and suggestions.

REFERENCES

[1] Alfred V. Aho. 2011. Ubiquity Symposium: Computation and Computational Thinking. *Ubiquity* 2011, January, Article 1 (Jan. 2011). https://doi.org/10.1145/1922681.1922682

[2] Michal Armoni. 2016. COMPUTING IN SCHOOLS: Computer Science, Computational Thinking, Programming, Coding: The Anomalies of Transitivity in K-12 Computer Science Education. *ACM Inroads* 7, 4 (Nov. 2016), 24–27. https://doi.org/10.1145/3011071

[3] Matt Bower and Katrina Falkner. 2015. Computational Thinking, the Notional Machine, Pre-service Teachers, and Research Opportunities. In *Proceedings of the 17th Australasian Computing Education Conference (ACE 2015)*, Vol. 27. 30.

[4] Karen Brennan and Mitchel Resnick. 2012. New frameworks for studying and assessing the development of computational thinking. In *Proceedings of the 2012 annual meeting of the American Educational Research Association, Vancouver, Canada*. 1–25.

[5] Barefoot CAS. 2014. Computational Thinking. (2014). Retrieved April 4, 2017 from http://barefootcas.org.uk/wp-content/uploads/2014/10/Computational-thinking-Barefoot-Computing.pdf

[6] Isabella Corradini, Michael Lodi, and Enrico Nardelli. 2017. Computational Thinking in Italian Schools: Quantitative Data and Teachers' Sentiment Analysis after Two Years of "Programma il Futuro" Project. In *Proceedings of the 2017 ACM Conference on Innovation and Technology in Computer Science Education (ITiCSE '17)*. ACM, New York, NY, USA. https://doi.org/10.1145/3059009.3059040

[7] Peter J. Denning. 2009. The Profession of IT: Beyond Computational Thinking. *Commun. ACM* 52, 6 (June 2009), 28–30. https://doi.org/10.1145/1516046.1516054

[8] Peter J. Denning, Matti Tedre, and Pat Yongpradit. 2017. Misconceptions About Computer Science. *Commun. ACM* 60, 3 (Feb. 2017), 31–33. https://doi.org/10.1145/3041047

[9] Caitlin Duncan, Tim Bell, and James Atlas. 2017. What Do the Teachers Think?: Introducing Computational Thinking in the Primary School Curriculum. In *Proceedings of the Nineteenth Australasian Computing Education Conference (ACE '17)*. ACM, New York, NY, USA, 65–74. https://doi.org/10.1145/3013499.3013506

[10] Informatics Europe and ACM Europe. 2013. Informatics education: Europe cannot afford to miss the boat. (2013). Retrieved April 4, 2017 from http://europe.acm.org/iereport/ACMandIEreport.pdf

[11] Google. 2017. Exploring Computational Thinking. (2017). Retrieved April 4, 2017 from http://g.co/exploringct

[12] Mark Guzdial. 2015. *Learner-Centered Design of Computing Education: Research on Computing for Everyone*. Morgan & Claypool Publishers. http://dx.doi.org/10.

[13] ISTE and CSTA. 2011. Computational Thinking teacher resources. (2011). Retrieved April 4, 2017 from https://c.ymcdn.com/sites/www.csteachers.org/resource/resmgr/472.11CTTeacherResources_2ed.pdf

[14] ISTE and CSTA. 2011. Operational Definition of Computational Thinking for K-12 Education. (2011). Retrieved April 4, 2017 from https://c.ymcdn.com/sites/www.csteachers.org/resource/resmgr/CompThinkingFlyer.pdf

[15] Enrico Nardelli and Giorgio Ventre. 2015. Introducing Computational Thinking in Italian Schools: A First Report on "Programma Il Futuro" Project. In *INTED2015 Proceedings (9th International Technology, Education and Development Conference)*. IATED, 7414–7421.

[16] Seymour Papert. 1980. *Mindstorms: Children, Computers, and Powerful Ideas*. Basic Books, Inc., New York, NY, USA.

[17] Seymour Papert. 1996. An exploration in the space of mathematics educations. *International Journal of Computers for Mathematical Learning* 1, 1 (1996), 95–123. https://doi.org/10.1007/BF00191473

[18] Roy D. Pea and D.Midian Kurland. 1984. On the cognitive effects of learning computer programming. *New Ideas in Psychology* 2, 2 (1984), 137 – 168. https://doi.org/10.1016/0732-118X(84)90018-7

[19] Juha Sorva. 2013. Notional Machines and Introductory Programming Education. *Trans. Comput. Educ.* 13, 2, Article 8 (July 2013), 31 pages. https://doi.org/10.1145/2483710.2483713

[20] Jeannette M. Wing. 2006. Computational Thinking. *Commun. ACM* 49, 3 (March 2006), 33–35. https://doi.org/10.1145/1118178.1118215

[21] Jeannette M. Wing. 2008. Computational thinking and thinking about computing. *Philosophical Transactions of the Royal Society A: Mathematical, Physical and Engineering Sciences* 366, 1881 (Oct 2008), 3717–3725. https://doi.org/10.1098/rsta.2008.0118

[22] Jeannette M. Wing. 2010. Computational Thinking: What and Why? *Link Magazine* (2010).

[23] Aman Yadav, Chris Mayfield, Ninger Zhou, Susanne Hambrusch, and John T. Korb. 2014. Computational Thinking in Elementary and Secondary Teacher Education. *Trans. Comput. Educ.* 14, 1, Article 5 (March 2014), 16 pages. https://doi.org/10.1145/2576872

[24] Aman Yadav, Ninger Zhou, Chris Mayfield, Susanne Hambrusch, and John T. Korb. 2011. Introducing Computational Thinking in Education Courses. In *Proceedings of the 42Nd ACM Technical Symposium on Computer Science Education (SIGCSE '11)*. ACM, New York, NY, USA, 465–470. https://doi.org/10.1145/1953163.1953297

2200/S00684ED1V01Y201511HCI033

Folk Pedagogy: Nobody Doesn't Like Active Learning

Kate Sanders
Rhode Island College
Providence, Rhode Island, USA
ksanders@ric.edu

Jonas Boustedt
University of Gävle
Gävle, Sweden
jbt@hig.se

Anna Eckerdal
Uppsala University
Uppsala, Sweden
Anna.Eckerdal@it.uu.se

Robert McCartney
University of Connecticut
Storrs, Connecticut, USA
robert@engr.uconn.edu

Carol Zander
Univ of Washington Bothell
Bothell, Washington, USA
zander@u.washington.edu

ABSTRACT

In a survey of the computing education community, many respondents suggested "active learning" as a teaching approach that would increase the likelihood of student success. In light of these responses, we analyze the way in which active learning is described in the computing-education literature. We find a strong consensus that active learning is good, but a lack of precision in how the term is used, often without definition, to describe instructional techniques, rather than student learning. In addition, active learning techniques are often discussed as if they were all equally effective.

We suggest that making clear distinctions, both between teaching techniques and active learning and among the teaching techniques, would be fruitful for both instructors and researchers. Finally, we propose some dimensions along which distinctions among techniques could usefully be made.

CCS CONCEPTS

• **Social and professional topics** → **Computer science education**;

KEYWORDS

Active learning; Activity; Folk pedagogy; Reflection; Social interaction; Techniques

ACM Reference format:
Kate Sanders, Jonas Boustedt, Anna Eckerdal, Robert McCartney, and Carol Zander. 2017. Folk Pedagogy: Nobody Doesn't Like Active Learning. In *Proceedings of ICER '17, Tacoma, WA, USA, August 18-20, 2017*, 10 pages.
https://doi.org/10.1145/3105726.3106192

1 INTRODUCTION

We recently surveyed the computing education community asking for faculty beliefs about teaching and learning [56]. In their responses to the question, "Identify an approach to teaching that you believe increases the likelihood of CS student success", many people mentioned active learning.

The belief that "active learning is good" appears to be part of the folk pedagogy of the computing education community. A folk pedagogy, as described by Bruner [9], is the teacher's understanding of students' minds and how they learn. Although the term "folk pedagogy" is often used pejoratively, we do not use it so. Here, it simply refers to beliefs about teaching and learning held by our community.

The nature of this particular belief is not immediately clear, however. If by "active learning", the respondents mean students actively engaging with a subject and reflecting on their own learning, the belief would be straightforward. But these were answers to a question about *teaching* approaches.

To further investigate this belief and its ramifications, we explored the computing education literature on active learning. In this paper, we report on an analysis of this literature. Specifically, our research questions are:

RQ1: How do computing education papers use the term "active learning"?

RQ2: How does the computing education literature expand on and/or modify the understanding of "active learning" found in the survey responses?

In Section 2, we discuss related work on active learning and literature reviews. In Section 3, we provide background on our survey results. In Section 4, we describe the way in which we collected and analyzed computing-education papers. Sections 5 and 6 address our findings with respect to our first and second research questions, respectively. In Section 7, we reflect on these results. Section 8 addresses possible limitations of the study. Finally, we conclude in Section 9 with a discussion of future work.

2 RELATED WORK

2.1 Active Learning

Bonwell and Eison, in an influential 1991 report, note that prior to that date, discussions of active learning in the education literature had "typically relied upon an intuitive understanding of the term" [7, p. 18]. They define active learning as anything that "involves students in doing things and thinking about the things they are doing" [7, p. 19].

Their definition combines two key elements: doing and reflection. The importance of both of these aspects of learning can be traced back to John Dewey, who argued that "methods which are permanently successful in formal education ... give the pupils something to do, not something to learn; and the doing is of such a nature as to demand thinking, or the intentional noting of connections; learning naturally results." [17, p. 154]. Similarly, Kolb's learning cycle includes both action and reflection [42]. The importance of action *and* reflection is further developed by Donald Schön [78].

Chi [10] proposed a distinction between three types of learners: "active", "constructive", and "interactive". She does not discuss the education literature on "active learning", but by the definitions discussed above, all three of Chi's categories would be considered types of active learning. For clarity, we refer to Chi's "active" learners as "active-only".

Chi's categories are based on observable student behavior. Active-only learners are doing something observable. This may be writing a program or a large team project, or it might even be something as small as looking at a book or a whiteboard, underlining part of their textbook, or doodling in the margins. Constructive learners satisfy the requirements for active-only, plus they are adding something to the knowledge they receive. And interactive learners can be "talking with another person (who can be a peer, a teacher, a tutor, a parent), responding to a system (such as an intelligent tutoring system, an animated agent), or interacting in some other physical way involving motor movements." [10, Section 1.1.3]. Chi conjectures that interactive learning is the most effective, followed by constructive, then active-only (which is still better than nothing).

For example, in terms of taking notes in lecture, a student would be inactive if not taking notes at all; active-only if taking verbatim notes; constructive if taking notes on the key points of the lecture, adding conclusions, questions, or reflections, etc.; and interactive if composing notes online in a shared GoogleDoc with another student in the same lecture.

Many active learning techniques involve social interaction. The value of social interaction in learning is supported by social constructivism [64]. This is implicitly highlighted in Page's thorough historical background on active learning. She found four common themes among the proponents of active learning, where one was "belief in the cognitive learning paradigm"[63]. Cognitive-development theory "views cooperation as an essential prerequisite for cognitive growth" [6, p. 29]. This might indicate that the social aspect of active learning emphasized in our study, is in fact included implicitly in Page's results.

There have been a number of meta-surveys and literature reviews of active learning research. For example, Freeman et al. [27]in a meta-study of active learning across the STEM disciplines, concludes that "Active learning increases student performance in science, engineering, and mathematics", without distinguishing among techniques. Michael [59], gives a more qualified yes, concluding that there is evidence that "active learning approaches" work, but cautions that "results from a particular student population ... may not transfer well to a different context" [59, p. 7]. Prince [70] provides

an excellent model of how to read the active learning literature in a survey addressed to engineering educators. He begins by carefully defining both active learning itself and the core features of the most common active learning approaches, discusses how we might measure whether a particular technique works, and carefully evaluates the evidence provided up to that point. He concludes that there was support for some aspect of each of the techniques he examined, but support varied from technique

2.2 Systematic Literature Reviews

One approach to analyzing research questions from the literature is systematic literature review [12, 41]. While more common in software research, these have been used in computing education as well, for example [15, 36, 62]. Key aspects of such a review are that it be defined around particular research questions, that the search be well-described, that the criteria for inclusion or exclusion be explicit, and that all of the included papers are included in the analysis. [41] provides a detailed set of guidelines for literature reviews in software engineering; [62] provides an example of a carefully-executed review.

3 THE SURVEY

The details of our survey are reported in an earlier paper, in which we examined the folk pedagogy surrounding the idea of a "geek gene" [56]. Briefly, we surveyed the computing-education community. We received a total of 141 responses from 13 different countries and six continents (North America, South America, Europe, Asia, Australia, and Zealandia). Each respondent had the opportunity to answer (up to five times) the question "Identify an approach to teaching that you believe increases the likelihood of CS student success" (the question most relevant to this paper). The 141 respondents provided a total of 205 answers to this question.

We used a qualitative content analysis to analyze these data. First, all of the authors reviewed all of the responses. Second, 2-3 authors re-examined each response and tagged all the responses that mentioned active learning explicitly or implicitly (by referring to an instructional technique commonly associated with active learning). Out of 205 answers, 122 referred to active learning either explicitly or implicitly.

Some explicit mentions of active learning gave no further explanation. Some added further details, for example, "Actively engage students through any number of active learning techniques. Make sure students understand they are responsible for their own learning, that you can't pour knowledge into their brains; it takes effort to learn." Others gave generalities, for example, "Provide an active learning style of teaching with a mixture of talking, hands-on programming or design, quizzes and group work." "Implicit" answers suggested specific techniques, such as using a flipped classroom, think-pair-share, Peer Instruction, or POGIL.

Some responses, but very few, connected active learning to underlying learning theories, for example, "Active learning with exercises that expose variations in the critical features of the concepts of [sic] being learnt."

Although this is not stated explicitly, active learning seems to be defined as "any teaching technique that is not lecture". Moreover, like "active learning is good", "lecturing is bad" seems to be part of our folk pedagogy. Another question asked the respondents about beliefs their colleagues have that they *didn't* share. According to the respondents, these "bad beliefs" included: "Lectures are an effective teaching technique", "Lecturing is a good way to teach computing", and "Lecturing is essential". One respondent extended his or her preference for active learning to classes of all sizes, rejecting a colleague's belief that "active learning is impossible in a large class".

4 METHODOLOGY

In order to examine the way in which authors in the computing education community view active learning, we systematically identified and collected computing education papers that discussed active learning. These were meant to be full papers, so we excluded abstracts, works in progress, and short descriptions of workshops and panel sessions. This was an iterative process.

A preliminary search for papers in Google Scholar containing the terms "active learning" and "computer science education" resulted in over 6000 results, many of them only peripherally related, sometimes because these terms were in a citation in the paper. To get a more focused set, we searched in the ACM Digital Library (full text collection), IEEE Xplore, and ERIC. It was still necessary to restrict our queries: in the ACM Digital Library there were 1073 papers with the term "active learning" in the text and 551 papers with "active learning" in the abstract; these included many machine learning papers. There were 340 papers with "active learning" and "computer science education" in the text; we further restricted the search to papers that had "active learning" in the author's keywords, and "computer science education" as a term in the paper's Computing Classification System (CCS) descriptor which is built from a limited vocabulary; Computer science education is a term in all ACM CCS versions since 1982. This resulted in 153 papers, which we further reduced to 128 by filtering out papers that had "(Abstract only)" in the title.

We used a similar query for IEEE Xplore: "active learning" in keywords, "computer science" in INSPEC controlled terms ("computer science education" was not in these terms), and retrieved 69 papers. We eliminated 9 of these that had "Work in progress" in their titles, leaving 60.

Finally, we used the ERIC education-literature database to search the journal *Computer Science Education*. Here we searched on "active learning" anywhere in the text of the article and restricted the search to that journal alone; this search yielded four additional papers.

Given this set of papers, we eliminated those that were not full papers (one or two pages that accompany posters or panel presentations); we found 28 of those in the ACM set. Finally we eliminated papers that were about active learning in a discipline other than computer science, such as signal processing or automation engineering (9 from IEEE set), and one paper (from ACM) that used active learning in the machine learning sense. This left us with our corpus of 154 papers, as summarized in Table 1. These papers were all published between 1998 and 2016; all of the searches were performed in December, 2016 and January, 2017.

These papers were each read by one or more of the authors of this paper. Among other things, we looked for whether (and how) active learning was defined, what active learning techniques were

Table 1: Paper totals from searches, and those eliminated by each criterion from each source.

Source	Initial	Abstract/Work in Progress	Not full	Out of area	Final set
ACM	153	25	28	1	99
IEEE	69	9	0	9	51
ERIC	4	0	0	0	4
total	226	34	28	10	154

reported, and what student activities were described. To try and add some structure to the set, two of the researchers analyzed of the papers by clustering the instructional techniques they described (the description of techniques was the focus of nearly all of the papers). The clustering was an "all in one" open card sort based on overall similarity, [75] done by two of the authors, who then discussed and resolved any differences in their sorts.

5 RQ1: WHAT IS ACTIVE LEARNING?

In this section, we discuss the various answers to the question "What is active learning?" that we found in the computing-education literature.

5.1 A Good Thing

In the papers we examined, we found a strong consensus that active learning is good. There were no papers arguing against active learning.[1]

5.2 Not Often Defined

To our surprise, we found little in the way of definitions, despite the fact that the earliest paper in our dataset was published several years after Bonwell and Eison [7] (and a considerable time after Dewey). A few do reference Bonwell and Eison, for example [2, 25]

Even without a definition some papers contain a more nuanced discussion of active learning, even arguing from a learning theory. One such example is [19]: "In active learning, the student is not merely a recipient of knowledge but, rather, takes an active role in his/her learning. The knowledge obtained in this manner is generally deeper and longer lasting than knowledge memorized as facts delivered via lectures." But some skip the definition and simply assert that active learning is effective (for example, Boyer et al. [8]). Often, papers that are focused on a particular instructional technique say (in effect) "Technique X is active learning" (as a stamp of approval for Technique X) and, without further discussion of active learning, focus on Technique X. Some papers only put active learning in the keywords and never refer to it later.

5.3 Rarely Based on Learning Theory

In addition to a lack of precise definitions, there are few references to educational theory. Some papers mention constructivism, see for example [19, 21, 32, 40, 72, 74]. Also mentioned are situated

---

[1] One interesting paper has appeared since our literature review, however, arguing not that active learning is ineffective, but that its implementation can have significant drawbacks: time management is more challenging for students, and, paradoxically, their freedom to allocate their own time to appropriate learning activities is reduced [65].

learning and student-centered learning [18], and sociocultural and constructivism theory [53].

Moreover, very few papers offer a theoretically based definition of active learning. One paper that does is Hazzan and Dubinsky [32]. The authors describe active learning with reference to Schön [78], writing that "learners are active to the extent which enables a reflective process". The importance of reflective processes in software development, the authors' research area, is "mainly based on Schön's Reflective Practitioner perspective" [32, p. 704].

5.4 Not Necessarily Reflective

In general, we found very few explicit mentions of reflection. One example was Bareiss and Radley [3]'s implementation of cognitive apprenticeship. Students were encouraged to "articulate their thought process" and later "what they have learned" and participated in a "reflection session" at the end of the semester. Miller et al. [60], in their work on Learning objects (T3), concluded their tutorials with a summary and hints for reflection. However, no details are given. Nguyen et al. [61] argue that PjBL (T19) will give the students "a 'learning-by-doing' experience" which includes several "learning modes", one of which is "Observing - Reflecting: learning through observing the work of others or contemplating on one's own work." There is, however, no detailed description on how this "learning mode" is implemented, observed, or evaluated. Martinez and Camacho [55] describe using a qualitative assessment in their cooperative learning-based teaching strategy (T17) which invited students to "reflect on their own learning and the group work." This is the extent of the description on how reflection is used.

5.5 A Set of Instructional Techniques

We did identify 38 distinct techniques that were said to be active learning. In the remainder of this section, we present these techniques (labeled "T1" through "T38") grouped by five themes: (delivering) lecture content outside of lecture; activities replacing lecture time; collaboration and social engagement, in or out of class; techniques borrowed from other disciplines; techniques borrowed from software development practices; and techniques that did not seem to share the characteristics we would expect from active learning.

5.5.1 Lecture content outside lecture. One way to replace or partially replace lecture is by moving material outside of the lecture time, and using lecture time for other activities. This may be complete, with all the lecture content presented elsewhere, or blended, with some of the lecture content replaced with in-class activities. [21, 31, 51]. The techniques given here are ones that are described as active, and do not include other common approaches like "assigned online videos" and "assigned readings from the textbook."

T1 E-books, which augment the normal content of a book with interactive features like embedded audio, video, slide shows, and image galleries. These may also include questions assessing reader understanding. [25, 26].

T2 Automated tutoring systems, which share many features with e-books, like generating and grading questions and providing feedback. [44]

T3 Learning Objects: a collection of content items, practice items, and assessment items that are organized around a single learning objective. Each learning object contains a tutorial, a set of interactive exercises, and an assessment [60].

T4 Visualizations and animations, [24, 82], which may also be part of E-books. These may be classified by the level of interactivity, as in [13].

T5 Online discussion forums, where students post questions or comments in a location where all students can see them, sometimes with a degree of anonymity. [76].

T6 Exploratory homeworks, an activity where the student enhances their textbook reading by interleaving programming exercises. [23]

T7 Active code reading, a web-based application supporting generation and delivery of quizzes designed to evaluate and improve code reading skills [33]

5.5.2 Activities during lecture time. Some of the activities we found were designed to be done during the class, to supplement or replace the lecture.

T8 "Fun" activities, such as puzzles, games, or toys [1, 73]

T9 Courses that require the students to be self-directed and independent [37].

T10 Integrating labs with lectures [8].

T11 Microlabs: 5-10-minute labs (opportunities to try out some code) incorporated into lectures [45].

T12 Prepare-Present-Positive feedback (3PF): teaching is done by students, and positive feedback given to the students – student prepares an instructor-assigned topic, presents to class, discussion follows, and instructor and class provide positive feedback to the student; aimed at low achieving students who are less likely to participate in active learning activities [72]

T13 Kinesthetic learning activities, which use physical activities to engage the students with classroom material. [4, 80]

T14 Role-playing activities, such as performing a live simulation of a recursive list [29].

T15 Tool-supported activities, including live coding, interactive lecture notes, and discussions [20]

5.5.3 Collaboration and social engagement. Many of the techniques involved work done by cooperating groups of students, not necessarily in class.

T16 Team-based learning (TBL): an evidence based collaborative learning teaching strategy designed around modules that are taught in a three-step cycle of preparation, in-class readiness testing, and application-focused exercise. [22, 47, 48]

T17 Cooperative learning in general; the educational use of small groups that allows students to work together to improve their own learning and that of their peers. [55]

T18 Jigsaw, a particular cooperative learning exercise, involves decomposing a problem into partial tasks, one of which is performed by each student in a team, who subsequently integrate their solutions. [69].

T19 Project-Based Learning (PjBL): students work in small collaborative groups on real-world projects. [61]

T20 Expo-based learning, an extension of problem-based learning (T25)where students present work to outside audiences to encourage social engagement. [74].

T21 Learning communities, where small groups of students are assigned to take all their classes together for one or more terms [34].

T22 Other collaborative activities mentioned were collaborative homework [2], collaborative problem-solving in lab [8], and collaborative note taking [39].

5.5.4 Techniques from other disciplines. Some of the approaches are well-established approaches from other disciplines.

T23 Think-pair-share: a collaborative learning strategy in which students work together to solve a problem or answer a question about an assigned reading. They do this by thinking individually about a topic or question, discussing this in pairs, then sharing their ideas with classmates. [43]

T24 Process Oriented Guided Inquiry Learning (POGIL), a team-based learning approach originally developed in Chemistry [46]. Activities are highly scripted and a facilitator helps students to go through a cycle of activities.

T25 Problem-based learning (PBL), an approach that has groups work on open-ended problems, originally from Medicine [74]. The computing version of this technique is said to include many different active-learning tactics: Think-pair-share, short project demonstrations, code dependency analysis and hands-on programming, research review and open discussion, assessment [52].

T26 Cognitive Apprenticeship: a master of a skill teaches that skill to an apprentice, acting more as a coach than a teacher while working on authentic tasks [3, 83].

T27 Peer Instruction (PI), an approach developed in Physics education: students use a device (often clickers) to answer multiple-choice questions anonymously, then discuss their answers with each other, then answer again. The whole class's answers are displayed anonymously (to the students) in the form of a bar graph [50, 68].

5.5.5 Software development techniques. Not surprisingly, a number of activities are modeled on software development approaches.

T28 Pair programming [57, 68]

T29 Extreme programming practices, including test-driven development, refactoring, collective ownership, continuous integration, and so forth. [58]

T30 Pre-Programming Analysis Guided Programming (PAGP) [38], an approach meant to mimic how an expert approaches a programming task.

T31 Large-scale systems projects, which have individual students develop complex systems in stages over a number of weeks. [77]

5.5.6 Instructor's philosophy/presentation. Some techniques listed as active learning do not necessarily involve any active work or reflection by students. They may reflect more of a change in the instructor's philosophy:

T32 Abductive learning: based on activities intended to trigger abduction, i.e. going from a set of specific observations to a more general theory, "the best possible explanation" [71]

T33 Inductive learning, where tasks are designed to teach particular lessons by side-effect. [79]

T34 Gamification of courses by applying game elements and digital game design techniques to non-game problems to increase student engagement. [66]

T35 Just-in-time teaching (JiTT), a strategy designed to promote the use of class time for more active learning. Students turn in homework before class, instructors grade it before class, and adapt their lectures accordingly [14, 54].

T36 Just-in-time-learning, which suggests that we let students learn by "Googling it", and adapt our teaching approaches to their habits. [5]

T37 Evidence based: constant monitoring of outcomes from assessment, e.g., quizzes, and resulting continuous improvement of the applied method [28].

T38 Storytelling to illustrate or reinforce concepts [67, 73].

6 RQ2: SURVEY DATA VS. LITERATURE

The computing-education literature generally confirmed what we saw in the survey data. "Active learning" doesn't refer to learning; instead, it is used as a shorthand for a collection of teaching techniques. Illustrating this failure to distinguish between what the instructor does and how the students might respond, one author reported on a class in which students "were taught using a high degree of active learning ..." [34, p. 3].

Like the survey data, the computing-education papers we read rarely define active learning and rarely reference the underlying educational theory. As in the pre-Bonwell-and-Eison education literature, authors rely on the readers' "intuitive understanding" of what the term means.

The computing-education literature enlarged the picture drawn by the survey data, adding many more teaching techniques to those mentioned in the survey data. While these activities give students "something to do" (in Dewey's terms), the question of whether they "demand thinking" is rarely addressed. Finally, some papers seem to assume that solitary work (for example, reading an e-book, or using automated tutoring systems, visualizations, or animations) can be active [23–26, 44, 60, 82]; others seem to imply that active learning must be social (see, e.g., [34]). Unlike Chi [10], the papers we read do not address these points directly, and as a result, leave the conflict unresolved.

7 DISCUSSION

Combining a clear definition of active learning with a distinction between techniques and student learning opens up new possibilities for research questions. For example, nearly all of the 38 techniques we found give the students something active to do. Do all activities work equally well? If not, could it be because some activities require the students to be more engaged than others? Because different students respond differently to different activities? Because some activities do not "demand thinking, or the intentional noting of connections" [17]? Can we characterize learning contexts where particular techniques work well?

In the remainder of this section, we consider four dimensions, each suggested by educational theory, along which techniques might differ, and where differences might lead to different outcomes.

The dimensions are: what the techniques involve in terms of activity, reflection, and social interaction, and whether they are distinctive to computing. We are not claiming that these factors *do* make a difference, simply that it might be interesting to explore whether they do.

7.1 How active are they, and what do they do?

Both the type and level of activity involved vary considerably from technique to technique. Types of activity include reading, writing, speaking, and performing. To give just a few examples: In an attempt to encourage active learning, students are asked to read e-books (T1), read code (T7), and view slide shows (T1). They are asked to write both long and short programs (T6, T11, T16, T19), collaborative class notes (T22), and posts to (and comments on) online discussion forums (T5). They are asked to perform skits (T14). They are asked to speak to individuals and small groups (T23, T27, T26, T28), to discuss decisions within their teams (T16), to formally present their work (T20), and even to teach part of the course material to their peers (T12). The activities include all three of Chi's types: active, constructive, and interactive [10].

The level of activity required varies equally widely. Some techniques, such as instructor story-telling (T38) or just-in-time teaching (T35), need nothing more than the students' attention – in Chi's terms, minimal activity. Online forums may function in this way for many students (those who read but do not post).

Other techniques are associated with a small amount of activity: an individual Microlab (T11), role-playing activity (T14), think-pair-share session (T23), or Peer Instruction (T27) discussion lasts for part of a class and requires only a little effort.

An individual session of pair programming (T28) is at an intermediate level. It involves a significant amount of effort, and there's little opportunity to slack off, but each session typically lasts for only one or two class periods.

For many of the small and intermediate-level activities, the overall activity level depends on how often they are used: the cumulative amount of activity could be quite large if they are used frequently.

Techniques that involve a high level of expected activity include long-term group activities, like Problem-Based Learning (T25), Team-based Learning (T16), POGIL (T24), Cognitive Apprenticeship (T26), and Project-based Learning (T19).

In some cases, the level of activity also depends on specific implementation details. Interactive visualizations can support a range of types of interactivity – from simple clicking to drive the animation, to running visualization on different inputs, to changing or creating the machine being visualized – which correspond to increasing amounts of engagement [13]. Storytelling as reported in our examples [67, 73] is low-activity since the stories are presented to the students, but the level of activity would be higher if the students were writing and presenting the stories.

Finally, it is possible (even likely) that the level of activity theoretically associated with an instructional technique is not the same as the level of activity observed in practice. Not every student posts equally often to an online forum or works equally hard on a team project. One question to explore might be whether some instructional techniques have a higher variance than others.

7.2 How reflective are they?

Even though the importance of action being combined with reflection is emphasized in the research literature, it can be lost in the work on active learning. A reason for this may be that reflection is not captured explicitly in the term itself. Another reason might be that activity is relatively easy to observe, and reflection less so.

What evidence would indicate that students might be reflecting? Suppose we take as a definition of "reflection" that students are thinking about what they're learning and making connections (in Dewey's terms), or adding to the knowledge they've been given (Chi's definition of constructive learners). Do all techniques incorporate or encourage reflection? Do they do so equally? In discussing these questions, we will adopt Chi's approach and look for observable evidence.

Like type and levels of activity, the amount of reflection associated with the instructional techniques varies widely. Some techniques simply modify lectures to make them more engaging or relevant. These techniques fall into Chi's "activity only" category: we can tell if the students are attentive, but generally not whether they are reflecting. Examples in our dataset include storytelling and just-in-time teaching. Live coding is another example, if students do not participate in the coding.

Some examples involve a few students being constructive and the rest being active-only. For example, students who design and present a skit show evidence of having added to what they know; those who watch only give evidence of paying attention.

Other techniques have students doing something more active, but still not explicitly reflecting. Jigsaw puzzles, games, and discussion forums – for those students who log on but do not post – fall into this category. These again are examples of active-only learning.

Some techniques fall into Chi's "constructive" category, in that reflection is an explicit part of the technique: think-pair-share and peer instruction, for example. Students who post to discussion forums may also provide observable evidence of reflection.

Many techniques fall into Chi's "interactive" category. Some of these involve interacting with other people face to face. These techniques include working with fellow students (Team-Based Learning (T16), Project and Problem-Based Learning (T19, T25), POGIL (T24), and other collaborative activities) and interacting with a mentor (Cognitive Apprenticeship (T26)).

Some techniques fall into Chi's "interactive" category even though they do not involve social interaction, because they involve "responding to a system (such as an intelligent tutoring system, an animated agent)" [Section 1.1.3] [10]. Reflection is common in these techniques, although rarely explicitly described as such in the literature. Often E-books (T1), tutoring systems (T2), active code reading (T7), and other ways of accessing content include questions that allow for students to reflect on what they have learned.

Pair programming is an intermediate case of "interactive" learning: two students are interacting with each other face to face, but they are focused on (indeed, likely facing) the computer that they share.

A lack of reflection is not an unavoidable part of these techniques. Techniques can be modified to add an explicit requirement for a written (or oral) reflection. In our data, Bareiss et al. [3], Miller et al. [60], Nguyen et al. [61], and Martinez and Camacho [55] all incorporate such a requirement. These techniques all involve interactive learning, but similar strategies could work for techniques that involve active-only learning.

7.3 How social are they?

The papers in our data set illustrate the use of social interaction in active learning. These social interactions vary widely. Some active-learning techniques may not involve social interaction at all, such as e-books (T1), automated tutoring systems (T2), and visualization/animation systems (T4). Some involve talking to one other person, such as think-pair-share (T23), pair programming (T28), and Cognitive Apprenticeship (T26). Many involve working together in small groups, for example Team-Based Learning (T16), Jigsaw (T18), POGIL (T24), the discussion phase of Peer Instruction (T27), and Problem-Based Learning (T25). At the opposite extreme, the audience for online discussion forums (T5), the question-answering phase of Peer Instruction (T27), and role-playing activities and skits (T14) is the whole class, and for Expo-Based Learning (T20), it may even be larger.

Interaction may be face to face or mediated by technology. Think-pair-share (T23) does not require any technology. Pair programming (T28) and Project-Based Learning (T19) focus on software development; for these techniques, the technology is the topic of the students' conversation. For online discussion forums (T5) and Peer Instruction (T27), by contrast, the technology is the infrastructure that makes the interaction possible, and the topic may be any course-related question.

Face-to-face communication is never anonymous, but technology mediated communication may be. For example, the question phases of Peer Instruction (T27) allow students to answer questions anonymously; and online discussion forums (T5) typically give students the option of posting anonymously. (By "anonymous" here, we mean "unknown to the student's peers"; these techniques do allow instructors to know who said what.)

Social interaction may be short-term or long. Think-pair-share (T23) and Peer Instruction (T27) typically involve a relatively brief interaction with one or two people who happen to be sitting nearby. The pairs in Pair Programming (T28) may work together for a week or longer. Other team projects may last an entire semester.

The interaction may be reciprocal or not. Examples of reciprocal communication include techniques like pair programming (T28), where the individuals take turns each explaining to the other what edits should be made to their program, and this turn-taking is carefully enforced. Similarly, in the question-answering phase of Peer Instruction (T27), everyone sees the bar graph that summarizes everyone else's answers. Discussion forums (T5) and group work are *potentially* reciprocal: that is, everyone has the opportunity to both talk and listen (though the speaking and listening may not actually be evenly shared). At the opposite extreme, techniques like Expo-Based Learning (T20) and role-playing (T14) are *not* reciprocal. Here, a small group performs in front of a much larger one.

The social interaction is most often with peers: this is the case for all of the examples mentioned in this section so far. One exception is cognitive apprenticeship (T26), where a student works closely with an instructor.

The quality of the interaction will also be affected by the degree to which it affects students' grades. With Peer Instruction (T27), in the typical answer-discussion-answer sequence, students are graded only on participation. At the opposite extreme, in a team project course, the stakes of social interaction are much greater; most, or even all, of the students' grades may depend on the students' ability to interact effectively.

7.4 How specific to computing are they?

Lave and Wenger [49] explain why it is important to work on authentic activities in their work on "Legitimate peripheral participation." Through authentic activities, novices become familiar with the vocabulary and tasks of the discipline. These activities are effective because they help the newcomer to become part of the community. Taking a holistic perspective on CS education, it is reasonable to argue for it as a *socialization* process. The social aspects of active learning, especially in authentic activities, seem to play an important role for socializing students into the computing community.

Active-learning techniques that are distinctive to computing include those involving coding, e.g., Active code reading (T7) or Live coding (T15). Pair programming (T28), Extreme programming (T29), PPAGP (T30), and Large-scale systems projects (T31) also involve coding or software design and are derived or adapted from professional software development practice.

All the active learning activities found in the Collaboration and social engagement grouping (T16-T22) in Section 5.5.4 – teamwork, projects, problem solving, etc. – although they are also found in other fields, are authentic computing activities.

On the other hand, the computing-education field is a relatively young discipline and borrows much from other disciplines. Section 5.5.4 specifically lists techniques from other disciplines (T23-T27): Think-pair-share, POGIL, PBL, Cognitive apprenticeship, and Peer Instruction.

Although interactive software was developed in computing, many techniques which involve generic electronic activities such as E-books (T1), Automated tutoring systems (T2), and Online discussion forums (T5), are used by other disciplines. While not specific to computing, Visualization/animation (T4), is more common in technical fields.

Similarly, activities replacing lecture, not involving coding, e.g., Puzzles, games, toys (T8), Role playing (T14), or Self-directed (T9) are also used in other disciplines.

7.5 Finally, about learning theories

There is a striking lack of learning theories in the papers in the present study. Theory may seem abstract, difficult, or irrelevant. But in this case, it is *useful.*

Many papers, both inside and outside of computing education research, treat active learning as a collection of teaching techniques. What nearly all of these techniques have in common is that the students are *doing* something: reading, writing, speaking, performing, almost anything but sitting and listening to a lecture. If you develop an intuitive understanding based on these papers, you may well come to believe that to promote active learning, all we need to do is to get students to be active.

But if we look at definitions of active learning in educational theory and cognitive science, we find that activity is only one of the essential parts (and activity can be as subtle as focusing your eyes on a particular part of the whiteboard). The other key part of active learning is that students must *think* about what they're doing – make connections, add to what they know, reflect [7, 17, 78].

Having this definition opens up new questions: which instructional techniques encourage – or demand – reflection? And what evidence would satisfy us? Theory also provides us with a framework for thinking about what might satisfy us that a particular technique does in fact "demand thinking" [10].

As Suppes [81] argues, "A powerful theory changes our perspective on what is important and what is superficial" (p. 4) and with theory, "what appear on the surface to be simple matters of empirical investigation, on a deeper view, prove to be complex and subtle".

8 THREATS TO VALIDITY

We were interested in the computing education community's beliefs about active learning. To this end, we set search criteria that would return papers that the authors considered to be about active learning, and operationalized this by requiring "active learning" to be in the author's keywords. Some papers that we would certainly consider to be about active learning, however, were excluded. Four examples:

(1) A paper about Treisman groups [11], a socially-interactive strategy for replacing homework, did not have Active learning in the keywords, but had it in the Abstract.
(2) A paper about Contributing student pedagogy [30] did not include Active learning in the keywords or abstract, although it is clear in the text that the authors consider it as an active learning technique.
(3) A paper about PeerWise [16], a widely-used system that enables students to contribute multiple-choice questions on course material to a shared database of questions, didn't mention active learning at all, rather it had "Contributing student" in the keywords and text.
(4) A paper about pedagogical code reviews [35] described it as an active learning technique in the abstract an the paper, but did not have Active learning in the keywords.

We don't believe, however, that missing some papers in the sample had much of an effect on our findings. The four papers cited above, along with the many other papers that focus on specific techniques without putting the term "active learning" in their keywords, support the consensus that active learning techniques are good, but do not change the folk pedagogy of the term itself.

9 CONCLUSIONS AND FUTURE WORK

In this paper, we report on an investigation into the folk pedagogy of computing education, specifically those beliefs surrounding active learning. Our data include the results of a faculty survey and a sample of computing education papers about active learning.

We found that, while there is a consensus that "active learning is good", there is often a lack of precision in how the term is used. We suggest that grounding investigations in the precise definitions of active learning to be found in educational theory would be helpful.

We have identified a gap in the computing education literature on active learning: few papers explicitly touch upon students' reflection, and even if they do, they may build their arguments on weak ground. Many papers give a detailed description of an active learning technique and seem to jump to the conclusion that the technique, since active, necessarily leads to good learning. Questions that could be addressed in future research are

- Which types of activity promote reflection?
- How can we better promote students' reflection while using (or enhancing) the different existing active learning techniques in our discipline?
- How can we evaluate the effect different kinds of reflection have on students' learning?

Chi [10] provides a framework for thinking about what evidence might satisfy us that a particular technique does in fact cause students to reflect.

Further, we argue that the instructional techniques associated with active learning vary widely, for example in the type and level of activity required and in whether or not they are distinctive to computing. In particular, the social aspect of active learning is prominent in the computing education literature, but the wide variety of types of social interaction have not been examined. Questions that could be addressed are:

- How are the different social interactions associated with different techniques experienced by students?
- Which groups of computing students benefit from which social learning activities, and which might be negatively affected?

Additionally, from a practical perspective,

- Can we characterize learning contexts where one activity, or one type of interaction might be more effective than another?

Finally, we speculate that some of the active-learning techniques developed by computing educators, such as pair programming, might be adapted for use in other fields – enabling computing education to repay some of our intellectual trade deficit vis à vis more mature education disciplines.

ACKNOWLEDGMENTS

Thank you to all of the people who responded to the original survey. We would also like to thank the reviewers of this paper for their questions and suggestions on how the paper could be improved.

REFERENCES

[1] Owen Astrachan. 1998. Concrete Teaching: Hooks and Props As Instructional Technology. *SIGCSE Bull.* 30, 3 (Aug. 1998), 21–24. DOI: http://dx.doi.org/10.1145/290320.283003 *[in dataset]*.

[2] Saurabh Bagchi, Mark C Johnson, and Somali Chaterji. 2008. Effects of types of active learning activity on two junior-level computer engineering courses *(FIE '08)*. IEEE, F2A–11. *[in dataset]*.

[3] Ray Bareiss and Martin Radley. 2010. Coaching via Cognitive Apprenticeship *(SIGCSE '10)*. ACM, 162–166. *[in dataset]*.

[4] Andrew Begel, Daniel D. Garcia, and Steven A. Wolfman. 2004. Kinesthetic Learning in the Classroom. *SIGCSE Bull.* 36, 1 (March 2004), 183–184. DOI: http://dx.doi.org/10.1145/1028174.971367

[5] Elizabeth Boese. 2016. Just-In-Time Learning for the Just Google It Era *(SIGCSE '16)*. ACM, 341–345. DOI: http://dx.doi.org/10.1145/2839509.2844583 *[in dataset]*.

[6] Curtis Jay Bonk and Donald J Cunningham. 1998. Searching for learner-centered, constructivist, and sociocultural components of collaborative educational learning tools. *Electronic collaborators: Learner-centered technologies for literacy, apprenticeship, and discourse* 25 (1998), 25–50.

[7] Charles C Bonwell and James A Eison. 1991. *Active Learning: Creating Excitement in the Classroom. 1991 ASHE-ERIC Higher Education Reports*. ERIC.

[8] Kristy Elizabeth Boyer, Rachael S Dwight, Carolyn S Miller, C Dianne Raubenheimer, Matthias F Stallmann, and Mladen A Vouk. 2007. A case for smaller class size with integrated lab for introductory computer science. *SIGCSE Bulletin* 39, 1 (2007), 341–345. *[in dataset]*.

[9] Jerome Bruner. 1996. Folk Pedagogy. In *The Culture of Education*. Harvard University Press, Chapter 2, 44–65.

[10] M.T.H. Chi. 2009. Active-Constructive-Interactive: A Conceptual Framework for Differentiating Learning Activities. *Topics in Cog. Sci.* 1, 1 (2009), 73–105. DOI: http://dx.doi.org/10.1111/j.1756-8765.2008.01005.x

[11] Donald Chinn, Kristofer Martin, and Catherine Spencer. 2007. Treisman Workshops and Student Performance in CS *(SIGCSE '07)*. 203–207.

[12] Tony Clear. 2012. Systematic Literature Reviews and Undergraduate Research. *ACM Inroads* 3, 4 (Dec. 2012), 10–11. DOI: http://dx.doi.org/10.1145/2381083.2381087

[13] Joshua J. Cogliati, Frances W. Goosey, Michael T. Grinder, Bradley A. Pascoe, Rockford J. Ross, and Cheston J. Williams. 2005. Realizing the Promise of Visualization in the Theory of Computing. *J. Educ. Resour. Comput.* 5, 2, Article 5 (June 2005). DOI: http://dx.doi.org/10.1145/1141904.1141909 *[in dataset]*.

[14] Janet Davis. 2009. Experiences with Just-in-time Teaching in Systems and Design Courses *(SIGCSE '09)*. ACM, 71–75. *[in dataset]*.

[15] Adrienne Decker, Monica M. McGill, and Amber Settle. 2016. Towards a Common Framework for Evaluating Computing Outreach Activities. In *Proceedings of the 47th ACM Technical Symposium on Computing Science Education (SIGCSE '16)*. ACM, 627–632. DOI: http://dx.doi.org/10.1145/2839509.2844567

[16] Paul Denny, John Hamer, Andrew Luxton-Reilly, and Helen Purchase. 2008. PeerWise: Students Sharing Their Multiple Choice Questions *(ICER '08)*. ACM, 51–58. DOI: http://dx.doi.org/10.1145/1404520.1404526

[17] John Dewey. 1916. *Democracy and Education: An introduction to the philosophy of education*. The Macmillan Company, New York.

[18] Janine DeWitt and Cynthia Cicalese. 2006. Contextual integration: a framework for presenting social, legal, and ethical content across the computer security and information assurance curriculum *(InfoSecCD '04)*. ACM, 30–40. *[in dataset]*.

[19] Cheryl A Dugas. 2008. No Computers? No Problem! Active and cooperative learning in an introductory computer science course *(FIE '08)*. IEEE, T3A–16. *[in dataset]*.

[20] Michael Ebert and Markus Ring. 2016. A presentation framework for programming in programing lectures *(EDUCON '16)*. IEEE, 369–374. *[in dataset]*.

[21] Rob Elliott. 2014. Do students like the flipped classroom? An investigation of student reaction to a flipped undergraduate IT course *(FIE '14)*. IEEE, 1–7. *[in dataset]*.

[22] Ashraf Elnagar and Mahir S Ali. 2013. Survey of student perceptions of a modified team based learning approach on an information technology course *(PICICT '13)*. IEEE, 22–27. *[in dataset]*.

[23] Sarah Esper, Beth Simon, and Quintin Cutts. 2012. Exploratory Homeworks: An Active Learning Tool for Textbook Reading *(ICER '12)*. ACM, 105–110. DOI: http://dx.doi.org/10.1145/2361276.2361297 *[in dataset]*.

[24] Nils Faltin. 1999. Designing Courseware on Algorithms for Active Learning with Virtual Board Games. *SIGCSE Bull.* 31, 3 (June 1999), 135–138. DOI: http://dx.doi.org/10.1145/384267.305894 *[in dataset]*.

[25] Tommy Färnqvist, Fredrik Heintz, Patrick Lambrix, Linda Mannila, and Chunyan Wang. 2016. Supporting Active Learning by Introducing an Interactive Teaching Tool in a Data Structures and Algorithms Course *(SIGCSE '16)*. ACM, 663–668. DOI: http://dx.doi.org/10.1145/2839509.2844653 *[in dataset]*.

[26] James B. Fenwick, Jr., Barry L. Kurtz, Philip Meznar, Reed Phillips, and Alex Weidner. 2013. Developing a Highly Interactive Ebook for CS Instruction *(SIGCSE '13)*. ACM, 135–140. DOI: http://dx.doi.org/10.1145/2445196.2445241 *[in dataset]*.

[27] S. Freeman, S.L. Eddy, M. McDonough, M. K. Smith, N. Okoroafor, H. Jordt, and M.P. Wenderotha. 2014. Active learning increases student performance in science, engineering, and mathematics. *Proc. Natl. Acad. Sci. USA* 111, 23 (2014), 8410–8415. DOI: http://dx.doi.org/10.1073/pnas.1319030111

[28] M. M. Fuad, D. Deb, and J. Etim. 2014. An evidence based learning and teaching strategy for computer science classrooms and its extension into a mobile classroom response system *(ICALT '14)*. IEEE, 149–153. *[in dataset]*.

[29] Michael Goldwasser and David Letscher. 2007. Teaching strategies for reinforcing structural recursion with lists *(SIGPLAN '07)*. ACM, 889–896. *[in dataset]*.

[30] John Hamer, Quintin Cutts, Jana Jackova, Andrew Luxton-Reilly, Robert McCartney, Helen Purchase, Charles Riedesel, Mara Saeli, Kate Sanders, and Judithe Sheard. 2008. Contributing Student Pedagogy. *SIGCSE Bull.* 40, 4 (Nov. 2008), 194–212. DOI: http://dx.doi.org/10.1145/1473195.1473242

[31] Yasuhiro Hayashi, Ken-Ichi Fukamachi, and Hiroshi Komatsugawa. 2015. Collaborative Learning in Computer Programming Courses That Adopted the Flipped Classroom *(LaTiCE '15)*. IEEE, 209–212. *[in dataset]*.

[32] Orit Hazzan and Yael Dubinsky. 2006. Teaching framework for software development methods *(ICSE '06)*. ACM, 703–706. *[in dataset]*.

[33] Daniel Malcolm Hoffman, Ming Lu, and Tim Pelton. 2011. A Web-based Generation and Delivery System for Active Code Reading *(SIGCSE '11)*. ACM, 483–488. *[in dataset]*.

[34] Trudy Howles. 2009. A Study of Attrition and the Use of Student Learning Communities in the Computer Science Introductory Programming Sequence. *Computer Science Education* 19, 1 (2009), 1–13. *[in dataset]*.

[35] Christopher D. Hundhausen, Anukrati Agrawal, and Pawan Agarwal. 2013. Talking About Code: Integrating Pedagogical Code Reviews into Early Computing Courses. *Trans. Comput. Educ.* 13, 3, Article 14 (Aug. 2013), 28 pages. DOI: http://dx.doi.org/10.1145/2499947.2499951

[36] Petri Ihantola, Tuukka Ahoniemi, Ville Karavirta, and Otto Seppälä. 2010. Review of Recent Systems for Automatic Assessment of Programming Assignments. In *Proceedings of the 10th Koli Calling International Conference on Computing Education Research (Koli Calling '10)*. ACM, 86–93. DOI: http://dx.doi.org/10.1145/1930464.1930480

[37] Ville Isomöttönen and Ville Tirronen. 2013. Teaching Programming by Emphasizing Self-direction: How Did Students React to the Active Role Required of Them? *Trans. Comput. Educ.* 13, 2, Article 6 (July 2013), 21 pages. DOI: http://dx.doi.org/10.1145/2483710.2483711

[38] Wei Jin. 2008. Pre-programming Analysis Tutors Help Students Learn Basic Programming Concepts *(SIGCSE '08)*. ACM, 276–280. *[in dataset]*.

[39] Michael Jonas. 2013. Group Note Taking in Mediawiki, a Collaborative Approach *(SIGITE '13)*. ACM, 131–132. DOI: http://dx.doi.org/10.1145/2512276.2512312

[40] Håkan Jonsson. 2015. Using flipped classroom, peer discussion, and just-in-time teaching to increase learning in a programming course *(FIE '15)*. IEEE, 1–9. *[in dataset]*.

[41] Barbara Kitchener and Stuart Charters. 2007. *Guidelines for performing Systematic Literature Reviews in Software Engineering, Version 2.3*. Technical Report EBSE Technical Report EBSE-2007-01. Software Engineering Group, School of Computer Science and Mathematics, Keele University and Department of Computer Science, University of Durham.

[42] D.A. Kolb. 1984. *Experiential learning: experience as the source of learning and development*. Prentice Hall, Englewood Cliffs, NJ.

[43] Aditi Kothiyal, Sahana Murthy, and Sridhar Iyer. 2014. Think-pair-share in a Large CS1 Class: Does Learning Really Happen? *(ITiCSE '14)*. ACM, 51–56. DOI: http://dx.doi.org/10.1145/2591708.2591739 *[in dataset]*.

[44] Amruth N. Kumar. 2005. Generation of Problems, Answers, Grade, and Feedback—case Study of a Fully Automated Tutor. *J. Educ. Resour. Comput.* 5, 3, Article 3 (2005). DOI: http://dx.doi.org/10.1145/1163405.1163408 *[in dataset]*.

[45] Barry L. Kurtz, James B. Fenwick, Rahman Tashakkori, Ahmad Esmail, and Stephen R. Tate. 2014. Active Learning During Lecture Using Tablets *(SIGCSE '14)*. ACM, 121–126. DOI: http://dx.doi.org/10.1145/2538862.2538907 *[in dataset]*.

[46] Clifton Kussmaul. 2012. Process oriented guided inquiry learning (POGIL) for computer science *(SIGCSE '12)*. ACM, 373–378. *[in dataset]*.

[47] Patricia Lasserre. 2009. Adaptation of Team-based Learning on a First Term Programming Class *(ITiCSE '09)*. ACM, 186–190. *[in dataset]*.

[48] Patricia Lasserre. 2009. Introduction to Team-based Learning *(WCCCE '09)*. ACM, 77–78.

[49] Jean Lave and Etienne Wenger. 2002. Legitimate peripheral participation in communities of practice. *Supporting lifelong learning* 1 (2002), 111–126.

[50] Cynthia Bailey Lee, Saturnino Garcia, and Leo Porter. 2013. Can Peer Instruction Be Effective in Upper-division Computer Science Courses? *Trans. Comput. Educ.* 13, 3, Article 12 (Aug. 2013), 22 pages. DOI: http://dx.doi.org/10.1145/2499947.2499949 *[in dataset]*.

[51] Mary Lou Maher, Celine Latulipe, Heather Lipford, and Audrey Rorrer. 2015. Flipped Classroom Strategies for CS Education *(SIGCSE '15)*. ACM, 218–223. DOI: http://dx.doi.org/10.1145/2676723.2677252 *[in dataset]*.

[52] E. Manogaran. 2013. ACt-PBL: An adaptive approach to teach multi-core computing in university education *(T4E '13)*. IEEE, 19–23. *[in dataset]*.

[53] Estefanía Martín, Carlos Lázaro, and Isidoro Hernán-Losada. 2010. Active learning in telecommunication engineering: A case study *(EDUCON '10)*. IEEE, 1555–1562. *[in dataset]*.

[54] Alexandra Martinez. 2012. Using JiTT in a Database Course *(SIGCSE '12)*. ACM, 367–372. DOI:http://dx.doi.org/10.1145/2157136.2157245 *[in dataset]*.

[55] Alexandra Martinez and Arturo Camacho. 2011. A Cooperative Learning-based Strategy for Teaching Relational Algebra *(ITiCSE '11)*. ACM, 263–267. *[in dataset]*.

[56] Robert McCartney, Jonas Boustedt, Anna Eckerdal, Kate Sanders, and Carol Zander. 2017. Folk Pedagogy and the Geek Gene: Geekiness Quotient. (2017). DOI:http://dx.doi.org/10.1145/3017680.3017746

[57] Charlie McDowell, Linda Werner, Heather E. Bullock, and Julian Fernald. 2006. Pair Programming Improves Student Retention, Confidence, and Program Quality. *Commun. ACM* 49, 8 (Aug. 2006), 90–95. DOI:http://dx.doi.org/10.1145/1145287.1145293

[58] Dawn McKinney and Leo F Denton. 2005. Affective assessment of team skills in agile CS1 labs: the good, the bad, and the ugly. *SIGCSE Bulletin* 37, 1 (2005), 465–469. *[in dataset]*.

[59] Joel Michael. 2006. Where's the evidence that active learning works? *Adv. Physiol. Educ.* 30 (2006), 159–167. DOI:http://dx.doi.org/10.1152/advan.00053.2006

[60] L. D. Miller, Leen-Kiat Soh, Gwen Nugent, Kevin Kupzyk, Leyla Masmaliyeva, and Ashok Samal. 2011. Evaluating the Use of Learning Objects in CS1 *(SIGCSE '11)*. ACM, 57–62. *[in dataset]*.

[61] Duc Man Nguyen, Tien Vu Truong, and Nguyen Bao Le. 2013. Deployment of capstone projects in software engineering education at duy tan university as part of a university-wide project-based learning effort *(LaTiCE '13)*. IEEE, 184–191. *[in dataset]*.

[62] Keith Nolan and Susan Bergin. 2016. The Role of Anxiety when Learning to Program: A Systematic Review of the Literature. In *Proceedings of the 16th Koli Calling International Conference on Computing Education Research (Koli Calling '16)*. ACM, 61–70. DOI:http://dx.doi.org/10.1145/2999541.2999557

[63] Marilyn Page. 1990. *Active Learning: historical and contemporary perspectives.* Master's thesis. University of Massachusetts, Amherst.

[64] A.S. Palincsar. 1998. Social Constructivist Perspectives on Teaching and Learning. *Annu. Rev. Psychol.* 49 (1998), 345–75.

[65] A. Pears, A. Nylén, and M. Daniels. 2016. A critical analysis of trends in student-centric engineering education and their implications for learning *(FIE)*. 1–7.

[66] Johanna Pirker, Maria Riffnaller-Schiefer, and Christian Gütl. 2014. Motivational Active Learning: Engaging University Students in Computer Science Education *(ITiCSE '14)*. ACM, 297–302. DOI:http://dx.doi.org/10.1145/2591708.2591750 *[in dataset]*.

[67] Shannon Pollard and Robert C Duvall. 2006. Everything I needed to know about teaching I learned in kindergarten: bringing elementary education techniques to undergraduate computer science classes. In *SIGCSE Bulletin*, Vol. 38. ACM, 224–228. *[in dataset]*.

[68] Leo Porter, Cynthia Bailey Lee, and Beth Simon. 2013. Halving Fail Rates Using Peer Instruction: A Study of Four Computer Science Courses *(SIGCSE '13)*. ACM, 177–182. DOI:http://dx.doi.org/10.1145/2445196.2445250 *[in dataset]*.

[69] J. A. Pow-Sang Portillo and P. G. Campos. 2009. The jigsaw technique: Experiences teaching analysis class diagrams *(Mexican International Conference on Computer Science)*. IEEE, 289–293. *[in dataset]*.

[70] Michael Prince. 2004. Does active learning work? A review of the research. *Journal of engineering education* 93, 3 (2004), 223–231.

[71] Atanas Radenski. 2007. Digital support for abductive learning in introductory computing courses. *SIGCSE Bulletin* 39, 1 (2007), 14–18. *[in dataset]*.

[72] Vijay T Raisinghani. 2013. 3Pf: Prepare-Present-Positive Feedback–An Active Learning Approach for Low Achievers *(T4E '13)*. IEEE, 1–8. *[in dataset]*.

[73] MRK Rao. 2006. Storytelling and puzzles in a software engineering course. *SIGCSE Bulletin* 38, 1 (2006), 418–422. *[in dataset]*.

[74] Mario Romero, Björn Thuresson, Christopher Peters, Filip Kis, Joe Coppard, Jonas Andrée, and Natalia Landazuri. 2014. Augmenting PBL with large public presentations: a case study in interactive graphics pedagogy *(ITiCSE '14)*. ACM, 15–20. *[in dataset]*.

[75] Gordon Rugg and Peter McGeorge. 2005. The sorting techniques: a tutorial paper on card sorts, picture sorts and item sorts. *Expert Systems* 22, 3 (2005), 94–107.

[76] Harry Budi Santoso and Eunice Sari. 2015. Transforming Undergraduate HCI Course in Indonesia: A Preliminary Study *(APCHIUX '15)*. ACM, 55–59. DOI:http://dx.doi.org/10.1145/2846439.2846451 *[in dataset]*.

[77] Shimon Schocken. 2012. Taming Complexity in Large-scale System Projects *(SIGCSE '12)*. ACM, 409–414. DOI:http://dx.doi.org/10.1145/2157136.2157259 *[in dataset]*.

[78] Donald A Schon. 1995. Educating the Reflective Legal Practitioner. *Clinical L. Rev.* 2 (1995), 231.

[79] Yvonne Sedelmaier and Dieter Landes. 2015. Active and Inductive Learning in Software Engineering Education *(ICSE '15)*. IEEE Press, 418–427. *[in dataset]*.

[80] Paolo AG Sivilotti and Scott M Pike. 2007. The suitability of kinesthetic learning activities for teaching distributed algorithms *(SIGCSE '07)*. ACM, 362–366. *[in dataset]*.

[81] Patrick Suppes. 1974. The Place of Theory in Educational Research 1. *Educational Researcher* 3, 6 (1974), 3–10.

[82] Andy Ju An Wang. 2005. Web-based Interactive Courseware for Information Security *(SIGITE '05)*. ACM, 199–204. DOI:http://dx.doi.org/10.1145/1095714.1095760 *[in dataset]*.

[83] Tom Wulf. 2005. Constructivist Approaches for Teaching Computer Programming *(SIGITE '05)*. ACM, 245–248. DOI:http://dx.doi.org/10.1145/1095714.1095771 *[in dataset]*.

Understanding the "Teacher Experience" in Primary and Secondary CS Professional Development

Tracie Evans Reding
University of Nebraska at Omaha
6001 Dodge Street
Omaha, NE 68182
treding@unomaha.edu

Brian Dorn
University of Nebraska at Omaha
6001 Dodge Street
Omaha, NE 68182
bdorn@unomaha.edu

ABSTRACT

The increasing awareness for the need of effective Computer Science Education (CSE) Professional Development (PD) at the K–12 grade levels has been demonstrated by the increase in grant funding for CSE PD programs, public awareness campaigns by industry, and scale-up initiatives in schools. While the increase in funding has led to increasing availability of PD programs, funding alone does not guarantee a successful experience for teachers. This study investigates the affective experiences of a cohort of ten in-service teachers (nine middle school and one high school) as they participate in an intensive, multi-faceted summer CSE PD program at a Midwestern metropolitan university in North America. Teachers' experiences were documented in their written daily journals, which were analyzed qualitatively using thematic and sentiment analysis techniques. We find five cognitive themes that recurred throughout the program along with sentiment values associated with daily activities. Through the examination of these results, recommendations regarding how to best engage teachers by understanding their concerns and affective responses are included to help design more effective CSE PD implementations.

CCS CONCEPTS

• **Social and professional topics → K-12 education; Computer science education;**

KEYWORDS

K–12 CS, Teacher Professional Development, Teacher Experience

1 INTRODUCTION

The importance of Computer Science (CS) in primary and secondary schools has been growing throughout the world. This was demonstrated by the tens of millions of students from more than 180 countries that participated in Code.org's hour of code during Computer Science Education Week in December of 2015, as well as the millions of dollars spent globally on CS Education teacher professional development grants, public awareness campaigns by industry, and scale-up initiatives in schools. While exposure and funding are great ways to pique interest, they do not necessarily increase student graduation rates in the area of CS, which is an area of concern.

In the U.S., Computer Science/Information Sciences have the highest attrition rates of all Science, Technology, Education, and Mathematics (STEM) fields of study [3], and in the U.K., CS has the highest dropout rate of all subjects [25]. While the causes of attrition tend to be complex, students' lack of pre-college preparation in such courses has been shown to impact their success in CS-related courses which can lead to dropping out [3]. Two key factors that consistently correlate with student achievement are teacher instructional practices and teacher content knowledge [17, 27]. These factors pose a particular problem when addressing CS in primary and secondary schools. Most primary and secondary teachers have never been exposed to CS-related content or CS-specific pedagogy, possibly due to the lack of prioritization of CS in the U.S. [20]. For these reasons, the importance of effective, Computer Science Education (CSE) Professional Development (PD) for in-service teachers is necessary in order to improve teacher CS content and pedagogic knowledge which will directly impact their students' CS successes in primary and secondary school.

The growing need for effective PD in general has gained a lot of popularity in recent years. There is a movement in education to steer away from the more traditional, one or two day formal presentation style of PD, informally known as "sit and get", to more effective PD where teachers play an active role in the learning and practicing of new pedagogical styles [4, 5]. Many authors have defined what effective PD looks like and have researched the characteristics of effective PD, but there are very few articles addressing the "teacher experience" of these new types of PD. Here, we refer to "teacher experience" in much the same way an interaction designer would use the term "user experience"–ie., capturing holisitic notions of emotional, social, and cultural factors related to a user's interaction with technology in addition to functionality and usability concerns. Here, we are concerned with similarly broad experiences of teachers engaged in a PD experience. It has been well established that PD and teaching in general is not only a cognitive endeavor but also an affective one [1, 13, 19]. Using journal entries from a cohort of teachers who participated in an intensive CSE PD experience, this study seeks to explore both the cognitive and affective elements of teachers' experiences by exploring two broad research questions:

RQ1: What are the cognitive themes that arise throughout an effective Computer Science Education PD program?

RQ2: What are the affective patterns that arise throughout an effective Computer Science Education PD program?

ICER'17, August 18–20, 2017, Tacoma, WA, USA.
© 2017 Copyright held by the owner/author(s). Publication rights licensed to ACM.
ISBN 978-1-4503-4968-0/17/08…$15.00
DOI: http://dx.doi.org/10.1145/3105726.3106185

2   RELATED WORK AND SPARCS PD

This section introduces recent CS PD programs that are widely regarded as effective, describes current challenges in implementing computing curricula, outlines our SPARCS program, and overviews research on the cognitive and affective aspects of teacher PD.

2.1   Effective PD

In a literature review of CSE PD programs between 2004 and 2014, Menekse summarized the findings of multiple PD studies and determined the qualities of effective programs as including collaboration between educators, adequate time for implementation and practice, active learning methods to demonstrate how to implement new teaching practices, emphasis on pedagogical content knowledge, follow-up support for teachers, and establishment of professional learning communities [16]. Recent CSE PD programs have incorporated all or most of the qualities of effective PD outlined by Menkse. For example, Georgia Computes implemented a Disciplinary Commons for Computing Educators (DCCE) where in-service high school computing teachers and undergraduate computing instructors convened at monthly meetings throughout the academic year and shared course portfolio reflections [18]. These monthly meetings promoted collaboration, sharing of pedagogical content knowledge, ongoing support of teachers, and the establishment of a professional learning community [18] which implements most of the qualities of effective PD. Later versions of the DCCE focused exclusively on high-school teachers due to the dissimilarity in the secondary and post-secondary teaching contexts. During the Exploring Computer Science (ECS) PD, teachers actively collaborate to develop and pilot their inquiry based lessons on a specific CS topic during the PD program which consists of a week long summer institute followed by quarterly academic year meetings and then a follow-up second summer institute [11]. Through this model, teachers collaborate, are provided significant time to practice, implement and refine their lessons, and address pedagogical content knowledge (PCK). Teachers are then given follow up support with academic year meetings and a second summer workshop.

2.2   Classroom Implementation Challenges

While emerging CSE PD programs are implementing many best practices of PD in order to get quality CS lessons into classrooms, there is little research focused on the current status of this implementation and the struggles/challenges associated with it. In a recent study, Sentance et al. [22] looked at the responses of over 300 teachers in the UK (mostly England) who were currently implementing Computing curriculum within their classes in order to identify both challenges and coping strategies used in the implementation of computing in their K-12 classrooms. The challenges teachers face when implementing computing in the UK classroom involve subject matter knowledge, approaches to teaching, assessment practices, and lack of resources, support, and time [22].

Introduction of novel teaching methods is often a component of innovative PD programs, and this adds additional complexity. For example, problem based learning (PBL) is often pointed to as a means to engage learners in solving real-world problems with computational tools. PBL focuses on student learning through the use of inquiry, where the curriculum is guided by a problem rather

than teacher-led presentation of content [14, 15]. A recent study by Girvan et al. examines the cognitive themes that teachers report while implementing education reforms [9]. These reforms introduced "21st Century Skills, Assessment for Learning, a flexible curriculum and a new focus on Information and Communications Technology (ICT)" and involved the use of learner-centered pedagogy similar to PBL [9]. The themes that were found in the Girvan study included concerns centered around the role of the teacher in a learner-centered classroom, student inexperience working in teams, lack of time needed for the lessons; insufficient support structures present through peers and administration; and the impact on student engagement and learning. Incorporating this knowledge of teacher concerns when implementing CS in the classroom and/or using a PBL approach in an effective PD model is necessary to its success.

2.3   SPARCS as Effective PD

In order to provide context for the basis of our study, it is necessary to highlight the goals and activities of the SPARCS[1]PD program. The SPARCS project has several anticipated outcomes as a result of the activities and outputs of the project including: increased teacher CS knowledge; enhanced school capacity for CS instruction; increased student CS knowledge; and increased student awareness of CS careers [23]. These outcomes are the result of an intensive summer PD program coupled with academic year meetings.

The focus of our study is on the summer portion of the PD and the experiences of the 10 teachers who voluntarily participated during summer 2016. Most of the teachers that participated in this PD were relatively inexperienced in both the content of CS and the instructional approach of PBL. Three of the ten teachers had some sort of formal training concerning CS, while seven of the teachers had no formal training in CS.

The SPARCS PD program embraces many of the best practices in designing effective PD programs described earlier [23]. The program began with a one week teacher institute that was a workshop with a focus on the basics of CS and PBL. While CS is the focus of the new content learned by the teachers, PBL is the new pedagogical approach learned by the teachers. The next activity was an individual online course with an emphasis on computational thinking and programming. The second teacher institute portion was also a week-long workshop which focused on the PBL lesson development. At the end of the summer portion of the program, there was a week-long student academy that functioned as a pilot run for the lessons that were developed the prior week. The total amount of time teachers spent on SPARCS related activities over the summer totalled a minimum of 100 hours. The total amount of face to face contact time with peers and PD facilitators which consisted of university personnel as well as Master Teachers was roughly 90 hours.

Throughout the program, teachers collaborated with one another to established a professional learning community during the teacher institute weeks, where they worked together to learn CS content and the basics of PBL, planned PBL based CS lessons, and co-taught these lessons during the student academy. The last two weeks of the teacher institute allowed time for teachers to plan, implement, and

---

[1]Strategic Problem-Based Approach to Rouse Computer Science

practice various aspects of their CS lessons. Piloting their lessons during the student academy week allowed teachers active learning experience on how to implement the lessons in their classrooms. The combination of learning CS content for themselves and using a PBL approach addressed the PCK component. While not discussed in this study, monthly meetings were held during the AY in which teachers came together with PD facilitators to work through their lessons and share their experiences.

2.4 Effective PD as Cognitive and Affective

The purpose of all adult learning experiences (including teacher PD) is to promote the acquisition and use of new knowledge, which is a complex enterprise considering knowledge itself is multifaceted and interrelated. There are three interdependent facets of knowledge and effective teacher training programs involve all three. The first facet is associated with the cognitive processes of learning and is known as explicit knowledge. Implicit knowledge is associated with behavior, actions, and accumulated experiences of the learning process. Finally, emancipatory knowledge is associated with the emotional component of learning [29].

Due to the interrelated nature of the facets of knowledge, PD is more than just learning new ideas about the practice of teaching; it also involves an affective component that plays a large part in how the teachers experience the PD and how the PD impacts their own emotions, beliefs, attitudes, and actions [12, 13]. "Emotions are important in adult learning because they can either impede or motivate learning" [7]. The importance of recognizing and understanding one's own emotions and feelings has been shown to be an important aspect of change [6]. The ability to use this understanding of emotions to guide our thinking and actions is known as Emotional Intelligence (EI) [21] and the improvement of EI has been shown to reduce job stress [28]. The first component of EI is known as self-awareness and involves the ability to recognize and understand personal moods, emotions, and drives [10].

In this study, we seek to identify not only the cognitive themes that teachers experience, but also the patterns of the affective component that arise during the SPARCS PD program. This understanding may help in the design of future CSE PD programs.

3 METHOD

Our phenomenological study uses the reflections of the teachers during the summer portion of the SPARCS PD program to gain insights into their experiences.

3.1 Teachers

A total of 10 teachers from the greater metropolitan area in the Midwestern United States. 4 different school districts were represented and all of the teachers were in-service teachers with a range of experience from 2 years to 27 years. The teachers were selected through a review process that looked at their resumes, applications, and letters of recommendation from their building administrators. Nine of the ten teachers were from schools whose students ranged in age from 12-14 (ie., middle school). One teacher was from a school whose students ranged in age from 14-18 (ie., high school). Table 1 provides an identifier for each teacher, years teaching, and subject taught for each teacher.

Table 1: Participant Teaching Experience

Participant ID	Years Teaching	Discipline
P1	20	Computer Applications
P2	2	Math
P3	3	Journalism
P4	17	Computer Applications
P5	17	Journalism
P6	27	Language Arts
P7	23	Computer Applications
P8	23	Science
P9	23	Computer Applications
P10	10	Science

3.2 Data Collection

Our study focuses on the teacher experience throughout the summer portion of the SPARCS program. Teachers were asked to complete a daily on-line journal during each of the three face-to-face weeks of the summer program: the Week 1 Teacher Institute, the Collaborative Lesson Planning Week, and the Student Academy week. Teachers were also asked to provide three journal reflections during the on-line course portion of the program, which took place between the teacher institute and lesson planning weeks. Prompts were given by the PD facilitators to help focus the teachers' reflections., examples of these sentence starters include "One thing I learned today..." and "One AHA moment I had today..." These written reflections comprise the data corpus used in our analyses.

3.3 Data Analysis

Due to the nature of our study seeking to understand the experiences of the teachers during the summer portion of the SPARCS PD program, qualitative approaches were used. This qualitative understanding involved both thematic coding and sentiment analysis as the analysis methods used in this phenomenological study. The first step concerning the thematic coding was the initial coding process of the teacher journal reflections. While the prompts that were provided to the teachers narrowed their reflections a bit, journal entries were analyzed by the first author using a constant comparative approach that drew on both open and axial coding [24]. This approach began with an initial analysis of one of the teacher's reflections which generated multiple codes. As other journals were analyzed, the initial codes were applied but new ones also emerged. Throughout the ongoing process, as more codes were generated, earlier journals that had already been analysed were revisited and recoded. When the first set of codes were finalized, individual codes were examined to ensure there was no repetition and those codes that were determined to be similar enough, were combined into one code. Next, a decision tree was used to group together similar codes in order to generate categories. These categories were then compared to one another in order to determine broader relationships that existed. These broader relationships were then identified as the major cognitive themes and are presented in section 4.1. It is useful to note that these themes are not meant to imply relative importance of topics or make clames of wide generalizability, but rather to uncover the range of variation expressed in the data.

The second portion of our study examined the affective experience of the teachers by performing a sentiment analysis on the reflections according to the journal entries associated with each day/assignment. Human raters were used for coding the sentiment of each entry as initial trials with algorithmic coding based on word polarity failed to adequately characterize posts. The sentiment analysis used in this study adapted the typical sentiment analysis model which includes data preparation, review analysis, sentiment classification, and results [2]. The first step was data preparation in which the researchers removed the unnecessary information not required for the analysis including the dates of the entries and the authors' names. The second step included review analysis which involved establishing interrater reliability to ensure the same score, either positive, neutral, or negative, would be assigned to the journal entries regardless of who was conducting the analysis. A randomized subset of 25 journal entries was analyzed independently by two raters and scores were compared. The first step was to determine subjectivity classification of each sentence. Sentences determined to be objective were given a neutral score and sentences determined to be subjective were assigned either a positive or negative score. Once each sentence of a teachers' journal entry was analyzed, a score was assigned to the overall journal entry based on the frequency of the three possible scores which had been assigned to each sentence of the entry. This was conducted for each of the 25 journal entries from the subset. This first rating produced a weighted kappa of 0.628. The major discrepancies involved differences in the subjectivity classification of some sentences. The raters then discussed this first subset of journal entries and resolved any discrepancies. A second randomized subset of 25 journal entries were then independently analyzed again by the two raters. This second rating produced a weighted kappa of 0.765, demonstrating acceptable agreement. Once this interrater reliability had been established, the next step of sentiment classifaction was performed by analysing each journal entry of a particular day using the same process as the interrater reliability method. Once all the journal entries were scored for the day, an overall score of sentiment for the day was assigned using the frequency of scores that were given to each journal entry. This was completed for every day of the SPARCS summer PD program and the results are presented in section 4.2.

4 RESULTS

4.1 Cognitive Themes

This section presents the experiences of the teachers that were consistently mentioned as they progressed through the SPARCS summer PD program. These themes include: PBL concerns; classroom realities; peer collaboration; impact on students; and personal learning. Quotes were selected to show a variety of voice in the data as well as to represent different views.

4.1.1 PBL Concerns. For all the teachers in the study, problem based learning was a new pedagogical approach and many concerns and questions were raised. The focus of the reflections changed throughout the program as the teachers became more familiar with PBL and shifted from learning about PBL to planning for PBL to implementing PBL. When PBL was first introduced, the comments centered around a more general understanding of PBL and brainstorming possible ways to incorporate PBL:

"One question I have is how to begin formulating an arsenal of 'problems' for kids to work to solve." P1

Once the teachers were engrossed in the planning of their PBL units, the comments became more specific and really focused on how to develop and create good problems/scenarios:

"What I struggled with most today is determining if our big hairy problems were good enough. I'm still somewhat confused about how to be sure the overall problem is a good one." P4

The teachers also questioned how students would react to the "learner-centered" approach:

"I believe my students will struggle with problem-based learning being rather unstructured." P9

"I feel the students will struggle because we are not giving them the framework." P10

Finally, during the student academy week where the teachers were piloting their lessons on actual students, their concerns became more specific and centered on student experience and classroom management. After Day 1 of the student academy, many of the teachers were initially worried about student "buy in:"

"I am not convinced that the students have bought into the problem..." P9

"The student feedback tells us some kids are still bored and not completely sold on the project." P4

But as the week progressed the overall perception of student engagement improved:

"There was a lot of ownership and buy-in from the students, and they seem really excited to work on their projects!" P5

Another concern that lessened over the course of the Student Academy was allowing the students to be in charge of their own learning:

"The kids are also feeling like we're giving them too much feedback and they want to have the freedom to work on their own." P4

"The feedback from the students and master teachers told me that we need to step back and give the time for the students to design and develop." P7

4.1.2 Connections with Classroom Realities. Another theme that was consistently mentioned was the notion of how to incorporate all the new ideas, methods, and resources learned into their classrooms. Teachers were constantly thinking about how these new resources would fit into their curriculum and the time required. During the first week when they were exposed to the new resources, many comments focused on a general application of the new resources into their curriculum:

"Where do I want to add this information, would it be possible to use on all assignments?" P10

"Is it possible (or even recommended) to try and include a [Computational Thinking Practice] into each unit, no matter the discipline?" P8

During the online course portion of the PD, the teachers became much more familiar with Scratch and StarLogo Nova. Once the teachers had more experience with these programs, their comments became much more specific to the possibility of implementing the different programs into their classrooms:

"The tutorials (Scratch) could easily be done as bell work, brain break, or finished early activities." P3

"I don't really have the time in class to teach them how to use the program." P6

During the collaborative lesson development week, teachers were placed in groups based on their shared content domains, and they developed a lesson to pilot the following week during the student academy. Teachers were explicitly making connection between the lessons they developed and implementing them into their own classes:

"I was really worried about how I would be able to take this project and make it work for my students but I think it's great!" P5

"We came up with some really great activities we can do in our classrooms." P3

The final week of the summer PD program was the Student Academy where teachers got to collaboratively teach the lesson they had developed during the prior week. The comments that came out of this week were no longer focused on curriculum fit but were specific to things they would change in their current lessons:

"I would like to have gone deeper into the design cycle because I feel students are unclear on why we use it." P7

"We may need to be more clear on the daily objectives...some students were getting ahead of themselves and starting to design projects today." P2

4.1.3 Peer Collaboration. Throughout the summer PD program, teachers spent three week working closely with one another. This peer collaboration was consistently mentioned and was a source of both support and struggle. During the first week when teachers were learning the new pedagogy and content together, comments were more focused on learning about one another:

"One thing I learned today our cohort of SPARCS teachers come from widely varied backgrounds but all are very eager to learn about Computer Science!" P7

When teachers returned for the collaborative lesson development week the comments were varied and toward the beginning of the week teachers were unclear about the purpose and their roles:

"I was left wondering how authentic is collaboration to the way most of us lesson plan?" P2

"I am still nervous about our individual responsibilities and how we'll get our parts to come together as one, solid theme." P4

Toward the end of the week, most nervousness concerning individual roles had subsided:

"I feel very comfortable with what parts I am in charge of and how my team supports each other during the lessons." P10

However, not all comments demonstrated an enjoyable collaborative experience:

"One of my issues may be that we are all strong classroom teachers and personalities and we sometimes just don't see things the same way." P1

During the Student Academy, some individuals' comments indicated that the collaboration was their favorite part of the summer, while others indicated that the collaboration was a struggle:

"I have enjoyed working with my colleagues." P7

"I enjoyed my team the most." P8

"Not all opinions are begin considered and there is still a bit of overlap when one teacher is attempting to instruct." P4

"The thing that is clearer for me today than it was yesterday is that teaching in a group of teachers is very difficult." P7

4.1.4 Personal Learning Experience. A unique aspect of SPARCS is that teachers not only learn a new pedagogical approach but they also learn new content. For SPARCS this new content included coding and computational thinking skills. The process of learning new content added an additional element of reflection. During the first week, most of the comments were more general comments toward learning the new resources:

"I am looking forward to learning more about this programming and modeling tool (StarLogo Nova)." P2

"One thing I learned today is how to use a flow chart and create an artifact prototype." P1

The online course portion of SPARCS prompted a lot more insights into the teachers' learning processes as well as empathizing with their students:

"I didn't know what to expect, but I picked up on the content (Scratch) more quickly than I thought." P3

"Even after I considered a project complete, I would keep thinking about how I could have made it better or how to make it function just a little differently." P9

"This ordeal has given me an insight into how kids sometimes feel when they're asked to work on a project idea of which they truly have no interest." P4

When the teachers returned and began collaborating on the lesson development, the reflections became very focused on what they needed to learn in order to develop an effective lesson for their students:

"I need to research our topic of Internet and online use for teens so I can develop a better pitch or scenario." P7

"I need to learn A LOT about our [Big Hairy Problem] - I need to investigate the learning objectives, think about the artifacts and experiences and basically figure out what directions need to be

provided and what guiding questions do we need to be prepared to answer." P8

The Student Academy week presented the teachers with plenty of learning opportunities. Many of the teachers commented on how they modified the lessons throughout the day as a result of learning what did and didn't work throughout the week:

"I really like the critical feedback from students and the master teachers because it helps to refine the lesson and make it better." P3

"After getting the feedback from the students on day two I think we need to be clearer and introduce our end product on the first day and review it daily so they know what is expected and they can be thinking about it through the week." P6

"I'm very impressed with how we changed our lesson throughout the day that addressed the needs of the students." P5

4.1.5 Student Impact. Throughout the entire SPARCS PD program the teachers always had their students in mind. They constantly wondered how to best incorporate the new resources in order to keep their students engaged and motivated. During the first week, teachers expressed excitement about using the new resources with their students:

"I can picture my kids getting into this and this is a great way to allow the art side to shine." P8

"I also really enjoyed working with Blocky Games. I got easily hooked and it is something our students would greatly enjoy." P9

During the online course portion of the PD, the teachers focused specifically on what they would have to do with the programs in order to make them accessible to the students:

"I would definitely have the program already coded and maybe the students just change one variable at a time but give them step-by-step directions or they will be lost." P10

"I really enjoyed the tutorials and began to see how my middle schools students would like them as well." P3

The Collaborative Lesson Development week began with many teachers expressing concern that students wouldn't find the lesson interesting or relevant:

"I'm still nervous about the kids not being excited about our activities." P4

"I'm still nervous about how the kids will respond." P1

But as the week progressed the teachers expressed excitement for their lessons being engaging for the students:

"I feel super excited about our lesson because it has the potential to be fun, engaging and will get kids excited about CS." P8

During the final week of the summer PD program, the teachers were very excited to see how well the students were engaged:

"I have enjoyed watching the students become invested in their projects. I was really impressed with how hard the students worked, even during the last group of the day." P9

"They seemed motivated and willing to share their ideas with each other." P6

While the teachers were noticing that students were engaged, they were also struggling with the time restraint impacts of the process on students:

"It looks like we will need to address the fact that they will more than likely have to be told once again that we will probably not finish our projects in time for Friday. I think this will be a challenge for the kids to accept." P5

Not only were teachers concerned about the impacts of the time restraints on the students, they also voiced concerns about their own limitations:

"I'm also new to computer science in general, so I struggled with asking kids questions that would encourage them to think about how to take their original ideas further." P9

4.2 Affective Patterns

While the cognitive themes experienced by the teachers of the SPARCS program provide necessary insight into what the teachers are concerned with as they progress through the program, their general attitude/emotional response is also important in order to provide a fuller picture of the experience. Table 2 provides the topics covered on a daily basis, along with the average sentiment value, either positive, neutral, or negative, of each day.

The affective patterns experienced by this cohort during the SPARCS PD program showed mostly positive responses during the initial week after starting off as neutral. These positive responses mostly centered on the following topics: connections of CS to the real world; exciting CS specific resources they can use in their classrooms; providing a general overview of what to expect in the coming weeks; and allowing for networking with fellow teachers.

During the next portion of the PD (the online course) affective responses were neutral and negative. Most of the negative responses referred to the difficulty of learning how to use the platforms, technical problems while working in the platforms, and difficulty making connections to using specific programs in their own classrooms.

The lesson development week began with negative responses focused on teacher insecurities in developing a "Big Hairy Problem" for the students to tackle. This was coupled with the difficulty of lesson planning in a group. As the week progressed and the teachers were able to develop a "Big Hairy Problem" and activities they felt the students would like, the responses became positive. As the teachers felt successful in their lesson planning, their responses became more positive.

The final week where the teachers piloted their lessons with actual students elicited positive responses during the entire week. The positive responses mostly referred to the amount of student engagement and enjoyment of the lessons. There were also positive responses concerning working with their colleagues.

5 DISCUSSION

The focus of our study was to examine the "teacher experience" during an effective CS PD program as both a cognitive and affective experience. Understanding the cognitive and affective experience

Table 2: PD Topics by Day/Unit

Day	Topics Covered	Avg Sentiment
Week 1		
Day 1	Personal introductions; SPARCS program expectations; what is CS?; CS in other topics	Neutral
Day 2	CS + X existing curriculum; Computational Artifacts	Positive
Day 3	Industry Field Trip	Positive
Day 4	Problem-Based Learning; Problem Solving Process; CS Unplugged	Neutral
Day 5	Intro to Scratch and StarLogo Nova	Positive
Online Course		
Entry 1	Scratch Assignments	Positive
Entry 2	Beginning of StarLogo Nova Assignments	Negative
Entry 3	Finishing StarLogo Nova Assignments	Neutral
Collaborative Lesson Planning Week		
Day 1	Develop and articulate "Big Hairy Problem" (BHP) for Student Academy Lesson; relate BHP to CTP's	Negative
Day 2	Refine BHP for Students Academy Lesson; relate BHP to CTP's; outline lessons activities for Student Academy Lesson	Neutral
Day 3	Articulate CTP's and CS learning objective of Student Academy Lesson; develop Student Academy lesson Days 1 and 2 framework	Positive
Day 4	Develop Student Academy lesson Days 3 and 4 framework	Positive
Day 5	Finalize preparation for Student Academy lesson; practice day 1 lesson	Positive
Student Academy Week		
Day 1	Implementation of Lesson developed during previous week	Positive
Day 2		Positive
Day 3		Positive
Day 4		Positive

of teachers during this PD aids in the successful design and implementation of further CSE PD programs. By raising awareness of these issues for both the PD facilitators and the teachers, some stress can be alleviated [28]. In order to investigate the teacher experience, qualitative analyses involving the constant comparative approach [24] and sentiment analysis were conducted. From these approaches, five major cognitive themes emerged, and the affective patterns associated with the daily activities were identified. The combination of the cognitive and affective insights gained from our study can act as a guide when planning and implementing future CSE PD programs.

5.1 Limitations

As with any qualitative study, a major limitation of this study is potential for researcher bias. While such inherent bias provides a specific lens through which the researchers interpret the experiences of the teachers, appropriate steps were taken to minimize the effect of this bias through the constant comparative approach [24] and establishing interrater reliability regarding what constitutes a

positive or negative post. Another limitation that must be noted is the use of prompts during the daily reflections. Admittedly, these prompts did narrow the scope of the content that was mentioned in the journals, but they also allowed for enough elaboration on the part of the teachers by remaining largely open-ended. It should also be noted that the teachers in this study voluntarily applied to be a part of this PD program and were reimbursed for their efforts so the teachers here may not be necessarily representative of the "average" in-service teacher.

5.2 Implications for PD Design

When comparing the results of this study with the Sentance [22] study (which focused on the challenged and strategies of teachers implementing CS in their classes) and the Girvan [9] study (which focused on the teacher experience of implementing a new student-centered pedagogical approach), there are many similarities. There are three major concerns teachers encountered in all three studies: comfort level, practical application, and student success. These concerns provide highlights of teacher experiences in PD programs that need to be considered when designing effective CSE PD programs:

Comfort Level: Teachers want to feel well-prepared for the implementation of the learned content and/or pedagogic approaches. They often experience insecurities surrounding their own CS content knowledge and/or ability to give up "control" in the classroom to allow for more student-centered learning. Not only should PD experiences incorporate new CS-specific learning, but they also should begin with making connections between teachers' current knowledge and CS principles/concepts. Highlighting connections between current classroom methodologies and the new pedagogic approaches also serves to improve comfort. Lastly, explicitly modeling "student-centered" approaches while implementing the PD program helps the teachers see the new pedagogic approach in practice and provides an example of how to implement it. Another method to improve the comfort level for teachers is to provide support structures. In order to increase their support structures it's important to allow for time to network with other teachers involved in the program. These relationships will be the foundation for support and resources that were previously lacking.

Practical Application: Teachers are constantly considering how the new learning can be adapted to their current classrooms relative to their specific content focus—which they typically do not associate with CS. Teachers are also concerned with the perceived limitations of time, resources, and support. Allowing teachers the time during PD experiences to map out the connections between their current content standards and CS standards allows them to identify optimal places in their curriculum in which to implement the CS lessons. Allowing for the teachers themselves to do this rather than being told is important for their buy-in. This connection made between their current curriculum and CS lessons provides a solid foundation for practical application as it demonstrates how the CS component can be smoothly integrated into their existing curriculum.

Student Success: Teachers want to make their lessons as engaging as possible for their students, and they are always focused on how the new learning can best be used to encourage student buy-in and success. PD facilitators should provide opportunities through which teachers can witness student engagement and success through the implementation of the objectives of the PD program. One example is to invite the teachers from the next cohort to attend a "student fair" where projects from the current cohort's students are on display. Another example is to have a student academy week where teachers pilot their lessons with actual students and can experience the student engagement directly.

The additional knowledge gained through this study was the sentiment associated with specific experiences throughout the SPARCS PD program. In order to make the PD experience as beneficial as possible it may be helpful to raise the teachers' awareness of possible affective experiences in order to increase their emotional intelligence which will in turn help alleviate some stress [28]. During the first week, the teachers' responses were generally positive. This initial positive experience is important to help with resilience when individuals are faced with negative experiences [26], which is what happened during the following portion of the program that consisted of the online course. During this second portion of the SPARCS PD program, affective responses progressed through neutral, negative, and back to neutral. These neutral and negative experiences are not necessarily obstacles to overcome but rather natural experiences of the learning process [8]. While such negative responses may be natural indicators of learning, it has been the experience of the facilitators of the SPARCS PD program that these responses should be addressed and discussed in order to move on to the next topic. The collaborative lesson planning week began with negative/neutral responses but ended positively. Informing the teachers that they will most likely struggle at the beginning of the lesson planning process but through the struggle, they will design a well-developed lesson that will engage the students will provide them with the acknowledgement of their emotional responses through the week. The final week involved the student academy in which teachers piloted their lessons with actual students. This entire week was overall very positive and most of the positive responses surrounded student engagement and learning. Again, it is important to end the summer program on a positive note so that when teachers face inevitable challenges implementing these lessons in the classroom, they can rely on these positive experiences to help them persevere [26].

Teachers face a multitude of challenges and emotional responses when learning and implementing new content and methodologies, and these experiences need to be recognized and addressed in order for teachers to feel supported and understood when trying the newly learned content and methods in their classrooms. It is necessary to keep the teacher experience in mind when developing CSE PD because how the teachers experience the PD program will have a major impact on how faithfully the objectives of the program are implemented. Effective CSE PD initiatives should begin seeking to understand the teacher experience more holistically in order to make the initiatives as beneficial as possible to all stakeholders.

ACKNOWLEDGMENTS

The authors sincerely thank the SPARCS teacher participants and master teachers, along with the other members of the SPARCS development team: Harvey Siy, Neal Grandgenett, Jong-Hoon Youn, Qiuming Zhu, and Carol Engelmann.

This work is funded in part by the U.S. National Science Foundation under grant DRL-1433788. Any opinions, findings, and conclusions, or recommendations expressed in this material are those of the authors and do not necessarily reflect the views of the NSF.

REFERENCES

[1] Beverley Bell and John Gilbert. 1994. Teacher development as professional, personal, and social development. *Teaching and teacher education* 10, 5 (1994), 483–497.
[2] Vrushali K. Bongirwar. 2015. A Survey on Sentence Level Sentiment Analysis. *International Journal of Computer Science Trends and Technology (IJCST)* 3 (2015), 110–113.
[3] Xianglei Chen. 2013. STEM Attrition: College Students' Paths into and out of STEM Fields. Statistical Analysis Report. NCES 2014-001. *National Center for Education Statistics* (2013).
[4] Christopher Day and Judyth Sachs. 2005. *International handbook on the continuing professional development of teachers*. McGraw-Hill Education (UK).
[5] Christopher Day, Judyth Sachs, C. Day, and J. Sachs. 2004. Professionalism, performativity and empowerment: discourses in the politics, policies and purposes of continuing professional development. *International handbook on the continuing professional development of teachers* (2004), 3–32.
[6] Rekha Dhingra and Bijender K. Punia. 2016. Relational Analysis of Emotional Intelligence and Change Management: A Suggestive Model for Enriching Change Management Skills. *Vision* 20, 4 (2016), 312–322.
[7] John M. Dirkx. 2001. The power of feelings: Emotion, imagination, and the construction of meaning in adult learning. *New directions for adult and continuing education* 2001, 89 (2001), 63–72.
[8] John M. Dirkx. 2008. The meaning and role of emotions in adult learning. *New directions for adult and continuing education* 2008, 120 (2008), 7–18.
[9] Carina Girvan, Claire Conneely, and Brendan Tangney. 2016. Extending experiential learning in teacher professional development. *Teaching and Teacher Education* 58 (2016), 129–139.
[10] Daniel Goleman. 2006. *Emotional intelligence*. Bantam.
[11] Joanna Goode, Jane Margolis, and Gail Chapman. 2014. Curriculum is not enough: The educational theory and research foundation of the exploring computer science professional development model. In *Proceedings of the 45th ACM technical symposium on Computer science education*. ACM, 493–498.
[12] Thomas R. Guskey. 2002. Professional development and teacher change. *Teachers and teaching* 8, 3 (2002), 381–391.
[13] Andy Hargreaves. 2005. *The emotions of teaching and educational change*. Springer, 278–295.
[14] Cindy E. Hmelo-Silver. 2004. Problem-based learning: What and how do students learn? *Educational psychology review* 16, 3 (2004), 235–266.
[15] Peter Kahn and Karen O'Rourke. 2005. Understanding enquiry-based learning. *Handbook of enquiry and problem-based learning–Irish case studies and international perspectives. Dublin: Centre for Excellence in Learning and Teaching, NUI Galway & All Ireland Society for Higher Education* (2005).
[16] Muhsin Menekse. 2015. Computer science teacher professional development in the United States: a review of studies published between 2004 and 2014. *Computer Science Education* 25, 4 (10/02 2015), 325–350. DOI:http://dx.doi.org/10.1080/08993408.2015.1111645 doi: 10.1080/08993408.2015.1111645.
[17] Johannes Metzler and Ludger Woessmann. 2012. The impact of teacher subject knowledge on student achievement: Evidence from within-teacher within-student variation. *Journal of Development Economics* 99, 2 (2012), 486–496.
[18] Briana B. Morrison, Lijun Ni, and Mark Guzdial. 2012. Adapting the disciplinary commons model for high school teachers: improving recruitment, creating community. In *Proceedings of the ninth annual international conference on International computing education research*. ACM, 47–54.
[19] Jennifer Nias. 1996. Thinking about feeling: The emotions in teaching. *Cambridge journal of education* 26, 3 (1996), 293–306.
[20] Tanys Roscorla. 2015. 3 Policay Barriers Facing Computer Science Education. (2015). http://www.centerdigitaled.com/k-12/3-Policy-Barriers-Facing-Computer-Science-Education.html
[21] Peter Salovey and John D. Mayer. 1990. Emotional intelligence. *Imagination, cognition and personality* 9, 3 (1990), 185–211.
[22] Sue Sentance and Andrew Csizmadia. 2017. Computing in the curriculum: Challenges and strategies from a teacher's perspective. *Education and Information Technologies* (2017), 1–27.
[23] Harvey Siy, Brian Dorn, Carol Engelmann, Neal Grandgenett, Tracie Reding, Jong-Hoon Youn, and Qiuming Zhu. 2017. SPARCS: A Personalized Problem-based Learning Approach for Developing Successful Computer Science Learning Experiences in Middle School. In *EIT'17: Proceedings of the IEEE International Conference on Electro Information Technology*.

[24] Anselm Strauss and Juliet Corbin. 1994. Grounded theory methodology. *Handbook of qualitative research* 17 (1994), 273–285.

[25] The Telegraph. 2016. University Degree Subjects with the Highest Dropout Rates. (2016).

[26] Michele M. Tugade and Barbara L. Fredrickson. 2004. Resilient individuals use positive emotions to bounce back from negative emotional experiences. *Journal of personality and social psychology* 86, 2 (2004), 320.

[27] Harold Wenglinsky. 2001. Teacher classroom practices and student performance: How schools can make a difference. *ETS Research Report Series* 2001, 2 (2001).

[28] N. Yamani, M. Shahabi, and F. Haghani. 2014. The relationship between emotional intelligence and job stress in the faculty of medicine in Isfahan University of Medical Sciences. *Journal of advances in medical education & professionalism* 2, 1 (Jan 2014), 20–26.

[29] Baiyin Yang. 2003. Toward a Holistic Theory of Knowledge and Adult Learning. *Human Resource Development Review* 2, 2 (2003), 106–129.

Using Tracing and Sketching to Solve Programming Problems

Replicating and Extending an Analysis of What Students Draw

Kathryn Cunningham
School of Interactive Computing
Georgia Institute of Technology
85 5th St NW
Atlanta, Georgia 30332
kcunningham@gatech.edu

Sarah Blanchard
School of Psychology
Georgia Institute of Technology
654 Cherry Street
Atlanta, Georgia 30332
sblanchard6@gatech.edu

Barbara Ericson, Mark Guzdial
School of Interactive Computing
Georgia Institute of Technology
85 5th St NW
Atlanta, Georgia 30332
{ericson,guzdial}@cc.gatech.edu

ABSTRACT

Sketching out a code trace is a cognitive assistance for programmers, student and professional. Previous research (Lister *et al.* 2004) showed that students who sketch a trace on paper had greater success on code 'reading' problems involving loops, arrays, and conditionals. We replicated this finding, and developed further categories of student sketching strategies. Our results support previous findings that students who don't sketch on code reading problems have a lower success rate than students who do sketch. We found that students who sketch incomplete traces also have a low success rate, similar to students who don't sketch at all. We categorized sketching strategies on new problem types (code writing, code ordering, and code fixing) and find that different types of sketching are used on these problems, not always with increased success. We ground our results in a theory of sketching as a method for distributing cognition and as a demonstration of the process of the notional machine.

CCS CONCEPTS

•Social and professional topics → Computing education; *CS1;*

KEYWORDS

CS1, novice programmers, tracing, sketching, notional machine, distributed cognition

1 INTRODUCTION

Introductory computing courses aim to teach students computing fundamentals through instruction on basic programming skills, syntax, and semantics [1]. Studies suggest these courses often fail to teach students how to successfully write code to solve basic problems [17, 27]. Many students reach the end of CS1 without being able to read and understand short pieces of code [14, 24].

Why do students struggle? Research suggests that the intrinsic cognitive load [23] of solving typical introductory programming problems may be higher than that of introductory problems in

ICER '17, August 18–20, 2017, Tacoma, WA, USA
© 2017 ACM. 978-1-4503-4968-0/17/08...$15.00
DOI: http://dx.doi.org/10.1145/3105726.3106190

other fields [18]. Also, students exhibit a wide range of misunderstandings about a crucial concept: the *notional machine* [22]. The notional machine is a theoretical construct representing the process through which a computer executes code of a particular language or paradigm [22]. An accurate understanding of the notional machine is central to a student's ability to trace and write code, since they must run code through their mental model of the notional machine in order to predict the outcome of that code's execution.

The understanding of the notional machine and the management of cognitive load are hidden mental processes. However, when students sketch out a problem-solving technique such as a code trace on paper, we can observe some signs of their cognition. Prior work in computing education research has used student drawings to identify misconceptions about variable assignment [15]. In educational psychology student sketches are also used to gauge understanding of concepts [3].

In this paper, we use the term **sketching** to describe a programmer's written visualizations of program state or any other computing process. Sketching may be most frequently associated with *code reading*, when students are likely to write down a trace of variable states. However, we purposefully keep the definition of sketching broad to cover many situations in which a student or professional programmer may take pencil to paper. Such tasks may include planning an algorithm, designing an object-oriented hierarchy, or annotating existing code.

Sketching may help students manage cognitive load while also demonstrating the student's understanding of the notional machine to themselves, peers, and instructors. Sketching requires that the student take an active role as they describe a computational process with their pen. Sketching the process of code execution, as during a trace, forces a student to ask themselves "what happens next?" as they draw each step of the notional machine.

This study investigates the following questions about sketching by CS1 students:

- *Are some sketching techniques more associated with correct problem-solving than others?*
- *Does sketching differ for different problem types, like reading, writing, fixing, and ordering code?*
- *What may influence students' sketching choices?*

2 BACKGROUND

2.1 Sketching in computing education research

The Leeds Working Group (LWG) at ITiCSE 2004 produced an influential multi-institutional, multi-national study analyzing the code reading skills of hundreds of students [14]. While outcomes were not as stark as those of the McCracken Working Group analysis at ITiCSE 2001 which evaluated code writing skills [17], the LWG found that CS1 students were challenged by many code reading problems involving loops, conditionals, and arrays. Their assessment involved two question types: code prediction problems where students determined the values of variables after code execution, and code completion problems where students chose pieces of code needed to complete a code snippet with certain functionality.

For a subset of participants, LWG researchers characterized and analyzed all notes and marks drawn on the test sheets. Certain sketches seemed more helpful than others. Tracing sketches that tracked multiple values of the same variable were most correlated with correct responses. When students left their paper blank, their success rate was lower than when any sketching type was employed. These findings suggest that sketching may support students' ability to solve code prediction and code completion problems.

Some members of the LWG took this analysis further [16]. Sketching amounts varied widely from institution to institution, from as as low as 28% of problems sketched to as high as 92%. Students consistently sketched more often on code prediction problems than on code completion problems.

Whalley *et al.* [29] analyzed student sketching on questions from the LWG analysis and on additional code reading question types. Like the LWG, they found that sketching is associated with more successful problem-solving. Different sketch types were more common on different problem types. The authors also noted that a minority of participants used the tracing sketch type demonstrated in their classroom. Lister et al. (2010) [13] also replicated the LWG's results about the success of tracing sketches and expressed a need for more fine-grained categories of sketched traces.

Researchers have reported that CS1 students' ability to sketch variable states correlates with their scores on other assessments. Such diagrams include "memory diagrams" [9], where differing shapes distinguish objects (circles), primitives and references (squares), and classes (diamonds). Similar results were observed with "object diagrams" [25], although Thomas *et al.* found that students were not more likely to use diagrams after they were introduced in class, and that using a diagram did not correlate with increased success for students with prior programming experience. Hertz and Jump used "trace-based-teaching" [8], a curricular method involving intricate sketched program traces, including details about variables' location in the stack or in the heap and variables' enclosing method call. Each class started with 20-30 minutes of tracing activities using these diagrams. They found that CS2 grades increased and dropout rates decreased after introduction of this technique.

2.2 Tracing and the notional machine

The idea of the notional machine was first proposed in 1986 [5], yet recent work [22] has made the notional machine a key framework for viewing how students understand computing. The notional machine is an abstraction of how the computer processes code, based in a particular language or paradigm. When a student writes code with an expected outcome or predicts the result of running a piece of code, the student runs that code through their mental model of the notional machine [22]. The understanding of the notional machine forms a hidden but crucial intermediate step in programming work.

When teachers understand the notional machine, it becomes clear what mental processes a student must learn. Effective classroom techniques assist students in defining and refining their mental models, and successful assessments allow teachers to gauge their students' depth of understanding of the notional machine.

Tracing code, which is stepping through the process of the notional machine, makes a student's mental model of the notional machine evident [22]. A teacher reviewing a sketch of a student's trace might be able to identify misconceptions and focus on improving the student's understanding. By creating a sketch of a code trace, students may be able to clarify and refine their mental model of the notional machine.

2.3 Sketching as distributed cognition

Intelligence is commonly considered a characteristic of an individual, and cognition is commonly considered a process of a single mind. However, from the perspective of *distributed cognition*, cognitive processes occur in a socio-technical system composed of humans, artifacts, and their interactions [10]. The sketch and the sketcher can be viewed as part of a distributed system that is performing cognition about programming. Together, the markings on the paper, the process of modifying the marks, and the cognition of the sketcher work to generate an answer.

Cognition can be off-loaded from a single mind with memory aides like diagrams and text, technological tools like measurement devices and data displays, and other individuals like teachers and peers [20]. Many introductory-level fields make effective use of drawing and sketching to help students work "smarter". Examples include structured long division calculations in elementary mathematics [12], the pushing electron formalism in organic chemistry [6], and force body diagrams in introductory physics [4].

A key insight from work in distributed cognition is that the design of visual aids can modify the amount and type of cognition a human must perform when interacting with the aid [10]. With the limited working memory that a student must use to run their mental model of the notional machine [26], effective off-loading is crucial. Some sketching methods may successfully offload more cognition from the human to the paper. Another sense of a sketch's effectiveness is greater correctness. Sketches may not always be highly successful at both. Single value tracing is a phenomenon noted by Vainio and Sajaniemi [28], where students only keep track of one "memory slot" that holds the most recently modified value. This trace has low cognitive load, but with its inaccurate representation of the notional machine, it produces incorrect results for all but the simplest problems.

3 EXPERIMENTAL DESIGN

CS1 students from a large research university in North America participated in a computer-mediated experiment, using their own laptops in a supervised setting. The experiment took place during the 10th week of a 16 week semester. The analysis presented here is from the pre-test portion of this experiment.

The test consisted of eight questions written in Python. It tested CS1 knowledge on lists, loops, and conditionals. As shown in Table

Table 1: Question types and grading strategies.

#	Type	Graded by
1	Reading - Prediction	Multiple choice
2	Reading - What code does	Multiple choice
3	Reading - Prediction	Multiple choice
4	Reading - Prediction	Multiple choice
5	Reading - Prediction	Multiple choice
6	Fixing	Rubric (12 point scale)
7	Ordering - 2D Parsons	Rubric (12 point scale)
8	Writing	Rubric (12 point scale)

What do a and b equal after the following code executes?

```
a = 10
b = 3
t = 0
for i in range(1,4):
    t = a
    a = i + b
    b = t - i
```

Figure 1: Wording of Problem 4

1, the test consisted of five multiple choice questions about code reading, one question about fixing code to meet a specification, one question involving ordering code in a two-dimensional Parsons problem with paired distractors [11, 19], and one question involving writing code to meet a specification. The code reading questions were of two types: four involved predicting the result of executing a code snippet (see Figure 1 for an example), while one involved determining what code does. The problems involving fixing, ordering, and writing code all contained sample input and output in the problem descriptions. The fix code and write code problems provided feedback to test-takers in the form of unit tests. Students were allowed a maximum of 45 minutes to complete the eight-question test: 15 minutes for the reading questions, 10 minutes for the fixing question, 10 minutes for the ordering question, and 10 minutes for the writing question.

During the test, participants were instructed to use provided pens and blank scratch paper (labeled with their unique identification number) if they wished to draw. Participants were instructed to return their scratch paper to the experiment administrators after completion of the test.

In this study, we examine scratch sheet and performance data. 159 participants attended the experiment. 24 participants were eliminated from the data set because they did not answer at least one of the questions or spent less than 30 seconds on trying to answer one of the fix code, order code, or write code problems.

4 REPLICATION OF THE LEEDS WORKING GROUP ANALYSIS

Our data provides the opportunity to replicate the Leeds Working Group (LWG) analysis on the use of sketching by CS1 students on code reading problems about loops, lists, and conditionals. We

present a replication of the key figure about sketching from the LWG study in Table 2. For this analysis, we used a random subset of the data: scratch sheets with even-numbered IDs (N=65).

4.0.1 Differences between studies. Minor procedural differences between the LWG study and the current study should be noted. In our computer-mediated experiment, students read questions on their laptop screen, sketched on a blank sheet of paper, and selected an answer by clicking a button on the screen. In the LWG study, participants sketched on paper that contained printed test questions, and chose their answer by circling a printed answer choice. While the LWG's questions were written in Java, this study used questions written in Python. Our participants were CS1 students a little more than halfway through their course, while Leeds Working Group students had recently completed or were near completion of CS1.

4.0.2 Sketch types. The LWG identified twelve types of sketching in their analysis. The following eight sketch types are used in this replication:

- *Blank Page (B)*: Nothing written at all.
- *Computation (C)*: An expression containing an operation such as addition or division. The operands may be two literal values or a value and a variable. The
- *Keeping Tally (K)*: Tally marks keeping track of the number of occurrences of something.
- *Number (N)*: A standalone value, or a variable and an associated single value.
- *Position (P)*: Indices are written on top of an array, assisting with lookup by index.
- *Trace (T)*: Multiple values of one or more variables are tracked by listing values near variable names. Previous values may be crossed out.
- *Synchronized Trace (S)*: Values of multiple variables are tracked, with the value of all variables re-written any time any variables changes.
- *Odd Trace (O)*: Multiple values of one or more variables are tracked, but in a way that is not T or S.

The computer-mediated nature of our experiment meant that some of the LWG sketch categorizations are not applicable because they require writing on or near pre-existing problem text. The categories *Alternate Answer (A)*: a different answer choice circled, *Underlined (U)*: part of the original problem text underlined, and *Ruled Out (X)*: one or more of the answer choices crossed out were not considered in this analysis. We also removed the *Extraneous Marks (E)* category, and instead did not record sketching that did not clearly fall into one of the other categories

We noticed some additional sketch types in our data that we created new categories for:

- *Describe (D)*: English words describing expected functionality of code.
- *Loop Variables (L)*: A listing of the loop variables returned by the range function[1] are written out. This provides a reminder of the value for each loop iteration.
- *Rewrite (R)*: Portions of code from the question are rewritten. Question information is then more easily accessible for tracing or other sketching.

---
[1]Used in Python for loops to generate index variable values

Table 2: Percentage of correct answers on code reading problems when students (N=65) use a particular LWG sketch type

Sketch Category	Current Study		LWG Study	
	% Correct	n	% Correct	n
Trace (T)	82.1	95	75	215
Computation (C)	78.7	61	60	30
Loop Variables (L)	77.3	44	-	-
Position (P)	66.7	9	64	75
Number (N)	65.3	118	70	189
Rewrite (R)	60.7	56	-	-
Blank (B)	60.7	135	50	256
Odd Trace (O)	55.6	9	78	23
Synchronized Trace (S)	-	0	77	73
Keep Tally (K)	-	0	100	6
Alternate answer (A)	-	-	69	26
X-ruled Out (X)	-	-	60	60
Underlined (U)	-	-	52	44

4.0.3 Coding the data. We created a coding system for each of the eleven categories and the first two authors coded the data. Inter-rater reliability on these sketching categories an 81% match across 20% of the data.

In the LWG study, sketching was performed on or near question text, making determination of which sketch belonged to which question straightforward. In our data, all problems were sketched on a single scratch sheet, requiring additional analysis to pair sketches with questions.

Noting the distinct variable names used in the different problems, we developed a coding scheme to determine which sketches belonged to which problems. The first two authors implemented this coding scheme to match sketches with questions, while leaving out sketches whose originating question was unclear. Inter-rater reliability on how each line of sketching was categorized was 95% across 20% of the data.

4.1 Not all sketching is created equal

We replicate the first major result of the LWG: different sketching types are associated with different rates of success. Students' average score across all code reading problems was 66.8%. However, the use of certain sketches like Trace and Computation was associated with higher than average success, while the use of Rewrite or Odd Trace was associated with lower than average success. Some methods of offloading cognition appear to be more helpful than others.

4.2 The sketch type "Trace" is the most successful

The LWG study identified three different types of tracing sketches, and found that they were the most highly associated with success out of all sketch types. In our data, one of those trace categories was the most successful category of all sketching categories (82.1% success rate), while the other two tracing categories were rarely

used. These results support the idea that tracing is a strong strategy for solving code reading problems.

4.3 No sketching at all is associated with lower success

While students who left problems blank did not score as poorly in our data as in the LWG study (61% vs 50%), they still scored poorly compared to other sketch categories. In the LWG study, leaving a problem blank was associated with the lowest average score of any sketch type, closely followed by Underlined. In our analysis it has the second lowest average score overall, tied with Rewrite. It should be noted that the category with the lowest score, Odd trace, has few data points. Choosing not to sketch is not a successful strategy for solving code reading problems.

4.4 Differences from LWG results

4.4.1 Odd Traces are not successful. In the LWG, the Odd Trace category was one of the sketch categories with the highest rate of success (78%). However, in our analysis, the technique had the lowest success rate (56%). In both studies, Odd Traces were rare, occurring in only 3% of all problems. Synchronized Traces were not found at all in our data.

It is possible that we interpreted the Odd Trace and Synchronized Trace categories differently than the LWG. It is also possible that our participants simply did not use those trace types, perhaps because they had never seen them. All our students attended a single institution, while participants in the LWG study attended a variety of institutions, and potentially saw a wider variety of sketching techniques.

In our data, Odd Traces tended to be less structured than Traces. It also was more difficult to determine which values were associated with which variable. Perhaps this lack of clarity was associated with more difficulty in tracking variable values.

4.4.2 Differences in non-tracing sketch types. While the most successful and least successful sketching techniques were consistent between our results and those of the LWG, other sketch types were observed at different rates and were associated with varying success.

This difference may be explained by differences in the problem types. In our data we did not observe certain sketch types, including Keep Tally. Keep Tally was rare in the LWG analysis; it may have been even less common in this data set because a counter variable only appeared in one problem in our test, while the LWG questions contained four problems with counters.

The difference could also be due to the difference in test-taking format. For example, the Position type was much more rare in our data than in that of the LWG. It is possible that creating this sketch required extra effort to copy down an array, rather than writing near a pre-printed array. The additional burden of this task may have made it less appealing. Alternatively, the questions in our experiment may have requires less complex patterns of indexing into arrays than those of the LWG, making it less likely that students sketch to assist with this task.

Table 3: Probability of getting problems right, with and without sketching.

Question	% Correct	% Who Sketched
1 - Predict	63.0	70.4
2 - What code does	78.5	20.0
3 - Predict	66.7	43.7
4 - Predict	75.6	94.8
5 - Predict	53.3	63.0
Fix	65.6	12.6
Order	96.5	3.0
Write	67.6	22.2

Table 4: Average score on code fixing, ordering, and writing problems when students (N=65) use a particular sketch type from the Leeds Working Group categorization.

Sketch Category	Average score (%)	Data Points
Write (W)	92.7	7
Describe (D)	81.4	14
Blank (B)	77.7	165
Number (N)	71.5	11
Rewrite (R)	65.0	6
Position (P)	40.0	1
Computation (C)	26.7	3

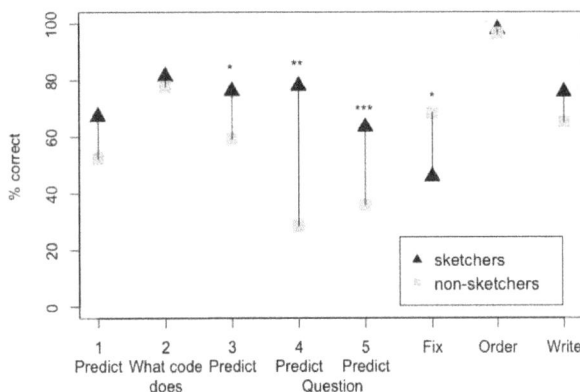

Figure 2: Differences in correctness between sketchers and non-sketchers (* = p <0.10, ** = p <0.05, *** = p <0.01 on Welch two Sample t-test)

4.5 Sketching to avoid split attention effect

Differences in sketches between this study and the LWG study shed light on differences in student cognition between a paper-based exam and a computer-based exam. Students frequently re-wrote pieces of code from questions on their scratch sheets, perhaps to manage issues related to the split attention effect [2]. While students in the LWG study could annotate printed code, in our study student sketches were separated from original problem text on the computer screen. In order to decrease this extrinsic cognitive load, students copied text to be closer to their other sketching.

Rewriting was not a highly successful sketching technique, however, with a success rate about the same as not sketching at all. It is possible that struggling students tried to use Rewrite to relieve some extrinsic cognitive load, but it was not a major assistance.

5   PROFILING SKETCH USE

We extend the LWG analysis to examine use of sketching more deeply, including on additional problem types: fixing code, ordering code, and writing code.

5.1   Some prediction problems trigger sketching more than others

Students chose to sketch the most for code tracing problems (1, 3, 4, and 5). However, even among code tracing problems, some problems were much more frequently sketched than others. 95% of students sketched on question 4, while 44% of students sketched on question 3 (see Table 3).

These differences may be explained by the number of variable states that students had to track in each problem. In question 4, three different variables were updated three times. In question 3, one variable was updated three times, and there were three comparisons. In that question, if students noticed that all comparisons would be false due to a code "error", they did not need to complete a trace. This supports the view that tracing is offloading cognition, which may be more necessary on some problems than others.

5.2   Sketching leads to better predictions

On code prediction problems, sketchers were more successful, sometimes dramatically so (Figure 2). On question 4, those who sketched performed nearly 50 percentage points higher than non-sketchers. For other prediction problems, the difference was 15-25 percentage points. For the problem where students described what a code snippet does, there was almost no difference between sketchers and non-sketchers.

The high rate of sketching on problem 4 suggests that students have some idea when it is a good idea to sketch, at least in cases of high cognitive load.

5.3   Sketching on fix, order, and write code problems

5.3.1 Sketching was associated with lower scores on the fix code problem. Surprisingly, students who sketched on the fix code problem had a lower average score than those who did not sketch (Figure 2) (46% vs 69%, p-value=0.06 on Welch two sample t-test). Only 12% of students sketched on this problem, and the most common sketch type used was Number (a sketch of a single value of a variable). No students chose to sketch a trace on this problem.

Students might have used sketching techniques like Trace fruitfully on the fix code problem, but they chose not to. Maybe they did not perceive the value of sketching when fixing code. Perhaps students' usual strategy when fixing code is to look for patterns, to match the code to their existing schema [21].

5.3.2 There was very little sketching on the order code problem. Only 3% of students sketched on this problem. Both sketchers and non-sketchers were highly successful (average score 97.9% and 96.5% respectively). No students chose to sketch a trace on this problem. Students' low amount of sketching on the order code problem may be further evidence of the low cognitive load of Parsons problems.

5.3.3 Different sketch types were used when writing code. 22% of students sketched on the code reading problem, they scored higher than their non-sketching peers, but not statistically significantly so (p = 0.34 on Welch two sample t-test). The most common sketching technique used was Describe, where students wrote the expected functionality of code on their scratch sheet. Second most common was the Write technique, where students wrote code to solve the problem on paper. This occurred even though students could write their code on the computer. Writers were highly successful, scoring an average of 92.7% (see Table 4). Writing sketches were only used on this problem. It is hard to say whether the increased success of sketchers is related to sketching itself, or an effect of time spent planning before implementing.

5.4 Sketchers take more time

Sketchers took more time than non-sketchers on code fixing (5.5 min vs 12.7 min, p <0.001 on Welch two sample t-test), code ordering (5.4 min vs 12.2 min, p <0.01 on Welch two sample t-test), and code writing problems (7.0 min vs 12.0 min, p <0.001 on Welch two sample t-test). Students who sketched on more code reading problems took more time to complete that part of the test. Correlation between the number of code reading problems sketched and time spent on the code reading questions has an r^2 of 0.64.

This raises the possibility that sketchers score more highly simply because they spend more time problem-solving. However, there is no correlation in our data between time taken and score for any of the problem types (r^2 <0.15 for all).

6 OBSERVING NEW SKETCH TYPES

We replicated the result that a tracing sketch type is highly correlated with correctness on code prediction problems. However, during our data analysis, we noticed that students used several distinct tracing sketch types not distinguished in the Leeds Working Group categorizations. These sketch types were most often used for problem 4, a code prediction problem involving complex variable assignment within the loop body (see Figure 1 for question text). This section explores why certain tracing types might be more representative of the notional machine. We compare the success of students using various techniques and discuss how different populations vary in their use of these sketch types.

6.1 Creating finer distinctions in the LWG sketching taxonomy

We identified four distinct sketching types, shown in Figures 3-6. All of the sketches are traces, involving the tracking of changing variable values over time. All these sketches would be categorized

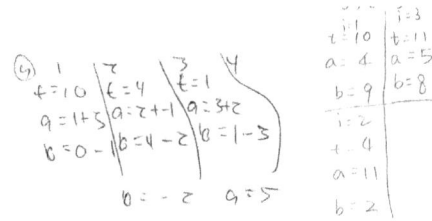

Figure 3: Examples of the "chunk" technique

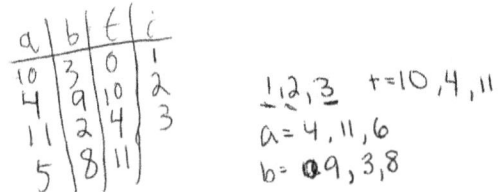

Figure 4: Examples of the "line" technique

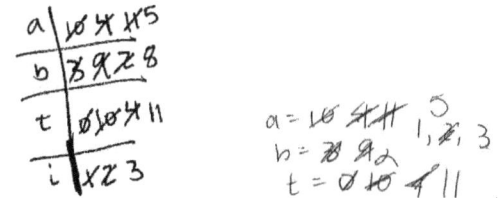

Figure 5: Examples of the "crossout" technique

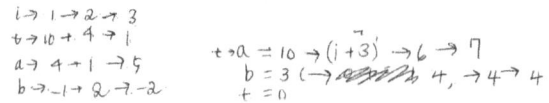

Figure 6: Examples of the "arrow flow" technique

as Trace (T) in the LWG analysis, but we felt their structures were distinct and that they should be distinguished.

6.1.1 Chunk. This sketch is identified by groupings of assignments, with variable names, equal signs, and the variable value re-written for each loop iteration.

6.1.2 Line. This sketch lists values in a series, following a variable name. The values may simply be written next to each other, or may be separated by commas.

6.1.3 Crossout. This sketch is distinguished by values that are crossed out, usually with a slash. Each variable is written once, with a series of values after it. The value at the end of the line is not crossed out.

6.1.4 Arrow Flow. In this sketch type, variable names are written once, and values are separated by arrows, drawn in the direction of newer values.

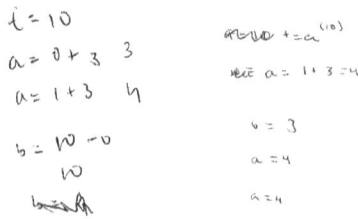

Figure 7: Examples of "incomplete" tracing sketches

6.2 Sketches are different in how they mirror the notional machine

The notional machines of major procedural programming languages share common operations when assignment of primitives is involved. During assignment, a variable's value is overwritten by the new value being assigned. Each variable can hold only one value at a time. Accurate sketching techniques for tracing are a demonstration of this action of the notional machine.

Some sketching techniques from our data seem to mirror the notional machine more clearly than others. Crossout, for instance, demonstrates that previous values are no longer accessible by a strike-through. It is hard to mistakenly use a prior value when it is clearly crossed out. For Line and Arrow Flow, if the sketcher understands that the value at the end of the line is the current value, the sketch communicates this same idea. In contrast to these three techniques, Chunk groups variable values together by the loop iteration when they are assigned. In order to find the most recent value, the student must consider both the current listing of values and the previous listing of values.

From this point of view, Crossout places the least cognitive demand on the sketcher as they act out the notional machine, because information about the most recent value is clearly presented. In contrast, Chunk requires more cognitive effort by the sketcher.

6.3 These tracing sketches were equally successful

We predicted that this cognitive demand would affect students' correctness when using these methods, so that Crossout would have a higher success rate than Chunk.

We coded tracing sketch types used on question 4 (n=135, interrater reliability on tracing type used was 93% across 20% of the data). In addition to the four tracing sketch types described in Section 5.1, we also created categories for Incomplete tracing sketches and Other tracing sketches. Incomplete traces did not have a clear sketching structure or include the majority of variable values. Other tracing sketches were traces that were organized and covered all values, but were not from the four main categories we identified. Students overwhelmingly used the chunk tracing method (53.3%), followed by the line tracing method (16.4%).

Difference in correctness on question 4 between students who used the four tracing types was not statistically significant. Students who used one of these methods performed similarly. Differences in representations of the notional machine did not significantly impact students' outcomes in this setting. However, if there were increased

Table 5: Percentage of correct answers based on tracing sketch type.

Sketch Type	% Correct	Count
Line	92.3	26
Chunk	82.4	77
Crossout	77.8	9
Arrow Flow	50.0	2
Other	50.0	2
None	37.5	8
Incomplete	9.1	11

Figure 8: Tracing technique used by the second instructor

time constraints or if students had less programming experience, we may be more likely to see differences between tracing sketches based on this variation in cognitive process.

6.4 Incomplete tracers and non-tracers were less successful

Students who used no tracing method or used an incomplete tracing method performed much more poorly on this question than students who used a complete tracing method. A statistically significant difference in correctness was found in comparisons between incomplete sketchers and Chunk, Line, and Crossout (p <0.001 on all on Fisher's exact test). A statistically significant difference in correctness was found in comparisons between non-sketchers and those using Chunk and Line (p <0.001 on Fishers Exact Test). The difference between non-sketchers and those using Crossout technique was significant at the lower bar of accepting an alpha value of 0.10 (p=0.06).

6.5 Instructors, TAs, and students trace differently

Instructors may influence a student's choice of technique. Participants in this experiment came from two sections of CS1, taught by two different lecturers following the same schedule. Students in these courses were each assigned to a weekly recitation, led by an undergraduate teaching assistant (TA). Both course instructors and 12 of the 17 TAs (70%) were interviewed to determine if they demonstrated tracing techniques similar to those described here (see Table 6).

One instructor self-reported use of Chunk and Line in her classroom, which were the two most commonly-used sketching techniques seen in our data. However, the second instructor self-reported use of a technique not observed in any student sketches,

Table 6: Tracing sketches used by TAs and students

Sketch Type	% of interviewed TAs (n)	% of students (n)
Chunk	16.7% (2)	57.0% (77)
Line	33.3% (4)	19.3% (26)
Crossout	41.7% (5)	6.7% (9)
Arrow flow	8.3% (1)	1.5% (2)
Total	100.0% (12)	84.4% (114)

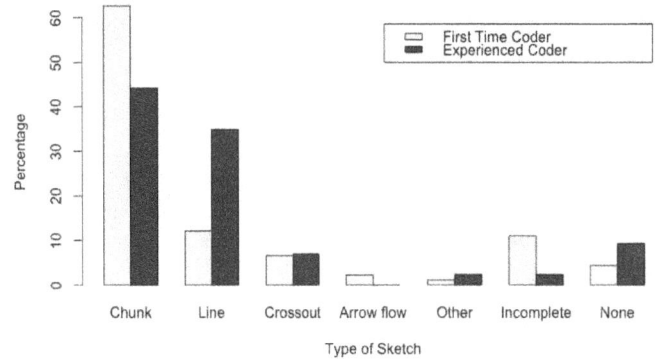

Figure 9: Tracing types used by first time coders and experienced coders

although 47% of participants were enrolled in this instructor's section. This technique involved a representation of variables as boxes, and the crossing out of prior values as variables took on new values (see Figure 8).

TAs also did not present standardized sketching techniques during recitations and office hours. Interviews with 12 of the 17 TAs showed that they used a wide variety of tracing sketches, although they favored Crossout and Line techniques (see Table 6).

We cannot determine why students used a certain technique without more information, but the data suggests interesting questions. Why did students use the techniques of the first instructor, but never the technique of the second instructor? Although Crossout was favored among TAs, why did students rarely use that technique?

It is possible that Crossout and the method used by the second instructor require more effort to sketch than Line or Chunk. Students may not view the extra effort of striking out values as being worth it, even if it does save cognition later. Even in the effort is similar, students may value sketches that better reflect code syntax.

6.6 Students with prior experience trace differently than first-time coders

Participants in this study were taking an introductory computer science class. However, a demographics survey revealed that 32.6% of participants had prior programming experience. When we categorized students based on programming experience, we found a significant difference in the distribution of tracing techniques used on multiple choice question 4. Students who had prior programming experience used Line much more than first time coders (see Figure 9). Experienced coders still used Chunk the most. Among the four tracing methods, there was a statistically significant difference in tracing technique use between experienced and new coders ($p < 0.01$ on Fisher's exact test).

Similarly, inexperienced coders used Chunk the most, but, unlike experienced coders, they use other coding types less. Instructor 1 stated in her interview that she felt Chunk was more appropriate for students new to programming, while Line was a better fit for students more comfortable with programming. This association seems to be reflected in our data.

Experienced coders used Incomplete much less than first time coders; however, experienced coders were more likely to use no tracing method at all. However, the difference was not statistically significant ($p = 0.11$ on Fisher's exact test).

7 CONCLUSION

Our results replicate the LWG's major findings on sketching, extend the LWG analysis to new problem types, and expand the taxonomy of sketches. We re-affirm that tracing is a successful sketch type for use on code reading problems, while not sketching at all has a low success rate. When tracing, completeness of tracing is more predictive of correctness than tracing strategy. Details of tracing sketches do not seem to make much difference.

Sketching is not as frequently used or as successful on code fixing, code ordering, and code writing problems. Sketches like tracing could certainly be used on these problems, such as for testing. Students may not associate sketching with these problem types as much as they do with code prediction. Alternatively, students may have used problem-solving strategies that are not well-represented in sketches, such as pattern-matching with known code patterns.

Our results are consistent with a view of sketching as a technique to distribute cognition and manage cognitive load. When students offload more cognition, as with complete trace sketches, they are more successful. However, such well-ordered sketches may only be possible with strong understanding of the notional machine. Students who do not sketch may lack fundamental knowledge of the notional machine, and are unable to use any sketching technique.

Besides assisting with problem-solving, sketching presents an opportunity for instructor observation and peer interaction. Sketching is visible and can be completed in a group setting. New K-12 computing teachers cite the lack of materials and techniques to aid them in the classroom as a major difficulty [7, 30]. Sketching research can lead to the development of engaging, active pedagogical techniques.

The success of sketching on certain problems, particularly tracing sketches for code prediction problems, supports the idea that all students should be taught a tracing sketch technique. Our results suggest that students' choice of technique is not a straightforward adaptation of their instructor's sketching. If we know more about why students choose a particular technique, we might be able to determine techniques students are most likely to adopt and complete.

ACKNOWLEDGMENTS

We are grateful to the anonymous reviewers, who provided detailed feedback and suggestions that improved this paper.

REFERENCES

[1] ACM/IEEE-CS Joint Task Force on Computing Curricula. 2013. *Computer Science Curricula 2013*. Technical Report. ACM Press and IEEE Computer Society Press. DOI : http://dx.doi.org/10.1145/2534860

[2] Paul Chandler and John Sweller. 1991. Cognitive load theory and the format of instruction. *Cognition and instruction* 8, 4 (1991), 293–332.

[3] Michelene TH Chi, Stephanie A Siler, Heisawn Jeong, Takashi Yamauchi, and Robert G Hausmann. 2001. Learning from human tutoring. *Cognitive Science* 25, 4 (2001), 471–533.

[4] Michelene T. H. Chi, Paul J. Feltovich, and Robert Glaser. 1981. Categorization and Representation of Physics Problems by Experts and Novices. *Cognitive Science* 5, 2 (1981), 121–152. DOI : http://dx.doi.org/10.1207/s15516709cog0502_2

[5] Benedict Du Boulay. 1986. Some Difficulties of Learning to Program. *Journal of Educational Computing Research* 2, 1 (1986), 57–73. DOI : http://dx.doi.org/10.2190/3LFX-9RRF-67T8-UVK9

[6] Robert Ferguson and George M. Bodner. 2008. Making sense of the arrow-pushing formalism among chemistry majors enrolled in organic chemistry. *Chem. Educ. Res. Pract.* 9 (2008), 102–113. Issue 2. DOI : http://dx.doi.org/10.1039/B806225K

[7] Mark Guzdial, Barbara Ericson, Tom McKlin, and Shelly Engelman. 2014. Georgia Computes! An Intervention in a US State, with Formal and Informal Education in a Policy Context. 14, 2 (2014).

[8] Matthew Hertz and Maria Jump. 2013. Trace-Based Teaching in Early Programming Courses. *Proceedings of the 44th ACM Technical Symposium on Computer Science Education* (2013), 561–566. DOI : http://dx.doi.org/10.1145/2445196.2445364

[9] Mark A. Holliday and David Luginbuhl. 2004. CS1 assessment using memory diagrams. *ACM SIGCSE Bulletin* 36, 1 (2004), 200. DOI : http://dx.doi.org/10.1145/1028174.971373

[10] Edwin Hutchins. 1995. How a cockpit remembers its speeds. *Cognitive science* 19, 3 (1995), 265–288.

[11] Petri Ihantola and Ville Karavirta. 2011. Two-dimensional parsonfis puzzles: The concept, tools, and first observations. *Journal of Information Technology Education* 10 (2011), 2011.

[12] Magdalene Lampert. 1992. Teaching and learning long division for understanding in school. In *Analysis of Arithmetic for Mathematics Teaching*, Rosemary A. Hattrup Gaea Leinhardt, Ralph Putnam (Ed.). Psychology Press, Chapter 4, 221–282.

[13] Raymond Lister, Tony Clear, Dennis J Bouvier, Paul Carter, Anna Eckerdal, Jana Jacková, Mike Lopez, Robert McCartney, Phil Robbins, Otto Seppälä, and others. 2010. Naturally occurring data as research instrument: analyzing examination responses to study the novice programmer. *ACM SIGCSE Bulletin* 41, 4 (2010), 156–173.

[14] Raymond Lister, Otto Seppälä, Beth Simon, Lynda Thomas, Elizabeth S. Adams, Sue Fitzgerald, William Fone, John Hamer, Morten Lindholm, Robert McCartney, Jan Erik Moström, and Kate Sanders. 2004. A multi-national study of reading and tracing skills in novice programmers. In *ACM SIGCSE Bulletin*, Vol. 36. 119–150. DOI : http://dx.doi.org/10.1145/1041624.1041673

[15] Linxiao Ma. 2007. *Investigating and improving novice programmers' mental models of programming concepts.* Ph.D. Dissertation. University of Strathclyde.

[16] Robert McCartney, Jan Erik Moström, Kate Sanders, and Otto Seppälä. 2004. Questions, Annotations, and Institutions: observations from a study of novice programmers. In *the Fourth Finnish/Baltic Sea Conference on Computer Science Education, October 1–3, 2004 in Koli, Finland*. Helsinki University of Technology, Department of Computer Science and Engineering, Laboratory of Information Processing Science, FINLAND, 11–19.

[17] Michael McCracken, Vicki Almstrum, Danny Diaz, Mark Guzdial, Dianne Hagan, Yifat Ben-David Kolikant, Cary Laxer, Lynda Thomas, Ian Utting, and Tadeusz

Wilusz. 2001. A Multi-national, Multi-institutional Study of Assessment of Programming Skills of First-year CS Students. *SIGCSE Bull.* 33, 4 (Dec. 2001), 125–180. DOI : http://dx.doi.org/10.1145/572139.572181

[18] Briana B. Morrison, Lauren E. Margulieux, and Mark Guzdial. 2015. Subgoals, Context, and Worked Examples in Learning Computing Problem Solving. In *Proceedings of the Eleventh Annual International Conference on International Computing Education Research (ICER '15)*. ACM, New York, NY, USA, 21–29. DOI : http://doi.acm.org/10.1145/2787622.2787733

[19] Dale Parsons and Patricia Haden. 2006. Parson's Programming Puzzles: A Fun and Effective Learning Tool for First Programming Courses. In *Proceedings of the 8th Australasian Conference on Computing Education - Volume 52 (ACE '06)*. Australian Computer Society, Inc., Darlinghurst, Australia, Australia, 157–163. http://dl.acm.org/citation.cfm?id=1151869.1151890

[20] Roy D Pea. 1993. Practices of distributed intelligence and designs for education. *Distributed cognitions: Psychological and educational considerations* 11 (1993).

[21] Robert S. Rist. 1989. Schema Creation in Programming. *Cognitive Science* 13, 3 (1989), 389–414. DOI : http://dx.doi.org/10.1207/s15516709cog1303_3

[22] Juha Sorva. 2013. Notional Machines and Introductory Programming Education. *Trans. Comput. Educ.* 13, 2, Article 8 (July 2013), 31 pages. DOI : http://dx.doi.org/10.1145/2483710.2483713

[23] John Sweller, Jeroen JG Van Merrienboer, and Fred GWC Paas. 1998. Cognitive architecture and instructional design. *Educational psychology review* 10, 3 (1998), 251–296.

[24] Allison Elliott Tew and Mark Guzdial. 2010. Developing a Validated Assessment of Fundamental CS1 Concepts. In *Proceedings of the 41st ACM Technical Symposium on Computer Science Education (SIGCSE '10)*. ACM, New York, NY, USA, 97–101. DOI : http://dx.doi.org/10.1145/1734263.1734297

[25] Lynda Thomas, Mark Ratcliffe, and Benjy Thomasson. 2004. Scaffolding with Object Diagrams in First Year Programming Classes: Some Unexpected Results. In *Proceedings of the 35th SIGCSE Technical Symposium on Computer Science Education (SIGCSE '04)*. ACM, New York, NY, USA, 250–254. DOI : http://dx.doi.org/10.1145/971300.971390

[26] Juhani E. Tuovinen. 2000. Optimising Student Cognitive Load in Computer Education. In *Proceedings of the Australasian Conference on Computing Education (ACSE '00)*. ACM, New York, NY, USA, 235–241. DOI : http://dx.doi.org/10.1145/359369.359405

[27] Ian Utting, Allison Elliott Tew, Mike McCracken, Lynda Thomas, Dennis Bouvier, Roger Frye, James Paterson, Michael Caspersen, Yifat Ben-David Kolikant, Juha Sorva, and Tadeusz Wilusz. 2013. A Fresh Look at Novice Programmers' Performance and Their Teachers' Expectations. In *Proceedings of the ITiCSE Working Group Reports Conference on Innovation and Technology in Computer Science Education - Working Group Reports (ITiCSE -WGR '13)*. ACM, New York, NY, USA, 15–32. DOI : http://dx.doi.org/10.1145/2543882.2543884

[28] Vesa Vainio and Jorma Sajaniemi. 2007. Factors in Novice Programmers' Poor Tracing Skills. *SIGCSE Bull.* 39, 3 (June 2007), 236–240. DOI : http://dx.doi.org/10.1145/1269900.1268853

[29] Jacqueline Whalley, Christine Prasad, and P. K. Ajith Kumar. 2007. Decoding Doodles: Novice Programmers and Their Annotations. In *Proceedings of the Ninth Australasian Conference on Computing Education - Volume 66 (ACE '07)*. Australian Computer Society, Inc., Darlinghurst, Australia, Australia, 171–178. http://dl.acm.org/citation.cfm?id=1273672.1273693

[30] Aman Yadav, Sarah Gretter, Susanne Hambrusch, and Phil Sands. 2017. Expanding computer science education in schools: understanding teacher experiences and challenges. *Computer Science Education* 26, 4 (2017), 235–254. DOI : http://dx.doi.org/10.1080/08993408.2016.1257418 arXiv:http://dx.doi.org/10.1080/08993408.2016.1257418

The Affordances and Constraints of Diagrams on Students' Reasoning about State Machines

Geoffrey L. Herman*
University of Illinois at Urbana-Champaign
201 N. Goodwin Ave
Urbana, IL 61801
glherman@illinois.edu

Dong San Choi
University of Illinois at Urbana-Champaign
1308 W. Main St.
Urbana, IL 61801
choi88@illinois.edu

ABSTRACT

While the concept of state is foundational to computing, students possess a myriad of misconceptions about it and the role it plays within computing systems. Research on students' misconceptions reveals that their ability to use conceptually appropriate information varies based on the task they are performing and the representational tools they are provided. Critically, the tacit information in these representations influences this process, hindering or helping students. In this paper, we present a qualitative research study, in which we interviewed 24 students as they transformed finite state machines into synchronous, sequential logic circuits. We found that students generally had profound skill with procedures. However, their ability to reason about the four components of state, next-state, inputs, and outputs, were constrained by the representations that they were given or created themselves. Conversely, the order in which students produced their drawings provided complementary insights into students conceptual understanding. These findings revealed that students possess conceptions of computers as input-output systems rather than state-based systems. We suggest potential interventions and future research based on these findings.

CCS CONCEPTS

• **Social and professional topics** → **Computer science education**; • **Hardware** → **Finite state machines; Sequential circuits**; • **Human-centered computing** → *Visualization systems and tools*;

KEYWORDS

State, Misconceptions, Visual Representations, Diagrams, Finite State Machines

1 INTRODUCTION

The concept of state and finite state machines (FSMs) undergirds computer architecture and programming practices [7, 8, 18, 22].

*Corresponding Author

Some have even argued that the concept of state is a threshold concept, a prerequisite concept without which students cannot truly understand how a computer operates [17, 20]. From this perspective, a computer has two fundamental operations, it 1) stores states and 2) manipulates those states in response to the systems' current state and inputs from users or other devices. This state information can also be used to derive system-level outputs to be used by other devices or users. While the concept of state is foundational to computing, students possess a myriad of misconceptions about state and how information is stored in a computer [15, 21].

In this paper, we examine how students reason about FSMs in the context of digital logic and synchronous, sequential logic circuits. State can be thought of functionally as all stored bits in a digital circuit [3, 27] or it can be thought of conceptually as all the necessary information about the past to account for a system's future behavior [28]. Prior studies have documented that students reveal multiple (as many as seven), mutually exclusive, conceptions of state when reasoning about digital logic circuits and computer architecture [15]. Students consider the state of the circuit to be its input bits, output bits, or some combination of those with the stored bits. It has been posited that state may be hard to learn, in part because instructors have so internalized the concept of state that they fail to make it explicit [7, 20].

The tacit nature of the state concept suggests that we should explore the ways in which state concepts are tacitly encoded within the representations used to teach finite state machines and their physical implementations, sequential logic circuits. In line with this, research on spatial reasoning and visual representations underscores that the tacit vs. explicit information that is presented in diagrams affects what information novices are able to learn [11]. We present a qualitative research study in which we interviewed students as they transformed FSM state diagrams into synchronous, sequential logic circuits. We specifically investigate two research questions, 1) What information about state is explicitly or tacitly encoded within traditional representations of finite state machines? and 2) How does this explicit versus tacit information affect how students reason about state?

2 LITERATURE REVIEW

We review literature on spatial reasoning and the effect of visualizations on students' reasoning. We then provide a brief background on FSMs and synchronous sequential logic circuits.

2.1 Making Vital Information in Diagrams Explicit Improves Students' Performance

Spatial reasoning skills are one of the strongest predictors of students' success in Science, Technology, Engineering, and Mathematics, including computer science [26]. The visual representations that we provide students can effect their ability to access the right concepts or procedures at the appropriate times [10, 11]. Hegarty argues that part of this challenge derives from the fact that visual representations of information (i.e., displays) tacitly encode vital information about how to interpret the display and thus require external conceptual understanding to be interpreted [4, 11]. For example, an arrow in a display may indicate motion of an object, draw attention to an object, indicate a force vector, or something entirely different [13]. Knowing which interpretation is correct likely depends on knowledge that is not encoded in the display. Additionally, a novice must also know when to appropriately aggregate objects into meta-objects or disassemble what appears to be a single object into several smaller objects.

Consider how chess experts are able to more quickly memorize the arrangement of chess pieces mid chess game but are unable to replicate this performance gain when the chess pieces are arranged randomly [5]. These experts have learned how to see configurations of pieces based on what known strategies those configurations enable rather than simply perceiving the individual pieces. Conversely, consider the challenges that students have when solving classical mechanics problems. When students are learning how to construct free body diagrams, they struggle to identify when/how to group multiple distinct bodies into a single "free body [24]."

Recent studies into students' interactions with displays has revealed that displays that are informationally equivalent to experts can lead to dramatically different student performance on what appear to be isomorphic tasks [10]. Consider the task of adding or subtracting two vectors. Vectors are often taught using three different types of displays: arrows with a magnitude on a grid, arrows with a magnitude and an angle from a reference point, or $\hat{i}, \hat{j}, \hat{k}$ format (i.e., $\vec{x} = 6\hat{i} + 8\hat{j}$). Each of these displays is informationally equivalent in that all information needed to derive one display is available in the other displays.

However, these displays make different information more or less explicit. The arrow magnitude displays make the magnitude and direction of the arrows explicit but requires the viewer to extract the component parts of the vector. In contrast, the $\hat{i}, \hat{j}, \hat{k}$ format makes the component parts of a vector explicit but the magnitude and direction implicit. When physics students were given these different types of displays, all students were able to reliably perform vector addition (e.g., 90% accuracy) when given $\hat{i}, \hat{j}, \hat{k}$ format [10]. In contrast, while the strong students could still reliably perform vector addition with the other display types, weaker students' performance dropped precipitously (50% with the magnitude and angle format and 25% with the magnitude and grid format). Because adding vectors depends on adding the vector components, the $\hat{i}, \hat{j}, \hat{k}$ format best helps students perform [10]. Parallel findings exist in other disciplines such as organic chemistry [12, 25].

There is a growing number of tools for visualizing how programs run and Sorva et al [23] provide an excellent review of these visualizations and their usefulness in helping students understand their code. For example, providing structured visualizations for tracing code has been found to improve students' ability to code and trace code [16]. Other studies have suggested that RAM diagrams that illustrate how memory is allocated may improve students' learning more than traditional trace tables [19].

2.2 Finite State Machine Displays

Digital logic instruction frequently progresses through a sequence of teaching a set of analysis tools (visualizations) that enable students to transform FSM *state diagrams* to *circuit diagrams* (See textbooks such as [3, 27, 28] for examples of this approach). Examples of these displays are illustrated in Figure 1). In this progression, students are first taught how to transform tabular representations such as truth tables (display 2 but without state variables) and Karnaugh maps (K-maps) into Boolean logic expressions (display 3) in the context of combinational circuits (stateless, input-output circuits). They are also then taught how to transform these Boolean logic expressions into logic gates in a circuit diagram (see the D-shaped and triangle-shaped objects in display 4). Finally, students are taught how to interpret state diagrams (display 1) and how to transform those diagrams into tabular representations.

Once students have learned how to use each display, they are expected to be able to transform first from a (1) state diagram to a (2) tabular representation, then to a (3) Boolean logic expression, and finally to a (4) circuit diagram in that order. Notably, each of these displays is informationally equivalent like the vector representations. However, it is generally easier to transform between adjacent displays (i.e., transforming between displays 1 and 2 or 3 and 4) than between distant displays (transforming between displays 1 and 3 or 2 and 4). Arguably, the rationale for even introducing all four display types is to make the process of translating from state diagrams to circuit diagrams a mechanistic one that reduces the likelihood of errors relative to translating directly from state diagrams to circuit diagrams without the intermediate displays.

As described earlier, a FSM does two things: store state and manipulate state. State diagrams illustrate this concept (see Figure 2) by displaying states as "bubbles" (e.g., circles labeled with letters). If the system is in a current state (e.g., state A), then the system will transition to a next state according to the value of the system input (the next-state will be A if the input is 0 and the next-state will be B if the input is 1). We will call this the "origin+transition=destination" algorithm. In a Moore model state machine, the output of the system is a function of the current state (e.g., the system output is 0 in state A and the system output is 1 in state B). To create a circuit implementation of the state machine, the state needs to be encoded into a set of bits (frequently represented using a vector of Q_i variables, see variable key in Figure 2). A minimal encoding will need $\lceil log_2 n \rceil$ state bits to encode n states. The system inputs and the system outputs are also encoded with bits.

The system can be represented using tabular representations or a system of Boolean expressions. The system input bits and state bits (e.g., x and $Q_1 Q_0$ respectively in Figure 1 displays 2 and 3) are treated as inputs in these representations and the system output and the system's next-state (e.g., z and $Q_1^+ Q_0^+$ respectively) are treated as outputs (i.e., the state and system inputs are treated as independent variables, while the next-state and system outputs are

Display 1: State Diagram

A – '-' seen
B – '0' seen
C – '01' seen
D – '010' seen

Display 2: Next-state Table

Current State		Input	Output	Next State	
Q_1	Q_0	x	z	Q_1^+	Q_0^+
0	0	0	0	0	1
0	0	1	0	0	0
0	1	0	0	0	1
0	1	1	0	1	0
1	0	0	0	1	1
1	0	1	0	0	0
1	1	0	1	0	1
1	1	1	1	1	0

Display 3: Boolean expression

$$Q_1^+ = Q_0 x + Q_1 \bar{Q_0} \bar{x}$$
$$Q_0^+ = \bar{x}$$
$$z = Q_1 Q_0$$

Display 4: Circuit Diagram

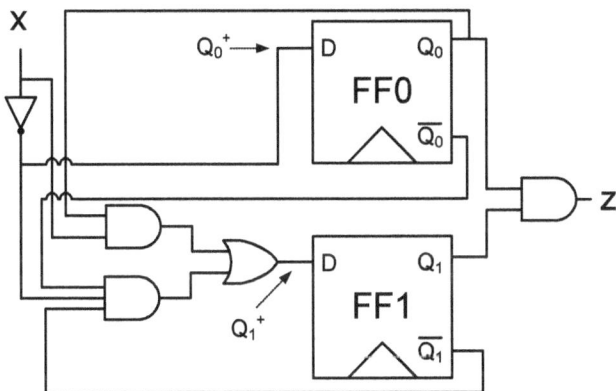

Figure 1: Examples of four displays used to teach finite state machines. Students are expected to be able to transform from the state diagram (display 1) through the other displays to design a circuit diagram (display 4).

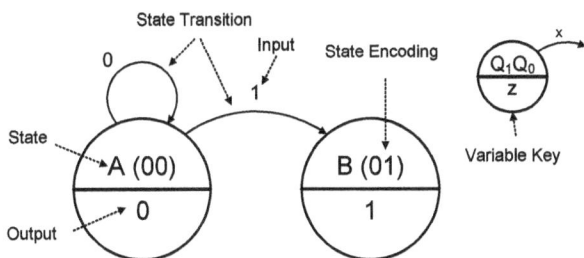

Figure 2: An example partial state diagram. Dotted arrows highlight which parts of the diagram correspond to which components of the state system.

Current state		Input	Next state (FF input)	
Q_1	Q_0	x	$Q_1^+ (D_1)$	$Q_1^+ (D_0)$
0	0	0	m_0	n_0
0	0	1	m_1	n_1
0	1	0	m_2	n_2
0	1	1	m_3	n_3
1	0	0	m_4	n_4
1	0	1	m_5	n_5
1	1	0	m_6	n_6
1	1	1	m_7	n_7

Q_1^+

$Q_1 Q_0$	00	01	11	10
x 0	m_0	m_1	m_3	m_2
1	m_4	m_5	m_7	m_6

Q_0^+

$Q_1 Q_0$	00	01	11	10
x 0	n_0	n_1	n_3	n_2
1	n_4	n_5	n_7	n_6

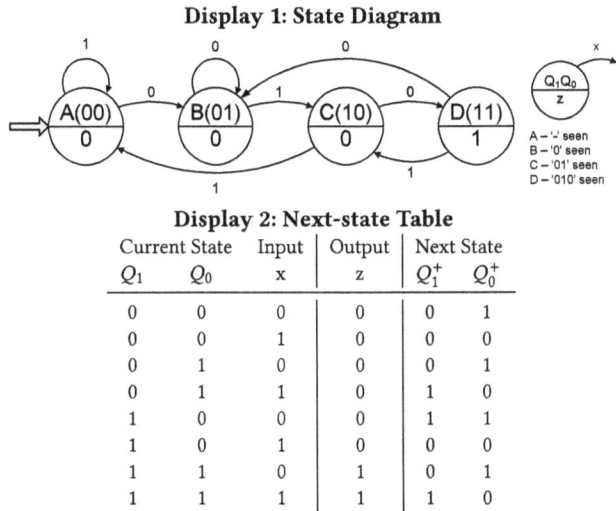

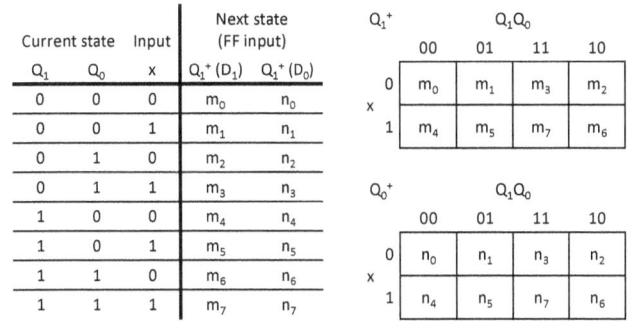

Figure 3: A next-state table (left) and two equivalent Karnaugh maps (right). m_i and n_i identify which rows of the table correspond to which cells in the Karnaugh maps.

dependent variables). The next-state variables have a superscript + to indicate the discrete-time-dependent relationship between the current state and next-state variables in sequential circuits.

Figure 1 display 2 shows a next-state table as an example tabular representation. A K-map is an alternate tabular representation that facilitates deriving minimal Boolean expressions (Boolean expressions with fewer operators and variables). There is a one-to-one mapping between the rows of a next-state table and the cells of a K-map (See Figure 3). A K-map is intended to be used with only one output variable at a time. While new outputs in a next-state table can be appended to an existing table by adding columns on the right, a new K-map needs to be drawn for each new output variable being analyzed.

In synchronous sequential circuits, the state encoding bits are stored in flip-flops (see boxes labeled FF in Figure 1). The current state of the system is the output of the flip-flops (e.g., Q_1, Q_0 in Figure 1 display 4). The system input is usually drawn on the left (e.g., x) and the system output on the right (e.g., z). The state bits are combined with the system input using logic gates to calculate the next-state of the system (e.g., the D inputs to the flip-flops).

3 METHODS

Because we knew of no prior research that specifically examined students' interactions with the aforementioned displays, we conducted a qualitative research study to develop rich descriptions of students' interactions. We used standard cognitive interview techniques and analyzed these interviews using the Constant Comparative Method [1].

3.1 Interview Protocol

During the interview, subjects were given a simple state diagram (see left diagram in Figure 4 in Section 4.1) for a sequential comparator that compares two streams of system input bits and sends a system output which indicates which stream has a greater value when interpreted as an integer. They were then asked to design a sequential circuit based on the diagram. Subjects were not told what approach to use during this task. After they finished designing the sequential circuit, subjects were then asked to draw the state diagram for a counter FSM (a canonical FSM that all subjects had previously been assigned to design in their coursework). Rather than let subjects design the sequential circuit for the counter FSM using the approach outlined in Figure 1, subjects were asked to simply sketch the final sequential circuit diagram using black boxes wherever needed (e.g., using a black box in place of logic gates for calculating the system output). Subjects were told to skip to the sequential circuit in the interest of time and because we had already seen how the subjects executed that process. This forced change in procedure enabled us to examine what type of information subjects could extract when transforming directly from a state diagram to a circuit diagram versus going though the series of three transformations (i.e., jumping from display 1 to 4 instead of stepping through from display 1 to 2 to 3 to 4).

3.2 Sampling and Data Collection

In Fall 2014 and Spring 2015, the authors interviewed 11 and 13 undergraduate students, respectively, who had just completed a large enrollment course in digital logic and computer architecture at Research University. Interviews were conducted until the interviewers perceived that each new interview provided no new insights into students' problem solving processes. The course taught FSMs using a method similar to that described in Section 2.2. All interviewed students (i.e., subjects) were traditional-age (18-22 years old), first- or second-year undergraduates majoring in electrical or computer engineering. The sample had 7 females and 17 males, reflecting the demographics of the department (14% female students). Students were recruited via e-mail solicitation after completing the aforementioned course.

Subjects were interviewed for one hour. Interviews were conducted in a think-aloud format: Subjects were instructed to vocalize their thoughts as they solved problems and responded to questions. They were told not to expect feedback during the interviews about whether their designs were valid, but to expect frequent requests to elaborate on what they were doing.

Interviews were conducted on a tablet computer running Windows 8. Subjects wrote in Microsoft OneNote using a digitizer stylus to draw. Interviews were recorded using Camtasia for screen capture and audio recording. Subjects were given a brief training exercise to familiarize them with the tablet computer and stylus interface. Subjects were paid $10 for their participation, and all subjects gave written consent to be interviewed under IRB approval.

3.3 Analysis

Interviews were analyzed using the Constant Comparative Method without an a priori coding scheme [1, 6], but with a structured method for ensuring that specific types of comparisons were made at each stage of the analysis process. Analysis was conducted by a team of two researchers. The researchers first analyzed the interviews independently to increase their familiarity with the data as well as to provide a record of personal observations and biases. The researchers directly coded (a qualitative research process for tagging data) the video data using MaxQDA. Team members then collaboratively reconciled codes and interpretations of subjects' statements and actions.

Analysis and comparisons were made along three units of analysis of different granularities: 1) the problem, 2) the transformation and 3) the statement.

Problem unit of analysis: Each subjects' approach to solving each problem was also described holistically. For example, did a subject invoke the concept of state when performing the procedures described in Section 2.2 during this problem? Did the subject analyze the system output bits separately from the next-state bits during this problem?

Transformation unit of analysis: We coded at what times each subject was transforming from one display to a different display. Codes included things like "State Diagram to Next-State Table" or "Boolean to Circuit."

Statement unit of analysis: Each statement a subject made or figure they drew was analyzed to document a subjects' conceptual understanding as revealed in the moment. For example, a subject might refer to the output of the circuit (O) as the next state (Q^+) revealing a contextual conflation of the two concepts.

The goal of the Constant Comparative Method is to make comparisons within and across these units of analysis to collect evidence for and against emergent themes and theories. In this analysis approach, the researchers focus on maintaining thick descriptions of observations to facilitate comparisons for as long as possible before reducing these observations to a strict coding scheme. After analyzing each of the interviews once, the researchers developed and finalized a coding scheme that captured core observations. The researchers applied this coding scheme to the data independently before comparing and reconciling any disagreements. The researchers had 92% inter-rater agreement after their independent coding and were able to reconcile all disagreements.

4 RESULTS

In accordance with our Constant Comparative Method, we first present our findings organized by the transformations that subjects performed during the interviews and the order in which they performed them. While the results are organized according to the transformations, the results draw upon the statement and problem units of analysis. We provide comparative analysis across transformations to explore effects of the tacit and explicit information in the different displays.

4.1 Transformation: State diagram to tabular representations

All subjects immediately attempted to transform the state diagram into a tabular representation, although one subject stopped almost immediately and began drawing his circuit diagram directly from the state diagram. Everyone was able to correctly articulate the "origin+transition=destination" algorithm (see Section 2.2). However, five of these subjects failed to use the tacit Q_i^+ variables for next-state and instead used the explicit c_i output variables (See right diagram in Figure 4). Additionally, three of the subjects who did use the tacit Q_i^+ variables applied the "origin+transition=destination" algorithm to both their next-state and output variables. In total, 8 of 23 subjects who completed a tabular representation mistakenly treated their output variables as if they were next-state variables.

Of the 23 subjects who used tabular representations, 18 first transformed the state diagram into a next-state table. Fifteen of these subjects then transformed their next-state table into a K-map (see Figure 3) while the other three began transforming their next-state

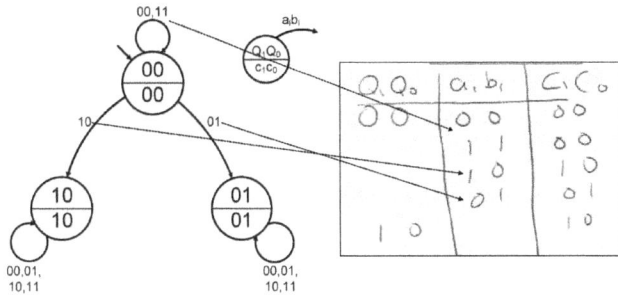

Figure 4: Left: Finite state diagram for a bit-serial comparator. Right: A subject's next-state table derived from the state diagram. Dotted arrows show how the subject transferred information from the state diagram to the next-state table.

tables into Boolean expressions or circuit diagrams. Five subjects first transformed the state diagram into a K-map directly, skipping the next-state table entirely. Notably, three subjects explicitly transformed their state diagram into a tabular representation twice, first transforming into a next-state table, then erasing the table, and then transforming into a K-map.

4.1.1 Transformation: State diagram to next-state table. When transforming the state diagram in Figure 4 to a next-state table, 16 of 18 subjects finished their next-state table (one switched to a K-map partway while the other skipped directly to drawing her circuit diagram). Of these 16 subjects, eight did not analyze the tacitly encoded state 11 (note: because the system uses 2 bits to encode the state, there will actually be four distinct states (2^2) in the physical circuit even if one of them is unreachable by the FSM algorithm). When drawing their next-state tables, some subjects drew a table with 16 rows with every possible encoding before performing their transformation while others drew their next-state tables as they analyzed the state transitions (notice how the next-state table in Figure 4 does not have any values listed for the inputs $a_i b_i$ for state 10). Only subjects who drew their next-state tables as they analyzed the state transitions forgot the 11 state. Subject created a new row in their next-state table for every state transition they analyzed. When there were no more state transitions to analyze, these subjects stopped creating new rows in their next-state table.

When performing this transformation, 7 of 18 subjects analyzed the state transitions in natural reading order, writing that the system would return to state 00 after an input of either 00 or 11 in state 00 (see dotted arrows in Figure 4). These subjects then analyzed the state transition from state 00 with input 10 and then the state transition with input 01. The remaining subjects use some variant of numeric order for analysis, analyzing the state transitions from $Q_1 Q_0 a_i b_i = 0000$ (binary 0) to $Q_1 Q_0 a_i b_i = 1111$ (binary 15).

4.1.2 Transformation: State diagram to Karnaugh map. Nineteen subjects used a K-map. When performing this transformation, only 1 out of 19 subjects did not analyze the tacitly encoded state 11. Many subjects even exclaimed something to the effect of "Oh! that's right. There's a 11 state" when performing this transformation. When drawing their K-maps, all 19 subjects fully drew all 16 cells of the K-map before filling in any of them cells.

When performing this transformation, 7 of 19 subjects analyzed the state transitions in natural reading order.

4.1.3 Comparing "State diagram to next-state table" with "State diagram to Karnaugh map". Only 50% of subjects analyzed the tacit 11 state when creating a next-state table but 95% of subjects analyzed the tacit state when creating a K-map. The one subject who failed to analyze the tacit 11 state was also the only subject to incorrectly draw a K-map, making a 4 × 3 grid rather than the required 4 × 4 grid. Notably, when using a K-map, the subjects always enumerated all possible combinations of state and input variables before beginning analysis, whereas when using a next-state table, more than half of the subjects enumerated combinations of state and input variables as they analyzed the state diagram.

Similar percentages of subjects used reading order analysis in both types of transformations ($39\% vs. 37\%$). However, five subjects revealed different analysis orders when transforming to a next-state table than when they transformed to a K-map. Four of these subjects used reading order analysis when transforming to a next-state table, but switched to a numeric order analysis when transforming to a K-map. Only one subject did the opposite.

4.2 Transformation: Tabular displays to Boolean expressions

Most subjects (22 of 24) transformed a tabular display into a Boolean expression. Of these subjects, 19 (86%) correctly performed these transformation. Two subjects could not remember the process for performing the transformation and did not write any Boolean expressions, despite efforts to remember. The remaining subject forgot to add NOT operators to two variables during the transformation (a mistake similar to changing the sign of a number).

4.3 Transformation: Tabular to circuit diagram

The two subjects who could not create Boolean expressions, both transformed their tabular representations into circuit diagrams. Both subjects used black boxes instead of logic gates and attempted to draw flip-flops but could not fully remember how they were drawn. Both subjects drew their approximations of a flip-flop first and then drew their next-state logic black boxes, progressing from left-to-right.

4.4 Transformation: Boolean expressions to circuit diagram

All 20 subjects who wrote Boolean expressions were able to correctly transform those expressions into a set of logic gates that implemented those expressions. However, seven of these subjects did not draw flip-flops as part of their circuit diagrams. Another two subjects attempted to draw flip-flops but drew them incorrectly.

When the 11 subjects who included correctly drawn flip-flops in their circuits drew their state diagrams, they began by drawing the flip-flops first (See Figure 5). After drawing the flip-flops, these subjects then transformed their Boolean expressions into logic gates. These subjects exhibited a "flip-flops to next-state logic" drawing order (See Figure 5). In contrast, eight of the nine subjects who failed to draw flip-flops correctly or at all, used a "left-to-right"

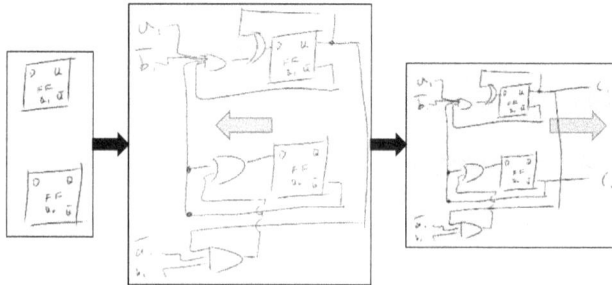

Figure 5: Example of a subject drawing their circuit diagram with flip-flops first. Left panel: Subject draws flip-flops. Middle panel: subjects adds next-state logic. Right panel: subject adds system outputs as dependent on current state.

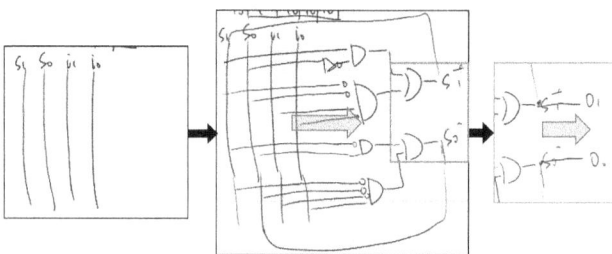

Figure 6: Example of a subject drawing their circuit diagram left-to-right without flip-flops. Left panel: Subject draws a set of rails, treating state ($S_1 S_0$) and input ($i_1 i_0$) variables as inputs. Middle panel: subject adds logic gates. Right panel: subject does not add flip-flops and adds system outputs as dependent on next state.

drawing order (see Figure 6). These subjects treated the independent variables of their Boolean expressions (state and system input bits) solely as inputs to their Boolean expressions. Some subjects even assigned state variables to rail notations, a notation typically reserved for system inputs (see the long vertical lines in Figure 6), explicitly treating state variables the same as system inputs. The one subject, who failed to draw flip-flops and did not use "left-to-right" drawing order, treated the OR logic gate (the D-shaped object with a curved concave left side) that would have been the fed into a flip-flop as if it was a flip-flop. He exhibited an "OR gate to next-state logic" drawing order.

When subjects failed to draw flip-flops, they labeled their current state variables on the left and their next-state variables on the right. Because the next-state variables were on the right, subjects would assign their output variables to be the same as or dependent on their next-state variables (see last panel of Figure 6) instead of being dependent on their current-state variables.

4.5 Comparing "state diagram to tabular" and "Boolean to circuit"

In the "state diagram to tabular" transformation (Section 4.1) and "Boolean to circuit" transformation (Section 4.4), we observed that some subjects either treated their next-state variables as equivalent

to their output variables or they treated their output variables as dependent on their next-state variables (see Figures 4 and 6).

4.6 Transformation: State diagram to circuit diagram

Only 21 of 24 subjects reached the final portion of the second interview question, translating directly from the state diagram to a circuit diagram. Three subjects got stuck when drawing the counter FSM (interview question 2). Of the 21 subjects who performed the state diagram to circuit diagram transformation, 20 included flip-flops in their circuit diagrams. The remaining subject simply described his circuit as a black box with logic gates inside. Of the 20 subjects who included flip-flops, 15 used the "flip-flops to next-state logic" drawing order. Two subjects began by drawing next-state logic black boxes before indicating that the current state and inputs would be fed into this black box. These subjects then showed that their next-state logic boxes fed into flip-flops. The remaining three did not draw flip-flops correctly and used a "left-to-right" drawing order.

Seven subjects also spontaneously performed transformations from state diagrams to circuit diagrams during the first, undirected problem. These subjects used the state diagram to determine that the final circuit would need flip-flops and immediately drew those flip-flops. Two of these subjects finished drawing these circuit diagrams directly from the state diagram. The remaining five subjects abandoned or erased their initial circuit diagrams and switched to transforming the state diagram into a tabular representation.

4.7 Comparing "State diagram to circuit" and "Boolean to circuit"

When transforming Boolean expressions into circuit diagrams, 35% of subjects failed to remember to use flip-flops in their final circuit diagrams. Notably, 2 of the 7 subjects who failed to remember flip-flops in their final circuit diagrams were also unable to design a counter FSM and could not progress to the final part of the interview. In contrast, only 5% of subjects failed to remember to use flip-flops when transforming state diagrams into circuit diagrams. Further 4 of 5 subjects who forgot to draw flip-flops during the Boolean to circuit transformation remembered to add flip-flops during the state diagram to circuit transformation. When reasoning about why they needed flip-flops, these subjects would appeal to the logarithmic relationship between the number of states and the number of flip-flops.

Across all transformations, a failure to include flip-flops or a failure to remember how they are structured was associated with a left-to-right drawing order. When subjects knew the structure of a flip-flop, they began by drawing the flip-flop first or by explicitly drawing attention to the next-state function of their logic circuit.

5 DISCUSSION

These findings suggest that the digital logic students in this study had strong procedural knowledge. The vast majority of subjects were able to accurately execute the procedures associated with transforming from one display type to another. Notably, subjects generally did not make mistakes on tasks that do not explicitly rely on the state concept to be solved correctly (i.e., next-state table to K-map, tabular representations to Boolean expressions, and Boolean expressions to logic gates). Students' mistakes primarily reflect an inability to access tacit information about the state concept or the distinct components of a state-based system.

5.1 Tacit information in the state diagram

The use of arrows to indicate transitions between state-like ideas can be found in a variety of contexts, from decision-making to the metamorphosis of animals. Students are able to successfully build on this knowledge to extract the "origin+transition=destination" algorithm for interpreting the state diagram. However, this study revealed three examples of tacit information in the state diagram that obscured domain-specific knowledge behind conventions: a tacit 11 state, a tacit variable assignment for the next-state, and a tacit relationship between the state and system output.

The clearest example of the relevance of tacit information is how 50% of subjects failed to think about the tacit 11 state when creating next-state tables but 95% mentioned it when creating K-maps. Many subjects created rows of their next-state tables on an "as-needed" basis. Consequently, the analysis of these subjects focused on the explicit states in the state diagram. This finding is reminiscent of the idea of Proof by Incomplete Enumeration previously found by Herman et al., in which students evaluate the goodness of their Boolean logic expressions based only on readily perceptible cases [14]. In contrast, when creating a K-map, subjects created the entire grid for the K-map, which incidentally makes the 11 state encoding explicit. Subjects were then forced to grapple with the existence of this tacit state and were able to handle it appropriately. Notably, the only subject who never analyzed the tacit 11 state was also the only subject to incorrectly draw a K-map. In this case, the explicit information provided by the K-map provided subjects with the missing information they needed to identify the tacit information in the state diagram.

One interesting thing to consider is why subjects drew their next-state tables on an "as-needed" basis rather than fully enumerating all state and input combinations before beginning analysis. One reason may be the amount of writing required to fully enumerate the combinations. To enumerate all combinations in a K-map requires the subject to write only 16 1's and 0's, but the next-state table would require writing 64 1's and 0's. The overhead of fully creating the next-state table may have been a deterrent. Alternatively, subjects used K-maps to derive Boolean expressions but never successfully did so with the next-state table. A K-map's topology is its primary affordance in deriving Boolean expressions, so subjects prioritized creating its full topology. In contrast, the next-state table appeared to either be a form of mental scratch work (many subjects erased their next-state tables before creating their K-maps) or as a means to the end of creating a K-map. It is possible that a combination of these two factors influenced these different behaviors with the different tabular representations.

Another tacit piece of information in the state diagram was the encoding for the next-state variables (Q_i^+). While subjects knew how to perform the "origin+transition=destination" procedure, they did not know to search for four unique sets of variables: one set each for the state, the next-state, the system input, and the system

output. Consequently, subjects were forced into situations where they either had to discover this missing information or had to incorrectly treat the next-state and output as the same thing.

Finally, the relationship between the state and system output is also tacit. In the given problem, the system output happens to have the same value as the state. The line dividing the state from the system output was insufficient to help the subjects understand the relationship between these two values, leading to subjects either ignoring the system output entirely or treating the system output as if it were the next-state. Because we only have data from this one problem, this finding is tenuous and will need to be investigated further in future studies that can compare the impact of different relationships between the values of the state and the system output.

These findings reveal a critical insight into students' conceptual understanding of state systems. Students' problem solving process is not guided by a strong conceptual framework that distinguishes and organizes four distinct constructs of state, next-state, system input, and system output. This finding aligns with prior findings by Herman et al. [15], but extends these findings by suggesting that the very representations we use to teach this topic may be in part responsible for students' failures to create this conceptual structure.

5.2 Explicit information in the state diagram and implicit information in Boolean expressions

A comparison of the "state diagram to circuit" and "Boolean to circuit" transformations reveals another set of tacit vs. explicit information that guides students' reasoning about state systems. In a state diagram, the number of states is an explicit piece of information. When transforming from a state diagram to a circuit, students readily determined the number of flip-flops in the circuit from the number of states using a logarithm. Seven subjects spontaneously performed this procedure when given the state diagram before determining their next-state logic. Additionally, four out of the five subjects who failed to include flip-flops in their first circuit added flip-flops to their second circuit when constrained to not use tabular representations. These subjects each invoked the logarithmic relationship in this context.

In contrast, the concept of state is tacit in the Boolean representation: System inputs and state variables are equivalently treated as equation inputs in Boolean expressions. Boolean expressions build on students' prior knowledge of algebra and combinational logic, which treat variables to the right of the equals sign as inputs and variables to the left of the equals sign as outputs. Because students are so adept at transforming Boolean expressions into logic gates, it is likely that subjects so automated this process that they simply executed the process, failing to extract the tacit information that state variables are not system inputs. Notably, when subjects made these mistakes, they were forced again into situations in which they either needed to discover the difference between system inputs and state or they needed to treat the next-state variables as if they were either the system output or the same as the state. Without flip-flops separating state and next-state, subjects had to incorrectly map distinct concepts onto the same wire.

This finding underscores that students' problem solving is not guided by a proper conceptual distinction of state, next-state, system inputs, and system outputs. Critically, subjects do not search the problem for this information, despite its central importance.

5.3 Reading order analysis and creation of displays

Many subjects analyzed the state transitions in natural reading order (top-left to bottom-right). This finding was particularly salient when students were creating the next-state tables on an "as needed" basis. Rather than create rows in the table in numeric order (i.e., 0000, 0001, 0010, 0011), subjects created rows in reading order (see Figure 4, notice the 0000, 0011, 0010, 0001 order). This ordering reinforces the observation that subjects may be treating next-state tables as mental scratchwork rather than systematically approaching the tool. Future research will need to explore more whether this type of reading order analysis is actually a detriment on students' performance.

Similarly, when subjects revealed a weak conceptual organization of the four distinct components of a state system, they also used a left-to-right drawing order associated with stateless, input-output systems. Students revealed this weak understanding by failing to add flip-flops to their circuits, drawing flip-flops incorrectly, or being unable to correctly name flip-flops. In contrast, when subjects revealed a strong connection of flip-flops to state and distinct from the other system components, they began their drawings by adding flip-flops first and then drawing next-state logic. Because the tabular representations and equations lack strong perceptual cues to help subjects distinguish between state and system inputs, students defaulted to using natural and mathematical reading schema to interpret their tables and equations.

This finding suggests again that students do not maintain strong conceptual distinctions between the four components of a state-based system and instead treat state systems as stateless, input-output systems. This finding also suggests that tracking the order in which students draw diagrams may provide insights into students' underlying conceptual understanding. Future studies will need to further investigate the robustness of this finding, but it could have implications for future research on students' cognitive processes as well as potentially new modes of assessment that can use the visible processes of students' drawings to diagnose hidden cognitive processes.

6 CONCLUSION AND IMPLICATIONS FOR INSTRUCTION

The core finding of this study is that many digital logic students do not develop a conceptual understanding of state-based systems that maintains a strong distinction between the four components of a state system: state, next-state, system input, and system output. Consequently, when subjects encountered representations that tacitly encoded elements of these distinctions, yet relied on these distinctions for correct interpretation, subjects made mistakes. This study suggests that the primary challenge for students learning digital logic and computer architecture may be that they simply have not created the conceptual distinctions necessary to navigate each new representation of a state machine.

One concern is that this lack of conceptual distinction may be a result of the current instructional model of digital logic. Current instructional models typically spend several lectures or weeks ingraining how to create logic gates from Boolean variables (e.g., [3, 27, 28]). It appears that this part of instruction is successful as students were adept at these skills. However, it appears that students' adeptness with these skills drowns out the need to extract the four distinct components from their Boolean expressions. The accurate and effortless creation of logic gates from Boolean expressions helps students remain oblivious to their mistakes. Since students can master the mechanistic parts of these transformations, perhaps we should begin with state-based systems and teach these mechanistic transformations in the context of a state-based system.

This suggestion certainly defies tradition, but it aligns with shifts in instructional models in other disciplines. For example, biology courses have shifted away from teaching taxonomies of species toward computationally modeling how species interact or develop [2]. The core idea behind such shifts is that a better understanding of basic skills or knowledge results from understanding how those skills and knowledge fit in the context of core concepts and models. In teaching students digital logic, our goal should be teach students how a computer functions. Much like how we can expect that any student who has taken an integrative biology course will have an understanding of predator-prey models, we should expect that our students should have an understanding of how to model state-based systems. If students cannot even consistently, correctly distinguish the components of this model after passing a digital logic course, is the current method of teaching FSMs only after students have mastered combinational logic really working?

While changing the fundamental organization by which we teach digital logic may be overwhelming, these results also suggest other, potentially simpler avenues for improving learning. Instruction could focus on helping students know how to interpret diagrams better or creating more informative diagrams that may help students perceive the different components of state. For example, adding the naming conventions of next-state variables to the legend of state diagrams may help students remember to consider these variables. The goal of this intervention is to aligning perceptually salient distinctions in our diagrams with conceptual important distinctions. Alternatively, using representations that constrain students to use expert-like problem solving schema (e.g., using K-maps which encourage full enumeration of input combinations) may accelerate students' learning and improving their performance [9].

Beyond the implications of these findings for digital logic instruction, these findings also suggest avenues for future research. What tacit information is hiding in the representations that we use in other computing topics such as programming? Are our canonical examples hiding essential information from novices, hindering their learning?

ACKNOWLEDGMENTS

This work was supported by the National Science Foundation under grant EEC 1429348. The opinions, findings, and conclusions do not necessarily reflect the views of the National Science Foundation or the author's institution.

REFERENCES

[1] H. Boeije. 2002. A purposeful approach to the constant comparative method in the analysis of qualitative interviews. *Quality & Quantity* 26 (2002), 391–409.

[2] C. A. Brewer and D. Smith (Eds.). 2009. *Vision and Change in Undergraduate Biology Education: A Call to Action.* American Association for the Advancement of Science, Washington, DC.

[3] S. Brown and Z. Vranesic. 2009. *Fundamentals of Digital Logic with VHDL Design.* McGraw-Hill, New York.

[4] M. Canham and M. Hegarty. 2010. Effects of knowledge and display design on comprehension of complex graphics. *Learning and Instruction* 20, 2 (2010), 155–166.

[5] W. G. Chase and H. A. Simon. 1973. Perception in chess. *Cognitive Psychology* 4 (1973), 55–81.

[6] J. Corbin and A. Strauss. 2007. *Basics of Qualitative Research: Techniques and Procedures for Developing Grounded Theory.* Sage, Thousand Oaks, CA.

[7] B. duBoulay. 1989. *Some difficulties learning to program.* Lawrence Erlbaum, Hillside, New Jersey.

[8] B. duBoulay, T. O'Shea, and J. Monk. 1989. *The black box inside the glass box: Presenting computing concepts to novices.* Lawrence Erlbaum, Hillside, New Jersey, 431–446.

[9] Robert J. Dufresne, William J. Gerace, Pamela T. Hardiman, and Jose P Mestre. 1992. Constraining novices to perform expert like problem analyses: Effects on schema acquisition. *Journal of the Learning Sciences* 2 (1992), 307–331.

[10] A. F. Heckler and T. M. Scaife. 2015. Adding and subtracting vectors: The problem with the arrow representation. *Physical Review Special Topics-Physics Education Research* 11 (2015), 010101.

[11] M. Hegarty. 2011. The cognitive science of visual-spatial displays: Implications for design. *Topics in Cognitive Science* 3 (2011), 446–474.

[12] M. Hegarty, M. Stieff, and B. L. Dixon. 2013. Cognitive change in mental models with experience in the domain of organic chemistry. *Journal of Cognitive Psychology* 25, 2 (2013), 220–228.

[13] J. Heiser and B. Tversky. 2006. Arrows in comprehending and producing mechanical diagrams. *Cognitive Science* 30 (2006), 587–592.

[14] G. L. Herman, M. C. Loui, L. Kaczmarczyk, and C. Zilles. 2012. Discovering the what and why of students' difficulties in Boolean logic. *ACM Transactions on Computing Education* 12, 1 (2012), 3:1–28.

[15] G. L. Herman, C. Zilles, and M. C. Loui. 2012. Flip-flops in students' conceptions of state. *IEEE Transactions on Education* 55, 1 (2012), 88–98.

[16] Matthew Hertz and Maria Jump. 2013. Trace-based Teaching in Early Programming Courses. In *Proceeding of the 44th ACM Technical Symposium on Computer Science Education (SIGCSE '13).* ACM, New York, NY, USA, 561–566. DOI: https://doi.org/10.1145/2445196.2445364

[17] Colleen M. Lewis. 2012. *Applications of Out-of-Domain Knowledge in Students' Reasoning about Computer Program State.* Ph.D. Dissertation.

[18] Colleen M. Lewis. 2012. The Importance of Students' Attention to Program State: A Case Study of Debugging Behavior. In *Proceedings of the Ninth Annual International Conference on International Computing Education Research (ICER '12).* ACM, New York, NY, USA, 127–134. DOI: https://doi.org/10.1145/2361276.2361301

[19] L. J. Mselle. 2010. Enhancing comprehension by using Random Access Memory (RAM) diagrams in teaching programming: Class experiment. In *Proceedings of the Psychology of Programming Interest Group (PPIG 2010).*

[20] D. Shinners-Kennedy. 2008. *The everydayness of threshold concepts: State as an example from computer science.* Sense, Rotterdam, The Netherlands, 119–128.

[21] Juha Sorva. 2007. Students' Understandings of Storing Objects. In *Proceedings of the Seventh Baltic Sea Conference on Computing Education Research - Volume 88 (Koli Calling '07).* Australian Computer Society, Inc., Darlinghurst, Australia, Australia, 127–135. http://dl.acm.org/citation.cfm?id=2449323.2449337

[22] Juha Sorva. 2013. Notional Machines and Introductory Programming Education. *Trans. Comput. Educ.* 13, 2, Article 8 (July 2013), 31 pages. DOI: https://doi.org/10.1145/2483710.2483713

[23] Juha Sorva, Ville Karavirta, and Lauri Malmi. 2013. A Review of Generic Program Visualization Systems for Introductory Programming Education. *Trans. Comput. Educ.* 13, 4, Article 15 (Nov. 2013), 64 pages. DOI: https://doi.org/10.1145/2490822

[24] P. S. Steif, J. Lobue, A. L. Fay, and L. B. Kara. 2010. Improving problem solving performance by inducing talk about salient problem features. *Journal of Engineering Education* 99 (2010), 135–142.

[25] M. Stieff, M. Hegarty, and G. Deslongchamps. 2011. Identifying representational competence with multi-representational displays. *Cognition and Instruction* 29 (2011), 123–145.

[26] D. H. Uttal and C. A. Cohen. 2012. *Spatial thinking and STEM education: When, Why, and How?* Vol. 57. 147–181.

[27] F. Vahid. 2006. *Digital Design.* Wiley, Hoboken, NJ.

[28] J. F. Wakerly. 2006. *Digital Design: Principles and Practices.* Prentice-Hall, Upper Saddle River, NJ.

K-8 Learning Trajectories Derived from Research Literature: Sequence, Repetition, Conditionals

Kathryn M. Rich
UChicago STEM Education
University of Chicago
kmrich@uchicago.edu

Carla Strickland
UChicago STEM Education
University of Chicago
castrickland@uchicago.edu

T. Andrew Binkowski
Department of Computer Science
University of Chicago
abinkowski@uchicago.edu

Cheryl Moran
UChicago STEM Education
University of Chicago
cgmoran@uchicago.edu

Diana Franklin
UChicago STEM Education
University of Chicago
dmfranklin@uchicago.edu

ABSTRACT

Computing curricula are being developed for elementary school classrooms, yet research evidence is scant for learning trajectories that drive curricular decisions about what topics should be addressed at each grade level, at what depth, and in what order. This study presents learning trajectories based on an in-depth review of over 100 scholarly articles in computer science education research. We present three levels of results. First, we present the characteristics of the 600+ learning goals and their research context that affected the learning trajectory creation process. Second, we describe our first three learning trajectories (Sequence, Repetition, and Conditionals), and the relationship between the learning goals and the resulting trajectories. Finally, we discuss the ways in which assumptions about the context (mathematics) and language (e.g., Scratch) directly influenced the trajectories.

CCS CONCEPTS

•Social and professional topics →Computational thinking; K-12 education;

KEYWORDS

K-6; Computational Thinking; Learning Trajectories

1 INTRODUCTION

Several school districts, including public schools in Chicago, New York City, and San Francisco, have begun CS for All initiatives that will bring computational thinking (CT) instruction to all students, elementary through high school. However, the knowledge to create research-based curricula - namely what, how, and when to teach CT material - is still emerging.

There exist two bodies of research literature to draw upon – one discussing what CT concepts students *should learn* [2, 22, 38] and the other exploring what students at different ages *did learn*

ICER'17, August 18-20, 2017, Tacoma, WA, USA.
© 2017 ACM. 978-1-4503-4968-0/17/08...$15.00
DOI: http://dx.doi.org/10.1145/3105726.3106166

through various CT-related activities [11, 12, 14, 16, 17, 20]. The wide breadth of literature presents a challenge: How do we extract cohesive learning trajectories for computational thinking concepts from a body of literature largely discussing individual, disconnected learning goals?

In this paper, we present the first three learning trajectories (Sequence, Repetition, and Conditionals) developed through analysis of over 100 published papers over the past decade. In particular, we make the following four contributions:

- Identify two study attributes common in current research literature that limit the studies' usefulness in creating full, empirically-supported learning trajectories.
- Articulate a decision-making process, grounded in education theory, to connect related learning goals.
- Present three learning trajectories and discuss their relationship to current literature.
- Discuss the ways in which assumptions about our context (integration with mathematics) and programming language (e.g., Scratch) directly influenced the trajectories.

The rest of the paper is organized as follows. We first present related work and our theoretical basis in Sections 2 and 3. We then describe our methods in Section 4. Section 5 analyzes attributes of the literature as it is relevant to this endeavor. Section 6 presents the learning trajectories, and Section 7 discusses the ways in which our assumptions influenced the trajectories. Finally, concluding thoughts are in Section 8.

2 BACKGROUND

Our project is based on prior work in computational thinking and is situated in particular curricular contexts.

2.1 Related Work

Wing's foundational paper describes computational thinking as "solving problems, designing systems, and understanding human behavior, by drawing on the concepts fundamental to computer science," noting connections between CT and problem-solving strategies of other disciplines [38]. These connections have been further described by Barr and Stephenson [3] in a report on efforts to develop a definition of CT that is "coupled with examples that demonstrate how computational thinking can be incorporated in the classroom."

A challenge in bringing CS/CT to all has been understanding what topics, to what depth, and in what order computational thinking can be taught at different grades. Different tools and approaches have been used to explore this issue. Early work explored using LOGO to teach a variety of content areas at different ages [7, 8, 30]. The reemergence of computing in elementary schools has largely focused on Scratch, a popular block-based language. Seiter [33] used existing Scratch projects across different grade levels to identify how computational thinking concepts varied by level in their Progression of Early Computational Thinking (PECT) Model. However, existence of a block in a project is not evidence of understanding the full meaning of the block, as Brennan et al. [5] found when interviewing Scratch contributors. Others have looked more directly at how CT content might be ordered. Dwyer et al. [11] explored lower anchor points and learning progressions for early work in algorithmic development, Franklin et al. [16] analyzed 4th, 5th, and 6th grade student work in sequence, events, and initialization, and Grover and Basu [20] explored student misconceptions of loops, variables, and Boolean logic.

2.2 Curricular Context

Learning trajectories influence curriculum, but they also are reciprocally influenced by curricular choices [9]. We made two curricular choices that influenced our trajectories.

Mathematics integrated with CT is a promising approach. Integration with a traditional subject connects new CT concepts to what students and teachers already know. Additionally, a large portion of the school day is already set aside for mathematics, allowing this new content to fit into an already-full K-5 curriculum, and there are many synergies between mathematics concepts and CT concepts.

Visual Block-Based Languages (VBBLs), such as Scratch [27], have become the language of choice for elementary level project-based curricula. The programming language and programming environment are the window through which learners interact with and learn about computational thinking. VBBLs are popular because they are used by dragging and dropping instructions (reducing syntax errors as well as typing, spelling, and memorization requirements) to create programs that involve the animation of 2-d images.

3 THEORETICAL BASIS

Our work was influenced by several bodies of work. First, we draw on the learning trajectory approach to defining and describing the components of a learning progression in a manner that makes it useful for guiding learning and instruction. Second, we draw on work reflecting a number of perspectives on how to organize and express the progression of topics at different ages (depicted four different ways in Figure 1).

3.1 Learning Trajectories

In our work, we use a learning trajectory (LT) approach. An LT is a map, or route, from knowledge that students bring to the classroom to more sophisticated and detailed understanding of a topic [9]. The starting point of the route is a crucial aspect of a trajectory; LTs are based on the assumption that their generation should be based on understanding of the current knowledge of the students being guided along the route [35] (a tenet of constructivism).

A learning trajectory begins as a thought experiment – a "hypothetical learning trajectory" in the words of Martin Simon [34] (p. 133) – that anticipates ways that students might be engaged in the kinds of thinking and learning necessary to move them toward the target understanding. These conjectures are then cyclically refined and tested in classrooms, with results with individual students or groups of students eventually being aggregated into a instructional sequence that might be considered "best-case" [9]. In this study, we attempted to synthesize scholarly literature to create initial hypothetical LTs to be tested in future work. A similar approach was used by Confrey, Maloney, and Corley [10], who developed learning trajectories by organizing and synthesizing the Common Core State Standards for Mathematics (CCSS-M), one of the most widely-adopted standards documents in U.S. education.

To operationalize the assembly of LTs from literature, we conceptualized LTs as having three parts: a set of learning goals, a developmentally appropriate path through those goals, and a set of illustrative activities that help students move along the path [9]. Our literature review process was designed with the aim of extracting information about these three elements from the articles reviewed. In this paper, we focus on the first two elements of learning trajectories: goals and pathways. Thorough discussion of tasks is beyond the scope of this paper.

3.2 Shapes of Learning Trajectories

Several theories of learning influenced the manner in which we organized our trajectories. The influence of each of these theories is described in Section 4.

First, learning progressions have been proposed that illustrate a path (or choice of paths) that a student goes through while developing understanding of a particular topic, with the final goal being some level of understanding appropriate to the student's age and experience [4]. This might lead to a trajectory with a shape as depicted in Figure 1a - largely linear with some choices in path.

Other scholars have made the argument that learning progression models, in general, are too simple to capture the learning process. Hammer and Sikorski [23] argue that a particular level of understanding requires different pieces of knowledge. These pieces of knowledge may not have a particular order and may be activated differently depending on the learning context. This perspective might lead to a trajectory more like Figure 1b, with many more independent pieces of knowledge that, once learned, result in a deeper or more complete understanding.

A third influence on the shape of our trajectories is theory inspiring spiral curricula, itself influenced by cognitive theory advanced by Jerome Bruner [6]. Bruner wrote, "We begin with the hypothesis that any subject can be taught in some intellectually honest form to any child at any stage of development." That is, complex topics can be simplified in various ways for young children. Those same topics are revisited multiple times, teaching more depth and complexity as students mature. In this case, the shape of a learning trajectory would look like Figure 1c, in which students revisit some of the same topics each year, building some new knowledge and complexity each time.

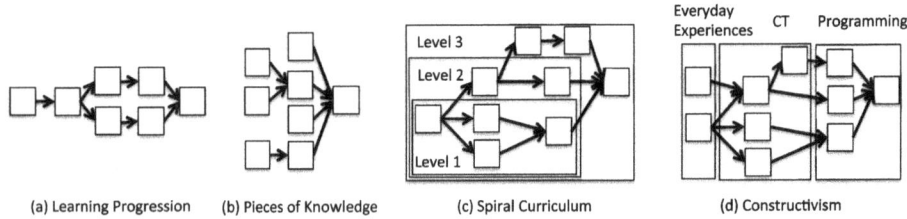

Figure 1: Shapes and Content of LTs as influenced by theoretical framings.

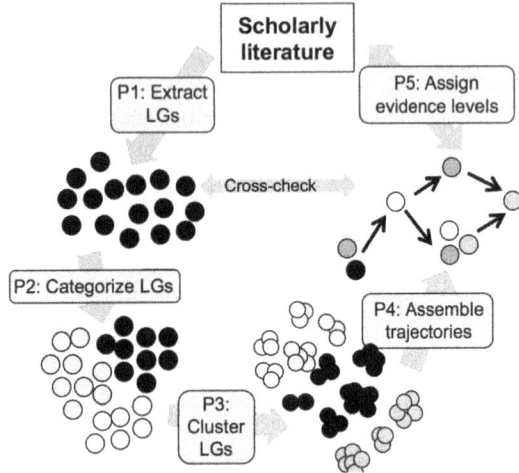

Figure 2: The learning trajectories creation process

Finally, our work is influenced by the constructivist assumption that all effective learning utilizes knowledge that learners already possess [34]. This perspective might lead to a trajectory that begins with everyday experiences, then "filters" them to identify the aspects that are most relevant to the new learning, gradually refining everyday knowledge to apply to academic topics of interest. For our work, we conceptualize the progression as starting with everyday experiences, proceeding to broad CT ideas, then applying those ideas to programming, as shown in Figure 1d.

4 METHODS

Our methods for building learning trajectories take place in five iterative phases: (1) extracting learning goals (LGs) from literature, (2) categorizing learning goals, (3) clustering learning goals, (4) assembling clusters into trajectories, and (5) assigning evidence levels to goals and relationships. We describe each of these phases in the sections that follow. The overall process is summarized in Figure 2.

Phase 1: Extracting Learning Goals from Literature

The literature search included all articles that cited Wing's [38] paper on computational thinking, keyword searches of the Educational Research Information Center (ERIC) database, and proceedings from the 2006–2016 Special Interest Group on Computer Science Education (SIGCSE) Technical Symposium and the Innovation and Technology in Computer Science Education (ITiCSE). Application of retention criteria described in [31] resulted in 108 articles.

Table 1: Concept categories for sorting learning goals

Concepts[21]
Abstraction and pattern generalization
Systematic processing of information
Symbol systems and representations
Algorithmic notions of flow of control
Structured problem decomposition
Iterative, recursive, and parallel thinking
Conditional logic
Efficiency and performance constraints
Debugging and systematic error detection

We define a learning goal as *any explicit statement or implicit endorsement of what students can or should be able to do in relation to computational thinking.* Example heuristics for identifying learning goals that meet this definition can be found in [31]. When possible, text was recorded verbatim from the article, aside from minor edits to be understood out of context. This process resulted in 671 learning goals.

Phase 2: Categorizing Learning Goals

As each learning goal was extracted from an article, it was categorized by concept and support type. Concepts, taken from [21], are listed in Table 1. The two support types are *student* and *theoretical.*

Student support: The authors describe evidence that students of particular ages were able to engage with the learning goal.

Theoretical support: The authors describe the goal and/or its appropriateness for students without citing any particular evidence other than their own expertise or work with learners outside the target student population (e.g., teachers or other adults).

Each article was independently reviewed by at least two researchers to extract and categorize learning goals. If intercoder agreement of at least 80% could not be reached through discussion, a third reader coded the LGs from the article independently and decided the remaining discrepancies.

Phase 3: Clustering Learning Goals

Learning goals were sorted into large groups according to combinations of concepts. In this paper, we discuss the set of LGs tagged as related to Conditional logic, Algorithmic notions of flow of control, or Iterative, recursive, and parallel thinking. We chose these particular concepts because they were widely discussed in the literature and had the most concrete learning goals, making them a useful starting point for refining our process. In future work, we plan to develop learning trajectories for the other aspects of CT articulated in Table 1.

Four researchers independently sorted this collection of LGs into categories, with no predetermined categories. The researchers then met to discuss what major themes emerged. Based on these thematic discussions, new categories were defined, and researchers independently re-sorted the original collection into these categories. Any LG that was sorted into the same category by at least three of the four researchers was retained, with any goals that did not meet this criteria removed from the collection. The resulting collections of goals were called clusters. This paper discussed the LTs created from three clusters: Sequence, Repetition, and Conditionals.

Phase 4: Assembling Clusters into Trajectories

We used a two-stage process to assemble each cluster of learning goals into a trajectory. Due to the limited information available within the literature (as discussed in Section 5), we gathered an interdisciplinary team consisting of experts in computer science, computational science, computer science education, mathematics education, and mathematics curriculum to agree upon decisions involving the trajectories.

First, we wrote "consensus goals" (CGs) to articulate big ideas expressed within a cluster and assigned to each CG the learning goals that supported it. An LG was characterized as directly supporting a CG if the CG could be considered a restatement of the LG. An LG was considered inferred support for the CG if it was not a direct restatement, but was more specific than the CG, represented an idea for which the CG was a prerequisite, or lacked sufficient detail to provide direct support.

Second, we attempted to articulate relationships and dependencies among the consensus goals that define potential pathways through the goals. To do so, we applied the theories discussed in Section 3.2 as follows. To apply the theory of learning progressions, we noted any study results that suggested a progression in difficulty (e.g., when students could complete one aspect of a task but not another), and used this information to place the less difficult ideas before the more difficult ideas.

We then adopted three general organizational heuristics based on the pieces-of-knowledge theory, spiral curriculum ideas, and constructivist assumptions, respectively:

1. Address and develop component ideas separately before expecting them to be applied in concert.

2. Identify the minimum knowledge needed to create an artifact applying a concept, and place this knowledge into a progression. Then add to the trajectory by adding alternative, branching paths that add layers of complexity to the use of the concept.

3. Begin with the ideas most closely connected to students' everyday lives, continue toward broad CT concepts, and finally apply CT to programming. In practice, this resulted in a pattern of addressing "unplugged" ideas before programming-specific ideas.

In addition to these heuristics, we also applied knowledge of mathematical skills, pedagogical approaches used in mathematics instruction, and likely programming languages that would be used in age-appropriate activities. We discuss the ways in which these assumptions influenced the resulting trajectories in Section 7.

Phase 5: Assigning Evidence Levels

A last cross-check was performed on all consensus goals with relevant learning goals to ensure that the CGs aligned with the original intent of the LGs.

The collection of learning goals supporting each consensus goal was examined. If at least one learning goal supporting a CG had student support, the CG was marked with student support; otherwise, the CG was marked with theoretical support. Any CGs without learning goals supporting them were removed. We also identified which arrows were supported by the literature and which were a result of professional judgement guided by the heuristics above.

5 LITERATURE ATTRIBUTES

In this section, we describe two attributes of the CS education literature that made it difficult to create empirically-supported learning trajectories.

Little research in K-6 has been performed on students deliberately chosen to have computing experience.

Only 14% of the studies that produced LGs with student support stated that the students had some programming/CT experience. The rest either stated that students had mixed experience (10%), unclear experience (43%), or no experience (33%). As a result of the low experience level of most study participants, similar goals have been attempted by students of disparate ages. For example, one study showed that eighth and ninth graders could decompose a game into a sequence of frames [32], while another showed that Kindergarteners can parse a sequence of events into component steps [14]. These goals could be generalized into the same consensus goal about parsing a large task into parts, but the wide range of grade levels gives little information about where this goal should be placed within an age-graded trajectory. In addition, the grade range in a study was sometimes too wide to be useful, such as an analysis of Scratch projects created by students aged 8–18 in an after-school program [28].

As a result, we were largely unable to use the ages or grade levels of students to inform the relationships between consensus goals. We instead relied heavily on our theoretical underpinnings to determine relationships among goals.

Most research in K-8 focuses on independent learning goals rather than the dependency between multiple learning goals

A related attribute of the literature is that most research (81%) focused on a single learning goal or independent learning goals rather than the relationship between multiple learning goals. For example, studies asked questions such as, did students learn how to think in parallel [19]? Or, are students able to create programs with Booleans, variables, conditionals, loops, functions, or events, which were the programming constructs taught [25]? This is related to the fact that most studies were on novice learners – most interventions were short, so students would not learn enough in a single intervention to study the relationships between different learning goals. This was another factor that led us to rely on educational theories to determine relationships among consensus goals.

6 LEARNING TRAJECTORIES

We now present three learning trajectories: Sequence, Repetition, and Conditionals. We begin by presenting numerical summaries of the trajectories, shown in Tables 2 and 3. Table 2 shows the number of learning goals in each cluster, detailing how many had student support and how many had theoretical support. In the

Table 2: Learning goals for each cluster

Trajectory	Total LGs (Student / Theoretical)	LGs used in trajectory
Sequence	48 (34/14)	37
Repetition	47 (30/17)	42
Conditionals	49 (34/15)	49

Table 3: CGs and arrows for each trajectory

Trajectory	Total CGs (Offline / Computer-based)	Total arrows	Literature-supported arrows
Sequence	10 (5/5)	11	3
Repetition	10 (5/5)	13	0
Conditionals	12 (6/6)	18	3

Table 4: Three LGs leading to one Sequence CG

LG1	Correctly sequence a set of computational instructions. [13]
LG2	"[P]ut instructions in the correct sequence". [1]
LG3	"[G]iven lines of pseudocode that need to be put in the correct order to solve a problem", put them in order. [24]
CG	The order in which instructions are carried out can affect the outcome.

cases of Sequence and Repetition, a handful of learning goals were discarded during the trajectory construction process due to being miscategorized or being identified as the same goal extracted twice from different reports of the same study. The number of LGs used to support the final trajectory is shown in the third column. All the LGs in the Conditionals cluster were used in the trajectory.

Table 3 shows the number of consensus goals and arrows in each trajectory, along with how many of the CGs are offline goals versus computer-based goals, and how many of the arrows were supported by information extracted from the literature.

Pictorial summaries of the trajectories are shown in Figures 3, 4, and 5. Gray boxes indicate offline, or "unplugged," CGs, while white boxes indicate computer-based CGs. Arrows indicate two types of relationships between consensus goals. First, a black arrow indicates that the understanding of the source box is necessary (or at least very helpful) to understand the destination box. Second, a grey arrow indicates that traversing through the previous box is *helpful*, but not always *necessary* to reach the destination box. These grey arrows are the beginnings of a spiral curriculum, allowing students to make multiple paths through the same material, gaining more understanding each time. Finally, information on the lower right-hand corner of each box indicates the number of LGs that were coalesced into this consensus goal and the stronger type of evidence found for a CG or relationship arrow (*S* for student support or *T* for theoretical support).

We now discuss each trajectory in more depth with details on the LT construction process, including an example of a set of learning goals that were coalesced into a single consensus goal, and a discussion of the ideas summarized in the trajectory.

6.1 Sequence

Construction Process The Sequence cluster included 48 learning goals, 34 with student support and 14 with theoretical support. Table 4 lists the three learning goals that were coalesced into the single "The order in which instructions are carried out can affect the outcome." consensus goal. This example shows two things. First, the three learning goals were nearly identical, discussing various activities involving putting instructions in order. Second, the consensus goal was expressed as an *understanding* goal rather than an *action* goal. To articulate the consensus goal, we determined a core knowledge students would either learn from or demonstrate their understanding of by performing the specified actions.

As the learning goals were synthesized into consensus goals, two big ideas emerged: Precision and Order, as seen in the two branches in Figure 3. Following Heuristic (1) discussed in Phase 4 of the Methods section, we placed CGs relating to each big idea separately before CGs that combined them. Following Heuristic (3), we articulated a path through each big idea that started with everyday knowledge, proceeded to CT, and later addressed programming. During this process, we also made use of three student-supported dependence relationships pulled from the literature.

In this trajectory, both the early, offline CT goals and the later programming goals are well-supported by LGs with student support. This was not the case for the other two trajectories, as discussed below.

Trajectory Description The Sequence trajectory begins with two branches: Precision and Order. The beginning treatment includes the Precision branch, whereas the intermediate treatment includes both branches and the coordination of the two ideas. Note that the arrows between consensus goals within the Precision branch are largely black, while the arrows within the Order branch are largely grey. This means that the Order branch shows a possible path, not a path based on strict dependencies. The order of CGs within the Order branch, as well as the choice to put this branch in the intermediate treatment instead of the beginning treatment, was influenced by our work in mathematics, as described in Section 7.

After the branches meet, our two subsequent consensus goals are springboards to other learning trajectories. "Some commands modify the default order of execution, altering when and which instructions are executed." leads to Repetition and Conditionals, described below. "The position of a new command can affect outcomes." describes the modification process, as opposed to creation process, of programming. This not only relates to understanding instructions and ordering, but it also relates to debugging techniques, the subject of a future learning trajectory not included in this paper. Due to the need for coordination with other topics, we place these CGs in the advanced treatment of Sequence.

6.2 Repetition

Construction Process The Repetition (iteration / loop) trajectory was assembled from 47 LGs, with a 30/17 split on student support vs. theoretical support. Table 5 lists the four LGs that were used to create one CG. This example illustrates the ways in which we inferred support from seemingly disparate LGs into one CG. LG1 articulates an understanding that restating instructions in fewer commands can be desirable, implying that children should know

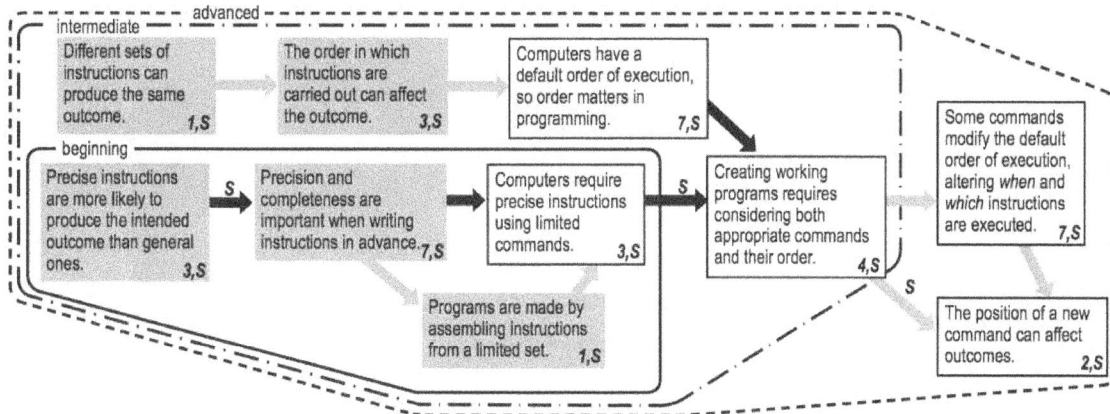

Figure 3: Sequence learning trajectory.

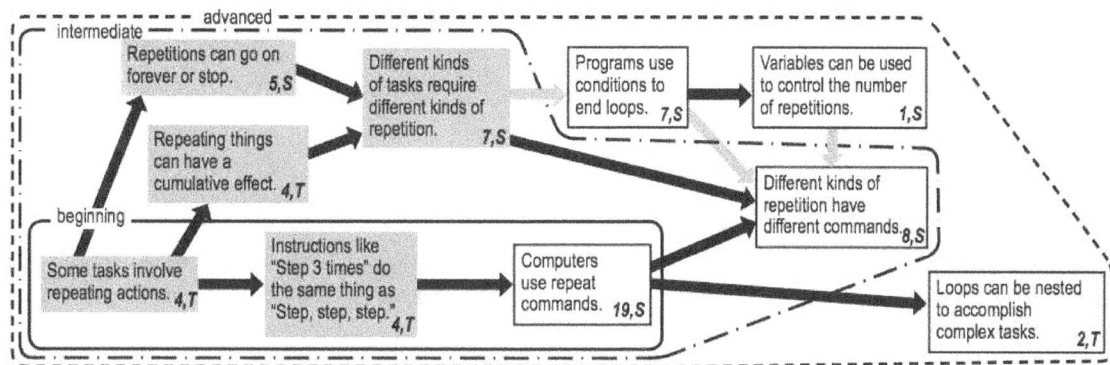

Figure 4: Repetition learning trajectory.

Table 5: Four LGs leading to one Repetition CG

LG1	Recognize when it is not desirable to "repeat code in the same project". [29]
LG2	Identify "loop constructs but not necessarily working code." [18]
LG3	Use "explicit looping". [22]
LG4	Use "loops" (as an example of abstraction). [3]
CG	Instructions like "Step 3 times" do the same thing as "Step, step, step."

how to do so. LG2 points out that students can be expected to think about a loop construct without using it in a program, implying that a broader, offline CT goal can appear before a programming goal. "Explicit looping" in LG3 refers to using repetition and being aware that you are doing so, implying that you should be able to express the repetition ideas explicitly. Finally, LG4 points out that using a loop requires abstraction, which we specify as identifying what repeats and how many times it should repeat. Thus we consider all of these LGs to be inferred support for the understanding of how to write instructions using repetition language.

Following Heuristic (3), the first CG in this trajectory relates to how repetition manifests in everyday life. The LT then proceeds towards broad CT ideas related to repetition and finally proceeds

to programming goals. Interestingly, we found that though approximately 64% of the LGs in this cluster had student support, these tended to support the five programming consensus goals – in particular, the CG about basic understanding and use of a loop command ("Computers use repeat commands."). We relied heavily on theoretical literature to articulate the early CGs, and defined the pathways based entirely on our heuristics.

Trajectory Description Figure 4 depicts the resulting Repetition learning trajectory. It begins with the idea that repetition is used for many tasks, then expands into three branches addressing broad CT ideas related to repetition. The first relates to expressing the need to repeat instructions via a simple, countable loop – this is what we suggest for beginners. The other two branches relate to recognizing the power of repetition ("Repeating things can have a cumulative effect.") and how and when to stop a repetition. At the end of the intermediate treatment, students have an understanding of how and when to use multiple kinds of loops. An advanced treatment introduces nested loops and using variables (and conditions) to control loops.

6.3 Conditionals

Construction Process The Conditionals trajectory was assembled from 49 LGs, with a 34/15 split on student support vs. theoretical

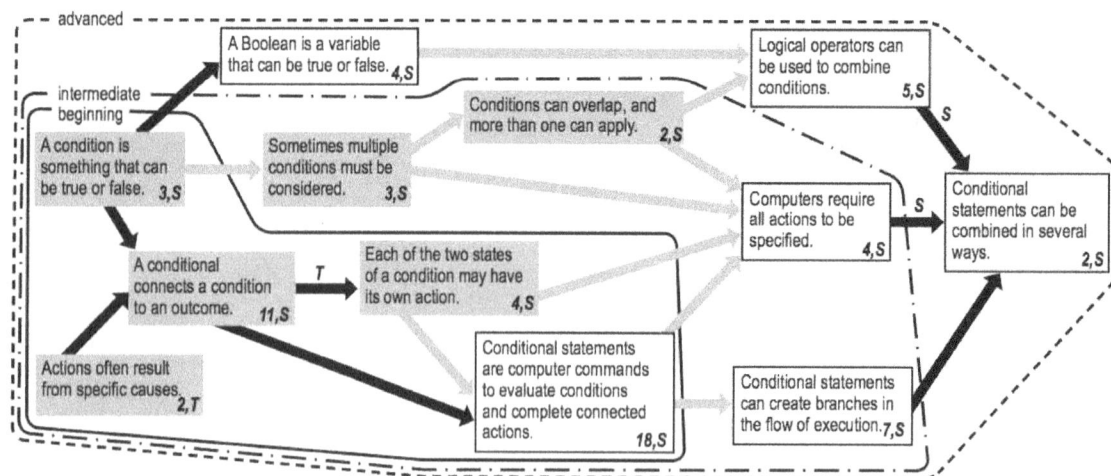

Figure 5: Conditionals learning trajectory.

Table 6: Four LGs leading to one Conditionals CG

LG1	Interpret the results of conditional statements [26]
LG2	Use an "if/else statement" [37]
LG3	Use an if/else statement [33]
LG4	"Write an algorithmic solution ... that takes into account all boundary conditions" [2]
CG	Each of the two conditional states may have its own action.

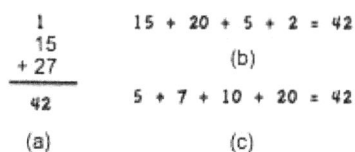

Figure 6: Three ways to add 15 + 27. (a) uses a rote process, whereas (b) and (c) show different orders and steps.

support. Table 6 lists the four LGs that were coalesced into "Each of the two states of a condition may have its own action." This example illustrates that the context of the trajectory is necessary to see the relationship between the LGs and the resulting CG. On its face, the LGs do not necessarily speak directly to the importance of considering the false state. However, this is what distinguishes this CG from its predecessors – other LGs referred only to an if statement or generally to conditionals. The presence of the else and the stated desire to take into account all boundary conditions resulted in a separate CG focused on paying special attention to considering the false state of a condition and specifying the else clause of a conditional.

Following Heuristic (3), we began the Conditionals LT with the basic understanding of cause and effect and of evaluating the truthfulness of a statement. Spiral curriculum ideas (Heuristic (2)) strongly influenced the shape of this trajectory, as analysis of the LGs in this cluster revealed many layers of complexity both in consideration of possible conditions and in how conditionals might be implemented.

Trajectory Description The Conditionals trajectory is spiraled to present three levels of advancement in understanding. At a beginning level, students learn the binary nature of conditions, the cause-and-effect connection between condition states and outcomes, and the commands necessary to use conditionals in a program. At this level of understanding, event-based programs could be used without explicit if-then statements. An intermediate treatment adds multiple conditions and overlapping conditions, requiring multiple or nested conditionals, as well as explicit if-then-else code that

breaks the sequential execution of a single code snippet. Finally, an advanced treatment introduces Boolean variables.

7 DISCUSSION

In the absence of evidence from the literature to order consensus goals, or when there were multiple reasonable possibilities, two extra pieces of information were used to influence the ordering: mathematics and programming language. In this section, we discuss more thoroughly specific examples of how mathematics and programming language assumptions influenced the decisions made.

7.1 Mathematics

Mathematics influenced our trajectories by providing an existing order in which CT concepts related to mathematics were introduced. In essence, where the CT literature was lacking in tying concepts to grade levels, mathematics instruction provided insight into existing expectations for students to use those concepts, even if they are not presented as such.

For example, in the Sequence LT presented in Section 6.1, which concept should be taught first – that different instructions can have the same outcome or that the order of instruction affects the outcome? That is, should understanding *instructions* come first or the effect of *order*? If we look to the CS K-12 Framework [15], we see that order comes first.

Research-supported pedagogical approaches to early exploration of mathematical operations, however, de-emphasize the importance of order of steps. A traditional approach to teaching two-digit addition is depicted in Figure 6a. To add 15 + 27, the digits in the

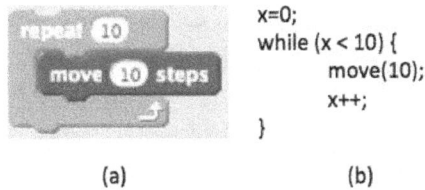

Figure 7: 10-iteration loop, (a) Scratch and (b) C.

Figure 8: Testing a pixel for black, (a) Scratch and (b) C.

ones places are added (5 + 7 = 12). We write the 2 in the ones column of the sum and carry the 1. Then 1 + 1 + 2 are added, resulting in 4. We write the 4 in the tens column to get the final answer of 42. This is a specific algorithm in which the order of the steps matters. However, another approach encourages students to explore the meaning of addition and invent their own methods for computation. As they gain understanding of the counting sequence, children often invent "jump" strategies such as jumping up 20 from 15, then jumping up 5 more, then 2 more, as shown in Figure 6b [36]. A different student may prefer to start from 0, then jump up by the ones (5 from 15 and 7 from 27) and then by the tens (10 from 15 and 20 from 27), as shown in Figure 6c. Both methods result in the same answer, 42. The additions could be performed in any order, and the numbers broken up in more than one way.

Now looking closely at the Order branch of the Sequence trajectory, we see that it reflects the order of math instruction, placing "Different sets of instructions can produce the same outcome." before "The order in which instructions are carried out can affect the outcome." Instead of the first puzzles in the code.org curriculum, in which students use forward and turn blocks to navigate a character through a maze with obstacles blocking all alternate paths, students would be given a project that is explicitly designed to allow multiple solutions. We do not have empirical evidence that would tell us which approach is better. Instead, we observe that the trajectory depicted in this paper is likely to align better with mathematics.

7.2 Programming Language

Finally, we found that assumptions about the programming language used in elementary school influenced the dependencies for the Repetition and Conditionals trajectories. In many languages used by college students and industry professionals, loops and conditionals are much more complex than in Scratch. In contrast, Scratch is specifically designed to provide "low floors and high ceilings." This means that while Scratch includes very sophisticated instructions that require knowledge of percentages, negative numbers, and variables, it also includes blocks with minimal requirements.

In Scratch, a programmer can set up a loop to execute 10 times by merely entering 10 as an argument into a repeat block. An equivalent loop in most languages, as shown in Figure 7, would require the use of variables and conditionals, both more advanced concepts than a simple repeat block. This means that to use a loop in a Scratch-like language, students need only be able to count – a Kindergarten skill. This is reflected in the beginning level of the Repetition trajectory. All that is necessary is to understand that "Step 3 times" is the same as "Step, step, step." This is the only prerequisite knowledge to using a simple repeat command; there are no connections between Conditionals and Repetition in early levels.

Likewise, a meaningful use of a conditional in conventional text-based languages requires variables and a comparison operator, as shown in Figure 8. Scratch, on the other hand, provides condition primitives such as "touching [other sprite]" or "touching [color]" in order to allow one to create code that reacts to conditions in the visual screen. This affects the Conditionals trajectory because students can use conditionals in the elementary level, yet Boolean variables can be delayed until the advanced level.

8 CONCLUSIONS

This paper presents detailed learning goals, and connections between them, for three CT concepts: Sequence, Repetition, and Conditionals. We provide insight into how these topics can be developed by harnessing knowledge from students' everyday experiences, potentially leading to broader understanding of how CT applies to the world than would result from teaching through programming alone. We also discuss how integration context and programming languages can influence (though not determine) learning trajectories.

This is merely a starting point. More empirical data is necessary to better understand the relative difficulty of different concepts, how they map to specific grade levels, and how they change based on integration with specific subjects. Finally, there are several more trajectories to be created, such as Debugging, Decomposition, and Abstraction.

ACKNOWLEDGMENTS

This material is based on work supported by the National Science Foundation under Award 1542828 and Award 1240985. Any opinions, findings, and conclusions or recommendations expressed are those of the authors and do not necessarily reflect those of the National Science Foundation.

REFERENCES

[1] Charoula Angeli, Joke Voogt, Andrew Fluck, Mary Webb, Margaret Cox, Joyce Malyn-Smith, and Jason Zagami. 2016. A K-6 computational thinking curriculum framework: implications for teacher knowledge. *Educational Technology & Society* 19, 3 (2016), 47–58.
[2] Michal Armoni and Judith Gal-Ezer. 2014. Early Computing Education: Why? What? When? Who? *ACM Inroads* 5, 4 (Dec. 2014), 54–59. DOI:http://dx.doi.org/10.1145/2684721.2684734
[3] Valerie Barr and Chris Stephenson. 2011. Bringing Computational Thinking to K-12: What is Involved and What is the Role of the Computer Science Education Community? *ACM Inroads* 2, 1 (Feb. 2011), 48–54. DOI:http://dx.doi.org/10.1145/1929887.1929905
[4] Michael T Battista. 2011. Conceptualizations and issues related to learning progressions, learning trajectories, and levels of sophistication. *The Mathematics Enthusiast* 8, 3 (2011), 507–570.

[5] Karen Brennan and Mitchel Resnick. 2012. New frameworks for studying and assessing the development of computational thinking. In *In AERA 2012*.

[6] Jerome Bruner. 1960. *The Process of Education*. The President and Fellows of Harvard College, Cambridge, MA, USA.

[7] Douglas H. Clements. 2002. Computers in Early Childhood Mathematics. *Contemporary Issues in Early Childhood* 3, 2 (2002), 160–181.

[8] Douglas H. Clements and J Sarama. 1997. Logo: A Decade of Progress. *Computers in Schools* 14, 1/2 (1997), 9–46.

[9] Douglas H. Clements and J Sarama. 2004. Learning Trajectories in Mathematics Education. *Mathematical Thinking and Learning* 6, 2 (2004), 81–89.

[10] Jere Confrey, Alan P. Maloney, and Andrew K. Corley. 2014. Learning trajectories: a framework for connecting standards with curriculum. *ZDM* 46, 5 (2014), 719–733. DOI:http://dx.doi.org/10.1007/s11858-014-0598-7

[11] Hilary Dwyer, Charlotte Hill, Stacey Carpenter, Danielle Harlow, and Diana Franklin. 2014. Identifying Elementary Students' Pre-instructional Ability to Develop Algorithms and Step-by-step Instructions. In *Proceedings of the 45th ACM Technical Symposium on Computer Science Education (SIGCSE '14)*. ACM, New York, NY, USA, 511–516. DOI:http://dx.doi.org/10.1145/2538862.2538905

[12] G Fessakis, E Gouli, and E Mavroudi. 2013. Problem Solving by 5-6 Years Old Kindergarten Children in a Computer Programming Environment: A Case Study. *Computers Education* 63 (April 2013), 87–97. https://www.learntechlib.org/p/132276

[13] Louise P Flannery and Marina Umaschi Bers. 2013. Letfis dance the firobot hokey-pokey!fi Childrenfis programming approaches and achievement throughout early cognitive development. *Journal of research on technology in education* 46, 1 (2013), 81–101.

[14] Louise P. Flannery, Brian Silverman, Elizabeth R. Kazakoff, Marina Umaschi Bers, Paula Bontá, and Mitchel Resnick. 2013. Designing ScratchJr: Support for Early Childhood Learning Through Computer Programming. In *Proceedings of the 12th International Conference on Interaction Design and Children (IDC '13)*. ACM, New York, NY, USA, 1–10. DOI:http://dx.doi.org/10.1145/2485760.2485785

[15] K-12 Computer Science Framework. 2016. K-12 Computer Science Framework. (2016). https://k12cs.org/

[16] Diana Franklin, Gabriela Skifstad, Reiny Rolock, Isha Mehrotra, Valerie Ding, Alexandria Hansen, David Weintrop, and Danielle Harlow. 2017. Using Upper-Elementary Student Performance to Understand Conceptual Sequencing in a Blocks-based Curriculum. In *Proceedings of the 2017 ACM SIGCSE Technical Symposium on Computer Science Education (SIGCSE '17)*. ACM, New York, NY, USA, 231–236. DOI:http://dx.doi.org/10.1145/3017680.3017760

[17] Michelle Friend and Robert Cutler. 2013. Efficient Egg Drop Contests: How Middle School Girls Think About Algorithmic Efficiency. In *Proceedings of the Ninth Annual International ACM Conference on International Computing Education Research (ICER '13)*. ACM, New York, NY, USA, 99–106. DOI:http://dx.doi.org/10.1145/2493394.2493413

[18] Ursula Fuller, Colin G Johnson, Tuukka Ahoniemi, Diana Cukierman, Isidoro Hernán-Losada, Jana Jackova, Essi Lahtinen, Tracy L Lewis, Donna McGee Thompson, Charles Riedesel, and others. 2007. Developing a computer science-specific learning taxonomy. In *ACM SIGCSE Bulletin*, Vol. 39. ACM, 152–170.

[19] Chris Gregg, Luther Tychonievich, James Cohoon, and Kim Hazelwood. 2012. EcoSim: a language and experience teaching parallel programming in elementary school. In *Proceedings of the 43rd ACM technical symposium on Computer Science Education*. ACM, 51–56.

[20] Shuchi Grover and Satabdi Basu. 2017. Measuring Student Learning in Introductory Block-Based Programming: Examining Misconceptions of Loops, Variables, and Boolean Logic. In *Proceedings of the 2017 ACM SIGCSE Technical Symposium on Computer Science Education (SIGCSE '17)*. ACM, New York, NY, USA, 267–272. DOI:http://dx.doi.org/10.1145/3017680.3017723

[21] Shuchi Grover and Roy Pea. 2013. Using a Discourse-intensive Pedagogy and Android's App Inventor for Introducing Computational Concepts to Middle School Students. In *Proceeding of the 44th ACM Technical Symposium on Computer*

[22] Mark Guzdial. 2008. Education: Paving the Way for Computational Thinking. *Commun. ACM* 51, 8 (Aug. 2008), 25–27. DOI:http://dx.doi.org/10.1145/1378704.1378713

[23] D. Hammer and T. Sikorski. 2015. Implications of complexity for research on learning progressions. *Science Education* 99, 3 (2015), 424–431.

[24] Celine Latulipe, N Bruce Long, and Carlos E Seminario. 2015. Structuring flipped classes with lightweight teams and gamification. In *Proceedings of the 46th ACM Technical Symposium on Computer Science Education*. ACM, 392–397.

[25] Michael J Lee, Faezeh Bahmani, Irwin Kwan, Jilian LaFerte, Polina Charters, Amber Horvath, Fanny Luor, Jill Cao, Catherine Law, Michael Beswetherick, and others. 2014. Principles of a debugging-first puzzle game for computing education. In *Visual Languages and Human-Centric Computing (VL/HCC), 2014 IEEE Symposium on*. IEEE, 57–64.

[26] Colleen M Lewis. 2010. How programming environment shapes perception, learning and goals: logo vs. scratch. In *Proceedings of the 41st ACM technical symposium on Computer science education*. ACM, 346–350.

[27] John Maloney, Mitchel Resnick, Natalie Rusk, Brian Silverman, and Evelyn Eastmond. 2010. The Scratch Programming Language and Environment. *Trans. Comput. Educ.* 10, 4, Article 16 (Nov. 2010), 15 pages. DOI:http://dx.doi.org/10.1145/1868358.1868363

[28] John H. Maloney, Kylie Peppler, Yasmin Kafai, Mitchel Resnick, and Natalie Rusk. 2008. Programming by Choice: Urban Youth Learning Programming with Scratch. In *Proceedings of the 39th SIGCSE Technical Symposium on Computer Science Education (SIGCSE '08)*. ACM, New York, NY, USA, 367–371. DOI:http://dx.doi.org/10.1145/1352135.1352260

[29] Jesús Moreno and Gregorio Robles. 2014. Automatic detection of bad programming habits in scratch: A preliminary study. In *Frontiers in Education Conference (FIE), 2014 IEEE*. IEEE, 1–4.

[30] Seymour Papert. 1980. *Mindstorms: Children, Computers, and Powerful Ideas*. Basic Books, Inc., New York, NY, USA.

[31] Kathryn Rich, Carla Strickland, and Diana Franklin. 2017. A Literature Review through the Lens of Computer Science Learning Goals Theorized and Explored in Research. In *Proceedings of the 2017 ACM SIGCSE Technical Symposium on Computer Science Education*. ACM, 495–500.

[32] Emmanuel Schanzer, Kathi Fisler, Shriram Krishnamurthi, and Matthias Felleisen. 2015. Transferring Skills at Solving Word Problems from Computing to Algebra Through Bootstrap. In *Proceedings of the 46th ACM Technical Symposium on Computer Science Education (SIGCSE '15)*. ACM, New York, NY, USA, 616–621. DOI:http://dx.doi.org/10.1145/2676723.2677238

[33] Linda Seiter and Brendan Foreman. 2013. Modeling the Learning Progressions of Computational Thinking of Primary Grade Students. In *Proceedings of the Ninth Annual International ACM Conference on International Computing Education Research (ICER '13)*. ACM, New York, NY, USA, 59–66. DOI:http://dx.doi.org/10.1145/2493394.2493403

[34] M. A. Simon. 1995. Reconstructing mathematics pedagogy from a constructivist perspective. *Journal for Research in Mathematics Education* (1995), 114–145.

[35] Martin A Simon and Ron Tzur. 2004. Explicating the role of mathematical tasks in conceptual learning: An elaboration of the hypothetical learning trajectory. *Mathematical thinking and learning* 6, 2 (2004), 91–104.

[36] Lieven Verschaffel, Brian Greer, and Erik De Corte. 2007. Whole number concepts and operations. In *Second handbook of research on mathematics teaching and learning*. Information Age Publishing, 557–628.

[37] Linda Werner, Jill Denner, and Shannon Campe. 2015. Children programming games: a strategy for measuring computational learning. *ACM Transactions on Computing Education (TOCE)* 14, 4 (2015), 24.

[38] Jeannette M. Wing. 2006. Computational Thinking. *Commun. ACM* 49, 3 (March 2006), 33–35. DOI:http://dx.doi.org/10.1145/1118178.1118215

Science Education (SIGCSE '13). ACM, New York, NY, USA, 723–728. DOI:http://dx.doi.org/10.1145/2445196.2445404

Quantifying Incremental Development Practices and Their Relationship to Procrastination

Ayaan M. Kazerouni, Stephen H. Edwards, and Clifford A. Shaffer

Department of Computer Science, Virginia Tech

Blacksburg, Virginia 24061

ayaan|s.edwards|shaffer@vt.edu

ABSTRACT

We present quantitative analyses performed on character-level program edit and execution data, collected in a junior-level data structures and algorithms course. The goal of this research is to determine whether proposed measures of student behaviors such as incremental development and procrastination during their program development process are significantly related to the correctness of final solutions, the time when work is completed, or the total time spent working on a solution. A dataset of 6.3 million fine-grained events collected from each student's local Eclipse environment is analyzed, including the edits made and events such as running the program or executing software tests. We examine four primary metrics proposed as part of previous work, and also examine variants and refinements that may be more effective. We quantify behaviors such as working early and often, frequency of program and test executions, and incremental writing of software tests. Projects where the author had an earlier mean time of edits were more likely to submit their projects earlier and to earn higher scores for correctness. Similarly earlier median time of edits to software tests was also associated with higher correctness scores. No significant relationships were found with incremental test writing or incremental checking of work using either interactive program launches or running of software tests, contrary to expectations. A preliminary prediction model with 69% accuracy suggests that the underlying metrics may support early prediction of student success on projects. Such metrics also can be used to give targeted feedback to help students improve their development practices.

KEYWORDS

Educational data mining, incremental development, metrics, software development process, IDE, Eclipse, plugin, DevEventTracker

1 INTRODUCTION

Every CS student eventually reaches a point in their coursework where they must begin using good program development practices if they are going to successfully complete their programming assignments. When this happens may depend on the individual's ability or prior experience. For some students, this may happen in a traditional CS1 or CS2 course. Others successfully pass through CS1 and CS2 without developing good project management practices, but then reach the limits of undisciplined development in a later course with larger programming assignments. At our University, students are required to take a junior-level Data Structures and Algorithms course, which we will call "CS3". Unfortunately, it is typical to see 25-30% of students each semester who either drop this course, or fail to earn a grade of C or better so they can progress to later courses.

Students in our CS3 course typically complete four significant programming assignments, each with a 3-4 week life cycle. While the raw code size of these projects is not hugely greater than those found in CS2, they are generally considered to be far more difficult. Possible reasons include less scaffolding in terms of design constraints, significant use of programming techniques such as recursion, dynamic memory allocation, and pointer manipulation, and file-based data access. Typically, these projects involve far more complicated design choices, and far greater need for a rigorous testing process than projects in earlier classes.

We believe that a lack of good project management skills may be a key contributing factor to poor outcomes on major programming projects such as these. Necessary skills include incremental development (writing, testing, and debugging small chunks of code at a time), effective time management, and effective software testing. Unfortunately, poor testing ability is common at many US universities [6, 18], and students often display a disinclination to practice regular testing as they work towards project completion [3].

We believe that changing student behavior in this regard will require changing the way this material is taught, practiced, and assessed. Learning any skill requires practice [17]. But without a mechanism to capture necessary details about each student's personal development process (in contrast to outcomes in terms of successful completion of projects on time), it is not possible to assess or give feedback on that process.

The goal of this research is to capture and analyze the information needed for interventions related to improved learning of project management skills. This requires that we both collect data, and use it to deduce behavior related to processes such as incremental development, testing, and time management. Eventually, we seek to "close the loop" by providing feedback in the form of carefully designed interventions that provide timely and effective guidance. But to accurately assess incremental development and procrastination, sufficient information about the detailed behavior of students during the development process is required. This level of information is not available if one only examines work students elect to submit for assessment as they near completion of an assignment, even when students are making frequent submissions in order to determine if their program passes instructor unit tests, as happens in our programming courses.

In previous work [15], we presented *DevEventTracker*, a plugin for the Eclipse Integrated Development Environment (IDE) that captures programming events in real time as students develop. The DevEventTracker plugin is based on the HackyStat project [14]. We employed this plugin to collect data in one semester of our CS 3 course involving 166 students over four assignments, producing a total of 546 final programs. The result was a dataset of nearly 6.3 million events capturing the details of student editing, compiling, execution, and testing activities. These data were used to calculate four metrics designed to cover the various dimensions of incremental development—working early and often, incrementally checking work via either interactive program launches or software test execution, and incrementally writing software tests. Such metrics allow instructors to assess aspects of a student's programming process and make it possible to provide guidance based on that assessment.

This work builds on [15], which described DevEventTracker's functionality, defined the calculation of the four metrics, and performed a preliminary qualitative evaluation of the validity of the measures using manual inspection of code snapshots, and using student interviews to compare metrics against student subjective experience. In this paper, we develop a quantitative evaluation of the four metrics with respect to three separate outcome measures:

(1) Which metrics are significantly related to project success, in terms of producing a solution that behaves correctly?
(2) Which metrics are significantly related to finishing solutions on time?
(3) Which metrics are significantly related to how much time is spent working?

By examining how the original four metrics relate to these outcomes, we also develop and evaluate refinements with the aim of better characterizing intuitive notions of good development practices and time management practices. By using an analysis of covariance with repeated measures, we perform within-subjects comparisons to account for varying performance traits of individual students. Finally, we consider how these metrics might be used to produce a predictive model indicating whether students might be successful on a project vs. struggling.

We begin the discussion in Section 2, which presents related work on capturing and quantifying the programming process. Our method is described in Section 3, with the corresponding analysis in Section 4. Section 5 discusses our results, and their impact is presented in Section 6.

2 RELATED WORK

There is a sizable body of literature on the modeling and assessment of the student programming process. Studies done in this area range in size from a few students working on small assignments in a controlled environment to several hundred students working on several projects over the course of a semester or year. The bulk of this work focuses on the needs and behaviors of students who are just learning to program, while our work is focused on more advanced programmers.

Jadud [12] focuses on modeling the programming process of novices in the BlueJ programming environment using their compilation behaviors. He uses this information to gain a 'rough sketch' of novice programming behavior in the classroom, describing the errors novices commonly run into, the time they typically spend programming before re-compiling, and the ways in which they respond to error messages from the IDE. Jadud also developed the Error Quotient [13], a $0 \rightarrow 1$ metric developed by taking into account the type, location, and frequency of syntax errors, used to characterize the novice programming process.

Watson, et al. [20] developed the Watwin Algorithm to score a student based on their programming process in an introductory programming course. Specifically, the Watwin Algorithm scores a student based on their ability to resolve a specific type of error, compared to the time taken by their peers. Evaluation of the score showed it to be a good predictor of performance, and an improvement from Jadud's Error Quotient.

Blackbox [2] is a perpetual data-collection project that collects programming process data about Java code written by worldwide users of the BlueJ IDE—a programming environment designed for novice programmers. Altadmri and Brown [1] use this dataset to gain an understanding of the common syntactic and semantic errors encountered by novice programmers and the times taken to address them.

More closely related to our work, Carter, et al. model the student programming process of CS2-level students using the Normalized Programming State Model (NPSM) [5]. The NPSM focuses on knowing the state of the program at key points in the development process (when the program is being edited, launched, or debugged). The NPSM was used to develop predictors and explain variance for various outcome variables like assignment performance and overall course performance, making use of a holistic representation of the programming process as well as sequences of transitions between states [4].

A significant portion of previous work attempts to model the programming process based on compilation (syntactic) errors, semantic errors, or both. The NPSM models the programming process in much finer detail than other work described above, but does not model incremental development. Attempts have been made to assess and reward students based on their software testing practices [6]. However, students are typically scored *after* a significant portion of work has been done (for example, when they make a submission to Web-CAT) [7]. This means that it cannot be used as the basis for a just-in-time intervention to nudge students back on track or change their ongoing behavior.

Helminen et al. [9] capture and analyze the programming process of students using an in-browser Python editor-and-console environment in a Web Software Development (WSD) course. Data is collected in the form of 'interaction traces'. In addition to exploring syntactic and semantic errors, they explore student testing behaviors, but focus on ad-hoc testing in the console, rather than formal unit or functional test writing. They also analyze and visualize problem-solving paths taken by students [10]. Backgrounds of students varied greatly: some had previous experience with both Python and web programming, and some had little prior programming experience. As such, the course seems to be at the CS1 level or below, though this is not explicitly stated. Some data were collected from a CS2 course, but the analysis was focused on data from the WSD course.

The NPSM work in particular is the most similar to our work discussed here. NPSM is focused on metrics of state transitions, which are abstracted from the clickstream. In contrast, our work is focused on metrics of activity type and dispersion. That is, we look at how much time or other definition of effort is being devoted to various aspects (solution development, test writing, testing, debugging), and how that effort is dispersed over time. we model the student programming process with a focus on deducing high-order behavior such as testing, incremental development, and procrastination. Further, we focus on post-CS2 students working on more complex projects. As such, our results present potential for application in professional settings as well.

3 METHOD

The data presented in this paper was obtained by administering data-collection to three sections of CS3 at Virginia Tech, a junior-level Data Structures and Algorithms course. Students programmed in Java using the Eclipse IDE. The programming projects were relatively large, with lifecycles typically 3 or 4 weeks long. We include data from all completed project submissions, including data from students who might have withdrawn from the course after completing a project. Data from students who did not give consent for their data to be used (less than 4%) were excluded from the analysis reported here. According to the points of granularity as defined in [11], our data are a combination of character-level edits, executions, and submissions. Further information about the data collection process can be found in [15].

Before undertaking analysis, some preprocessing and filtering was necessary to only include data generated while students were actually working toward project completion. During our qualitative evaluation, we found that some students tend to open their Eclipse projects and make some edits several days after projects had been graded and their final work had been submitted. While there is educational value to such activities, they are not part of the process of developing their final solution. We excluded these edits from our analysis since they are clearly not part of the organic development process for a project, and tend to corrupt the incremental development scores due to the large amount of time between project completion and these after-the-fact activities. We also excluded projects that were worked on for less than 1 hour (that is, projects started by students but with no meaningful attempt to finish).

We use intervals between event timestamps to calculate the time spent on projects. We break up the project into *work sessions* that are separated by at least 1 hour of inactivity, and add up the times for each work session. This ensures that time calculations are not inflated by long periods of inactivity where no actual work is being done.

After filtering, the dataset consists of the work of 162 students working on 545 programming projects turned in to four assignments. Not every student completed every assignment, since some students dropped the course, and others may have missed an assignment for personal reasons. Project correctness was measured as the percentage of instructor-written software tests used as the reference for grading correctness in each assignment. We do not

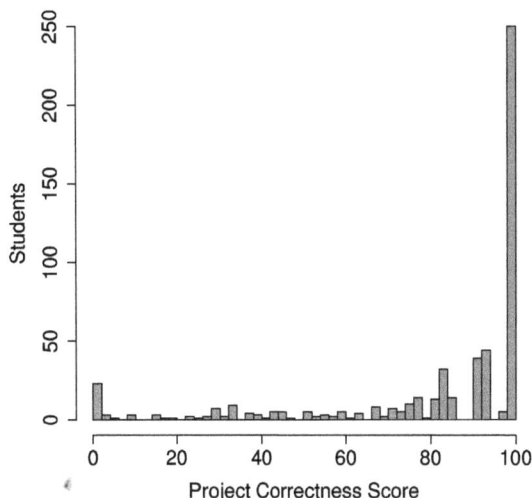

Figure 1: Distribution of correctness scores.

include bonuses/penalties due to early or late completion, manual grading criteria, or conformance to coding style standards when examining correctness. Results for all statistical tests use $\alpha = 0.05$ to determine significance unless otherwise noted.

To assess program correctness, a key outcome under consideration, we measure the percentage of instructor-written reference tests that a student's final solution passes. By examining the distribution of correctness scores over the class, there is a clear separation between students who are able to successfully "solve" a problem by creating a working solution, and those who create buggy or incorrect solutions.

Figure 1 shows the distribution of correctness scores. There is a clear trough just under a perfect score, with approximately half (47%) of the class scoring very close to perfect, and the remainder (53%) scoring noticeably lower. By choosing a cutoff of 95%, we can partition the class into projects that have successfully "solved" the behavior required for an assignment, and those that have imperfect solutions. As a result, we will examine differences in key metrics between projects that achieve this threshold and those that do not.

4 ANALYSIS

In this section, we analyze the various metrics derived from the extensive log data collected by DevEventTracker. We investigate the relationships our metrics have with the key outcome variables of project correctness, time spent on the project, and time of completion. The analyses are presented as a method of evaluating our metrics' relationships with various aspects of the programming process, particularly those that would be affected by the practice of incremental development.

4.1 Working Early and Often

A previous study by Edwards et al. [8] found that students who began submitting their work earlier also tended to score better

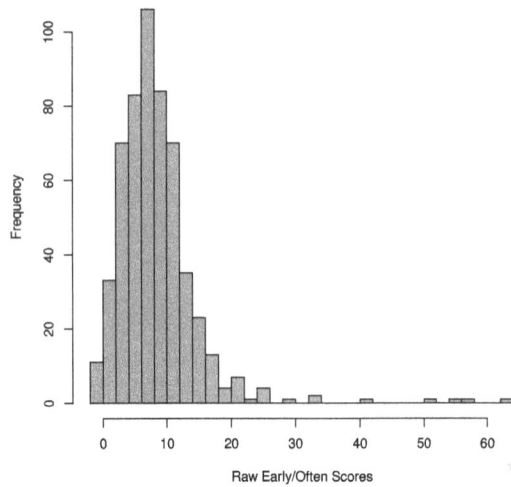

Figure 2: Distribution of Early/Often scores—the mean number of days before the deadline when editing occurred.

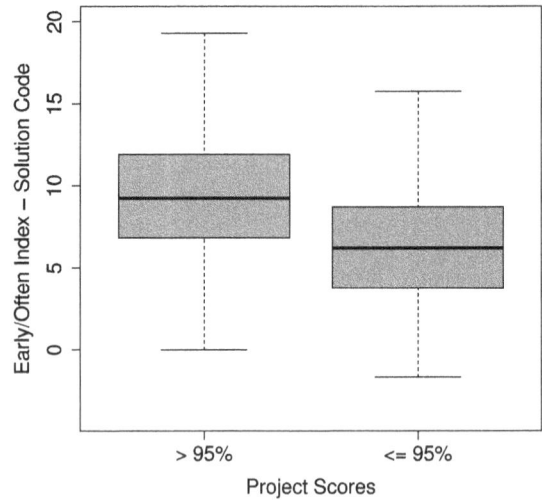

Figure 3: Comparison of solution edit times between projects that correctly solved an assignment, and those that did not.

on the project, with no significant difference in the time spent on the project. This is consistent with research on procrastination that indicates procrastination can lower scores. However, with DevEventTracker data, we have the ability to examine all programming activity, back to the initial creation of the student's project. In previous work [15], we defined the *Early/Often Index* as a way of using this data to capture the intuitive notion of procrastination. If E is the set of all edits events, then the Early/Often Index is defined as:

$$earlyOften(E) = \frac{\sum_{e \in E} size(e) * daysToDeadline(e)}{\sum_{e \in E} size(e)}$$

This definition amounts to the mean edit time, across all individual character-level changes in the project, with time measured relative to the assignment deadline—the average time at which a given character was edited. Since this measure is a time-based average, we present it as a (real) number of days, representing the mean number of days before the deadline across all character-level edits.

For this measure, we chose the mean because it is a common measure of central tendency, and it can be more sensitive to potential skew in the data. In this case, because skew can play an important role, where procrastination leads to larger edits late in the development period, the mean may provide greater discrimination. Students who work early and often will receive higher scores for this metric (representing more days in advance of the deadline) than students who tend to do more work close to the project deadline. Figure 2 shows the distribution of early-often scores across the data set.

While [15] define only the mean, following this strategy, we also can calculate an edit median in a similar way. Because skewness is an important consideration in the distribution of times for student development actions, we also considered using *Pearson's second coefficient of skewness* to characterize lopsided spread. Pearson's

coefficient is defined as $(mean - median) * 3/\sigma$, and gives a measure of skew normalized into units based on the standard deviation, with the sign of the measure indicating the direction of the skew. However, since this coefficient is a linear combination of the mean and median, it does not add explanatory power to any linear regression models. Instead, we opt to use both mean and median together, which captures this same notion of skewness.

Further, while both means and medians can be calculated across all edits, we also can calculate these measures separately for edits to software tests and for edits to the solution code. These measures help give an idea of *when* code is typically written for a project. Nevertheless, they are highly correlated, with R = 0.87 between the solution edit time mean and median, R = 0.91 between the solution edit time mean and the test edit time mean, and R = 0.84 between the test edit time mean and median. Still, we investigated all four for completeness.

To test for relationships with the outcome variables, we used a mixed model ANCOVA. Means and medians for both solution editing and software test editing were used as continuous independent variables, and were all simultaneously treated as covariates with the dependent variable of interest. Students served as subjects, and assignments were treated as repeated measures (with unequal variances) on the same subject, to perform within-subjects comparisons in the ANCOVA.

With respect to project correctness, we used the percentage of instructor-written software tests that the student's final solution could pass as the dependent variable in the ANCOVA. We found that solution mean edit times were significantly related to project correctness (F = 16.2, p < 0.0001). In other words, students who worked on their solution earlier were more likely to produce more correct programs. This is consistent with the earlier result from

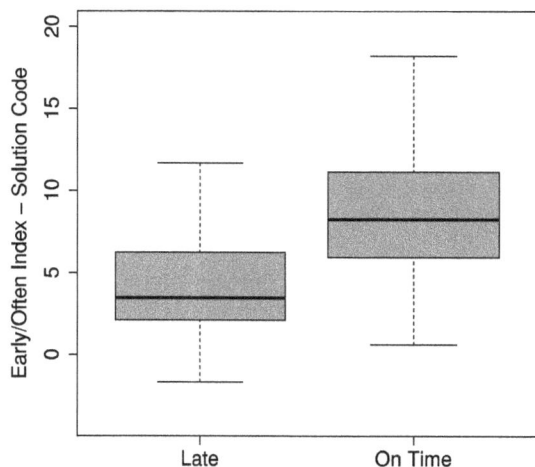

Figure 4: Comparison of solution edit times between projects that were on time versus late.

[8], but now using actual development log data instead of just submitted work. Figure 3 illustrates this relationship by showing the distribution of solution mean edit times for projects with greater than 95% correctness scores versus those with lower scores. Note that when both the solution edit mean and median times were considered, the median was not significant (F = 0.73, p = 0.39). The same ANCOVA indicated that the test edit median time was also significantly related to project correctness (F = 10.0, p = 0.0018; the mean was not significant, F = 0.06, p = 0.80). These differences were present, even when controlling for student variability using a within-subjects test, indicating that these differences were not simply due to individual student traits.

With respect to finish times, we used the number of hours before the deadline when the student's final work was submitted as the dependent variable in the ANCOVA. We found that both solution mean edit times (F = 55.9, p < 0.0001) and solution median edit times (F = 28.7, p < 0.0001) were significantly related to finish time, with earlier early/often scores corresponding to earlier finish times. This is as one would expect, since working earlier does allow a greater opportunity to finish earlier. This is also similar to the results in [8], where earlier submission times were associated with earlier completion times. Figure 4 illustrates this relationship by showing the distribution of solution mean edit times for projects that were completed on time versus late.

Finally, with respect to total time spent working, we used the number of hours spent as the dependent variable in the ANCOVA. We found that only the test edit time median (F = 10.8, p = 0.001) was significantly related to total time spent, with earlier edit times associated with slightly longer total time spent. It is notable that the median (not mean) was significant in this case, since the median is less sensitive to skewing when there are outliers very early in the development process but more editing occurs in a smaller

time frame closer to the deadline. The median edit time marks the point at which half of the edit activity has already been completed, regardless of its distribution over time. One might interpret this to mean that students who do a significant portion of the work earlier have more opportunities to invest time on the project later. Or, instead, it may be that students who start very early have to spend more time figuring out details that are only clarified in the assignment specification for everyone else at a later date. By performing a similar repeated measures ANCOVA to examine the relationship between time spent and program correctness, we find no evidence of a significant relationship (F = 1.9, p = 0.17).

In summary, projects with high early/often scores (more specifically, solution edit mean times) tended to be more correct and to be finished earlier. While earlier median edit times for software tests were associated with students who spent more time on their projects, this was not directly associated with higher scores. Our calculation of time spent on a project is more accurate than the previous study. Instead of using first and last submission times as proxies for beginning and completing a project, DevEventTracker allows us to get the *actual time spent* developing the project, by giving us work session information directly from students' local Eclipse environments.

4.2 Test Writing

Incremental test writing—that is, writing software tests to check your own work as you go—is another development practice we wished to examine. One aspect of test writing has already been discussed in Section 4.1: the test edit time mean (and median). Those measures capture part of what it means to "test early", but do not directly capture how close in time the writing of code and tests happen.

It is also worth noting here the relationship with *test-driven development* (TDD). In current practice, most developers interpret TDD to require writing the software tests for a feature *first*, before writing the corresponding piece of the solution. Here we are using a less stringent notion for incremental testing: whether you write the test or the solution first is less important than whether you do them together, in small chunks. In other words, we are more interested in indicating when students practice a "code a little, test a little" style of programming, regardless of whether they strictly write tests before writing solution code.

To capture this notion, the *Incremental Test Writing* measure is defined [15] as the difference between the mean time of solution edits and the mean time of test edits. A small number indicates that the central tendency for test editing somewhat closely follows the central tendency for solution editing, while a much larger value indicates that test editing on average occurs closer to the end of development—that is, noticeably after the bulk of the solution code was written. While this metric is calculated as a combination of early/often indices for test code and solution code, it is important to note that it has nothing to with procrastination. It is only concerned with assessing how regularly the student writes tests during the project life cycle, regardless of when in the life cycle this occurs. If $SE \subset E$ is the set of all solution edits and $TE \subset E$ is the set of all test edits, then Incremental Test Writing can be calculated as:

$$incTestWriting(E) = earlyOften(SE) - earlyOften(TE)$$

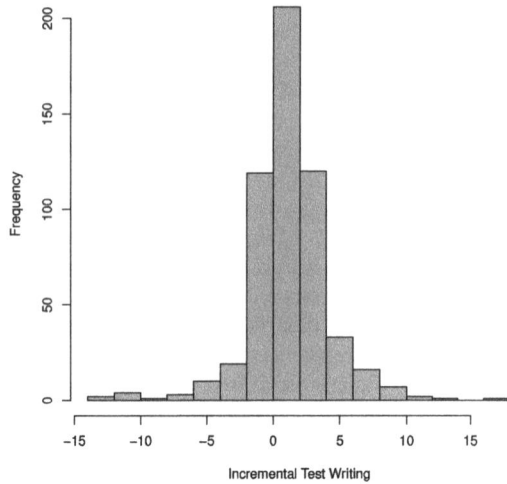

Figure 5: Distribution of Incremental Test Writing scores—the number of days that test writing occurs after solution writing, on average.

Figure 5 shows the distribution of Incremental Test Writing scores across all projects.

As with the early/often means and medians, for incremental test writing we used the same mixed model ANCOVA with assignments as repeated measures over students as subjects. With the incremental test writing metric as a continuous independent variable, we found no evidence for a relationship with project correctness (F = 2.54, p = 0.11), finish time (F = 0.17, p = 0.68), or time spent (F = 0.29, p = 0.59). From the data, it appears that the median time of test edits is more important than that test edits be "close" to solution edits, since test edit median time is significantly associated with project correctness.

At the same time, the DevEventTracker data can be used to provide visual analysis of a student's programming process. Helping students to visualize their own programming process and to compare that against their peers might encourage them to introspectively consider where improvements could be made. This could provide useful feedback during project life cycles. Figures 6, 7 and 8 show "skyline plots" of the programming process for projects with varying levels of incremental test writing and procrastination. The plots depict step-functions for the amount of test code and solution code written over time. The width of each step is the length of the work session, and the height (from the x-axis) is the amount of code written in each work session. Each work session is separated by at least 3 hours of inactivity [1]. Therefore, work sessions that look as though they lasted multiple days (particularly in Figures 6 and 7), appear because the student settled down to work on the project multiple times, without stopping for a period of at least 3 hours.

---

[1] This is less granular than the threshold of 1 hour used to calculate time spent on projects, which results in more cluttered visualizations that are harder to understand.

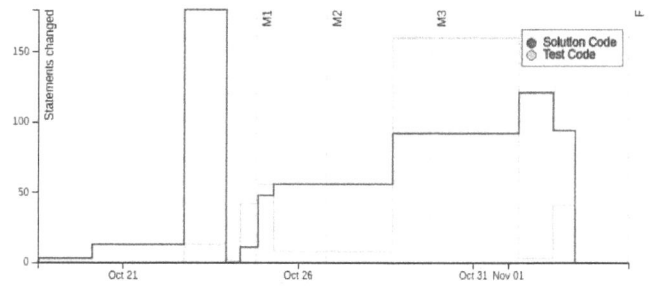

Figure 6: An example of a project with unsatisfactory test writing—notice the spike in the amount of test code written as the due date approaches. This project was in the 45th percentile for Incremental Test Writing, and in the 49th percentile for the Early/Often Index.

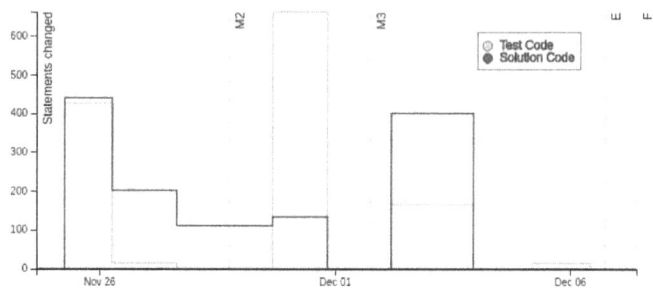

Figure 7: An example of a project with an intermediate metric score for test writing, with room for improvement. Notice the irregular bursts of test code writing, and that work started after the first Milestone was due. This project was in the 64th percentile for Incremental Test Writing, and in the 69th percentile for the Early/Often Index.

The dashed vertical lines represent project milestone due dates (**M1**, **M2**, and **M3**). These milestones are intermediate due dates, with minor grade penalties attached if a given milestone's requirements are not met by the due date. Typically, milestones are defined in terms of some number of reference tests passed, and percentage of solution code lines covered by student unit tests. Dashed vertical lines are also shown for (**E**), the "early bonus deadline" (students who make their final submission by this deadline are given a bonus in their total project score), and the actual project deadline (**F**).

4.3 Program and Test Launches

Another key notion of working incrementally is self-checking one's work periodically, as each small chunk nears completion. This might be done by writing and running software tests as one develops, for students who practice incremental testing. Alternatively, it might also involve interactively running a program to confirm its behavior manually. While proponents of TDD argue persuasively that interactive execution is not as effective for checking behaviors, in designing our incremental development metrics we chose to include both possibilities.

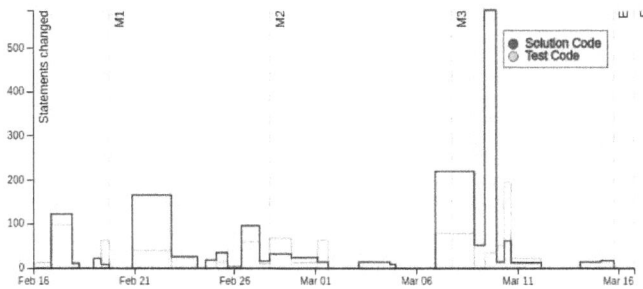

Figure 8: An example of a project with model scores under the test writing metric—notice how the test code and solution code follow similar patterns over time. This project was in 90+ percentile for both Incremental Test Writing and the Early/Often Index.

The DevEventTracker plugin tracks both interactive program launches and software test executions, and also records the pass/fail outcomes of software tests, providing all of this information in the logged data for analysis. The metrics originally presented in [15] included two aimed at capturing the amount of code students typically write before either launching the program interactively or running software tests on it.

The incrementalChecking metric [15] considers the time between an individual character-level edit action and the next subsequent program launch or test execution. It is the mean of these times over all edits, representing the average amount of time that passes between a code edit and the next program launch or test execution. Using the same ANCOVA analysis procedure, we found no evidence for a significant relationship between this measure and project correctness, time of completion, or time spent.

The incrementalTestChecking metric [15] is almost identical, except that it only considers software test executions and does not count any interactive program launches. While we advocate software testing in CS3 (and also in CS1 and CS2), experience suggests that at least some students do not follow it, and in proposing measures we wanted to account for students who self-checked their work without using software tests. However, it turned out that the event data showed students used software test executions much more commonly than interactive program launches. Test launches were significantly more frequent than normal program launches ($t = 13.977, p¡0.0001$, test $= 229.23$, normal $= 55.66$). 83% of projects had more test launches than solution launches, and test launches made up approximately 80% of all launches across projects.

Nevertheless, when examining the relationships between the incrementalTestChecking and the identified outcome variables, we found no evidence for a significant relationship with project correctness, time of completion, or time spent. We explored alternative measures, including mean and median times for both interactive program launches and software test executions relative to the due date, and also found no significant relationships.

5 DISCUSSION

Quantifying the programming process in terms of incremental development and procrastination is a non-trivial task, primarily because of the lack of ground truth against which to judge any metrics. However, our suite of metrics have provided some encouraging qualitative as well as quantitative results. However, based on this study, we can formulate answers to the research questions posed in Section 1.

(1) Which metrics are significantly related to project success, in terms of producing a solution that behaves correctly?

In this study, we measured project success using the percentage of instructor-written reference tests passed by a student's final submission for an assignment. We found a statistically significant relationship between project correctness and the mean edit times for solution edits, and also the median edit times for test edits. These metrics provide a quantified representation of procrastination, and these findings are in keeping with well-known effects of procrastination while working toward project completion [19]. However, we did not find significant relationships with the incremental test writing metric, or with either incremental checking metric based on when students launched their programs (or tests).

(2) Which metrics are significantly related to finishing solutions on time?

In this study, we measured finish times using the time of submission by a student of their final work on an assignment. Both solution mean and median edit times were significantly related to finish times. Again, these results are consistent with the known effects of procrastination. Better performance on the Early/Often Index is related with a higher likelihood of completing a project on time, regardless of the amount of time spent on a project. These findings align with a separate study that measured procrastination and its impact on project performance, using a different data source, suggesting that the Early/Often Index is an accurate measure of procrastination [8]. At the same time, we did not find significant relationships with the incremental test writing metric, or with either incremental checking metric.

(3) Which metrics are significantly related to how much time is spent working?

Although there was no evidence for a relationship between time spent and project correctness, we did find a significant relationship between the median time for test edits and total time spent. This result was not observed in prior work, although it is based on more accurate, finer-grained data collected over the whole development cycle, rather than only timestamps of submission attempts made by students as they near completion of their work. It is plausible that this effect may be related to the larger span of opportunities available over the longer period of time between project initiation and the deadline for students who start earlier, although more work would be needed to confirm this. Yet, since there is no evidence for a relation between time spent and project correctness, this extra time does not appear to translate directly into a grade advantage. Instead, it may simply mean more time to work at a slower pace under less stressful conditions, and more time for reflection while working.

6 APPLICABILITY

In this section we discuss methods by which our metrics could be used to support class interventions. To support possible interventions it is necessary to develop a predictive model based on these metrics. While complete predictive model development is outside the scope of this paper, we did explore predicting program correctness prediction in particular. Because both solution edit mean times and test edit median times were significant, we constructed a response surface model using these two as continuous independent variables, with project correctness score as the continuous dependent variable to be predicted. This model was statistically significantly related to correctness scores, and we used its prediction equation as the input to generate a partition model used to classify program solutions as either "solved" (in the group scoring greater than 95% correctness) or not. This predictive model was 69% accurate at classifying the students in our sample (where SE represents all solution edits and TE represents all test edits):

$$(0.733 + 0.022 * \text{earlyOften}(SE) - 0.007 * \text{medianTime}(TE)) > 0.83$$

While this is by no means a validated prediction model, it suggests that such models can achieve some degree of accuracy. Further, if project size can be estimated, medians (or approximations of means) can also be estimated. Since successful (solved) project solutions have mean edit times more than a week ahead of deadlines, it should be possible to predict performance with some degree of accuracy with some degree of lead time before the deadline. Developing and validating an appropriate model is important future work, although this paper lays the necessary groundwork by identifying the measures most appropriate for use in such a model. There are also many potential interventions that could be driven by such a predictive model.

Adaptive emails: Previous work [16] has discussed the effects of interventions with adaptive feedback on students' procrastination behaviors and project performance. Students were sent emails with feedback generated from data about their last submitted work, and the effects were positive when compared to a control group. Our suite of metrics could be applied in a similar fashion. The feedback generated from data made available by DevEventTracker could be far more specific than that reported in [16].

A learning dashboard: Visualizations such as those seen in Figures 6, 7, and 8 could be part of a web-based learning dashboard. Graphs showing the progression of solution code and test code over time could be automatically generated for each student, providing visual feedback of their programming process.

A leaderboard: The information described above could also be presented in a way that relates the individual's performance to the rest of the class. Making students aware of their standing in the class could provide more incentive for self-improvement than simply informing them of their own programming practices.

Project grade: A portion of the project grade is already allocated based on things other than correctness, such as the percentage of code covered by students' own tests, and the quality of the comments and program style. A natural step is to allocate a portion of the project grade based on an assessment of incremental development and time management practices. However, this opens up some possibilities for gaming the system to artificially raise the

metrics, so work would need to be done to make the metrics robust to these activities.

7 CONCLUSIONS AND FUTURE WORK

In this paper, we built on previous work [15] that enabled us to collect fine-grained programming process data from students' local Eclipse environments. In order to accurately assess abstract concepts like incremental development and procrastination, we developed a set of four metrics that we believe cover different dimensions of both concepts. We built on previous qualitative evaluations by conducting a quantitative analysis to investigate the relationships our metrics have with three identified outcome variables, and we used these results to make a case for the accuracy and correctness of our calculations.

We found a number of significant relationships between our metrics and project correctness, time of completion, and total time spent working on the project. Although we hoped to characterize the effects of incremental development actions, it appears that the most significant effects come from effective time management practices—that is, working on a project early and often, as characterized by mean and median edit times for solution code and for test code, and thus avoiding the pitfalls of procrastination. Unfortunately, other metrics regarding incremental test writing, or incremental self-checking of work using interactive program launches or execution of software tests were not significant. Those implications are discussed in Section 5. These relationships are not novel ones uncovered by our metrics. Rather, we take advantage of their intuitive and well-known nature to provide legitimacy to our metrics. The key issue is that these metrics provide an opportunity for meaningful feedback to students, either in an on-going basis during a project's development cycle, or as assessment feedback.

This research is a work in progress, and naturally there is room for improvement and future work. The most important next step is to develop and validate a predictive model that can be used for applying interventions. This can be followed by evaluation of the effectiveness of interventions, which can be measured in terms of the metrics found to be significant in this paper.

In addition, the DevEventTracker data is rich enough that this work barely touches the surface. It offers the possibility to examine the effects of debugger use, on its own or in relation to testing activities; examine issues regarding test quality, and what role it plays in self-checking or incremental development; examine predicting time to completion, to keep students informed of when they are likely to finish or whether they are likely to be late, with as much advance notice as possible; and perform deeper examinations of code changes captured in the git snapshots that track the event stream collected by DevEventTracker. All these and more are enabled by this style of data collection, which helps to open new avenues of data-driven research about student programming activities.

8 ACKNOWLEDGEMENTS

This work is supported in part by the National Science Foundation under grants DUE-1245334 and DUE-1625425. Any opinions, findings, conclusions, or recommendations expressed in this material are those of the authors and do not necessarily reflect the views of the National Science Foundation.

REFERENCES

[1] Amjad Altadmri and Neil C.C. Brown. 2015. 37 Million Compilations: Investigating Novice Programming Mistakes in Large-Scale Student Data. In *Proceedings of the 46th ACM Technical Symposium on Computer Science Education (SIGCSE '15)*. ACM, New York, NY, USA, 522–527. DOI:https://doi.org/10.1145/2676723.2677258

[2] Neil Christopher Charles Brown, Michael Kölling, Davin McCall, and Ian Utting. 2014. Blackbox: A Large Scale Repository of Novice Programmers' Activity. In *Proceedings of the 45th ACM Technical Symposium on Computer Science Education (SIGCSE '14)*. ACM, New York, NY, USA, 223–228. DOI:https://doi.org/10.1145/2538862.2538924

[3] Kevin Buffardi and Stephen H. Edwards. 2014. A Formative Study of Influences on Student Testing Behaviors. In *Proceedings of the 45th ACM Technical Symposium on Computer Science Education (SIGCSE '14)*. ACM, New York, NY, USA, 597–602. DOI:https://doi.org/10.1145/2538862.2538982

[4] Adam Scott Carter and Christopher David Hundhausen. 2017. Using Programming Process Data to Detect Differences in Students' Patterns of Programming. In *Proceedings of the 2017 ACM SIGCSE Technical Symposium on Computer Science Education (SIGCSE '17)*. ACM, New York, NY, USA, 105–110. DOI:https://doi.org/10.1145/3017680.3017785

[5] Adam S. Carter, Christopher D. Hundhausen, and Olusola Adesope. 2015. The Normalized Programming State Model: Predicting Student Performance in Computing Courses Based on Programming Behavior. In *Proceedings of the Eleventh Annual International Conference on International Computing Education Research (ICER '15)*. ACM, New York, NY, USA, 141–150. DOI:https://doi.org/10.1145/2787622.2787710

[6] Stephen H. Edwards. 2003. Improving Student Performance by Evaluating How Well Students Test Their Own Programs. *J. Educ. Resour. Comput.* 3, 3, Article 1 (Sept. 2003). DOI:https://doi.org/10.1145/1029994.1029995

[7] Stephen H. Edwards and Manuel A. Perez-Quinones. 2008. Web-CAT: Automatically Grading Programming Assignments. In *Proceedings of the 13th Annual Conference on Innovation and Technology in Computer Science Education (ITiCSE '08)*. ACM, New York, NY, USA, 328–328. DOI:https://doi.org/10.1145/1384271.1384371

[8] Stephen H. Edwards, Jason Snyder, Manuel A. Pérez-Quiñones, Anthony Allevato, Dongkwan Kim, and Betsy Tretola. 2009. Comparing Effective and Ineffective Behaviors of Student Programmers. In *Proceedings of the Fifth International Workshop on Computing Education Research Workshop (ICER '09)*. ACM, New York, NY, USA, 3–14. DOI:https://doi.org/10.1145/1584322.1584325

[9] Juha Helminen, Petri Ihantola, and Ville Karavirta. 2013. Recording and Analyzing In-browser Programming Sessions. In *Proceedings of the 13th Koli Calling International Conference on Computing Education Research (Koli Calling '13)*. ACM, New York, NY, USA, 13–22. DOI:https://doi.org/10.1145/2526968.2526970

[10] Juha Helminen, Petri Ihantola, Ville Karavirta, and Lauri Malmi. 2012. How Do Students Solve Parsons Programming Problems?: An Analysis of Interaction Traces. In *Proceedings of the Ninth Annual International Conference on International Computing Education Research (ICER '12)*. ACM, New York, NY, USA, 119–126. DOI:https://doi.org/10.1145/2361276.2361300

[11] Petri Ihantola, Arto Vihavainen, Alireza Ahadi, Matthew Butler, Jürgen Börstler, Stephen H. Edwards, Essi Isohanni, Ari Korhonen, Andrew Petersen, Kelly Rivers, Miguel Ángel Rubio, Judy Sheard, Bronius Skupas, Jaime Spacco, Claudia Szabo, and Daniel Toll. 2015. Educational Data Mining and Learning Analytics in Programming: Literature Review and Case Studies. In *Proceedings of the 2015 ITiCSE on Working Group Reports (ITICSE-WGR '15)*. ACM, New York, NY, USA, 41–63. DOI:https://doi.org/10.1145/2858796.2858798

[12] Matthew C Jadud. 2005. A First Look at Novice Compilation Behaviour Using BlueJ. *Computer Science Education* 15, 1 (2005), 25–40.

[13] Matthew C. Jadud. 2006. Methods and Tools for Exploring Novice Compilation Behaviour. In *Proceedings of the Second International Workshop on Computing Education Research (ICER '06)*. ACM, New York, NY, USA, 73–84. DOI:https://doi.org/10.1145/1151588.1151600

[14] Philip M Johnson, Hongbing Kou, Joy M Agustin, Qin Zhang, Aaron Kagawa, and Takuya Yamashita. 2004. Practical automated process and product metric collection and analysis in a classroom setting: Lessons learned from Hackystat-UH. In *Proceedings of the 2004 International Symposium on Empirical Software Engineering, ISESE'04*. 136–144.

[15] Ayaan M. Kazerouni, Stephen H. Edwards, T. Simin Hall, and Clifford A. Shaffer. 2017. DevEventTracker: Tracking development events to assess incremental development and procrastination. In *Proceedings of the 2017 ACM Conference on Innovation and Technology in Computer Science Education (ITiSCE '17)*. ACM, New York, NY, USA. DOI:https://doi.org/10.1145/2361276.2361300

[16] Joshua Martin, Stephen H. Edwards, and Clfford A. Shaffer. 2015. The Effects of Procrastination Interventions on Programming Project Success. In *Proceedings of the Eleventh Annual International Conference on International Computing Education Research (ICER '15)*. ACM, New York, NY, USA, 3–11. DOI:https://doi.org/10.1145/2787622.2787730

[17] Allen Newell, Paul S Rosenbloom, and JR Anderson. 1981. Mechanisms of skill acquisition and the law of practice. *Cognitive skills and their acquisition* 1 (1981), 1–55.

[18] Jaime Spacco and William Pugh. 2006. Helping Students Appreciate Test-driven Development (TDD). In *Companion to the 21st ACM SIGPLAN Symposium on Object-oriented Programming Systems, Languages, and Applications (OOPSLA '06)*. ACM, New York, NY, USA, 907–913. DOI:https://doi.org/10.1145/1176617.1176743

[19] Piers Steel. 2007. The nature of procrastination: a meta-analytic and theoretical review of quintessential self-regulatory failure. (2007).

[20] C. Watson, F. W. B. Li, and J. L. Godwin. 2013. Predicting Performance in an Introductory Programming Course by Logging and Analyzing Student Programming Behavior. In *2013 IEEE 13th International Conference on Advanced Learning Technologies*. 319–323. DOI:https://doi.org/10.1109/ICALT.2013.99

Comparison of Time Metrics in Programming

Juho Leinonen
University of Helsinki
Helsinki, Finland
juho.leinonen@helsinki.fi

Leo Leppänen
University of Helsinki
Helsinki, Finland
leo.leppanen@helsinki.fi

Petri Ihantola
Tampere University of Technology
Tampere, Finland
petri.ihantola@tut.fi

Arto Hellas
University of Helsinki
Helsinki, Finland
arto.hellas@cs.helsinki.fi

ABSTRACT

Research on the indicators of student performance in introductory programming courses has traditionally focused on individual metrics and specific behaviors. These metrics include the amount of time and the quantity of steps such as code compilations, the number of completed assignments, and metrics that one cannot acquire from a programming environment. However, the differences in the predictive powers of different metrics and the cross-metric correlations are unclear, and thus there is no generally preferred metric of choice for examining time on task or effort in programming.

In this work, we contribute to the stream of research on student time on task indicators through the analysis of a multi-source dataset that contains information about students' use of a programming environment, their use of the learning material as well as self-reported data on the amount of time that the students invested in the course and per-assignment perceptions on workload, educational value and difficulty. We compare and contrast metrics from the dataset with course performance. Our results indicate that traditionally used metrics from the same data source tend to form clusters that are highly correlated with each other, but correlate poorly with metrics from other data sources. Thus, researchers should utilize multiple data sources to gain a more accurate picture of students' learning.

1 INTRODUCTION

The amount of practice it takes to become an expert has intrigued researchers for decades. General rules, such as the 10-year rule [11, 32] and the 10,000-hour rule [11, 14, 28], have been developed to estimate how laborious it is to master a skill. The rules have been fine-tuned along the way, for example by only taking deliberate practice [11] into account. While more recent research [24] has somewhat criticized these rules that promise mastery within a fixed-time period, there is no denying that the use of time on the

task must have at least some kind of an effect on learning the task – one cannot become a master without practice.

A rising field within computer science education research is research based on logs of the students' programming process [17]. These logs can be very fine-grained, including information even on single keystrokes the students type while completing course activities [35]. One of the main advantages of fine-grained programming logs is the wide range of research that can be conducted with such data. For example, fine-grained log data can be aggregated into complex formats such as typing profiles [20], used to study the programming behavior of students [10], and estimate the time and effort students spend on assignments [33, 34]. In practice, data with finer granularity provides, among other things, information on how the students have reached a solution instead of just showing what the students' solutions are – this information can be used to even determine if the students have collaborated during the process [16].

The metrics that can be derived from programming logs have been used to detect struggling students in need of an intervention [1, 26]. The total time students spend on programming assignments has been found to correlate with course scores by Munson [26]. However, as programming logs only include indirect information on time, estimating the time that students actually use on an assignment is challenging [27]. For example, Munson [26] calculated the time between first and last compilations of an assignment to estimate the time that students spent on a single exercise. Murphy et al. [27] assumed that all compile events within 30 minutes of each other belong to the same programming session while Toll et al. [34] allowed up to 15-minute breaks within a single session. Additionally, both Murphy et al. [27] and Munson [26] assume that students are working on the assignment and not engaging in off-task behavior in-between compilations in a single session.

However, when only programming logs are considered, it is impossible to know what students do in-between compile events. There are many types of off-task behavior that the students might engage in – some that should be counted as practice towards the course such as studying the course material, and some that probably should not such as browsing social media. This means that additional information aside from programming logs should be considered. Even then, it is hard to know what type of metrics would be most suitable for measuring time. For example, if there are two time-like metrics available, even if they appear quite similar, there could be great differences in what they measure, which means that the results of a study could be totally different depending on the chosen metric.

In this work, we study time and time-like metrics derived from three separate data sources: programming logs, online material usage logs, and questionnaire answers. We look into how the metrics correlate with each other at three granularities: within a single assignment, within a single course component, and over the whole course. We are interested in learning whether some of the studied metrics could be replaced by other metrics, i.e. whether they have a strong correlation.

This article continues as follows. In Section 2 we go over some of the relevant background literature. In Section 3 we lay out the design of this research, first listing our research questions (Section 3.1), then describing the context of the study (Section 3.2), where the data for it is from (Section 3.3) and the methods we use to answer the research questions (Section 3.4). Sections 4 and 5 describe and discuss our results, respectively, with Section 5.1 describing the limitations of this work. Finally, Section 6 draws final conclusions from the results of this study.

2 BACKGROUND

2.1 Time on Task and Learning

Time on task is a term from pedagogy that refers to the amount of time that is spent on learning related activities. This period of time – as it is by definition spent actively on learning – is considered to be one of the most important factors to learning.

Tracing the origins of the notion is challenging. One of the earlier notions of the phenomenon comes from Ebbinghaus [9], who in the late 19th century acknowledged the phenomenon and sought to understand it more deeply by asking if the relationship was linear. In a series of memory experiments that involved memorizing nonsense syllable sequences, he observed that the time spent on memorizing the sequences did indeed have a near-linear relationship with the amount of remembered syllables. In another experiment where the syllable sequences were split into subsequences that were first learned and then combined, he observed that the total time spent on learning the whole task was not reduced. This led to the formation of the *total time hypothesis*, which states that a fixed amount of time is necessary to learn a fixed amount of material no matter how the task is divided.

Ebbinghaus was also one of the first to study the benefits of distributed practice versus massed practice. He studied the memorization task over a series of days, where the memorized syllable series was repeated a changing number of times, and observed that learning was most effective when distributed. That is, the total time spent on memorizing a series of syllables was longer if the memorization process was crammed together when compared to distributing the practice over multiple days.

Whilst subsequent research has shown the benefits of time on task and spaced practice over massed practice over and over again [2, 6], students' decisions on how to study are influenced by numerous competing factors. As a consequence, massed practice is often preferred over spaced practice, even when students have explicitly been given feedback on their better performance with spaced practice [18].

This observation on some preferring to use non-optimal learning practices lends directly to the studies conducted by Ericsson et al. [11]. They studied the practice of expert violinists, and noted that the high-performing individuals had a habit of deliberately focusing on the areas that they were lacking in instead of simply practicing the songs over and over again. They suggested that in order to truly excel at something, one must "step outside the comfort zone" and deliberately practice the challenging activities over and over again – something that many choose not to do.

Whilst Ericsson observed that developing expertise takes years, neither Ebbinghaus nor Ericsson claimed that each individual would learn at the same pace. The observation that the speed of learning varies among individuals [4, 37] has led to the development of teaching approaches that take this variety into account, including the Mastery Learning approach [3], where students are expected to master the current tasks before they are allowed to advance to the next tasks.

2.2 Factors Affecting Performance in Programming Courses

Factors affecting students' performance in programming courses have traditionally been studied with the purpose of being able to predict the students' performance. In this line of research, a myriad of predictors ranging from students' affective states [31], students' programming behavior [8, 10, 12, 13, 21, 27, 38] to complex programming process based metrics [5, 20, 30] have been constructed. Research has also been invested in analyzing and reviewing different metrics for student performance [39]. Much of the research on performance in programming courses has been aimed at identifying at-risk students early enough to intervene and help the students learn the course contents and thus pass the course [1, 26].

Murphy et al. [27] have developed a tool called Retina to give both students and instructors a better idea of how students are performing on the course. The tool offers information on errors made on exercises, but also information on how much time it takes on average to complete each exercise. They note that it is practically impossible to know the exact amount of time that students work on assignments solely based on programming log data.

Several studies have highlighted time as an integral factor in course success. For example, Watson et al. [39] found that in addition to an metric constructed from sequential compilation events [38], the percentage of time that students spent on resolving errors in a programming lab was indicative of their future performance in the course. They studied 38 traditional and 12 new metrics of student success. The new metrics were solely based on programming log data whilst the traditional metrics were based on for example student background variables such as previous programming experience and questionnaire answers.

An emerging field of detecting at-risk students is using machine learning methods instead of relying on the educator for noticing struggling students [1, 26]. Recently, Munson [26] studied automated metrics for assessing novice programmers' performance early enough in the course for an intervention. Munson derived numerous metrics from programming logs and analyzed their correlations with course scores and each other. The metrics included session time, error, edit, and compile related measurements. He found that especially total session time, i.e. the amount of time the student spent programming, had a moderate positive correlation with course scores. Additionally, the amount of changes to the source code had a similar positive correlation with course scores. Interestingly, total session time and the amount of change events were highly correlated, which could indicate that the amount of changes to the source code is a good metric for time. However, as partial correlations between the metrics were not studied, it remains possible that the correlation could be at least partially explained by other variables that correlate with both the amount of changes and total session time.

As noted by Ihantola et al. [17], it is questionable whether specialized metrics generalize to other contexts as many studies are conducted within a single course at a single institution with custom metrics, which makes it hard to replicate such studies. Even with an increasing amount of research conducted based on time and effort metrics derived from programming logs, there are no standardized metrics for measuring time based on these logs. It is also unclear how such metrics are related to each other.

3 METHODOLOGY

3.1 Research Questions

The overview of the background literature in Section 2 paints a picture where a large amount of research has focused on two types of predictors of student success. Some predictors are essentially metrics of "quality" such as the amount of errors in program code, whilst other predictors are essentially metrics of time and effort in that they measure how much work or time or effort the student put into studying, for example by calculating the amount of changes to the source code or estimating the time spent based on timestamps.

This raises a question: how are these different time-like metrics related to each other? To allow for a better understanding and comparison of results from different studies, we take a look at correlations between a certain group of time-like metrics available to us and answer the following research questions:

RQ1: How do common time and time related metrics correlate on a per-assignment basis?

RQ2: How do common time and time related metrics correlate within larger course components?

RQ3: How do common time and time related metrics correlate over the whole course?

3.2 Context of the Study

The data for this study has been gathered from two introductory programming courses organized at University of Helsinki, a research-oriented university in Europe. The courses were held during spring and fall of 2016 and one of the authors of this paper is also responsible for organizing both courses. The programming language that is taught in the course is Java, and the contents of the course are similar to many other introductory programming courses offered at universities: variables, input/output, selection, objects, lists, sorting, and searching. The courses lasted for seven weeks each.

The teaching method in the course expects that the majority of the time in the course is spent on working on programming assignments. To provide support, the computer science department offers open labs with a total of 70 computer seats and additional places for those with laptops. Instructors and teaching assistants attend the open labs providing support (for additional details, see [19]).

The course is mandatory for students majoring in computer science, and they are expected to take it in the first teaching period of their first year. Other students can take it if they feel that it would benefit their studies, or if they are considering computer science as a potential minor subject. Non-CS students often take the course later in their studies, for example in the second year. During spring 2016, the course was graded using a pen-and-paper exam and a computer-based exam, and during fall 2016, the course was graded using three take-home exams. The course grading schemes were slightly different, but approximately 40% of the overall course mark comes from the exams, and 60% comes from working on sets of individual programming assignments and pair-programming assignments.

3.3 Data Sources and Variables

During the courses, participants provided data through many avenues. The students used the NetBeans IDE with the Test My Code (TMC) -plugin [36] as they worked on the programming assignments. The plugin recorded the students' programming process and automatically assessed the correctness of students' submissions. For each submitted assignment that was solved correctly, the students were asked to rate the difficulty, workload, and educational value of the assignment. Additionally, the online learning material that the students used stored details on their use of the material, and finally, questionnaires were administered to gather data regarding the students' weekly use of time in the course.

3.3.1 Working Environment and Assessment Server. The NetBeans IDE with TMC provides the functionality needed to download and submit programming assignments, as well as the typical programming environment functionality such as running and testing the code that one is working on. The students were able to run assignment specific test suites that gave them feedback on what parts of the assignment were correctly implemented and provided hints towards solving some of the simpler and more common mistakes.

The environment was augmented to record and store the students' working process data on each programming project that was related to a programming assignment on the course. The data includes timestamps for every modification that the students do on the programming assignment templates as well as project specific actions such as running the code, testing the code and submitting the project. Whenever the student submitted an assignment to the server, a set of unit tests was run on the assignment. Once the unit tests were executed, feedback on the correctness of the student's solution so far was provided back to the student. Multiple submissions were allowed and there was no penalty associated with submitting incomplete or incorrect solutions.

The programming process data was further analyzed by extracting assignment specific information that contains (1) total time spent on each assignment, (2) total active time spent on each assignment, (3) number of code edit events, (4) number of paste events, (5) number of times that the assignment was run, (6) number of times that the assignment was tested, (7) number of times that the assignment was submitted, (8) number of times the students used the debug functionality of the IDE, (9) the number of times the IDE either gained or lost focus, (10) sum of counts 3 through 9, and (11) the average typing speed of the student.

The total time spent on the assignment was calculated based on the first event and the last event where the student modified the source code similar to Munson's work [26]. The total active time was the same, but excluding pauses longer than 3 minutes. The average typing speed was calculated by extracting all intervals between edit events (that is, individual key presses) between 10 and 750 milliseconds in length similar to Longi et al. [23].

3.3.2   Online Course Material Usage Data. The course used an online ebook with embedded assignment descriptions. The ebook was divided into seven course components, each containing theory, program snippets, worked examples and assignment descriptions for the specific week of the course. The course components were long HTML pages; each page can be considered an analogue to a chapter of a traditional textbook. The online ebook used a JavaScript library that stores information on the use of the materials [22].

The stored data includes information on each time when a user scrolls the page, or stays in the same location of the page for a predefined time interval or a "tick", and can be used to measure the amount of time a user spends at different parts of the online material. If the user spent more than three minutes on the same exact location without moving, the JavaScript library stopped storing the events until the next time that the user became active.

Weekly information on the amount of scroll events and ticks on the material was extracted for the analysis.

3.3.3   Questionnaire Data. After completing an assignment, the students were prompted for information on the assignment. The per-submission questionnaires contained three specific questions, one each regarding the educational value, difficulty and workload of the assignment. Answers to each of these were provided on a 5-step Likert-scale with 1 indicating "not at all" and 5 "extremely". The participants were also able to provide feedback in a free text form, but these textual answers were not analyzed as a part of this study. The students were not required to answer these questionnaires and were not incentivized to answer them.

Furthermore, at the end of each week, the students were asked to provide a self-estimate of the time they had spent working on the course during that week.

3.3.4   Course Exam. During spring 2016, the course had both a pen-and-paper exam as well as a computer exam, and during fall 2016, three computer exams were administered. As the courses had a different number of exams, administered using different means and with different questions, we use only the combined exam scores for both courses as variables in this study. That is, each student has a single variable that contains how many points the student obtained overall in all the assignments of all the exams of the respective course.

3.3.5   Summary. A summarizing listing of the variables used in this study – grouped by source – is provided as Table 1.

Overall, 406 students participated in the courses in total. After excluding the students who chose to opt out from the study, who had participated in the same programming course previously, and who did not answer at least a single self-report questionnaire, a total of 309 students was left for the analysis.

Table 1: A listing of the variables and their sources used in the study

Source	Variable
Process data	Time spent on each assignment
Process data	Active time spent on each assignment
Process data	Edit event count
Process data	Paste event count
Process data	Run event count
Process data	Test event count
Process data	Submit event count
Process data	Debug event count
Process data	Focus changes
Process data	Event count
Process data	Average typing speed
Assessment	Assignment correctness
Assessment	Points from assignments
Material	Weekly scroll event count
Material	Weekly tick event count
Exams	Total exam points
Questionnaire	Assignment-specific perceived educational value
Questionnaire	Assignment-specific perceived difficulty
Questionnaire	Assignment-specific perceived workload
Questionnaire	Estimated time spent on course each week

3.4   Method

The data from the sources described in the previous subsection were combined into a singular data set. For each research question, the data was normalized to have 0 mean and variance of 1 within the corresponding groups: within each assignment for the first research question, within each course component for the second research question, and finally over the whole course for the third research question. The questionnaire data was left unnormalized.

In the case of the first research question, our data includes students who did not answer the questionnaires. In the data set used to answer research question two, students who did not answer the questionnaires were excluded.

From these normalized data sets, correlations were calculated between all pairs of variables. After that, correlation matrices were reordered by using hierarchical clustering[1] to facilitate visual analysis of the results. Finally, partial correlations between all variable pairs were estimated from the previously calculated correlation matrix[2] so that the effects of all other variables were excluded.

We use Spearman's rank correlation coefficient to measure relatedness between our variables since some of the correlations are nonlinear. Unlike Pearson's correlation coefficient, which measures *linear* relation, Spearman's rank correlation coefficient measures how well the relation between the two variables is explainable by a *monotonic* function [15]. As an added benefit, Spearman's rank correlation coefficient does not require the variables to be normally distributed and is as such more resilient towards outliers [25].

All calculated p-values were corrected for multiple comparisons using the Bonferroni correction [7], which controls the familywise

---

[1]https://cran.r-project.org/web/packages/corrplot/
[2]https://cran.r-project.org/web/packages/corpcor/

error rate of multiple comparisons. The correction simply modifies the threshold of statistical significance from $\alpha = 0.05$ to α/n, where n is the number of comparisons made. Essentially, the Bonferroni correction is used to avoid finding correlations based on random chance due to the large amount of pairwise correlations that are studied in this work.

4 RESULTS

Our results are presented visually in Figures 1–6. Non-significant correlations in Figures 1, 3 and 5 are excluded and shown as crosses, other correlations are statistically significant after Bonferroni correction. The size of the diagonal correlations (correlation of the variable with itself, i.e. $r = 1$) can be used for visually estimating the strength of the other correlations.

4.1 Per-Assignment Results

In order to answer the first research question, "How do common time and time related metrics correlate on a per-assignment basis?", we observe the pairwise correlations plotted in Figures 1 and 2. These correspond to students' effort during individual assignments.

Figure 1 presents the full correlations between all pairs of variables in the data. We note that the graph contains multiple clusters wherein the variables are highly correlated with each other. The largest of these is the cluster in the top-left corner of the graph, where active work time, total count of source code events, count of code edit events, number of times the program was run and number of focus change events are all correlated with each other positively (correlations range between $r = .4$ and $r = .9$). Specifically, active time correlates with total count of source code events ($r = .79$), edit event count ($r = .72$), run event count ($r = .53$) and focus change event count ($r = .54$). These same variables are then mildly correlated with student perceptions of educational value, workload and difficulty, as well as number of paste events (these correlations range between $r = .15$ and $r = .3$).

Next up, the number of times the debug feature was used is correlated positively with the total time (including pauses) used on the assignment ($r = .4$). Both of these are then negatively correlated with maximum assignment correctness ($r = -.25, r = -.35$). Finally, a cluster of positive correlations forms between student perceptions of educational value, workload and difficulty (these correlations range between $r = .5$ and $r = .8$).

Observing the pairwise partial correlations where all other variables have been used as control variables (see Figure 2), we notice essentially the same clusters, albeit with significantly weaker correlations. The total event count and code edit counts are very strongly correlated ($r = .9$), as are student perceptions of difficulty and workload ($r = .7$). We note that typing speed is unsurprisingly negatively correlated with total time spent ($r = -.3$), as is the count of paste events with the count of code edit events ($r = -.3$). The negative correlation between assignment correctness and total time is essentially unaffected compared to the full correlations.

One additional change from the full correlations is the new negative correlation between number of edits and number of focus changes ($r = -.3$).

4.2 Per-Week Results

For the second research question, "How do common time and time related metrics correlate within larger course components?" we observe the pairwise correlations plotted in Figures 3 and 4. These correspond to students' effort within single weeks of the studied course.

The full correlations in Figure 3 are largely similar to those presented in Figure 1. Similar clusters form in both between largely the same variables. Perhaps the clearest difference is that the negative correlations with assignment correctness disappear when inspecting a course week instead of single assignments. Instead, we see a new medium-strength correlation between assignment correctness and edit count ($r = .41$), submission count ($r = .38$), event count ($r = .35$) and active time ($r = .34$). We furthermore note that both scroll and tick counts retrieved from material usage metrics ($r = .73$) are correlated with the larger cluster of programming environment count (these correlations range between $r = .3$ and $r = .5$). An additional value representing students' self-reported weekly time on the course is also included – the correlation between the self-reported time and active time is $r = .5$.

Continuing to the partial correlations presented in Figure 4, we note that it, too, is very similar to Figure 2. We note that the only negative correlation of any significance is between the number of edits and the number of focus changes ($r = -.33$). This same correlation was present in the per-assignment partial correlations. Compared to the full correlations, the correlations between the learning material event counts and the programming environment event counts essentially disappear when partial correlations are considered, as do the correlations with the students' self-reported total time.

4.3 Full Course Results

For the third research question, "How do common time and time related metrics correlate over the whole course?", we observe Figures 5 and 6.

Figure 5 presents the full correlations over the combined data set that includes both courses. The plot contains two larger striking features: first of all, almost everything is correlated with almost everything else. Secondly, the only outliers regarding that are total time spent – which does not correlate with exam scores or assignment correctness – and exam scores. Exam scores show a relatively strong correlation with assignment correctness ($r = .6$), which is easily understandable. Interestingly, while exam scores do correlate positively with active time ($r = .2$), the correlation with total time is not statistically significant when corrected.

Figure 6 shows the partial correlations between all variable pairs over the complete courses. These results seem to be largely in line with those presented in relation to the other partial correlation plots. We note that the number of negatively correlated pairs is, however, slightly larger than previously. Assignment correctness is negatively correlated with the programming environment event count ($r = -.24$). The number of source code edits is also negatively correlated with the number of focus changes to and from the programming environment ($r = -.25$) and the number of paste events ($r = -.25$). Peculiarly, the time spent in the course ebook

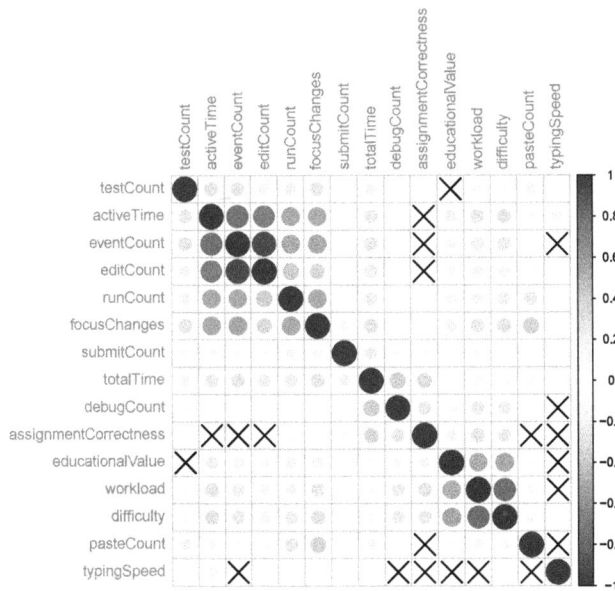

Figure 1: Per-assignment Spearman-correlations with significances corrected using the Bonferroni correction for multiple comparisons. Size and color of circles indicate the Spearman correlation coefficient. Crosses indicate that the correlation is not statistically significant.

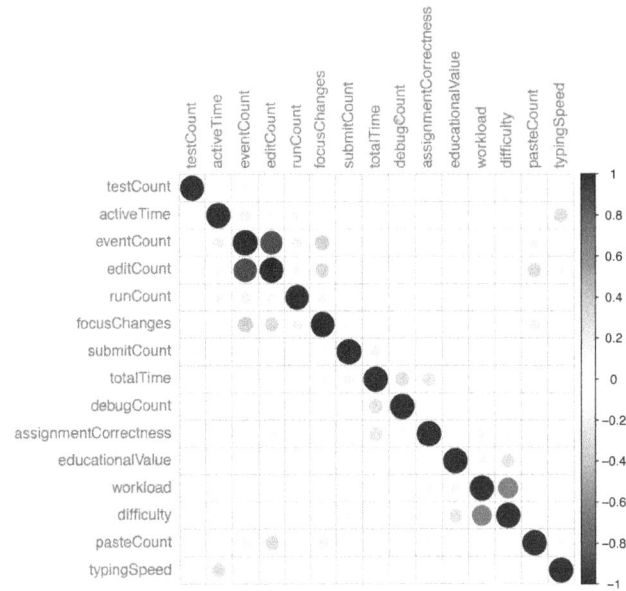

Figure 2: Pairwise per assignment partial Spearman-correlations controlled for all the other variables. Size and color of circles indicate the Spearman correlation coefficient.

(tick count) is very slightly negatively correlated with total time spent on assignments ($r = -.14$).

In the partial correlations, the exam scores are positively correlated with assignment correctness ($r = .44$), and slightly correlated with the number of paste events ($r = .19$). They also show a very slight negative correlation with total time ($r = -.12$), but this correlation was not statistically significant as a full correlation.

5 DISCUSSION

Our results show that there is a large amount of correlation within certain variable clusters. Events recorded within the programming environment tend to correlate, as do events recorded from the learning material. Due to this, it is important to look at partial correlations of the variables. Essentially, partial correlations are used to study whether any two variables correlate when controlling for other variables in the data set.

The largest cluster of highly-correlating variables we observed consisted of variables collected from the IDE the students used. First of all, active programming time is highly correlated with the number of actions taken in the programming environment and the number of code edits. It is also relatively well correlated with the count of program runs and changes of focus either out of or to the programming environment. These together form a large cluster of variables that are well-correlated with each other.

At the same time, this first cluster is only slightly correlated with the counts of test runs, debug usage, total time (including pauses),

number of paste events and the number of times the code is submitted. There is also very little correlation between this cluster of variables and the perceived amounts of educational value, workload or difficulty for each assignment.

When partial correlations are considered, this cluster essentially reduces to a strong correlation between the total number of events and code edits. This indicates that most of the actions taken by the students in the programming environment are edits to code.

While these relations – as well as the negative correlation between the typing speed and the amount of active time – are somewhat self-evident they do suggest that the analytical methods are correct. Thus, these "trivial" results support the existence of the more curious phenomena we observe next.

One such curious phenomenon is the negative correlation between the numbers of edits and focus changes that is also visible when corrected for the other variables. This indicates that the students who do more changes to their code tend to not change in and out of their editor as much as students with less changes to their code. One possible explanation for this is that some students tend to tinker their code in the editor if they are having trouble whereas others go to the material for help [29].

Also curious is the behavior of the number of debug events: it is negatively correlated with assignment correctness, perceived educational value, workload and difficulty. While the first one is explainable by the fact that struggling students are likely to both use the debug tool and abandon an assignment before finishing it completely, the negative correlations with perceptions regarding

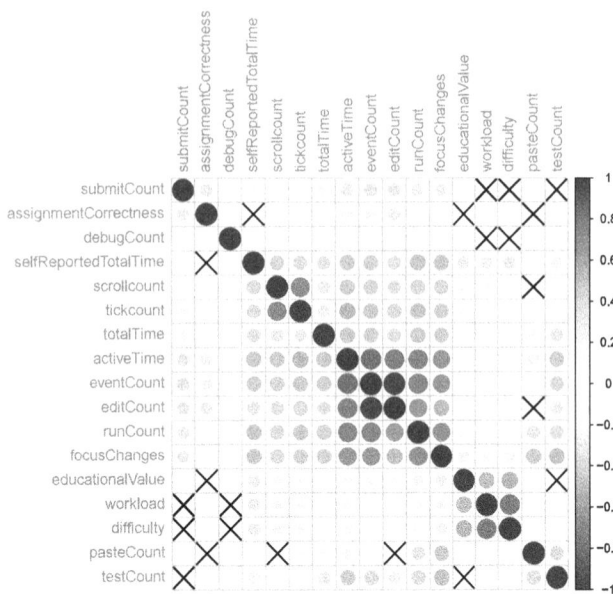

Figure 3: Within week, i.e. per course component Spearman-correlations with significances corrected using the Bonferroni correction for multiple comparisons. Size and color of circles indicate the Spearman correlation coefficient. Crosses indicate that the correlation is not statistically significant.

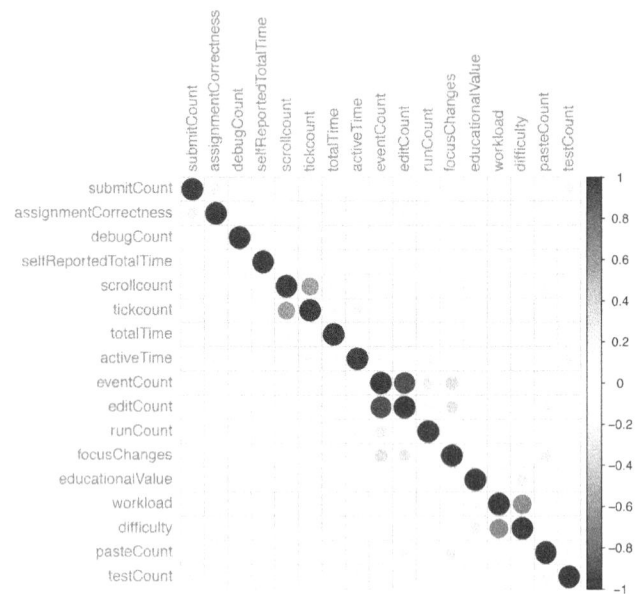

Figure 4: Pairwise within week, i.e. per course component partial Spearman-correlations between the tested variables controlled for all the other variables. Size and color of circles indicate the Spearman correlation coefficient.

the assignment are not as intuitive. One possible explanation is that the debug feature is mostly used by advanced students, or in other words, students who do not struggle with the assignments and want to understand the functionality of the programs better.

We further note that while perceived educational value, workload and difficulty are correlated in the full correlation analysis, partial correlation analysis indicates that perceived educational value is only very slightly correlated with the others when partial correlations are observed. In other words, assignments that are difficult or laborious are not necessarily beneficial for learning, and beneficial assignments do not need to be laborious or difficult. Additionally, these self-reported metrics, including the self-reported hours spent each week, did not have significant correlations with other metrics when examining the partial correlations, which raises questions about the validity of self-reported metrics altogether.

We failed to find any significant partial correlations between metrics obtained from the ebook-like learning material and the programming environment. Our belief is that this is partially due to focusing on too coarse grained data – it is likely that different students spend different proportions of time in different learning environments and material locations. Thus, effort should not be estimated solely based on the total study time, as even small pauses can account for large variations in learning outcomes [21]. Moreover, it is also important to know what the time is spent on – for example, knowledge on which material paragraphs the students spend their time on could provide additional insights on the students' struggles [22].

Interestingly, essentially none of the variables are strongly correlated with exam scores: exam scores are most strongly correlated with assignment correctness and slightly correlated with paste counts, number of assignment submissions, active programming time, number of programming events and code edit event counts. When partial correlations are considered, only assignment correctness and paste counts are correlated in any significant magnitude with exam scores. Based on this, it seems that in our context, it would not be sensible to conduct interventions based on time related metrics alone without additional proof of the student needing help – however, it is also possible that the change from the pen-and-paper -based exam to the computer exam has influenced the overall exam data.

5.1 Limitations

One of the core limitations of this work is that the data comes from a type of a university course with high attrition rates. In our context where over 400 students were initially active, data from marginally over 300 was used. We excluded information from students who chose to not participate in the study, who did not answer any of the questionnaires, and who potentially had e.g. JavaScript blocking scripts on their computers (students with practically no data from the material logging component). This means that there is a risk of selection bias. However, we tried to combat these problems by normalizing the data whenever possible so that the metrics would be comparable as well as taking averages instead of summing so that missing data points (e.g. a student not answering a questionnaire) would not affect the results as much.

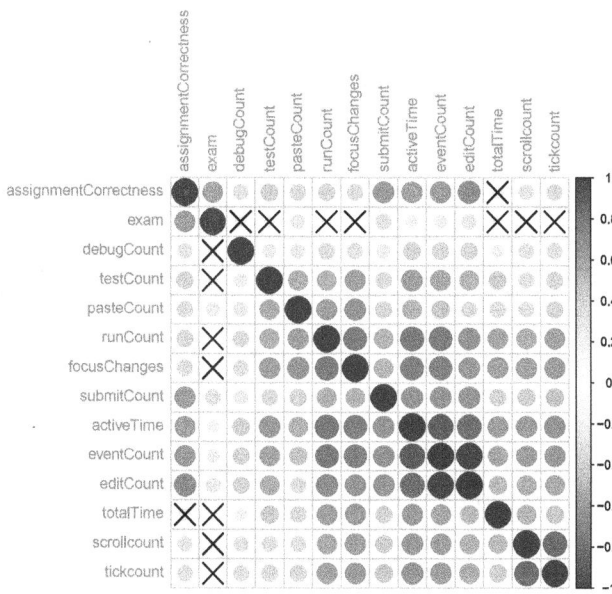

Figure 5: Full course Spearman-correlations with significances corrected using the Bonferroni correction for multiple comparisons. Size and color of circles indicate the Spearman correlation coefficient. Crosses indicate that the correlation is not statistically significant.

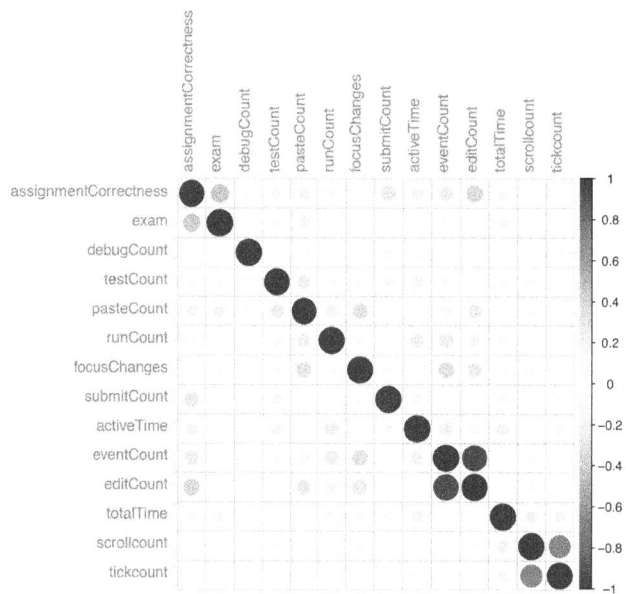

Figure 6: Full course partial pairwise Spearman-correlations between the tested variables controlled for all the other variables. Size and color of circles indicate the Spearman correlation coefficient.

A concern for the external validity and generalizability of the study arises from the fact that all the data used in this study comes from a single university. We sought to combat this by including data from multiple course instances, but acknowledge that the course content is the same. We encourage fellow researchers to replicate our study in their context, and are willing to provide support and the necessary tools to do so.

Additionally, the course material usage data might differ depending on the specifications of the resolution of the screen of the user as the JavaScript library used to study material usage tracks things visible on the user's screen. A larger screen with a higher resolution can have more content on the screen at the same time. Thus, users with low-resolution monitors might have more scroll events compared to users with high-resolution screens.

6 CONCLUSIONS

In this work, we looked at different time metrics from multiple different data sources. We calculated the correlations between the metrics within single assignments, single thematically coherent course components, and over the whole course. We found that many of the metrics form clusters indicating possible redundancy. Further analysis of partial correlations revealed that some metrics are indeed most likely redundant, for example students' self-reported workload and difficulty.

With this work, we have sought to bring attention to the myriad of variables that can potentially be used to measure students' activity and time usage in the course. If this multitude of factors is not taken into account, the best case scenario is that separate research streams that study these variables merely create redundancy as research groups report on distinct but highly correlated variables as all explaining some other variable. In the worst case, strands of research that in actuality describe the same underlying phenomena are not recognized as related if they use slightly different – but in actuality highly related – variables as both the explaining and explained variables.

Interestingly, we found that exam scores are not strongly correlated with any of the studied metrics. Based on our results, when corrected for independence, the self-reported educational value of an assignment does not have a strong correlation with assignment difficulty and workload, which indicates that an assignment can be educational even if it is not laborious. Additionally, we noticed that material usage metrics do not have significant correlations with metrics built from programming logs. This means that in order to get an accurate picture of students' learning, data from all the learning environments the students use should be combined.

As part of our future work, we are interested in combining student background information with the data studied here. For example, there could be differences in how well certain metrics perform depending on factors such as previous programming experience. Additionally, we are interested in building predictive models based on the time-like metrics examined in this study.

ACKNOWLEDGEMENTS

This work was partially funded by Academy of Finland under grant number 303694 *Skills, education and the future of work.*

REFERENCES

[1] Alireza Ahadi, Raymond Lister, Heikki Haapala, and Arto Vihavainen. 2015. Exploring machine learning methods to automatically identify students in need of assistance. In *Proceedings of the Eleventh Annual International Conference on International Computing Education Research.* ACM, 121–130.

[2] AD Baddeley and DJA Longman. 1978. The influence of length and frequency of training session on the rate of learning to type. *Ergonomics* 21, 8 (1978), 627–635.

[3] Benjamin S Bloom. 1974. Time and learning. *American psychologist* 29, 9 (1974), 682.

[4] John B Carroll. 1963. A model of school learning. *Teachers college record* (1963).

[5] Adam S Carter, Christopher D Hundhausen, and Olusola Adesope. 2015. The normalized programming state model: Predicting student performance in computing courses based on programming behavior. In *Proceedings of the eleventh annual International Conference on International Computing Education Research.* ACM, 141–150.

[6] John Dunlosky, Katherine A Rawson, Elizabeth J Marsh, Mitchell J Nathan, and Daniel T Willingham. 2013. Improving students' learning with effective learning techniques: Promising directions from cognitive and educational psychology. *Psychological Science in the Public Interest* 14, 1 (2013), 4–58.

[7] Olive Jean Dunn. 1961. Multiple comparisons among means. *J. Amer. Statist. Assoc.* 56, 293 (1961), 52–64.

[8] Gregory Dyke. 2011. Which aspects of novice programmers' usage of an IDE predict learning outcomes. In *Proceedings of the 42nd ACM technical symposium on Computer science education.* ACM, 505–510.

[9] Herm Ebbinghaus. 1885. Ueber das Gedächtnis. (1885).

[10] Stephen H Edwards, Jason Snyder, Manuel A Pérez-Quiñones, Anthony Allevato, Dongkwan Kim, and Betsy Tretola. 2009. Comparing effective and ineffective behaviors of student programmers. In *Proceedings of the fifth international workshop on Computing education research workshop.* ACM, 3–14.

[11] K Anders Ericsson, Ralf T Krampe, and Clemens Tesch-Römer. 1993. The role of deliberate practice in the acquisition of expert performance. *Psychological review* 100, 3 (1993), 363.

[12] Anthony Estey and Yvonne Coady. 2016. Can Interaction Patterns with Supplemental Study Tools Predict Outcomes in CS1?. In *Proceedings of the 2016 ACM Conference on Innovation and Technology in Computer Science Education.* ACM, 236–241.

[13] Anthony Estey, Hieke Keuning, and Yvonne Coady. 2017. Automatically Classifying Students in Need of Support by Detecting Changes in Programming Behaviour. In *Proceedings of the 2017 ACM SIGCSE Technical Symposium on Computer Science Education.* ACM, 189–194.

[14] Malcolm Gladwell. 2008. The 10 000 hour-rule. In *Outliers: the story of success.* Little, Brown and Company, New York, 35–68.

[15] J Hauke and T Kossowski. 2011. Comparison of values of Pearson's and Spearman's correlation coefficient on the same sets of data. *Quaestiones Geographicae* 30, 2 (2011).

[16] Arto Hellas, Juho Leinonen, and Petri Ihantola. 2017. Plagiarism in Take-home Exams: Help-seeking, Collaboration, and Systematic Cheating. In *Proceedings of the 2017 ACM Conference on Innovation and Technology in Computer Science Education.* ACM, 238–243.

[17] Petri Ihantola, Arto Vihavainen, Alireza Ahadi, Matthew Butler, Jürgen Börstler, Stephen H Edwards, Essi Isohanni, Ari Korhonen, Andrew Petersen, Kelly Rivers, and others. 2015. Educational data mining and learning analytics in programming: Literature review and case studies. In *Proceedings of the 2015 ITiCSE on Working Group Reports.* ACM, 41–63.

[18] Nate Kornell and Robert A Bjork. 2007. The promise and perils of self-regulated study. *Psychonomic Bulletin & Review* 14, 2 (2007), 219–224.

[19] Jaakko Kurhila and Arto Vihavainen. 2011. Management, Structures and Tools to Scale Up Personal Advising in Large Programming Courses. In *Proceedings of the 2011 Conference on Information Technology Education (SIGITE '11).* ACM, New York, NY, USA, 3–8. DOI: http://dx.doi.org/10.1145/2047594.2047596

[20] Juho Leinonen, Krista Longi, Arto Klami, and Arto Vihavainen. 2016. Automatic inference of programming performance and experience from typing patterns. In

Proceedings of the 47th ACM Technical Symposium on Computing Science Education. ACM, 132–137.

[21] Leo Leppänen, Juho Leinonen, and Arto Hellas. 2016. Pauses and spacing in learning to program. In *Proceedings of the 16th Koli Calling International Conference on Computing Education Research.* ACM, 41–50.

[22] Leo Leppänen, Juho Leinonen, Petri Ihantola, and Arto Hellas. 2017. Using and collecting fine-grained usage data to improve online learning materials. In *Proceedings of the 39th International Conference on Software Engineering: Software Engineering and Education Track.* IEEE Press, 4–12.

[23] Krista Longi, Juho Leinonen, Henrik Nygren, Joni Salmi, Arto Klami, and Arto Vihavainen. 2015. Identification of programmers from typing patterns. In *Proceedings of the 15th Koli Calling Conference on Computing Education Research.* ACM, 60–67.

[24] Brooke N Macnamara, David Z Hambrick, and Frederick L Oswald. 2014. Deliberate practice and performance in music, games, sports, education, and professions a meta-analysis. *Psychological science* 25, 8 (2014), 1608–1618.

[25] MM Mukaka. 2012. A guide to appropriate use of correlation coefficient in medical research. *Malawi Medical Journal* 24, 3 (2012), 69–71.

[26] Jonathan P Munson. 2017. Metrics for timely assessment of novice programmers. *Journal of Computing Sciences in Colleges* 32, 3 (2017), 136–148.

[27] Christian Murphy, Gail Kaiser, Kristin Loveland, and Sahar Hasan. 2009. Retina: helping students and instructors based on observed programming activities. *ACM SIGCSE Bulletin* 41, 1 (2009), 178–182.

[28] David A Omahen. 2009. The 10 000-hour rule and residency training. *Canadian Medical Association Journal* 180, 12 (2009), 1272–1272.

[29] David N Perkins, Chris Hancock, Renee Hobbs, Fay Martin, and Rebecca Simmons. 1986. Conditions of learning in novice programmers. *Journal of Educational Computing Research* 2, 1 (1986), 37–55.

[30] Andrew Petersen, Jaime Spacco, and Arto Vihavainen. 2015. An exploration of error quotient in multiple contexts. In *Proceedings of the 15th Koli Calling Conference on Computing Education Research.* ACM, 77–86.

[31] Ma Mercedes T Rodrigo, Ryan S Baker, Matthew C Jadud, Anna Christine M Amarra, Thomas Dy, Maria Beatriz V Espejo-Lahoz, Sheryl Ann L Lim, Sheila AMS Pascua, Jessica O Sugay, and Emily S Tabanao. 2009. Affective and behavioral predictors of novice programmer achievement. In *ACM SIGCSE Bulletin*, Vol. 41. ACM, 156–160.

[32] Herbert Simon and William Chase. 1988. Skill in chess. In *Computer chess compendium.* Springer, 175–188.

[33] Daniel Toll. 2016. *Measuring Programming Assignment Effort.* Ph.D. Dissertation. Faculty of Technology, Linnaeus University.

[34] Daniel Toll, Tobias Olsson, Morgan Ericsson, and Anna Wingkvist. 2016. Fine-grained recording of student programming sessions to improve teaching and time estimations. In *International Journal of Engineering, Science and Innovative Technology*, Vol. 32. 1069–1077.

[35] Arto Vihavainen, Matti Luukkainen, and Petri Ihantola. 2014. Analysis of source code snapshot granularity levels. In *Proceedings of the 15th Annual Conference on Information technology education.* ACM, 21–26.

[36] Arto Vihavainen, Thomas Vikberg, Matti Luukkainen, and Martin Pärtel. 2013. Scaffolding students' learning using test my code. In *Proceedings of the 18th ACM conference on Innovation and technology in computer science education.* ACM, 117–122.

[37] Herbert J Walberg. 1988. Synthesis of research on time and learning. *Educational leadership* 45, 6 (1988), 76–85.

[38] Christopher Watson, Frederick WB Li, and Jamie L Godwin. 2013. Predicting performance in an introductory programming course by logging and analyzing student programming behavior. In *Advanced Learning Technologies (ICALT), 2013 IEEE 13th International Conference on.* IEEE, 319–323.

[39] Christopher Watson, Frederick WB Li, and Jamie L Godwin. 2014. No tests required: comparing traditional and dynamic predictors of programming success. In *Proceedings of the 45th ACM technical symposium on Computer science education.* ACM, 469–474.

Principled Assessment of Student Learning in High School Computer Science

Eric Snow
SRI International
Menlo Park, CA
USA
eric.snow@sri.com

Daisy Rutstein
SRI International
Menlo Park, CA
USA
daisy.rutstein@sri.com

Marie Bienkowski
SRI International
Menlo Park, CA
USA
marie.bienkowski@sri.com

Yuning Xu
SRI International
Menlo Park, CA
USA
yuning.xu@sri.com

ABSTRACT

As K-12 computer science (CS) initiatives scale throughout the U.S., educators face increasing pressure from their school systems to provide evidence about student learning on hard-to-measure CS outcomes. At the same time, researchers studying curriculum implementation and student learning want reliable measures of how students apply their CS knowledge. This paper describes a two-year validation study focused on end-of-unit and cumulative assessments for Exploring Computer Science, an introductory high school CS curriculum. To develop the assessments, we applied a principled methodology called Evidence-Centered Design (ECD) to (1) work with various stakeholders to identify the important computer science skills to measure, (2) map those skills to a model of evidence that can support inferences about those skills, and (3) develop assessment tasks that elicit that evidence. Using ECD, we created assessments that measure the practices of computational thinking, in contrast to assessments that only measure CS conceptual knowledge. We iteratively developed and piloted the assessments with 941 students over two years and collected three types of validity evidence based on contemporary psychometric standards: test content, internal structure, and student response processes. Results show that reliability was moderate to high for each of the unit assessments; the assessment tasks within each assessment are well aligned with each other and with the targeted learning goals; and average

scores were in the 60 to 70 percent range. These results indicate that the assessments validly measure students' computational thinking practices covered in the introductory CS curriculum. We discuss the broader issues we faced of balancing the need to use the assessment results for evaluation and research, and demands from teachers for use in the classroom.

CCS CONCEPTS

• **Social and professional topics~Computational thinking**; • **Social and professional topics~Student assessment**

KEYWORDS

Assessment, Test Validity, High School Computer Science, Computational Thinking Practices

ACM Reference format:

E. Snow, D. Rutstein, M. Bienkowski, and Y. Xu. 2017. Principled Assessment of Student Learning in High School Computer Science. In *Proceedings of International Conference on Computer Science Education Research, Tacoma, WA USA, August 2017 (ICER'17)*, 8 pages.

DOI: http://dx.doi.org/10.1145/3105726.3106186

1 INTRODUCTION

Computer science (CS) is spreading throughout the US K-12 system, with full, yearlong classes being offered in secondary schools. Moving from the informal, afterschool context into this higher accountability realm means that the demand for measures that support valid inferences about student learning increases. As computer science course outcomes become more consequential—for example, counting as credit for graduation or being required for graduation—the demand for and on assessments will increase [1]. For introductory courses, the focus has been on attracting students to the CS pipeline, and prior research into the effectiveness of these courses has focused primarily on measuring student attitudes and interests [2,3]. In academic settings, however, stakeholders want to know what knowledge and skills students are developing: teachers in the introductory courses because they want to adapt their instruction as needed; principals because they want to determine whether they are offering rigorous courses; and teachers in later, more advanced high school courses because they want to determine the extent to which students are prepared for advanced work and where they will need extra help.

CS education research that studies effective teaching and learning also relies on effective measures of learning—whether that be teacher or student learning. If we want to understand the factors that impact learning, we need to gather evidence via assessments that support valid inferences about student learning.

But assessing student learning is not simple. Often, measures of learning are created by an instructor's instincts that the tasks they provide to the student are really eliciting evidence of what they deem to be important. While this might be the case for formative purposes, it may not hold when it comes to reliably measuring student learning on more complex computational thinking (CT) practices that require both CS content knowledge and application of that knowledge, especially if the results are used to report evidence to stakeholders outside the classroom.

In this paper, we describe the results of a two-year study focused on creating and validating end-of-unit and cumulative assessments for an introductory high school CS curriculum. The curriculum we are working with, Exploring Computer Science (ECS, exploringcs.org), provides high school teachers with more than just a pre-AP computer science course. It also supports a way of looking at learning that combines computer science content with inquiry teaching and learning. Inquiry-based teaching emphasizes active student engagement, classroom and individual sensemaking, creativity, collaboration, self-determination, and self-monitoring. ECS provides a good survey of issues in computer science without overly focusing on programming and does not shy away from advanced topics in computer engineering, discrete mathematics, and limits of computing. ECS is currently being implemented across the United States.

2 BACKGROUND AND RELATED WORK

2.1 Computational Thinking Practices

The focus of the recent infusion of CS into U.S. K-12 is less on programming and more on foundational skills. Spurred in part by efforts to define computational thinking (CT) [4], these foundational skills have been identified and cataloged in various efforts, including the CT practices of computing as the foundation for the Advanced Placement (AP) Computer Science Principles course (AP CSP) [5]; a synthesis of elements from the long history of research in programming [6]; and framing CS in the context of the Next Generation Science Standards and science learning [7-11]. Capstone efforts in the U.S. resulted in the recent Computer Science Teachers Association (CSTA) Standards [12] and the K-12 CS Framework [13].

Overall, CT is a core skill set for CS, and can be broadly viewed as the intellectual and reasoning skills needed to master and apply algorithmic thinking, pattern recognition, abstraction, decomposition, and other computational techniques to problems and projects in a wide range of fields. The new AP CSP identifies six CT practices as the core activities that expert computer scientists engage in (much as the Next Generation Science standards, NGSS, offers disciplinary practices). This "work of experts" reflects skills that students should be able to do, show, and explain their thinking about. First, students should be able to create computational artifacts—they should not simply solve

problems, but also be engaged in creative expression. Second, students should be able to analyze existing artifacts in light of their understanding of computation. Third is applying abstraction to simplify complexity. Fourth is analyzing the effects of computing—on society, science, and cultural areas. Fifth and sixth are the social practices of computing, communicating and working in teams.

CT practices constitute a high but important bar to reach for in assessments. They also reflect a broader shift in the science and engineering fields away from measurements of factual knowledge and toward knowledge and skill application. For example, the 2014 Technology and Engineering Literacy Assessment given under the U.S. National Assessment of Educational Progress (NAEP), was specifically designed to measure how well students can apply principles of engineering and technology to real-life situations [14], and student performed a variety of interactive tasks to demonstrate these skills. The science education community similarly recommends that assessments for NGSS require students to use and apply core ideas and crosscutting concepts in the context of disciplinary practices [15]. These assessments represent a shift away from measures of factual knowledge and toward using and applying knowledge to understand the world and solve problems. The authentic practices of these science and technology disciplines are central to student sense making.

2.2 Assessing Programming and Computational Thinking Practices in K-12

There are no comprehensive assessment frameworks for CT practices for K-12 computer science [16,1]. Without such frameworks, it is difficult to know how to measure what really matters, and assessments can end up being too closely tied to particular courses. To measure CT practices effectively, we need to begin to identify what to measure and build up empirical support and validity evidence to support inferences about student learning. Related work in K-12 assessment has measured CT in many ways, described below.

2.2.1 K-12 Assessment. Measuring CT in K-12 has its roots in the studies of programming by young learners. Many of the efforts in assessment of programming (and even CT) look for evidence of student learning in the final product of students' programming efforts on a given assignment or across a course [17] or in open-ended game design tasks [18]. Others rely on traditional multiple-choice questions or descriptive open-ended items [19]—not a rich way to capture practices—or interviews with students which are time consuming and not scalable.

Sometimes, students' use of programming constructs (such as methods in object-oriented programming languages) in a program is used to infer their knowledge of some higher-level CT skills, such as abstraction, modeling, or algorithmic thinking [20]. The difficulty of relying on only the presence or absence of programming constructs as evidence of learning is that research has shown that just using the constructs is not enough evidence: children may use code without understanding what it does [21,22]. For open-ended interactive media or game assignments, assessment generally involves looking for the presence of programming constructs in code [23], or defining measures such as computational game sophistication [24], which consist of programming constructs, constellations of these constructs called patterns, and game mechanics. Researchers have also looked for the presence of more abstract CT patterns in game design code that reflect abstract actions in the game, such as diffusion, collision, and transportation [18].

Looking at the code students produce during open-ended game design is one approach. Another is to place a student in a situation deliberately designed to elicit the desired practices. Such performance tasks can be explicitly designed to measure specific practices. Webb measured practices in an authentic performance task, asking middle-school students who had had 10 hours of instruction in game-based programming to find and fix a buggy program [25]. Building off this work, Denner and Werner [20] created the Fairy Assessment for middle school students that also had find-fault type of problems as well as modifying a given program to meet a new specification.

Brennan and Resnick [21] used multiple approaches to assess student's learning, in informal settings as they created interactive media through programming. They studied four computational practices using artifact-based interviews and design scenarios. The design scenarios were similar to the fault-finding and fixing describe previously, as students were given a program, and asked to explain it, extend it, fix it, and add a new feature.

2.2.2 Advanced Placement CS Principles Assessment. ECS is designed as an introduction to computer science that may come, for some students, before an advanced placement course. Therefore, it is important that ECS has a measurement system similar to the College Board's AP CSP course, to keep consistency between the two levels of courses. CSP's assessment is multi-part, consisting of performance tasks, delivered as a through-course assessment and an end-of-course exam consisting of multiple choice and short response items. As we will discuss later, we did not choose the multiple-choice form for our assessments, but the expectations placed on students in our tests ask them to evaluate and explain their work, and these skills are aligned with similar demands in the CSP performance tasks (as described in the rubrics in [26,27]).

2.2.3 Postsecondary. In postsecondary education, students often take assessments that are developed by their instructors. However, the CS education community has made an effort to create programming language-independent assessments. In CS0 and CS1 (the basic and introductory courses), such assessments have been developed and are in various stages of being evaluated [28-30].

2.3 Evidence-Centered Design

If valid assessment of student's CT practices requires deliberate design of assessments tasks, we need to employ design methods that are systematic and produce the required evidence of student learning. In the remainder of this section, we present background on the methods we used to design assessments for Exploring Computer Science (ECS).

2.3.1 Systematic Design. Evidence-Centered Design (ECD) is a systematic design process that improves the coherence of assessments by explicitly linking particular features of tasks, the evidence of student performances generated by those tasks, and the knowledge and skills implicated by that evidence [31-33]. ECD is especially helpful when the knowledge and skills to be measured are complex, multistep performances such as those required in CT. The ECD process typically occurs across layers of iteration and refinement, each layer representing a part of the work of building and testing an evidence argument.

2.3.2 Domain Analysis. In the domain analysis layer, assessment developers and domain experts identify and analyze the domains, constructs, and underlying skills of interest. The analyses include the ways people acquire and use the knowledge and skills, the situations under which this knowledge is used, and indicators of successful application of the knowledge. Typical sources of information used in domain analysis include existing domain and construct definitions, content and practice standards, curriculum documents, relevant research findings, especially regarding validity, and assessment instruments. Practitioner judgement is also important. Typical outcomes of the domain analysis layer include lists of concepts and principles in the domain(s) being analyzed that are organized as an assessment framework that lays out constructs, measurement approaches, and templates that guide task design.

2.3.3. Domain Modeling. In the domain modeling layer, developers organize information from the domain analysis using a design pattern [34]. Design patterns are structured narratives that fully lay out an assessment argument. They specify (1) the knowledge, skills, and other attributes one wants to address, (2) potential observations and work products that can provide evidence about acquisition of this knowledge or skill, (3) potential rubrics to evaluate student performances on the tasks, and (4) features of task situations that enable the student to provide this evidence. When completed, a design pattern makes the relationships among these elements of an assessment blueprint explicit.

2.3.4. Conceptual assessment framework. Another layer in ECD is the conceptual framework, and developing this requires a designer to specify the constructs of interest (what knowledge and skills) and the activity to be performed. These two parts are linked by an evidence model that specifies how student performances are evaluated to yield observed data, and also by measurement models that connect the observed data to the constructs of interest.

Other layers in ECD encompass additional work related to assessment design and development, including the specification of the tasks, the development of models to collect and analyze evidence and assessment delivery.

2.4 Test Validity

ECD helps us build an assessment argument and design assessments. The next classic challenge in assessment is drawing accurate inferences about what students know and can do based on test scores and other proxies of authentic practices. The latest thinking in test validity [35,36] focuses on supporting these inferences through collecting and integrating different types of evidence. In this paper we report on three types of validity evidence: (1) test content, (2) internal structure, and (3) student response processes.

2.4.1 Validity Evidence Based on Test Content. The content of a test can be thought of as the 'operationalization' of one or more selected constructs situated within a larger domain of interest. We establish validity based on test content by analyzing how well the test content represents the content domain(s). Evidence based on test content reflects the degree to which the test content represents, underrepresents, or is irrelevant to the content domain. This kind of evidence typically comes from expert and practitioner judgments of how well the test items represent the target construct(s) [37]. Within the ECD framework, we establish validity evidence based on test content through domain analysis and modeling.

2.4.2 Validity Evidence Based on Internal Structure. We establish evidence based on internal structure by examining the extent to which the relationships among test items conform to how the construct has been modeled during assessment development. Of particular interest is the distributions of responses to individual items and the statistical characteristics of the items. For example, are the items that are designed to be harder or easier to complete actually harder or easier for students to complete? Do students who, in general, score higher on the construct also score higher on each item [35, 37-38]?

Current conceptions of test validity see reliability as integral to validity [35]. Specifically, estimates of test score reliability play an important role in accurately using evidence based on internal structure to investigate the validity of assumptions and inferences underlying test score interpretations. An inference commonly made for an assessments designed to measure only one theoretical construct is that students can be reliably distinguished by latent proficiency scores representing the construct. If latent proficiency cannot be accurately estimated based on observed test scores then it calls into question the validity of this important structural inference.

2.4.3 Validity Evidence Based on Student Response Processes. We establish evidence based on response processes by closely examining the fit between how students think through responding to test items and the theory of the construct(s) being measured. The construct(s) is made manifest in the test items so it is possible to determine the extent to which responses elicited by the items are consistent with the expected responses (from theory). Evidence based on response processes is typically collected by asking students to think-aloud as they complete the test items and to reflect on their decision and challenges following completion of the test items [35, 39-41].

3 METHODS

3.1 Analyzing and Modeling the CT Practices Domain for ECS

For this project, our ECD *domain analysis* focused on how CT practices are represented in the ECS curriculum. We reviewed the CT practices design patterns from prior work [7], the learning objectives and lesson activities specified in the ECS curriculum, and obtained input from the curriculum design team and experienced ECS teachers. Two computer science content experts, two learning sciences experts, and one assessment expert reviewed the summary from the domain analysis.

The results from the domain analysis gave us the information we needed to specify the focal knowledge and skills underlying the four focal ECS curriculum units in ECD *domain modeling.* These ECS knowledge and skills represent a link between the specific content of the curriculum and the broader CT practices described in 2.1. While the CT practices are general and can be instantiated in many different curricula and contexts, the knowledge and skills at the curriculum unit level are at a finer grain size and are focused on (but are not identical to) the particular learning objectives for that unit. The different units of the ECS curriculum emphasize different CT practices, but all practices are represented across the four units for which we developed assessments.

As we specified the knowledge and skills, we also specified features related to how these could be assessed. In particular, we identified characteristic features of tasks (features that any task that measures them must have) and variable feature of tasks (ways that the tasks can vary but still measure the knowledge and skills). This specification forces us to be explicit about what the task must contain and also prepares us for ways to make new, related tasks by varying features. During this domain modeling, we also create examples of the types of responses students might produce (e.g., explanations or matching) and what quality of their response will be used to score the response (e.g., the amount of detail provided, the accuracy of the response, or the degree to which their explanation supports their claim).

3.2 Developing Assessments of CT Practices for ECS

Once the features of the tasks were specified in domain modeling, we developed tasks using these as a guide. We use the term "task" to represent a scenario with a related set of questions. We chose scenario-based tasks for the assessment format for ECS because they allowed us to present more authentic situations to students [42]. We developed assessment tasks for the first four units ECS.

3.2.1 Developing Assessment Tasks. First, we selected skills to measure and specified a scenario. We required that scenarios be something that most students could relate to and provide opportunities to measure the skills of interest. We developed test items around the scenario to measure the skills. The number of test items for a scenario ranged from 1 to 6 with most scenarios having 3 or 4 items.

We considered Bloom's taxonomy when developing the questions. One of the issues we heard from teachers was that while they had some assessments that aligned to the *remembering* and *understanding* levels of Bloom's taxonomy, they had difficulty assessing the higher levels. Our assessments therefore focused on the *applying, analyzing,* and *evaluating* levels [43]. These levels align well with our focus on CT practices. The 'creating' level of Bloom's taxonomy is covered in the curriculum through the projects that students create.

As an example of how we measured these higher levels of Bloom's taxonomy, in one of the tasks from Unit 1 (shown in Figure 1) we provide students with instructions that they can give to a robot to pick out clothes. The instructions are intentionally vague and subjective. Students are asked to evaluate the instructions, and then modify them to create instructions more appropriate for a computer. The task measures student's skills to *evaluate* the language to decide if it is appropriate for instructions to a computer.

2. Carla programmed a robot to select clothes for her. The robot is able to move around the room, open and close doors, and pick up and drop objects.

Carla's Closet

Below is a set of instructions for the robot once the robot is inside the closet:
1. Take out the top pair of pants from the left side of the third shelf down.
2. Take out a T-shirt.
3. Take out the hat from the top shelf that matches the outfit.

Figure 1: Sample Item - Carla's Closet.

3.2.2 Rubrics for Scoring for Researchers and Teachers. Assessment tasks need a model for interpreting student responses, so we developed scoring rubrics that focused on the quality of the student responses. Rubrics ranged from 1 to 3 points depending on the complexity of the response. As an example, Figure 2 shows the rubric for the item from Figure 1 that defines each possible score point. We developed two versions of the rubrics. The first was a quick guide for scorers who were familiar with the rubrics. The second version, designed for teachers, was a detailed rubric that had further clarification and examples of student responses for the different score points. These rubrics were included in the expert review (described next) so that experts could use them to judge the alignment of tasks to skills being measured.

Sample Responses

2-Point Sample Response 1

For sample response 1,

a) Student selects "Take out a t-shirt" and correctly explains that the instruction does not say exactly what type of t-shirt.

b) Student correctly re-writes step to include location of where the shirt to select is in the closet.

a)	**Step:** Take out a t-shirt A robot would have difficulty completing this step because the instructions don't say what exact type of shirt. You can have many types of shirts in the closet. Shirts come in different colors, styles, and sizes.
b)	Take out first t-shirt from the right hanging on hanger.

1-Point Sample Response 2

For sample response 2,

a) 1pt: Student "Take out the hat from the top shelf that matches the outfit" and correctly explains a robot does not have fashion sense or knows how to determine to match a hat with an outfit.

b) 0pts: Student incorrectly re-writes step which specifies clothing item, but does not give precise/complete instructions about hat selection.

a)	**Step:** Take out the hat from the top shelf that matches the outfit. A robot wouldn't have a fashion sense, or know how to determine which hat would match. It wouldn't have a mind of its own.
b)	Take out the hat that matches the red shirt.

0-Point Sample Response 4

For sample response 4,

a) Student "Take out a t-shirt" and provides an incomplete explanation.

b) Student incorrectly re-writes step with vague instructions.

a)	**Step:** Take out a t-shirt How would a robot know what shirt to pick? Maybe the classmate or the person who made the robot thinks a different shirt is better. Or the shirt might not match the outfit.
b)	Select the most appropriate shirt for my outfit.

Figure 2: Sample Rubric - Carla's Closet.

3.3 Piloting and Refining Assessments of CT Practices for ECS

We collected validity evidence based on test content and student responses processes during the pilot testing to help us refine and improve the assessments. For validity evidence based on test content, we conducted an expert review of the alignment between the knowledge and skills, the curriculum learning goals, and CT practices. For validity evidence based on student response processes, we conducted cognitive think-aloud interviews with a subset of students participating in the pilot testing activities.

The first year of piloting occurred during 2014-2015 school year, and the second during 2015-2016. The cognitive interviews and first year of piloting gave us feedback to revise the assessments. Based on this, additional tasks, including some parallel tasks, were developed. The parallel tasks were designed to help us test two tasks simultaneously. The focus of the second year of piloting was to determine which tasks would be retained for the final form of the test and to obtain validity evidence.

3.3.1 Expert Review. Our expert review helped make sure that the knowledge and skills covered the constructs of interest (and no others). The reviewers included ECS curriculum authors and experts in CS learning. Reviews occurred after each task revision to ensure that any changes had not changed the alignment. Alignment issues were addressed by revising the tasks so that they were well aligned to specific knowledge and skills. These reviews add to the validity evidence based on test content.

3.3.2 Cognitive Think-Aloud Interviews. Before the first round of piloting, we performed cognitive interviews with 8 students. We had students read the scenario out loud and talk through their solution. Observers took notes on areas in which the students struggled either with the interpretation of the question or with determining how to answer it. This information was used to guide questions revisions to reduce confusion and to ensure that the tasks had no constructs that would cause variance among students that was irrelevant to the targeted knowledge and skills.

3.3.3 Pilot Sample and Process. ECS teachers from across the U.S. including Los Angeles, Chicago, and New York participated in the pilot. For each pilot, teachers administered each unit assessment when they finished teaching that unit. The cumulative assessment was administered after the fourth unit assessment. The students in these classes were mostly 9th and 10th graders with limited or no prior experience with computer science. Teachers returned the assessments along with a feedback survey. This feedback was used when making revisions.

3.4 Scoring and Inter-Rater Reliability

In both pilots a set of researchers were trained on the rubrics. The training involved a leader walking the scorers through the rubric and defining each score points. The scorers then talked through the scoring of a set of student responses. Next, a random set of student responses were scored as a group with discussions on each response. Each scorer then scored a common set of student responses on their own. Scores on this second set were reviewed as a group and any disagreements were discussed. Once all scorers were comfortable with the rubric and were reaching agreement, they scored on their own.

Each assessment was scored by two different scorers with a third scorer scoring if there were discrepancies in the scores. Overall the inter-rater reliability was high, with over 90% agreement between raters for most of the tasks. Tasks for which the reliability was lower were revised either by modifying the item to clarify what was expected or by modifying the rubric. Revisions from the 2014-2015 pilot year were made based on the item statistics (e.g., looking at items that had either very high or very low difficulty) and by examining the student responses. Questions that did not seem to be eliciting the desired evidence due to misinterpretation of the problem were revised. The results from the 2015-2016 school year (discussed below) were used to identify the final set of tasks for each of these units.

4 ANALYSIS AND RESULTS

In the 2015-2016 pilot year of the ECS assessment, five assessments were piloted: one for each of the four units, covering different curriculum content on CT, as well as one cumulative assessment covering core content from the ECS Units 1-4.

Two forms were developed (Form A and Form B) for the Unit 1, Unit 3, Unit 4, and cumulative assessments. Different forms were used so that we could pilot parallel versions of some of the tasks as well as to pilot new tasks. Unit 2 had new tasks that were piloted, but no parallel tasks were developed and therefore only one form (Form A) was included in the pilot. For each Unit, students within each classroom were randomly assigned one of the forms.

Table 1 presents a summary of assessment information by Unit and Form. In each assessment, there were 8-10 tasks. Each of the tasks included a scenario and a set of one to six items (or individual questions) related to that scenario. Within each Unit (except for Unit 2), there were a subset of common tasks across Forms A and B. The total number of possible points of the assessments ranged from 21.00 to 33.00.

Table 1: Summary of Assessment Information

Assessment	Content	Form	# of Tasks	# of Common Tasks	# of Items	Total Points	# of Teachers	# of Students
Unit 1	Human-Computer Interaction	Form A	10	6	22	29.00	5	59
		Form B	10		22	29.00	5	53
Unit 2	Problem Solving	Form A	10	-	24	29.50	5	163
Unit 3	Web Design	Form A	8	5	19	27.00	12	189
		Form B	8		20	31.00	12	208
Unit 4	Introduction to Programming	Form A	9	7	21	33.00	13	192
		Form B	8		19	30.00	13	196
Cumulative	Units 1-4	Form A	6	2	17	21.00	7	139
		Form B	7		19	22.00	7	142

A total of 513 students and 16 teachers from 12 schools took at least one of the assessments. In this sample, we had 33.47% female students and 59.55% males. Around half of the students were Hispanic/Latino (49.28%). The sample size for each assessment is presented in the last column of Table 1. Overall students had average total scores in the 60 to 70 percent range across the assessments. For all assessments, distributions of student scores were slightly negatively skewed, indicating more students scored at the high end of the score distributions.

We compared student performance by their demographic background and different levels of computer experience for each assessment. Female and male students had comparable average scores on seven of the nine assessments. For the Unit 4 Form A and Cumulative Form B assessments, the average scores of males were significantly higher than average scores of females. On Unit 4 Form A, Males scored 62.50% of the total points on average while females scored 55.61% ($F(1, 175) = 4.34$, $p = .04$). The percentages on Cumulative Form B were 65.42% and 58.67% for males and females ($F(1,133) = 4.33$, $p = .04$), respectively. In these two assessments, the numbers of male students were twice as many as the females.

Comparisons of students in difference grade levels indicated a negative relationship between grade and assessment performance. Descriptively, students in higher (10th–12th) grades tended to perform worse than students in lower (7th–9th) grades on all assessments. This could be because younger students who enrolled in ECS may be higher achieving overall than those who elected to take ECS later in high school. Hypothesis tests were not conducted for comparing grade levels because of the disparate sample sizes. For the same reason, we did not conduct hypothesis tests for comparing ethnicity groups. Observations of the total score distributions did not reveal a consistent pattern of ethnicity difference across the assessments.

We surveyed students on how much they learned computers from different sources and how frequently they engaged in various type of computer activities. Student performance on the unit where they first used computers was found to be positively related to the degree that they learn computers in a formal setting (e.g., school and after-school program). Also, students' frequency of conducting specific activities such as programming and designing webpages was positively related to their performance on assessments with related topics.

4.1 Validity Evidence Based Internal Structure

We computed Cronbach's alpha to evaluate internal consistency reliability, or the degree to which tasks within each unit assessment are all measuring one general construct. As shown in Table 2, the coefficient ranged from .66 to .84 at the test level except for one form. These results indicated moderate to high levels of reliability for the assessments. The one form that had low reliability was Unit 4 Form A. Removing one item from the form increased the reliability to be in the moderate range. The item was a new item and was removed from future versions of the assessment.

To further investigate the internal structures of the assessments, we conducted exploratory factor analysis for categorical variables at both the task level and the item level. We explored the number of factors (i.e., the number of concepts measured in each assessment in our context) by synthesizing our knowledge of the tasks/items and evidence from the statistical tests. Each form of Units 1-4 was found to measure one or two underlying constructs, meaning the assessment tasks are well aligned with the learning goals. The cumulative assessments were found to measure multiple constructs that align with expectations as this assessment was designed to cover content from multiple units. For all the assessments, the achieved factor structures accounted for a substantial proportion of task covariance in the data (ranging from .30 - .47). The majority of the assessment tasks had factor loadings greater than .40.

Table 2 also presents the difficulty index at the assessment and task levels, as well as the averaged discrimination index at the task level. The difficulty index for a dichotomously scored task is the percent of students who received a correct score. For polytomously scored tasks and the assessment level, difficulty is calculated as the average task/assessment score dividing by the full points. The discrimination index defines the degree to which the task separates the high performing students (top 25% on total score) from the low performing students (bottom 25% on total score). Higher difficulty index values indicate easier levels of the tasks and higher discrimination values indicate better separation of students at different ability levels. The results in Table 2 show that overall the assessments had moderate difficulty levels, with the index ranging from .58 to .67. The average task discrimination was moderate. Analysis at the task and the item levels revealed high discriminating power for tasks/items with medium levels of difficulty. For all assessments, tasks/items that were too difficult and/or not discriminating were replaced or revised.

Table 2: Validity Evidence Based on Internal Structure

		# of Students	Cronbach's Alpha	Assessment Difficulty	Task Difficulty Min	Task Difficulty Max	Average Task Discrimination
Unit 1	Form A	59	.82	.67	.10	.86	.37
	Form B	53	.83	.58	.06	.85	.50
Unit 2	Form A	163	.84	.63	.45	.83	.55
Unit 3	Form A	189	.69	.67	.41	.83	.44
	Form B	208	.69	.64	.46	.82	.44
Unit 4	Form A	192	.49	.59	.58	.91	.44
	Form B	196	.76	.62	.31	.91	.46
Cumulative	Form A	139	.66	.65	.50	.74	.32
	Form B	142	.68	.64	.45	.77	.34

These results indicate that the assessments were well suited to be used in the classroom. Additionally, the evidence shows that they were well aligned with the learning goals within units. The internal structure of the assessments aligned with expectations.

5 DISCUSSION

Our study shows how applying ECD to analyze and model CT practices and to create assessments helped us develop validity evidence based on test content, internal structure, and student response processes.

The validity evidence based on internal structure is particularly promising. While each ECS unit covers multiple topics and concepts, the unit assessments are designed to measure the main construct underlying each unit (e.g., Unit 2 is focused on solving problems with algorithms). The moderate to high reliability coefficients and the results of the factor analysis indicate that the tasks within each unit assessment are all measuring one general construct, which is consistent with the structure of the curriculum. Additionally, analysis at the task and item levels revealed high discriminating power for tasks with medium levels of difficulty. This indicates that the assessments are best suited for differentiating students of average ability on the CT practices being measured. Finally, while students had average total scores in the 60 to 70 percent range across the assessments, total scores on each assessment were distributed across the possible range of the points. The results further support the use of the assessments for measuring student CT practices in classrooms.

These results are promising and lend strong empirical support to the intended uses of the assessments. We are now using the results to inform additional research in assessment development and validation. First, we are developing additional assessment tasks, particularly those with easy and hard levels of difficulty. This will improve the utility of the assessments to measure CT practices across a wider range of ability levels. Second, the results presented here focus on the generation of task and item characteristics using classical test theory. Third, while our analysis indicated comparable performance among gender and ethnicity groups, it is important to recall that these findings are based on a sample of 12 schools and approximately 500 students, which limits the generalizability of our current validity evidence based on internal structure. Of particular interest is whether these results will hold in a larger sample of students and schools drawn from different contexts than those represented in our sample.

6 CONCLUSION

Measuring the *application* of CS knowledge and skills is important for scaling ECS. This study is an important effort to apply principled assessment design methods and contemporary test-validity standards to guide the development, piloting and validation of assessments of CT practices.

We sought to build on prior work in two important ways. First, we modeled the CT practices explicitly for assessment development purposes, specifying ECS learning objectives as more detailed knowledge and skills and then linking these to guidance on what counts as evidence and how to elicit that evidence in assessment situations. From this we developed assessment design patterns that guide the development of assessments aligned with both the curriculum and broader CT practices that match the broad ECS learning objectives. Second, we gathered validity evidence based on current test validity standards that provide empirical support for the inferences to be drawn from student performance on the assessment.

Our findings support use of the assessments by both educators measuring students' CT practices and by researchers studying curriculum implementation and student learning in introductory high school computer science. Feedback from teachers and fellow researchers has been very positive, and teachers are continuing to use our assessments for measuring students in their classrooms. Developing more measures for teachers to use will provide them with the supports they need to help their students grow as computer scientists.

A significant contribution of this work is the set of assessment design patterns that guided the development of the ECS assessments. ECS teachers and other stakeholder groups can use these design patterns to develop new and novel assessment items for use in their classroom or in research on the impact of the ECS curriculum on students' CT practices. A forthcoming technical report (to be released on pact.sri.com) will detail the development of the ECS assessment design patterns and how they were used to develop the ECS assessment items. The ECS design patterns were based on a more general set of design patterns not specific to CTPs in ECS, but to CTPs in the secondary CS domain [7]. Secondary CS teachers and other stakeholders can use these design patterns to develop novel assessment items measuring CTPs aligned with their own curricula.

ACKNOWLEDGMENTS

This work was conducted with support from the National Science Foundation under contract numbers, CNS-1132232, CNS-1240625, and DRL-1418149. We thank the ECS curriculum developers, teachers and students who participated in our pilot work.

REFERENCES

[1] Aman Yadav, David Burkhart, Daniel Moix, Eric Snow, Padmaja Bandaru, and Lissa Clayborn. 2015. *Sowing the Seeds: A Landscape Study on Assessment in Secondary Computer Science Education.* Comp. Sci. Teachers Assn., NY, NY. Retrieved January 18, 2016 from http://csta.acm.org/Research/sub/Projects/ResearchFiles/AssessmentStudy2015.pdf

[2] Joanna Goode, Gail Chapman, and Jane Margolis. 2012. Beyond curriculum: the exploring computer science program. *ACM Inroads* 3, 2: 47–53.

[3] Brenda Castro, Terrence Diaz, Marissa Gee, Rebekah Justice, David Kwan, Preethi Seshadri, and Zachary Dodds. 2016. *MyCS at 5: Assessing a Middle-years CS Curriculum.* 558–563. https://doi.org/10.1145/2839509.2844643

[4] Jeannette M Wing. 2008. Computational thinking and thinking about computing. Philosophical Transactions of the Royal Society A: Mathematical, Physical and Engineering Sciences 366, 1881: 3717–3725. https://doi.org/10.1098/rsta.2008.0118

[5] Andrea Arpaci-Dusseau, Owen Astrachan, Dwight Barnett, Matthew Bauer, Marilyn Carrell, Rebecca Dovi, Baker Franke, Christina Gardner, Jeff Gray, Jean Griffin, Richard Kick, Andy Kuemmel, Ralph Morelli, Deepa Muralidhar, Rebecca Brook Osborne, and Chinma Uche. 2013. Computer science principles: analysis of a proposed advanced placement course. In Proceeding of the 44th

ACM technical symposium on Computer science education (SIGCSE), 251–256. https://doi.org/10.1145/2445196.2445273

[6] Shuchi Grover and Roy Pea. 2013. Computational Thinking in K–12 A Review of the State of the Field. *Educational Researcher* 42, 1: 38–43. https://doi.org/10.3102/0013189X12463051

[7] Marie Bienkowski, Eric Snow, Daisy Rutstein, and Shuchi Grover. 2015. Assessment design patterns for computational thinking practices in secondary computer science: A first look. SRI technical report. Menlo Park, CA: SRI International. Retrieved from http://pact.sri.com/resources.html.

[8] Irene Lee, Fred Martin, and Katie Apone. 2014. Integrating Computational Thinking Across the K–8 Curriculum. *ACM Inroads* 5, 4: 64–71. https://doi.org/10.1145/2684721.2684736

[9] Pratim Sengupta, John S. Kinnebrew, Satabdi Basu, Gautam Biswas, and Douglas Clark. 2013. Integrating computational thinking with K-12 science education using agent-based computation: A theoretical framework. *Education and Information Technologies* 18, 2: 351–380. https://doi.org/10.1007/s10639-012-9240-x

[10] Cary Sneider, Chris Stephenson, Bruce Schafer, and Larry Flick. 2014. Exploring the science framework and NGSS: Computational thinking in the science classroom. *Science Scope* 38, 10–15.

[11] Uri Wilensky, Corey E Brady, and Michael S Horn. 2014. Fostering computational literacy in science classrooms. *Communications of the ACM* 57, 8: 24–28. https://doi.org/10.1145/2633031

[12] CSTA Standards Task Force. 2016. [Interim] CSTA K-12 Computer Science Standards: Revised 2016. Retrieved April 13, 2017 from https://c.ymcdn.com/sites/www.csteachers.org/resource/resmgr/Docs/Standards/2016StandardsRevision/INTERIM_StandardsFINAL_07222.pdf

[13] K-12 CS Framework Committee. 2016. K-12 Computer Science Framework. Retrieved April 11, 2017 from http://www.k12cs.org.

[14] National Assessment Governing Board. 2014. Abridged Technology and Engineering Literacy Framework for the 2014 National Assessment of Educational Progress. Retrieved April 13, 2017 from https://www.nagb.org/content/nagb/assets/documents/publications/frameworks/technology/2014-technology-framework-abridged.pdf

[15] National Research Council. 2014. *Developing Assessments for the Next Generation Science Standards*. The National Academies Press., Washington DC. Retrieved April 13, 2017 from https://www.nap.edu/catalog/18409/developing-assessments-for-the-next-generation-science-standards

[16] Cameron Wilson, Leigh Ann Sudol, Chris Stephenson, and Mark Stehlik. 2010. Running on empty: The failure to teach K-12 computer science in the digital age. Association for Computing Machinery/Computer Science Teachers Association. Retrieved from http://runningonempty.acm.org/fullreport2.pdf

[17] Linda Seiter and Brendan Foreman. 2013. Modeling the learning progressions of computational thinking of primary grade students. Proceedings of the Ninth Annual Conference on International Computing Education Research (ICER '13) 59-66. https://doi.org/10.1145/2493394.2493403

[18] Kyu Han Koh, Ashok Basawapatna, Vicki Bennett, and Alex Repenning. 2010. Towards the Automatic Recognition of Computational Thinking for Adaptive Visual Language Learning. In *2010 IEEE Symposium on Visual Languages and Human-Centric Computing*, 59–66. https://doi.org/10.1109/VLHCC.2010.17

[19] Iris Zur-Bargury, Bazil Pârv, and Dvir Lanzberg. 2013. A Nationwide Exam As a Tool for Improving a New Curriculum. In Proceedings of the 18th ACM Conference on Innovation and Technology in Computer Science Education (ITiCSE '13), 267–272. https://doi.org/10.1145/2462476.2462479

[20] Linda Werner, Jill Denner, Shannon Campe, and Damon Chizuru Kawamoto. 2012. The Fairy Performance Assessment: Measuring Computational Thinking in Middle School. In Proceedings of the 43rd ACM Technical Symposium on Computer Science Education (SIGCSE '12), 215–220. https://doi.org/10.1145/2157136.2157200

[21] Karen Brennan and Mitchel Resnick. 2012. New frameworks for studying and assessing the development of computational thinking. In *Proceedings of the 2012 annual meeting of the American Educational* Research Association, Vancouver, Canada. Retrieved December 7, 2015 from http://scratched.gse.harvard.edu/ct/files/AERA2012.pdf

[22] Brian Dorn, Allison Elliot Tew, and Mark Guzdial. 2007. Introductory Computing Construct Use in an End-User Programming Community. In IEEE Symposium on Visual Languages and Human-Centric Computing (VL/HCC 2007), 27–32. https://doi.org/10.1109/VLHCC.2007.35

[23] John H. Maloney, Kylie Peppler, Yasmin Kafai, Mitchel Resnick, and Natalie Rusk. 2008. Programming by Choice: Urban Youth Learning Programming with Scratch. In Proceedings of the 39th SIGCSE Technical Symposium on Computer Science Education (SIGCSE '08), 367–371. https://doi.org/10.1145/1352135.1352260

[24] Linda Werner, Jill Denner, and Shannon Campe. (2014). Children Programming Games: A Strategy for Measuring Computational Learning. Transactions on Computing Education, 14(4), 24:1–24:22. https://doi.org/10.1145/2677091

[25] David C. Webb. 2010. Troubleshooting assessment: an authentic problem solving activity for IT education. Procedia - Social and Behavioral Sciences 9: 903–907. https://doi.org/10.1016/j.sbspro.2010.12.256

[26] College Board. 2016a. AP® Computer Science Principles 2016 Pilot Scoring Commentary: Performance Task: Explore—Impact of Computing Innovations. Retrieved April 14, 2017 from https://secure-media.collegeboard.org/digitalServices/pdf/ap/high-explore-sample-commentary.pdf

[27] College Board. 2016b. AP® Computer Science Principles 2016 Scoring Commentary: Performance Task: Create—Applications From Ideas. Retrieved April 14, 2017 from https://secure-media.collegeboard.org/digitalServices/pdf/ap/create-sample-tasks-commentary.pdf

[28] Michael McCracken, Vicki Almstrum, Danny Diaz, Mark Guzdial, Dianne Hagan, Yifat Ben-David Kolikant, Cary Laxer, Lynda Thomas, Ian Utting, and Tadeusz Wilusz. 2001. A multi-national, multi-institutional study of assessment of programming skills of first-year CS students. In *Working group reports from ITiCSE on Innovation and technology in computer science education* (ITiCSE-WGR '01), 125–180. https://doi.org/10.1145/572133.572137

[29] Allison Elliott Tew and Mark Guzdial. 2010. Developing a Validated Assessment of Fundamental CS1 Concepts. In Proceedings of the 41st ACM Technical Symposium on Computer Science Education (SIGCSE '10), 97–101. https://doi.org/10.1145/1734263.1734297

[30] Geoffrey L. Herman, Michael C. Loui, and Craig Zilles. 2010. Creating the Digital Logic Concept Inventory. In Proceedings of the 41st ACM Technical Symposium on Computer Science Education (SIGCSE '10), 102–106. https://doi.org/10.1145/1734263.1734298

[31] Robert J. Mislevy and Geneva D. Haertel. 2006. Implications of Evidence-Centered Design for Educational Testing. Educational Measurement: Issues and Practice 25, 4: 6–20.

[32] Robert J. Mislevy and Michelle Riconscente. 2006. Evidence-centered Assessment Design: Layers, Concepts, and Terminology. In S. Downing & T. Haladyna (Eds.), Handbook of Test Development. 61-90. Mahwah, NJ: Erlbaum.

[33] Robert J. Mislevy, Linda S. Steinberg and Russell Almond. 2003. On the Structure of Educational Assessments. Los Angeles, CA: Center for the Study of Evaluation, National Center for Research on Evaluation, Standards, and Student Testing, Graduate School of Education & Information Studies, University of California, Los Angeles.

[34] Min Liu and Geneva Haertel. 2011. Design Patterns: A Tool to Support Assessment Task Authoring (Large-Scale Assessment Technical Report 11). Menlo Park, CA: SRI International.

[35] American Educational Research Association (AERA), American Psychological Association (APA), and National Council on Measurement in Education (NCME). 1999. Standards for educational and psychological testing. Retrieved from http://www.apa.org/science/programs/testing/standards.aspx

[36] Robert L. Brennan. 2006. Educational Measurement. American Council on Education, Praeger Publishers, Westport, CT.

[37] Joanna S. Gorin. 2006. Test Design with Cognition in Mind. Educational Measurement: Issues and Practice 25, 4: 21–35.

[38] Mark Wilson. 2005. Constructing measures: An item response modeling approach. Lawrence Erlbaum Associates, Mahwah, NJ.

[39] K. Anders Ericsson and Herbert A. Simon. 1993. Protocol analysis: Verbal reports as data. MIT Press, Cambridge, MA.

[40] Maarten W. van Someren, Yvonne F. Barnard, and Jacobijn A. C. Sandberg. 1994. The Think Aloud Method: A Practical Guide to Modelling Cognitive Processes. Academic Press.

[41] Gordon B. Willis. 2005. Cognitive interviewing: A tool for improving questionnaire design. Sage, Thousand Oaks, CA.

[42] Dennis Fulkerson, Paul Nichols, Kathleen Haynie, and Robert Mislevy. 2009. Narrative Structures in the Development of Scenario-Based Science Assessments (Large-Scale Assessment Technical Report 3). Menlo Park, CA: SRI International.

[43] Lorin W. Anderson. 2005. Objectives, evaluation, and the improvement of education. Studies in Educational Evaluation 31, 2–3: 102–113. https://doi.org/10.1016/j.stueduc.2005.05.004

An Instrument to Assess Self-Efficacy in Introductory Algorithms Courses

Holger Danielsiek
Department of Computer Science
Westfälische Wilhelms-Universität
Münster, Einsteinstr. 62,
48149 Münster, Germany
holger.danielsiek@uni-muenster.de

Laura Toma
Department of Computer Science
Bowdoin College
8650 College Station
Brunswick, ME 04011, USA
ltoma@bowdoin.edu

Jan Vahrenhold
Department of Computer Science
Westfälische Wilhelms-Universität
Münster, Einsteinstr. 62,
48149 Münster, Germany
jan.vahrenhold@uni-muenster.de

ABSTRACT

We report on the development and validation of an instrument to assess self-efficacy in an introductory algorithms course. The instrument was designed based upon previous work by Ramalingam and Wiedenbeck and evaluated in a multi-institutional setup. We performed statistical evaluations of the scores obtained using this instrument and compared our findings with validated psychometric measures. These analyses show our findings to be consistent with self-efficacy theory and thus suggest construct validity.

CCS CONCEPTS

• **Social and professional topics** → **Computer science education**; *Student assessment*;

KEYWORDS

Computer Science Education; Self-Efficacy; Algorithms

1 INTRODUCTION

Self-efficacy, introduced by Bandura [2], is a self-belief concept to which, among other effects, considerable influences on academic achievement have been attributed—see, e.g., Pajares and Schunk [31] and the references therein. According to Bandura, self-efficacy, i.e., the expectation of personal efficacy, determines "whether coping behavior will be initiated, how much effort will be expended, and how long it will be sustained in the fact of obstacles and aversive experiences" [2, p. 191]. In the light of recent reports regarding mental problems and decreasing resilience among college students [19, 40], a positive correlation between self-efficacy and coping behaviour makes investigating self-efficacy in undergraduate computing classes worthwhile not only from a purely achievement-oriented point-of-view.

It has been argued that self-efficacy can be influenced by corresponding teaching methods—see, e.g., [1, 35, 42] and the references therein. For the development and assessment of such methods, validated instruments for measuring self-efficacy are needed. While Bandura describes the concept of self-efficacy in a domain-unspecific way, it is apparent that coping strategies and techniques for domain-specific challenges should be assessed with domain-specific instruments. It could be argued that developing a course-specific self-efficacy instrument for every single course in the curriculum might not be needed. Given, however, that AP courses or computer science classes in higher secondary education usually focus on programming and programming-related constructs, an algorithms course is likely to pose challenges even to those with prior experience in computer science. Hence, even students who entered college well-prepared may need to overcome obstacles and experience averse situations. For understanding how to cope with this, an instrument specific to to course it is applied in is mandatory.

Even though self-efficacy influences academic achievement, efficacy expectations alone are not sufficient [2, 25]. In addition to efficacy expectations, matching outcome expectations are needed. An outcome expectation is concerned with believing that a certain behaviour will result in a certain outcome, whereas an efficacy expectation is concerned with believing that one can execute a certain behaviour (that potentially leads to a certain outcome) [2]. Put differently, outcome expectations are needed to align one's behaviors with a certain goal, but it is a different issue to be convinced that one can actually do what is needed to reach these goals. In our study, we focused on efficacy expectations.

Self-efficacy does not necessarily manifest itself in "heightened grades" but can be seen as "an important measure of what students 'get'" [42, p. 374] from a class. Consequently, measuring self-efficacy is different from measuring academic performance.

Our research question was how to develop and conceptually validate an instrument to assess self-efficacy in the context of an algorithms course. We discuss the design of such an instrument, an exploratory factor analysis along with an investigation of the internal consistency, and—through comparing our findings with self-efficacy theory and other measures—its construct validity. As the validation of such an instrument usually takes multiple iterations, the research questions of identifying factors that influence the measured construct and of developing corresponding interventions could not be addressed during the first stages of the development reported upon here and thus are subject of future work.

2 RELATED WORK

The concept of self-efficacy has received a considerable amount of attention in educational psychology (see, e.g., [31] and the references therein): according to Google Scholar, Bandura's seminal paper has been cited over 43,000 times. In contrast, the systematic study of self-efficacy has received comparatively little attention in computer science education with an exclusive focus on introductory programming self-efficacy. Ramalingam and Wiedenbeck [36] developed a 32-item instrument for measuring computer programming self-efficacy. This instrument has subscales for four empirically derived factors, interpreted as "Independence and Persistence", "Simple Programming Tasks", "Self-Regulation", and "Complex Programming Tasks" [36]. Using this instrument, Zingaro [42] showed that peer instruction positively contributes to self-efficacy in a CS1 course. Ramalingam et al. [35] built upon their previous work to link previous experiences, self-efficacy, and mental models as factors influencing the performance in an introductory programming course. Another self-efficacy scale was developed by Quade [34], this scale, however, is not specific to course contents and instead includes more general academic and career expectations. In a small-scale, qualitative study, Kinnunen and Simon [24] investigated the self-efficacy of computer science freshmen using a grounded-theory approach; they focussed on the role of programming assignments.

The *growth mindset*-theory [14] has been the subject of a number of recent papers in the computing education research community, e.g., [28, 38]. This theory is concerned with whether or not a learner believes that intelligence and abilities can be developed. This theory is related to self-efficacy, there are, however, important differences: For example, a learner may have a fixed mindset, i.e., believe that abilities and inteligence are inherited and cannot be changed, but still report a high self-efficacy for certain tasks. On the other hand, a growth mindset supports the development of self-efficacy and vice versa—see the literature review by Farrington et al. [15].

3 PARTICIPANTS AND ADMINISTRATION

When composing the study group for developing an instrument to assess the self-efficacy in algorithms, we had to balance different aspects: on one hand, a large enough population should be considered to work in similar conditions as Ramalingam and Wiedenbeck who used $n = 421$ responses for the design of their scales. On the other hand, noting that Ramalingam and Wiedenbeck aggregated "eight sections [...] taught by seven different instructors" [36, p. 369] we also aimed at using courses taught by different instructors to reduce possible bias. Taking into account both enrollment measures and mission goals (the two of the four criteria suggested by Rawson et al. [37] relevant for our context), we ended up with four different participating institutions. Three of these (Bowdoin College, Washington & Lee University, and Williams College) are located in the United States, the other institution (Westfälische Wilhelms-Universität Münster) is located in Europe. The three US schools have been rated consistently among the top undergraduate institutions, the computer science department at Westfälische Wilhelms-Universität Münster has a comparable department size and similar enrollment measures and student-to-faculty ratio as the other institutions. All instructors were tenured research faculty; the second author taught the course at Bowdoin College.

The fact that this set of participants is not representative of the general student population was a deliberate design choice. Due to the relative homogeneity of the student population, more external factors could be ruled out for examining the construct validity of the instrument. Moreover, self-efficacy theory predicts that gains will be stronger for those with low initial self-efficacy [2]. Hence, an instrument that is developed based upon data from participants assumed to show a relatively high initial self-efficacy[1] and that then can be shown to be sensitive to even small changes, is of additional value. When interpreting the results of future applications of the instrument, however, the characteristics of the respective study group should be kept in mind.

The size of the student population from which fully completed responses were obtained during the pre-course study that led to the construction of the subscales for our instrument was $n_{\text{pre-course}} = 362$. Of these, 53 participants were from US institutions while 309 participants were from Westfälische Wilhelms-Universität Münster. The large number of students from Westfälische Wilhelms-Universität Münster is explained by the fact that the algorithms course is a second-semester course attended by a variety of non-majors, including students with Mathematics, Physics, or Business Information Management majors; all students had taken the same "Introduction to Programming" course in the preceding term and, hence, were indistinguishable from the point of previous exposure to computer science concepts in college. The US students had taken "Introduction to Computer Science" and "Data Structures" courses prior to the "Algorithms" courses considered. For the validity of the study, we note that with the exception of dynamic programming (see Section 6) all students were exposed to the same concepts, algorithms, and competence requirements.

The instrument was administered in-class and in a paper-based form as the experiences from a small pilot study as well as from other surveys led to expect a high response rate. On each sheet of paper, the students were asked to give a one-way hashcode based upon information privy to the students only; this code was used to match the otherwise anonymous responses from the pre-course survey and the post-course survey. The pre-course surveys were administered during the first week of classes, the post-course surveys were administered during the last week of classes.

As participation was voluntary and, more importantly, attendance in class was not required, we had $n_{\text{post-course}} = 130$ responses to the post-course questionnaires. The number of matched answers from all pre- and post-course questionnaires was $n_{\text{matched}} = 107$ (28 US/79 European). Preempting the analyses detailed in Section 6 where we will present the pre- and post-course scores in aggregated form, i.e., for all participants, and detailed by continent, we note that the nominal imbalance of the study population did not affect the (significance) of the results reported.

4 DESIGN OF THE INSTRUMENT

In the design of our instrument, we started from the scale provided by Ramalingam and Wiedenbeck [36]. We examined each item and checked whether the constructs behind it could be transferred to an algorithms course. This led to the exclusion of almost half of the items that referred, e.g., to the usage of reserved words in a

---

[1]Table 4 indeed shows rather high initial scores.

programming language, the object-oriented paradigm, or using third-party functions or libraries. We also decided not to restate the "self-regulation" subscale in the context of algorithms as, after Ramalingam and Wiedenbeck's paper, self-determination theory has led to validated psychometric instrument for measuring self-regulation [4]; also, the concept of a "deadline for a programming project" [36] has no direct counterpart in an algorithms course.

Depending on the school and the preferences of instructors, the main focus of an algorithms course may vary between the details of the implementation in a particular programming language to formal proofs of correctness. Furthermore, it is not uncommon in Europe to teach both data structures and (non-advanced) algorithms in one course and defer more advanced topics, such as dynamic programming or randomization to upper-level courses. Each instructor may have personal preferences for which algorithms to explain in more detail. Finally, the assignment of algorithms to a particular introductory course is not fully agreed upon even within the scope of the ACM computing curriculum [21].

To make our instrument as broadly applicable as possible, we thus decided to not focus on particular algorithms, e.g., Quicksort or the Floyd-Warshall algorithm. Doing so, we also tried to avoid the pitfall of soliciting a self-reported assessment of very specific skills such as executing a particular algorithm as opposed to the intended self-reported self-efficacy related to a more general understanding of topics in algorithms. Based upon curricular aspects and previous work on topics in algorithms prone to misconceptions [17, 39], we constructed items pertaining to runtime analysis, divide-and-conquer, and dynamic programming; see Table 1.

We deliberately decided to only include items that could be operationalized easily. In particular, even though part of the motivation to perform well in an algorithms course is that major companies include "problem solving" items in their assessments, we refrained from including more generic "problem solving" or "abstraction" items into our instrument.[2] A very practical reason for this is that the instrument, just like Ramalingam and Wiedenbeck's instrument, was designed to be administered at a very basic college level or maybe even advanced placement level and thus should be refined to very basic aspects. More importantly, though, recent research on abstraction in computer science classes shows "a strong tendency, by many senior students, to remain on low levels of abstraction, even after realizing abstraction in a variety of CS courses" [18, p. 242] and identifies a lack of practicing abstraction in algorithms courses. Also, the development of abstraction strategies appears to take a longer time than the course of a semester [32].

The existence of a "problem solving" scale in Mathematics seems to contradict the above reasoning. Indeed, Pajares and Miller [30] report having used Dowling's *Mathematics Confidence Scale* [12]; another set of items has been proposed by Dunham [13]. A closer look at these items, however, reveals that the term "problem solving" is used differently: the items in Dunham's scale present a mathematical problem of the form "Solve $\frac{2}{x+3} - 2 > 0$" [13, p. 123] and ask the subject about the confidence of correctly selecting one of five given answers. The items in Dowling's scale[3] are of the form "A living room set consisting of one sofa and one chair is priced

at \$200. If the price of the sofa is 50% more than the price of the chair, find the price of the sofa" [20, Table 3]. In contrast, the task of "solving a problem" in an algorithms course usually includes modeling the problem, devising an algorithm (or another mathematical construct), proving its correctness, and then applying it to the given setting, see, e.g., [18]. Hence, our above reasoning stands.

As discussed above, Ramalingam and Wiedenbeck had identified "Independence and Persistence" as the factor with the highest Eigenvector. The corresponding items concerned "completing a programming project" with various levels of support. We addressed this by constructing items for both algorithm design and runtime analysis that assumed matching levels of available support. A small-scale pilot study at Bowdoin College (Fall 2015) showed that administering the instrument did not pose organizational obstacles. Also, no student reported difficulties regarding understanding the items.

5 EXPLORATORY FACTOR ANALYSIS

To assess the construct validity of our instrument and to be able to better interpret the results, we followed Ramalingam and Wiedenbeck and performed an exploratory factor analysis of the pre-course data.[4] In line with the previous approach, data was extracted using principal axis factoring and, as the factors could not be expected to be independent, a direct oblimin factor rotation.

With 21 items and $n_{\text{pre-course}} = 362$ responses to the pre-course questionnaire, the overall Kaiser-Meyer-Olkin (KMO) measure was 0.908 with individual KMO measures all greater than 0.846, classifications of "meritious" to "marvellous" [22]. Bartlett's Test of Sphericity was statistically significant ($p < 0.001$, $\chi^2 = 6027.217$), indicating that the data was likely factorizable. The analysis revealed four factors with Eigenvalues greater than 1 which explained 44.3%, 9.3%, 7.9%, and 4.7% of the total variance, respectively. Together, these factors explained 66.3% of the total variance. These factors met the interpretability criterion and were thus retained.

The interpretation of the data was consistent with what the instrument was designed to measure indicating construct validity. The data showed strong loading of items referring to designing an algorithm with varying degrees of support on Factor 1. This "Algorithm Design" factor accounted for 44.3% of the variance and included an item referring to finding counterexamples for an algorithm known to be incorrect; this item, however, has a low loading factor of 0.390. Five items referring to understanding and applying the divide-and-conquer and the dynamic programming paradigm strongly loaded on Factor 2. This factor accounted for 9.3% of the variance and is referred to as "Advanced Paradigms". Four items referring to analyzing the runtime of an algorithm with varying degrees of support strongly loaded on Factor 3. This factor accounted for 7.9% of the variance and is referred to as "Runtime Analysis". The remaining six items, referring to producing and tracing pseudocode, strongly loaded on Factor 4. This factor accounted for 4.7% of the variance and is referred to as "Pseudocode Writing and Tracing".

The details, given in Table 1, also show that there are two items with low primary loadings: the primary loading of Item 10 "Mentally trace through the execution of an iterative algorithm given to me" (Factor "Pseudocode Writing and Tracing") is only marginally

---

[2]This is in contrast to a deliberately generic instrument to assess self-efficacy in Engineering Design [7].

[3]We report on Hackett and Betz' adaptation [20].

[4]All statistical analyses reported upon were performed using IBM SPSS™ 24 using 95% confidence intervals.

No.	Item Description	I	II	III	IV	h^2	M	SD
Factor 1: Algorithm Design ($\alpha = 0.898$)								
6	Come up with an algorithm if I could call someone for help if I got stuck.	**.916**	-.044	.051	.004	.757	5.27	1.310
7	Come up with an algorithm once someone helped me get started.	**.856**	-.043	-.043	-.007	.734	5.17	1.311
8	Come up with an algorithm if I had a lot of time.	**.830**	-.057	-.094	-.035	.704	<u>5.35</u>	1.335
4	Organize and design an algorithm in a modular manner.	**.624**	.210	.068	.031	.533	*4.15*	1.505
9	Find ways of overcoming the problem if I got stuck while coming up with an algorithm.	**.444**	.087	-.222	.182	.591	4.42	1.311
15	Come up with a counterexample for an algorithm known to be incorrect.	**.390**	.158	-.144	.169	.483	4.20	1.427
Factor 2: Advanced Paradigms ($\alpha = 0.881$)								
18	Understand the dynamic programming paradigm.	-.077	**.943**	-.032	-.025	.834	3.43	1.725
19	Comprehend a dynamic programming algorithm.	-.023	**.942**	.040	-.041	.818	3.43	1.673
20	Write down a recursive definition of the optimal solution for a dynamic program.	.042	**.799**	-.009	-.070	.645	*3.02*	1.536
17	Understand the divide-and-conquer paradigm.	.091	**.506**	-.096	.196	.505	<u>4.99</u>	1.541
5	Comprehend a complex divide-and-conquer algorithm.	.303	**.362**	-.064	.191	.532	3.90	1.720
Factor 3: Runtime Analysis ($\alpha = 0.929$)								
12	Analyze the running time of an algorithm once someone else helped me get started.	.040	-.045	**-.937**	-.058	.843	<u>4.59</u>	1.481
13	Analyze the running time of an algorithm if I had a lot of time to do so.	.005	-.005	**-.914**	-.028	.843	<u>4.59</u>	1.481
11	Analyze the running time of an algorithm if I could call someone for help if I got stuck.	-.063	-.009	**-.912**	-.014	.755	4.56	1.557
14	Find ways of overcoming the problem if I got stuck at a point while analyzing the running time of the algorithm.	.016	.084	**-.746**	.059	.677	*4.11*	1.448
Factor 4: Pseudocode Writing and Tracing ($\alpha = 0.871$)								
1	Write a pseudocode description for computing the average of three numbers.	-.117	-.055	.041	**.984**	.801	<u>5.77</u>	1.432
2	Write a pseudocode description for solving a small problem that is familiar to me.	-.029	-.069	-.005	**.940**	.823	5.68	1.294
3	Write a pseudocode description for solving a reasonably complex problem that is only vaguely familiar to me.	.198	.023	.014	**.665**	.637	4.38	1.410
16	Write a pseudocode description for sorting n numbers.	.143	.100	-.045	**.549**	.505	4.99	1.541
21	Write a pseudocode description for binary search in an ordered array of n numbers.	.077	.236	-.156	**.364**	.415	*4.06*	1.788
10	Mentally trace through the execution of an iterative algorithm given to me.	.261	.026	-.276	**.307**	.501	5.14	1.418

Table 1: Factor pattern coefficients, communality estimates, means, and standard deviations for the algorithms self-efficacy items ($n_{\text{pre-course}} = 362$). For each item, the highest factor pattern coefficient above 0.300 is shown in bold. For each of the resulting factors, alpha reliability estimates are given in parentheses. The underlined means display the highest value in each factor which represents the most confident item within this factor. The lowest mean is displayed in italics.

	Mean	SD	Factor 1	Factor 2	Factor 3	Factor 4
Algorithm Design	4.758	1.114	1.000			
Advanced Paradigms	3.585	1.420	0.559**	1.000		
Runtime Analysis	4.470	1.366	0.593**	0.468**	1.000	
Pseudocode Writing and Tracing	5.004	1.160	0.688**	0.475**	0.529**	1.000

Table 2: Spearman's rank-correlation coefficients for the exploratory factor analysis from the pre-course data ($n_{\text{pre-course}} = 362$; **: correlation significant at $p < 0.01$).

in excess of 0.3. However, as the next highest loading was well below 0.3, we decided not to omit this items and its assignment to the factor. For Item 5 "Comprehend a complex divide-and-conquer algorithm", both the primary loading (0.362; Factor "Advanced Paradigms") and the secondary loading (0.302; Factor "Algorithm Design") were higher than 0.3. However, the secondary loading was only marginally higher that this threshold value, the primary loading was roughly 20% higher than the secondary loading. As, in

Group	n	All Items					Excluding Dynamic Programming Items				
		μ_{pre}	μ_{post}	δ_μ	t	p	μ_{pre}	μ_{post}	δ_μ	t	p
ALL	107	4.56 (1.00)	5.37 (0.95)	0.81 (0.86)	9.714	< 0.0005	4.81 (1.02)	5.55 (0.92)	0.74 (0.85)	8.977	< 0.0005
US	28	4.70 (0.98)	5.97 (0.76)	1.27 (0.87)	7.642	< 0.0005	5.08 (1.05)	5.95 (0.78)	0.87 (0.93)	4.936	< 0.0005
Europe	79	4.50 (1.01)	5.15 (0.91)	0.65 (0.81)	7.180	< 0.0005	4.71 (1.00)	5.41 (0.93)	0.69 (0.82)	7.486	< 0.0005

Table 3: Results of running a paired t-test on the $n = n_{matched} = 107$ differences between pre- and post-course scores (average over all items). Both mean and standard deviation (in parentheses) are given. Results are reported for the scores derived from all items and the scores derived without the items referring to Dynamic Programming.

addition, the inspection of the items in each group confirmed that the Item 5 corresponded to Item 17 which had a clearly higher loading on the "Advanced Paradigms" Factor than on the "Algorithm Design" factor, we decided to also keep Item 5 in the instrument and assign it to the "Advanced Paradigms" factor.

The reliability of the scores, measured by Cronbach's Alpha, was 0.938 with reliability of the four factors ranging between 0.871 and 0.929. This is slightly less than the reliability of Ramalingam and Wiedenbeck's scores but still high enough to meet clinical standards [5]. The scale showed a high re-test validity in the $n_{post-course} = 130$ post-course responses: the reliability of all scores was 0.950 with the reliability of the four factors ranging between 0.868 and 0.931.

To possibly account for differences between the institutions, we attempted to separately extract factors based upon the US and European data. However, the data quality for the $n_{post-course,US} = 32$ US responses was too low (KMO measure: 0.684) to yield reliable results. Thus, we used the above factors derived from all pre-course responses. Table 2 presents the descriptive statistics of the empirically-derived factors and their correlations.

Naturally, the above factors could also be used with different weights that reflect their relative importance for a certain outcome.

6 ANALYSES

We discuss the results of applying the scale and the factors obtained by our exploratory factor analysis. To assess construct validity of our instrument, we relate our findings to self-efficacy theory.

Pre-/Post-Course. According to general self-efficacy theory and previous studies on self-efficacy, an increase in self-efficacy is to be expected over the course of a semester. To verify this, we analyzed the change in the overall, i.e., averaged over all 21 items, pre-course and post-course scores.

According to Fay and Proschan, one should use a t-test "whenever the difference in means is desired for interpretation of the data" [16, p. 19]. Analyzing the data showed two outliers that were more than 1.5 box-lengths from the edge of the box in a boxplot. The first of these values corresponded an increase from 1.5 (pre-course) to 5.85 (post-course). Further inspection revealed that this student had indicated a low confidence ("1") on all items containing technical terms specific to the design and analysis of algorithms. It appears that this student had responded to the cue "If a specific

term or task is totally unfamiliar to you, e.g., because it has not been discussed in class, yet, please mark 1" (this cue also had been used by Ramalingam and Wiedenbeck [36, p. 372]), hence, the value was kept in the analysis. The second of these values corresponded to a decrease from 5.0 (pre-course) to 1.16 (post-course). Even though this value was extreme, we could not dismiss the data point as some of the entries were larger than 1 indicating that the student had not simply given an unreflected, default answer.

To assess the influence of the second of these outliers, we ran a t-test with and without this data point included. In both cases, normality was confirmed using a visual inspection of a Normal Q-Q plot.[5] Including the second outlier, the scores increased by 0.812 (95% CI, 0.646 to 0.978) from pre-course to post-course, the increase was statistically significant, $t(106) = 9.714$, $p < 0.0005$. Excluding the second outlier, the scores increased by 0.846 (95% CI, 0.692 to 0.999) from pre-course to post-course, the increase was statistically significant, $t(105) = 10.952$, $p < 0.0005$. We concluded that keeping the extreme outlier did not affect the type or significance of the change and retained it as well.

We then separately investigated the descriptive statistics and the change in scores for the three US institutions[6] and the European institution. For the three US institutions, there were no outliers in the data, as assessed by inspection of a boxplot for values greater than 1.5 box-lengths from the edge of the box. The differences in scores were normally distributed as assessed by visual inspection of a Normal Q-Q plot and the Shapiro-Wilk test ($n = 28$, $p = 0.926$). The scores increased by 1.26 (95% CI, 0.927 to 1.607) from pre-course to post-course, the increase was statistically significant, $t(27) = 7.642$, $p < 0.0005$.

For the European institution, Shapiro-Wilk test failed to confirm normality due to the presence of the extreme outlier discussed above ($n = 79$, $p = 0.004$). Following the above line of reasoning, however, we confirmed normality using visual inspection of a Normal Q-Q plot and kept the data point.[7] The scores increased by 0.651 (95%

---

[5]The second outlier, however, caused the Shapiro-Wilk test to fail ($n = 107$, $p < 0.001$); deleting this data point would have resulted in the Shapiro-Wilk test confirming normality as well ($n = 106$, $p = 0.165$).
[6]Due to the small sample sizes at each institution and as the courses had been selected to be comparable (see Section 3), we did not perform separate analyses for each institution.
[7]Deleting the extreme data point would have resulted in passing the Shapiro-Wilk test as well ($n = 78$, $p = 0.244$).

Group	n	Pre-Course Self-Efficacy				Post-Course Self-Efficacy			
		Algorithm Design	Advanced Paradigms	Runtime Analysis	Pseudocode Write/Trace	Algorithm Design	Advanced Paradigms	Runtime Analysis	Pseudocode Write/Trace
US female	8	4.85 (1.61)	2.73 (1.56)	5.53 (1.07)	5.60 (0.77)	5.77 (1.00)	6.15 (0.99)	6.03 (0.94)	6.27 (0.62)
US male	20	4.85 (1.22)	3.14 (1.21)	4.90 (1.81)	5.75 (0.72)	5.82 (0.84)	5.89 (0.70)	5.55 (1.19)	6.36 (0.73)
US	28	4.85 (1.31)	3.02 (1.31)	5.08 (1.64)	5.71 (0.72)	5.80 (0.87)	5.96 (1.13)	5.68 (0.69)	6.33 (0.76)
Europe	79	4.84 (1.04)	3.63 (1.45)	4.32 (1.33)	5.01 (1.11)	5.30 (1.05)	4.81 (1.20)	5.13 (1.27)	5.75 (0.94)
ALL	107	4.85 (1.12)	3.48 (1.44)	4.53 (1.45)	5.19 (1.06)	5.43 (1.03)	4.72 (1.32)	5.28 (1.25)	5.91 (0.91)

Table 4: Descriptive statistics for various demographic groups. For each factor, mean and standard deviation (in parentheses) are given. The European course did not cover Dynamic Programming, hence, the post-course scores for the "Advanced Paradigms" self-efficacy factor are considerably lower.

CI, 0.470 to 0.831) from pre-course to post-course, the increase was statistically significant, $t(78) = 7.180, p < 0.0005$.

The t-values given indicate that the increase in scores was higher for the US institutions than for the European institutions. However, it is important to note that the curriculum for the European course did not contain dynamic programming as this topic was handled in an advanced algorithms course. Instead, the course covered several data structures topics not contained in the curricula for the US courses. Filtering out the three items related to dynamic programming, the analysis showed the changes to be much more consistent across institutions: the scores for the US courses increased by 0.871 (95% CI, 0.509 to 1.23; $t(27) = 4.936, p < 0.0005$) and the scores for the European institution increased by 0.694 (95% CI, 0.510 to 0.879; $t(78) = 7.486, p < 0.0005$). Thus, the influence of the two subgroups (US vs. European) did not affect the overall outcome or its significance: Table 3 show that a statistically significant increase could be found for both the whole population and individual groups.

Self-Efficacy Gain for Quartile Groups. Given that only few, if any, students have been exposed to the topics covered in an algorithms course before, it can be assumed that a low initial self-efficacy is not attributed to previous aversive experience. In line with Ramalingam and Wiedenbeck, we thus conjectured that the largest gain in self-efficacy would be observed for those with a low initial self-efficacy.

To investigate this hypothesis, we conducted a one-way ANOVA ($\alpha = 0.05$) to determine whether the difference in pre-course and post-course scores was different for the groups determined by the pre-course scores' quartiles. The group corresponding to the lowest quartile contained 27 participants, the other groups, in increasing order of quartiles, contained 31, 23, and 26, participants, respectively. As discussed above, the data set contained two outliers, one of which could be traced back to apparently erring on the side of caution and checking "not at all confident" for every single item on the pre-course questionnaire, hence, resulting in a extremely large increase in self-efficacy. The other participant showed an extreme drop in self-efficacy, which we have been unable to explain so far. Thus, the data of both participants was retained. Homogeneity of variance,

as assessed by Levene's test for equality of variances ($p = 0.076$), was observed. Data is presented as mean ± standard deviation.

The increase in self-efficacy was statistically significantly different for the four groups ($F(3, 103) = 9.974, p < 0.001$, partial $\eta^2 = 0.363$). The differences increased from the first (1.46 ± 0.85), to second (0.76 ± 0.98), to third (0.67 ± 0.52), to fourth (0.32 ± 0.58) groups, in that order. Tukey post hoc analysis revealed that the increase from the first to the second (-0.69, 95% CI (-1.22 to -0.16), $p = 0.005$), from the first to the third (-0.77, 95% CI (-1.35 to -0.21), $p = 0.002$), and from the first to the fourth group (-1.13, 95% CI (-1.69 to -0.57), $p < 0.001$) was statistically significant.

Gender. Responding to the literature on gender differences regarding self-assessment in computing [3, 8, 11], we followed up by a one-way ANOVA ($\alpha = 0.05$) for both the overall scores (averaged over all items) as well as for each of the factors. As we only had access to the the gender information of $n_{gender} = 28$ US participants, the population studied was rather small. Normality for the change in scores was assessed using a Shapiro-Wilk test within each group ($p > 0.05$). There was homogeneity of variances, as assessed by Levene's test for equality of variances ($p = 0.340$). However, no statistically significant differences between the group of $n_{female,US} = 8$ female participants and the groups of $n_{male,US} = 20$ male participants ($F(1, 26) = 0.130, p = 0.721$) could be detected; the same holds on the level of the factors. This is consistent with the findings of Ramalingam and Wiedenbeck who could not find a statistically significant difference between (much larger groups of) female and male students w.r.t. computer programming self-efficacy. Their hypothesis that "females entering computer science are members of a self-selected group that tends to have high mathematics [...] experience" [36, p. 379] is supported by Beyer [3] who reported (slightly) higher Math ACT scores for both major and non-major female students in introductory programming courses.

Pre-/Post-Midterm. In each of the US courses considered in this study, students had to take a midterm exam. Since the midterm exam was the first major formal feedback putting self-efficacy in

	Mean	SD	Self-Efficacy	Perceived Competence	Interest/Enjoyment	Pressure/Tension
Self-Efficacy	5.761	0.853	1.000			
Perceived Competence	4.147	1.479	0.629**	1.000		
Interest/Enjoyment	4.326	1.132	0.527**	0.662**	1.000	
Pressure/Tension	4.116	1.601	-0.335*	-0.604**	-0.280	1.000

Table 5: Spearman's rank-correlation coefficient for post-midterm self-efficacy and factors from the *Intrinsic Motivation Inventory* (n_{midterm} = 46; *: correlation significant at $p < 0.05$; **: correlation significant at $p < 0.01$).

context with actual performance, we administered our instrument immediately before and after the midterm exam.

The changes as reported by our instrument could not be shown to be statistically significant: 12 of the $n_{\text{midterm,matched}}$ = 23 students for which we had complete data saw an increase in self-efficacy while 11 participants saw a decrease. In the light of self-efficacy theory, this is rather unsurprising, since taking this first algorithms exam could either reinforce existing self-efficacy, show performance accomplishments, or give demotivating, negative feedback. Consistent with self-efficacy theory, the gain in self-efficacy from this first calibration point until the end of the course was statistically significant again as assessed by a Wilcoxon signed-rank test[8] ($n = 23$, $n_{\text{incr}} = 16$, $n_{\text{decr}} = 5$, $n_{\text{tie}} = 2$, $z = 2.714$, $p = 0.007$, $r = 0.40$). This can be related to both performance accomplishments later in the course and vicarious experiences as "seeing others perform threatening activities without adverse conditions [...] [can convince observers that they can] achieve at least some improvement" [2, p. 197]. We conjecture that the small class sizes at the participating US institutions favoured closely observing vicarious experiences.

We relate these observations to the findings by Lishinski et al. [26]. In their research on general self-efficacy in an introductory programming course, they observed the influence of performance feedback on the development of self-efficacy. As they used a general self-efficacy scale taken from the *Motivated Strategies for Learning Questionnaire*, this similarity in observations supports convergent construct validity. Lishinski et al. also found female students to exhibit different development patterns than male students: female students were reported to adjust their self-efficacy before the midterm exams while male students started adjusting their self-efficacy after this point. In our analyses using a one-way ANOVA, however, we could not detect statistically significant differences between male and female students for the changes in scores from pre-course to pre-midterm ($F(1, 21) = 0.21$, $p = 0.887$) and post-midterm to post-course ($F(1, 21) = 0.75$, $p = 0.786$). We hypothesize these divergent observations to be related to the different nature of the introductory programming course studied by Lishinski et al. and the introductory algorithms courses studied by us: female students have been reported to have less confidence in their computing ability than male students [3], also it is known that programming-heavy courses and their assignments induce an emotional burden [23]. Combining these two factors with the fact that the midterm was the first feedback that might positively influence self-efficacy can explain the observations of Lishinski et al.. At the same time, these factors and the self-selection also reported by Beyer et al. [3] is suited to

explain why no such gender-based difference could be observed in our study of a much more math-oriented algorithms courses.

For assessing motivational aspects that may influence the self-efficacy after the midterm, we administered a 12-item questionnaire together with the post-midterm questionnaire. The subscales in this instrument were taken from the *Intrinsic Motivation Inventory*—see, e.g., [10]—and referred to "Interest/Enjoyment", "Perceived Competence", and "Pressure/Tension". These scores were checked for correlations with the post-midterm self-efficacy scores as measured by our instrument. Not all variables were normally distributed (Shapiro-Wilk test, $p < 0.05$), so Spearman rank-order correlations were computed. Preliminary analyses showed all relations to be monotonic as assessed by scatterplot.

Table 5 shows that both the "Interest/Enjoyment" and the "Perceived Competence" scores positively correlate with the post-midterm self-efficacy (n_{midterm} = 46). Conversely, the "Pressure/Tension" scores negatively correlate with post-midterm self-efficacy. This is in line with Bandura's theory about the correlations between performance accomplishment and self-efficacy on one hand and emotional arousal and self-efficacy on the other hand [2, p. 195ff.].

In addition, we compared these motivational scores with self-reported midterm graded obtained as part of the post-course evaluation. Reporting these grades was optional, hence, not all students chosen to do so ($n_{\text{reported-grades}}$ = 28). As already observed by Wilson and Shrock [41], no statistically significant correlation between grades and self-efficacy (as reported immediately after having completed the exam) could be observed (Spearman's rank-order, $r_s(28) = -0.203$, $p = 0.300$). Running a Spearman's rank-order correlation on "Pressure/Tension" and self-reported grades, however, showed a rather strong correlation ($r_s(28) = 0.545$, $p = 0.003$). As the grades were coded inverted, i.e., $A = 1$, $B = 2$, and $C = 3$, this shows that high pressure/tension correlated with a low grade. This is of particular interest, as all midterm exams were take-home exams, i.e., it can be assumed that time pressure played a much weaker role than for in-class exams.

7 CONSTRUCT VALIDITY

The validation of an instrument usually requires multiple iterations during which the instrument may be refined. In the context of this paper, we only report on our preliminary steps to assess construct validity. In the previous section, we have discussed how the changes in pre- and post-scores related to general self-efficacy theory. To further investigate construct validity, we followed Peter [33] who distinguishes four aspects of construct validity: reliability, convergent validity, divergent validity, and nomological validity.

---

[8]Due to the small number of subjects for which data was available, we decided not to use a *t*-test.

The reliability, i.e., how much the instrument is correlated with itself was assessed through the alpha reliabilities within the factors (between 0.871 and 0.929, see Table 1) and the statistically significant correlations between the factors (see Table 2). Both measures showed the necessary reliability conditions to be fulfilled.

As the proposed instrument is, to the best of the authors' knowledge, the first instrument directed towards assessing self-efficacy in the domain of introductory algorithms, a multitrait-multimethod matrix [6], the standard method to assess convergent and divergent validity, could not be computed. Instead, we tried to establish nomological and discriminant validity by relating the obtained scores and other psychometric scores obtained together with the algorithms pre-course questionnaire. As in no case all variables were normally distributed (Shapiro-Wilk test, $p < 0.05$), all correlations were computed as Spearman's rank correlations.

Computer Programming Self-Efficacy. This score was determined by administering the instrument developed by Ramalingam and Wiedenbeck [36]. This instrument was administered in all courses together with our instrument during the pre-course tests. Where needed, we restated the items in terms of the programming language used in the preceding programming course. We found a strong positive correlation between programming self-efficacy and algorithms self-efficacy, ($r_s(99) = 0.772, p < 0.001$). At first, this may seem to indicate that the two instrument measure the same construct more than nomological expectations would indicate and, hence, that our instrument is not course-specific enough. However, previous research showed a correlation between performance in introductory programming and introductory algorithms courses [9] indicating that also self-efficacy in these areas may be correlated.

Moreover, divergence was found during the factor analysis. In the original paper, Ramalingam and Wiedenbeck had worked with items asking for the confidence to "complete a programming project" given various degrees of support. These items had been found to constitute a factor labeled "Independence and Persistence". In the design of our instrument, we had restated these items both the "come up with an algorithm" context (Items 6–8) and "analyze the running time" context (Items 11–13). Our exploratory factor analysis (using the same methodology as Ramalingam and Wiedenbeck) clearly separated these two instantiations of Ramalingam and Wiedenbecks' "Independence and Persistence" factor. Instead, the analysis grouped them with different other items indicating that at least on subscale levels the instruments were not measuring identical constructs. We leave to future work whether the domain-specifics overshadow the interpretation of Ramalingam and Wiedenbeck or whether their interpretation of this factor should be revisited.

Self-Regulation. As mentioned in the introduction, we had not included self-regulation items in our instrument. Instead, this score was determined using ten items from Black and Deci's validated scale [4]. Six of these items referred to "Autonomous Regulation", the remaining four items referred to (externally) "Controlled Regulation". We compared these scores with the scores for the "Self-Regulation" factor as determined by Ramalingam and Wiedenbeck's instrument (see above). While positive correlations could be found between this factor and both autonomous and controlled regulation as well as the sum of these, none of these were statistically significant. Again, this suggests a discrimination of our instrument

against the instrument proposed by Ramalingam and Wiedenbeck. Also, the missing convergence between Black and Deci's instrument and the "Self-Regulation" factor of Ramalingam and Wiedenbeck raises interesting revalidation questions for future work.

Personality Traits. According to O'Connor and Paunonen [29], the "Conscientiousness" and "Openness to Experience" personality traits are positively associated with academic success. As self-efficacy has been associated with academic success as well [30, 31], we thus investigated whether nomological validity, i.e., a "relationship between measures purported to assess different (but conceptually related) constructs" [33, p. 137f.] could be established. Personality traits scores were determined using sixteen "Conscientiousness" items and eight "Openness to Experience" items from the NEO personality inventory [27]. We found positive correlations between "Conscientiousness" and both programming self-efficacy ($r_s(99) = 0.383, p < 0.001$) and post-course algorithms self-efficacy ($r_s(99) = 0.322, p = 0.001$); correlation to pre-course algorithms self-efficacy was weaker ($r_s(99) = 0.200, p < 0.05$). "Openness to Experience" was positively correlated to pre-course ($r_s(99) = 0.272, p = 0.006$) and post-course ($r_s(99) = 0.300, p = 0.003$) algorithms self-efficacy; correlation to programming self-efficacy was weaker ($r_s(99) = 0.272, p = 0.012$). These findings are consistent with the interpretation of "Conscientiousness" in terms of motivation and the weaker role of "Openness to Experience" as discussed by O'Connor and Paunonen [29]; thus suggesting nomological validity.

Summary. Summarizing the analyses reported in this section, we conclude that reliability could be confirmed statistically and supporting evidence for nomological validity (through other psychometric score) and divergent validity (through comparison with programming self-efficacy and general self-regulation) can be reported. Due to the lack of alternative instruments, convergent validity could not be examined beyond comparing our instrument with an instrument to assess programming self-efficacy.

8 CONCLUSIONS

We have developed an instrument geared towards assessing self-efficacy in an introductory algorithms course. An exploratory factor analysis showed four main factors which we interpret as "Algorithm Design", "Advanced Paradigms", "Runtime Analysis" and "Pseudocode Writing and Tracing". The results of statistical analyses on the first application of this instrument suggest construct validity with respect to general self-efficacy theory. Additional support for construct validity comes from correlations with related psychological factors, such as motivation and personality traits.

To strengthen the validity argument and to increase the confidence in making judgements using this instrument in broader student populations, we plan to extend the context of applicability and to apply this instrument at institutions with a broader range of selectivity. Also, we aim at identifying topics and corresponding items for which extreme changes or no changes at all can be observed when assessing self-efficacy; this will enable us to examine the influence of teaching methodologies on algorithms self-efficacy.

Acknowledgments. We thank the participating instructors for their cooperation and B. Köpcke and J. Seep for entering the data. This work was partially supported by the German Federal Ministry of Education and Research (grant 01PB14007A).

REFERENCES

[1] A. R. Artino Jr. Academic self-efficacy: from educational theory to instructional practice. *Perspectives in Medical Education*, 1:76–85, 2012.

[2] A. Bandura. Self-efficacy: Toward a unifying theory of behavioral change. *Psychological Review*, 84(2):191–215, 1977.

[3] S. Beyer, K. Rynes, J. Perrault, K. Hay, and S. Haller. Gender differences in computer science students. In S. Grissom, D. Knox, D. Joyce, and W. Dann, editors, *Proceedings of the 34th SIGCSE Technical Symposium on Computer Science Education*, pages 49–53. ACM Press, 2003.

[4] A. E. Black and E. L. Deci. The effects of instructors' autonomy support and students' autonomous motivation on learning organic chemistry: A self-determination theory perspective. *Science Education*, 84(6):740–756, Nov. 2000.

[5] J. M. Bland and D. G. Altman. Statistics notes: Cronbach's alpha. *British Medical Journal*, 314:572, Feb. 1997.

[6] D. T. Campbell and D. W. Fiske. Convergent and discriminant validation by the multitrait-multimethod matrix. *Psychological Bulletin*, 56(2):81–105, Mar. 1959.

[7] A. R. Carberry, H.-S. Lee, and M. W. Ohland. Measuring engineering design self-efficacy. *Journal of Engineering Education*, 99(1):71–79, Jan. 2010.

[8] J. M. Cohoon. Gendered experiences of computing graduate programs. In I. Russell, S. M. Haller, J. D. Dougherty, and S. H. Rodger, editors, *Proceedings of the 38th SIGCSE Technical Symposium on Computer Science Education*, pages 546–550. ACM Press, 2007.

[9] H. Danielsiek and J. Vahrenhold. Stay on these roads: Potential factors indicating students' performance in a CS2 course. In C. Alphonce, J. Tims, M. E. Caspersen, and S. Edwards, editors, *Proceedings of the 47th SIGCSE Technical Symposium on Computer Science Education (SICGSE 2016)*, pages 12–17. ACM Press, 2016.

[10] E. L. Deci, H. Eghari, B. C. Patrick, and D. R. Leone. Facilitating internalization: The self-determination theory perspective. *Journal of Personality*, 62(1):119–142, Dec. 1994.

[11] P. Denny, A. Luxton-Reilly, J. Hamer, D. B. Dahlstrom, and H. C. Purchase. Self-predicted and actual performance in an introductory programming course. In R. Ayfer, J. Impagliazzo, and C. Laxer, editors, *Proceedings of the 15th Annual SIGCSE Conference on Innovation and Technology in Computer Science Education, ITiCSE 2010*, pages 118–122, New York City, 2010. ACM.

[12] D. M. Dowling. *The Development of a Mathematics Confidence Scale and Its Application in the Study of Confidence in Women College Students*. PhD thesis, Ohio State University, 1978.

[13] P. H. Dunham. *Mathematical Confidence and Performance in Technology-Enhanced Precalculus: Gender-Related Differences*. PhD thesis, Ohio State University, 1990.

[14] C. S. Dweck. *Self-theories: Their role in motivation, personality, and development*. Psychology Press, Philadelphia, PA, 1999.

[15] C. A. Farrington, M. Roderick, E. Allensworth, J. Nagaoka, T. S. Keyes, D. W. Johnson, and N. O. Beechum. *Teaching adolescents to become learners. The role of noncognitive factors in shaping school performance: A critical literature review*. University of Chicago Consortium on Chicago School Research, Chicago, 2012.

[16] M. P. Fay and M. A. Proschan. Wilcoxon-Mann-Whitney or t-test? on assumptions for hypothesis testing and multiple interpretations of decision rules. *Statistics Surveys*, 4:1–39, 2010.

[17] J. Gal-Ezer and E. Zur. The efficiency of algorithms – misconceptions. *Computers & Education*, 42:215–226, 2004.

[18] D. Ginat and Y. Blau. Multiple levels of abstraction in algorithmic problem solving. In M. E. Caspersen, S. Edwards, T. Barnes, and D. D. Garcia, editors, *Proceedings of the 48th SIGCSE Technical Symposium on Computer Science Education (SICGSE 2017)*, pages 237–242. ACM Press, 2017.

[19] P. Gray. Declining student resilience: A serious problem for colleges. *Psychology Today*, 2015. Blog post (Sep. 22): https://www.psychologytoday.com/blog/freedom-learn/201509/declining-student-resilience-serious-problem-colleges.

[20] G. Hackett and N. E. Betz. Mathematics self-efficacy expectations, math performance, and the consideration of math-related majors. Paper presented at the Annual Meeting of the American Educational Research Association, Mar. 1982. 42 pages.

[21] M. Hertz. What do CS1 and CS2 mean?: Investigating differences in the early courses. In T. Cortina and E. Walker, editors, *Proceedings of the 41st SIGCSE Technical Symposium on Computer Science Education (SIGCSE 2010)*, pages 199–203. ACM Press, 2010.

[22] H. F. Kaiser and J. Rice. Little Jiffy, Mark IV. *Educational and Psychological Measurement*, 34(1):111–117, Sept. 1974.

[23] P. Kinnunen and B. Simon. Experiencing programming assignments in CS1: the emotional toll. In M. E. Caspersen, M. J. Clancy, and K. Sanders, editors, *Proceedings of the 6th International Workshop on Computing Education Research (ICER 2010)*, pages 77–86. ACM Press, 2010.

[24] P. Kinnunen and B. Simon. CS majors' self-efficacy perceptions in CS1: Results in light of social cognitive theory. In M. E. Caspersen, A. Clear, and K. Sanders, editors, *Proceedings of the 7th International Workshop on Computing Education Research (ICER 2011)*, pages 19–26. ACM Press, 2011.

[25] R. W. Lent and S. D. Brown. Towards a unifying social cognitive theory of career and academic interest, choice, and performance. *Journal of Vocational Behavior*, 45(1):79–122, 1994.

[26] A. Lishinski, A. Yadav, J. Good, and R. Enbody. Learning to program: Gender differences and interactive effects of students' motivation, goals, and self-efficacy on performance. In J. Sheard, J. Tenenberg, D. Chinn, and B. Dorn, editors, *Proceedings of the 2016 ACM Conference on International Computing Education Research (ICER 2016)*, pages 221–220. ACM Press, 2016.

[27] J. L. Maples, L. Guan, N. T. Carter, and J. D. Miller. A test of the international personality item pool representation of the revised NEO personality inventory and development of a 120-item IPIP-based measure of the five-factor model. *Psychological Assessment*, 26(4):1070–1084, Dec. 2014.

[28] L. Murphy and L. Thomas. Dangers of a fixed mindset: Implications of self-theories research for computer science education. In J. Amillo, C. Laxer, E. M. Ruiz, and A. Young, editors, *Proceedings of the 13th Annual SIGCSE Conference on Innovation and Technology in Computer Science Education, ITiCSE 2008*, pages 271–275, New York City, 2008. ACM.

[29] M. C. O'Connor and S. V. Paunonen. Big five personality predictors of post-secondary academic performance. *Personality and Individual Differences*, 43(5):971–990, 2007.

[30] F. Pajares and M. D. Miller. Role of self-efficacy and self-concept beliefs in mathematical problem solving: A path analysis. *Journal of Educational Psychology*, 86(2):193–203, 1994.

[31] F. Pajares and D. H. Schunk. Self-beliefs and school success: Self-efficacy, self-concept, and school achievement. In R. Riding and S. Rayner, editors, *Perception*, pages 239–266. Ablex Publishing, London, 2001.

[32] J. Perrenet and E. Kaasenbrood. Levels of abstraction in students' understanding of the concept of algorithm: the qualitative perspective. In R. Davoli, M. Goldweber, and P. Salomoni, editors, *Proceedings of the 11th Annual SIGCSE Conference on Innovation and Technology in Computer Science Education, ITiCSE 2006*, pages 270–274, New York City, 2006. ACM.

[33] J. P. Peter. Construct validity: A review of basic issues and marketing practices. *Journal of Marketing Research*, 18(2):133–145, May 1981.

[34] A. Quade. Development and validation of a computer science self-efficacy scale for CS0 courses and the group analysis of CS0 student self-efficacy. In *Proceedings of the International Conference on Information Technology: Computers and Communications (ITCCi03)*, pages 60–64. IEEE Computer Society, 2003.

[35] V. Ramalingam, D. LaBelle, and S. Wiedenbeck. Self-efficacy and mental models in learning to program. In R. D. Boyle, M. Clark, and A. Kumar, editors, *Proceedings of the 9th Annual SIGCSE Conference on Innovation and Technology in Computer Science Education, ITiCSE 2004*, pages 171–175, New York City, 2004. ACM.

[36] V. Ramalingam and S. Wiedenbeck. Development and validation of scores on a computer programming self-efficacy scale and groups analyses of novice programmer self-efficacy. *Journal of Educational Computing Research*, 19(4):367–381, Dec. 1998.

[37] T. M. Rawson, D. P. Hoyt, and D. J. Teeter. Identifying "comparable" insitutions. *Research in Higher Education*, 18(3):299–310, 1983.

[38] B. Simon, B. Hanks, L. Murphy, S. Fitzgerald, R. McCauley, L. Thomas, and C. Zander. Saying isn't necessarily believing: influencing self-theories in computing. In M. E. Caspersen, R. Lister, and M. Clancy, editors, *Proceedings of the Fourth International Computing Education Research Workshop, ICER 2008*, pages 173–184, New York City, 2008. ACM.

[39] J. Vahrenhold and W. Paul. Developing and validating test items for first-year computer science courses. *Computer Science Education*, 24(4):304–333, Dec. 2014.

[40] R. Wilcon. An epidemic of anguish: Overwhelmed by demand for mental-health care, colleges face conflicts in choosing how to respond. *Higher Education Chronicle*, 2015. Aug. 21, http://chronicle.com/article/An-Epidemic-of-Anguish/232721.

[41] B. C. Wilson and S. Shrock. Contributing to success in an introductory computer science course: A study of twelve factors. In H. M. Walker, R. A. McCauley, J. L. Gersting, and I. Russell, editors, *Proceedings of the 32nd SIGCSE Technical Symposium on Computer Science Education*, pages 184–188. ACM Press, 2001.

[42] D. Zingaro. Peer instruction contributes to success in CS1. In J. D. Dougherty, K. Nagel, A. Decker, and K. Eiselt, editors, *Proceedings of the 45th SIGCSE Technical Symposium on Computer Science Education (SICGSE 2014)*, pages 373–378. ACM Press, 2014.

Dual Modality Code Explanations for Novices: Unexpected Results

Briana B. Morrison
University of Nebraska at Omaha
6001 Dodge Street
Omaha, NE 68182
bbmorrison@unomaha.edu

ABSTRACT

The research in both cognitive load theory and multimedia principles for learning indicates presenting information using both diagrams and accompanying audio explanations yields better learning performance than using diagrams with text explanations. While this is a common practice in introductory programming courses, often called "live coding," it has yet to be empirically tested. This paper reports on an experiment to determine if auditory explanations of code result in improved learning performance over written explanations. Students were shown videos explaining short code segments one of three ways: text only explanations, auditory only explanations, or both text and auditory explanations, thus replicating experiments from other domains. The results from this study do not support the findings from other disciplines and we offer explanations for why this may be the case.

CCS CONCEPTS

• **Social and professional topics** → **K-12 education**; **Computer science education**;

KEYWORDS

cognitive load; modality; live coding

1 INTRODUCTION

Cognitive load theory (CLT) describes the role of the learner's memory during the learning process. The central problem identified by CLT is that learning is impaired when the total amount of processing requirements exceeds the limited capacity of working memory [43]. By minimizing undesirable loads within the instructional materials, the learner's memory can hold more relevant information, thereby improving the effectiveness of the learning process.

CLT has been used to explain key research findings. One example of this is the *split-attention effect*. Some worked examples have been found to be ineffective for improving learning. This occurs when learners have to split their attention between at least two sources of information, each of which is necessary for learning the material. This can occur when the information for learning is split into different pieces which are separated spatially or temporally.

The information in the pieces is required to learn the material and each piece would make no sense alone. Because the learner must integrate all the disparate sources of information, the cognitive load to do so is unnecessarily high when the sources are separated by space or time. Having to switch focus and attention between two or more sources requires information to be maintained in working memory while searching and processing interacting elements in the linked source. Sweller states that "cognitive load theory does not distinguish between text and diagrams, text and text, or diagrams and diagrams" as contributors to a split-attention effect. [50, p.98]

Another recognized research finding has been labelled the *modality effect*. Modality is a particular form of sensory perception. In this context it pertains to how the information within the instructional materials is delivered to the learner. The modality effect occurs when the information to be learned is being delivered through multiple sensory channels –namely the auditory and visual channels. While the modality effect has been well documented as effective in other disciplines, it has yet to be empirically tested within the domain of computer science and introductory programming. Instructors presenting code in class often utilize dual modality: while code is displayed via a shared display, the instructor explains the code verbally. The students may concentrate on looking at code while the instructor explains the code. This removes the split-attention problem of a textbook. Intuitively we may believe this is an effective pedagogical technique and aids in student learning by reducing cognitive load, but what evidence do we have?

This paper reports on a study designed to empirically test the modality effect in computer science, specifically introductory programming. Given trends toward active learning classrooms and research for multimedia instructional design, we developed instructional material in an online format. All available recommendations for designing the instructional materials were used to create videos explaining small code examples in one of three formats: 1) auditory only explanations, 2) text only explanations, or 3) auditory and text explanations. This experiment design is a replication of studies conducted in other disciplines which confirmed the modality effect. We sought to answer the research question: **Does altering the modality (text, oral, both) of code explanations improve student learning as measured by retention and transfer questions?** Before the study we had two hypotheses: 1) Students receiving oral explanations will demonstrate better retention of the material, and 2) Students receiving both oral and text explanations will demonstrate the worst retention of the material. These hypotheses correspond with previous research findings. First we present the background literature in which this study is grounded. We then present the study method followed by the data analysis and results. We conclude with a discussion of the results and the implications for the research community and instructors.

2 BACKGROUND

To understand the basis for the study, we present a brief overview of Cognitive Load Theory followed by measurement techniques of cognitive load. Then previous research on the modality effect is discussed. We conclude with a summary of the necessary conditions in order to produce the modality effect.

2.1 Cognitive Load Theory

According to the original definition of CLT [51, 56, 63], instruction can impose three different types of cognitive load on a student's working memory: intrinsic load, extraneous load, and germane load. Intrinsic load (IL) is defined as a combination of the innate difficulty of the material being learned as well as the learner's characteristics [28]. A topic is considered to have a high IL if the material being learned is interconnected; that is, learning requires processing several elements simultaneously to understand their relations and interactions [55]. Intrinsic load can also vary with the domain expertise and previous knowledge of the learner [53] in that learners with a higher level of previous knowledge may chunk the material differently than novices [8], allowing them to hold more information in working memory. Extraneous load (EL) is the load placed on working memory that does not contribute directly toward the learning of the material –for example, the resources consumed while understanding poorly written text or diagrams without sufficient clarity [28]. The IL and EL are the factors that can be controlled through instructional design. The final category is that of germane load (GL) which are the instructional features that are *necessary* for learning the material [28]. One of the assumptions of original CLT is that these three components are additive [44]. If the extraneous load is using most of the capacity in working memory, little can be devoted to the germane load. However, the more recent consensus among researchers is that the three components –intrinsic, extraneous, and germane –are not additive to an overall sum [24]. Researchers now consider that cognitive load consists of the use of resources, both germane and extraneous. It is now believed that instructional material can help to reduce the extraneous load and minimize the intrinsic load thus leaving the remaining working memory free for learning [52].

2.2 Measuring Cognitive Load

Since the identification of CLT, researchers have searched for a means to measure cognitive load. To date, this has been accomplished through indirect, subjective, and direct measures. Indirect measures of cognitive load use production system models [4, 49] or learner performance indicators [11, 12] including error rates [4, 5]. Subjective measures of cognitive load include survey instruments that ask users to assess their mental effort [38, 40, 42, p.429]. The subjective rating scale has been shown to be the most sensitive measure available to differentiate the cognitive load imposed by different instructional methods [53] and have been consistent in matching performance data predicted by CLT [33]. The subjective scale has been used extensively to measure the relative cognitive load of different instructional methods with over 25 studies having used it between 1992 and 2002 [37]. Another subjective measurement is an efficiency measure for cognitive load [39], which combines both mental effort with task performance indicators. Over 30 cognitive load theory related studies have used this efficiency measure [61].

Two basic means of measuring cognitive load through direct measures have been used in research: using a dual task [9, 13, 60] and physiological measurements such as measurements of heart rates [41], pupillary response [59], EEGs [2], and eye tracking [58, 62].

Several researchers have attempted to distinguish between and measure the different types of cognitive load. Ayres attempted to keep the extraneous cognitive load (EL) constant between treatments thus attributing the differences to a change in intrinsic load (IL) [3]. DeLeeuw and Mayer used a mixed approach (both subjective measures and a secondary task method) to investigate if different instruments could measure the three loads separately [15]. The results indicated that different measures do tap into different processes and show varying sensitivities. In an attempt to measure the different cognitive load categories, Gerjets, Scheiter, and Catrambone selected three items from the NASA-TLX [21] associated with task demands [16, 17]. The researchers argued that the three items selected (mental and physical activity required, effort to understand the contents, and navigational demands of the learning environment) could be mapped to the intrinsic, germane, and extraneous loads, respectively. The test manipulated the complexity of worked examples. While the groups with the highest learning outcomes reported the lowest cognitive load, there was no corroborating evidence that the three measures corresponded to the different types of cognitive load as proposed.

In 2013, Leppink et al.[28] developed an instrument specifically for measuring different types of cognitive load which consists of a ten question subjective survey. This study revealed that none of the existing survey tools adequately separated the three types of cognitive load in that each had significant cross-loading between factors. However the newly developed survey yielded results that were consistent with outcomes based on CLT. Leppink et al. [29] extended their 2013 work by adapting the survey instrument to another domain, that of learning languages, and replicated their analyses. These new findings reinforce the strong support for the survey measuring both intrinsic and extraneous load, but found less support for the direct measure of germane load. In 2014, Morrison et al. [35] adapted the Leppink survey instrument to the programming domain and provided initial validation. This is the instrument used in this study.

2.3 Modality Effect Research

Research in both cognitive load theory [54] and multimedia principles for learning [31] indicates presenting information using both diagrams with audio explanations yields better learning performance than using diagrams with text explanations. According to the available models of multimedia learning [32, 45], cognitive processing of related text and pictures involves the selection and organization of the relevant elements of visual and auditory information, resulting in a coherent unified representation. All this is processed in the learner's working memory. CLT argues that limited working memory can be effectively expanded by using more than one presentation modality.

Working memory consists of three subsystems: a phonological loop, a visuospatial sketchpad, and a central executive [6]. The phonological loop processes auditory information while the visuospatial sketchpad processes pictorial or written information. Because these are separate processes, we can assume that each have capacity and duration limitations. In some situations we can effectively increase the capacity of working memory by utilizing both processors.

In [36], the authors found that a visually presented geometry diagram, combined with aurally presented statements, enhanced learning compared to a conventional, visual-only presentation. In a split-attention situation, increasing effective working memory by using more than one modality produced a positive effect on learning. In [57], the authors used elementary electrical engineering instructions to show that an audio/visual diagram format was superior to purely visual instructions. The cognitive load measurement tool [42] was used to support the suggestion that the effect can be attributed to cognitive load factors. In [26] the authors confirmed that a dual-mode presentation of instructional information is a viable alternative to physical integration of all written materials (eliminating split-attention) within an elementary electrical engineering domain. In addition, Mayer [32] presents evidence of several studies done in the multimedia medium with animated videos and spoken explanations and reveals findings which indicate that the spoken explanation was only effective when done simultaneously rather than sequentially with the visually presented information. Kalyuga [25] provides an overview of all modality studies alongside instructional implications.

One modality study in computer science [48] involved students debugging introductory programs with a modified development environment that used auditory cues. Students were assigned to one specific modality interface (text only, auditory only, or both) and asked to complete comprehension questions and debugging tasks. No statistical significance between the modalities existed for the comprehension questions, but the auditory only interface was statistically worse for the debugging tasks. This study did not involve learning new material but only performance on tasks previously learned.

There are limitations as to when the modality effect will affect learning. Textual information presented in spoken form will not generate a modality effect if it merely re-describes a diagram. The information presented in the diagram and the textual information must be unintelligible by themselves. If a diagram and text are being used, both must contain information that requires learners to refer to the other source in order to enable comprehension [54].

Ginns conducted a meta-analysis of modality effects based on 43 different experiments [18]. The meta-analysis generally supported the positive effects of dual-modality presentations. However, two major moderators were found: the level of element interactivity and the pacing of the presentation. Generally, only problems with a high level of element interactivity will benefit from a dual-modality presentation. The benefit of a dual-modality presentation can be lost, however, if the interactivity is excessively high. Strong effects of a dual-modality presentation were found only under system-paced conditions or fixed timings.

2.4 Summary

Given that research shows the modality effect is present in some instances while not in others, we sought to design the instructional materials for this study to result in a modality effect. In other words, we attempted to follow all recommendations to cause the modality effect to occur. In essence, this study is a replication of [26, 36, 57] within the computer programming domain. Using the known limitations of when the modality effect occurs, examples were specifically

selected and instructional materials developed with the expectation that the experiment would show that the modality effect holds with novice programmers.

Sweller et al. [54] list the following conditions required to obtain the modality effect:

- Diagrammatic and textual information must refer to each other and be unintelligible unless they are processed together.
- Element interactivity must be high, but not excessive.
- Auditory text should be limited. Any lengthy, complex text should be written, not spoken.
- If the diagrams are complex, cuing or signaling may be required so that learners can focus on the appropriate portion of the diagram and not be forced to search for the relevant piece.

In this experiment, the code and the explanations are separate pieces of information for the learner that need to be processed together to be understood. Learners for this experiment are complete novices, with many having never seen any code before. It is expected that seeing only the source code or hearing only the explanation would not be enough information to acquire the desired knowledge. Source code elements, or tokens, are highly interactive as they depend upon each other to be understood and interpreted. The explanations were designed to be simple and limited. Signaling was utilized during the explanations to illustrate the line of code being explained. Explanations were not strictly line by line or top-down, but done in chunks of program execution.

We have limited evidence that people see code segments more as a diagram rather than text to be read [20]. We know that expert programmers do not read a program line by line to understand it [10]. Instead, they group the lines of code into 'chunks' which represent a purpose. This is similar to what chess grand masters do when they see a chess board [19], or what physics experts do when examining a diagram by classifying the problem by the components within the diagram ([7, 54]). Jeffries suggests that novices may begin by reading code segments as text [22], however eye-tracking data suggests that novices transition to an expert style of viewing code as they learn [34].

3 STUDY METHOD

We designed a series of videos, each with the purpose of explaining a single segment of code written in Python. Three different introductory programming topics were addressed: assignment with mathematical operators, nested selection (if) statements, and finding an element within a collection (using a for loop). In addition, an appropriate context or real life scenario was derived to motivate the problem. In video 1, the problem is summing lines of an invoice, calculating the tax due and then the final total for the invoice. In the second video, the code determines whether or not a donor and recipient have compatible blood types. The final video presents how to find the next possible movie time from a list of movie times.

3.1 Instructional Materials

Within each video, the problem was presented followed by an explanation of the code. Each explanation presented the overall solution outline followed by an explanation of each line of code, much like an instructor would do in class. Each video then concluded with an explanation of one or more traces of execution of the code with sample values.

Recipient	Donor O−	O+	A−	A+	B−	B+	AB−	AB+
O−	✓	✗	✗	✗	✗	✗	✗	✗
O+	✓	✓	✗	✗	✗	✗	✗	✗
A−	✓	✗	✓	✗	✗	✗	✗	✗
A+	✓	✓	✓	✗	✗	✗	✗	✗
B−	✓	✗	✗	✓	✓	✗	✗	✗
B+	✓	✓	✗	✗	✓	✓	✗	✗
AB−	✓	✗	✓	✗	✓	✗	✓	✗
AB+	✓	✓	✓	✓	✓	✓	✓	✓

Red blood cell compatibility table

Figure 1: Red Blood Cell Compatibility Table

After each video the participant was asked a series of questions. The first question always asked the purpose of the code segment for verification of understanding. This was followed by one or more recall questions concerning the purpose of variables or interpretation of a given line of code. One or more application questions were then presented, asking the participant to predict the output for a segment of code from the original example. The last questions were transfer questions, asking the learner to apply their new knowledge to novel problems. All transfer questions were taken in their original form or adapted from [1]. A final question allowed the participant to indicate if there were any technical issues with the video. This added up to a total of eight questions after each video.

3.1.1 Video 1. The first example is straightforward using mathematical operators and the assignment statement to compute the total price from quantities and prices in an invoice. After the video there were four recall questions concerning the purpose of the code, number of invoice lines processed, and the purpose of variables. There was one application question concerning the ability of a variable to appear on both sides of an assignment type. This was followed by two transfer questions involving assignment statements only. The final question asked about technical difficulties.

3.1.2 Video 2. The second example involves nested selection statements and determining if a donor's and recipient's blood types are compatible, including the Rh factor. Participants were shown the problem definition along with a chart indicating blood type compatibility (Figure 1). Two examples were described on how to read and interpret the table. The code was then explained, followed with two examples tracing through the code, one for a compatibility match and one for an incompatible match. Recall questions covered the purpose of the code, possible values for a boolean variable, the name of the function, and the second thing checked for blood compatibility. The one application question involved tracing a portion of the nested selection statements. Two transfer questions were then asked, both with nested selections statements. The final question asked about technical difficulties.

This second example was written to include a "main" program along with a function call and function definition. This was done purposefully to allow for easy changing of the values of the variables for compatibility testing.

```
qty = 15
price = 15.67
amt = qty * price
total = amt
qty = 250
price = 0.32
amt = qty * price
total = total + amt
tax = total * 0.08
total = total + tax
```

Figure 2: Signaling Example

3.1.3 Video 3. The third video describes finding the next possible movie time from a list of non-sequential movie times and involved a loop. The participant was given the problem definition and an outline of the solution approach followed by an explanation of the code. The video concluded by tracing through two executions with sample values. The recall questions for this video were the purpose of the code, understanding the solution, and representation of the data. The application question asked the user to determine what would happen if all the movie times had already passed for the day. There were the usual three transfer questions and the final question on technical difficulties. All loops in the example and questions used the `for` loop format.

3.1.4 Design Considerations. It should be noted that the videos were designed with the purpose of minimizing cognitive load. During the explanation of the code, there was signaling indicating which line or lines were being discussed (Figure 2). When examples were being traced, the variable values and results of comparisons were integrated into the code diagram (Figure 3). There were no code comments for the first video, minimal (2 lines) of comments for the second video, and only a few lines of comments for the third and most complex video.

For each problem solved, the exercise was presented and followed by an algorithm, then the initial code. After the explanation of the code, a sample trace using test values was explained. The second example given in each video allowed a pause for participants to attempt to trace through the code on their own before the solution was presented.

A script for the code explanation was written for each problem. For each video, three different versions were created: one with an audio only code explanation (no text explanation other than

```
def match (recipientType, recipientRh, donorType, donorRh):
    <lines 2-13>                                      ("B", 0, "O", 0)
#now consider Rh;
    if compatible == True:        to match with blood types that match
      if donorRh == 1:            orRh is +, then recipientRh must be +
        if recipientRh == 1:
            compatible = True
        else:
            compatible = False
    return compatible
```

Figure 3: Code Tracing Example

the code), one with a text only explanation (no sound), and one that combined both the text explanation and the audio explanation simultaneously. (See Figure 4 to illustrate the text only condition.) The line(s) of code currently being explained was highlighted in all three treatments. At the conclusion of each video, a summary page was presented.

The time, with one exception, was controlled for within each treatment and participants were instructed not to pause the videos except where instructed. The time spent on each screen was constant for all three versions. It was determined how long it took to read the current text on the screen using the reading time of an average 17 year old (plus a slight delay), and the audio was controlled to match that time. The one exception was when the participant was asked to trace through the code for the second example in each video. The instructions asked the user to pause the video while the code was showing and walk through the example. They were asked to continue the video when they knew the expected output.

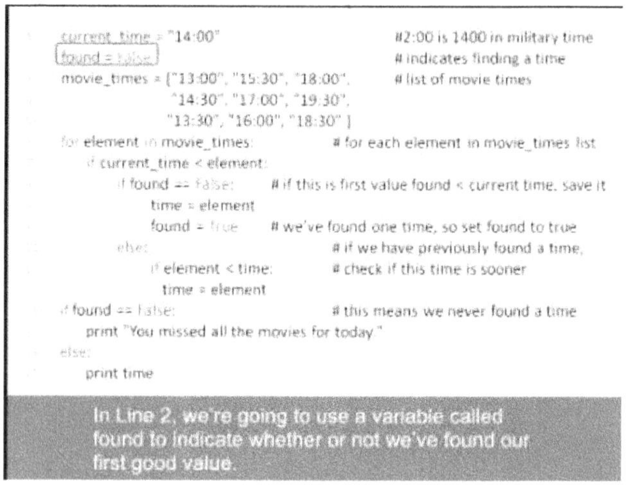

3.2 Participants

Participants were recruited from introductory programming courses or breadth-first (CS0) courses at multiple universities in the southeast United States via the internet or class announcements. Having read and given consent, participants were given a pre-test in order to eliminate those that had too much programming knowledge. Based upon the day of their birth, they were assigned to one of the three study conditions (audio only, text only, or both audio and text). After viewing each video they were asked to complete the CS cognitive load questionnaire [35], followed by a series of questions designed to determine how much information they recalled, how much they could apply, and how well they could transfer the knowledge. The only compensation participants received was an entry into a raffle for an Amazon gift card. At the conclusion of watching the videos, they were asked a series of demographic questions. The demographic questions were moved to the end to prevent stereotype threat [46, 47]. For the participants that answered the demographic questions, the average age of participants whose data was analyzed was 21.04, with a minimum of 18 and a maximum of 42. The median age was 19. In terms of their native language, 39 of the participants spoke English, 6 spoke Dutch, 2 spoke Korean, and 8 spoke other languages.

4 DATA ANALYSIS AND RESULTS

Data was collected from August 13, 2014 to November 29, 2014. See Table 1 for participant numbers and Table 2 for participants disaggregated by treatment.

Many participants did not view all three videos (Figure 5). Participants were given the option to quit the study after answering questions for each video. When piloting this study, the most common complaint was the overall length of the study, which caused participants to exit before completion. To improve participation, the incentive for the participants was changed to one raffle entry for each video and set of questions completed, and an extra raffle entry if all three videos were completed. If the participant chose to quit after answering questions for a video they were routed to the demographic questions in an effort to collect that information from all participants. Generally, if the participant continued on to the second video, they watched all three videos.

```
current_time = "14:00"              #2:00 is 1400 in military time
found = false                        # indicates finding a time
movie_times = ["13:00", "15:30", "18:00",   # list of movie times
               "14:30", "17:00", "19:30",
               "13:30", "16:00", "18:30" ]
for element in movie_times:          # for each element in movie_times list
    if current_time < element:
        if found == false:           # if this is first value found < current time, save it
            time = element
            found = true             # we've found one time, so set found to true
        else:                        # if we have previously found a time,
            if element < time:       # check if this time is sooner
                time = element
if found == false:                   # this means we never found a time
    print "You missed all the movies for today."
else:
    print time
```

In Line 2, we're going to use a variable called found to indicate whether or not we've found our first good value.

Figure 4: Modality Study Example

Day of the month was used to randomly assign participants to a treatment because the survey package used, SurveyMonkey, did not support random assignment of participants to treatments. This resulted in an unequal assignment of participants to treatments. 36 participants were assigned to the text group, 30 were assigned to the audio group, but only 22 were assigned to the "both" group. Thus for the text only group, 62% of the participants assigned to the treatment went on to watch the first video and have their data analyzed. For the audio only group, 80% of the participants completed the first video and had data analyzed. However for the "both" treatment, only 50% of the participants assigned to the treatment had their data analyzed. This may be because these participants found having both video and audio explanations confusing or experienced cognitive overload and thus chose to end their participation in the experiment early.

The average and standard deviation were calculated for the cognitive load components for each video per treatment (Table 3). In

Table 1: Participant Numbers

	N	Comment
Consented	141	
Non blank answers	99	Participants with all blanks removed
Novices (pre-test)	88	Those with a score of 67% or better (6 out of 9 possible points) were eliminated for having too much knowledge
Assigned treatment	77	Birth date question answered
Answered post video	61	Answered all video questions
Demographic data	55	Answered demographic data

Table 2: Participants by Treatment

Treatment	N
Audio	24
Text	26
Both	11

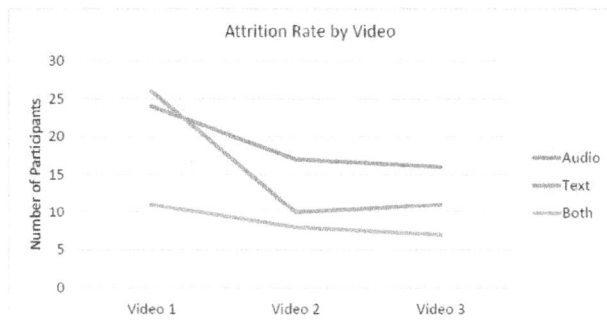

Figure 5: Participant Attrition by Video

Table 3: Cognitive Load Components by Video / Treatment

Treatment		Video 1	Video 2	Video 3
Audio	N	24	17	16
	IL avg (stddev)	3.35 (3.12)	4.69 (3.50)	3.92 (2.70)
	EL avg (stddev)	1.75 (2.05)	1.85 (2.38)	2.23 (2.78)
	GL avg (stddev)	6.10 (2.77)	5.18 (3.36)	6.09 (2.93)
Text	N	26	10	11
	IL avg (stddev)	3.31 (3.05)	4.27 (2.32)	4.27 (2.54)
	EL avg (stddev)	2.94 (2.88)	3.17 (2.55)	2.85 (2.44)
	GL avg (stddev)	6.04 (2.88)	5.5 (2.36)	5.34 (2.56)
Both	N	11	8	7
	IL avg (stddev)	2.55 (3.08)	3.92 (3.02)	2.62 (2.27)
	EL avg (stddev)	1.70 (2.04)	1.96 (2.06)	2.10 (2.76)
	GL avg (stddev)	6.14 (2.51)	6.34 (2.06)	6.46 (2.3)

all three groups the germane load (GL) was perceived as the highest component and the extraneous load (EL) was perceived as the lowest component. In addition video 2 consistently had the highest, intrinsic load (IL) measure. A statistical analysis was performed to determine if correlations existed between the cognitive load factors and treatment and all results were statistically insignificant (IL, $p = .375$, EL, $p = .715$, GL, $p = .628$).

Using learning performance as an indirect measure of cognitive load, we looked at the post-test results. The post-test questions for each video were scored for correctness by the author. For the open-ended purpose question, a rubric was developed and answers were scored for correctness out of 4 points. For multi-select multiple-choice questions, the number of incorrect choices was subtracted from the number of correct choices to get a final score. The results for each video by treatment can be seen in Table 4. For the purpose question, the average score (out of 4) is given along with the percentage of answers that were completely correct. The remaining questions were multiple choice questions and the percentage of correct answers are given.

A statistical analysis was done to determine if any correlations existed between treatment and participant performance. All results were statistically insignificant. There was no main effect for treatment, $F_{(2, 52)} = 0.178$, MSE = 1.145, $p = .837$.

We grouped the results by question type to explore if there was a difference in performance based on treatment and question type. Recall that based on prior research, we would expect the audio

Table 4: Post Test Results of Modality Study

		Treatment		
		Audio	Text	Both
Video 1	Purpose (% correct)	3.13 (54)	2.57 (42)	2.46 (27)
	first question (% correct)	46	23	18
	second question	83	46	64
	third question	50	46	45
	fourth question	42	23	45
	fifth question	33	38	36
	sixth question	17	46	36
Video 2	Purpose (% correct)	3.06 (65)	3.4 (80)	3.5 (88)
	first question	47	60	50
	second question	47	20	75
	third question	82	100	75
	fourth question	47	90	50
	fifth question	6	40	25
	sixth question	41	60	38
Video 3	Purpose (% correct)	3.29 (56)	2.91 (64)	2.29 (29)
	first question	56	73	57
	second question	19	9	0
	third question	75	73	43
	fourth question	44	55	43
	fifth question	19	18	29
	sixth question	19	27	29

only condition to perform the best in general and the group that received explanations in both audio and text to perform the worst.

As can be seen in Figure 6 which examines only the purpose question, video 2 had the best performance even though it was the longest video. While video 1 displays the expected performance based on treatment, the other videos do not. In fact, video 2 shows the exact opposite performance of what would be expected from prior research. In looking at the questions that asked learners to recall learned information (Figure 7), the average performance across all three videos is the expected result. However, in looking at each individual video, the results do not match prior research. It is interesting to note that video 3, arguably considered the most difficult concept (loops), had the best performance for both the audio and text groups. The final category of questions asked learners to transfer their newly acquired knowledge to novel problems and can be seen in Figure 8. None of the groups performed particularly well on the transfer problems, with a maximum of 50%. Interestingly, the text only group performed the best on the transfer questions.

The results from this study do not match what was found in the original studies and what we expected to find in this study. In the auditory only group, the code explanations were given aurally only along with color coded signaling. This was the group that was expected to have the best performance, especially with recall questions. If the modality principle was to hold in computer science, the audio treatment participants should have scored significantly higher statistically than the other two groups. The group that received both written text and an auditory explanation was expected to perform the worst on the learning performance tasks. While we expected these predictions to hold for all three videos, it should have held for at least the first and most simple of the videos, but it did not.

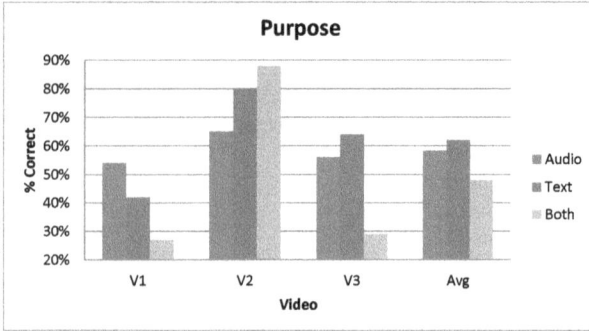

Figure 6: Performance on Purpose Question by Treatment

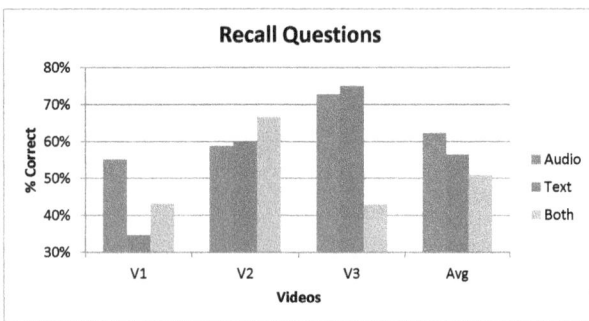

Figure 7: Performance on Recall Questions by Treatment

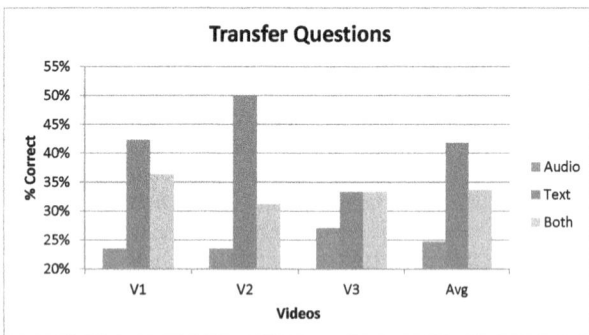

Figure 8: Performance on Transfer Questions by Treatment

To answer the research question, **we find no evidence to support either hypothesis: H1: Students receiving oral explanations will demonstrate better retention. H2: Students receiving both oral and text explanations will demonstrate the worst retention.** We find no evidence that altering the modality (text, oral, both) of code explanations improves student learning as measured by retention and transfer questions.

5 DISCUSSION

Seeing that the anticipated results were not obtained, we must examine if it is because the modality principle does not hold within

the programming domain or if there are other explanations. It is possible the unanticipated results were obtained due to low and uneven participant rates. It may be possible to obtain the predicted results with additional and more evenly distributed participants across the treatment conditions. While care was taken to design the instructional material to produce the modality effect, it is possible that one of the recommendations may have been violated. We will examine each one in turn.

5.1 Separate Information

The recommendation to create a modality effect is that diagrammatic and textual information refer to each other and be unintelligible unless they are processed together. Kalyuga [23] posits two conditions when the modality effect may not be found: (1) when equivalent auditory and visual explanations are presented concurrently, and (2) when the instructional format is not matched to learner experience. While we attempted to ensure that the audio and text explanations were synchronized, there were two comments indicating that the participants' native language was not English and they were unable to keep up with the speed of the information presented. One of the participants was in the audio only group and the other was in the text only group. We do not believe this to be a likely explanation of the results.

5.2 Element Interactivity

It is recommended that element interactivity must be high, but not excessive. Certainly the elements of program code rely upon each other indicating interactivity between the elements. However, examples were chosen to limit the number of elements having to be retained in memory at a single time. The least amount of interactivity occurred in video 1, which had the worst overall performance on the recall questions (Figure 7). Therefore we do not believe this to be a likely explanation of the results.

5.3 Limit Auditory Length

The recommendation is that auditory text should be limited and that any lengthy, complex text should be written, not spoken. This recommendation is because of the transient effect [27, 64], or the amount of time auditory information can be retained. The participants in the study were novices with minimal computing knowledge (only those that failed the pre-test had data analyzed). It is possible that even the easiest and shortest of the videos overloaded their cognitive mental processing abilities. Knowing that we can only hold information in memory for no longer than 20 seconds [14], the videos may have been too long for the participants to comprehend and understand all the material asked of them. Video 1 was 5 minutes long; the second video was almost 23 minutes long and video 3 was 12 minutes long.

However in [27] the modality effect occurred when the videos were *longer* (going from 605 seconds to 867 seconds) but with fewer words (668 words to 576 words). In Leahy and Sweller's second experiment the explanation was simplified into smaller segments and less complex sentences. For this experiment, video 1 contained 528 words in 14 slides, video 2 contained 3167 words in 63 slides, and video 3 contained 1901 words in 33 slides. While videos 2 and 3 were lengthy in both time and words, video 1 was completely in line with those used in previous studies which reported these values and thus should have produced the modality effect.

Video 2 produced the most correct answers for the purpose question, even though it was the longest of the three videos. This would seem to contradict the transient effect. However, it may be due to the length of the video that the purpose was cemented in the learner's memory (more time on task). The text only explanation group performed the best on the transfer questions (Figure 8) which lends support that complex material should be written for better learning concerning transfer. It is unclear the role that auditory length plays in producing the modality effect in programming examples.

5.4 Complex Diagrams

If diagrams are complex, cuing or signaling may be required. This was accounted for within the videos through both cuing and signaling (Figures 2 and 3). It is also possible that no modality effect was found due to the complexity of the material. Kalyuga [25] provides an excellent overview of the modality effect and studies which find and do not find the modality effect in an effort to identify factors influencing its existence. The one consistent finding is to not use spoken explanations for any material which is highly complex. In this study, it could be reasoned that learning programming is so complex that no modality effect was found. However, if the material is truly inherently complex then the text only group should have performed better. This also did not occur, lending support that complexity of the diagrams or examples did not cause the unanticipated results.

5.5 Other Possible Explanations

Each video was designed to be a replacement for an in class lecture for that content topic. It is possible that each example was overreaching in its goal. Instead of trying to instruct an entire topic in a single video, it may be more effective to concentrate on a small piece of a topic per video. In other words, rather than covering every possible aspect of a selection statement, it may be more effective to have a shorter video that only explains what happens when a conditional expression evaluates to true in a selection statement. Then, a separate video describes when it evaluates to false, and yet another video for a nested selection statement. This would make each video much shorter and allow for progressive building of the information. This approach would support limiting the length of the auditory information.

Another possibility may be that novice programmers do not view code as a diagram. As Morgan et. al state, "Little is known about the progression of the process involved as novices become experts."[34, p. 15]. The code most likely to be viewed as a diagram was within video 2 as it had a method/function call (or two separate sections) and would require just-in-time inquiries about the code, as predicted by [30], though questions related to video 2 did not yield a learning performance any better than the others.

To summarize, there are several possible explanations why the results from this experiment did not confirm the results from other disciplines. However, we have no definitive answer on whether there was a confounding variable causing the unanticipated results or if the modality principle does not hold for programming. This leads to the need for additional research.

6 FUTURE STUDIES

Below are a few different possible next steps to attempt to determine when, if, and how the modality principle applies to introductory programming:

- Think Aloud Study: Recruit a minimum of three participants for each treatment and have them watch the instructional videos used in this study. Instead of controlling for time, the researcher could pause the video at different times and ask the participant to describe aloud about what they have learned, what they can remember, and probe about possible transient effects. As the participants are answering the post video questions, they would be prompted to think aloud their thought process on how they are arriving at their answers. By capturing information during the learning and assessment process we may be able to more accurately determine what is occurring and explain the unanticipated results.
- Restructure the Videos: It may be possible to rework one of the three videos into separate and more distinct content topics as described previously. Another set of of participants could be recruited to determine if shortening the videos and scaling back the content makes a difference in the overall results.
- Use other measurement techniques to determine the cognitive load. We may be able to use eye-tracking to determine exactly where the learners are looking on the screen to determine how they view code segments. We may also be able to determine exactly when and where the cognitive processing is occurring by examining the frequency and duration of gaze at specific areas of interest within the code segment.

7 CONCLUSION

It is possible that the modality effect does not hold within learning programming, but we cannot conclude that based on this study alone. This initial evidence indicates that simply replicating existing studies is not enough. Instead, more information is needed on several topics. First, the transient effect within programming should be studied to determine at what point the learner begins to lose information. Exactly how much content can be explained in a single audio explanation should be evaluated as well. It may be possible to cover only the most simple, straightforward case for a control structure without deviating to the exceptions or even including a trace of code. Additional studies using other measurement techniques, such as eye-tracking, may be utilized to more precisely pinpoint when and where the cognitive processing occurs.

Knowing whether or not the modality effect holds in programming is important to all those teaching and developing instructional materials for introductory programming. In traditional classrooms many instructors do "live coding," assuming that presenting the code on the overhead display and explaining the code is an effective pedagogical technique. Instructional programming videos consistently show the code with verbal explanations and expect students to learn and retain the information. Yet as this study illustrates, we still have no empirical evidence that this dual modality teaching technique is effective for learners of introductory programming. More studies should be conducted.

ACKNOWLEDGMENTS

The author thanks the students who participated in the study and their instructors who helped to recruit them. Thanks also to my advisor, Mark Guzdial, under whose guidance this study was conducted. Many thanks to the reviewers whose suggestions made this a better paper.

REFERENCES

[1] Alireza Ahadi and Raymond Lister. 2013. Geek genes, prior knowledge, stumbling points and learning edge momentum: parts of the one elephant?. In *Proceedings of the ninth annual international ACM conference on International computing education research*. ACM, 123–128. http://dl.acm.org/citation.cfm?id=2493416

[2] Pavlo D Antonenko and Dale S Niederhauser. 2010. The influence of leads on cognitive load and learning in a hypertext environment. *Computers in Human Behavior* 26, 2 (2010), 140–150.

[3] Paul Ayres. 2006. Using subjective measures to detect variations of intrinsic cognitive load within problems. *Learning and Instruction* 16, 5 (2006), 389 – 400.

[4] Paul Ayres and John Sweller. 1990. Locus of difficulty in multistage mathematics problems. *The American Journal of Psychology* (1990).

[5] Paul L Ayres. 2001. Systematic mathematical errors and cognitive load. *Contemporary Educational Psychology* 26, 2 (2001), 227–248.

[6] Alan Baddeley. 1986. *Working Memory*. Oxford University Press.

[7] J. Bransford. 2000. *How people learn: Brain, mind, experience, and school*. National Academies Press. http://books.google.com/books?hl=en&lr=lang_en&id=WaCW7i92lYkC&oi=fnd&pg=PA1&dq=How+people+learn&ots=JsRMAzrP8r&sig=q_klm0JlS2ATIqrFP-CnnXCsE64

[8] John D. Bransford, Ann L. Brown, and Rodney R. Cocking. 2000. *How People Learn: Brain, Mind, Experience, and School* (expanded ed.). National Academy Press, Washington, D.C.

[9] Roland Brunken, Jan L Plass, and Detlev Leutner. 2003. Direct measurement of cognitive load in multimedia learning. *Educational Psychologist* 38, 1 (2003), 53–61.

[10] S. N. Cant, D. Ross Jeffery, and Brian Henderson-Sellers. 1995. A conceptual model of cognitive complexity of elements of the programming process. *Information and Software Technology* 37, 7 (1995), 351–362. http://www.sciencedirect.com/science/article/pii/095058499591491H

[11] Paul Chandler and John Sweller. 1991. Cognitive load theory and the format of instruction. *Cognition and instruction* 8, 4 (1991), 293–332.

[12] Paul Chandler and John Sweller. 1992. The split-attention effect as a factor in the design of instruction. *British Journal of Educational Psychology* 62, 2 (1992), 233–246.

[13] Paul Chandler and John Sweller. 1996. Cognitive load while learning to use a computer program. *Applied cognitive psychology* 10, 2 (1996), 151–170.

[14] N. Cowan. 2010. The magical mystery four how is working memory capacity limited, and why? *Current directions in psychological science* 19, 1 (2010), 51–57.

[15] Krista E DeLeeuw and Richard E Mayer. 2008. A comparison of three measures of cognitive load: Evidence for separable measures of intrinsic, extraneous, and germane load. *J. of Educational Psychology* 100, 1 (2008), 223.

[16] Peter Gerjets, Katharina Scheiter, and Richard Catrambone. 2004. Designing instructional examples to reduce intrinsic cognitive load: Molar versus modular presentation of solution procedures. *Instructional Science* 32, 1-2 (2004), 33–58.

[17] Peter Gerjets, Katharina Scheiter, and Richard Catrambone. 2006. Can learning from molar and modular worked examples be enhanced by providing instructional explanations and prompting self-explanations? *Learning and Instruction* 16, 2 (2006), 104–121.

[18] Paul Ginns. 2005. Meta-analysis of the modality effect. *Learning and Instruction* 15, 4 (2005), 313–331. http://www.sciencedirect.com/science/article/pii/S0959475205000459

[19] Fernand Gobet and Herbert A. Simon. 1998. Expert chess memory: Revisiting the chunking hypothesis. *Memory* 6, 3 (1998), 225–255. http://www.tandfonline.com/doi/abs/10.1080/741942359

[20] M. E. Hansen, A. Lumsdaine, and R. L. Goldstone. 2013. An experiment on the cognitive complexity of code. In *Proceedings of the Thirty-Fifth Annual Conference of the Cognitive Science Society*.

[21] Sandra G Hart and Lowell E Staveland. 1988. Development of NASA-TLX (Task Load Index): Results of empirical and theoretical research. *Advances in psychology* 52 (1988), 139–183.

[22] Robin Jeffries. 1982. A comparison of the debugging behavior of expert and novice programmers. In *Proceedings of AERA annual meeting*.

[23] Slava Kalyuga. 2000. When using sound with a text or picture is not beneficial for learning. *Australasian Journal of Educational Technology* 16, 2 (2000). http://ascilite.org.au/ajet/submission/index.php/AJET/article/view/1829

[24] Slava Kalyuga. 2011. Cognitive load theory: How many types of load does it really need? *Educational Psychology Review* 23, 1 (2011), 1–19. http://link.springer.com/article/10.1007/s10648-010-9150-7

[25] Slava Kalyuga. 2012. Instructional benefits of spoken words: A review of cognitive load factors. *Educational Research Review* 7, 2 (2012), 145–159. http://www.

sciencedirect.com/science/article/pii/S1747938X11000546

[26] Slava Kalyuga, Paul Chandler, and John Sweller. 1999. Managing split-attention and redundancy in multimedia instruction. *Applied cognitive psychology* 13, 4 (1999), 351–371. http://www.researchgate.net/profile/Paul_Chandler3/publication/238680916_Managing_split-attention_and_redundancy_in_multimedia_instruction/links/0a85e5300f4b3b95d6000000.pdf

[27] Wayne Leahy and John Sweller. 2011. Cognitive load theory, modality of presentation and the transient information effect. *Applied Cognitive Psychology* 25, 6 (2011), 943–951. http://onlinelibrary.wiley.com/doi/10.1002/acp.1787/pdf

[28] Jimmie Leppink, Fred Paas, Cees PM Van der Vleuten, Tamara Van Gog, and Jeroen JG Van Merriënboer. 2013. Development of an instrument for measuring different types of cognitive load. *Behavior research methods* 45, 4 (2013), 1058–1072.

[29] Jimmie Leppink, Fred Paas, Tamara van Gog, Cees PM van der Vleuten, and Jeroen JG van Merriënboer. 2014. Effects of pairs of problems and examples on task performance and different types of cognitive load. *Learning and Instruction* 30 (2014), 32–42.

[30] Stanley Letovsky, Jeannine Pinto, Robin Lampert, and Elliot Soloway. 1987. A cognitive analysis of a code inspection. In *Empirical studies of programmers: second workshop*. Ablex Publishing Corp., 231–247.

[31] R. E. Mayer. 2002. Multimedia learning. *Psychology of Learning and Motivation* 41 (2002), 85–139. http://www.sciencedirect.com/science/article/pii/S0079742102800056

[32] Richard E. Mayer. 2009. *Multi-Media Learning* (2nd ed.). Cambridge Univ Press.

[33] Roxana Moreno. 2004. Decreasing cognitive load for novice students: Effects of explanatory versus corrective feedback in discovery-based multimedia. *Instructional science* 32, 1-2 (2004), 99–113.

[34] Andrew Morgan, Bonita Sharif, and Martha E Crosby. 2015. Understanding a novice programmerâĂŹs progression of reading and summarizing source code. *Eye Movements in Programming Education II: Analyzing the NoviceâĂŹs Gaze* (2015), 13.

[35] Briana B. Morrison, Brian Dorn, and Mark Guzdial. 2014. Measuring cognitive load in introductory CS: adaptation of an instrument. In *Proceedings of the tenth annual conference on International computing education research*. ACM, 131–138. http://dl.acm.org/citation.cfm?id=2632348

[36] Seyed Yaghoub Mousavi, Renae Low, and John Sweller. 1995. Reducing cognitive load by mixing auditory and visual presentation modes. *Journal of educational psychology* 87, 2 (1995), 319. http://psycnet.apa.org/journals/edu/87/2/319/

[37] Fred Paas, Juhani E Tuovinen, Huib Tabbers, and Pascal WM Van Gerven. 2003. Cognitive load measurement as a means to advance cognitive load theory. *Educational psychologist* 38, 1 (2003), 63–71.

[38] Fred G Paas. 1992. Training strategies for attaining transfer of problem-solving skill in statistics: A cognitive-load approach. *J. of educational psychology* 84, 4 (1992), 429.

[39] Fred GWC Paas and Jeroen JG Van Merriënboer. 1993. The efficiency of instructional conditions: An approach to combine mental effort and performance measures. *Human Factors: The Journal of the Human Factors and Ergonomics Society* 35, 4 (1993), 737–743.

[40] Fred GWC Paas and Jeroen JG Van Merriënboer. 1994. Variability of worked examples and transfer of geometrical problem-solving skills: A cognitive-load approach. *Journal of educational psychology* 86, 1 (1994), 122.

[41] Fred GWC Paas and Jeroen JG Van Merriënboer. 1994. Variability of worked examples and transfer of geometrical problem-solving skills: A cognitive-load approach. *Journal of educational psychology* 86, 1 (1994), 122.

[42] Fred GWC Paas, Jeroen JG Van Merriënboer, and Jos J Adam. 1994. Measurement of cognitive load in instructional research. *Perceptual and motor skills* 79, 1 (1994), 419–430.

[43] Jan L Plass, Roxana Moreno, and Roland Brünken. 2010. *Cognitive load theory*. Cambridge University Press.

[44] Jan L Plass, Roxana Moreno, and Roland Brünken. 2010. *Cognitive load theory*. Cambridge University Press.

[45] Wolfgang Schnotz. 2005. An integrated model of text and picture comprehension. *The Cambridge handbook of multimedia learning* (2005), 49–69. https://books.google.com/books?hl=en&lr=&id=Cvw6BAAAQBAJ&oi=fnd&pg=PA72&dq=schnotz+2005&ots=HuUbWczY_Q&sig=keMb_F17xn6jwCMemW8k7LHNt0M

[46] Claude M. Steele and Joshua Aronson. 1995. Stereotype threat and the intellectual test performance of African Americans. *Journal of personality and social psychology* 69, 5 (1995), 797. http://psycnet.apa.org/journals/psp/69/5/797/

[47] Claude M. Steele, Steven J. Spencer, and Joshua Aronson. 2002. Contending with group image: The psychology of stereotype and social identity threat. *Advances in experimental social psychology* 34 (2002), 379–440. http://www.sciencedirect.com/science/article/pii/S0065260102800090

[48] Andreas Stefik and Ed Gellenbeck. 2009. Using spoken text to aid debugging: An empirical study. In *Program Comprehension, 2009. ICPC'09. IEEE 17th International Conference on*. IEEE, 110–119.

[49] John Sweller. 1988. Cognitive load during problem solving: Effects on learning. *Cognitive science* 12, 2 (1988), 257–285.

[50] John Sweller. 1999. *Instructional Design in Technical Areas*. Australian Education Review, No. 43. ERIC. http://eric.ed.gov/?id=ED431763

[51] John Sweller. 2010. Element interactivity and intrinsic, extraneous, and germane cognitive load. *Educational Psychology Review* 22, 2 (2010), 123–138.

[52] John Sweller. 2010. Element interactivity and intrinsic, extraneous, and germane cognitive load. *Educational psychology review* 22, 2 (2010), 123–138. http://link.springer.com/article/10.1007/s10648-010-9128-5

[53] John Sweller, Paul Ayres, and Slava Kalyuga. 2011. *Cognitive load theory*. Vol. 1. Springer.

[54] John Sweller, Paul Ayres, and Slava Kalyuga. 2011. *Cognitive load theory*. Vol. 1. Springer.

[55] John Sweller and Paul Chandler. 1994. Why some material is difficult to learn. *Cognition and instruction* 12, 3 (1994), 185–233.

[56] John Sweller, Jeroen JG Van Merriënboer, and Fred GWC Paas. 1998. Cognitive architecture and instructional design. *Educational psychology review* 10, 3 (1998), 251–296.

[57] Sharon Tindall-Ford, Paul Chandler, and John Sweller. 1997. When two sensory modes are better than one. *Journal of experimental psychology: Applied* 3, 4 (1997), 257. http://psycnet.apa.org/journals/xap/3/4/257/

[58] Geoffrey Underwood, Lorraine Jebbett, and Katharine Roberts. 2004. Inspecting pictures for information to verify a sentence: Eye movements in general encoding and in focused search. *Quarterly Journal of Experimental Psychology Section A* 57, 1 (2004), 165–182.

[59] Pascal WM Van Gerven, Fred Paas, Jeroen JG Van Merriënboer, and Henk G Schmidt. 2004. Memory load and the cognitive pupillary response in aging. *Psychophysiology* 41, 2 (2004), 167–174.

[60] Pascal WM van Gerven, Fred Paas, Jeroen JG van Merriënboer, and Henk G Schmidt. 2006. Modality and variability as factors in training the elderly. *Applied cognitive psychology* 20, 3 (2006), 311–320.

[61] Tamara Van Gog and Fred Paas. 2008. Instructional efficiency: Revisiting the original construct in educational research. *Educational Psychologist* 43, 1 (2008), 16–26.

[62] Tamara van Gog and Katharina Scheiter. 2010. Eye tracking as a tool to study and enhance multimedia learning. *Learning and Instruction* 20, 2 (2010), 95–99.

[63] Jeroen JG Van Merriënboer and John Sweller. 2005. Cognitive load theory and complex learning: Recent developments and future directions. *Educational psychology review* 17, 2 (2005), 147–177.

[64] Anna Wong, Wayne Leahy, Nadine Marcus, and John Sweller. 2012. Cognitive load theory, the transient information effect and e-learning. *Learning and Instruction* 22, 6 (2012), 449–457. http://www.sciencedirect.com/science/article/pii/S0959475212000369

Computing Mentorship in a Software Boomtown: Relationships to Adolescent Interest and Beliefs

Andrew J. Ko
The Information School, DUB Group
University of Washington
Seattle, WA
ajko@uw.edu

Katie Davis
The Information School, DUB Group
University of Washington
Seattle, WA
kdavis78@uw.edu

ABSTRACT

Prior work on adolescent interest development shows that mentorship can promote interest in a subject while reshaping beliefs about the subject. To what extent do these same effects occur in computing, where interest and beliefs have traditionally been negative? We conducted two studies of the Puget Sound region in the United States, surveying and teaching 57 diverse adolescents with interests in computing. In the first study, we found that interest in computing was strongly related to having a mentoring relationship and not to gender or socioeconomic status. Teens with mentors also engaged in significantly more computing education and had more diverse beliefs about peers who engaged in computing education. The second study reinforced this finding, showing that teens who took a class from an instructor who aimed to become students' teacher-mentor had significantly greater positive changes in interest in computing than those who already had a mentor. These findings, while correlational, suggest that mentors can play a key role in promoting adolescent interest in computing.

KEYWORDS

Computing education, mentorship, interest development

1 INTRODUCTION

Prior work has shown that diverse adolescent populations around the world continue to view computing as boring, antisocial, irrelevant, male, and competitive [6, 8, 20, 24, 25, 35, 35–37, 44, 52]. To address this, multiple efforts worldwide aim to engage adolescents in computing education with the goal of overcoming these views, developing *interest* in computing.

Sustaining this interest, however, requires more than just initial engagement. Theories of interest development, for example, view interest as something initially triggered by events such as an in-class activity, and afterwards, as something that is maintained over time, first externally by the learning environment and then individually through intrinsic motivation, values, and identity [26]. From this view, developing adolescent interest in computing is first a matter of *triggering* interest through experiences like Hour of Code or a

ICER'17, August 18-20, 2017, Tacoma, WA, USA.
© 2017 Copyright held by the owner/author(s). Publication rights licensed to ACM.
978-1-4503-4968-0/17/08...$15.00
DOI: http://dx.doi.org/10.1145/3105726.3106177

parent enrolling a child in a computing camp and then a matter of maintaining and developing it through coursework, projects, and community engagement.

Mentors can play a key role in both triggering and maintaining adolescent interest. They can devise learning experiences to situationally maintain interest and they can also encourage further learning, connecting learning to adolescents' identities, shifting situational interest into individual interest [26]. For example, studies of technology fluency (which have investigated coding among other technology skills) have found that parents can play mentoring roles in the development of technology skills, advancing their children's learning through parent-child collaborations [4]. These relationships are associated with adolescents' deeper expertise and positive attitudes toward technology.

Parents, of course, are only one kind of mentor. Dawson, for example, conceptualizes mentorship broadly [12], describing it as both formal relationships between younger and older individuals, but also relationships between individuals of all ages with widely varying formality and levels of engagement. Lave and Wenger treat mentorship similarly, describing apprenticeship as a form of peer mentorship that develops skill and knowledge [34].

Unfortunately, there is little prior work on informal mentoring [1]. Prior work has shown that many youth have some kind of informal mentor [5], and that these mentors can be central to youths' lives [32], but only a few works investigate computing. For example, Barron et al.'s investigation of parent-mentors only considered a few adolescents learning to code [4] and Ko's study of computing autobiographies only reported a few students mentioning mentoring relationships as part of their developed interest in computing [33]. Most prior work has instead focused on *formal* mentoring in the workplace (e.g., [28, 29]) and in educational contexts with at-risk learners (e.g., [38, 51]. This trend is also true of research on mentoring in computer science in higher education, which has found that strong communication skills and an appropriate personality fit are key [39, 42, 49], mirroring more general research on formal mentoring [23, 30]. By following these practices, CS faculty can influence enrollment decisions [45], increase retention [10, 21], and produce more effective learning [16]. Formal peer mentoring, in contrast is fraught with challenges [27], but can improve learners' sense of community [14].

While all of this prior work *suggests* that mentorship may be an effective contributor to developing adolescents' interest in computing, there has been little systematic investigation into the relationships between computing mentoring, interest, and beliefs among youth. Specifically:

- RQ1: To what extent is mentorship related to positive beliefs about computing, interest in computing, and engagement in computing education?
- RQ2: What relationship does acquiring a computing mentor have with interest in computing?

Studying these question is complex. As Renninger and Hidi discuss in their review of conceptualizations of interest, researchers have only just begun to develop systematic, consistent conceptualizations of interest [43], providing few methods or measurements that control for interacting roles of age, identity, cognitive development, and learning context. Moreover, conducting longitudinal controlled experiments on the effects of mentorship is not only challenging, but premature, without first establishing the potential effects of computing mentorship. Therefore, our goal was to measure these potential effects and do so in a community near universal access to computing education and an abundance of potential computing mentors, partially mitigating confounding factors such as access to computing education and availability of mentors. While these methods cannot show that mentorship was a *cause* of the beliefs and interests we observed in either study, we hope that they provide insight into the potential effects of mentorship in computing education, laying a foundation for further investigation.

2 APPROACH

Our approach to investigating these two questions was to study adolescent experiences with computing mentorship in the Seattle metropolitan area in Washington state in the United States (also known as the Puget Sound region). Seattle is unique in that while it only has tens of thousands of students, it also has over 90,000 professional software engineers, possibly providing most students with access to potential computing mentors. Moreover, public and private schools in the region also provide near universal access to both formal computing education in secondary school, each offering at least one if not more computer science courses, some with dedicated CS instructors, some who primarily teach math, science, or technology, and some who are industry volunteers through programs like TEALS (Microsoft's Technology Education and Literacy in Schools program). The city also is full of *informal* learning opportunities, including adolescent coding camps designed to develop interest. Dozens of companies including Microsoft, Google, and Zillow also sponsor frequent day or week-long computing education events for teens across the region. Finally, Seattle is unique in that it is also one of the most highly educated and wealthy cities in the U.S. and yet still contains socioeconomic diversity due to the significant influx of immigrants and refugees relative to its size. These conditions made it possible to explore more idealized conditions for mentorship, mitigating structural inequities in access to learning and mentorship, while also preserving socioeconomic diversity and a degree of racial diversity and segregation. Therefore, our exploratory study is as much an investigation into the unique conditions in Seattle as it is a study of mentorship.

In this context, we conducted two studies. First, we surveyed two socioeconomically and racially diverse groups of high school students. One group of students enrolled in a 1-week, half-day web design course through a fee-based summer camp program sponsored by the University of Washington, which tends to attract upper-middle class White and Asian students from Seattle's wealthier neighborhoods and suburbs. The other group was enrolled in a federally-funded Upward Bound program, a first-generation college preparation program that recruits from three of south Seattle's public high schools, which tend to enroll racially diverse immigrant youth living in neighborhoods with low socioeconomic status. We asked students about beliefs, interests, and mentorship relationships. We then taught the Upward Bound students in a six-week course that framed the instructor as an informal computing mentor, investigating the potential for his mentorship to strengthen students' situational interest in computing.

3 STUDY 1: MENTORSHIP, BELIEFS, ENGAGEMENT, AND INTEREST

The goal of our first study was to investigate adolescents' computing mentoring relationships, their beliefs about computing, and their interest in computing.

3.1 Method

3.1.1 Population and Sampling. Our target population was adolescents aged 14-18 living in Seattle or the broader Puget Sound region. Our objective was to recruit as diverse a group of teens as possible, across race, age, gender, socioeconomic status, geography, and school. To do so, we offered two types of summer coding classes. One was a university-based Upward Bound program. Upward Bound (UB) is a federally funded college preparation program that helps high school students who are low-income and/or have no parent with a bachelor's degree enter college. There are currently 826 programs in the U.S., many of which have existed since the 1964 Economic Opportunity Act that founded them. The program we worked with serves three urban south Seattle public high schools. The program serves about 125 students per year. The program is free; students receive lunch money and a stipend to attend. In 2016, 79% were both low-income and first-generation immigrants, 50% identified as female, 35% as South Asian, 19% as African, 16% as Asian, 14% as Hispanic/Latino, 10% as Black, 4% as two or more races, and 2% as White. The program's high school graduation rate is 98% and its college graduation rate is consistently above 60%, with many alumni pursuing graduate studies. Therefore, the program primarily serves the high-achieving end of Seattle's lower income schools.

The UB program offers a full summer curriculum that includes afternoon electives. We offered a course titled "Web Design" with an enrollment limit of 25. The course description made no mention of "coding." Students could choose between it and electives in ballroom dancing, swimming, or music. Program administrators solicited student preferences and then randomly assigned students to their 1st and 2nd choices, ensuring a balance along racial and gender lines; however, administrators also encouraged students to focus on classes that would satisfy graduation requirements, and so most students who enrolled in the class had an existing interest in computing. The UB class was 6 weeks, 4 days per week, and 36 hours total. We describe the class in detail later.

Our 2nd class was two sections of a 5-day, 3-hours per day coding camp (also titled "Web Design" and using the same UB course description) offered through a university-based summer youth (SY)

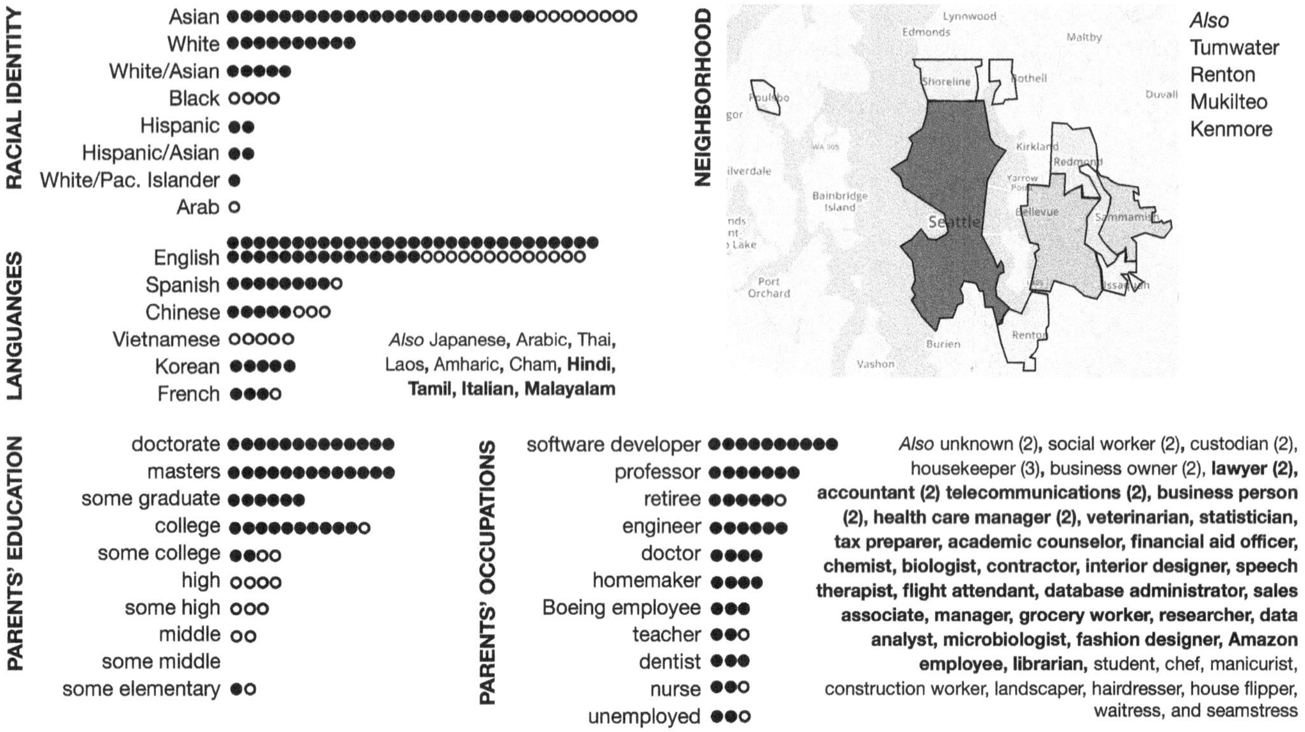

Figure 1: Student demographics. Students could choose multiple races and languages, one parent education level, one city, and up to two guardian occupations. Dark circles and bold text are SY students, white circles and non-bold text are UB students.

program. This program markets to teachers in Seattle's wealthier north suburbs and the eastern suburbs of Bellevue, Redmond, and Kirkland. These classes tend to attract youth from upper-middle class families. Teachers distribute camp information to parents, who enroll their teens. The course had a registration fee of $275 for the week, providing a barrier to enrollment for lower-income students (though the program had a limited budget for financial assistance). Our class's fee was comparable to other half-day camps in the city. We offered two sections: one in the morning and one in the afternoon, with an enrollment limit of 25 each.

3.1.2 Participants. We successfully enrolled 57 teens across both classes. We filled both SY camps, but had several last minute cancellations, resulting in 44 total enrolled students. Our UB class had room for 25, but we only enrolled 13, two of whom dropped the class in favor of ballroom dance, but still filled out our survey.

Despite the enrollment challenges, our sample was still diverse along many dimensions. Students were 39% female and aged 14-17 (median 15). As shown in Figure 1, students were all fluent in English, but most were bilingual (12 reported never speaking English at home), most identified as White or Asian, many had highly educated parents but across a diversity of occupations, and students came from across the region, but primarily Seattle.

As with any sample, there were several biases. All students reported wanting to go to college, despite Seattle Public's 2015 high school dropout rate of 22%. Over 75% of students had a parent with a bachelor's degree, which is higher than the city's 2015 count of 54% of residents over age 25 with a bachelor's degree. (Seattle

has one of the highest education rates of any U.S. city, and so the region already skewed toward high educational attainment.) Seattle's racial demographics are also unique, with many low-income recent Asian immigrants, and many affluent Hispanic families. The resulting sample is therefore reflective of the city's mix of educated professional families and its recent immigrant families.

3.1.3 Data Collection. We began all classes by having students fill out a web-based survey. Both classes were held in adjacent computer labs on a university campus, roughly identical in layout and identical in hardware. Students took approximately 30 minutes to complete the survey. It began with demographic information (age in years, neighborhood they lived in, school and grade they would enter in the fall). Next, to obtain data on students' interests broadly, we asked students about their academic plans, asking whether they planned to go to college and measuring students' possible selves [41], responding to the prompt *"Describe your vision of your life at the age of 25, assuming everything goes well. Who are you? What will you have achieved? What will your goals be?"* This question allowed us to understand students' interests, identities, and motivations. The survey then probed for interest in computing (detailed shortly), followed by beliefs about peers engaged in computing education and about software developers.

The end of the survey probed identity (to avoid potential stereotype threats [47], as questions about identity can influence how respondents describe their interests, prior knowledge, and ability). We asked for students' languages that they speak fluently, ordered from most to least fluent. We also asked them to note which language they spoke most at home. We then asked for racial identity (following the latest U.S. census recommendations found at *census.gov/topics/population/race/about.html*), gender, and socioeconomic status. Measuring socioeconomic status (SES), which is viewed as a combination of education, income, and occupation, is non-trivial [19]. However, there is evidence that parents' educational attainment is highly predictive of youth SES in adulthood [17]. Therefore, following the latest best practices on SES measurement [31], we asked students *"How many years of school has your most educated parent or guardian completed (0-25 years)? (0=no school, 5=finished elementary school, 8=finished middle school, 12=finished high school, 16=finished college, more than 16 means graduate school)."* We also asked students to identify their parent and/or guardians' occupations to help us understand their parents' occupational proximity to the software industry.

3.2 Results

3.2.1 Access to Computing Mentors. We first consider the degree to which students reported access to potential computing mentors. Of all students, 49 (89%) reported knowing someone who knew "how to code." This did not vary by SES (*F*(1,55)=.86, p=.36), gender (*Fisher's*, p=.72), or UB/SY class (*Fisher's*, p=.37). Students reported their relationships with these individuals as friends (17), fathers (16), teachers (9), brothers (4), uncles (3), cousins (2), a mentor, a neighbor, a friend's sibling, a parent's friend, a sister, and a tutor.

To analyze the nature of students' relationships with these individuals, we analyzed the students' descriptions for qualities of mentoring. Although the literature on mentorship has not yet agreed upon a theoretical account of mentoring, there are four facets that consistently arise in the mentoring literature [11]: 1) psychological and emotional support, 2) support for goal setting and career selection, 3) teaching of academic subject knowledge, and 4) framing of the mentor as a role model. We liberally operationalized computing mentoring relationships as any relationship that a student described that included one or more of these facets, including descriptions of explicit encouragement, learning activities, including explicit instruction, help enrolling in classes, visits to workplaces, role modeling and the fostering of other mentoring relationships. We treated all other relationships (including those with individuals who knew how to code) as non-mentoring relationships (for example, many described fathers, friends, and brothers who never explained their software development jobs or attempted to teach them anything about computing). Based on this definition, 24 (42%) of the students described having at least one computing mentoring relationship. Whether a student had a mentor did not differ by SES (*F*(1,55)=.87, p=.36), gender (*Fisher's*, p=.17), or UB/SY class (*Fisher's*, p=.2).

Students with mentors described a wide range of mentoring relationships:

"My dad is a professor in biology here at the university and he has been teaching me python recently." (SY, White male, 16)

"One of my best friends is very interested in programming, and has taught me some basics about HTML5" (SY, White male, 14)

"My dads friend sister works in Microsoft and he's a developer we only got to talk about her job a little bit, she took me on a tour of

the campus and saw what people do there. it was pretty cool" (UB, Black female, 17)

"In the past few summers, I had a private computer programming therapist... She taught me new programs and new coding. She didn't do it this year because now she's going to college." (SY, White/Asian male, 14)

"My mom is a website developer, she teaches me about the tools she uses. My dad, writes code in java. My friends taught me how to program also" (SY, White male, 17)

"My cousin wants to be a computer science major in college and runs a club at her school called "Girls Who Code." She encourages me to try coding. " (SY, White/Asian male, 16)

"My dad is a software engineer and he frequently talks to me about his job. He has enrolled me in several classes and in our free time, he often teaches me. " (SY, Asian female, 14)

"My neighbor Laura who did APCS and really enjoyed it and introduced me to it." (SY, Hispanic female, 15)

3.2.2 Beliefs about Computing Education and Software Developers. Next, we turn to the beliefs that students reported about computing and computing education. We first asked students, *What kinds of students take your school's technology courses?* In their responses we saw few of the beliefs reported in prior work (e.g., [3, 36]), in which adolescents attributed student interest in computing to gender or intelligence. Organizing their free responses by the specific words they used, we found that students described students who engaged in computing education as "anyone" (17), "people who love computers" (9), "overachievers" (6), "people who want good jobs" (5), "people who are required to" (5), "slackers" (3), "Asians" (2), "boys," "girls," "cool people," "game lovers," and "loners." Eight students said they were unsure about who takes CS because they were new to their school.

When we considered the beliefs reported by students with and without mentors, there were only minor differences. Of students without mentors, 33% described students who took computing courses as "anyone" and 18% were unsure, whereas of the students *with* mentors, only 25% reported "anyone" and 8% were unsure. However, the students with mentors had more diverse beliefs that differed from those without mentors, including "boys," "girls," and "cool people."

In addition to beliefs about their peers who engaged in computing education, we also considered students' beliefs about professional software developers, asking students *"What characteristics do you think someone must have to be a software developer?"* Adjectives used by more than 10% of students *without* mentors included "creative," "patient," "smart," "hard-working," "intelligent", and "perseverant," all mentioned by more than 10% of students. Students *with* mentors used largely the same language, but unlike students without mentors, also used the adjectives "logical", "collaborative," "enthusiastic," and "precise."

We also asked students *"What do you think software developers do at work?"* Most students, regardless of whether they had a computing mentor, believed that developers "code all day," "go to a few meetings," and "think of product ideas." Most students did not describe the collaborative aspects of the job, portraying a typical day as a solitary one. We also asked students *"What must someone do to become a software developer?"* Responses universally mentioned taking courses and practicing extensively, as in this representative response: *"They need to learn about coding and practice it until it becomes as easy as breathing"* (UB, Vietnamese male, 15).

3.2.3 Engagement in Computing Education.

Next we consider students' engagement in computing education and its relationship to students' access to computing mentors. We asked students to list all of the technology courses that their school offers, what kinds of students take those technology courses, and whether they had taken those courses. We also asked if they had used other online learning technologies to learn to code.

Of the 57 students, 50 (88%) could name at least one computing course in their school. There were no significant relationships between the number of courses known and SES ($r(55)$=.07, p=.60), gender ($F(1,55)$=2.5, p=.12), UB/SY class ($F(1,55)$=.84, p=.36), or whether a student had a computing mentor ($F(1,55)$=0.24, p=.63). We confirmed that the schools of the 7 students who could not name a computing class *did* offer one in the year prior; they were just not aware of it because they were incoming freshmen or had recently moved. Of these 7 students, 6 did not report having a computing mentor.

We asked students what CS courses or learning experiences they had engaged in. Twenty-seven (47%) reported having already engaged in some kind of computing education. Of these students, 89% (24 students) had taken an elective class at school. Who had taken a course did not differ by SES ($F(1,55)$=1.1, p=.29), gender (*Fisher's*, p=.10), or UB/SY class (*Fisher's*, p=1.0). Courses taken *did* differ significantly by whether a student had a computing mentor ($F(1,55)$=4.44, p=0.04); 16 students (67%) with a mentor had taken at least one class (and only 3 of these reported that their sole mentor was their teacher), compared to 27% of students without a mentor.

Only 4 students mentioned engaging in informal learning. One read a Python book over the summer; one started but did not complete a Codecademy Java tutorial; one started but did not complete a Codecademy JavaScript tutorial; and one had completed a series of Udacity online classes and Codecademy tutorials. Three of these four students reported having a computing mentor.

Despite only half of the students mentioning that they had engaged in computing education, when we asked students to list the programming languages that they had encountered, 42 (74%) mentioned having encountered at least one. Students mentioned familiarity with Scratch (28), HTML (19), Java (18), JavaScript (12), Python (12), CSS (8), Excel (8), C/C++ (6), Minecraft mods (7), Kodu (4), C# (2), Processing, Alice, Ruby, Go, Swift, Lua, and PHP. There were no trends in who had encountered a language by SES ($F(1,55)$=1.2, p=.28), gender (*Fisher's*, p=.22), or UB/SY class (*Fisher's*, p=.29). However, students with computing mentors reported encountering significantly more programming languages ($F(1,55)$=11.4, p=0.001), with 92% of students with a mentor encountering at least one language, compared to only 40% of students without a mentor.

3.2.4 Interest.

We now turn to students' interest in computing. According to our adopted theoretical framework [26], students' engagement in computing education and access to mentors would have triggered and maintained interest in computing. We would therefore expect that there would be a strong relationship

Table 1: Linear regression predicting interest. *=p<.05.

	B	SE B	β
Gender	.234	.316	.098
SES	.097	.070	.177
# PL encountered	.131	.071	.254
Had mentor	.623	.319	.265*

between mentorship, engagement in computing education, and interest. Prior work would also suggest a relationship between gender and cultural factors, mediated by beliefs and access [36, 37].

To investigate interest, we first analyzed the *possible selves* [41] that students described, inspecting them for interests. Although 13 students wrote that they were unsure about their careers and 15 mentioned computing careers (software developer (8), game developer (5), and web developer (2)), the other 30 described diverse interests: including doctor (6), writer (2), mechanical engineer (2), aeronautical engineer, autism activist, bioengineer, businessman, computer engineer, drug researcher, Ethiopian politician, illustrator, and several other distinct professions. This variety suggests that most of the students did not enroll in our courses because they were explicitly interested in computing as a career.

To measure students' interest in computing, we adapted the scale used by Oh et al. [40], presenting the following five items on a 7-point Likert scale: 1) *I'm interested in taking courses that help me learn to code*, 2) *I am interested in careers that allow me to use coding skills*, 3) *I would like to learn to code because it will help me prepare for college*, 4) *I would like to learn to code because it will help me get a good job*, and 5) *I would like to learn to code because it will help me create new technologies*. We mapped each response to a -3 to 3 scale and computed the mean of the five items.

Interest in computing skewed positive. The mean response was 1.1 and ranged from -2 to 3, suggesting most teens viewed computing as an interesting, valuable subject to learn. Only 10 students (18%) had attitudes below 0 on the scale, including 5 of 11 (45%) of the UB students and 5 of 46 (12%) of the SY students. This was consistent with the reasons that students listed for enrolling, which included: "I'm interested" (28), "parents wanted me to" (9), "seemed useful" (7), "curious about the topic" (3), "friends encouraged me" (2), "bored this summer" (2), "placed by counselor" (2), "retake" (2), "avoiding physical activity," and "for credit."

To test the relationship between mentorship and interest in computing, we built a linear regression. For predictors, we included gender, since prior work has observed significant disinterest from girls because of the culture of computing education (e.g., [37]). We included number of programming languages encountered as an indicator of prior learning about computing. We included SES, as prior work has shown that higher SES is related to higher academic ambitions [46]. And finally, we included whether the student reported a mentoring relationship, given its clear relationship to interest reported in prior work [4, 26] and many students had described it as a significant factor in their interest. The interest scale and the predictor variables satisfied the assumptions for a linear regression.

Table 1 shows our resulting model, which explained a significant proportion of the variance in interest (R^2=.223, $F(4,52)$=3.72, p=.01).

Gender, SES, and programming languages encountered did not explain a significant proportion of variance in interest, but having a computing mentor did, and was responsible for a 0.623 increase on the -3 to 3 computing interest scale.

4 STUDY 2: FORMING COMPUTING MENTORING RELATIONSHIPS

The results of Study 1 suggested that the most significant factor related to interest in computing was mentoring. However, this study did not allow us to observe mentoring relationships being formed, or the possible effects of acquiring a mentor on change in interest. Therefore, in Study 2 we taught the 6-week UB class with the explicit goal of the instructor (the 1st author) to develop informal computing mentoring relationships with each of the 11 students. To do this, the instructor aimed to give the students an accurate portrayal of the web development communities of practice [34], while developing a sincere interest in each individual student's learning, leveraging his decade of experience as a teacher and 5 years of experience as a professional web developer.

4.1 Course Design

Throughout the course, we attempted to follow best practices from education and computing education. The class was only 11 students, reducing the negative effects of large class sizes (e.g., [2]). The instructor followed the best practices of classroom management [18]. For example, because the class was in a computer lab, he managed student attention by creating separate spaces for lecture and computer-based learning to prevent students from being distracted. He established and enforced clear rules of conduct, preventing disruptions. He also followed the evidence-based practice of learner-centered teacher-student relationships [9], attempting to create authentic relationships in which students were trusted, given responsibility, spoken to honestly and warmly and treated with dignity. This approach was consistent with the tone of instruction throughout the rest of the UB program. In addition, the class followed NCWIT's inclusive learning practices (*ncwit.org/resources/type/promising-practices*), explicitly discussing stereotype threat, imposter syndrome, and theories of intelligence in the context of the software industry, computing education, and in the classroom. The instructor also followed NCWIT's practice of intentional role modeling (based on studies such as [48]), 1) explaining what made his role as a practitioner relevant to their learning, 2) describing his personal history and how it related to the students' experiences, 3) speaking about his strengths and weaknesses and how they related to his expertise, and 4) showing them how he attained his position.

Our instruction was also informed by communities of practice theory [50], as prior work has explored in computing education [13, 22]. In this theory, a newcomer's purpose is to learn to talk and do as the community does, acquiring the norms, practices, skills, and tools that the community uses to do its work. In our class, we followed the practices described in prior work (e.g., [7, 22]), having students use authentic web development tools of GitHub, JSFiddle, and Bootstrap, but scaffolding them to facilitate learning. We introduced the students to three experienced web developers who had worked at local companies. We showed the students the diversity of software companies in the Puget Sound region, teaching them about the dozens of large companies and their different corporate cultures and values, but also the hundreds of software startups. Across four reading assignments, students reflected on equity in computing education, reading the White House press release on the CS for All initiative, Chapter 4 of Stuck in the Shallow End [36] (which covers preparatory privilege), a viral blog post by a female software engineer on imposter syndrome in the software industry, and a case study written by the 1st author about his experiences at a software startup.

We designed a 3-week project in which the students designed and developed a website individually or in teams, creating something personally meaningful. The class involved 6 projects across the 11 students. They chose diverse topics, including an informational site about Ethiopian culture, practical applications of the philosophy of ethics in everyday high school life, a youth book recommendation site, a site to help high school students reduce stress and avoid procrastination, a site for sharing trends in athletic shoes, a site for sharing life hacks that make high school easier, and a site for surviving junior-year humanities courses. Throughout 3 weeks of web development, the instructor provided individual help, offering constructive, guiding feedback about each student's efforts. He also required students to provide weekly peer evaluation about their teammates' collaboration skills.

The instructor taught students about pathways to joining web development communities of practice, giving detailed information about what kind of education was required, what types of jobs and companies hire web developers, and what kinds of people currently pursue these pathways, including his own path. The web developers who visited the class also talked about the pathways that they took, what they regretted about their path, and what surprised them as they followed their path.

In the context of the pedagogical strategies and content described above, the instructors' mentorship formation strategies included the following: 1) talking each day to each student about their progress on learning, 2) in these conversations, explicitly linking their progress to the goals they reported in their possible selves, and 3) at the end of the course, having an explicit mentoring conversation with each student individually, offering to help them with their college applications, connect them with further computing education experiences, and answer their questions over email as they approached college.

Finally, at the end of the course, the instructor gave students the survey from Study 1, excluding redundant demographic questions.

4.2 Results

UB student interest in computing changed significantly, moving from a mean of 0.5 to 1.35 (t(10)=2.9, p=.016). None of the students began at the top of the interest scale and all but one had an increase toward neutral or positive interest.

Students' descriptions of their possible selves at the end of the class revealed some reasons for these changes. Six of the 11 students were still sure they wanted to be doctors, lawyers, software developers, and pharmacists. However, 5 of the 11 students described substantially different possible selves, incorporating computing into their identities. One student who was particularly engaged in

Table 2: An ordinal regression predicting change in interest in computing. *=p<.05.

	B	SE B	Wald	β
Interest before class	-0.46	0.25	3.49	.06
Male	4.05	2.27	3.18	.07
SES	-0.21	0.58	0.13	.71
# PL encountered	-0.67	0.67	0.99	.32
No mentor	5.79	2.82	4.21	.04*
Midterm	-0.43	0.19	4.97	.16

class went from being generically interested in medicine to wanting to strengthen her coding and drawing skills, both of which she explored in the design and implementation of her team's website. One went from wanting to be a doctor to wanting to first study computer science to make money, then use the money to go to medical school to study ophthalmology. Another student who was particularly adept at learning JavaScript went from describing his future as *"a blank canvas"* to wanting to study computer science and aviation, because *"perhaps those fields need someone to write programs to analyze data and make better equipment"* (UB, Asian male, age 15). Yet another student came into the class with strong web development skills from a prior course but low self-efficacy due to a bad teamwork experience. After working independently on his project, he left the class confident in his skills and said he was now considering computer science as a major.

To investigate what was related to these changes, we built a regression similar to that in Study 1, but this time predicting *change* in interest from several factors. We included the same factors from before: number of programming languages encountered before the class as an indicator of prior knowledge, gender, SES, and whether a student had a mentor. However, we also included interest in computing prior to the class (as this would likely contribute to interest after the class) and the students' scores on their final exam (as success in CS classes can greatly influence interest [33]). Change in interest violated normality assumptions for a linear regression, and so we built an ordinal regression model instead, computing the difference in the pre and post sum of Likert items.

Table 2 shows the resulting model. The model explained a significant amount of the variance in change in post-class computing interest (χ^2=21.8, p=.001, Cox and Snell R^2=.86). In this model, not having a mentor before the class was significantly related to positive changes in interest in computing.

When we asked the students to explain how the class influenced their interest in computing, if at all, their explanations included many references to the instructor, and particularly to the inclusive learning environment:

"This class helped me understand what jobs involved with tech would look like and how it's not just a lonely person in the basement." (UB, Asian male, 15)

"The readings from this summer encouraged me to acquire technology skills since President Obama plans to enforce Computer Science classes and it seemed to be possible for anyone to learn once they get past imposter syndrome like that one woman in the reading." (UB, Asian male, 16)

"This class has greatly influenced my attitude towards coding. It allowed me to look past the stereotype that I never realized." (UB, Asian male, 16)

"You definitely changed what I thought about computer science and web design. I love designing things, but I never thought one day I could design my own website in 6 weeks. The environment and class made class more enjoyable for me. This environment made me want to be part of it. Unlike classes where you feel like you aren't needed. Lastly, you taught me the thought and idea of what technology skills can do for you in the future even if it's in the medical field. That makes me want to continue learning." (UB, Asian female, 16)

Students' reflections on the reading assignments revealed similar shifts in interest. For example, one of the readings was a blog post by a woman who started as a web developer and faced imposter syndrome, but eventually realized that failure was part of every developer's job. Two girls were surprised:

"Learning to code is intimidating because it's like learning a foreign language...When I feel frustrated, I start to feel like I don't belong in the class. I start to question whether I should pursue a career where I would never be able to master a subject. Technology is always changing, and I have to ask myself if I would feel comfortable learning something new every day for the rest of my life. I now know it's normal to feel uncomfortable when you are learning something new and that is why I believe I will have the perseverance to learn as much as I can about web design." (UB, Asian female, 15)

"When I first took web design, I thought the guys would be experts in this. Because I know guys who knew a lot about computer [sic] and how it works. So in the beginning I was a bit intimidated until I learned that all of us know nothing about web design. It made me less scared when I want to ask a question about web design." (UB, Asian female, 16)

Three of the students that did not have mentors prior continued to engage the instructor as a mentor after the class ended. One sought advice on computing-related summer jobs and at the time of this writing is participating in a Girls Who Code camp as an instructor upon the instructor's recommendation. Another sought advice on how to engage in computing research as an incoming university freshman and is now participating in a first-generation college student research mentorship program. A third sought advice on what to study to combine computing and medicine.

5 DISCUSSION

Our results contribute the following discoveries about Puget Sound teens with interests in computing:

- Teens can have mentoring relationships with a range of people, including friends, parents, siblings, cousins, teachers, and even neighbors.
- Teens' beliefs about peers who engage in computing education were mostly positive, describing high-achieving youth of any gender, race, or ethnicity.
- Teens' beliefs about software developers described developers as creative, patient, intelligent, hard-working, and perseverant people.
- Beliefs held by those with mentors were more diverse and had greater depth than those without mentors.

- While most teens knew about computing education opportunities regardless of whether they had a mentor, having a mentor was related to engaging in more of them and encountering more programming languages.
- While most teens expressed interest in computing as a skill, subject, and career, teens with mentors reported stronger interest regardless of gender or socioeconomic status.
- Teens that reported the first author as a teacher-mentor reported significantly higher changes in interest in computing than students that already had mentors, regardless of gender, socioeconomic status, performance in class, prior knowledge, or prior interest.

There are many ways to interpret these results. First and foremost, none of these results are causal. It is possible, for example, that students who developed interests in computing did so without mentors (for example, through Code.org's Hour of Code or some other compulsory learning setting) and then sought mentors in their social networks. It is also possible that interest was entirely mentorship driven, with mentors proactively triggering the students' interest in computing and then maintaining it through subsequent activities. Students' self-reports about their mentoring relationships suggest the latter was more likely than the former, as most students with mentors described fathers and siblings proactively introducing them to computing.

Similarly, our efforts to *form* a mentoring relationships with the UB students may have not been the *cause* of students' increased interest in computing. Students may have had other experiences in the summer that developed interest in computing, such as the college prep class that encouraged the UB students to develop their career interests. It may have been the *combined* effect of mentorship and career interest reflection that produced the increases in interest. The ability to form a mentoring relationship with the Asian students may have also been mediated by the somewhat Asian appearance of the instructor. That said, prior work on role models suggests that identity matters less in recruiting than in retention [15].

Our study has limited generalizability, first and foremost because of the sampling biases in our data. At the time of our study, there were tens of thousands of high school students in the Puget Sound metropolitan area and we only learned about 57 of them. Our claims are limited to the types of students who enroll in UB (low income, first-generation college students), and the types of students who enroll in the SY camps that we offered (students with highly educated parents interested in their teens learning to code). We did not study any low-income students who were not college bound, nor did we study middle-class students who did not have sufficient prior interests (or parents with sufficient interest) to enroll in our web design courses. There were also likely structural inequities that prevented the full population of students of being aware of our classes, limiting participation from teens in lower SES, lower educational attainment families.

There is also little evidence to claim generality of our results to other regions in the world. For example, even regions that share some features to the Puget Sound such as Silicon Valley have other features that could have changed our findings: it is more diverse racially and socioeconomically than Seattle, not to mention an order of magnitude larger in population. Moreover, it is unclear how our results would generalize to regions that do not have vibrant software industries or universal access to computing education.

Our measurements relied on self-report surveys and scales that can be sensitive to the timing of self-report, introducing some threats to construct validity. Moreover, while most of the measurements in the surveys were taken from validated scales, not all of them were, and so some of the data may not accurately reflect the phenomena we intended to study. Moreover, we used regressions to investigate predictors of interest, which only suggest correlation.

In light of these multiple interpretations and limitations, the need for future work is extensive. Studies should investigate the causal effects of mentorship, for example, through formal mentorship programs, exploring the potential for virtuous cycles of mentorship-triggered interest and learner-driven interest maintenance. Future studies should investigate the granular effects of specific forms of mentorship, such as the explicit instruction by parents and siblings that students reported. Studies should also investigate the specific effects of mentorship on other constructs such as changes in identity and shifting of beliefs, especially in settings with the more negative beliefs we did not observe.

In addition to developing a better theoretical account of computing mentorship, there are also numerous design questions about how to structure mentorship in computing. For instance, are adults, siblings, friends, or teachers better or worse positioned to mentor adolescents about computing? Are teacher-mentors scalable, given typical class sizes in public schools? What kinds of skills do mentors need to be credible and relevant to teens? Would recent high school graduates pursuing computing be effective mentors? Is remote mentorship feasible, especially in light of the majority of regions in the world having substantially fewer mentors than regions like the Puget Sound? These alternatives suggest that increasing interest in computing, even in the presence of universal access to learning opportunities, may require significant investments from the computing community to increase interest and engagement in computing education. Recent efforts like *NextBillion.org*, which helps connects people with disabilities to industry professionals is one example of what such efforts might entail.

ACKNOWLEDGMENTS

This material is based upon work supported by Microsoft, Google, Adobe, and the National Science Foundation under Grant No. 1539179, 1314399, 1240786, and 1153625.

REFERENCES

[1] Tammy D. Allen and Lillian T. Eby. 2011. *The Blackwell handbook of mentoring: A multiple perspectives approach*. John Wiley & Sons, USA.
[2] Joshua D Angrist and Victor Lavy. 1999. Using Maimonides' rule to estimate the effect of class size on scholastic achievement. *The Quarterly Journal of Economics* 114, 2 (1999), 533–575.
[3] Louise Archer and Hiromi Yamashita. 2003. 'Knowing their limits'? Identities, inequalities and inner city school leavers' post-16 aspirations. *Journal of Education Policy* 18, 1 (2003), 53–69.
[4] Brigid Barron, Caitlin Kennedy Martin, Lori Takeuchi, and Rachel Fithian. 2009. Parents as learning partners in the development of technological fluency. *International Journal of Learning and Media* 1, 2 (2009), 55–77.
[5] Margaret R Beam, Chuansheng Chen, and Ellen Greenberger. 2002. The nature of adolescents' relationships with their "very important" non-parental adults. *American Journal of Community Psychology* 30, 2 (2002), 305–325.
[6] Lori Carter. 2006. Why students with an apparent aptitude for computer science don't choose to major in computer science. *SIGCSE Bulletin* 38, 1 (2006), 27–31.

[7] Gwo-Dong Chen, Liang-Yi Li, and Chin-Yea Wang. 2012. A Community of Practice Approach to Learning Programming. *Turkish Online Journal of Educational Technology-TOJET* 11, 2 (2012), 15–26.

[8] Sapna Cheryan, Benjamin J Drury, and Marissa Vichayapai. 2013. Enduring influence of stereotypical computer science role models on womenfis academic aspirations. *Psychology of Women Quarterly* 37, 1 (2013), 72–79.

[9] Jeffrey Cornelius-White. 2007. Learner-centered teacher-student relationships are effective: A meta-analysis. *Review of educational research* 77, 1 (2007), 113–143.

[10] A Craig. 1998. Peer mentoring female computing students–does it make a difference?. In *Proceedings of the 3rd Australasian conference on Computer science education*. ACM, USA, 41–47.

[11] Gloria Crisp and Irene Cruz. 2009. Mentoring college students: A critical review of the literature between 1990 and 2007. *Research in higher education* 50, 6 (2009), 525–545.

[12] Phillip Dawson. 2014. Beyond a definition: Toward a framework for designing and specifying mentoring models. *Educational Researcher* 43, 3 (2014), 137–145.

[13] Betsy DiSalvo, Mark Guzdial, Amy Bruckman, and Tom McKlin. 2014. Saving face while geeking out: Video game testing as a justification for learning computer science. *Journal of the Learning Sciences* 23, 3 (2014), 272–315.

[14] Peggy Doerschuk. 2004. A research and mentoring program for undergraduate women in computer science. In *Frontiers in Education*. IEEE, USA, S2H-7–12.

[15] Benjamin J Drury, John Oliver Siy, and Sapna Cheryan. 2011. When do female role models benefit women? The importance of differentiating recruitment from retention in STEM. *Psychological Inquiry* 22, 4 (2011), 265–269.

[16] Daryl D'Souza, Margaret Hamilton, James Harland, Peter Muir, Charles Thevathayan, and Cecily Walker. 2008. Transforming learning of programming: a mentoring project. In *Conference on Australasian Computing Education*. Australian Computer Society, Inc., Australia, 75–84.

[17] Eric F Dubow, Paul Boxer, and L Rowell Huesmann. 2009. Long-term effects of parentsfi education on childrenfis educational and occupational success: Mediation by family interactions, child aggression, and teenage aspirations. *Merrill-Palmer quarterly (Wayne State University. Press)* 55, 3 (2009), 224.

[18] Carolyn M Evertson and Carol S Weinstein. 2013. *Handbook of classroom management: Research, practice, and contemporary issues*. Routledge, England.

[19] Arline T Geronimus, John Bound, and Lisa J Neidert. 1996. On the validity of using census geocode characteristics to proxy individual socioeconomic characteristics. *J. Amer. Statist. Assoc.* 91, 434 (1996), 529–537.

[20] Tony Greening. 1998. Computer science: through the eyes of potential students. In *Australasian conference on Computer science education*. ACM, New York, 145–154.

[21] Denise Gürer and Tracy Camp. 2002. An ACM-W literature review on women in computing. *ACM SIGCSE Bulletin* 34, 2 (2002), 121–127.

[22] Mark Guzdial and Allison Elliott Tew. 2006. Imagineering inauthentic legitimate peripheral participation: an instructional design approach for motivating computing education. In *ACM International Workshop on Computing Education Research*. ACM, New York, 51–58.

[23] John C. Hall. 2003. *Mentoring and Young People: A Literature Review*. ERIC, USA.

[24] Michael Hewner. 2013. Undergraduate conceptions of the field of computer science. In *ACM International Computing Education Research*. ACM, New York, 107–114.

[25] Michael Hewner and Mark Guzdial. 2008. Attitudes about computing in postsecondary graduates. In *ACM International Workshop on Computing Education Research*. ACM, New York, 71–78.

[26] Suzanne Hidi and K Ann Renninger. 2006. The four-phase model of interest development. *Educational psychologist* 41, 2 (2006), 111–127.

[27] Mark A Holliday and David R Luginbuhl. 2004. Peer-centered service learning. In *Frontiers in Education*. IEEE, USA, F3E-1–6.

[28] Beth K Humberd and Elizabeth D Rouse. 2016. Seeing you in me and me in you: Personal identification in the phases of mentoring relationships. *Academy of Management Review* 41, 3 (2016), 435–455.

[29] David Marshall Hunt and Carol Michael. 1983. Mentorship: A career training and development tool. *Academy of management Review* 8, 3 (1983), 475–485.

[30] Thomas E. Keller. 2005. The stages and development of mentoring relationships. *Handbook of youth mentoring* 1 (2005), 82–99.

[31] Harold R Kerbo. 1996. *Social stratification and inequality: Class conflict in historical and comparative perspective*. McGraw-Hill College, New York.

[32] Rhodes Jean E. Klaw, Elena L. and Louise F. Fitzgerald. 2003. Natural mentors in the lives of African American adolescent mothers: Tracking relationships over time. *Journal of Youth and Adolescence* 32, 3 (2003), 223–232.

[33] Andrew J Ko. 2009. Attitudes and self-efficacy in young adults' computing autobiographies. In *IEEE Symposium on Visual Languages and Human-Centric Computing*. IEEE, New Jersey, 67–74.

[34] Jean Lave and Etienne Wenger. 1991. *Situated learning: Legitimate peripheral participation*. Cambridge university press, Cambridge.

[35] Colleen M Lewis, Ruth E Anderson, and Ken Yasuhara. 2016. I Don't Code All Day: Fitting in Computer Science When the Stereotypes Don't Fit. In *ACM Conference on International Computing Education Research*. ACM, New York, 23–32.

[36] Jane Margolis, Rachel Estrella, Joanna Goode, Jennifer Jellison Holme, and Kim Nao. 2010. *Stuck in the shallow end: Education, race, and computing*. MIT Press, Cambridge, MA.

[37] Jane Margolis and Allan Fisher. 2003. *Unlocking the clubhouse: Women in computing*. MIT press, Cambridge, MA.

[38] J Mitchell Miller, JC Barnes, Holly Ventura Miller, and Layla McKinnon. 2013. Exploring the link between mentoring program structure & success rates: Results from a national survey. *American Journal of Criminal Justice* 38, 3 (2013), 439–456.

[39] Emma Norling. 1995. Encouraging networking through informal mentoring: a look at a newly-established mentor scheme. In *Second Australasian Women in Engineering Forum*. RMIT, Australia.

[40] Youn Joo Oh, Yueming Jia, Mhora Lorentson, and Frank LaBanca. 2013. Development of the educational and career interest scale in science, technology, and mathematics for high school students. *Journal of Science Education and Technology* 22, 5 (2013), 780–790.

[41] Becky Wai-Ling Packard and Paul F Conway. 2006. Methodological choice and its consequences for possible selves research. *Identity* 6, 3 (2006), 251–271.

[42] SS Pisimisi and MG Ioannides. 2005. Developing mentoring relationships to support the careers of women in electrical engineering and computer technologies. An analysis on mentors' competencies. *European journal of engineering education* 30, 4 (2005), 477–486.

[43] K Ann Renninger and Suzanne Hidi. 2011. Revisiting the conceptualization, measurement, and generation of interest. *Educational Psychologist* 46, 3 (2011), 168–184.

[44] Ashley Robinson, Manuel A Pérez-Quiñones, and Glenda Scales. 2015. Understanding the attitudes of African American middle school girls toward computer science. In *Research in Equity and Sustained Participation in Engineering, Computing, and Technology (RESPECT), 2015*. IEEE, New York, 1–8.

[45] Amber Settle, Sarah Pieczynski, Liz Friedman, and Nathan Kizior. 2013. Evaluating a Prospective Student Mentoring Program. In *International Conference on Frontiers in Education: Computer Science and Computer Engineering (FECS)*. IEEE, USA, 1.

[46] Selcuk R Sirin. 2005. Socioeconomic status and academic achievement: A meta-analytic review of research. *Review of educational research* 75, 3 (2005), 417–453.

[47] Claude M Steele and Joshua Aronson. 1995. Stereotype threat and the intellectual test performance of African Americans. *Journal of personality and social psychology* 69, 5 (1995), 797.

[48] Gloria Childress Townsend. 1996. Viewing video-taped role models improves female attitudes toward computer science. *ACM SIGCSE Bulletin* 28, 1 (1996), 42–46.

[49] Gloria Childress Townsend. 2002. People who make a difference: mentors and role models. *ACM SIGCSE Bulletin* 34, 2 (2002), 57–61.

[50] Etienne Wenger, Richard Arnold McDermott, and William Snyder. 2002. *Cultivating communities of practice: A guide to managing knowledge*. Harvard Business Press, Cambridge, MA.

[51] Sarah Wood and Evan Mayo-Wilson. 2012. School-based mentoring for adolescents: A systematic review and meta-analysis. *Research on Social Work Practice* 22, 3 (2012), 257–269.

[52] Sarita Yardi and Amy Bruckman. 2007. What is computing?: bridging the gap between teenagers' perceptions and graduate students' experiences. In *ACM International Workshop on Computing Education Research*. ACM, New York, 39–50.

Barriers Faced by Coding Bootcamp Students

Kyle Thayer
Paul G. Allen School of Computer Science & Engineering
University of Washington
Seattle, WA 98105
kthayer@cs.washington.edu

Andrew J. Ko
The Information School
University of Washington
Seattle, WA 98105
ajko@uw.edu

ABSTRACT

Coding bootcamps are a new and understudied way of training new software developers. To learn about the barriers bootcamp students face, we interviewed twenty-six coding bootcamp students and analyzed the interviews using the *Communities of Practice* framework. We found that bootcamps can be part of an alternate path into the software industry and they provided a second chance for those who missed computing education opportunities earlier, particularly for women. While bootcamps represented a second chance, students entering the industry through bootcamps faced great personal costs and risks, often including significant time, money and effort spent before, during, and after their bootcamps. Though the coursework of bootcamps only ranged from three to six months, career change could take students a year or more, with some students even attending sections of multiple bootcamps.

CCS CONCEPTS

•**Social and professional topics** → **Computing education;** *Employment issues;* Adult education;

KEYWORDS

Coding bootcamps; computer science education; career change; communities of practice

1 INTRODUCTION

Demand for software developers is expected to grow 17% in the US between 2014 and 2024 [3]. In response to this, more people are graduating from undergraduate computer science (CS) programs (Figure 1), while others are learning software development from online tutorials, Massive Open Online Courses (MOOCs), and now fast-paced coding bootcamps [1, 17]. Coding bootcamps have grown rapidly in the US and Canada since 2013 (Figure 1) and serve a different population than undergraduate programs [19].

In spite of the growth of bootcamps, we know little about the barriers bootcamp students face, as previous reports on bootcamps have only focused on the logistics of bootcamps [18, 22], or the demographics and success rate of their graduates [19]. Research in computing education and career change suggests several barriers bootcamp students might face. For example, in various computing education contexts (high schools, colleges and universities), societal

ICER '17, August 18-20, 2017, Tacoma, WA, USA.
© 2017 Copyright held by the owner/author(s). 978-1-4503-4968-0/17/08.
DOI: http://dx.doi.org/10.1145/3105726.3106176

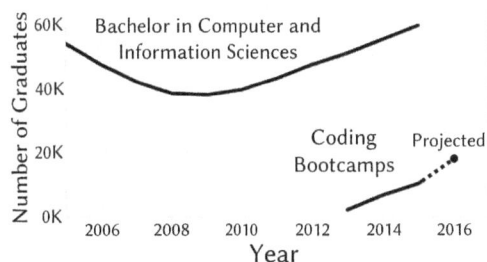

Figure 1: Yearly US bachelor in computer and information science graduation rate (by end of academic year) [14], along with yearly coding bootcamp actual and projected graduation rate in the US and Canada [18].

pressures cause divisions in who is encouraged to use computers and who is made to feel welcome in computing classes, in particular excluding female, black and latino/a students [2, 5, 12, 13]. In computing classes, students face stereotypes of what it takes to be a "real" programmer [5, 10, 12, 13] and those who feel belonging, comfort and confidence are better able to succeed [21, 27]. Similarly, people changing careers face barriers of confidence, gender, age, and educational level [4, 15, 20] while also facing pressures due to lost income and the effect of lost income on family [15, 20].

We hypothesized that the barriers faced in other computing education and career change contexts would also be faced by bootcamp students as they went through bootcamps and sought jobs in the software industry. We therefore interviewed 26 current and former bootcamp students to ask about their stories and the barriers they faced. Our participants represented eight bootcamps and a range of trajectories and stages, from early in a bootcamp to having finished. After considering frameworks for learning [8, 9, 24] and career change [20, 23], we decided to analyze our data with *Communities of Practice* [24] and concepts from the career change literature.

2 RELATED WORK

2.1 Communities of Practice

Communities of practice are "groups of people who share a concern or a passion for something they do and learn how to do it better as they interact regularly" [25]. These communities can range from formal such as a work team in an office, or informal such as a clique of students. We considered each bootcamp as its own community of practice and software industry jobs as communities of practice tied together in a *constellation of practice* [24].

The *Communities of Practice* framework [24] provided several useful concepts for analyzing and framing our results.[1] Communities of practice have community defined *boundaries* (both *formal*

---

[1] Since Wenger[24] rarely includes formal definitions of his terms, we provide our own.

like member lists and *informal* like specialized jargon) which define what is *inside, outside* and at the *periphery* of the community. For joining a community, these boundaries must be *negotiated* with the community and are one type of barrier to entry. An individual's relationship with a community evolves over time as part of their *learning trajectory* [24]. As individuals belong to multiple communities of practice simultaneously, they face conflicting meanings and practices. The *Communities of Practice* framework has been used to understand the design of schools and businesses [24], apprenticeships [9], career change [26], involvement in Open Source communities [28], identity formation [16], and course design [7].

2.2 Barriers in Career Change

Another concept we used for analyzing barriers was *personal obstacles*,[2] which came from the career change literature. People changing careers face *personal obstacles* that include age, gender, financial considerations around temporary lost income (especially when they had dependent spouses or children), education level, personality and confidence [4, 15, 20].

2.3 Barriers in Computing Education

Previous studies on barriers in computing education have mostly focused on barriers students face in choosing and continuing CS studies in high school, college and university settings. In *Unlocking the Clubhouse* [13], Margolis and Fisher found barriers for women in undergraduate CS that included admissions (*formal boundary*), gender divides in computer use from a young age, stereotypes of who a "real" programmer is (e.g., anti-social), expected background experience and a belief in a "natural" ability to understand computers (*informal boundaries*). They also found women faced barriers of lost confidence and lack of social support (*personal obstacles*). *Stuck in the Shallow End: Education, Race and Computing* by Margolis, Estrella, et al. [12] examined the racial gap in high school CS, finding barriers that included lack of access to classes (*formal boundary*), cultural expectations on who the classes were for, feelings of isolation in classes, divisions within classes between those who "have it or don't have it" (*informal boundaries*), and lack of social support (*personal obstacle*). Additional studies found participation and success in computing programs depended on background experience [2, 27], comfort level [27], sense of belonging and stereotypes (disproportionately negatively affecting women) [2, 5, 10, 16], view of self as an "insider" [21], and believed role of luck [27].

In addition to these studies, there have been posters, marketing reports and commissioned reports on bootcamps [11, 18, 19, 22]. In the US and Canada in 2016, bootcamps had an average tuition of $11,451 and length of 13 weeks [18]. Bootcamp graduates were diverse in backgrounds (54% had previous full-time employment and 40% had never programmed before) and diverse in gender (43% were female, compared to the 16% of CS graduates) [19]. A report on international bootcamps briefly mentioned students may face *formal boundaries* (admissions, payment, and graduation), *informal boundaries* (gender), and *personal obstacles* (intensity, time, location, and family support), but it didn't provide details [22].

3 METHOD

To study barriers in bootcamps and the software industry, we interviewed current and former students of bootcamps, focusing on bootcamps in the Puget Sound area (Washington, USA). We defined coding bootcamps as non-university programs that offered full-time, in-person, short-term (months-long) software development training. This excluded weekend, night, and part-time classes, strictly online bootcamps and any program that takes more than one year. We also excluded bootcamps that were not primarily targeted for software engineering jobs (e.g., data science, UX).

We found an initial group of bootcamp students through personal connections, LinkedIn, and a weekend programming class. From there we used stratified snowball sampling to find a range of bootcamp students. We focused on recruiting participants from different bootcamps, at different stages (*in bootcamp, post-bootcamp, job hunting, in job, no longer searching for a job*), as well as diversity in race and gender. We conducted 26 interviews and had at least two students from each of six full-time bootcamps in the Puget Sound area: Ada Developers Academy, Code Fellows, Coding Dojo, Dev Bootcamp, Galvanize, and General Assembly, as well as one student each from two out of state bootcamps. We had at least ten females and eight males.[3] We had students who were Black, White, Asian, Latino/a, and at least five who were more than one race or ethnicity. The youngest participant (who we know the age of) started a bootcamp at age 18, and the oldest at 39. We also interviewed students who identified as straight and as gay.

We developed a semi-structured interview protocol consisting of twenty-five questions divided into four sections: *background, deciding to attend a bootcamp, changes in views and goals*, and *how they perceive their experience in relation to others'*. We piloted and refined the questions with the help of someone changing careers into the software industry, though not through a bootcamp. The length of the interviews ranged from 24 to 94 minutes with a median length of 43 minutes. After completing the interviews, we transcribed them, removed personally identifiable information, and deleted the recordings.

From the interviews, we created chronological *coding bootcamp trajectories* and *software development trajectories* for each participant. We categorized the pieces of each trajectory by how they related to the community of practice. We then coded all discussions of *formal boundaries* (e.g., admissions, graduation, and hiring), *informal boundaries* (e.g., fitting in, unstated expectations, and group dynamics) with respect to the two communities of practice. We also did this for discussions of *personal obstacles*, which we defined as obstacles to negotiating community boundaries that were not concerns of the community (e.g., personal financial burdens and relational costs). We then synthesized the results in each category.

4 RESULTS

Because the coding bootcamp students we talked to viewed entering the software industry as their high-level goal (with bootcamps as a means to that end), we first discuss students' software industry trajectories and then discuss how students' bootcamp experiences

---

[2]*Personal obstacles* is our term combining "personal factors" and "obstacles" [15, 20].

[3]We did not ask for demographic information in some interviews. For those, we counted any statements participants made which stated or implied their demographics.

related to these trajectories. We include quotes throughout, selectively omitting identifying information to preserve anonymity, and making minor edits for clarity. Any emotions reported are those explicitly stated by participants.

4.1 Participant Learning Trajectories

4.1.1 Software Industry Learning Trajectories. For each participant, we mapped each step of their *software industry trajectories* chronologically using the following four levels of involvement in the software industry: *unrelated activities* (e.g., other education, jobs), *preparation to enter the software industry* (e.g., classes, bootcamps, building a portfolio), *partial employment as a software developer* (e.g., contracts, internships), and *full employment as a software developer* (the stated goal of all participants).[4] Figure 2 shows the variety of our participants' trajectories. For example, participants P1, P2 and P3 went from unrelated education and careers into full employment while P26 returned to their former career after failing to get employment as a software developer. Nineteen participants took online courses, ten took separate in-person classes, and P5, P8 and P13 had degrees in CS before starting a bootcamp. Participants P18, P22, and P23 attended more than one bootcamp and participants P13, P14, P15, and P24 did not finish a bootcamp and had no plans to. Participants P19, P20 and P21 went to a bootcamp that had a built-in internship.

4.1.2 Coding Bootcamp Learning Trajectories.[5] Since the stated goal of coding bootcamps was to prepare students for entering the software industry, students' trajectories through bootcamps were a part of their trajectories into the software industry. Because of this, most students' bootcamp trajectories appear much like the first half of their software industry trajectories, so we do not show them here. Some students took actions to prepare for the software industry before starting a bootcamp, which incidentally also helped prepare them for their bootcamps. Other students prepared specifically for bootcamps, including P22, who attended the intro section of one bootcamp in order to improve their chances of getting into another bootcamp. While attending bootcamps, some students felt the tests, assignments and even bootcamp graduation did not align with their software industry trajectory. Because of this perceived misalignment, P25 took a break from the bootcamp to study more, P13 quit their bootcamp, and P6 suggested ignoring some bootcamp content and deadlines. After graduating from a bootcamp, some students continued to be involved through residencies (free space and time for building portfolios), paid TA positions, and alumni networks.

4.2 Barriers in the Software Industry

Having seen students' diverse software industry and bootcamp trajectories, we now focus on the boundaries and personal obstacles they faced in the context of their software industry trajectories.

4.2.1 Formal Boundaries. Bootcamp students universally reported wanting a full-time jobs in the software industry. Getting

---

[4]Mapping the learning trajectories of our participants into these categories was mostly straightforward, though there were occasions where chronology was unclear.
[5]In discussing bootcamps, it should be noted that bootcamps are new and changing rapidly, with students mentioning significant changes in courses, content, and social dynamics between cohorts or even within their own journey through a bootcamp.

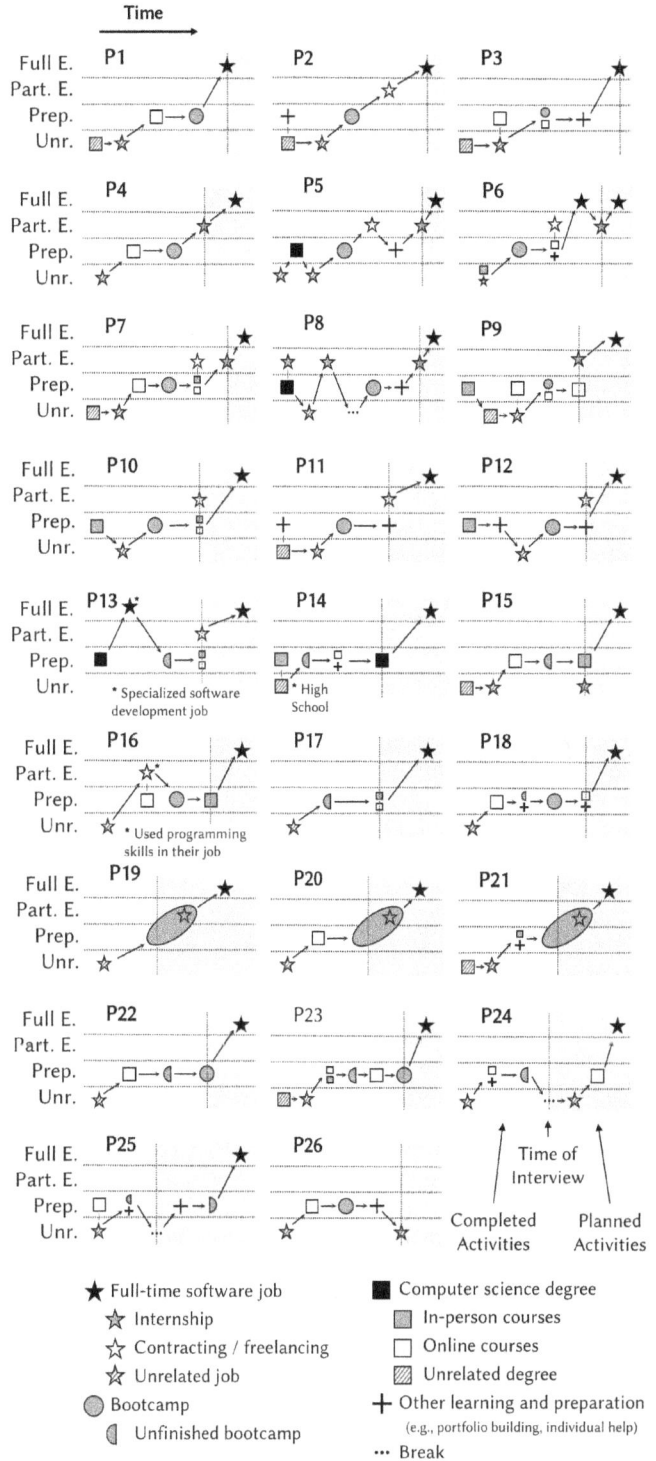

Figure 2: Software industry trajectories for all participants. Each graph show a participant's chronological activities in four levels of increasing software industry involvement: *unrelated* (Unr.), *preparation* (Prep.), *partial employment* (Part. E.), and *full employment* (Full E.). Participants are sorted by industry involvement at time of interview.

these jobs meant getting and passing job interviews. In their attempts cross these boundaries, four of our participants mentioned not understanding why they passed or failed interviews. This uncertainty was compounded by interviewers being unwilling to share their decision making process. As P5 said:

> [The problem is] not understanding what I'm doing wrong. [...] I would ask [interviewers], "Please give me feedback. What can I do better next time?" But I wouldn't get a response.

In spite of some uncertainty, bootcamp students mentioned several key factors in getting and passing job interviews.

The first was relevant educational credentials. While three of our participants had degrees in CS (bachelor's or associate's), the rest did not. Some of our participants chose to attend a bootcamp as a way of getting relevant educational credentials that would help with job interviews. P6 believed their bootcamp did just that, but several of our participants felt that bootcamp certificates were looked down on by employers. P3 said there was a "stigma" against bootcamp certificates and P26 explained:

> [I thought bootcamps] represented a vocational training standard, that it's somehow equivalent to going to nursing school and getting a certificate that says, "I'm qualified to be an entry level nurse." [...] It simply doesn't work that way.

Second, bootcamp graduates talked about the need to get initial software industry work experience (six participants describe this with a version of the phrase "get a foot in the door"). To get initial experience, some bootcamp graduates found paid contracting work and internships. Six participants were in internships and three were in a bootcamp that included internships. We believe our data over-represents internships since several participants were recruited through others in the same internship and we heard little else about internships besides how most were not open to bootcamp graduates (P16 said, "A lot of the internships [...] only want college-aged computer science students.").

Third, several of our participants mentioned the importance of online portfolios in getting a job. Some said their bootcamps gave them enough time, knowledge, and projects for their portfolio, while others used additional time and effort after graduation.

Fourth, in order to find job openings and meet recruiters, our participants talked about the need to network by going to tech meetups and hackathons, applying for jobs, and using LinkedIn and bootcamp Slack channels. P8 had a programming background, but chose to attend a bootcamp in part for the networking and P3 believed networking made a large difference in getting a job:

> Some people were always behind in their coding, but they got jobs straight away because they had the networking connections.

Fifth, our participants emphasized the importance of interviewing skills, especially the skill of "whiteboarding" (eight students used a variation of that word) an interview technique, often requiring knowledge of data structures and algorithms. Some students approved of the whiteboarding training at their bootcamps, while others felt they needed more practice than their bootcamp gave them. Students used a variety of methods to get more whiteboarding

practice, from online courses, to whiteboarding practice meetups, to non-bootcamp in-person classes.

Besides whiteboarding skills, several of our participants mentioned soft skills interviewers were looking for. P10 mentioned needing to be "a cool person," and P1 listed several specific factors:

> I felt when I was in interviews they were saying that they want someone with strong communication skills and someone who's easy to work with, a team player, who took instruction well.

4.2.2 Informal Boundaries. Our participants' discussion of informal boundaries fell into three categories: *knowledge, identity,* and *belonging.* The *knowledge* expected of a software developer included "learning to learn," meaning the ability to learn new programming languages and libraries from documentation, tutorials, and websites like StackOverflow. Twelve students mentioned this concept. P7 said this was the skill they wanted out of a bootcamp and most said this was something their bootcamp taught them, though P22 was annoyed with how this was taught:

> So they're trying to get you into this mentality of you have to read all the documentation. They sit back in the background [to let students read the documentation], and what annoys me is that I've paid a lot of money so that I could have somebody there to teach it to me.

Another piece of knowledge expected of software developers was knowing popular technologies and practices. P12 mentioned learning at their bootcamp about programming tools like Git and Slack, while P22 said they went to a bootcamp because they "wanted to learn the technologies that are up-and-coming."

The second category of informal boundaries was *identity.* Some students said they had difficulties in claiming an identity as a software developer and felt *impostor syndrome.*[6] Impostor syndrome was mentioned by seven of our participants (though one said they didn't struggle with it). One student (no CS degree) said that even after working as a software developer for about six months, they "still don't feel like an established developer." P2 said their bootcamp encouraged them to publicly claim the title of "web developers:"

> At the end of the first week they said, "Bring up your LinkedIn profiles [...] and change [your title] to web developer." And we're all like, "What? You've got to be kidding me. We're not web developers yet." And her point was that until you start thinking of yourself as one, then nobody else is going to.

The third category of informal boundaries was *belonging,* or fitting in among software developers. This included needing to know "the terms that interviewers are looking for," (P7) and handling "the social aspects that allow you to be a part of this group" (P5). One of the most mentioned aspects of fitting in was the lack of women. One participant (male, CS degree) said his current work environment was "all white dudes." Another participant (female, no CS degree) worried about how to handle a male-only work environment:

> In an actual job [when] I'm the only woman on the team, how do I do that?

---

[6]Impostor syndrome is when someone falsely believes that they are not competent and that they have fooled anyone who thinks they are [6].

Several participants said gender dynamics played into why they did not learn software development earlier. One participant (female, no CS degree) said:

> I never thought when I was younger that women could be programmers. That's just something that everybody knew, I guess.

Another participant (female, no CS degree) said her bootcamp provided a second chance to become a software developer:

> I'm a good example of somebody who easily could've gotten into this field the first time around. When I was in college [...] it just wasn't floated as something I could do. Nobody ever said, "Oh, you can't be a computer scientist." But nobody ever said, "Oh, you can be a computer scientist," either.

Race also came up as an element of fitting in. One Black participant (female, no CS degree) mentioned the lack of diversity at her current company:

> Especially at [my company], I felt like a lot of the software engineers I had seen are white or Indian or Asian. I see very few women, I see very few black people, so it's hard,

An Asian participant (male, no CS degree) said he was used to being a minority, but in the "programming world [he] wasn't a minority anymore," and a Latino participant (male, CS degree) said his race was less of an issue in Seattle and in the software industry than in his hometown:

> [In my hometown] it always felt like [...] I was just the brown guy. [...] Coming out here, people are a lot more open minded and they don't care what you are, they just care what you're doing.

Besides race and gender, the perception of software developers as nerdy or intelligent played a role in fitting in. P25 said:

> I started [learning to code] online. But it was so foreign to me that I'm like, "Okay, these are just for nerdy people. There's no way I'm gonna be able to."

Similarly, P2 perceived back-end programmers as "really technical people who eat Linux for breakfast," and then was surprised to find they also enjoyed back-end programming.

For others, the perceived nerdiness and intelligence of software developers was a desirable feature. One (female, no CS degree) had negative experiences with the online gaming culture, and needed to "start learning if [the software industry] is a community I can stand." She said:

> When I actually went [to a tech meetup, the fact that I was new] wasn't any kind of barrier, [...] people were actually supportive.

P16 felt similarly about meeting software developers:

> You know, when I went to a lot of events before I started bootcamps, I thought, [...] "I feel like I fit in with the curiosity and, for the most part, level of intelligence," even though I didn't have any of [programming] skills yet.

4.2.3 Bootcamps' Role in Negotiating Boundaries.
Bootcamp students had to negotiate both formal and informal boundaries in the software industry, and our participants expressed different views on how attending bootcamps contributed to this process.

Some participants believed their bootcamps were successful in getting them what they needed to know, such as P4:

> I would say that going to [my bootcamp] was probably the best decision that I've ever made [...]. Going from not knowing anything about coding [six months earlier] to being here today is pretty ridiculous…I love [my bootcamp].

Some were upset with their bootcamps. P12 said some from their cohort "want[ed] to do a class action lawsuit," and P26 said, "if I were able to do it all over again, I absolutely would not go."

Others had mixed feelings, such as P16, who said bootcamps and other classes were "just steps along the path [into the software industry] that every person has to find," and another participant (male, CS degree), who said:

> I feel very confident being able to get a job now. And I do attribute it to how things went while I was at [my bootcamp]. But [...] I withhold some judgment on how good [my bootcamp] is at producing employment for people on a broader scale.

Several students were skeptical of the success rates their bootcamps advertised. One (female, CS degree) questioned whether contracting work was being counted as success and P11 said their contracting work was announced as successful employment. One bootcamp had a (later discontinued) job guarantee program with strict requirements which one student (male, no CS degree) missed at the end. Another student thought these strict requirements were used to make the bootcamp success rate look better.

4.2.4 Personal Obstacles.
Bootcamp students also faced *personal obstacles* in entering the software industry. Most of these personal obstacles stemmed from the time it took to transition into the software industry. While a number of students told us they chose bootcamps because they provided a faster route to a job than a degree, many still found time to be an obstacle. Students could spend a year or more when including the time spent learning programming before their bootcamp, or learning more and seeking full-time jobs after graduation (Table 1)[7]. Many felt their bootcamps had not communicated accurately about the time needed. P16 said, "I wish I had known before I started [the bootcamp] that it could take a really long time." In addition to losing time in the career change process, the career change also could mean loss of previous career and educational investments, like P9 said:

> I knew if I went into coding, I would be making my bachelor's degree obsolete. And that was a hard thing.

Financial costs were a personal obstacle for students trying to enter the software industry. These costs came from bootcamp tuition and prolonged unemployment. P1 said, "the cost became more of an obstacle after graduation, when I was on the job search," and another participant (male, CS degree) said he was surprised by this cost:

> When I [started the bootcamp, I] was really surprised [that after] almost four months [...] there was a decent number of [the previous cohort] still not having jobs. [...] I certainly hadn't factored that into my finances.

---

[7]Our participants did not always tell us how much time they spent on different activities, particularly with activities before bootcamps.

Table 1: Times spent before and after bootcamps

	Time spent before bootcamp	Time from graduation to job		Time from graduation to our interview (no job)	
	Classes (no CS degrees)	Full-time job	Internship	With some contracting	With no contracting
Time Range	3 months - 6 years	2 - 5 months	0 - 1.5 years	3 - 12 months	1 week - 9+ months
Median Time	9 months	2 months	1 week	5.5 months	2.5 months
Participant #s	9, 16, 20, 26	1, 2, 3, 6,	4, 5, 7, 8, 9	10, 11, 12, 13	15, 16, 17, 18, 26

These financial obstacles were mitigated in various ways. Some participants had a spouse who supported them. One participant went back to part-time work after their bootcamp while continuing to study on their own. Bootcamps sometimes offered partial solutions through paid TA positions that graduates could take while they were job-hunting. Some students still struggled tremendously. P26, who could not find a job after attending, said:

> I have been so distressed by [the bootcamp and job search]. I have put everything on hold. My house is for sale. My whole life is in shambles because of this. The whole thing has pretty much derailed my career, derailed my life. I spent tens of thousands of dollars pursuing this.

Another participant (female, no CS degree) said:

> To be extremely honest, in choosing this path, I've come the closest to being homeless that I've ever been.

The obstacles of time and money could be compounded for those with families. One participant told us about the nine months following bootcamp graduation:

> I pretty much devoted my time to [my bootcamp's] prescribed job hunting methods, which means financially, I have no money. [...] And that [sacrifice] reflects on my family because now we're low on funds [...] and now instead of selling our house and buying a house, we're selling our house to pay the debt that we're in and then go rent until I can find a job.

In addition to time and money were several other obstacles. Finding support of family and friends was an obstacle for some, including one participant (female, no CS degree) who said:

> My friends and family [...] have known me until that point as nonprofit lady who did informal education and experiential education. So when I said, "I'm doing this program so I can be a software developer," they'd just look at me like, [...] "You doing tech? We just don't get it."

Location was another. Though some said the software industry opened opportunities to live where they wanted, others had to leave friends and family. As one participant (female, no CS degree) said:

> I love [my state]. I have a house there. And my husband's currently there. I wanna go back, but at the same time, [my internship in Washington is at] one of the top tech companies in the United States.

Another set of obstacles involved motivation. Several students mentioned the difficulty of maintaining focus while learning software development outside of a bootcamp. For example, P10 said:

> I didn't want to commit towards something that I wasn't passionate about, and regular school is boring. [...] I

needed to go to a bootcamp, because it's going to keep me focused.

Motivation to persevere on the job hunt was an obstacle for some, like P5, who said they applied to 100 different jobs and P1, who described job hunting as "dehumanizing."

Finally, confidence was an obstacle for some students, which was previously discussed in terms of impostor syndrome in 4.2.2. For some students, attending a bootcamp increased their confidence, (P1 said "[My bootcamp] made me very confident about my ability to achieve the goals that I've set for myself as long as I work hard."), while others lost confidence in a bootcamp (P18 said, "My confidence went downhill after that month at [the bootcamp].").

4.3 Barriers in Coding Bootcamps

We now turn from the barriers students faced in entering the software industry to those they faced specifically in bootcamps.

4.3.1 Formal Boundaries. Formal boundaries in bootcamps included admissions, payment, co-location, and bootcamp stages. Admission to a bootcamp could be permissive (one student said their bootcamp had "no entrance exam or anything [...] they'll take literally anyone.") or strict, such as the first one P10 applied to:

> It's super competitive. The acceptance rate I think is 2% [...] I didn't get in, which is fine. So that's why I went to [another bootcamp].

After admission, all bootcamps required in-person attendance (at least for some sections of the bootcamp) and significant payment. One bootcamp had no tuition, but for the others, our participants mentioned prices from $10,000 to $20,000. Some bootcamps offered scholarships and some allowed students to pay partial tuition for only attending part of the bootcamp. During the bootcamp, courses or stages were formal boundaries marking progress. Some bootcamps had tests that had to be passed in order to advance. When students graduated, they could stay involved through alumni networks, residencies, and TA positions.

4.3.2 Informal Boundaries. Informal boundaries within bootcamps were often similar to those in the software industry (4.2.2), particularly those of race, gender, expectations around knowledge, impostor syndrome and the perceived "nerdiness" and "intelligence" of software developers. For example, the demographic makeup of many bootcamps had a lack of women and minorities like the software industry. P24 said that there were only two women in their cohort, and another (male, CS degree) described the ways his cohort was homogeneous:

> Almost everyone was in a really tight age band. It was a bunch of people that were 27 years old. Everybody

was white. Everybody was middle-class, wealthy though there were a couple outliers. […] The only way that [my bootcamp] was diversifying at all from the current demographic of people in software was there were a lot of women there.

On the other hand, some bootcamps pushed for more diversity. For example, one bootcamp only accepted women and people of non-binary gender, and at least two bootcamps had built-in training around diversity and empathy. One (female, no CS degree) explained how welcoming she felt her bootcamp cohort was:

There are [many] of us that come from poor backgrounds. There are a number of us that are Latina. […] [My bootcamp] is the first place where I felt that owning different identities and being different is okay.

A different kind of diversity at bootcamps was in students' relations to programmers. Though we did not specifically ask, we found that at least four students were married to programmers, and another seven had parents, siblings or friends who were programmers. One student (male, CS degree) said:

Yes, [there are] women being involved in programming, but the women the bootcamps are drawing in right now are from the same social sphere as the current programmers.

As with diversity, the informal boundaries around perceptions of "nerdiness" and "intelligence" showed up in bootcamps. For example, P22 said they had difficulty relating to classmates who were gamers. Similarly, students mentioned feeling impostor syndrome in their bootcamps. In particular, several students mentioned their cohorts being divide into two groups. There were different descriptions of the divide based on one or more factors including effort, "being good at school" (P16), being "tech savvy" (P3), and seven people mentioned a divide based on "background" and previous "experience" with programming, such as P18:

It was divided, the class. Those with experience, I think, they were looking down at [those of us without experience] because maybe there were certain things we were supposed to know and we didn't.

Another participant (female) saw this divide from the other side:

A lot of [the other students] don't have the experience that I have. I have a degree in computer science, I have 10 years-plus experience in a job market. […] A lot of people are coming from accounting, or something else completely unrelated [and] are probably are going to have a way harder time than I am.

This divide was difficult for some students. For example, P25 talked about a student who was having trouble and then quit:

To me what was most sad was not the fact that he quit, [but that] he felt he was dumb and not smart enough to do it.

To cope with this divide, some students tried to reach out within their cohort, like P12 who hung out with more experienced programmers, even though they did not feel like they fit in with them.

Though some students talked about divided classrooms, other students mentioned group bonds that formed in their bootcamp. P5 mentioned making close friends at their bootcamp and P9 said at

their bootcamp, "everybody knows what's going on with everybody else. It was a very close-knit experience."

One final informal boundary faced by students was access to teachers. While some participants at some bootcamps said their teachers were helpful and engaged with everyone, other participants felt differently, such as one (female, no CS degree), who said "I felt uncomfortable asking questions [of the teachers]." One (no CS degree) had a particularly bad experience with asking for help:

There was this one time where my database wouldn't work because I hadn't capitalized a letter and I asked one of the assistant teachers about that and he thought it was ridiculous that I made a mistake about this capital letter.

Some participants saw bias in who their teachers spent time with. One participant (male, no CS degree) believed some women were getting extra attention and another (female, no CS degree) said extra help was "reserved for people who were on the upper-end of class." TAs provided a middle ground of access between students and teachers, though opinions ranged from, "It's very nice that we have TAs" (female, no CS degree), to "The TAs were not helpful whatsoever" (female, no CS degree).

4.3.3 Personal Obstacles. Many of the personal obstacles faced by bootcamp students in their software industry trajectories (4.2.4) overlap with those they faced in attending and succeeding in bootcamps, such as time, money, impostor syndrome, and location. For example, just as location was an obstacle for some jobs, one participant (female, no CS degree) moved away from her husband to attend a bootcamp.

The ways personal obstacles were unique in bootcamps revolved around what eight students described as the "intensity" of the bootcamps. The intensity started with a large percentage of students' weekly time spent on the full-time portion of their bootcamps.[8] One participant (female, no CS degree) said that the official weekly schedule of her bootcamp was eleven hour days, six days a week, while P18 talked of even longer days:

Ten, twelve hours at least per day, and sometimes fourteen or sixteen hours […] and no weekends because we had assignments.

This time spent gave our participants very little time to do other things in their life. One (female, no CS degree) talked about the resulting state of her home and hygiene:

I did all my laundry this weekend, for the first time in like a month, because I was out of everything. My kitchen is a disaster. My whole house is just a mess. Anything that is not directly related to [the bootcamp] or to keeping me up and functioning, just goes by the wayside. […] I don't remember the last time I had a shower.

The time spent at bootcamps added financial obstacles beyond just tuition and costs of living. Students were not able to hold jobs for full-time portion of their bootcamps and P9 said financial difficulties caused some people to drop out of their bootcamps.

The intense time commitment of bootcamps also meant students lost time with friends (P11: "I had to tell pretty much everyone in my immediate intimate circle, 'I'm probably going to disappear.' "),

---

[8]Some bootcamps were broken into stages and they allowed or required the early stages to be taken online or as night classes.

partners (P21: "My poor boyfriend. I see him so rarely.") and family (P12: "I didn't spend time with my family at all for a month."). Also, similar to the software industry trajectories 4.2.4, some students faced obstacles in getting social support for attending bootcamps.

The intensity and speed at which material had to be learned at bootcamps could be very stressful for students. P11 said everyone else in their cohort broke down and cried at some point and one participant (female, no CS degree) said how this affected her "brain power:"

> Sometimes I'm just so burnt out, I can't even think. I can't process. Somebody asked me, "What'd you have for dinner last night?" I'm like, "I don't know. I dumped all that."

To succeed in the intense bootcamp environment, several participants said students needed confidence, commitment, and determination. P2 said, "What's going to make or break your success [in a bootcamp] is how nice you are to yourself when you're frustrated." Another (female, no CS degree) got help from her husband:

> I learned more from coming home and my husband teaching me algorithms and how to approach a certain problem than [from the] teaching in class.

The intensity of bootcamps also had an effect on some students' health. Two students mentioned how their diet had suffered (E.g., P5: "When I first started doing this, I didn't really eat or drink too much.") and three participants mentioned their lack of sleep while attending a bootcamp. P12 talked about getting sick:

> When I was in college, when I got sick, I could take some time off. At work, I got sick and they'd rather me stay home. Here, when I got sick, I needed to still show up because one day of missing a class is a lot.

5 DISCUSSION

Unlike prior reports on bootcamps [18, 18, 22] our study is the first to explore the experiences and perspectives of bootcamp students.

Our investigation provided a long, chronological perspective of several adults' attempts to enter the software industry (Fig. 2), and showed how bootcamps provided a second chance. In particular, some women, as in previous research [2, 5, 13], either had not thought programming was something for them or had been scared off by the lack of women in CS. When attempting to enter the software industry through bootcamps, many of our participants, perhaps due to their independence and experience or because of misalignments between bootcamps and the software industry, made use of additional time and resources outside of their bootcamps or even attended sections of multiple bootcamps. For these students, bootcamps were just one step on a longer path to cross the formal and informal boundaries into the software industry, with the bootcamp providing focus, peers, networking and a set curriculum.

The informal community boundaries bootcamp students faced mirror prior work on computing education in high schools, colleges, and universities, such as those around race, gender, and previous experiences [2, 12, 13, 27]. Some, though, found different bootcamps (or cohorts) to be more open and inclusive. This could partially explain how coding bootcamps have achieved near gender parity [19] and may provide insights on how other computing programs can increase diverse engagement. Stereotypes of "nerdiness" and "intelligence" also formed informal boundaries for bootcamp students,

as found elsewhere [2, 5, 10]. The class divide, largely attributed to previous experience, also matched other contexts [12, 13, 21].

Bootcamp students faced significant personal costs when attending bootcamps and changing careers. Some costs, like financial and family concerns, match what has been found in other career change contexts [15, 20]. Beyond those, the intensity of bootcamps and the career change time required significant perseverance and confidence, while leaving little time for relationships and self-care.

Though bootcamps offered more diverse graduates to the software industry, it was these diverse students who were taking on large costs and risks with few guarantees. Only one bootcamp had tuition covered by the industry, and several students doubted the success rates posted by their bootcamps. Additionally, students struggled with finishing their bootcamps, learning the material, knowing what was required to get a job, and a perceived "stigma" against coding bootcamp graduates. Some of our participants found full-time work despite these struggles (many were enthusiastic about their bootcamps), while others struggled or failed. These risks and costs may limit the diversity in background and financial status of those who attempt and succeed in entering the software industry through bootcamps. If coding bootcamps address the difficulties faced by their students and the industry takes on more of the risks and costs, then bootcamps have the potential to expand the pipeline into the software industry with more diverse talent, while personally benefiting many more students to come.

6 LIMITATIONS AND FUTURE WORK

Our research focused on a small sample of students in coding bootcamps in one part of only one country. Other students may have had different experiences, especially in other bootcamps, in other places, and in other times. Additionally, while our stratified snowball sampling provided a range of experiences, we can make few claims about the commonality of experiences or causality.

Our interviews were also limited. We did not ask for a full chronology of events, which may have left gaps in the learning trajectories, and students may have answered differently with a different interviewer (all interviews were done by a white male with a CS background). More perspectives would give further context on bootcamps, such as from classroom observations and the views of bootcamp organizers and teachers, and those making hiring decisions in the software industry. Additionally, our use of prior frameworks in analyzing results could distort student perspectives.

To further understand the role of bootcamps in meeting demand for software developers, our results suggest future studies in the quality and content of instruction, the structural inequities within bootcamps and the software industry, and the downstream differences in long-term careers between software developers with CS degrees and with bootcamp training.

7 ACKNOWLEDGMENTS

We appreciate input from Kristen Thayer, Katharina Reinecke, Daniel Epstein, Trevor Perrier, Amanda Swearngin, Fahad Pervaiz, Harrison Kwik, Leanne Hwa, and Alex Tan. This material is based upon work supported by Microsoft, Google, Adobe, and the National Science Foundation under Grant No. 1539179, 1314399, 1240786, and 1153625.

REFERENCES

[1] 2016. Stack Overflow developer survey 2016 results. (2016). http://stackoverflow.com/research/developer-survey-2016

[2] Maureen Biggers, Anne Brauer, and Tuba Yilmaz. 2008. Student perceptions of computer science: A retention study comparing graduating seniors with CS leavers. In *Proceedings of the 39th SIGCSE Technical Symposium on Computer Science Education (SIGCSE '08)*. ACM, New York, NY, USA, 402–406. https://doi.org/10.1145/1352135.1352274

[3] Bureau of Labor Statistics. 2015. *Software developers.* Technical Report. U.S. Department of Labor, Occupational Outlook Handbook, 2016-17 Edition. https://www.bls.gov/ooh/computer-and-information-technology/software-developers.htm

[4] Sally A. Carless and Jessica L. Arnup. 2011. A longitudinal study of the determinants and outcomes of career change. *Journal of Vocational Behavior* 78, 1 (Feb. 2011), 80–91. https://doi.org/10.1016/j.jvb.2010.09.002

[5] Sapna Cheryan, Victoria C. Plaut, Caitlin Handron, and Lauren Hudson. 2013. The stereotypical computer scientist: Gendered media representations as a barrier to inclusion for women. *Sex roles* 69, 1-2 (2013), 58–71. http://link.springer.com/article/10.1007/s11199-013-0296-x

[6] Pauline Rose Clance and Suzanne A. Imes. 1978. The imposter phenomenon in high achieving women: Dynamics and therapeutic intervention. *Psychotherapy: Theory, Research and Practice* 15, 3 (1978), 241–247. http://www.suzanneimes.com/wp-content/uploads/2012/09/ImposterPhenomenon.pdf

[7] Mark Guzdial and Allison Elliott Tew. 2006. Imagineering inauthentic legitimate peripheral participation: An instructional design approach for motivating computing education. In *Proceedings of the Second International Workshop on Computing Education Research (ICER '06)*. ACM, New York, NY, USA, 51–58. https://doi.org/10.1145/1151588.1151597

[8] Mizuko Ito, Kris Gutirrez, Sonia Livingstone, Bill Penuel, Jean Rhodes, Katie Salen, Juliet Schor, Julian Sefton-Green, and S. Craig Watkins. 2013. *Connected Learning.* BookBaby, Cork.

[9] Jean Lave and Etienne Wenger. 1991. *Situated learning: Legitimate peripheral participation.* Cambridge university press.

[10] Colleen M. Lewis, Ruth E. Anderson, and Ken Yasuhara. 2016. "I Don't Code All Day": Fitting in Computer Science When the Stereotypes Don't Fit. In *Proceedings of the 2016 ACM Conference on International Computing Education Research (ICER '16)*. ACM, New York, NY, USA, 23–32. https://doi.org/10.1145/2960310.2960332

[11] Louise Ann Lyon, Quinn Burke, Jill Denner, and Jim Bowring. 2017. Should your college computer science program partner with a coding boot camp?. In *Proceedings of the 2017 ACM SIGCSE Technical Symposium on Computer Science Education (SIGCSE '17)*. ACM, New York, NY, USA, 712–712. https://doi.org/10.1145/3017680.3022401

[12] Jane Margolis, Rachel Estrella, Joanna Goode, Jennifer Jellison Holme, and Kim Nao. 2010. *Stuck in the shallow end: Education, race, and computing.* MIT Press.

[13] Jane Margolis and Allan Fisher. 2003. *Unlocking the clubhouse: Women in computing.* MIT press.

[14] National Center for Education Statistics. 2016. Digest of Education Statistics, 2016. (2016). https://nces.ed.gov/programs/digest/d16/tables/dt16_322.10.asp?current=yes

[15] Jerome Neapolitan. 1980. Occupational change in mid-career: An exploratory investigation. *Journal of Vocational Behavior* 16, 2 (April 1980), 212–225. https://doi.org/10.1016/0001-8791(80)90052-4

[16] A. K. Peters and A. Pears. 2013. Engagement in Computer Science and IT – What! A Matter of Identity?. In *2013 Learning and Teaching in Computing and Engineering*. 114–121. https://doi.org/10.1109/LaTiCE.2013.42

[17] Quincy Larson. 2016. We asked 15,000 people who they are, and how they fire learning to code. (May 2016). https://medium.freecodecamp.com/we-asked-15-000-people-who-they-are-and-how-theyre-learning-to-code-4104e29b2781

[18] Course Report. 2016. 2016 Coding Bootcamp Market Size Study. (June 2016). https://www.coursereport.com/reports/2016-coding-bootcamp-market-size-research

[19] Course Report. 2016. 2016 Course Report alumni outcomes & demographics study. (Sept. 2016). https://www.coursereport.com/reports/2016-coding-bootcamp-job-placement-demographics-report

[20] Susan R. Rhodes and Mildred Doering. 1983. An integrated model of career change. *Academy of Management Review* 8, 4 (Oct. 1983), 631–639. https://doi.org/10.5465/AMR.1983.4284666

[21] Carsten Schulte and Maria Knobelsdorf. 2007. Attitudes towards computer science-computing experiences as a starting point and barrier to computer science. In *Proceedings of the Third International Workshop on Computing Education Research (ICER '07)*. ACM, New York, NY, USA, 27–38. https://doi.org/10.1145/1288580.1288585

[22] Araba Sey and Maria Garrido. 2016. *Coding bootcamps: A strategy for youth employment in developing countries.* Research Report. Technology & Social Change Group, University of Washington. http://tascha.uw.edu/publications/coding-bootcamps-a-strategy-for-youth-employment-in-developing-countries/

[23] Roslyn Smart and Candida Peterson. 1997. Super's Career Stages and the Decision to Change Careers. *Journal of Vocational Behavior* 51, 3 (Dec. 1997), 358–374. https://doi.org/10.1006/jvbe.1996.1544

[24] Etienne Wenger. 1998. *Communities of practice: Learning, meaning, and identity.* Cambridge university press.

[25] Etienne Wenger-Trayner and Beverly Wenger-Trayner. 2015. Communities of practice a brief introduction. (April 2015). http://wenger-trayner.com/wp-content/uploads/2015/04/07-Brief-introduction-to-communities-of-practice.pdf

[26] Judy Williams. 2010. Constructing a new professional identity: Career change into teaching. *Teaching and Teacher Education* 26, 3 (April 2010), 639–647. https://doi.org/10.1016/j.tate.2009.09.016

[27] Brenda Cantwell Wilson and Sharon Shrock. 2001. Contributing to success in an introductory computer science course: A study of twelve factors. In *Proceedings of the Thirty-second SIGCSE Technical Symposium on Computer Science Education (SIGCSE '01)*. ACM, New York, NY, USA, 184–188. https://doi.org/10.1145/364447.364581

[28] Yunwen Ye and Kouichi Kishida. 2003. Toward an understanding of the motivation of open source software developers. In *Proceedings of the 25th International Conference on Software Engineering (ICSE '03)*. IEEE Computer Society, Washington, DC, USA, 419–429. http://dl.acm.org/citation.cfm?id=776816.776867

Hack.edu: Examining How College Hackathons Are Perceived By Student Attendees and Non-Attendees

Jeremy Warner
UC Berkeley
Berkeley, CA, USA
jeremy.warner@berkeley.edu

Philip J. Guo
UC San Diego
La Jolla, CA, USA
pg@ucsd.edu

ABSTRACT

College hackathons have become popular in the past decade, with tens of thousands of students now participating each year across hundreds of campuses. Since hackathons are informal learning environments where students learn and practice coding without any faculty supervision, they are an important site for computing education researchers to study as a complement to studying formal classroom learning environments. However, despite their popularity, little is known about why students choose to attend these events, what they gain from attending, and conversely, why others choose *not* to attend. This paper presents a mixed methods study that examines student perceptions of college hackathons by focusing on three main questions: 1.) Why are students motivated to attend hackathons? 2.) What kind of learning environment do these events provide? 3.) What factors discourage students from attending? Through semi-structured interviews with six college hackathon attendees (50% female), direct observation at a hackathon, and 256 survey responses from college students (42% female), we discovered that students were motivated to attend for both social and technical reasons, that the format generated excitement and focus, and that learning occurred incidentally, opportunistically, and from peers. Those who chose not to attend or had negative experiences cited discouraging factors such as physical discomfort, lack of substance, an overly competitive climate, an unwelcoming culture, and fears of not having enough prior experience. We conclude by discussing ideas for making college hackathons more broadly inclusive and welcoming in light of our study's findings.

CCS CONCEPTS

• **Computers in Society** → General;

KEYWORDS

college hackathon; informal learning; situated learning

1 INTRODUCTION

A hackathon is an event where people gather in one location to create prototype software projects within a short time period, usually from one day to one week. This term originated in 1999 when OpenBSD and Sun Microsystems hosted hackathons for developers to create software on their respective platforms [6]. These events have become popular over the past decade and now exist in several forms: 1.) Technology companies host hackathons to promote their APIs [11, 22], 2.) open-source software projects host hackathons to make concentrated bursts of progress [6, 30], 3.) governments and nonprofits host civic hackathons to create technologies for social good [7, 21], and 4.) colleges host hackathons for students [24].

One of the most prominent types of hackathons to arise in recent years is the *college hackathon*, which is usually a 24- to 36-hour event held on a college campus where students create software projects ("hacks") and optionally compete for prizes. Hundreds of students travel to attend large hackathons at schools such as MIT, UPenn, and the University of Michigan, with their bus or plane fares paid by corporate sponsors who view these events as recruiting opportunities. College hackathons started in the U.S. in 2010 [18] and have now become popular enough that there is an organization, Major League Hacking [5], that tracks the status and progress of attendees throughout each "season" (i.e., semester).

In 2016, Major League Hacking sponsored over 200 college hackathons with over 65,000 total participants [5, 24]. We also found that hackathons have occurred at all 47 of the 47 top-ranked computer science departments in the U.S., according to the U.S. News Top 40 rankings [2] (there are 47 since eight schools tied for rank 40). Press articles [24] and personal anecdotes indicate that hackathons are now well-advertised social events in computer science departments, with students viewing them as opportunities for project-based learning, socializing, community-building, and job hunting.

However, despite the rapidly rising popularity of hackathons on college campuses around the world, little is known about why many students choose to attend them, why they find it engaging to spend their weekends coding intensively, what they gain from attending, and, conversely, why other students choose not to attend.

Researchers have recently begun to study corporate [22], scientific [30], and civic [7, 15, 21] hackathons, which are attended mostly by working professionals. Our paper complements this existing literature by presenting one of the first studies of college hackathons. Since these events are popular on-campus venues for informal and situated learning [23] where students learn about programming-related technologies from each other without any faculty supervision, college hackathons are an important yet underexplored site for computing education researchers to study as a complement to studying formal classroom learning environments.

In this paper, we focused our exploratory study on surfacing the perceptions of both students who attended and those who chose not to attend college hackathons. To get a broad range of opinions, we used data from semi-structured interviews with six attendees (3 female, 3 male), direct observation at a hackathon in our university, and 256 survey responses from U.S. college students (42% female).

We found that students were motivated to attend hackathons for both social and technical reasons, that the unique time-limited environment generated excitement and helped them focus intensely, and that learning occurred incidentally, opportunistically, and mostly from peers. Those who chose not to attend or had negative experiences at hackathons mentioned discouraging factors such as physical discomfort, an emphasis on making superficial demos rather than substantive technologies, an overly competitive climate, fears of not having enough prior programming experience to meaningfully contribute, and a sometimes-unwelcoming culture.

We conclude by suggesting ways to make college hackathons more inclusive and welcoming. As hackathons continue moving toward the mainstream of computer science student culture at universities around the world [24], it is important to broaden participation because these are not merely venues for socializing and learning, but are also potential job-seeking opportunities as more companies start recruiting from hackathons in lieu of traditional on-campus career fairs [24]. A lack of inclusion at these events means that certain groups (e.g., women, underrepresented minorities) miss out on opportunities for learning, networking, and jobs.

The contributions of this paper are:

- One of the first studies of college hackathons, which contributes to computing education research by documenting how students informally learn and practice coding at a type of event that is now popular across many campuses.

- Student perceptions of college hackathons, including motivations for attending and not attending, how and what they learned, lasting impacts, and criticisms, based on interviews with 6 students and 256 survey responses.

- Recommendations for improving college hackathons to make them more inclusive and welcoming.

2 BACKGROUND

2.1 Related Work

Despite increasingly frequent mentions of hackathons in popular press articles [11, 12, 24], there have been relatively few academic studies of hackathons. Most of these prior studies have focused on hackathons organized by corporations, nonprofits, and governments rather than those by and for college students. For instance, Komssi et al. performed a case study of five hackathons hosted at an enterprise software company to prototype potential product ideas [22]. They found that these events are effective for getting people from different parts of the company to cross-fertilize expertise with one another. Irani documented her experiences as a participant-observer in a five-day civic hackathon in India to generate ideas for open governance [21]. She found that it infused participants with an energetic, entrepreneurial, action-oriented spirit to solving social problems, spurred by the urgency of a short time limit. Ames et al. studied the use of evangelistic metaphors to encourage volunteer participation in a civic hackathon for disaster relief technologies [7]. Trainer et al. studied team formation, social tie building, and follow-up routines at three scientific hackathons attended by professional scientists and research programmers [30]. They found that different

ways of organizing hackathons (i.e., how teams are formed) resulted in tradeoffs between participants building stronger social ties and more effectively advancing preset technical goals.

In the computing education literature, the few known studies of college hackathons have all been performed by the organizers of these events. For instance, in the StitchFest project [29], researchers created a specialized wearable devices hackathon to broaden participation amongst women in computing, and then studied its 33 attendees. Anslow et al. [8] wrote up an experience report on organizing specialized data science hackathons ("datathons") for teaching students data science as a supplement to university data science curricula. Nandi and Mandernach [28] organized a series of larger general-purpose hackathons at their university and performed a quantitative analysis of those events by documenting attendee majors, Git source code commit logs, and effects on attendee GPAs.

Unlike these prior studies, to our knowledge, we are the first to investigate college hackathons as third-party outside observers rather than as organizers. We are also the first to study non-participation to understand why students choose not to attend hackathons.

More broadly, our work relates to studies of informal learning of programming. For instance, Dorn and Guzdial studied graphic and web designers learning end-user programming outside of university settings [16, 17]. Boustedt, McCartney, et al. studied CS students' perceptions of and motivations for self-directed learning [10, 27].

2.2 What are College Hackathons?

Before presenting our study, we first provide background information on what college hackathons are and who attends them.

In the rest of this paper we will use the term "hackathon" to refer exclusively to college hackathons. In addition, note that although student groups also organize smaller niche hackathons for specific purposes (e.g., learning to use a certain technology or focusing on a specific underrepresented group), in this paper we use "hackathon" to refer to the larger-scale general-purpose hackathons that are the most popular instances of this event format.

A hackathon is a 24- to 36-hour free weekend event hosted in a large indoor open space within a college campus. Although these events are organized by students, corporate sponsors pay for food, prizes, and transportation. In return, they get publicity and access to participants for recruiting. At the start of the event, participants mingle, start forming teams, and brainstorm project ideas. Most of the participants' time is spent coding ("hacking") to produce prototype apps. There are sometimes technical talks in classrooms, social events such as games, giveaways of free gifts such as company-sponsored water bottles and shirts, and company representatives walking around to mentor or recruit. At the end of the event, teams can optionally present their project to a panel of judges to compete for prizes. Sometimes winners receive immediate internship or job offers at sponsoring companies [24].

Hackathons started in the Northeastern United States in 2010 [18] and spread across U.S. college campuses. Major League Hacking [5] (MLH) tracked data on over 200 hackathons in 2016, and we found that all 47 of the 47 top-ranked U.S. computer science departments [2] have hosted their own hackathons. Many more colleges host smaller hackathons that are not tracked by MLH. Most attract around 100 participants, but the largest can attract well over 1,000.

Hackathons have also spread to other countries [5], but we do not have detailed data on their growth at non-U.S. campuses.

For large general-purpose college hackathons, many participants are undergraduate students who travel to attend via carpool, bus, or plane, with their transportation costs reimbursed by corporate sponsors [18]. According to self-reported interests on participants' Devpost [3] profiles, web programming is currently the most popular interest, followed by mobile programming on Android/iOS.

2.3 Theoretical Framework

The theory of situated learning [23] provides a framework for contextualizing our study. Situated learning posits that people are motivated to learn by doing authentic hands-on activities that bring them closer to joining a desired community of practice. We found that hackathons represent such a type of activity for some students in computer science (CS) and related majors.

Situated learning requires the activity to be *authentic*: learners want to feel like they are working with real tools that professionals in their field use, not just "toy" environments designed for pedagogy [19]. In the context of software-focused hackathons for CS students, this means getting the chance to use programming languages, libraries, frameworks, APIs, and tech platforms that are now the most popular in industry to develop prototypes of industry-relevant projects.

This theory also describes how some people are motivated to learn to join a *community of practice* of professionals in their field and to acquire the values of that community. Many CS students today want to join a community of professional web and mobile application developers at top tech startups and big companies (e.g., Google, Facebook). The presence of professional software engineers attending college hackathons as mentors, guest speakers, and judges gives students an opportunity to interact with and learn from experts in their intended community of practice. In addition, students can learn from more experienced peers on their teams who have done internships at these tech companies.

More broadly, situated learning is loosely related to *social learning theory* [9], which posits that learning occurs within a social context where people directly observe and imitate others around them, often without formal instructional procedures. A hackathon provides one such social context for students to learn technology-related topics from peers.

Finally, although we observed instances of situated learning in our study, we could not see longitudinal effects associated with some aspects of this theory since hackathons are – by definition – short-lived events. For instance, we did not see legitimate peripheral participation, where newcomers gradually move toward the center of a community of practice by taking on core responsibilities over time. Thus, this framework should be used only as an informal lens for our study, but cannot encompass all of our findings.

3 RESEARCH QUESTIONS

Our study examines students' perceptions of college hackathons by focusing on three questions:

1.) Why are students motivated to attend college hackathons?
2.) What kind of learning environment do these events provide?
3.) What factors discourage students from attending?

4 METHODS

To discover students' expectations for and experiences at hackathons, we first performed a qualitative case study by gathering data using semi-structured interviews and direct observations at a college hackathon. Then as a follow-up study, we surfaced the opposite perspective – why students do not like to participate in these hackathons – via an online survey sent to four U.S. universities.

4.1 Case Study of Six Hackathon Attendees

We performed a qualitative case study [31] on students selected from the population of undergraduates at the University of Rochester (a mid-sized Ph.D.-granting U.S. university) who had registered to attend our university's annual hackathon. We emailed the registration list to ask for unpaid volunteers for our study. Then to maximize the diversity of perspectives, we selected six subjects to balance both gender (3 female, 3 male) and amount of prior hackathon experience (3 with no prior experience, 2 with some experience at 2–3 prior hackathons, 1 with lots of experience at 5 prior hackathons). Here are the pseudonyms for the six case study subjects, coded by both gender and ascending experience level:

Pseudonym:	Male			Female		
	M1	M2	M3	F1	F2	F3
# hackathons attended:	0	3	5	0	0	2

All six subjects were undergraduate computer science majors, which is the primary target audience for these kinds of hackathons.

4.2 Interviews and Direct Observations

We conducted three sets of 30-minute interviews with each subject: 1.) one week before our university's hackathon, 2.) one week afterward, and 3.) one month afterward. The first author also observed them working during the hackathon.

The design of our interview questions was initially inspired by prior studies of college hackathons [8, 28, 29] and by the theory of situated learning (Section 2.3). In addition, as each round of interview and observation notes arrived, our research team iteratively coded [14] them to identify common themes, which further refined the list of questions we asked in the next round.

Pre-hackathon expectations interview: This was conducted the week before the hackathon. Its purpose was to assess expectations leading up to the event. We asked the following questions, although each individual conversation was semi-structured and ended up covering different topics:

- What do think the point of hackathons are?
- Why do you want to go to this upcoming hackathon?
- What do you hope to gain from attending the hackathon?
- Do you already have project ideas or team members?
- Who are you hoping to learn from at this event?
- Are you nervous about any aspects of this hackathon?

Direct observations at hackathon: The first author attended our university's hackathon, observed those six students at work throughout the event, and took field notes. This event was a 36-hour hackathon that started on Friday evening at 5pm and ended on Sunday at noon (with 7 hours for sleeping). There were 84 total participants from eight universities, and nearly everyone was an undergraduate student. The first author struck a balance between being unobtrusive and inquisitive, using their judgment of etiquette from having attended previous hackathons. Since the venue was small (a ground-floor lobby in a single building), the first author was easily able to rotate among the six subjects to observe them at work throughout the course of the event.

Post-hackathon reflection interview: This was conducted the week after the hackathon so that memories were still fresh on subjects' minds. Its purpose was to assess what each subject learned from the event and how their experiences matched prior expectations. Thus, many of our questions followed up on those from the pre-hackathon expectations interview:

- What project did you end up working on?
- Who did you end up learning from?
- What did you end up learning? Anything unexpected?
- What (if anything) has changed about your initial perceptions of hackathons?
- What was most memorable about this hackathon?
- How did attending this hackathon affect your confidence in your coding abilities?

Follow-up lasting-impact interview: This final interview was conducted one month after the hackathon to assess how much of a lasting impact the event had on subjects after they had returned to the routine of school work for a month. We directed this conversation around the following questions:

- What new skills did you learn at the hackathon? (We wanted to see what they remembered one month later.)
- How do you think you will use these skills in the future?
- What criticisms (if any) do you have of hackathons after attending this one? Do you remember any discouraging moments?

4.3 Follow-Up Survey of Hackathon Criticisms

After analyzing data from the six case study subjects, we found their sentiments about hackathons to be mostly positive, since they all chose to attend and were enthusiastic enough to volunteer for our study. Some did express criticism of hackathons, though. Thus, we wanted to dig deeper in that direction by soliciting a broader range of criticisms from students who either chose not to attend these events or who did not have positive experiences there. To achieve this goal, we sent a short survey to undergraduate computer science department mailing lists at four Ph.D.-granting U.S. universities (located in the northeast, south, west, and northwest regions, respectively). Our survey had only three questions:

- If you have never attended a college hackathon, what factors discouraged you from attending? (open-ended)
- If you have attended college hackathons before but did not enjoy the experience, what aspects of the event felt discouraging to you? (open-ended)
- What is your gender? {female, male, other, decline to state}

Since this was a follow-up supplemental survey, we purposely kept it very short and focused to elicit only the information needed to supplement our main interviews and direct observations. We also instructed students to respond only if they were critical of hackathons. We received 256 responses (42% from women).

4.4 Data Collection and Analysis

The first author, who conducted all of the interviews and direct observations, was an undergraduate student who has attended six prior hackathons. While this was beneficial for making subjects feel comfortable talking candidly with someone whom they considered a peer, there is the chance that the first author injected their own biases into field notes. To reduce this risk, we instructed them to write down only raw observations without any interpretation. Then the first author coded the data together side-by-side with a professor who had no prior hackathon experience. Having two coders with varying backgrounds with respect to hackathons provided natural checks and balances throughout the coding process.

Since this was an open-ended qualitative case study, we adopted a grounded approach [14] to code for recurring themes across interviews, direct observations, and survey responses. Two researchers iteratively determined a set of codes together by tallying repeated mentions of themes across these data sources, guided by the frame of situated learning (Section 2.3) and by the first author's personal experiences at hackathons.

5 RESULTS

Based on qualitative data from interviews, observations, and surveys, we present findings on why students are motivated to attend hackathons, in what ways they learn throughout these events, and the main kinds of criticisms from both attendees and non-attendees.

5.1 Mostly-Social Motivations for Attending

We found that students often had social motivations for going to hackathons. The six subjects in our case study primarily viewed our university's hackathon as a weekend social event to attend with their friends and a place to hang out with like-minded people. Many mid-sized to large hackathons like the one we studied are intercollegiate social events where coordinators organize buses to bring students from nearby schools. Students take advantage of this opportunity to travel for free with their friends to see new places and meet new people. M3 summed up his motivations for attending our university's hackathon as: *"You get to be a part of a fun exciting environment, be encouraged to focus intently on a creative solution, meet new people, learn new technology, possibly travel someplace new, and take advantage of company swag [free gift items]."*

In the pre-hackathon interviews, no one felt nervous about finding teammates or a project to work on once they arrived. In fact, M1, M3, and F3 mentioned the social appeal of meeting new people there. Nobody expected to work alone at the event; they knew that hackathons provide group formation activities at the beginning to help attendees find teammates. Prior to attending, M1 and F2 already formed a team with friends from classes, while the other four subjects expected to find teammates there.

Only the most experienced subject mentioned being excited about technical opportunities in addition to social ones. M3, who had attended 5 prior hackathons, said that he was excited to gain access to software development kits, APIs, and hardware provided by sponsoring companies, as well as getting a chance to chat with employees from those companies who attend as mentors. Students could borrow a variety of hardware for the duration of the event. For instance, our university's hackathon featured Pebble smartwatches, 3D printers, Myo gesture control armbands, and Arduinos.

5.2 Situated and Social Learning

Situated and social learning (Section 2.3) emerged as major themes. Attendees had the chance to learn via working on software projects alongside their peers in an informal co-located setting without faculty supervision. In our post-hackathon interviews, subjects' memories about what software prototypes they built at the event were not nearly as salient as what and how they learned there. We classified subjects' recollections about learning into three categories: as being incidental, opportunistic, and from peers.

Incidental: Subjects mentioned learning technical skills at the hackathon as a side effect of trying to get their projects into a properly working state. During pre-hackathon interviews, only F1 mentioned that her goal was to attend to learn a specific skill – web programming from Codecademy (codecademy.com) tutorials – which she ended up doing. Everyone else focused their pre-interview conversation on what they wanted to *do* at the hackathon rather than what they wanted to explicitly learn. Yet at the event, we often observed them learning as a byproduct of doing. Pervasive examples of incidental learning included participants learning how to use software tools such as the Git version control system, how to upload their code to GitHub, how to share files with their teammates using Dropbox, how to deploy code to servers, and how to write Bash scripts to automate command-line tasks. Since these tools helped teams become more productive, members taught one another how to use them on-demand out of necessity as they encountered roadblocks in their projects.

Opportunistic: Attendees also learned opportunistically – taking advantage of short-lived ephemeral opportunities at the hackathon to direct their learning toward sometimes unexpected paths. For example, M3 started the event by working on a web programming project (an RSS feed generator) but saw that Pebble smartwatches were available to borrow at the hackathon venue. He then switched his project to hacking on a smartwatch app, opportunistically learning the Pebble API by reading online tutorials. He enjoyed this impromptu detour, but during the post-hackathon interview, he mentioned that one downside of this ad-hoc approach is that he would not get to reinforce those skills later since he did not own a Pebble smartwatch himself.

From peers: During pre-hackathon interviews, subjects described their perceptions of how learning occurs at these venues, and the theme of peers came up several times. For instance, M1 said that the *"learning style consists of goal-oriented peer learning."* M3 said that *"hackathons specialize in small group learning, and you feed off of your teammates' energies and enthusiasm."* And F3 said, *"hackathons are peer based, [with a] much more democratic learning style."*

Hackathons foster peer-based learning by having students work in teams; many do not allow individual projects to be submitted for judging. Although several mentors from companies and student hacking groups were present at our university's hackathon, there were not enough to help everyone. Less experienced attendees were especially reluctant to approach mentors for help, so they ended up learning more from peers.

Even the attendees who worked alone benefited from the presence of peers. For instance, F1 worked by herself on basic web programming tutorials from Codecademy. However, she felt comfortable asking for help from peers around her. She said that since the hackathon provided a social context where everyone was doing open-ended technical work, it did not feel awkward to approach people to ask questions about programming. In contrast, she said she would be reluctant to suddenly strike up a conversation about programming while socializing on campus; even if students were working on class assignments together, she felt it would be hard to get them to take a break to help her with unrelated topics.

During post-hackathon interviews, several subjects mentioned peer learning as a memorable part of the event. F2 reported that she learned how to work better in groups, how to split up work, and how to integrate different components under intense time pressure. She also did lots of pair programming to see how others approached the problem and learned by observing more experienced peers. F1, a first-time hackathon attendee, said she looked forward to attending more hackathons next semester based on this experience since she had fun learning while "goofing off" with peers at the same time, which was made possible by the lack of authority figures present.

5.3 Authenticity of Hackathons Versus Classes

During post-hackathon interviews, some subjects reflected on the differences between the learning environments in hackathons and in formal university classes. One emergent theme related to our lens of situated learning (Section 2.3) was *authenticity* – subjects perceived the hackathon environment to be more authentic than university classes in emulating a real-world tech company workplace. They enjoyed the chance to create projects at the hackathon using the latest industry-standard technologies, often provided by sponsoring companies and personally introduced to them by employees from those companies who attended as mentors. In contrast, they said how course curricula created by university professors are usually slower to update to the latest programming languages, libraries, frameworks, and APIs popular in industry today. M3 also mentioned the fact that *"you can actually get HIRED [by a sponsoring company] from doing well at a hackathon, which you can't get in the classroom."*

Subjects also mentioned how, in stark contrast to classes, students fully determine what and how they learn at a hackathon. They pointed out that professors are not present, which again simulates a more authentic work environment. F1 summarized the differences as: *"[at a hackathon] learning by example and experimentation instead of top down lecture style. Very hands on."* F3 said: *"Hackathons are very open ended, you are simply given space, resources, mentors, as well as access to peer mentors, and then encouraged to do something you think is awesome."*

However, they mentioned that the downside was that there is no formal structure or pedagogy at a hackathon, which can be detrimental to effective learning. M3 said that, unlike classes, there is no time for reflection and expert feedback in a hackathon, since there is no professional instructor whose job it is to give feedback to students. He continued, *"The main source of feedback is the current functionality of your project, and your peers' perceptions of it."*

Another difference between working on projects at a hackathon and in a class is the time dimension: Rather than lasting for several months, a hackathon lasts for 36 hours at most. Thus, students must pick up and apply newly-learned knowledge immediately rather than waiting for the next assignment or exam to get feedback.

F2 summarized the differences in formats as: *"A hackathon provides more creative freedom with projects, shorter time period than classes, and less concern about learning material deeply. I just want to focus on getting [projects] working. There is also no grade, so you don't face the academic pressure of the classroom. At a hackathon, people will be willing to collaborate and share what they are working on more since they are not working on the same project or for grades."*

Regarding the lack of grades, M1 pointed out that at a hackathon, one can experience *"failure without actual failure,"* so attendees can take on riskier projects without fears of receiving a failing grade if their attempts do not succeed.

Finally, some attendees bridged hackathons and classes by using their time at the hackathon to work on class projects. For example, M1 went to the hackathon with a friend and planned to use that time to make progress on a class project. Since it was his first hackathon, he was apprehensive about not being able to meaningfully contribute to a team there, but he still wanted to attend to experience the event.

Related to our lens of situated learning, we observed how these students' desire to join a community of practice of professional programmers motivates them to seek out *authenticity* in their university CS education [19]. They want to learn the latest programming languages, tools, APIs, and frameworks that industry practitioners use. They also reported that, in contrast to many computer science courses taught by professors, which are usually more theoretical or conceptual, hackathons offer a concentrated time and space where they could learn these more practical topics from their peers and from industry practitioners. Although professors are de facto authority figures in university classroom settings, the majority of students do not actually aspire to join the community of practice of college professors. Instead, their role models are older students who have obtained internships at top companies and current employees at those companies, who are often present at hackathons to show them the more pragmatic aspects of software development.

5.4 Lasting Impacts of Attending

During our follow-up interviews (one month after the hackathon) we asked subjects about what knowledge they retained from the event. Subjects could not vividly recall any of the specific skills they learned. Many remembered the event as a blur, with only vague recollections of the general kinds of topics they had learned. They attributed this lack of retention to the learning being *incidental* – they were focused on immersing themselves in the 36-hour experience and had no set curriculum, exams, or follow-up lessons to reinforce their knowledge like they would have in a class. One exception was F3, who purposely set out to learn the Scala programming language during her hackathon project because she knew that she would use it at her upcoming internship.

The most salient lasting impact was not about specific technical skills but rather on students' improved confidence about their own coding abilities. First-time attendee F1 said that *"going to this hackathon improved my self-confidence. I know a lot more than I thought I knew, and feel more normalcy with respect to peers."* F2 reported feeling more confident about working with others on a team. F3 felt that the environment was helpful and supportive for making progress on her technical interests and improving self-efficacy. We

a.) *"If you have attended hackathons before but did not enjoy the experience, what aspects of the event felt discouraging to you?"*

Total: N=126	Male: N=81	Female: N=43
Discomfort (35%)	Discomfort (33%)	Discomfort (40%)
Novice fears (28%)	Novice fears (22%)	Novice fears (37%)
No team/idea (21%)	No substance (20%)	No team/idea (33%)*
No substance (15%)	Competitive (20%)*	Hacker culture (16%)*
Competitive (14%)	No team/idea (15%)*	No substance (7%)
No time (10%)	No time (11%)	No time (7%)
Hacker culture (8%)	Hacker culture (2%)*	Competitive (5%)*

b.) *"If you have never attended a college hackathon, what factors discouraged you from attending?"*

Total: N=130	Male: N=61	Female: N=65
Novice fears (48%)	No time (51%)	Novice fears (65%)*
No time (43%)	Novice fears (33%)*	No time (35%)
No team/idea (22%)	No team/idea (18%)	No team/idea (26%)
Discomfort (11%)	Discomfort (8%)	Discomfort (14%)
Hacker culture (5%)	Competitive (3%)	Hacker culture (8%)
Competitive (5%)	Hacker culture (2%)	Competitive (6%)
No substance (2%)	No substance (2%)	No substance (2%)

Table 1: Summary of responses to both survey questions. Each column adds up to more than 100% since some responses contained more than one category. Chi-square statistically significant differences between genders for each category at $p < .05$ marked as * (e.g., Competitive: 20% vs. 5%). Six respondents identified as neither male nor female.

noticed that only the three female subjects reported this effect, but our sample size is far too small to make any meaningful generalizations. Based on these observations, though, we believe that the effect of hackathon attendance on CS student self-efficacy would be an interesting direction for future work.

5.5 Attendees' Criticisms of Hackathons

The mostly-positive sentiments reported by the six case study subjects prompted us to dig deeper to uncover the opposite perspective: students' criticisms of hackathons. From analyzing responses to a follow-up survey we sent to four U.S. universities, we grouped attendees' criticisms into seven categories. Table 1a shows how frequently each category was mentioned in the 126 survey responses to the question: "If you have attended hackathons before but did not enjoy the experience, what aspects of the event felt discouraging to you?" We present them here in descending order of prevalence:

Discomfort: The most common criticism amongst attendees was physical discomfort. Students cited lack of sleep, bad sleeping accommodations on gymnasium floors or dorm couches, unhealthy free food, and lack of personal hygiene of some participants as being uncomfortable. Also, they experienced discomfort and stress due to the time pressures of working intensely over an entire weekend and the loud ambiance of hundreds of students in a crowded space.

Novice fears: The next most common criticism was about the lack of support for novices. Some novices felt uncomfortable about not having enough technical skills to contribute meaningfully to projects and feared becoming "dead weight" on their team. They also mentioned how hackathons were not the ideal learning environment for novices, since they provide no pedagogical structure. There are technical talks, but those are usually for advertising a sponsoring company's products or APIs, not to guide novices step by step like a formal class would do. Mentors are practitioners and not trained educators, so they might not be good at explaining fundamental CS1-type concepts. Asking for help can be intimidating, especially as a novice in a room filled with more experienced hackers busy working on their projects.

No team or idea: Attendees who did not come to the hackathon already with a team or idea often had a hard time finding teams. Women reported this problem over twice as frequently as men (33% vs. 15%, chi-square test $\chi^2(1, N = 126) = 4.3, p = .038$). Teams also dissolved mid-way through the event due to ideas fizzling out, team members being flaky, or members not getting along. One survey respondent wrote: *"Going to Hackathons with students from [my university] and teaming up with them has always been discouraging as they would just give up on the project half way through and rather focus on going around the town."*

No substance: 15% of respondents noted how hackathons incentivized building flashy app demos rather than creating something more substantive and longer-lasting using computer science principles, since judges (often from companies) are more impressed by cool-looking demos. One wrote, *"because there are so many corporate sponsors, students tend to be dissuaded from building meaningful products and instead build toward whichever sponsor has the most attractive prize."* Also, some mentioned how hackathons do not teach rigorous software engineering practices; there are no instructors to critique the technical architecture of one's project, or how maintainable and robust the code is.

Overly competitive: Although submitting projects for judging is optional, some participants felt like the presence of cash prizes and company recruiters made the atmosphere overly competitive: e.g., *"The emphasis on huge prizes lessens the joy I get from hacking. I'd rather hack at a small, no frills, no prizes hackathon with close friends than go to a huge competition where I feel like I'm part of a herd of cattle whose job is to listen to propaganda from sponsors."*

Table 1a shows that men mentioned the overly competitive problem four times more often than women did (20% of men versus 5% of women, chi-square test $\chi^2(1, N = 126) = 4.0, p = .045$). One possible explanation is that more male participants viewed hackathons as a coding contest and cared more about winning, rather than viewing them as recreational social events.

No time: 10% of respondents regretted giving up an entire weekend to attend a hackathon, which is time that they could have spent catching up on sleep, attending social activities, and making progress on homework. One respondent wrote, *"Giving up an entire weekend to travel and work was tiring, making it tough to justify going to more in the future given my other commitments, both academic and otherwise."*

Hacker culture: 16% of female attendees cited the presence of "hacker culture" [26] or a "hardcore" ethos [20] as discouraging and sometimes even hostile; only 2% of male attendees mentioned this problem ($\chi^2(1, N = 126) = 6.0, p = .01$). One woman wrote, *"Arrogant students, mostly male, who act haughty and patronizing because*

I don't know some obscure JavaScript framework. I feel alienated by these types of people, and also alienated by the images of The Hacker stereotype these Hackathon marketing teams perpetuate."

5.6 Why Some Students Choose Not to Attend

Since hackathons are now becoming prevalent across college campuses, we wanted to also investigate why students who know about these events choose *not* to attend. Table 1b summarizes 130 survey responses we received to the question: "If you have never attended a college hackathon, what factors discouraged you from attending?" Note that these respondents all knew about hackathons; otherwise they would not have written responses about discouraging factors.

The most common discouraging factor was "novice fears," with women twice as likely to mention it as men (65% vs. 33%, $\chi^2(1, N = 130) = 11.5, p = .001$). For instance, one woman wrote, *"Being afraid that my skills are not enough to actually accomplish anything or that, if I do ask for help, I would be seen as incompetent or bad at programming."* This could be a manifestation of the well-documented gender confidence gap amongst computer science students [20].

The rest of Table 1b shows that even though these respondents had never attended hackathons, they still mentioned all of the same discouraging factors as the attendees did. One possible explanation is that these students heard about what happens at hackathons from peers who have attended, which led them to form those same negative preconceptions that discourage them from attending.

However, note that this is still a self-selected sample of non-attendee respondents; many other college students do not attend hackathons likely because they do not know much about them, or they do not have strong enough opinions to report in a survey.

6 STUDY LIMITATIONS

We performed a case study on six students who all attended a hackathon and who were willing to undergo three interviews. This volunteer sample may be biased toward more social or autodidactic students. To compensate, we obtained a broader set of perspectives by surveying 256 CS students at four U.S. universities. As with any case study, we cannot guarantee that its subjects are representative of all college hackathon attendees, but we strove to achieve some level of diversity along two dimensions: gender and amount of prior hackathon experience. Also, our findings may not generalize to smaller niche hackathons, those with specialized themes, or those that do not involve corporate sponsors.

Additionally, since the focus of this study was not on detailed demographic effects, we collected some data on gender but did not investigate race, ethnicity, or socioeconomic status. All case study subjects were either white or Asian. We also did not investigate the possible effects of intersectionality [13] (e.g., the experiences of women who are also underrepresented minorities). All data were collected from four-year Ph.D.-granting U.S. universities, so other types of higher education institutions were not represented.

Finally, our study is exploratory and high-level in nature because it is one of the first to investigate general college hackathons. Thus, we did not focus on the challenges faced by specific groups of students (e.g., women, underrepresented minorities, first-generation college students) in detail. Targeted follow-up studies are needed to uncover the deeper and richer nuances behind their experiences.

7 DISCUSSION

Relationship to prior work: As the first known study of college hackathons performed by outside researchers rather than by the organizers themselves, our findings about the energy and enthusiasm generated by these events, along with their abundant informal learning opportunities, corroborate similar findings from past hackathon organizers [8, 28, 29]. We deepened these prior results by making ties to situated learning theory, especially highlighting attendees' desires to join a community of practice of professional programmers and perceiving hackathons as more authentic learning environments than classes (Section 5.3). We also augmented prior studies with new perspectives from hundreds of students who either did not enjoy or did not attend hackathons (Table 1).

Implications for teaching: An ongoing challenge in computing education is how to balance teaching the foundational theoretical concepts of computer science with the pragmatic (but fast-changing) programming skills that students want to learn to get jobs. How can some positive elements of hackathons be infused into traditional university classes? One idea is for classes to hold mini-hack-days for students to implement small open-ended projects using concepts from those classes. Case study subject F1 mentioned that a *"hackathon is a time for implementation of theoretical concepts learned in class, so professors should support this type of thing."* M1 pointed out the importance of experiencing *"failure without actual failure"*, so hack-day assessments should be formative and not high-stakes. Another advantage of adapting hackathons into existing classes is the possibility of follow-up feedback and iteration after the events are over, which is lacking in current hackathons.

Implications for computing education research: Our high-level exploratory study only scratches the surface on investigating the recent phenomenon of college hackathons, so follow-up computing education research is needed to hone in on questions such as: What are the longer-lasting impacts of hackathons on students' self-efficacy and future job success? How do hackathons relate to the rich ecosystem of other informal computing learning environments on campuses such as student-run makerspaces and hobby computing clubs? How effective are hackathons at fostering rigorous learning and retention rather than simply serving a sociotechnical purpose? What randomized controlled experiments can we perform at hackathons to isolate the efficacy of specific event components?

Making hackathons more inclusive and welcoming: Given their recent popularity, it is critical to take steps to make hackathons more inclusive and welcoming. Although these have always been desirable goals for any computing-related event, they are now becoming urgent as hackathons move toward mainstream CS student culture. Students now view them not only as social and learning opportunities, but also as venues to obtain coveted job offers in lieu of attending career fairs [24]. As companies are recruiting more out of hackathons, lack of inclusion at these events means that certain groups (e.g., women, underrepresented minorities) are at more of a disadvantage when job hunting. It is no longer a matter of having fun at a social gathering; jobs are at stake.

The challenges faced by female computer science students have been well-documented [20, 26]. Our case study subjects and survey respondents corroborated these prior findings with their concerns that hackathons embody a type of geeky environment that implicitly excludes women and underrepresented minorities. In our survey, "hacker culture" was cited far more often by women than men as discouraging them from attending. Subjects F1 and F3 suggested that holding women-only hackathons and having more female mentors at existing hackathons would help, although those would only be first steps toward making them feel more welcoming. Another idea was for hackathons to follow the example of diversity-focused industry technology conferences by implementing codes of conduct [1, 4] with zero-tolerance policies for exclusionary behavior.

Making hackathons more generally welcoming for novices can also broaden participation, since students from underrepresented groups likely come into college with less prior programming experience [25, 26, 29]. In our survey, both men and women cited "novice fears" as a discouraging factor, although women were twice as likely to mention it. One way to make these events more novice-friendly is to add lightweight pedagogical structure such as distinct phases and checkpoints, with expert feedback given along the way. Hackathons are now largely unstructured, so novices can easily feel lost. However, adding such structure requires trained mentors to attend. One idea is for organizers to recruit from their school's computer science TA (teaching assistant) and LA (lab assistant) populations. Many current mentors are software developers from sponsoring companies who are not trained as educators and who have implicit incentives to advertise their own company's products rather than helping students learn generalizable knowledge.

Finally, as college hackathons grow more popular, they attract more corporate sponsorship. And as companies offer larger prizes and greater prospects of job offers, some students in our survey felt that hackathons are losing their original spirit of making creative technological hacks and are turning into full-fledged competitions. Our survey respondents cited "too competitive" and "no substance" (i.e., making flashy demos just to impress judges) as discouraging factors. We acknowledge that it can be hard for organizers to resist the allure of prestigious companies offering increasing amounts of funding to grow these events, but it is also critical to keep an eye on the core values – collaboration, informal learning, community building – that benefit students and not simply sponsors. Scaling gracefully is an ongoing challenge: How can organizers preserve the maker ethos of small-scale events while growing to hundreds of participants? They could potentially limit sponsor involvement, use funding to pay instructors to come as mentors rather than company representatives, and put modest caps on prizes.

8 CONCLUSION AND FUTURE DIRECTIONS

We have presented one of the first academic studies of college hackathons, which documents student perceptions of these now-popular events from both sides: those who participated and those who chose *not* to participate. Given the growing popularity of hackathons, how should computing educators view them – as threats to traditional CS education or as exciting new opportunities for combining the theoretical with the practical in a situated learning environment? If hackathons are indeed here to stay, then how can we make them more inclusive and welcoming so that more students benefit? And how can they potentially influence traditional classroom teaching? We hope this paper sparks discussion of these questions and more.

REFERENCES

[1] 2013. PyCon Code of Conduct for the Python community conference. https://github.com/python/pycon-code-of-conduct. (March 2013). Accessed: 2016-04-01.

[2] 2014. U.S. News and World Report: Computer Science Rankings. http://grad-schools.usnews.rankingsandreviews.com/best-graduate-schools/top-science-schools/computer-science-rankings. (2014). Accessed: 2016-04-01.

[3] 2015. Devpost - Hackathons, App Contests, and Hackers. http://devpost.com/. (2015). Accessed: 2016-04-01.

[4] 2015. Google Groups: A Code of Conduct for the Go community. https://goo.gl/RSJsRf. (June 2015). Accessed: 2016-04-01.

[5] 2016. About Major League Hacking. https://mlh.io/about. (2016). Accessed: 2016-04-01.

[6] 2016. OpenBSD hackathons. openbsd.org/hackathons.html. (April 2016). Accessed: 2016-04-01.

[7] Morgan G. Ames, Daniela K. Rosner, and Ingrid Erickson. 2015. Worship, Faith, and Evangelism: Religion As an Ideological Lens for Engineering Worlds. In *Proceedings of the 18th ACM Conference on Computer Supported Cooperative Work & Social Computing (CSCW '15)*. 69–81.

[8] Craig Anslow, John Brosz, Frank Maurer, and Mike Boyes. 2016. Datathons: An Experience Report of Data Hackathons for Data Science Education. In *Proceedings of the 47th ACM Technical Symposium on Computing Science Education (SIGCSE '16)*. ACM, New York, NY, USA, 615–620. DOI:https://doi.org/10.1145/2839509.2844568

[9] Albert Bandura. 1977. *Social Learning Theory*. Prentice Hall.

[10] Jonas Boustedt, Anna Eckerdal, Robert McCartney, Kate Sanders, Lynda Thomas, and Carol Zander. 2011. Students' Perceptions of the Differences Between Formal and Informal Learning. In *Proceedings of the Seventh International Workshop on Computing Education Research (ICER '11)*. ACM, New York, NY, USA, 61–68. DOI:https://doi.org/10.1145/2016911.2016926

[11] Alexandra Chang. 2012. Deep inside a Facebook hackathon, where the future of social media begins. *Wired* (July 2012).

[12] Lizette Chapman. 2017. These Hackathon Hustlers Make Their Living From Corporate Coding Contests. *Bloomberg Technology* (April 2017).

[13] Patricia H. Collins. 2015. Intersectionality's Definitional Dilemmas. *Annual Review of Sociology* 41, 1 (2015), 1–20.

[14] Juliet M. Corbin and Anselm L. Strauss. 2008. *Basics of qualitative research: techniques and procedures for developing grounded theory*. SAGE Publications, Inc.

[15] Carl DiSalvo, Melissa Gregg, and Thomas Lodato. 2014. Building Belonging. *interactions* 21, 4 (July 2014), 58–61.

[16] Brian Dorn and Mark Guzdial. 2006. Graphic Designers Who Program As Informal Computer Science Learners. In *Proceedings of the Second International Workshop on Computing Education Research (ICER '06)*. ACM, New York, NY, USA, 127–134. DOI:https://doi.org/10.1145/1151588.1151608

[17] Brian Dorn and Mark Guzdial. 2010. Discovering Computing: Perspectives of Web Designers. In *Proceedings of the Sixth International Workshop on Computing Education Research (ICER '10)*. ACM, New York, NY, USA, 23–30. DOI:https://doi.org/10.1145/1839594.1839600

[18] Jon Gottfried. 2014. A brief history of hackathons (lecture video). http://youtu.be/Zr6VPAe9CKU. (March 2014). Accessed: 2016-04-01.

[19] Mark Guzdial. 2015. Learner-Centered Design of Computing Education: Research on Computing for Everyone. *Synthesis Lectures on Human-Centered Informatics* 8, 6 (2015), 1–165.

[20] Lilly Irani. 2004. Understanding Gender and Confidence in CS Course Culture. In *Proceedings of the 35th SIGCSE Technical Symposium on Computer Science Education (SIGCSE '04)*. ACM, New York, NY, USA.

[21] Lilly Irani. 2015. Hackathons and the Making of Entrepreneurial Citizenship. *Science, Technology & Human Values* (2015).

[22] Marko Komssi, Danielle Pichlis, Mikko Raatikainen, Klas Kindström, and Janne Järvinen. 2014. What are hackathons for? *IEEE Software* PP, 99 (May 2014).

[23] J. Lave and E. Wenger. 1991. *Situated Learning: Legitimate Peripheral Participation*. Cambridge University Press.

[24] Steven Leckart. 2015. The Hackathon Fast Track, From Campus to Silicon Valley. *New York Times* (April 2015).

[25] Jane Margolis. 2008. *Stuck in the Shallow End: Education, Race, and Computing*. MIT Press.

[26] Jane Margolis and Allan Fisher. 2003. *Unlocking the Clubhouse: Women in Computing*. MIT Press.

[27] Robert McCartney, Jonas Boustedt, Anna Eckerdal, Kate Sanders, Lynda Thomas, and Carol Zander. 2016. Why Computing Students Learn on Their Own: Motivation for Self-Directed Learning of Computing. *Trans. Comput. Educ.* 16, 1, Article 2 (Jan. 2016), 18 pages. DOI:https://doi.org/10.1145/2747008

[28] Arnab Nandi and Meris Mandernach. 2016. Hackathons As an Informal Learning Platform. In *Proceedings of the 47th ACM Technical Symposium on Computing Science Education (SIGCSE '16)*. ACM, New York, NY, USA, 346–351. DOI:https://doi.org/10.1145/2839509.2844590

[29] Gabriela T. Richard, Yasmin B. Kafai, Barrie Adleberg, and Orkan Telhan. 2015. StitchFest: Diversifying a College Hackathon to Broaden Participation and Perceptions in Computing. In *Proceedings of the 46th ACM Technical Symposium on Computer Science Education (SIGCSE '15)*. 114–119.

[30] Erik H. Trainer, Arun Kalyanasundaram, Chalalai Chaihirunkarn, and James D. Herbsleb. 2016. How to Hackathon: Socio-technical Tradeoffs in Brief, Intensive Collocation. In *Proceedings of the 19th ACM Conference on Computer Supported Cooperative Work & Social Computing (CSCW '16)*.

[31] Robert K. Yin. 1989. *Case Study Research: Design and Methods*. SAGE Publications, Inc.

Codification Pedagogy for Introductory Courses

Rita Garcia
University of Adelaide
Adelaide, SA, Australia
rita.garcia@adelaide.edu.au

ABSTRACT

Codification is a legal term defining the process of ordering rules corresponding to a plan. This term is applicable to Software Development to describe the ordering of program requirements into coding tasks. Codification is a meta-skill taught in advanced Software Engineering courses for large collaborative projects, though novices lack the experience to transfer this skill to small-scale assignments. As a result, novices form their own approach, potentially contributing to poor learning behaviors, poor self-efficacy, and course attrition. My research investigates an approach for introductory courses, enabling novices to plan before they implement a solution. The approach uses Socratic questions and Parsons Problems to relate the student's current knowledge base to the assignment. The hypothesis is that the pedagogy will reduce misconceptions about the assignment and enable students to create an ordered plan without extraneous cognitive load. The research explores this approach without adding objectives to the curriculum, or increasing the teacher's workload. Further investigation will be made to apply the pedagogy to other science, technology, engineering, and mathematics (STEM) disciplines.

CCS CONCEPTS

• **Applied computing → Education**; *Computer-assisted instruction*; *E-learning*; Computer-managed instruction;

KEYWORDS

Program Comprehension; Codification; Teaching Pedagogy

1 PROGRAM CONTEXT

I am a first year PhD Research Candidate at the University of Adelaide and part of the Computer Science Education Research group. My interest in helping students learn how to problem solve began when I had the opportunity to teach while pursuing my Masters Thesis at the University of California, Santa Cruz. My thesis supported assignment completion using scaffolding in an Integrated Development Environment. It was trialled in a lab environment where I observed students discussing ways to improve their solutions. I had not observed this behavior in prior courses, and encouraged me to continue in the field of Computer Science Education.

I am currently applying the research within edX, a Massive Open Online Course (MOOC). The pedagogy is encapsulated within a plugin utilizing a Parsons Problems framework that allows students to order requirements to compose the design plan interactively. Work has begun on the plugin to make it compatible with edX's Learning Tools Interoperability (LTI) component. My intention is to pilot the research in the Spring 2018 semester. Afterwards, I will collect and compare results from a previous semester to further explore ways to enhance the teaching strategy. If findings are positive, I will evaluate my research for other STEM disciplines. My goal is to complete my Major Review in the middle of 2018 and defend my PhD in Spring 2020.

2 CONTEXT AND MOTIVATION

Novices are not taught in introductory courses skills to partition textual description into a set of steps to create a program. The inability to form a plan might contribute to frustration, poor self-efficacy, and course attrition. These meta-skills are addressed in higher level courses for large-scale software projects developed in a team environment. However, transferring this skill can be difficult for a novice working in isolation with little programming experience.

Trying to incorporate codification into course curriculums might be a challenge, since students are overwhelmed with new concepts, and might not fully understand these meta-skills due to lack of experience. Additionally, instructors are overloaded with a full curriculum, focused on teaching the primary objectives.

I believe my research can help novices identify requirements needed to develop a plan, and allow them to focus more on the learning objectives leading to improved solutions. The intention is to not increase students' cognitive load, while minimizing instructors' preparation time when creating the instructional material.

3 BACKGROUND & RELATED WORK

Teaching programming to novices is difficult because they have a limited knowledge base to relate to core concepts, making it difficult for them to identify requirements, create plans, and form a mental model representing code [4]. Schulte et al. describe methods to facilitate program comprehension to form a 'mental representation'. My work will approach program comprehension similarly, but for requirement identification.

To better relate the problem to the student's existing knowledge base, my work utilizes scaffolding [2], allowing students to focus on tasks while reducing extraneous cognitive load. Caspersen et al. also suggest reducing scaffolding when students gain experience, to encourage independent learning. My scaffolding approach uses effective questioning [1], to guide students through the problem-solving process by self-explaining for requirement identification.

Self-explanation is done through Socratic questions [5] for a deeper understanding of the problem.

After the student analyzes the problem, they have the opportunity to construct an ordered plan using Parsons Problems [3], an effective learning tool currently used by students to arrange fragments of code into a program. A similar arranging process is utilized in my research, except the fragments to order are requirements, rather than code.

4 STATEMENT OF THESIS/PROBLEM

Does codification scaffolding teach novices the meta-skills needed to develop ordered plans for a programming solution? I will develop a pedagogy used within an online introductory course to assist with planning assignment solutions, with surveys given to students and the teacher upon completion. The data collected is students' responses to design questions and logged interaction, where logged information can be evaluated during the semester to provide a correlation between students' performance and how well they planned the assignment. After the initial trial, feedback will be included to improve the learning experience. I will also examine extending the pedagogy to other STEM disciplines.

5 RESEARCH GOALS & METHODS

The goals of this research is to investigate a pedagogy to help novices during the design phase decompose a problem into a series of solutions, order solutions for implementation, and reduce cognitive load to focus on primary tasks.

The pedagogy resides between the assignment description and implementation, to get students thinking of how to implement code. The approach guides students through a series of questions designed to encourage reflection and relate their knowledge base to the problem for deeper understanding. The research provides scaffolding to support self-explanation and help novices design an ordered plan to then use to write code.

We can measure success by comparing students' final solutions with a previous semester taught without the pedagogy. Data collected includes students' surveys and logged interactions, where surveys measure frustration and opinions on effectiveness, and logged information provides insight into usage. An interview will also be conducted with the instructor for their perspective on students' improvement, along with additional work from the instructor to support the research.

6 DISSERTATION STATUS

I have identified an introductory programming course to pilot my research. This is a MOOC course offered at the University of Adelaide. The customized plugin needs to be developed using edX's XBlocks API and a Parsons Problems framework, js-parsons. When the pilot begins, I will monitor students' usage throughout the semester. At the conclusion of the course, I will evaluate ways to improve the learning approach by incorporating feedback.

7 EXPECTED CONTRIBUTIONS

The field of Software Engineering stresses the importance of developing design specifications for on-time product development with accurate requirements. However, software development meta-skills are not present in introductory courses, which can potentially lead to poor learning behaviors. The lack of problem solving guidance may contribute towards students' misconceptions and frustration with software assignments, potentially leading to poorly constructed solutions, self-efficacy, and class attrition. More research is needed to determine how novices perform when taught codification. If my research is positive, this pedagogy will be evaluated for other STEM disciplines.

8 DISCUSSION TOPICS

I have two research topics I would like to focus on with the Doctoral Consortium discussants. Firstly, the questioning approach used within the plugin. I am currently investigating three approaches: Self-Explanation, Self-Reflection, and Socratic questioning. I have not decided on a method.

My second topic is the data analysis, with respect to the growth in the students' metacognitive skills. I do not believe students' grades can solely determine metacognitive growth. Rather, I believe additional analysis of students' answers to the plugin's questions will show growth, and I have yet to determine the best analysis approach.

REFERENCES

[1] K. Boyer, W. Lahti, R. Phillips, M. Wallis, M. Vouk, and J. Lester. Principles of asking effective questions during student problem solving. In *Proceedings of the 41st ACM Technical Symposium on Computer Science Education*, 460–464, 2010.

[2] M. Caspersen, and J. Bennedsen. Instructional design of a programming course – A learning theoretic approach. In *Proceedings of the 3rd International Workshop on Computing Education Research*, 111–122, 2007.

[3] B. Morrison, L. Margulieux, B. Ericson, and M. Guzdial. Subgoals help students solve parsons problems. In *Proceedings of the 47th ACM Technical Symposium on Computer Science Education*, 42–47, 2016.

[4] C. Schulte, T. Busjahn, T. Clear, J. Paterson, and A. Taherkhani. An introduction to program comprehension for computer science educators. In *Proceedings of the 2010 ITiCSE Working Group*, 65–86, 2010.

[5] J. Wilson. A socratic approach to helping novice programmers debug programs. In *Proceedings of the 18th SIGCSE Technical Symposium on Computer Science Education*, 179–182, 1987.

Developing Teachers As Computational Participants

Daniel Hickmott

School of Education, University of Newcastle, Australia

Daniel.Hickmott@uon.edu.au

ABSTRACT

This document briefly explains the context, motivations, background and research design of a PhD project titled *"Developing Teachers as Computational Participants"*. This PhD project will explore how Australian Primary School teachers learn and teach the *core CS skills* (*computational thinking, computer programming* and *systems thinking*), their experiences implementing lessons that impart these skills and the challenges they encounter when implementing these lessons.

CCS CONCEPTS

• **Social and professional topics → Computational thinking; K-12 education;**

KEYWORDS

constructionism; computational participation; teacher professional development; primary school

1 PROGRAM CONTEXT

I am a full-time student in the Doctor of Philosophy (Education) program in the School of Education at the University of Newcastle, Australia. As of June 2017, I have been in the program for a year and four months. I have just completed my confirmation and am planning to complete my dissertation over the next two years (Australian PhDs are typically three to three and a half years full-time).

2 CONTEXT AND MOTIVATION

Several countries, such as England and New Zealand, have recently begun to shift the focus of their ICT curricula from the teaching of software applications, to the teaching of skills that will allow students to create and implement their own digital solutions [6]. These skills include: *computer programming, computational thinking* and *systems thinking*, which are referred to as the *core CS skills* in this study. In Australia, the Digital Technologies subject area has recently been introduced as part of the national curriculum, which will involve the compulsory teaching of the *core CS skills* to all students from the first year of schooling (Foundation) to their tenth year (Year 10).

Introducing the compulsory teaching of the *core CS skills* presents a major challenge for teachers, particularly for those that teach at a primary school level. The majority of Australian primary school teachers are generalist teachers [5] and are unlikely to have learned about the *core CS skills* in their formal education. Professional development (PD) programs, such as face-to-face workshops and online courses, have been developed as one approach to address this challenge. However, there is currently limited research into the effect of these programs on teachers' knowledge of the *core CS skills*, their self-efficacy towards learning and teaching these skills, and the pedagogical practices teachers use to impart these skills, particularly in the Australian context.

3 BACKGROUND & RELATED WORK

Computational participation is a frame for teaching and learning *computer programming*, which was introduced in the book *Connected Code* [3]. In *Connected Code*, Yasmin Kafai and Quinn Burke argue that students should not be taught *computer programming* solely with the aim to develop them as logical and rigorous *computational thinkers*, but instead with the aim to develop them as *computational participants* who understand the technical, social and cultural aspects of computing. The design of the *computational participation* frame has been influenced by the *Constructionism* learning theory [2], which underpins this project's theoretical framework. The central assumption of *Constructionism* is that students learn best when they construct physical and/or digital artefacts that can be shared with others.

There has been limited research conducted into PD programs that have been designed with a Constructionist lens on learning. Karen Brennan has developed a model of PD called *ScratchEd* [1], which is one example of a PD program designed in this way. The analysis conducted by Brennan has mainly been qualitative and has largely been concerned with how educators balance learners' structure and agency when teaching *computer programming*. However, in addition to qualitative analysis, this research project involves quantitative analysis of teachers' levels of knowledge of the *core CS skills*, self efficacy and pedagogical practices. The quality of pedagogical practices will be quantified by applying the *Quality Teaching Framework* [4], which is a validated model for examining teachers' practices.

4 STATEMENT OF THESIS/PROBLEM

The overall aim of this project is to understand how Australian primary school teachers learn and teach the *core CS skills*. It is intended that the model of PD developed in this project could be adapted by other PD providers and that the findings from the online survey will be available to policy makers, to help them design PD that is appropriate for teachers' current levels of knowledge of the *core CS skills*.

ICER '17, August 18-20, 2017, Tacoma, WA, USA

© 2017 Copyright held by the owner/author(s).

ACM ISBN 978-1-4503-4968-0/17/08.

https://doi.org/10.1145/3105726.3105728

5 RESEARCH GOALS & METHODS

The goal of this research project is to answer four main research questions, which are listed later in this section. The project consists of three separate stages, which will be preceded by the design of a pilot survey. These stages, and the pilot survey design, are briefly described in the following paragraphs.

Pilot Survey Design: Currently, a survey is being designed that will be piloted during Stage 1 of the project. This survey will collect information about teachers' demographics and the pedagogical practices they use when teaching the *core CS skills* to their students. The survey will also contain scales for measuring the teachers' self-efficacy towards computational thinking and their levels of knowledge of the *core CS skills.*

Stage 1 (PD Program): A PD program will be run as part of the project, designed with *computational participation* as a guiding framework. There will be 2 parts of the program, each of which will be 10 weeks in duration and that will involve weekly 2 hour after-school tutorial sessions.

Stage 2 (Interviews): Follow-up interviews with participants of the PD program will be conducted three months after the PD program has completed, in July 2018.

Stage 3 (Online Survey): The pilot survey will be reworked, and refined, as a result of analysis of the data collected in Stages 1 and 2 of the project. The reworked survey will be distributed nationally through an online survey platform in October 2018.

The following paragraphs state each of the project's research questions and briefly describe the methods of analysis that will be used on the data collected in the above three project stages, to answer each of the research questions.

Research Question 1: *"What are the levels of knowledge, self-efficacy and perceived pedagogical practices of Australian Primary School teachers, with respect to the Core CS Skills?"*

The first research question is an overarching research question. Answering this question will mainly involve quantitative analysis. Descriptive and inferential statistics will be performed on the responses to the online survey (Stage 3) to answer this question. Analysis conducted during Stages 1 and 2 will also inform the answer to this question.

Research Question 2: *"To what extent does Australian Primary School teachers' knowledge, self-efficacy and pedagogical practices, with respect to the Core CS Skills, change as a result of completing a professional development program developed with computational participation as a guiding framework?"*

This question will be answered by analysing collected data with a mixed methods approach. The survey responses and lesson plans, collected in Stage 1, will be analysed with descriptive and inferential statistics. Thematic analysis will be performed on the lessons and journal submissions collected in Stage 1. The results from the quantitative and qualitative analysis will be compared and contrasted, in order to answer the second research question.

Research Question 3: *"How do Australian Primary School teachers experience the elements of computational participation when taking part in the professional development program and when applying ideas from the program in their classrooms?"*

Answering the third research question will only involve qualitative analysis. Thematic analysis will be performed on the teachers'

journal submissions (collected in part 2 of Stage 1) and interviews (conducted in Stage 2).

Research Question 4: *"What challenges do Australian Primary School teachers encounter in their classroom experiences of implementing the Digital Technologies curriculum?"*

This question will be answered by analysing data with a mixed methods approach. Thematic analysis will be performed on the journal submissions (collected in part 2 of Stage 1) and interviews (conducted in Stage 2). Descriptive and inferential statistics will be performed on the online survey responses, to discover the challenges teachers commonly encounter when implementing Digital Technologies subject lessons.

6 DISSERTATION STATUS

I am currently designing the pilot survey and will begin collecting data in October 2017. I am in the early stages of the project and have started writing the *Introduction, Literature Review* and *Methodology* sections.

7 EXPECTED CONTRIBUTIONS

The following four contributions will be able to used by computing education PD providers and teacher educators to adapt for their own programs. The first expected contribution is a model of PD, that will be designed with *computational participation* as a guiding framework. The second expected contribution is a validated instrument for measuring teachers' understanding of the *core CS skills.* The third expected contribution is an understanding of the challenges Australian primary teachers encounter when implementing Digital Technologies lessons. The fourth expected contribution will be an understanding of Australian primary school teachers' levels of knowledge, self efficacy and pedagogical practices, with respect to the *core CS skills.*

8 DOCTORAL CONSORTIUM

I am hoping that, by participating the ICER Doctoral Consortium, I will get feedback about my proposed methodology and suggestions for improving my pilot survey's design. I would also like to meet other doctoral students and discuss their research with them, as I rarely get the opportunity to discuss computing education with fellow doctoral students and faculty at my institution. These discussions could broaden my understanding of computing education and could also foster future, international collaborations in this research area.

REFERENCES

[1] Karen Brennan. 2015. Beyond Technocentrism. *Constructivist Foundations* 10, 3 (2015), 289–296.
[2] Idit Harel and Seymour Papert. 1991. *Constructionism.* Ablex Publishing.
[3] Yasmin B Kafai and Quinn Burke. 2014. *Connected code: Why children need to learn programming.* Mit Press.
[4] James G. Ladwig. 2007. Modelling Pedagogy in Australian School Reform. *Pedagogies: An International Journal* 2, 2 (2007), 57–76.
[5] Rebecca Vivian, Katrina Falkner, and Nickolas Falkner. 2014. Addressing the challenges of a new digital technologies curriculum: MOOCs as a scalable solution for teacher professional development. *Research in Learning Technology* 22 (2014).
[6] Mary Webb, Niki Davis, Tim Bell, Yaacov J. Katz, Nicholas Reynolds, Dianne P. Chambers, and Maciej M. Sysło. 2017. Computer science in K-12 school curricula of the 21st century: Why, what and when? *Education and Information Technologies* 22, 2 (2017), 445–468.

Understanding and Supporting Better Pairings for CS1 Students

L Hobbes LeGault
University of Wisconsin—Madison
Department of Computer Sciences
Madison, WI
legault@wisc.edu

ABSTRACT

Introduction to programming courses employ pair programming with benefits to both students and instructors. When selecting their own partners, students without extant support or social networks are at a significant disadvantage relative to well-connected students. The present work will use individual and pair programming activities to create a matching program to suggest effective programming partners to students, with the goal of improving the experience of partner work in introductory CS classes. In doing so, we will explore the relevant matching traits in productive pairs and gain a deeper understanding of (un)productive pair partnerships.

CCS CONCEPTS

• **Social and professional topics** → **Computer science education**;

KEYWORDS

pair programming; diversity; equity

1 PROGRAM CONTEXT

I began my graduate work in Computer Sciences in a graphics lab, completed my master's thesis in optimization, and, after a brief hiatus, began my doctoral research in genetics-based bioinformatics. Throughout the entire process, however, I continued to serve as an instructor for the department. In 2014, I accepted a position as a faculty associate instructor for the department, and my bioinformatics project was discontinued shortly thereafter. At the time, there was no educational research emphasis in the department.

As I continued to work toward improving the introductory programming sequence, I met with my current advisor, Matthew Berland, and beginning in 2016, we agreed to formalize my educational research work into a dissertation project. I am still very new to CS Education Research as a formal field, but I am committed to it. The ICER doctoral consortium is an excellent opportunity for me to get pointers to relevant literature and network within the field.

2 CONTEXT AND MOTIVATION

Introductory programming courses very frequently encourage or even require students to work with partners. For faculty, the benefit is a reduction in grading load; for students, the benefit (ideally) comes from the collaboration itself. In theory, students make connections with other students who are interested in programming, they work through problems with a person whose understanding level is very near to their own, they divide the workload, and they then must articulate their own understanding rather than leaving it implicit, which can reinforce learning, particularly in weaker students [3].

That these benefits exist is established [5], but they are not universally applicable to any given pair of students. My research hypothesis is, succinctly, that "not all pairs are created equally," and, in my work, I investigate an optimal, automated partner recommendation algorithm that analyzes individual student work and preferences to suggest productive partnerships with other students.

Typically, partners in CS courses are either randomly-assigned or self-selected. If randomly assigned, every student stands an equal (potentially high) chance of entering into an unproductive partnership. If self-selected, students with preexisting networks in the subject area are at an advantage — an unfair bias against students in already under-represented groups. Obviously neither solution is optimal: with random assignment, there is a fair chance of hobbling class productivity in general; with self-selection, the students who need the most help may be more likely to be in unproductive partnerships.

To place all students on a level footing, with the additional benefit of providing students with repetitive coding practice, I am creating a tool to analyze how students in a given pairing make mistakes and solve problems in order to automatically recommend other students within the course as productive programming partners. This would remove any burden of such matchmaking from instructors, while allowing students to make informed choices about their partners even if they do not have any prior connections with other students in the course.

If successful, I anticipate using this tool heavily within my own courses, and other instructors have expressed enthusiastic interest in generalizing it to other courses and content.

3 BACKGROUND AND RELATED WORK

Recent CS educational research has established the utility of pair programming (PP) in introductory courses.

The systematic literature review in [5] synthesizes research done through 2011. Primarily it establishes that across research, PP has many positive benefits versus individual work, but also investigates several related subquestions. Of particular relevance to my research are the studies of factors influencing pair compatibility. Of most significance were actual or perceived skill levels (similar being better) and student personality (different being better).

More recent studies concur with these findings. Reinforcing the utility of the PP paradigm, a 2015 study [3] randomly assigned non-CS majors to either a traditional or PP lab. Students using the PP paradigm saw considerably increased attendance rates and improved performance, particularly among students on the lower end (C vs DF) of the grading scale. In particular, 15% more students in the PP cohort achieved a C or better than in the traditional cohort.

Examining additional factors which might influence pair compatibility, the study in [4] investigated racial differences while the study in [1] examined gender differences. For example, there was a marked qualitative difference in the experience of female-identified participants, who reported feeling much more comfortable and confident when working with another female. We propose to use the existing research on pair compatibility to create an initial pairing algorithm, which will continuously refine its performance by analyzing student inputs.

4 STATEMENT OF THESIS/PROBLEM

Given that not all working partnerships are created equal, how can we use machine learning algorithms to automatically recognize and recommend well-matched partnerships to students?

- Gather data on problem-solving process of students working individually and in pairs.
- Analyze data to uncover features of individuals who have worked well together, and suggest novel partnerships based on this analysis.
- Follow up on the success of resultant partnerships and refine analysis accordingly.

5 RESEARCH GOALS & METHODS

The primary goal of the research is the creation of a tool for automatic matchmaking of individual students into productive pairs for pair programming. Other goals include:

- Quantification and classification of discovered matching traits in compatible individuals
- Analysis of chosen partnerships and the traits that individuals prioritize when selecting a partner

The first stage of the research has been implementing a basic tool for assessing pair programming strategies and looking at qualitative versus quantitative measures of effectiveness. This version of the tool involved only a single task, a block-based programming language with 10 maze problems intended to be completed in pairs, followed by subjective evaluations of the experience for each partner. In addition to simple completion (success/failure) logs for each level, data was also gathered on every action taken within the programming space.

This version of the tool was tested by a small group of non-students before it was rolled out to an intro course of 300+ students in spring 2017. The data from the intro course run will be analyzed this summer to contrast the differences between quantitative success and qualitative satisfaction with PP.

The next version of the tool will include anonymized user profiles for students, individual programming activities, and multiple choice questions for assessing basic personality traits. I hope to track longitudinal development of skills with the goal of assessing and correlating individual performance with PP activities.

6 DISSERTATION STATUS

I have designed the tool and implemented a working alpha which includes a partner-based exercise in solving mazes using a block-based programming language (Blockly [2]). I have gathered data from this version of the tool in both a small pilot test and an IRB-approved pilot test on a class of about 300 students in spring 2017. Analysis and submission of an article on this data is slated for later this summer.

Further development on the tool enabling longitudinal analysis of individual programming behavior and analysis of data produced is projected for summer and fall 2017. Partnership analysis and algorithm refinement is projected for fall 2017 and spring 2018.

Thesis document outline is complete, with rough draft completion projected for summer 2017. Defense of the final dissertation is projected for summer 2018.

7 EXPECTED CONTRIBUTIONS

Upon successful completion of this research, I anticipate findings about how productive pairings work (and do not work); a functional prototype of a tool to assist instructors and students alike in a more optimal assignment of students to programming pairs; and a deeper understanding of the processes behind un/productive pairings in introductory CS classes.

REFERENCES

[1] Kyungsub Stephen Choi. 2015. A Comparative Analysis of Different Gender Pair Combinations in Pair Programming. *Behav. Inf. Technol.* 34, 8 (Aug. 2015), 825–837. https://doi.org/10.1080/0144929X.2014.937460
[2] Google Developers. 2016. Blockly. (2016). http://developers.google.com/blockly/
[3] Clem O'Donnell, Jim Buckley, Abdulhussain Mahdi, John Nelson, and Michael English. 2015. Evaluating Pair-Programming for Non-Computer Science Major Students. In *Proceedings of the 46th ACM Technical Symposium on Computer Science Education (SIGCSE '15)*. ACM, New York, NY, USA, 569–574. https://doi.org/10.1145/2676723.2677289
[4] Omar Ruvalcaba, Linda Werner, and Jill Denner. 2016. Observations of Pair Programming: Variations in Collaboration Across Demographic Groups. In *Proceedings of the 47th ACM Technical Symposium on Computing Science Education (SIGCSE '16)*. ACM, New York, NY, USA, 90–95. https://doi.org/10.1145/2839509.2844558
[5] Norsaremah Salleh, Emilia Mendes, and John Grundy. 2011. Empirical Studies of Pair Programming for CS/SE Teaching in Higher Education: A Systematic Literature Review. *IEEE Trans. Softw. Eng.* 37, 4 (July 2011), 509–525. https://doi.org/10.1109/TSE.2010.59

Physical Computing as an Inquiry Working Technique

Sandra Schulz
Humboldt-Universität zu Berlin
Department of Computer Science
Unter den Linden 6
Berlin, Germany 10099
saschulz@informatik.hu-berlin.de

ABSTRACT

Physical computing is receiving much attention in the shape of numerous variations of devices. This trend is apparent in computer science education from kindergarten to university. To improve the implementation of physical computing in secondary school I observe student's process of problem solving when they use physical computing devices. To successfully implement this in schools, it appears to be valuable to investigate problems that occur during the the process and to develop supporting material. These topics are the foci of my doctoral project and will be figured out with results from scientific inquiry. Particularly building on the experiment as an inquiry working technique.

CCS CONCEPTS

• **Social and professional topics** → **K-12 education**; • **Computer systems organization** → **Robotics**; *Robotic components*;

KEYWORDS

Computer Science Education; Physical Computing; Inquiry Learning

ACM Reference format:
Sandra Schulz. 2017. Physical Computing as an Inquiry Working Technique. In *Proceedings of ICER '17, Tacoma, WA, USA, August 18-20, 2017*, 2 pages.
https://doi.org/10.1145/3105726.3105730

1 PROGRAM CONTEXT

In January 2017 I started my 3rd year as a doctoral student at Humboldt-Universität zu Berlin in Germany. My advisor is Prof. Dr. Niels Pinkwart as the head of the "computer science education/computer science and society" chair. I am funded by a grant from Humboldt-ProMINT-Kolleg, an integrated STEM research group. It is also a structured doctoral program I am participating in and evaluating. Enabled by this colleague I went abroad for 3 months, starting in winter 2016 to conduct research at Carnegie Mellon University in Pittsburgh.

In the last two years I conducted an intensive literature review in computer science and natural science on concerning to this research area. Building on this, I explored the physical computing process

through qualitative studies, and am analyzing data. Afterwards a design for the final studies needs to be developed in fall this year.

2 CONTEXT AND MOTIVATION

The research on problem solving in natural sciences is well established and there are some supporting mechanisms which seems to be similar to problem solving in computer science. The experiment as an inquiry working technique is additionally very similar to the physical computing (PhC) process.

My motivation is twofold: 1) if it is possible to find evidence for the similarity of the scientific inquiry (SI) process and the PhC process, results from science can be adapted for computer science education (CS Ed). So we do not need to start from scratch in PhC research. 2) the research questions tackle hurdles for a successful implementation of PhC in school, and potentially in STEM subjects. This approach is aiming to enhance PhC research building on existing results.

3 BACKGROUND & RELATED WORK

In the literature, PhC is defined as "creating a conversation between the physical world and the virtual world of the computer" [4][p. xix]. The authors describe an interactive system consisting of sensors, actuators and a mircocontroller or mini computer, controlling received data and resulting aimed feedback. This is the case for example for Arduino mircocontrollers or robots.

From the science perspective, Klahr and Dunbar observed the scientific reasoning process (SDDS model), a base for following inquiry models [3]. The SDDS model contains to search in a hypothesis space and an experimental space. This means to first construct a hypothesis, test the hypothesis and draw conclusions based on data. The process is divided into phases and subphases, where the occurring order or integrity can vary. SI encompasses working techniques like experimentation and is known to be an important competence in science and needs to be improved [2].

The general idea of combining scientific inquiry (SI) and physical computing is not completely new, but not fully analyzed either. Blikstein [1] suggested a combination of the simulated and real world through PhC devices in an experimental setting. Therefore a robot programmed with LOGO like language was used for the intervention. He stated that with this approach models can be validated which leads to to a deeper understanding of scientific phenomena. Afterwards, Sullivan [7] pointed out that the necessary skills during robotics activities and scientific inquiry are similar. We can conclude that there is enormous potential in combining of both domains.

4 STATEMENT OF THESIS/PROBLEM

The results from literature lead us to the approach to investigate the deeper structure of PhC to compare the processes of PhC and SI. If both processes share substantial phases we probably can adapt findings from scientific inquiry research. This could be problems students have during the activity and also scaffolds for the process. PhC could be an interdisciplinary working technique to improve computer science and science skills.

5 RESEARCH GOALS & METHODS

To reach the goal to compare a science and a PhC process, the first hurdle was to construct a PhC process model, based on the limited literature.

An empirical analysis in a learning scenario was conducted to support and adapt the theoretical PhC process model (RQ1). According to results from SI, students have some problems to complete the SI process successfully. We will search for some of the common problems from SI in the PhC. The focus has been on the transition of performing a program to the evaluation of outcomes. In respect to the qualitative data, a preliminary categorization of occurring problems is figured out (RQ2, paper in preparation). The information about problems and investigating connected problem sources leads to RQ3. Building on this, an approach to support students during PhC activities will be developed.

One approach could be to open the "black box" of the PhC device and address the concrete problem sources, based on the components hardware, software and environment.

The research questions are:

RQ1 Do the similarities of the physical computing and scientific inquiry processes even support the theory that physical computing is a working technique in scientific inquiry? What are the similarities and differences?

RQ2 Which problems do students have to tackle and how can the problem sources be categorized?

RQ3 How effective is it to open the black box of a physical computing device in the evaluation phase to externalize the problem sources for students?

The 1st and 2nd research questions are (almost) tackled through qualitative studies. I recorded data from students working with LEGO Mindstorms robots and Arduinos. The students were video recorded while solving some tasks with the devices. The videos were transcribed and analyzed with a qualitative content analysis. A task with an Arduino could be to give different outputs regarding to the intensity of light in the environment. Using this data, I observed the process the students went through in solving PhC tasks. In the same data set student's problems became visible. Thereby I am already categorizing occurring problems and figure out appropriate hints for students how to tackle the problems.

Building on these hints I am considering to test them in a classroom setting. One methodological problem here is a lack in test instruments.

6 DISSERTATION STATUS

In 2015 I started with an exploratory study and reached preliminary results supporting the hypothesis that PhC tasks can be suitable to improve science learning as well as computer science competences [5]. I already tackled the first research question and published the results at a peer-reviewed conference [6]. An essential result is that the PhC process can be divided in the phases preparation, implementation, performance and evaluation, similar to SI. Both processes share an essential structure. As result of the conducted studies, there are results for the second research question and initial hints how to support the occurring problems students have. This time I am evaluating this data to give an answer regarding to RQ2. I plan to conduct further studies concerning RQ3. These will be designed in fall of 2017. After possible follow-up studies and the evaluation of gathered data, I plan to finish my doctoral studies in the mid of 2018.

I hope to get feedback from the ICER community regarding to the planned methods tackling the third research question. The most important issue is to find adequate indicators within qualitative video data to assess student learning. The participation in the conference would be important for me to receive some last hints before conducting final studies and finishing my dissertation. Additionally, I aspire to connect myself with the worldwide computer science education community.

7 EXPECTED CONTRIBUTIONS

By tackling my research questions I will provide a strong theoretical and empirical base for PhC through the connection of computer science and scientific inquiry. This creates a new facet of PhC research, that focuses on the concrete process and occurring problems during PhC tasks. This can effect the construction of new PhC devices and tasks, enabling an experimental approach in computer science in general.

Furthermore my research is directly influencing computer science education in school. An overview concerning occurring problems and suitable scaffolds will be constructed in my dissertation.

REFERENCES

[1] Paulo Blikstein and Uri Wilensky. 2007. Bifocal modeling: a framework for combining computer modeling, robotics and real-world sensing. In *annual meeting of the American Educational Research Association (AERA 2007), Chicago, USA.* Citeseer.

[2] National Research Council et al. 2012. *A framework for K-12 science education: Practices, crosscutting concepts, and core ideas.* National Academies Press.

[3] David Klahr and Kevin Dunbar. 1988. Dual space search during scientific reasoning. *Cognitive science* 12, 1 (1988), 1–48.

[4] Dan O'Sullivan and Tom Igoe. 2004. *Physical computing: sensing and controlling the physical world with computers.* Course Technology Press.

[5] Sandra Schulz and Niels Pinkwart. 2015. Physical Computing in STEM Education. In *Proceedings of the Workshop in Primary and Secondary Computing Education (WiPSCE '15).* ACM, New York, NY, USA, 134–135.

[6] Sandra Schulz and Niels Pinkwart. 2016. Towards Supporting Scientific Inquiry in Computer Science Education. In *Proceedings of the 11th Workshop in Primary and Secondary Computing Education (WiPSCE '16).* ACM, New York, NY, USA, 45–53.

[7] Florence R. Sullivan. 2008. Robotics and science literacy: Thinking skills, science process skills and systems understanding. *Journal of Research in Science Teaching* 45, 3 (2008), 373–394.

Towards a Fine-grained Analysis of Complexity of Programming Tasks

Rodrigo Duran
Aalto University
Department of Computer Science
P.O.Box 15400
Aalto, Finland 00076
rodrigo.duran@aalto.fi

ABSTRACT

Bloom's and SOLO taxonomies have been used to describe the complexity of computer science tasks and student's outcome. However, using these taxonomies have coarse granularity and programming tasks with very different demands could be equally classified at the same level. My research proposes a new framework using Neo-Piagetian stages of development based on the Model of Hierarchical Complexity (MHC) that enable formal definition and fine-grained evaluation of programming tasks nuances in paradigms, languages, and constructs. By empirically validating the model, I expect it to be a valuable tool to provide best practices to develop pedagogical approaches and tools.

CCS CONCEPTS

• **Social and professional topics** → **Computer science education**; *Model curricula*; Student assessment;

KEYWORDS

Task complexity; Model of Hierarchical Complexity; Neo-Piagetian stages.

1 PROGRAM CONTEXT

I am a full-time Ph.D. student in my 2nd year of studies toward the doctoral degree in Computer Science Education at Aalto University under supervision of Prof. Lauri Malmi. I'm completing my credits requirements and working on refining my research goals and methods, as I intend to apply to my pre-examination in fall 2019 and defend my dissertation in winter 2020. The status of my work is on a preliminary state, so it is crucial to me to discuss and receive constructive quality feedback on my assumptions, hypotheses and research methods used in my work.

2 CONTEXT AND MOTIVATION

When evaluating different programming tasks, how can we say that one is more complex than the other? Can paradigms and languages make tasks less complex? In fact, a more pertinent question is: how to define complexity itself?

ICER '17, August 18-20, 2017, Tacoma, WA, USA
ACM ISBN 978-1-4503-4968-0/17/08.
https://doi.org/10.1145/3105726.3105731

Computing Education Researchers (CER) applied different methods, mostly related to Bloom's and SOLO taxonomies, to quantify the complexity of the factors that make learning to program such a difficult task [5, 7]. Although the approaches using these taxonomies achieved varying degrees of success, using these taxonomies has not enabled researchers to perform a fine-grained analysis of the nuances in programming tasks. How to quantify the complexity of tasks itself and how programming languages, constructs, and paradigms have an impact in this complexity?

Literature, in general, agrees that implementing a solution to a problem in a programming language is highly complex and is rated very high (as much as "creating" in the Bloom's revised taxonomy). However, not every programming task has the same complexity in every language and paradigm. It is only reasonable to assume that solving the Rainfall Problem [8] is more complex than filtering the even numbers in an array. Nevertheless, can we measure how programs are related to each other? If we solve the Rainfall Problem using different languages and programming constructs, does make it less complex in a given approach?

Having a more formal and reliable method with appropriate granularity levels to evaluate the complexity of tasks and CS students stage of cognitive development and carefully matching them could lead to better designed learning materials and tools and a smoother linear learning curve in CS courses.

3 BACKGROUND & RELATED WORK

Quantifying the complexity of a problem and its solution in a programming language is not trivial. Besides the methods using Bloom's and SOLO taxonomies, Lister [4] presented a more general model with a sequence of actions of increasing complexity using Neo-Piagetian stage theory to interpret cognitive stages of development, providing evidence of an order of programming skills.

Aiming to provide a formal definition and more reliable methods to define and measure stages of cognitive development, the Model of Hierarchical Complexity (MHC) is a Neo-Piagetian and quantitative behavioral-developmental theory that can be used to analyze the complexity of tasks [3]. The model is based on the assumption that a large number of tasks exist and that these tasks occur in sequences that can be ordered as to their complexity. The MHC postulates that the development of competency results from the mastery of tasks that occur in a sequence from least to most hierarchically complex [6]. *Actions* are defined as behavioral events that produce outcomes. A *task* can be defined as a set of required actions that obtain an objective. The scaling of the tasks is operationalized by formally describing tasks in an Order of Hierarchical Complexity

(OHC), "...*measured by the number of recursions that the coordinating actions must perform on a set of primary elements. Recursion refers to the process by which the output of the lower-order actions forms the input of the higher-order actions*" [2]. Orders have *subtasks* and *subsubtasks* between them. Subtask actions organize only one action from the same order and one or more from previous orders [1].

How these actions and tasks are represented in programming? Soloway [8] has addressed the issue of how plans and *schemas* are a central component in learning how to program. In his article, Soloway already discusses that plans could be used as the most abstract description level of a task, and how the general plan composition can be used to compare different tasks, as long as they have isomorphic structures.

Formally, for a task to be more hierarchically complex than another, the new task must meet three requirements [3]: (1) A more hierarchically complex task and its required actions are defined in terms of two or more less hierarchically complex tasks; (2) The more hierarchically complex task organizes or coordinates two or more less complex actions; (3) The coordination of actions that occurs has to be non-arbitrary. Since MHC strongly relies on the formal definition of the relationship of tasks and not in direct evaluation of performance of subjects, Commons et al. [2] used a Rasch Scale Stages Score (RSSS) on balance beam tasks to validate the model, showing that it is very accurate in predicting the scaled scores, sequentiality of stages, clustering of same complexity tasks and intermediate performance of subjects.

4 STATEMENT OF THE THESIS/PROBLEM

My work aims to develop a framework to formally define and measure the complexity of programming tasks allowing researchers to capture the fine-grained specificities of programming languages and paradigms. I want to empirically validate the framework comparing student's performance on tasks with varying levels of complexity and investigate how different languages, paradigms, and constructs can impact the theoretical complexity of the task and student's performance.

5 RESEARCH GOALS & METHODS

Formally define a framework to measure the complexity of programming tasks: Complexity of the tasks will be formally defined in terms of *plan schema* structures and MHC. As programming tasks can be expressed using different structures, I will create a complexity hierarchy tree for three contexts: functional paradigm with Scala, object-oriented paradigm with Java and imperative paradigm with Python. The tasks will be selected based on their relevance on literature or predominance on popular problems databases [1].

Validate the framework with empirical results: The validation of the model will have three dimensions: the proposed theoretical hierarchy tree, an empirical Rasch analysis and a Cognitive Load Measurement test using collected data from Aalto University undergraduate students from three CS courses solving the proposed tasks in each of the given contexts.

Propose a pedagogical approach based on task's order of complexity: Since the MHC postulates that competency develops through tasks of increasing order of complexity [6], I will use the

results of my work to propose best practices to create a linear complexity sequence of examples using a language and paradigm with measured lower average complexity levels.

6 DISSERTATION STATUS

At the present moment, I'm in the process of formalizing the predicted order of complexity of tasks in paradigms and languages and selecting the tasks that will be theoretically measured and later applied to the selected cohorts.

7 EXPECTED CONTRIBUTIONS

By providing a more objective, reliable and fine-grained framework to classify programming tasks by order of complexity, I expect that the results of my research could have an impact in pedagogical approaches, particularly in introductory courses, helping educators to develop practices in line with the expected development level of beginners, creating a more linear learning curve in CS programming courses. This could support the process of choosing the language and paradigm of instruction, programming structures (loops, higher-order functions, library functions) used to teach concepts, as well improve the design of learning materials that take that measured complexity into account.

8 DOCTORAL CONSORTIUM CONTRIBUTION

I would like to discuss the methods that will be used to develop the programming complexity model based on the MHC framework. Open questions: should I create a generic model for plans, independent of language/paradigm, or focus on specific implementations of these plans using programming constructs? How this model interact with other learning theories? How is MHC related with Cognitive Load Theory? Can we unify those theories in a coherent model of how programming learning happens? How different scholar levels (K-12, for example) could show different stages of development and how these results could lead to adapted practices and development tools to teach programming in these settings?

REFERENCES

[1] Michael Lamport Commons, Robin Gane-McCalla, Cory David Barked, and Eva Yujia Li. 2014. The model of hierarchical complexity as a measurement system. *Behavioral Development Bulletin* 19, 3 (2014), 9.

[2] Michael Lamport Commons, Eric Andrew Goodheart, Alexander Pekker, Theo Linda Dawson, Karen Draney, and Kathryn Marie Adams. 2008. Using Rasch scaled stage scores to validate orders of hierarchical complexity of balance beam task sequences. *Journal of Applied Measurement* 9, 2 (2008), 182.

[3] Michael Lamport Commons, Edward James Trudeau, Sharon Anne Stein, Francis Asbury Richards, and Sharon R Krause. 1998. Hierarchical complexity of tasks shows the existence of developmental stages. *Developmental Review* 18, 3 (1998), 237–278.

[4] Raymond Lister. 2011. Concrete and Other Neo-Piagetian Forms of Reasoning in the Novice Programmer. *Proceedings of the Thirteenth Australasian Computing Education Conference* Ace (2011), 9–18.

[5] Raymond Lister and John Leaney. 2003. Introductory programming, criterion-referencing, and bloom. *ACM SIGCSE Bulletin* 35, 1 (2003), 143–147.

[6] Patrice Marie Miller and Darlene Crone-Todd. 2016. Comparing different ways of using the model of hierarchical complexity to evaluate graduate students. *Behavioral Development Bulletin* 21, 2 (2016), 223.

[7] Judy Sheard, Angela Carbone, Raymond Lister, Beth Simon, Errol Thompson, and Jacqueline L Whalley. 2008. Going SOLO to assess novice programmers. In *ACM SIGCSE Bulletin*, Vol. 40. ACM, 209–213.

[8] Elliot Soloway. 1986. Learning to program= learning to construct mechanisms and explanations. *Commun. ACM* 29, 9 (1986), 850–858.

---

[1] https://projecteuler.net/archives

Student Modeling Based on Fine-Grained Programming Process Snapshots

Juho Leinonen
University of Helsinki
Helsinki, Finland
juho.leinonen@helsinki.fi

ABSTRACT

I am studying the use of fine-grained programming process data for student modeling. The initial plan is to construct different types of program state representations such as Abstract Syntax Trees (ASTs) from the data. These program state representations could be used for both automatically inferring knowledge components that the students are trying to learn as well as for modeling students' knowledge on those specific components.

KEYWORDS

student modeling; programming snapshots; programming process data; educational data mining

1 PROGRAM CONTEXT

At the University of Helsinki, we collect fine-grained data from the students' programming process [11]. On each key-press within the programming environment, information on time, assignment, student and the source code modification is stored. In previous research, we have observed that students' programming experience can be partially inferred based on this fine-grained data [6]. My plan is to investigate whether more fine-grained knowledge could be also inferred from the data, such as the mastery of specific knowledge components. Studies along this topic have previously been conducted by, for example, Rivers et al. [8], Hosseini et al. [3], and Yudelson et al. [13]

Essentially, what is remaining in my PhD is 1) to define knowledge components based on the process states either automatically or manually and then 2) use these knowledge components and information on students' success (e.g. whether the code compiles or the assignment is proceeding to a desired direction) as an input for student modeling algorithms such as Bayesian Knowledge Tracing [2, 14] and Performance Factors Analysis [7], and possibly implement novel student modeling techniques that better utilize the high granularity of the data. It is likely, however, that this will be an iterative process.

ICER'17, August 18-20, 2017, Tacoma, WA, USA.
© 2017 Copyright held by the owner/author(s). 978-1-4503-4968-0/17/08.
DOI: http://dx.doi.org/10.1145/3105726.3105732

2 CONTEXT AND MOTIVATION

Our research group organizes the CS1 courses at the University of Helsinki and facilitates introductory programming courses throughout Finland in high schools and other universities and colleges. We also offer a MOOC with thousands of participants each year. For the time being, the courses are not too adaptive. All the students regardless of whether they study at the University or at a high-school have the same exercises, the same material, and the same support on the course. As the students' backgrounds vary a lot, especially in our MOOCs, the differences between the learners should be taken into account, and the material and the assignments should be adapted based on the students' knowledge and learning rate.

The data used in my PhD comes from these courses. In addition to the fine-grained programming process data that is being collected using a tool called Test My Code [12], we collect material usage data and voluntary demographic data such as students' gender, level of education, and age.

The current Test My Code -plugin evaluates only the functionality of the program. However, the correctness of the functionality is only a proxy for learning: it is possible that a knowledgeable student and a struggling student end up with the same solution, but took drastically different paths to achieve the solution. As we have the process data, we would like to be able to better utilize the information of the process by which the solution is constructed in addition to the end solution. This would allow us to e.g. give extra assignments to struggling students, while knowledgeable students would not need to complete assignments about a topic they already master.

3 BACKGROUND & RELATED WORK

A recent literature review that analyzed data collection in the context of computing education found that only 76 out of over 3500 articles included automatic programming process data gathering [5]. Rivers and Koedinger have developed a programming tutor that automatically generates hints based on abstract syntax trees which are built based on programming code [9]. Similarly, abstract syntax trees could be built based on students' programming snapshots and used for knowledge estimations as automatic hint generation and knowledge estimation are inherently examining the same problem – is the student struggling with a concept or not. More recently, Rivers et al. [8] studied learning curve analysis for estimating students' knowledge of KCs. They note that a lot of previous research has focused on compilation errors, and suggest that research on estimating students' knowledge based on their code (and not compilation status) should be conducted. A similar observation was made by Hosseini et al. when they studied the programming paths of students in our data [3].

Preliminary results that have been achieved in a research collaboration between University of Helsinki, University of Pittsburgh, and Carnegie Mellon University have shown that domain models can be extracted from our data and that the programming process data can be used for student modeling [13]. In my PhD, I am building on those results.

4 PROBLEM STATEMENT, RESEARCH GOALS & METHODS, AND EXPECTED CONTRIBUTIONS

In my PhD work, I hope to facilitate adaptiveness on our courses. To make the courses adaptive, we need to be able to model students' knowledge, as one of the main objectives of adaptiveness is to provide the students material and exercises that are suitable to them in regards to their current knowledge. On one hand, we want that the exercises and materials are not too hard for the student, so that they are able to learn the concepts. However, we also do not want to give out exercises or materials that the students already master as it is possibly demotivational.

While similar research has been conducted previously, research into how to model students' knowledge based on the whole programming process is still in its infancy. I have the following research objectives for my PhD thesis: 1) Construct a domain model (set of knowledge components) that describes the content the students are supposed to learn based on snapshot level data; 2) Estimate students' knowledge of course concepts based on their programming process.

To achieve these objectives, I will use the study by Yudelson et al. [13] as a starting point, and build on their work by examining other student modeling methods in addition to the Rasch model [10] and the Additive Factors Model [1]. In order to use the snapshots as input for student modeling algorithms, they need to be aggregated. Our plan is to build ASTs out of the snapshots and define KCs based on these ASTs. We could then examine sub-ASTs and see which constructs / KCs the students are struggling with by e.g. examining whether sub-ASTs compile or are correct by some other evaluation metrics.

The main contribution of my PhD is that students' learning is improved on courses where fine-grained programming snapshots are being collected. Other people in our research group are developing systems that could use the knowledge estimations for making the course contents adaptive.

5 DISSERTATION STATUS

Although I am officially a first-year PhD student, I have been working with the snapshot data already during my BSc and MSc studies on multiple publications. Additionally, I have studied relevant research which has allowed me to formulate the research objectives of my thesis. I have not yet started working on the AST construction or student modeling aspects; however, our group has an existing codebase for the purpose from previous work on CFAST [4]. I have an outline of my PhD thesis completed. My expected graduation is in late 2018 or early 2019.

6 EXPECTATIONS FROM THE DC

The data I have is very fine-grained as it contains every keystroke the students type when completing the programming assignments. I wish to discuss possible aspects that this kind of fine-grained data might have that could be used for estimating students' knowledge. For example, what parts of the programming process would be most relevant for estimating knowledge of specific knowledge components and skills. Additionally, I would appreciate ideas on what would be the best way to aggregate the data into suitable input for existing student modeling algorithms such as BKT [2, 14] or PFA [7]. For example, we want to retain the fine-grained aspects of the data, but individual programming process snapshots are hard to classify to just successes and failures as required by PFA. As I am in my first-year of PhD studies, I have plenty of time to revise and improve my plans for my PhD thesis. Furthermore, in addition to student modeling, fine-grained data could be used to infer other information about the students that could be used to facilitate learning, e.g. metacognitive strategies.

Lastly, I want to get acquainted with the ICER community as I will be attending many CSEd conferences in the next four years.

REFERENCES

[1] H. Cen, K. Koedinger, and B. Junker. Comparing two irt models for conjunctive skills. In *Intelligent tutoring systems*, pages 796–798. Springer, 2008.

[2] A. T. Corbett and J. R. Anderson. Knowledge tracing: Modeling the acquisition of procedural knowledge. *User modeling and user-adapted interaction*, 4(4):253–278, 1994.

[3] R. Hosseini, A. Vihavainen, and P. Brusilovsky. Exploring problem solving paths in a java programming course. 2014.

[4] D. Hovemeyer, A. Hellas, A. Petersen, and J. Spacco. Control-flow-only abstract syntax trees for analyzing students' programming progress. In *Proc. of the 2016 ACM Conference on International Computing Education Research*, pages 63–72. ACM, 2016.

[5] P. Ihantola, A. Vihavainen, A. Ahadi, M. Butler, J. Börstler, S. H. Edwards, E. Isohanni, A. Korhonen, A. Petersen, K. Rivers, M. A. Rubio, J. Sheard, B. Skupas, J. Spacco, C. Szabo, and D. Toll. Educational data mining and learning analytics in programming: Literature review and case studies. In *Proc. of the 2015 ITiCSE on Working Group Reports*, ITICSE-WGR '15, pages 41–63, New York, NY, USA, 2015. ACM.

[6] J. Leinonen, K. Longi, A. Klami, and A. Vihavainen. Automatic inference of programming performance and experience from typing patterns. In *Proc. of the 47th ACM Technical Symposium on Computing Science Education*, SIGCSE '16, pages 132–137, New York, NY, USA, 2016. ACM.

[7] P. I. Pavlik Jr, H. Cen, and K. R. Koedinger. Performance factors analysis–a new alternative to knowledge tracing. *Online Submission*, 2009.

[8] K. Rivers, E. Harpstead, and K. Koedinger. Learning curve analysis for programming: Which concepts do students struggle with? In *Proc. of the 2016 ACM Conference on International Computing Education Research*, pages 143–151. ACM, 2016.

[9] K. Rivers and K. R. Koedinger. Automating hint generation with solution space path construction. In *International Conference on Intelligent Tutoring Systems*, pages 329–339. Springer, 2014.

[10] W. J. van der Linden and R. K. Hambleton. *Handbook of modern item response theory*. Springer Science & Business Media, 2013.

[11] A. Vihavainen, M. Luukkainen, and P. Ihantola. Analysis of source code snapshot granularity levels. In *Proc. of the 15th Annual Conference on Information technology education*, pages 21–26. ACM, 2014.

[12] A. Vihavainen, T. Vikberg, M. Luukkainen, and M. Pärtel. Scaffolding students' learning using test my code. In *Proc. of the 18th ACM Conference on Innovation and Technology in Computer Science Education*, ITiCSE '13, pages 117–122, New York, NY, USA, 2013. ACM.

[13] M. Yudelson, R. Hosseini, A. Vihavainen, and P. Brusilovsky. Investigating automated student modeling in a java mooc. In *Educational Data Mining 2014*, 2014.

[14] M. V. Yudelson, K. R. Koedinger, and G. J. Gordon. Individualized bayesian knowledge tracing models. In *International Conference on Artificial Intelligence in Education*, pages 171–180. Springer, 2013.

Using Discernment Activities to Promote Skill Retention from Programming and Software Tutorials

Hilarie Nickerson
University of Colorado — Boulder
Computer Science & Cognitive Science
Boulder, CO 80309
USA
hnickerson@colorado.edu

ABSTRACT

Short self-guided tutorials for individuals who wish to create computational artifacts often emphasize activity completion, providing an immediate sense of accomplishment but failing to promote sustainable gains in learning. However, to be successful in subsequent endeavors, it is essential that these learners develop robust skills. By incorporating principles from Bransford & Schwarz's Preparation for Future Learning framework, interactive tutorials should be able to promote the acquisition of durable and adaptive abilities.

1 PROGRAM CONTEXT

I am close to submitting my dissertation proposal for a joint PhD in computer science and cognitive science at the University of Colorado – Boulder, advised by Alexander Repenning. For my area exam in human-centered computing I developed a 39 page synthesis paper entitled *Examining learning transfer in human-centered computing contexts*. During the past several years I have also been a graduate assistant with Scalable Game Design (SGD), a computer science education research project co-led by my advisor and by education faculty member David Webb.

My dissertation research, which arises from my interest in the cognitive basis for learning transfer and expertise development, is exploring how long-term learning outcomes for users of self-guided programming and software tutorials can be improved. One promising approach appears to be to incorporate activities through which learners strengthen their mental models by developing the ability to discern important features of the subject matter. I am now identifying key principles that underlie the methods described in the literature, which often rely on peer learning, and will repurpose them for interactive computer-based tutorials for individuals. To serve as testbeds for comparing discernment-based and procedural tutorial structures, I have selected specific SGD activities, one emphasizing programming and the other design. I have also worked out

selected details of my testing methodology, which will include laboratory, online, and classroom components.

2 CONTEXT AND MOTIVATION

As computational thinking and coding are becoming critical job skills, there is an increasing need for introductory experiences that provide exposure to computing to engage interest, as well as for more advanced learning options. At the same time, students and workers must still become familiar with the use of existing software. Both productivity and design applications can play a supporting role in programming endeavors. Individuals may be taught about coding and software use in group settings, ranging from K–12 classrooms to coding bootcamps, or learn on their own. Numerous providers such as Code.org, Khan Academy, and Udacity now provide self-instruction resources for learners who vary greatly with respect to age group and experience level. In addition, software vendors supply tutorials for their products, as do user group members and other enthusiasts. Many of these experiences emphasize activity completion and provide learners with an immediate sense of accomplishment and competence.

While the hope is that individuals will later be able to perform the activities covered in such tutorials unaided, and also use their abilities to achieve related goals, in reality the type of guidance provided in many tutorials for computational artifact development is not specifically designed to foster longer-term skill retention and transfer. Alternative approaches to tutorial design could result in more sustainable gains in learning, reducing the need for later help-seeking. Furthermore, since the coding or software use activity takes place in a computing environment, an opportunity exists for tutorials to check for the presence of early indicators that learners will acquire durable and adaptive abilities and to steer them accordingly.

3 BACKGROUND & RELATED WORK

As a prerequisite for developing coding proficiency or skill with software tools, users must become capable of recognizing and appreciating the features of the languages or applications that they work with. According to the situative view of learning and transfer, situational features serve as affordances for action [1]. From that perspective, knowing about the existence and operational characteristics of a feature is not sufficient; rather, user knowledge should incorporate a feature's purpose and eventually allow users to determine how features might be combined to achieve desired outcomes of some complexity. A fundamental difficulty with practice-oriented, step-by-step instructions, even when accompanied by supporting explanations, is that they do not require a great deal of mental engagement. Therefore, users may have difficulty recollecting important aspects of the features covered in tutorials offered in this format, such as how they contributed to accomplishing the focal task and how to use them in a coordinated fashion.

Active learning that asks more of users can promote deeper conceptual understanding and more highly elaborated knowledge, making later recall and transfer more likely. In particular, elaboration of mental models with important information about situational features occurs when learners participate in comparison activities through which they begin to *discern* similarities and differences [2, 3]. Two approaches that induce learners to attend to areas of contrast have emerged, primarily from research in the disciplines of mathematics, physics, and world languages. One approach entails providing specific examples that can be compared, and the other promotes comparison between student-invented and established disciplinary approaches [2, 3, 4]. It remains to be seen whether these methods, which often incorporate classroom-based peer discussion that assists learners to gain insights from multiple viewpoints, can translate successfully to self-guided environments for computing instruction.

The Preparation for Future Learning (PFL) framework [2] has served as an important source of ideas about discernment for later researchers, and it possesses additional characteristics of interest with respect to computational artifact tutorials. Discernment-oriented activities are viewed as catalysts that ready learners to gain a more sophisticated understanding of new material than would otherwise be possible, thereby preparing them to undertake progressively more challenging endeavors. PFL also incorporates checks for increasing understanding that precedes and predicts full skill mastery, providing information that can contribute to decisions about readiness to engage in more advanced work. Integrating PFL concepts with other design practices that are currently recommended for computing tutorials (e.g., [5]) is a promising idea for promoting more enduring learning outcomes.

4 PROBLEM STATEMENT & RESEARCH PLAN

The big picture question: How can principles drawn from the PFL framework be applied within self-guided tutorials to support robust learning? I will investigate:

Q1: Can discernment activities increase learner sensitivity to the existence and appropriate use of essential affordances within computational artifact development environments?

Q2: Do tutorials that incorporate discernment activities to increase affordance sensitivity lead to measurable differences in long-term skill retention and transfer outcomes?

Q3: What learner behaviors that are indicative of increasing conceptual understanding of essential affordances predict later mastery of related skills?

My research plan includes the following goals:

Develop guidelines for constructing discernment-based activities that are suitable for inclusion in self-guided tutorials. By reviewing past studies that have described such activities in classrooms and intelligent tutoring systems, I have begun to derive their most important attributes. Through further literature review I will continue to expand this list of studies, refine my understanding, and produce applicable guidelines.

Develop and pilot two sets of parallel tutorials that use discernment-based and step-by-step approaches. For each kind of activity (programming, design software use), one tutorial will be fully step-by-step, and the other a derivative that substitutes discernment-based instruction with respect to specific features.

Ascertain short- and long-term performance outcomes from tutorial use. Through three studies—laboratory (college students), online (mixed-age students), and classroom (middle school students pursuing independent projects)—I will test affordance sensitivity and long-term performance. Both qualitative and quantitative measures are planned.

Identify early learner behaviors that predict later skill mastery. As the studies progress, I will look for predictive information in the collected data, examining relationships among learner behaviors, immediate post-test results, and long-term outcomes.

Through participation in the ICER Doctoral Consortium I seek input on research participant pre- and post-assessments, as well as general thoughts on learning through tutorials.

5 EXPECTED CONTRIBUTIONS

This investigation has the potential to yield several contributions in learning science and computing education. The first is a set of broad guidelines for discernment activities in interactive, self-guided tutorials. Next, using these guidelines to develop tutorials for creating computational artifacts is expected to produce users who more deeply understand the features that they employ, both individually and together, and who are more likely to retain this knowledge. Finally, in keeping with the developmental aspect of the PFL framework, this research should provide insight into early indicators of learning progress during tutorial use. In future work I hope to explore how programmatically examining these indicators could automate the delivery of individualized scaffolding.

REFERENCES

[1] James G. Greeno, David R. Smith, and Joyce L. Moore. 1993. Transfer of situated learning. In *Transfer on Trial: Intelligence, Cognition, and Instruction*, Douglas K. Detterman and Robert J. Sternberg (Eds.). Ablex Publishing Corporation, Norwood, NJ, 99-167.
[2] John D. Bransford and Daniel L. Schwartz. 1999. Rethinking transfer: A simple proposal with multiple implications. *Rev. Res. Educ.* 24, 61-100.
[3] Ference Marton. 2006. Sameness and difference in transfer. *J. Learn. Sci.* 15, 4, 499–535.
[4] Manu Kapur and Katerine Bielaczyc. 2012. Designing for productive failure. *J. Learn. Sci.* 21, 1, 45–83.
[5] Ada S. Kim and Andrew J. Ko. 2017. A pedagogical analysis of online coding tutorials. In *SIGCSE '17: Proceedings of the 2017 ACM SIGCSE Technical Symposium on Computer Science Education.* ACM, New York, NY, 321-326.

Using Mediational Means during Learning and Understanding of Proof Assignments from Theory of Computation

Christiane Frede
Universität Hamburg
Department of Informatics
Vogt-Kölln-Straße 30
22527 Hamburg, Germany
frede@informatik.uni-hamburg.de

ABSTRACT

There is a lack of empirically validated studies about how students solve proof assignments in their Theory of Computation (ToC) courses. I want to get detailed insights about the nature of students' difficulties with this field of computer science (CS). To gather data, I want to perform several qualitative studies investigating how undergraduate CS majors solve assignments in individually-formed study groups. I will use Distributed Cognition Theory (DCOG) as the underlying theoretical framework and understand cognitive processes as an interplay between several humans, their environment, resources and tools/mediational means. In the context of ToC, tools/mediational means are all mathematical inscriptions, definitions and concepts as well as natural language or physical media like pen & paper or whiteboards. The goal of this dissertation is to understand how student groups use provided and their own mediational means and whether they are successful during solving proof assignments.

KEYWORDS

CS Education; Theory of computation; observational study; qualitative research; distributed cognition theory; tools

1 PROGRAM CONTEXT

I have completed the first year of my PhD program in the research group Computer Science Education at Universität Hamburg, Germany. As common in Germany, I am not enrolled in a PhD program but work as a research associate at the university. I intend to finish my work in late 2019. Until now, I have set my focus on finding an appropriate evaluation method and sharping my research questions. Now, I have to plan my studies with regard to location and thematic focus.

2 CONTEXT AND MOTIVATION

In the course of their undergraduate program, computer science (CS) majors usually are required to take courses in Theory of Computation (ToC). Several pedagogical approaches are built on

hypotheses that students' difficulties with ToC are mainly caused by lack of interest and motivation, e.g. [6], [11]. Because none of these assumptions has been empirically validated I want to get detailed insights about the nature of students' difficulties during creating and understanding proof assignments. This student-oriented research can prove more sustainable insights and help to develop pedagogy that better addresses students' needs.

3 BACKGROUND & RELATED WORK

Like stated before, we are lacking empirical studies about the way students are learning ToC. I found only two studies focusing precisely on this matter [1], [8] and therefore read the lack of additional studies as a call to action for CS education research in this field.

During my master thesis finished in March 2016 I designed a qualitative study investigating how three individually-formed study groups of undergraduate CS majors developed proofs to show NP-completeness. The research design was a triangulation approach consisting of a non-participatory observation and a qualitative interview. The research questions dealt with *1) how students use mathematical inscriptions in the course of working on their assignment* and *2) how and by which means do students assure themselves that their approach is correct*. Due to the limited time frame this research could only give little insight in the students' working process but the results indicate that the observed students lack the working proficiency and methods for completing the task at hand instead of motivation and general understanding of the topics [5]. Another master thesis in our research group showed similar results while using another assignment and topic as well as another evaluation method.

I have built my research on an understanding of teaching and learning shaped by Distributed Cognition Theory (DCOG) [2]. This theoretical framework has its roots in the Activity Theory that describes *activity* as the interaction of people with the world in which they live [13]. The tools that mediate between the people and the world [[4], p.10] could be understood as *mediational means* [10], [14]. DCOG was used in investigating collaborative learning and working processes before [1], [5] and sets the focus to understand cognitive processes as an interplay between several humans, their environment, resources and mediational means instead of assuming that all cognitive processes are only taking place in the individuals' head. To understand students' activities of problem-solving and knowledge representations during proof development and students' problems with ToC, I think it is helpful to include the whole cognitive system of which the students are part. Relating to mediational means, this includes their individually-formed study groups, their collaboration and interactions with each other, the abstract mathematical inscriptions and notations that are designed to represented theoretical objects and connections as well as physical objects they use during their learning process.

4 STATEMENT OF THESIS/PROBLEM

In my further research I would like to investigate whether the results and problems found during my master thesis appear by more student groups and different topics in the area of ToC and also compare it to other computer science fields. Furthermore, I would like to widen the used research questions not only to mathematical inscription investigated during my master thesis but more mediational means available for the students. In the end, I want to provide a base building on an empirical research for other researchers and lecturers to improve the teaching of ToC.

5 RESEARCH GOALS & METHODS

I want to understand how students use mediational means during their working process of solving proof assignments and whether they are successfully using it. It is common that students have to solve assignments in individually-formed study groups. Because I do not want to interfere their natural working process, I decided for non-participating observational studies. Due to the group work, I have natural think-aloud sessions. To capture every interaction within the group and with the tools, I will attend the group sessions silent and use videography with several cameras in the room. For clarifying unclear statements, I will use qualitative interviewing after the students ended their assignments. I want to evaluate the data as objective as possible. Therefore, I am researching for an adequate method, I am thinking about using qualitative content analysis [7] or interaction analysis [3] but this is not finally decided (should be in August).

With the help of my data I want to answer the following research questions:

- How do students organize their working process during individually-formed study groups?

- How do students solve assignments from ToC courses and what problems do they face?

- How do students use mediational means in the course of working on their proof assignments from the perspective of distributed cognition theory?

6 DISSERTATION STATUS

I have researched methodologies regarding the problems I faced during my master thesis. I also set the focus from mathematical inscriptions to all mediational means students can use during proof assignments and expanded my observational studies by using videography to capture all interactions in a better way than just observing live. I want to produce a time schedule for my studies until August.

7 EXPECTED CONTRIBUTIONS

I want to give an empirically validated insight in how student groups try to solve proof assignments in ToC and especially how they use provided and their own mediational means to experience the exercises as a whole not only considering the outcome. I want to understand what the definite available problems are during the working processes. Further research and work shall be able to build on the results and allows other pedagogical approaches.

8 FEEDBACK FROM THE DOCTORAL CONSORTIUM

I hope to get feedback about my research design and study design out of the doctoral consortium. Furthermore, I would like to share experiences about videography and methods used to evaluate and analyze videos, e.g. interaction analysis.

REFERENCES

[1] Deitrick, E., Shapiro, B., Ahrens, M., Fiebrink, R., Lehrman, P., and Farooq, S. 2015. Using Distributed Cognition Theory to Analyze Collaborative Computer Science Learning. In *Proceedings of the eleventh annual International Conference on Computing Education Research.* ICER '15. ACM, 51-60.

[2] Hollan, J., Hutchins, E., & Kirsh, D. (2000). Distributed cognition: toward a new foundation for human-computer interaction research. *ACM Transactions on Computer-Human Interaction (TOCHI)*, 7(2), 174-196.Kaptelinin, V., & Nardi, B. A. (2006). Acting with technology: Activity theory and interaction design. MIT press.

[3] Jordan, B., & Henderson, A. (1995). Interaction analysis: Foundations and practice. The journal of the learning sciences, 4(1), 39-103.

[4] Kaptelinin, V., & Nardi, B. A. (2006). Acting with technology: Activity theory and interaction design. MIT press.

[5] Knobelsdorf, M. and Frede, C.. 2016. Analyzing Student Practices in Theory of Computation in Light of Distributed Cognition Theory. *In Proceedings of the 2016 ACM Conference on International Computing Education Research (ICER '16).* ACM, New York, NY, USA, 73-81.

[6] Korte, L., Anderson, S., Pain, H., and Good, J. 2007. Learning by game-building: a novel approach to theoretical computer science education. In *Proceedings of the 12th annual SIGCSE conference on Innovation and technology in computer science education.* ITiCSE '07. ACM, 53-57.

[7] Mayring, P. (2014). Qualitative content analysis: theoretical foundation, basic procedures and software solution.

[8] Parker, M. and Lewis, C. 2014. What makes big-O analysis difficult: understanding how students understand runtime analysis. *Journal of Computing Sciences in Colleges.*29, 4, 164-174.

[9] Pillay, N. 2009. Learning Difficulties Experienced by Students in a Course on Formal Languages and Automata Theory. *SIGCSE Bulletin.* 41, 4, 48-52.

[10] Säljö, R. 1998. Learning as the use of tools: a sociocultural perspective on the human-technology link. *In Learning with computers.* Littleton, K. and Light, P., Ed. Routledge, New York, 144-161

[11] Sigman, S. 2007. Engaging students in formal language theory and theory of computation. *SIGCSE Bulletin.* 39, 1, 450-453.

[12] Tenenberg, J. and Knobelsdorf, M. 2013. Out of our minds: a review of sociocultural cognition theory. *Computer Science Education.* 24, 1, 1-24.

[13] Vygotsky, L. S. 1978. Mind in Society: The Development of Higher Psychological Processes: Harvard University Press

[14] Wertsch, J. V. 1993. Voices of the Mind: Sociocultural Approach to Mediated Action. Harvard University Press

Hands-on in Computer Programming Education

Kristina von Hausswolff

Department of Information Technology, Uppsala University

Box 337, SE-751 05 Uppsala, Sweden

kristina.von.hausswolff@it.uu.se

ABSTRACT

More and a wider range of students are learning to program as part of their formal education in Sweden as well as in other countries. In computer programming as in other laboratory subjects, the student's active learning in the form of physical motor movement is important. Nevertheless, there are gaps in understanding how, when, and why practical hands-on learning has positive effects. To study the effects of hands-on for novices leaning to program, an experiment in a controlled setting is planned, along with an in-depth study in an authentic classroom setting. The theoretical and methodological basis is a pragmatic view of knowledge and learning, resulting in a mixed methodology approach. This research aims at getting insights that could inform teachers in the CS classroom in making appropriate didactical decisions, both at university level and in upper secondary school. Another more general aim is to understand the reasons for why hands-on is beneficial for learning.

CCS CONCEPTS

• **Social and professional topics → Computing education**

KEYWORDS

Novice programming; practice; pragmatism; pair programming

1 PROGRAM CONTEXT

I am a PhD student in Computer Science with specialization in Computer Science Education Research at Uppsala University, Sweden. The PhD program follows common Swedish form, meaning a four-year salary position that includes course work equivalent to 60 weeks full time. I started in September 2016 and is a member of UpCERG, the Uppsala Computing Education Research Group, which currently includes eight senior researchers and five PhD students.

My PhD work is part of a national multi-institutional research project funded by the Swedish Research Council, consisting of four senior researchers and two PhD students from Uppsala University, Karolinska Institutet (KI), and KTH Royal

Institute of Technology. The research is in the domain of novice programming at the university and upper secondary school levels. The specific focus is on exploring the effects and potential roles of "hands-on" interaction with the computer using the keyboard, when learning programming for the first time. To examine this, we plan to do a controlled experiment of students learning to program for the first time, controlling the variable "hands on". Inspired by pair programming, half of the students are programming "hand-on", using the keyboard, while the other half is involved in the learning process in all other respects (problem-solving, discussion), that is, "hands-off". Our multidisciplinary project will further conduct detailed studies of the phenomenon of "hands-on", by means of fMRI scanning and also in a naturalistic setting. However, the fMRI studies are separate from my research.

2 CONTEXT AND MOTIVATION

More and a wider range of students are learning to program as part of their formal education, as countries such as Sweden continue to increase the amount of programming in various curricula. The decision in spring 2017 by the Swedish Government to include more programming in the curriculum for upper secondary school highlights the need for knowledge about teaching and learning programming.

Student's active learning in the form of physical motor movement is positive for knowledge retrieval. The positive effects are thus not only in terms of practical skills, but also of declarative (conceptual) knowledge. Nevertheless, there are gaps in understanding how, when, and why practical hands-on learning has these positive effects [1]. These gaps become especially important when considering that, in practice, it is common for students to work in pairs where one student is more hands-on than the other. Novice programming is a topic of ongoing interest within the area of computer science education. This research aims to contribute to the understanding of teacher described difficulties experienced by students when learning to program.

3 BACKGROUND & RELATED WORK

The embrace of the practice in education is not a new phenomenon. The pragmatic thinker and educationalist John Dewey argues practical action as necessary part of knowledge acquisition in his action and communication theory [2]. There is now empirical evidence that hands-on is an important factor for successfully learning of computer programming [3]. Students' reported time hands-on correlated highly with learning outcomes in a novice programming course at the university level. The complex and intertwining dependencies between practice and theory in the computer lab is further examined by Eckerdal [4]. Of further interest is that program comprehension has been examined using brain scanning, getting a picture of neural activation obtained with fMRI. Siegmund et al. [5] concluded that brain regions, related to working memory, attention, and language processing were activated when programmers try to understand code segments. Specific effects of hand-on is however unexplored in this context.

4 STATEMENT OF THESIS/PROBLEM

The area of my research is the role of practice in learning programming in an educational setting. My focus is on why and how hands-on comes into play. Hands-on experience of programming is an integrated part of learning the subject, and the role of student engagement, motivation, and the interaction between students are all factors that play a part in the whole of the learning experience. The problem area of the thesis is both to understand different factors behind the beneficial effects of hands-on, and also to studying hands-on experience in an actual educational setting. My research is aimed at gaining knowledge in this area to inform decision about curriculum design as well as didactic decisions in the CS classroom.

5 RESEARCH GOALS & METHODS

The broader project has two overarching research questions:
- RQ1: How does hands-on influence students' learning of computer programming with regard to some aspects of relevance for learning outcome?
- RQ2: How do students experience hands-on learning and its impact on their practical knowledge and conceptual understanding?

My research is concerned with both of these questions. I will try to single out correlations between a number of factors related to learning. Factors of interest are (reported) motivation, engagement in the task, stress in the learning situation, brain activities, and long-time memory. The goal is to be able to sketch a model of hands-on learning in a pair programming setting with the correlations of important factors. The model will then be tested in a naturalistic setting (answering RQ2). My theoretical standpoint is a pragmatic view of knowledge, which influences the choice of mixed methodology in answering the research questions. This entails a three-hour teaching session using Java, with students with no prior programming experience. Hands-on (writing on the keyboard) will be the independent variable, which half of the participants in the study will do. Data of both quantitative and qualitative character will be collected and analyzed within the framework of mixed methodology. In RQ2, a qualitative education research approach will be used to address the question of how hands-on learning is experienced by students in an authentic classroom setting. Another group of students taking an introductory programming class at a Swedish university will be studied throughout their whole course. Specific methods involved will range over test results analysis, interviews, filming the interaction in pair programming exercises and field observation. The idea is that answers to the two research questions will mutually provide context for and new perspectives on each other.

6 DISSERTATION STATUS

The teaching session of three hours has been developed along with a corresponding knowledge test. Both the lesson plan and the knowledge test have been tested as part of a pre-study, with special emphasis on a rigorous validation procedure for measuring the relevant knowledge. Findings of this pre-study are presently being analyzed and documented and the plan is to publish the results as an in-progress paper during the fall of 2017. The pre-study included 60 upper secondary school students with no prior experience of programming and showed that an effect of the hands-on variable on knowledge could be measured after the three hour session. Another pre-study, related to university students' experiences in a classroom setting related to hands-on and pair programming, was also conducted during 2017. The main finding of this second pre-study is the importance of available resources directed at the immediate problem at hand, including the importance of timing—which could be framed in terms of the Deweyan concept of inquiry. The interaction within a student pair doing pair programming also played a part in who gets to program hands-on. The plan now is to start the controlled study in the fall of 2017 and the authentic classroom study in the spring of 2018.

There are several topics interesting to discuss related to my current dissertation status: pragmatism as a theory of knowledge for computer science education, difficulties and challenges in applying mixed methodology, and non-language dependent methods when investigation novice programming.

7 EXPECTED CONTRIBUTIONS

One expected contribution is connecting the learning outcomes in programming to the hands-on experience, and building a model for how and why this is important. This could give knowledge important to the classroom situation and to the design of curriculum. Furthermore, this research could be important to education in other subjects where hands-on experience plays a significant part, e.g. in science education. A model of hands-on in CS education (programming) could possibly also serve as a hypothesis model for other areas and inspire further research.

REFERENCES

[1] J. Minogue and M. G. Jones. 2006. Haptics in edu: Exploring an untapped sensory modality. *Review of Educational Research*, 76, 3 (2006), 317–348
[2] G. Biesta and N. Burbules. 2003. *Pragmatism and educational research*. Lanham, MD: Rowman & Littlefield
[3] L. J Höök and A. Eckerdal. 2015. On the bimodality in an introductory programming course: An analysis of student performance factors. *Proceedings of the 2015 International Conference on Learning and Teaching in Computing and Engineering*, Taipei, Taiwan, IEEE. DOI: 10.1109/LaTiCE.2015.25
[4] A. Eckerdal. 2015. Relating theory and practice in laboratory work: A variation theoretical study. *Studies in Higher Education*, 40, 5, (2015), 867–880. DOI: http://dx.doi.org/10.1080/03075079.2013.857652
[5] J. Siegmund, C. Kästner, S. Apel, C. Parnin, A. Bethmann, T. Leich, G. Saake and A. Brechmann. 2014. Understanding understanding source code with functional magnetic resonance imaging, *Proceedings of the 36th International Conference on Software Engineering*, Hyderabad, India: ACM, 378–389

Growth Mindset in Computational Thinking Teaching and Teacher Training

Michael Lodi

Dep. of Computer Science and Engineering (DISI)
University of Bologna, Italy
michael.lodi2@unibo.it

ABSTRACT

Teacher training in computational thinking is becoming more and more important, as many countries are introducing it at all K-12 school levels. Introductory programming courses are known to be difficult and some studies suggest they foster a fixed-mindset views of intelligence, reinforcing the idea that only some people have the so called "geek gene". This is particularly dangerous if thought by future school teachers. Interventions to stimulate "CS growth mindset" in students and their teachers are fundamental and worth CS education research.

KEYWORDS

Computational Thinking; Growth Mindset; Teacher Training

1 PROGRAM CONTEXT

I'm halfway through the first year of the three-year PhD program in Computer Science and Engineering at University of Bologna, Italy. I anticipate to pass qualifying exams within Summer 2017. I have to make my thesis proposal within January 2018 and work on it full time (except for the yearly 60 hours of teaching assistance) till November 2019. For my Master Thesis I worked on a literature review of Computational Thinking and on the cognitive difficulties of learning to program. In the first months of PhD I worked on teacher training: I analyzed [2] teachers' sentiment about Programma il Futuro project and their conceptions and misconceptions [3] about computational thinking. Moreover I'm analyzing data on the effects of a "Creative Computing" course on Primary Education Major students' growth mindset, with promising preliminary results.

2 CONTEXT AND MOTIVATION

In the last decade, *computational thinking* has been recognized as a fundamental skill for everyone, not just for computer scientists [12]. Many countries in the world are making efforts to include it in the school curriculum, at all K-12 levels.

In Italy, the recent school system reform explicitly states that it is mandatory to develop students' digital skills, with particular attention to the development of *computational thinking*. In perspective, computational thinking is going to be introduced in Italian teaching curriculum. These pushes to teach computational thinking,

mainly through teaching programming ("coding"), give rise to the necessity of an urgent plan for teacher training, both for pre-service and in-service ones, and especially for Primary School teachers, that - in Italy - are mostly female and generally not trained to teach computer science fundamentals.

Learning to program may appear a too challenging task, achievable only from those with a so called "geek gene" [10]. Moreover, stereotypes lead to consider computer scientists as singularly focused, asocial, competitive, male figures [9].

Students and teachers have different personal ideas ("implicit theories") about their intellectual abilities. Some believe their intelligence is a fixed trait (like eye color or height when adult), and they can't do much to change it: they have an *entity theory of intelligence*, otherwise stated a *fixed mindset*. Some other believe that intelligence can be developed with study and effort (like muscles being trained): they have an *incremental theory of intelligence*, also called a *growth mindset*. Mindsets theory is a fundamental result of Carol Dweck's research [5]. In many studies she showed, among other things, that students' mindset can predict their achievement - especially in Math and Science [6] and their ability to cope with challenges. Moreover, female students with growth mindset showed less susceptibility to negative effects of stereotypes about women and Math [8].

3 BACKGROUND & RELATED WORK

As known, the term *computational thinking* (CT) was brought to the attention of our community by Jeannette Wing [12], that later defined it as "the thought processes involved in formulating problems and their solutions so that the solutions are represented in a form that can be effectively carried out by an information-processing agent" [13]. How to effectively teach computational thinking is highly debated, but the most popular methodology at the moment is to teach programming (with languages and environments suitable for different learners).

Dweck's studies on growth mindset are based on three decades of research. Students with growth mindset show learning-oriented goals (not afraid to ask and make errors, in order to learn) and a mastery-oriented responses (greater effort and new strategies) to challenges and setbacks, while students with fixed mindset show performance goals ("appear intelligent", so avoiding difficult tasks) and and helpless response to challenges (e.g. giving up or blaming teachers for their failure). Growth mindset can be positively conveyed by explicitly teaching students about mindsets, brain plasticity and the idea that intelligence can be trained; by portraying challenges and mistakes as highly valued; by praising process, and give constructive feedback rather than praising the person or being judgmental. Moreover, specific suggestions to stimulate a "Math

ICER'17, August 18-20, 2017, Tacoma, WA, USA.
© 2017 Copyright held by the owner/author(s). 978-1-4503-4968-0/17/08.
DOI: http://dx.doi.org/10.1145/3105726.3105736

growth mindset" includes giving rich open tasks, that require effort, reasoning, creativity [1]. Teachers' conceptions are crucial: growth minded people are more supportive with students, give encouragement and suggest positive strategies to deal with problems; by contrast, fixed minded people give students simple comfort and fixed messages and tend to help boys significantly more than girls [6].

Only a few studies have been conducted to assess and/or alter students' mindset before and after a programming course. Simon et al. [11] tried a small intervention in CS1 classes to change mindset of students form CS Majors and Minors, but they obtained mixed results. Cutts et al. [4] performed three structured interventions into an introductory programming course, gaining significant improvement in growth mindset level of students and also a positive correlation with their test scores. By contrast, Flanigan et al. [7] analyzed (without intervention) changes in students of CS courses across the semester, finding a significant increase in fixed mindset and a significant decrease in growth mindset.

4 STATEMENT OF THESIS/PROBLEM

A general research question of my work is: *What are the relationships between Growth Mindset, Computational Thinking Teaching and Computational Thinking Teacher Training?* Specifically some sub-problems to address are:

- What are the effects of computational thinking introductory courses on teachers and students mindsets?
- What are the effects of teachers mindset (in particular regarding CS) on students learning of computational thinking?
- What specific aspects of computational thinking / computer science / programming induce a more fixed mindset? And what aspects induce a growth mindset?
- Can computational thinking specifically designed activities help to induce a "CS growth mindset" in teachers and in their students?

5 RESEARCH GOALS & METHODS

Pre and post questionnaires that measure growth mindset of participants (K-12 students or Education Majors students or in-service teachers) before and after an intervention (a computational thinking course) using well validated growth mindset scales will be administered; control groups (e.g. other Education Major students that don't follow the course with intervention) are foreseen.

Qualitative research approaches, like grounded theory, with interviews and open-ended questions deep analysis will be used to determine which specific aspects of computational thinking can increase (or decrease) growth mindset in participants.

Classroom experimentation (both in K-12 schools and in teacher training courses) to validate proposed materials will be conducted and mindset changes measured.

6 DISSERTATION STATUS

The literature review on CT and the work on teachers' conceptions can become part of the introductory chapters of my thesis, while the data I'm collecting on growth mindset will be part of the experimental chapters: a preliminary analysis gives promising results in leveraging teachers mindset. I plan to find out what aspects of the course are useful to induce a growth mindset, and then to propose and test a series of ad-hoc materials to be used in teacher training courses and/or in schools.

7 EXPECTED CONTRIBUTIONS

Growth mindset has been recognized as a crucial aspect to foster students' success and to reduce gender and social gap. General interventions to increase growth mindset have been proposed. Moreover, people can have fixed mindset related to specific disciplines like Math or Computer Science that are typically connected with fixed views of "being or not being predisposed", so specific interventions can help to modify these ideas. Finally, teachers' mindsets have a profound impact on students' mindset development and success in the discipline, so specific teacher training interventions must be designed and tested.

8 EXPECTED LEARNING FROM DC

I think attending ICER Doctoral Consortium 2017 is a great opportunity to grow as a researcher.

My background is in (theoretical) computer science, and only in the last part of my Master Degree I started to get used to social and educational research methods: I really look forward to learning more about education research from participants with different backgrounds.

Moreover, in Italy CS Education is not (yet) a trending topic for academic career in CS, so I hope to broaden my views on which specific topics are worth to be investigated in this field.

REFERENCES

[1] Jo Boaler. 2013. Ability and mathematics: the mindset revolution that is reshaping education. In *Forum*, Vol. 55. Symposium Journals, 143–152.
[2] Isabella Corradini, Michael Lodi, and Enrico Nardelli. 2017. Computational Thinking in Italian Schools: Quantitative Data and Teachers' Sentiment Analysis after Two Years of "Programma il Futuro" Project *(ITiCSE '17)*. ACM, New York, NY, USA.
[3] Isabella Corradini, Michael Lodi, and Enrico Nardelli. 2017. Conceptions and Misconceptions about Computational Thinking among Italian Primary School Teachers *(ICER '17)*. ACM, New York, NY, USA.
[4] Quintin Cutts, Emily Cutts, Stephen Draper, Patrick O'Donnell, and Peter Saffrey. 2010. Manipulating mindset to positively influence introductory programming performance. *SIGCSE '10* (2010). https://doi.org/10.1145/1734263.1734409
[5] Carol S Dweck. 2000. *Self-theories: Their role in motivation, personality, and development.* Psychology Press.
[6] Carol S Dweck. 2008. Mindsets and Math/Science Achievement. *The Opportunity Equation* (2008).
[7] Abraham E. Flanigan, Markeya S. Peteranetz, Duane F. Shell, and Leen-Kiat Soh. 2015. Exploring Changes in Computer Science Students' Implicit Theories of Intelligence Across the Semester. *ICER '15* (2015). https://doi.org/10.1145/2787622.2787722
[8] Catherine Good, Aneeta Rattan, and Carol S. Dweck. 2012. Why do women opt out? Sense of belonging and women's representation in mathematics. *Journal of Personality and Social Psychology* 102, 4 (2012), 700–717. https://doi.org/10.1037/a0026659
[9] Colleen M. Lewis, Ruth E. Anderson, and Ken Yasuhara. 2016. "I Don't Code All Day". *ICER '16* (2016). https://doi.org/10.1145/2960310.2960332
[10] Elizabeth Patitsas, Jesse Berlin, Michelle Craig, and Steve Easterbrook. 2016. Evidence That Computer Science Grades Are Not Bimodal *(ICER '16)*. ACM, NY, USA, 9. https://doi.org/10.1145/2960310.2960312
[11] Beth Simon, Brian Hanks, Laurie Murphy, Sue Fitzgerald, Renée McCauley, Lynda Thomas, and Carol Zander. 2008. Saying isn't necessarily believing. *ICER '08* (2008). https://doi.org/10.1145/1404520.1404537
[12] Jeannette M. Wing. 2006. Computational Thinking. *Commun. ACM* 49, 3 (March 2006), 33–35. https://doi.org/10.1145/1118178.1118215
[13] Jeannette M. Wing. 2010. Computational Thinking: What and Why? *Link Magazine* (2010).

Studying Professional Identity in Software Engineering

Rick Parker

Department of Computer Science, Institute of Cognitive Science

University of Colorado

Boulder, Colorado, USA

rick.parker@colorado.edu

ABSTRACT

I am investigating the role of undergraduate formation of professional identity during the school-to-work transition of software engineers, with emphasis on the senior capstone experience. The social construct of professional identity represents the sense of connection between an individual and their profession. Professional identity is linked to persistence and to decreased likelihood of burnout. Improving our understanding of the influence of professional identity formation during the school-to-work transition may inform teaching practices earlier in the undergraduate program, and may guide organizations in adjusting how they work with new graduates.

CCS CONCEPTS

• **Social and professional topics** → **Software engineering education**; **Computing profession**; • **Applied computing** → *Collaborative learning*;

KEYWORDS

Capstone, communities of practice, professional identity, concerns-based adoption.

ACM Reference format:

Rick Parker. 2017. Studying Professional Identity in Software Engineering. In *Proceedings of ICER '17, Tacoma, WA, USA, August 18-20, 2017,* 2 pages.

https://doi.org/10.1145/3105726.3105737

1 PROGRAM CONTEXT

I am beginning the fifth year of my PhD studies at the University of Colorado. I am enrolled in the combined Computer Science and Cognitive Science PhD program, which supports integration of education and philosophy with my CS background.

2 RESEARCH CONTEXT AND MOTIVATION

My university has offered the CS senior capstone course in software engineering since the 1987-88 academic year, as part of facilitating the school-to-work transition of its graduates into their computing professions. Student teams work with industry sponsors to develop software solutions to real-world needs. I seek to understand in greater depth how this authentic, project-based learning experience benefits the formation of a professional identity for our undergraduate students.

Formation of professional identity may begin as early as secondary school when students decide on their undergraduate major [4], and continues through and beyond the academic setting [7]. Researchers in other professions have linked poor or weak formation of professional identity to increased likelihood to experience burnout and failure to persist in the profession [3]. Research into withdrawal from the computing major noted similar outcomes for many students [5].

3 BACKGROUND AND RELATED WORK

The role that the Senior Project capstone serves is that of introducing computing students into the practice of software engineering, with tools and techniques of the profession. I am using Wenger's Communities of Practice (CoP) theory to understand identity as a social construct emerging from individuals' participation across multiple communities [13]. I combine CoP and identity research with the Concerns-Based Adoption Model (CBAM) from the education research community [6]. CBAM provides a continuum of concerns that change in accordance with the level of adoption of a given teaching practice [6]. I am developing an evidence-based instrument to measure student concerns during their school-to-work transition and the adoption of a professional identity.

Investigations of professional identity rely heavily on qualitative methods, including interviews [7, 12], observations of team interactions [8], construction of narratives [2], and essays [11].

Through narratives, Dziallas & Fincher focused their analysis on the role of the "year in industry" experience in influencing graduateness [2]. The authors referred to the industry experience as a turning point for the individuals' trajectory of participation with respect to the community of practice [2].

Through essays and interviews, Peters & Pears explored early identity formation during introductory computing courses [11]. The authors note that misalignment or lack of professional identity at this early stage is linked to lack of engagement and persistence [11].

Through iterative interviews of senior capstone students throughout the academic year, Tomer & Mishra identified a cycle of professional identity formation, wherein the participant revisited and "morphed" their concept of what it means to be a professional [12]. Nyström conducted longitudinal interviews as participants moved from the senior year of their program into their early career, and similarly noted that professional identity is not strongly differentiated in students [7]. O'Connor's discourse analysis of student team interactions during the senior project indicate that various trigger events can cause a shift in the expressed identity [8].

4 PROBLEMS, GOALS, AND METHODS

I am studying formation of professional identity during the school-to-work transition of undergraduates in software engineering. Questions guiding my research are:

RQ1 What characteristics or cognitive dispositions differentiate academic identity from professional identity in software engineering?

RQ2 What academic and social practices indicate professional identity in software engineering?

RQ3 What concerns indicate formation of professional identity in software engineering?

Study 1 [9, 10] sheds light on the cognitive dispositions of undergraduate students during their capstone experience. I conducted 11 semi-structured qualitative interviews after the CS senior projects course, each lasting about 45 minutes. By performing thematic coding [1], analysis focused on student perceptions of the capstone experience as offering knowledge integration, shifting the authority role from academic to professional, and their own transformative agency to shape the project experience [9]. Additional analysis focused on the role of emotion in the senior capstone experience [10]. Specific roles identified were student perceptions of sponsor emotional investment during project pitching and evaluation, varied student emotions throughout their project experience, and emotional investment in project outcomes [10].

Study 2 examines student perceptions of professional labels and professional behaviors. Informed by the interview data from study 1, I developed a quantitative survey to explore the strength of professional identity in CS undergraduate students. The survey was piloted by distributing it to 1500 CS undergraduate students, resulting in 120 responses (8% response rate). The survey asks participants to consider how well professional labels, such as "software engineer", describe them and describe how their peers view them. The survey further explores professional behaviors by asking participants to consider how they engage in specific practices. Based on preliminary analysis, a statistically significant difference has been observed in how professional labels are claimed between students who have been enrolled in the capstone course and those who have not. No statistical difference has been observed based on gender, age, or enrollment in Bachelor of Science versus Bachelor of Arts CS degrees. This suggests that the capstone experience does have an impact on professional identity. To move forward, the survey will be refined and redistributed in the fall, with added incentives to improve response rate.

Study 3 will conduct interviews with students focusing on their concerns about adoption of their CS major and a professional identity. Results will be coded following the CBAM coding scheme [6], to establish a continuum of concerns relevant to the computing profession and to software engineering. The results of this coding process will support creation of a survey instrument to target concerns related to adoption of professional identity in computing.

5 DISSERTATION STATUS

I have completed my coursework and my comprehensive exams. I was awarded a summer research fellowship from the CS department to focus solely on preparation and defense of my dissertation proposal, with anticipated defense of that material in September 2017. Completion of dissertation work is tentatively anticipated for the latter half of 2018.

6 EXPECTED CONTRIBUTIONS

Deepening our understanding of the influence of the formation of professional identity may inform teaching practices earlier in the academic coursework, and may support individuals moving through the transition from academia into a position in industry. Findings may inform our understanding of similar processes with respect to other professions. The development of a Concerns-Based Model of Adoption of Professional Identity offers an instrument to assess an individual's progression towards an established professional identity.

7 EXPECTATIONS FOR THE CONSORTIUM

By participating in the doctoral consortium, I hope to receive guidance on strengthening connections between the sections of my research plan. In particular, the links between motivation, theory, related work, and the methodologies used to answer research questions needs to be coherent and sufficient to form a cohesive plan of research. At this stage of my dissertation work, I will also benefit from insights into exploring RQ3 about student concerns related to professional identity formation, as this work is still in development.

REFERENCES

[1] Virginia Braun and Victoria Clarke. 2006. Using thematic analysis in psychology. *Qualitative Research in Psychology* 3, 2 (2006), 77–101.

[2] Sebastian Dziallas and Sally Fincher. 2016. Aspects of graduateness in computing students' narratives. In *Proceedings of the 2016 ACM Conference on International Computing Education Research*. ACM, ACM, 181–190.

[3] John E Hofman and Liya Kremer. 1985. Teachers' professional identity and burn-out. *Research in Education* 34 (1985), 89.

[4] Dorthe Høj Jensen and Jolanda Jetten. 2016. The importance of developing students' academic and professional identities in higher education. *Journal of College Student Development* 57, 8 (2016), 1027–1042.

[5] Jane Margolis and Allan Fisher. 2003. *Unlocking the Clubhouse: Women in Computing*. MIT press.

[6] Beulah W Newlove and Gene E Hall. 1976. *A Manual for Assessing Open-Ended Statements of Concern About an Innovation*. ERIC.

[7] Sofia Nyström. 2009. The dynamics of professional identity formation: Graduates' transitions from higher education to working life. *Vocations and Learning* 2, 1 (2009), 1–18.

[8] Kevin O'Connor. 2001. Contextualization and the negotiation of social identities in a geographically distributed situated learning project. *Linguistics and Education* 12, 3 (2001), 285–308.

[9] Rick Parker. 2016. Student perceptions of success in computer science senior capstone projects. In *Proceedings of the 47th ACM Technical Symposium on Computing Science Education*. ACM, ACM, 689–689.

[10] Rick Parker. 2017. How do you feel: Affective expressions from computer science senior capstone projects. In *Learning and Teaching in Computing and Engineering (LaTiCE), 2017*. IEEE, IEEE, 57–64.

[11] Anne-Kathrin Peters and Arnold Pears. 2013. Engagement in computer science and IT–What! A matter of identity?. In *Learning and Teaching in Computing and Engineering (LaTiCE), 2013*. IEEE, IEEE, 114–121.

[12] Gunjan Tomer and Sushanta Kumar Mishra. 2016. Professional identity construction among software engineering students: A study in India. *Information Technology & People* 29, 1 (2016), 146–172.

[13] Etienne Wenger. 1998. *Communities of Practice: Learning, Meaning, and Identity*. Cambridge University Press.

Towards Understanding Student's Mental Effort in Block-Based Programming Environments Using Electroencephalogram (EEG)

Yerika Jimenez

University of Florida 432 Newell Dr,

Gainesville, FL, 326011, USA

jimenyer@ufl.edu

ABSTRACT

Block-based programming environments such as Scratch and App Inventor are currently being used by millions of students around the world. Although block-based programming environments were created to make computing concepts simpler for students to understand and visualize, students continue to struggle with understanding some basic Computer Science (CS) concepts [1]. My research focuses on understanding how students interact and learn computing concepts in block-based programming environments from a cognitive perspective. In particular, I am using neurophysiological devices, electroencephalography (EEG), to measures students' mental efforts that is attention and perception during programming tasks.

Keywords

Mental effort; Computer Science Concepts; CS Learning

1. PROGRAM CONTEXT

I have recently completed my third year of study in the Human-Centered Computing (HCC) doctoral program at the University of Florida. I have successfully completed all my coursework and passed my qualifying exam. I will be proposing my dissertation in Fall 2017, and I expect to defend my dissertation in Spring 2019. I recently conducted a research study that focuses on understanding how much mental effort novice programmers use as they interact and learn computer science concepts within a block-based programming environment. I am currently analyzing the data collected from this study and I plan to use the findings to refine my dissertation research questions and studies.

2. CONTEXT AND MOTIVATION

The US has recently begun scaling up efforts to increase access to CS into K-12 classrooms and many teachers are turning to block-based programming environments to minimize the syntax and conceptual challenges students often encounter in text-based languages. While visual programming language designers have created block-based programming environments to make programming easier for students of all ages [2], we have not evaluated the learning challenges or burden that these environments may have on students.

Recently, the VL/HCC community has called for guidelines and suggestions to improve the design of these learning environments and to better understand the unique challenges that students face when using and learning with these tools [3]. Researchers at the 2014 Computing Education Summit suggested that the field's next big challenges are understanding how students learn to program, how to promote learning for all people (especially K-12), and how to support personalized student CS learning [4]. At the same time, former, US President, Barack Obama announced the launch of the Brain Research through Advancing Innovative Neuroethologies (BRAIN) Initiative. This bold new initiative is focused on revolutionizing our understanding of the human brain, and it supports research to "better understand how we think, learn and remember" [5]. To date, most brain-based research has been focused on math and problem-solving contexts [6] and little research has been conducted on how students learn and cognitively process computer science content.

The goal of my dissertation research is to leverage advances in EEG research to explore how students learn CS concepts, write programs, and complete programming tasks in block-based programming environments.

3. BACKGROUND & RELATED WORK

Historically research on block-based programming has found that block-based environments provide positive engagement and attitudinal effects on novices who are learning to program [7]. More recently, research on block-based programming environments has focused on the learning challenges that students encounter when learning CS concepts [1,8]. Meerbaurm-Salant et al., [8], found that students using Scratch understood bounded loops and conditional loops but had difficulty understanding initialization, variables, and concurrency. Meerbaurn-Salant et al., suggested that students might fail to understand these concepts because they are abstract and required the use of several Scratch blocks. Lewis's [1] comparison of Logo and Scratch found that students understand programming concepts differently depending on the visual nature of a particular block-based programming environment. In particular, they found that 6th-grade students appeared to better understand loop construct when using Logo, but the construct of conditionals better in Scratch [1]. Thus, a systematic investigation of the affordances of block-based programming environments for supporting CS learning can improve our understanding how students are learning.

CS ED researchers have used different techniques to access and understand students programming knowledge such as content analysis of artifacts, and independent learning assessments [9]. These techniques provide researchers with valuable patterns of conceptual understanding and programing performance. However, these techniques only provide a snapshot of the student and not the cognitive process they engaged in to solve the problems. Thus, it is challenging to understand the real-time

ICER '17, August 18-20, 2017, Tacoma, WA, USA

© 2017 Copyright is held by the owner/author(s).

ACM ISBN 978-1-4503-4968-0/17/08.

http://dx.doi.org/10.1145/3105726.3105738

challenges students encounter and how to provide the best scaffolding.

Research focused on students' cognitive processing of computer science content currently uses data collected from self-reported cognitive load surveys and cognitive walkthroughs to understand how students solve problems [9]. Morrison et al., researched students' perceived cognitive load or mental effort levels during two lectures using a self-reported cognitive survey [9]. They found that students perceived higher mental efforts while performing a task that required them to understand and use three CS concepts at the same time [9]. However, cognitive load surveys are a post hoc assessment of the cognitive load students experience and their self-reported nature means they are largely dependent on the reflective ability of the student. Measurement of cognitive load using cognitive walkthroughs of students during the learning task have been found to add to students' mental efforts as they are trying to explain their rationale and process [8]. Thus, these techniques by themselves are inadequate for understanding the factors that affect students' cognitive load. However, use of neurophysiological devices such as EEG, can be used to capture real-time data about how students are engaging with content [10]. Measures of student's mental effort provided by EEG allow us to understand the students' cognitive activity and working memory load as they interact with the interface and perform programming tasks while learning CS in block-based programming environments. Using EEG in conjunction with think-aloud techniques and learning assessments will allow us to see students' mental efforts challenges in real time, allowing us to see where in the task a student is experiencing high mental efforts.

4. STATEMENT OF THESIS/PROBLEM

My research aims to explore the mental effort students engage in while learning to program in block-based learning environments. Through my dissertation research, I aim to answer the following research questions: **RQ 1:** How much mental effort are students exhibiting while performing CS learning tasks while using block-based programming environments? and in what areas do students exhibit the highest mental effort? **RQ 2:** What CS concepts do students experience high mental effort? Why? **RQ 3:** What factors affect students' mental effort while learning CS? e.i programming tasks, programming environments, conceptual understanding.

5. RESEARCH GOALS & METHODS

I will use a mixed method research approach that includes qualitative, quantitative, and psychophysiological methods and techniques to answer these research questions. Due to the growing emphasis on integrating CS in high school, the target population for this research is high school students. The research plan described in this section is composed of two phases. *Phase 1* is divided into collecting data of student learning from two studies: Laboratory and Classroom. These studies will identify the depth of student learning as well as successes and challenges students encounter while using block-based programming environments to learn basic CS concepts and completing authentic activities/tasks in Scratch. In particular, I seek to identify specific aspects of learning activities and tool interactions that negatively impact student engagement. The goal of these studies is to understand how students are learning CS concepts and how they are interacting with Scratch. **Study 1** is a lab-based study where students will be asked to interact and perform authentic tasks with Scratch. While students are interacting, and performing tasks their EEG data will be recorded. **Study 2** is a classroom-based study that uses observation methods to understand how students interact and perform authentic tasks within Scratch a block-based environment. *Phase 2* - After students in Study 1 and 2 finish interacting and performing authentic programming tasks, I will interview them using a think-aloud protocol to understand what they were focused on and any areas of challenge or frustration in the programing environment, programming tasks, and their conceptual understanding.

6. DISSERTATION STATUS

I am currently drafting my dissertation proposal. Attending the ICER doctoral consortium will provide me the opportunity to further refine my research questions and study design. In particular, I look forward to feedback on my approach and data collection methods from consortium attendees and faculty mentors.

7. EXPECTED CONTRIBUTIONS

Contributions of my dissertation research to the CS ED field: (1) Baseline EEG measurements of students learning CS in terms of positive and negative engagement. (2) A list of CS concepts through which students experience high levels of mental effort and reasons why they experience these; (3) Factors that contribute to students learning challenges in block-based programming environments.

REFERENCES

[1] Lewis, C. M. How programming environment shapes perception, learning and goals: logo vs. scratch. In Proceedings of the 41st ACM technical symposium on Computer science education (2010), 346-350.

[2] Resnick, M., Maloney, J., Monroy-Hernández, A., Rusk, N., Eastmond, E., Brennan, K., & Kafai, Y. Scratch: programming for all. Communications of the ACM 52, 2 (2009), 60-67.

[3] Blocks and Beyond. http://cs.wellesley.edu/~blocks-and-beyond/.

[4] Cooper, S., Bookey, L., & GruenBaum, P. "Future directions in computing education summit part one: important computing education research questions," Orlando, FL, Rep. CS-TR-14-0108-SC, (2014).

[5] [BRAIN Initiative. www.braininitiative.nih.gov

[6] Ambrus, A. Teaching Mathematical Problem-Solving with the Brain in Mind: How can opening a closed problem help?. CEPS Journal: Center for Educational Policy Studies Journal, 4(2) 2014), 105-120.

[7] Ericson, B., & McKlin, T. Effective and sustainable computing summer camps. In Proceedings of the 43rd ACM technical symposium on Computer Science Education (2012), 289-294.

[8] Meerbaum-Salant, O., Armoni, M., & Ben-Ari, M. Learning computer science concepts with scratch. In Proceedings of the Sixth international workshop on Computing education research (2010), 69-76.

[9] Morrison, B. B., Dorn, B., & Guzdial, M. Measuring cognitive load in introductory CS: adaptation of an instrument. In Proceedings of the tenth annual conference on International computing education research (2014), 131-138.

[10] van Gog, T., & Paas, F. Cognitive load measurement. In Encyclopedia of the Sciences of Learning. In Springer US (2012), 599 - 601.

Comprehension-First Pedagogy and Adaptive, Intrinsically Motivated Tutorials

Greg L. Nelson
University of Washington
Paul G. Allen School of Computer Science, DUB Group
Seattle, Washington 98195

ABSTRACT

Two large multinational studies show more than 60% of students incorrectly answer questions about the execution of basic programs. How can we improve program comprehension learning outcomes, and does that improve program writing learning outcomes? Nearly all prior tools and approaches have been evaluated in a *writing*-focused pedagogical context. People receive instruction on a programming construct's syntax and semantics, practice by writing code, then advance to the next construct (roughly a spiral syntax approach). In contrast, little work has explored a *comprehension*-first pedagogy, teaching and assessing *program semantics*—how static code causes dynamic computer behavior—*before* teaching learners to write code. I hypothesize this pedagogy improves program comprehension and writing learning outcomes, and that an adaptive curriculum of programs that aligns with the learner's interests and assessed knowledge further improves outcomes. Towards that goal, I built and evaluated a comprehension-first tutorial (PLTutor) with a fixed, non-adaptive curriculum, showing 60% higher learning gains (3.9 vs 2.4 on the SCS1) than the writing-focused tutorial Codecademy. I'm looking for new ideas (such as more social elements (theories, design, etc)), prior work, or methods to inform my thesis proposal and committee selection.

KEYWORDS

program comprehension, pedagogy, curriculum, motivation

1 PROGRAM CONTEXT

I am a PhD student in Computer Science at the University of Washington, near the end of my fourth year. I first-authored one paper as my qualifying project [6]. My next milestone is forming my committee and submitting a dissertation proposal, then I need to complete two more papers in order to form my thesis and write my dissertation.

2 CONTEXT AND MOTIVATION

Programming requires many complex skills, including planning, program design, and problem domain knowledge. It also fundamentally requires knowledge of how programs execute (e.g. [7]). Unfortunately, many learners still struggle to master even basic program comprehension skills: two large multinational studies show

more than 60% of students incorrectly answer questions about the execution of basic programs (e.g. [5]). A core practical question for CS education is "How can we improve program comprehension learning outcomes, and does that improve program writing learning outcomes?"; more theoretically, "How and why do learning outcomes vary for different pedagogies?"

3 BACKGROUND & RELATED WORK

Program visualization tools (e.g. [8]) may improve comprehension, but these approaches have been evaluated in a *writing*-focused pedagogical context. Prior work in compre-hension-first pedagogy proposes some approaches and curricular ordering (e.g. [3]), but lacks implementations and evaluations on learning outcomes, or has limitations in their evaluations or the breadth of what is taught (e.g. [2]).

Within pedagogy, curriculum (what is taught and when) substantially affects learning. Some math computer tutors (e.g. [1]) synthesize a curriculum based on learning performance, but no work exists for comprehension tutorials.

In addition to pedagogy and knowledge-appropriate curriculum, motivation and engagement affect learning; prior tutorial work investigated extrinsic engagement strategies like using a fictional narrative for debugging [4] or gamifying program comprehension into puzzle tasks [2]. Building on intrinsic motivation directly by showing programs that match the interests or goals of learners remains unexplored.

4 STATEMENT OF THESIS/PROBLEM

I hypothesize: A comprehension-first pedagogy improves program comprehension and writing learning outcomes, and an adaptive curriculum of programs that aligns with the learner's interests and assessed knowledge further improves outcomes. For the first part, I built a comprehension-first tutorial (PLTutor) [6]. PLTutor works like a debugger which also shows instruction and assessments as one steps through each program in a curriculum of example programs. I compared PLTutor to a writing-focused tutorial (Codecademy). When given in the first week of a CS1 course, after 4.3 hours of use, PLTutor had 60% higher average learning gains on the SCS1 (gain of 3.89 vs. 2.42 out of 27 questions). These gains predicted midterm grades (R^2=.64) only for PLTutor participants, and had less variation and no failures (10% in the Codecademy group failed). Still, users noted excessive practice for concepts they had already mastered. In an at-home discretionary setting, PLTutor had a 40% completion rate, perhaps from poor engagement. These observations lead to the two research questions below, followed by my working hypotheses and technical and design challenges for each.

ICER'17, August 18-20, 2017, Tacoma, WA, USA.
© 2017 Copyright held by the owner/author(s). 978-1-4503-4968-0/17/08.
DOI: http://dx.doi.org/10.1145/3105726.3105739

To reduce excessive practice, **RQ1**: How do we model and assess learner's knowledge of program comprehension to make an adaptive curriculum? **H1**: The task of learners filling in values in the execution of a program has enough granularity to usefully assess their current knowledge (I have started modeling knowledge as paths through the interpreter for the language [6]). Searching in a researcher-crafted set of example programs (or by synthesizing programs), based on a model of the learner's knowledge, algorithms can choose the next program to show and identify parts of programs to assess, until learning is complete. Key design and technical problems include: **RQ1.1**: How to map a program to the interpreter paths it covers? **RQ1.2**: How to use assessment results to update our model of a learner's knowledge? **RQ1.3**: How to create and train an algorithm to sequence and advance in the curriculum to the next concept, given the learner's knowledge?

To improve engagement and completion rates for discretionary use, **RQ2**: How do we model and assess learner's interests to make an engaging program comprehension learning experience using intrinsic motivation? **H2**: Compared to using a fictional game narrative (as found in an educational game (e.g. [4])) , learning outcomes will be higher using a curriculum that adapts to the learner's outside interests and uses personally interesting example programs. Key design and technical problems include: **RQ2.1**: How do we characterize learner's interests? **RQ2.2**: Can we make and search a fixed large library of interesting example programs using metadata, that also meet curriculum needs (the program can have knowledge-appropriate content for learning highlighted and assessed)? **RQ2.3**: What is the trade-off between showing interesting programs with more context (that really work using advanced features they do not understand yet) vs. useful but simple programs showing raw capability (like drawing art, generating music, or posting to social media)? Does just stepping over advanced code work or does it confuse the learner?

5 RESEARCH GOALS & METHODS

I will use design-based research methods and mixed method evaluations to answer my research questions. For RQ1, I will create and add a personalized curriculum to PLTutor for one language (Javascript), and give it at the start of a CS1 class to learners, in a joint between- and within-subject comparison study. Each half of the concepts will be taught with an adaptive or non-adaptive curriculum (creating a 2 X 2 design), measuring learning outcomes immediately after and later in their CS1 class.

I will measure learning outcomes by pre- and post-tests of comprehension and writing skills using a spectrum of tasks (from near to far transfer/use of comprehension skills, culminating in open-ended writing tasks) and by triangulating quantitative and qualitative assessment methods (performance and time spent on assessment tasks, think-alouds for tasks, and interviews about learner's experiences and strategies). As tasks, I will assess program comprehension performance using validated CS1 assessments (like the SCS1), as well as knowledge recall (performance on tracing assessments at a later time) and availability (using think-alouds during tasks to see their strategies and infer knowledge used). I will then explore how this knowledge affects writing skills by measuring near transfer from comprehension skills (performance on identifying where an

error is in some code), as well as far transfer (think-aloud debugging task), and writing task performance (using think-aloud tasks).

To answer RQ2, I will first personally tutor people from diverse backgrounds, trying to assess and match interests (a kind of wizard of oz study where I author and choose programs to show in PLTutor, while recording myself and learners). Given initial results on effectiveness using motivation/interest surveys and learning outcomes, I will look for patterns for how an algorithm could do this, build one, and evaluate it with a between-subjects design comparing PLTutor with it vs. with a fictional narrative.

6 EXPECTED CONTRIBUTIONS

By building a self-contained tool to teach program comprehension, we might scale learning so anyone (with some basic background knowledge) can learn to read code. My tool may also build a solid foundation for learning code writing, reducing failures in CS1 (as my initial study showed [6]).

7 CONSORTIUM GOALS

While I have sketched out research questions and designs for my work, this represents one path to continue my work, and I seek other promising directions I might take. For example, the tutorial genre tends to be one tutorial to one learner; in what ways might one design for more social aspects and what theories might one draw on? I would appreciate information about prior work, particularly unpublished or "failed" prior work in related areas. Finally, with respect to methods, what are the best ways to measure comprehension skill and are there any validated methods for doing so?

ACKNOWLEDGMENTS

This material is based upon work supported by the National Science Foundation Graduate Research Fellowship Program under Grant No. 12566082. Any opinions, findings, and conclusions or recommendations expressed in this material are those of the author(s) and do not necessarily reflect the views of the NSF.

REFERENCES

[1] Erik Andersen, Sumit Gulwani, and Zoran Popovic. 2013. A trace-based framework for analyzing and synthesizing educational progressions. In *ACM SIGCHI Conferenc.*
[2] Ian Arawjo, Cheng-yao Wang, Andrew C Myers, Erik Andersen, and François Guimbretière. 2017. Teaching Programming with Gamified Semantics. In *ACM SIGCHI Conference.*
[3] Lionel Deimel and David Moffat. 1982. A More Analytical Approach to Teaching the Introductory Programming Course. In *Proceedings of the National Educational Computing Conference.* 114–118.
[4] Michael J. Lee, Andrew J. Ko, and Irwin Kwan. 2013. In-game assessments increase novice programmers' engagement and level completion speed. *ICER* (2013).
[5] Michael McCracken, Tadeusz Wilusz, Vicki Almstrum, Danny Diaz, Mark Guzdial, Dianne Hagan, Yifat Ben-David Kolikant, Cary Laxer, Lynda Thomas, and Ian Utting. 2001. A multi-national, multi-institutional study of assessment of programming skills of first-year CS students. *ACM SIGCSE Bulletin* 33, 4 (2001).
[6] Greg L. Nelson, Benjamin Xie, and Andy. J. Ko. In submission. Comprehension First: Evaluating a Novel Pedagogy and Tutoring System for Program Tracing in CS1. (In submission).
[7] Michael O'Brien. 2003. *Software Comprehension - A review and research direction.* Technical Report UL-CSIS-03-3. University of Limerick. 1–29 pages.
[8] Juha Sorva and Teemu Sirkia. 2010. UUhistle: a software tool for visual program simulation. *Proceedings of the 10th Koli Calling International Conference on Computing Education Research Koli Calling 10* (2010), 49–54.

Explicitly Teaching Metacognitive and Self-Regulation Skills in Computing

Dastyni Loksa
Information School
University of Washington
Seattle, Washington
dloksa@uw.edu

ABSTRACT

Current computing education practices do not support the diversity of students who want to learn how to code equally, leaving those who encounter barriers to struggle. For instance, students with underdeveloped metacognitive and self-regulation skills, or whose skills do not easily transfer to programming struggle to develop them on their own. The high attrition rates in CS represent a loss of talent, creativity, and innovation for the discipline which we could capture. If we could support all students equally, we would increase diversity in the field while better meeting the growing need for computer scientists.

CCS CONCEPTS

• **Social and professional topics** → **Computing education;**

KEYWORDS

Programming; Problem solving; Metacognition; Self-regulation; Equity

ACM Reference format:
Dastyni Loksa. 2017. Explicitly Teaching Metacognitive and Self-Regulation Skills in Computing. In *Proceedings of ICER '17, Tacoma, WA, USA, August 18-20, 2017,* 2 pages.
https://doi.org/10.1145/3105726.3105740

1 PROGRAM CONTEXT

I am a forth year information science PhD candidate at the University of Washington's Information school. I have completed preliminary work and am preparing propose my dissertation in the Fall of 2017.

2 CONTEXT AND MOTIVATION

We are making great efforts to meet the growing demands for computer scientists by broadening participation and access to CS education, but this is not enough. Initiatives like CS For All seek to make CS accessible to all students. Increasing awareness and access to CS education helps involve more students but, the ability to support and retain such a diverse set of students in CS education

is also crucial. Many students are already interested and engaged in learning how to code but drop out or fail at high rates. To retain students CS education needs to be equitable, supporting students of all backgrounds, identities, levels prior knowledge, and levels of problem solving and self-regulation skills. Currently, some students are being supported and succeed but, as attrition rates show, many interested students encounter barriers and struggle.

My work focuses on making CS education more equitable, supporting all students by introducing explicit teaching of the cognitive problem solving skills required in programming into CS curriculum. By explicitly teaching the cognitive skills necessary for students to solve programming problems, we need not rely on them having strong and/or transferable domain knowledge, problem solving skills, or self-regulation skills. This explicit teaching also demystifies the 'magic' behind how programmers write code. It shows learners that solving programming problems and writing code is a skill that can be practiced and learned rather than some innate talent that only a few possess. This knowledge makes programming appear more attainable helping learners envision themselves coding despite stereotypes, supporting and encouraging anyone who is motivated to learn.

3 BACKGROUND & RELATED WORK

While prior work has investigated many aspects of programming problem solving, methods of teaching the metacognitive and self-regulation processes in programming has received little attention. Some studies do attempt to train participants to use self-regulation strategies such as self-explanation [1] or using sub-goal labels [5]. However, these studies focus on *supporting* learning, implicitly guiding the development problem solving skills, rather than explicitly *teaching* the cognitive skills needed to get from a problem prompt through constructing a solution. The most relevant related work is that of Linn and Clancy [2] which investigates the use of case studies, highly structured worked examples accompanied with an expert's rationale. These case studies model an expert solving programming problems. While beneficial, case studies are information dense and require studying many case studies to cover the variety of programming problems students will face.

My prior work draws upon work in learning sciences, educational psychology, and computing education to identify, understand, develop and investigate methods for explicitly teaching the cognitive skills necessary to craft programming solutions to open ended problems. One study defined programming problem solving as six nominally sequential but iterative activities: interpreting the problem prompt, searching for analogous problems, searching for possible solutions, evaluating possible solutions, implementing a solution, evaluating implemented solution [3]. In this study we explicitly taught these activities, provided a handout of the activities, prompted learners to track their progress through them, and prompted learners to describe their problem solving state when requesting help. We found that this promoted greater problem solving success, gains in productivity, increased participant self-efficacy and avoided growth mindset erosion typically found in CS1 courses.

In my latest work [4] I analyzed current programming education content genres' ability to support learning process, introduced a new genre of process-based worked examples, described a method of delivering those examples, and investigated the effect of process-based worked examples on novices' problem solving. I found that four genres of programming instruction content are lacking theoretically important elements for teaching problem solving and even a brief exposure to a few process-based worked examples increased self-regulation in students.

4 STATEMENT OF THESIS/PROBLEM

Following from my prior work I propose to incorporate explicit metacognitive and self-regulation instruction into a formal web development course. This course was selected because it directly follows completing a CS2 level course. This project will investigate to what extent the effects of explicit problem solving instruction found in previous studies (greater problem solving success, increased self-efficacy, and stabilized growth mindset) are found in a formal education setting with students who have already completed a CS2 level course.

I hypothesize that the more participants engage with process-based worked examples the better they will be able to articulate problem solving strategies, will increase their self-efficacy, and achieve higher problem solving success.

5 METHOD

To investigate my research question I will run a controlled experiment. I am partnering with four instructors who are each teaching one section of a client side web development course during the autumn quarter of 2017. Two sections of the course will be control groups, while the other two sections will be the experimental groups, incorporating the intervention. The format of the course such that students will complete a programming assignment each week of the ten week course.

The intervention for this experiment is having students study process-based worked examples delivered online using the Problem Solving Tutor prior to beginning programming assignments. Both the process-based worked examples and the Problem Solving Tutor are described in prior work [4]. The control group will receive instructions to use a specific worked example before beginning their second, fourth, sixth and eighth programming assignments. To provide extrinsic motivation, use of the worked examples will be mandatory to receive a grade for their assignment. I will develop examples to use a context that corresponds to the course content so that each depicts a problem that is isomorphic to the problem addressed in the corresponding assignment.

To collect student demographics, measure starting and continuing self-efficacy, growth mindset, and measure articulation of problem solving strategies I will administer surveys adapted from prior work. Students will take an initial survey after they complete their first programming assignment. On this survey students will report their demographics (eg. age, gender, major, programming experience), programming self-efficacy, growth mindset and reflect on their first problem solving assignment answering the question, "What was the hardest part, and how did you solve it?" To control for starting self-regulation skills students will also reflect on a previously encountered programming problem. Students will complete subsequent surveys after completing each of their other programming assignments. These subsequent surveys ask students to report current programming self-efficacy and growth mindset and to reflect on the corresponding assignment.

To answer my research question, I will work with instructors to create opportunities to measure problem solving success as part of the assignment grading process.

6 EXPECTED CONTRIBUTIONS

I expect my primary contribution to be additional evidence that learners benefit from explicit instruction on metacognitive and self-regulation processes and that this holds true even for students beyond CS2 level courses. Additionally, I will be contributing insight into how, and when students develop helpful self-regulation behaviors, evidence of the effect of a new genre of instructional content focused on this explicit instruction and one example of how to integrate this content into a current formal education settings.

7 TOPICS OF INTEREST

I look forward to discussing methods for measuring problem solving success, metacognition and self-regulation as well as innovative designs for investigating them.

REFERENCES

[1] Katerine Bielaczyc, Peter L. Pirolli, and Ann L. Brown. 1995. Training in self-explanation and self-regulation strategies: Investigating the effects of knowledge acquisition activities on problem solving. 13, 2 (1995), 221–252.

[2] Marcia C. Linn and Michael J. Clancy. 1992. Can experts' explanations help students develop program design skills? International Journal of Man-Machine Studies. 36, 4 (1992), 511–551.

[3] Dastyni Loksa, Andrew J. Ko, Will Jernigan, Alannah Oleson, Christopher J. Mendez, and Margaret M. Burnett. 2016. Programming, Problem Solving, and Self-Awareness: Effects of Explicit Guidance. In CHI. ACM.

[4] Dastyni Loksa, Andrew J. Ko, Alexandra Rowell, William Menten-Weil, Dakota Miller, and Harrison Kwik. 2017. Beyond Example Code: Process-based Worked Examples for CS Education (ICER (in submission)). ACM.

[5] Briana B. Morrison, Lauren E. Margulieux, and Mark Guzdial. 2015. Subgoals, Context, and Worked Examples in Learning Computing Problem Solving (ICER). ACM, 21–29.

Active Learning Design Patterns for CS Education

Nasrin Dehbozorgi

UNC, Charlotte
9201 University City Blvd
Charlotte, NC, 28223, USA
Ndehbozo@uncc.edu

ABSTRACT

Successful implementation of active learning depends on a wide range of practical tactics. In this work, we adopt pedagogical design patterns to bridge between theory and best practices of active learning. This offers practical solutions for known problems in implementing active learning in Computer Science Education (CSE). We believe these patterns would help instructors customize and apply the best practices in active learning CSE. The patterns can be applied iteratively and adaptively for designing course materials and activities to achieve desired goals, depending on the context of the course. Pedagogical design patterns can help educators share their teaching design ideas in a structured style as well as provide a framework for thinking about and comparing design decisions. Another contribution of this work will be the practical and theoretical distinctions between activity-based teams and project-based teams in CSE.

KEYWORDS

Computer Science Education; Activity based learning; Project based learning; Active learning; Pedagogical design patterns

1 PROGRAM CONTEXT

This research is within the context of 'The Connected Learner' project [8]. The key goal of The Connected Learner project is to increase the quality of education provided for computing students. To achieve the goal of this project, my contribution is to identify the emerging design patterns and create repositories of teaching practices and pedagogical design patterns in CSE.

2 CONTEXT AND MOTIVATION

The context of this research is the development of a better understanding of active learning by identifying problem-solution pairs that can help CS faculty and students change and build

new expectations about the learning practices. Our motivation is to formulate patterns for active learning in CSE, similar to using design patterns in software engineering as a formal language to define successful ways to solve recurring problems.

3 BACKGROUND AND RELATED WORK

Active learning techniques and pedagogical design patterns are being applied by educators as methods for designing and delivering content in CSE. Active learning and learning from peers are innovations in education that are receiving the attention of researchers and instructors in CSE [1]. As opposed to traditional lecture, active learning requires students to do meaningful activities and more importantly reflect on what they are doing, thus engages students in the process of learning and makes them active learners [2]. It is reported that active learning particularly in CS education improves students' critical thinking and problem-solving skills as well as long term knowledge retention by 70% [3,4]. Pedagogical design patterns are a suggested method for effective record and dissemination of active learning [5]. Design patterns help educators to share their design ideas in a structured style and also provide a framework for thinking about and comparing design decisions. They are effective in describing problems and solutions, thereby relating very specifically to the issues a faculty faces in implementing effective active learning practices.

4 STATEMENT OF THESIS/PROBLEM

The problem this research addresses is the lack of understanding of best practice and effective use of active learning in CSE. A successful implementation of active learning requires structured and goal orientated practices with appropriate assessment methods. Although research shows students' performance and concept inventories increase in active learning [6], however, partial implementation of active learning might not result in desired outcomes. Therefore, in order to help students learn better and retain the course materials in active learning classes, a wide spectrum of context-related activities need to be designed, applied, and evaluated. The problem and critical issue is the 'design' of activities for successful implementation of active learning. Although educators have addressed diverse problems and solutions of CSE in the form of design patterns, to the best of our knowledge, the proposed patterns do not address all aspects of problems throughout the curriculum and there exist some gaps in mapping the problems to different dimensions related to each problem. Moreover, there is not a coherent model and language to share the design ideas consistently.

5 RESEARCH GOALS AND METHODS

The goal of this research is to capture the pedagogical tactics that are applicable in active learning in CS education in the form of design patterns through a common language. Corresponding methods will be identified to show the effectiveness of applying the emerged patterns from students' and instructors' perspective. Moreover, some techniques will be applied to define the relationships among the developed design patterns and determine the sequence of patterns to be applied for addressing certain problems. We believe creating a generic design pattern model and a pattern language will help develop a coherent set of patterns which in turn, would assist educators in sharing and disseminating a wide spectrum of techniques in active learning for CSE. The method being applied in this research is to build an abstract model for identifying the active learning pedagogical framework based on Goodyear's model [5]. This hierarchical framework includes four levels, which are: 'philosophy', 'high level pedagogy', 'pedagogical strategy' and the 'pedagogical tactics' [5]. In order to define and formulate the 'pedagogical tactics' the idea of design patterns will be applied. A multidimensional design pattern model will be proposed, to formulate emerging design patterns from the literature and the empirical evidences. The proposed design patterns offer best practices of active learning tactics for delivering content as well assessment methods (summative and formative). These design patterns have the flexibility to be combined and applied in different orders (sequential or parallel) to achieve certain pedagogic goals.

6 DESERTATION STATUS

Based on Goodyear [5] and Alexander [7] we have developed a multidimensional design pattern model, which includes dimensions to address the details of problems and solution in different contexts. This model also offers a rationale that connects research-based evidence with experiential knowledge; which enables us to show how active and collaborative learning is different to current practice in team based learning and lecture format classes. Three abstractions have been identified to categorized the emerged design patterns: Activity Based Learning (ABL), Project Based Learning (PBL) and Active Learning (AL) patterns. The ABL category address the problems in forming teams in active learning classes to accomplish certain structured tasks. The main focus of forming ABL teams is to help students learn new concepts, which is more applicable in introductory courses. The PBL patterns address the challenges about forming teams in capstone courses where students are supposed to apply what they have learned to a real-world project or problem. The PBL patterns are mainly applicable in higher level courses. Finally, we have the AL patterns, which address a spectrum of diverse active learning tactics that can be applied throughout the curriculum. The AL patterns are further

categorized into several sub-domains such as: preparation for class activities, different assessment techniques (summative and formative), in class activities, lecturing methods and social aspects in active learning. We have held several workshops with faculty in the College of Computing and Informatics to identify the emerging design patterns based on the practices of active learning in our college. Currently we have developed 50 patterns in three domains of ABL, PBL and AL. Three concepts maps have been developed for each domain, in order to show the relationships among the patterns in each abstraction. These concept maps help in relating the patterns to each other and in adopting different pathways for implementing active learning techniques. In the next workshop, we are going to evaluate the emerged design patterns from the instructor's perspective. Standard methods of evaluating students' performance and perception will be identified and applied to measure the effectiveness of these design patterns. Finally, we aim to generate a pattern language based on the proposed design patterns. This will help us expand the domain of the design patterns from pedagogic tactics to achieve the higher-level goals in the suggested active learning pedagogical framework.

7 EXPECTED CONTRIBUTIONS

The expected contribution of this research is a set of pedagogical design patterns that have emerged from active learning practices and are evaluated by CS faculty. These design patterns, which are developed based on a multi-dimensional model, are tools to share the design ideas of active learning practices in CSE to improve the quality of active learning practices. We believe a successful active learning implementation would improve students' performance and perception, which will result in higher retention rate in CSE. Another contribution of this work will be the practical and theoretical distinction between activity-based teams and project-based teams in CS education.

REFERENCES

[1] M. L. Maher, C. Latulipe,, H. Lipford, A. Rorrer. 2015. Flipped Classroom Strategies for CS Education, In Proceedings of the 46th ACM Technical Symposium on Computer Science Education. pp. 218-223.
[2] M. Prince. 2004. Does Active Learning Work? A Review of the Research, Journal of Engineering Education, 93:223-231.
[3] S. Pulimood, U. Wolz. 2008. Problem Solving in Community: A Necessary Shift in CS Pedagogy, In Proceedings of the 39th SIGCSE technical symposium on Computer Science Education, pp.210-214.
[4] T. Briggs. 2005. Techniques for active learning in CS courses. Journal of Computing Sciences in Colleges, 156–165.
[5] P. Goodyear, P. 2004. Patterns, pattern languages and educational design. Learning, 339–347.
[6] S. Freeman, S. L., Eddy, M. McDonough, M. K. Smith, N. Okoroafor, H. Jordt, & M. P. Wenderoth. 2014. Active learning increases student performance in science, engineering, and mathematics. Proc Natl Acad Sci U S A, 111(23), 8410–8415.
[7] C. Alexander, et. al. 1997. A Pattern Language: Towns, Buildings, Construction, Oxford University Press.
[8] M. L. Maher, B. Cukic, L. Mays, S. Rogelberg, C. Latulipe, J. Payton, T. Frevert. 2016. The Connected Learner: Engaging Faculty to Connect Computing Students to Peers, Profession and Purpose. 2016 IEEE Frontiers in Education, FIE 2016

Improving the Learning Experiences of First-Year Computer Science Students with Empathetic IDEs

Carla De Lira

Human-centered Environments for Learning and Programming (HELP) Lab
School of Electrical Engineering and Computer Science
Washington State University, Pullman, WA, USA
carla.delira@wsu.edu

ABSTRACT

Computer science has the highest dropout rate among undergraduate STEM degree programs [5]. This is especially concerning, given that computer science-related jobs are projected to grow 12% in the next six years [2]. One contributing factor is that media representations of computer science can lead underrepresented groups to perceive themselves as unfit for the discipline, and ultimately to drop out [4]. To address this concern, I propose an empathetic IDE model that uses affective computing technologies to promote empathy among computer science students. A quasi-experimental research design will be used to evaluate the model's effectiveness in fostering a supportive community between instructors and students. By leveraging emotional learning process data as a form of constant feedback to both instructors and students, this research can gain new insights into how to improve learning environments for computer science students with or without affective computing technologies.

CCS CONCEPTS

• **Social & Professional** → **Computing Education** → **Computer education programs**; Computer science education.

KEYWORDS

Learning analytics; affective computing; empathy in computer science; computer science education

1 PROGRAM CONTEXT

I recently completed my second year as a Ph.D. student in computer science at Washington State University, with a research focus on learning analytics. At WSU, Ph.D. students must pass a qualifying and preliminary exam, and complete required coursework, in order to attain "all but dissertation" status. I have passed my qualifying exam and am in the process of preparing my dissertation proposal for the preliminary exam.

2 INTRODUCTION

Over the next six years, it is predicted that there will be more jobs available than graduating computer science students can fill

[2]. Unfortunately, computer science degree programs suffer from notoriously high attrition rates [5]. A 2013 study that tracked students from 2003-2009 revealed that computer and information science degree programs have the largest dropout percentage of all STEM degrees [5]. One approach to improving retention rates is to develop learning environments that are more welcoming to underrepresented groups who commonly leave computing degree programs due to feeling unwelcomed and socially isolated [4]. To that end, I believe affective computing environments can play an important role. Affective computing environments collect data on, and analyze, factors that influence, emotion during the learning process [1,6,7]. Insights revealed through emotional learning process data can provide a more holistic picture of computer science students' learning experiences. Empathy among students and instructors can translate into students' developing more positive attitudes toward themselves and their learning experiences, which can in turn influence their motivation and ability to achieve academic success [3]. Emotional learning process data can provide a foundation for higher-quality instruction that is sensitive to both their emotional and academic needs. Through learning environments that provide access to affective states, we can explore a fundamental research question: *How to use emotional learning process data to capture and improve the experiences of instructors and students in computer science courses?*

3 BACKGROUND & RELATED WORK

Undergraduate computer science degree programs can sometimes be unwelcoming to students of different backgrounds, who may feel uncomfortable and excluded. These feelings may stem from students' insecurities regarding their programming skills, or from an insensitivity to students' different cultural backgrounds [4]. The presence of empathy in students' learning environments can promote positive emotions of belonging, which can provide students with focus and motivation to learn [4]. Empathy, when integrated into a pedagogical model, can strengthen student-instructor and student-student interactions, which can, in turn, promote help-seeking, help-giving, and student rapport [6]. To design a learning environment that is conducive to empathy by establishing trust with and among students, we can integrate Carl Rogers' person-centered approach from psychology into pedagogical models for computing education [3].

Studies of affect in computing education have typically been built upon technologies that are invasive to students' workflows, since they prompt students for emotion disclosure [1,7]. To date, non-invasive affective technologies (e.g., heartrate monitors, eye trackers) have not been used in computer science education, even though such technologies have been shown to help improve instruction by unobtrusively collecting emotion data that can be leveraged to improve learning [6].

Complementing my lab's studies of social and programming process data [9], my dissertation will consider emotional data to provide a more holistic view of a computing students' learning experiences. These data can be used to design and evaluate a pedagogical model that leverages emotional data to enable instructors to view and respond to a class's emotional climate, i.e. its collective affective states. The goal of this model is to create a more supportive learning environment through empathy, leading to more positive learning experiences and higher retention rates, especially in underrepresented groups.

4 STATEMENT OF THESIS/PROBLEM

One approach to addressing the high attrition rates in computing degree programs is to better understand students' emotional experiences as they engage in computing tasks, and ultimately to design pedagogical approaches that promote more positive learning experiences. My dissertation proposes an empathetic IDE model that both non-invasively collects emotional learning process data and provides both students and instructors with means of accessing a class's emotional climate. I argue that such model could 1) help students and instructors to better understand and communicate with each other, and 2) promote collaborative learning of class material.

The Empathetic IDE Model instruments the students' IDE with a tool to monitor affective states as students code. The tool will also render data visualizations of the class's emotional climate, while preserving anonymity [6]. These data visualizations will serve as valuable feedback to students and instructors, who can leverage them to improve their learning and teaching processes by heeding students' needs. The ability to view and leverage the emotional climate of a class raises research questions that will be central to my dissertation:

RQ1. How should a class's emotional climate be gauged, and how should it be visually presented, to affect positive changes in teaching and learning?

RQ2. How does access to emotional data affect a student's learning process, ability to complete assignments, and ability to persist in a degree program?

RQ3. How can access to emotional data impact improve an instructor's teaching and responsiveness to student needs?

5 RESEARCH GOALS & METHODS

My proposed research will proceed in two phases: 1) the design and implementation of an IDE plugin to collect emotional data and present it to instructors and students, and 2) an empirical study to evaluate the Empathetic IDE Model. Design and implementation will be aligned with affective computing technologies used in previous studies [1,6,7] with modifications to ensure that they are non-invasive to workflow. An iterative, user-centered design process will be used to ensure that the IDE plug-in is highly usable and effectively presents relevant emotional data. The design and implementation phase will

facilitate the collection and visualization of data on students' affective states, thus enabling me to address **RQ1**.

In the evaluation phase, I will conduct a quasi-experiment using a matched comparison group design. Data on a control and treatment group of first year computer science students will be collected within two semesters. This design will allow me to assess the model's effectiveness by comparing a traditional class against a class that uses the IDE plugin. In order to address **RQ2**, I will measure three dependent variables: (a) emotional changes, (b) intention to persist, and (c) assignment grades. Questionnaires administered on an assignment-by-assignment basis and IDE plugin collecting log data, such as each student's emotions, can enable me to explore these dependent variables and how emotions and grades are related to a student's motivation to persist in a computer science program. Interviews with randomly-selected students will enable me to collect qualitative data to help explain these quantitative measures. To address **RQ3**, I will use periodic interviews with instructors to qualitatively consider changes to instructors' teaching approaches brought about their consideration of emotional data.

6 DISSERTATION STATUS

I am in the process of writing an early draft of my dissertation proposal. So far, I have conducted an extensive literature review and developed a preliminary research design. In the near future, I plan to develop pilot study materials and begin prototyping the IDE plug-in. My goal is to complete my preliminary exam and dissertation proposal by the spring of 2018. My projected graduation date is the summer of 2019.

7 EXPECTED CONTRIBUTIONS

This dissertation will offer new insights into how data on student emotions can promote an effective learning environment within computing education. For example, the results could reveal what kinds of instructor actions might lead to positive emotional changes and improved learning processes and outcomes. By leveraging affective computing technologies, this study could inspire a more student-centered pedagogy that helps computer science students better self-regulate through an understanding of their emotions. This research will benefit computer science educators by providing a practical model for tailoring their instruction based on data on their students' emotional states.

REFERENCES

[1]   L. Shen, M. Wang, and R. Shen, "Affective e-Learning: Using 'Emotional' Data to Improve Learning in Pervasive Learning Environment," Journal of Educational Technology & Society, 2009.

[2]   "Computer and Information Technology Occupations: Occupational Outlook Handbook: U.S. Bureau of Labor Statistics." [Online].

[3]   N. Feschbach and S. Feshbach, "Empathy and Education," in The Social Neuroscience of Empathy, The MIT Press, 2009.

[4]   L. J. Barker and K. Garvin-Doxas, "Making Visible the Behaviors that Influence Learning Environment: A Qualitative Exploration of Computer Science Classrooms," Computer Science Education, 2004.

[5]   "STEM Attrition: College Students' Paths into and Out of STEM Fields," 26-Nov-2013. [Online].

[6]   M. Alsmeyer, R. Luckin, J. Good, and E. Harris, "Supporting affective communication in the classroom with the Subtle Stone," International Journal of Learning Technology, 2009.

[7]   S. D'Mello and A. Graesser, "The half-life of cognitive affective states during complex learning," Cognition and Emotion, 2011.

[8]   Hundhausen, C.D., Carter, A.S. and Adesope, O. 2015. Supporting Programming Assignments with Activity Streams: An Empirical Study. Proc. 2015 SIGCSE Symposium on Computer Science Education, 2015.

Hybrid Environments: A Bridge from Blocks to Text

Jeremiah Blanchard
Department of CISE
University of Florida
Gainesville, FL, USA
jblanch@cise.ufl.edu

ABSTRACT

Hybrid, dual-modality programming environments provide both blocks-based and text-based interfaces for programming. While previous research investigated the transition from visual to textual environments, few studies considered these hybrid environments. The purpose of this dissertation is to explore how hybrid programming environments impact computer science competency, confidence, and interest in computer science among students when moving from blocks-based environments to text-based languages. Exploring these questions will help us understand which hybrid environments are effective, in which contexts they are effective, and if they can improve on current approaches to CS instruction.

KEYWORDS

Computer Science Education; programming environments; programming languages; novice programming; hybrid programming environments.

1 PROGRAM CONTEXT

I have passed the University of Florida CISE department's Qualifying Exam. I recently conducted a study investigating the effects of hybrid environments on student competency and attitudes. The study compared students in text-based and blocks-based instructional conditions. I plan to propose in fall 2017.

2 CONTEXT AND MOTIVATION

Computer science is increasingly taught in K-12 education, making it important to find approaches that are accessible to younger audiences. Learning CS can be challenging as it requires developing several skills, including computational thinking, programming, and algorithm use [1]. These abilities are distinct and carry unique cognitive loads [2]. Visual languages and environments have been developed to address syntax challenges and accessibility. However, interviews with students suggest some learners have difficulty moving from blocks-based environments to text-based languages [3]. Learners may also perceive the programming experience as inauthentic [4].

ICER '17, August 18-20, 2017, Tacoma, WA, USA
© 2017 Copyright is held by the owner/author(s).
ACM ISBN 978-1-4503-4968-0/17/08.
http://dx.doi.org/10.1145/3105726.3105743

Hybrid blocks-text programming environments, having representations in text and blocks, allow quick transition between blocks and text, these environments may help learners overcome actual and/or perceived difficulties of text-based languages. As hybrid environments are relatively new, studies of their effectiveness are limited. If we establish that hybrid environments provide an effective bridge between blocks-based environments and text languages, they can serve as a scaffolding when moving from basic CS principles introduced in blocks to more advanced CS topics that require text languages in practice.

3 BACKGROUND AND RELATED WORK

Several environments will translate from blocks to text, such as Alice 3's translation of blocks to Java code [5]. Others also translate from text to blocks. One such environment is Pencil Code and its Droplet Editor, which let users go between blocks- and text- representations at any time [6]. In doing so, Pencil Code lets users move from blocks to text at their own pace. Studies of bi-directional hybrid environments are limited but promising. Bau et al. showed that students use text representation more often over time, suggesting they use the text mode more often with experience [6]. Weintrop studied students starting in blocks, text, or hybrid versions of Pencil Code's JavaScript variant before moving to text-based Java instruction [7]. His work showed that students who began in a blocks-based environment or worked in the bidirectional hybrid environment scored similarly [7]. However, unlike blocks-based environment students, hybrid environment students had an increase in interest in taking computer science courses in the future after switching to text.

Weintrop's work provides a foundation for future work. One open question is whether changing languages (from JavaScript to Java) impacts competency learning and motivations to engage in CS in the future. Changing languages requires learning not just new syntax, but also control structures, potentially increasing cognitive load on learners and impacting perceptions and learning.

4 QUESTIONS, GOALS, & METHODS

4.1 Goals & Questions

Goals
My goals include measuring comparative differences in attitudes and competency regarding computer science among learners who learn computer science via different conditions (text, blocks-to-text, and blocks-to-hybrid-to-text). In addition, I seek to measure how students' attitudes regarding CS, especially confidence in their ability and future interest, are impacted by learning environments.

Questions

When used as a bridge between blocks and text, how do hybrid environments impact student competency and perception as compared to unbridged transitions and learning purely in text?

1.0 How do hybrid environments impact student learning of CS competencies?

    1.1 How do conditions (blocks, text, and hybrid) impact student learning in CS generally and on specific topics?

    1.2 What challenges do students encounter when programming in blocks and text and when transitioning?

2.0 How do hybrid environments impact student perceptions of computer science and their abilities?

    2.1 How do hybrid environments impact student confidence?

    2.2 How do hybrid environments impact interest in CS?

4.2 Methods

4.2.1 Environment

Pencil Code actively developed, but its language support was limited to JavaScript, whose syntax can be very complex, and CoffeeScript, which has limited use in industry and academia. By comparison, Python has been recognized as an effective learning language [8] which is in common production use. My initial work involved integration of a Python runtime into Pencil Code.

4.2.2 Instruments

To measure student attitudes and competency, I developed both (1) a survey to identify changes to and differences in attitudes regarding computer science, and (2) a series of assessments in multiple, comparable formats (blocks, text, and mixed-mode variants). The assessment drew from question styles and competencies outlined in the SCS1 [9] and Computer Science Principles manual [10], while the survey instrument was based on prior research on gauging attitudes about computing [11,12].

Study Design

I conducted an initial study at a middle school over five weeks. Six classes of about 30 students each were taught the fundamentals of computer science and the Python language in customized versions of Pencil Code. Students were divided into three conditions of about 60 students (two classes) each. Students in the text-condition, the control, learned exclusively in text. Those in the blocks-condition experimental group began in blocks before transitioning directly to text, while a hybrid-condition group began in blocks but moved into the hybrid environment before transitioning to text. Both experimental groups transitioned to text at the midpoint. Students in all groups were assessed and surveyed at the beginning, midpoint (just before the transition in experimental groups), and end of the study. The pre-assessment used only blocks-based questions, the mid-assessment varied according to group condition (blocks, mixed, and text respectively), and the post-assessment used only text. Based on the outcomes of this study, a follow-up study is also planned next year that will follow a similar design but over a longer instructional period.

5 DISSERTATION STATUS

The dissertation proposal is in its early stages of development. I am outlining and drafting the first version. Results from the initial study will also be incorporated. In late 2017, I will my dissertation. In spring of 2018, I am planning a follow-up study to build on the initial study's results. A complete draft of the dissertation will be done in the summer/fall of 2018, followed by several months of iteration. I expect to defend my dissertation in the spring or summer of 2019 to complete my PhD studies.

6 CONSORTIUM GOALS

My goals at the consortium are to connect with other CS education researchers in order to learn about and understand strands of research currently underway. It is also an opportunity to receive constructive feedback on my dissertation's topic (hybrid environments), specificity (focus on bridging), and study designs. Knowing about ongoing research and hearing feedback will aid exploration of research questions and the design of future studies.

7 EXPECTED CONTRIBUTIONS

Research to show impacts of hybrid environments on learners of CS would be a valuable contribution to CS education. This research will identify benefits and drawbacks of using hybrid environments as a bridge from blocks and text. It will provide a statistical comparison of learning outcomes and attitudes in students who transition from blocks to text via a hybrid environment versus those who do not. By identifying contexts in which hybrid environments are effective, this dissertation will provide a key foundation for further research into hybrid environments.

REFERENCES

[1] JTF on Computing Curricula - ACM/IEEE-CS, 2013. *Computer Science Curricula 2013: Curriculum Guidelines for Undergraduate Degree Programs in Computer Science*, 13-14. Retrieved from http://www.acm.org.

[2] J. Sweller, "Cognitive Load During Problem Solving: Effects on Learning," *Cogn. Sci.*, vol. 12, no. 2, pp. 257–285, 1988.

[3] D. J. Malan and H. H. Leitner, "Scratch for Budding Computer Scientists," in *Proc. SIGCSE2007*, (2007), 223–227.

[4] D. Weintrop and U. Wilensky, "To block or not to block? That is the question," In *Proc. IDC2015*, (2015), 199–208.

[5] W. Dann, D. Cosgrove, and D. Slater, "Mediated transfer: Alice 3 to Java," in *Proc. SIGCSE2012*, (2012), 141–146.

[6] D. Bau, D. A. Bau, C. S. Pickens, and M. Dawson, "Pencil Code: Block Code for a Text World," in *Proc. IDC2015*, (2015), 445–448.

[7] D. Weintrop, "Modality Matters: Understanding the Effects of Programming Language Representation in High School Computer Science Classrooms," Ph.D. dissertation, Northwestern University, 2016.

[8] R. J. Enbody, W. F. Punch, and M. McCullen, "Python CS1 as preparation for C++ CS2," *ACM SIGCSE Bull.*, vol. 41, no. 1, pp. 116–120, 2009.

[9] M. C. Parker and M. Guzdial, "Replication, Validation, and Use of a Language Independent CS1 Knowledge Assessment," *Proc.ITiCSE2016*, (2016), 93-101.

[10] College Board, 2017. "AP Computer Science Principles Course and Exam Descrption," 85-124. Retrieved from http://www.collegeboard.org.

[11] Marcu, Gabriela, et al. "Design and evaluation of a computer science and engineering course for middle school girls." In *Proc. SIGCSE2010*, (2010).

[12] B. Dorn and A. E. Tew. "Empirical Validation and Application of the Computing Attitudes Survey," *Computer Science Education*, 25(1):1-36, 2015.

Determining if Spatial Reasoning is Required to Learn CS

Amber Solomon
Georgia Institute of Technology
85 5th Street NW
Atlanta, GA 30308
asolomon30@gatech.edu

ABSTRACT

Spatial reasoning may be a strong predictor for a career in Computer Science (CS) [9]. However, it is unclear why and how spatial abilities lead to success in CS. Investigating the role of spatial reasoning in learning CS may be important for broadening participation. Most students who excel in CS are white males or students from a high socioeconomic status (SES) [2, 5]. These same students typically score higher on spatial reasoning tests than their peers [1]. Thus spatial reasoning may be another factor preventing marginalized communities from succeeding in CS.

CCS CONCEPTS

•Social and professional topics → Computer science education;

KEYWORDS

Spatial reasoning; marginalized communities

ACM Reference format:
Amber Solomon. 2017. Determining if Spatial Reasoning is Required to Learn CS. In *Proceedings of ICER'17, August 18-20, 2017, Tacoma, WA, USA.*, , 2 pages.
DOI: http://dx.doi.org/10.1145/3105726.3105744

1 PROGRAM CONTEXT

I have completed my second year of the Human-Centered Computing (HCC) Ph.D. program at Georgia Tech. I passed my qualifying exam in Spring 2017 and hope to finish all coursework and propose by Spring 2018. I expect to defend my dissertation by Spring 2020. I have worked on many research projects since entering the program. During my first year of the program, I worked on a project to understand the effects of using design studio pedagogy in a computer science (CS) classroom [9]. I also worked on a study to understand the role gestures can play in learning CS.

I am currently determining research questions pertaining to marginalized communities, spatial reasoning, and performance in CS. I am working on a study to understand the relationship between socioeconomic status (SES), access to CS learning opportunities in high school, spatial ability, and performance in CS.

2 CONTEXT AND MOTIVATION

Students with good spatial reasoning are a strong predictor for a career in CS [9]. Spatial reasoning is a cognitive characteristic that measures one's ability to conceptualize the spatial relations between objects [7]. It concerns the locations of objects, their shapes, their relations to each other, and the paths they take as they move [7]. However, it is unclear exactly why and how spatial abilities lead to success in CS.

Investigating the role of spatial reasoning in learning CS is important for broadening participation. Most students who excel in CS are white males or students from a high SES [2, 5]. White males and high SES students also typically score higher on spatial reasoning tests than their peers [1]. Spatial reasoning may thus be a factor inhibiting marginalized communities (e.g. women, Latinx, African Americans, and low SES) from succeeding in CS.

A typical intervention would suggest that marginalized communities should just receive spatial reasoning training in programming courses. This should cause these students to succeed in CS. However, Hansen [3] suggests most efforts to diversify are likely to fail since they do not address the individual learning needs of the student. Interventions should pay attention to details like how students learn and think to improve achievement and retention. Spatial reasoning training may not be enough to broaden participation and help these communities succeed in CS.

Spatial reasoning may currently be a requirement to learn CS. Most students that succeed in CS may use spatial reasoning as a technique to understand code. Furthermore, CS classrooms may privilege those with good spatial reasoning. The CS classroom uses very spatial language to describe many concepts. For example, a multi-dimensional array could be described as a 2D sequence of variables. The way the concepts of branching or if statements are described may require students to visualize the "jumps" in the code when a statement is true or false. However, spatial reasoning could possibly not be a requirement for success in CS if content were presented differently.

Research suggests that members of marginalized communities use different techniques to understand in classroom settings [3, 8]. Women, minorities, and low SES may not excel in CS because concepts in the classroom are not presented in effective ways that match their ways of understanding. Instead of making these students have good spatial reasoning, the CS classroom should change to support their ways of knowing.

3 BACKGROUND & RELATED WORK

Several researchers have explored the relationship between spatial reasoning and student programming ability. Cooper et al. [1] conducted a study with high school students and found a correlation exists between receiving training in spatial skills and improved student performance in introductory computing. This improvement occurred for students of different ethnicities and across different SES. Mayer et al. ran a study in Basic and found that "success in learning Basic was related to general intellectual ability, especially logical reasoning and spatial ability [6]." Jones and Burnett [4] found participants with high spatial abilities completed code exercises faster than those with lower spatial abilities. They also suggested spatial reasoning may help students navigate code and form mental models of code execution.

This research has suggested spatial reasoning may be a requirement for learning CS and a technique students use to learn CS. My research, however, argues that CS can possibly be taught in a way that does not require spatial reasoning.

4 STATEMENT OF THESIS/PROBLEM

This research will explore potential relationships between spatial reasoning and performance in CS. Potential research questions could be expansive:

- What is the relationship between spatial reasoning and CS performance?
- What are the different techniques students use to learn CS?
- What does it mean to teach to privilege spatial reasoning?
- How do we design a classroom environment to best teach students who have different ways of understanding?

5 RESEARCH GOALS & METHODS

To create an appropriate intervention, it is important to understand if good spatial reasoning is necessary to learn CS. Using college students from diverse backgrounds (e.g. different SES, race, gender, etc), statistical analyses using scores on spatial reasoning tests and CS performance can help determine a relationship between the variables. CS performance can be measured using the validated CS measure, SCS1. This would be the first step in determining if spatial reasoning is required to learn CS. Once doing that study, then it must be determined what it means to teach to privilege those with good spatial abilities and if there is a way to teach that does not require good spatial abilities. To do this I could do a study where I would be an objective observer of introductory CS courses. I would analyze the language used to describe concepts by the teachers and in books, and other course content, to see if very spatial language is used.

From there I would need to determine what does a non-spatial required CS course look like. Understanding how diverse students currently understand CS and the techniques they use to learn would be helpful for this. Once understanding this, a proof of concept can be done to determine if spatial reasoning is required. I would teach one concept, for example arrays, and see if there is a difference in performance.

6 DISSERTATION STATUS

I recently passed my qualifying exams for my Ph.D. program in Spring 2017. I hope to propose my dissertation by Spring 2018. My expectation from participating in this consortium is to have a better understanding of how to design the studies for this research and to learn about other work that could impact my own.

Broadening participation is an ongoing effort in CS Education. It is important to understand factors inhibiting marginalized communities from succeeding in CS and designing interventions so that these communities can succeed in CS. Discussions and insights from this workshop can also provide understanding for how to use different methods, theories, data analysis techniques, etc. for my research to help broaden participation.

7 EXPECTED CONTRIBUTIONS

From conducting this research I hope to understand some of the factors inhibiting success in CS Ed for marginalized communities. The major contributions of this work to CS Ed research include a better understanding of the techniques students use to learn CS, different pedagogies for teaching to different ways of understanding and knowing in CS, and broadening participation in CS by supporting different ways of understanding and knowing.

REFERENCES

[1] Stephen Cooper, Karen Wang, Maya Israni, and Sheryl Sorby. 2015. Spatial skills training in introductory computing. In *Proceedings of the eleventh annual International Conference on International Computing Education Research*. ACM, 13–20.
[2] Maryanne Fisher, Anthony Cox, and Lin Zhao. 2006. Using sex differences to link spatial cognition and program comprehension. In *Software Maintenance, 2006. ICSM'06. 22nd IEEE International Conference on*. IEEE, 289–298.
[3] John W Hansen. 1995. Student cognitive styles in postsecondary technology programs. (1995).
[4] Sue Jones and Gary Burnett. 2008. Spatial ability and learning to program. (2008).
[5] Susan C Levine, Marina Vasilyeva, Stella F Lourenco, Nora S Newcombe, and Janellen Huttenlocher. 2005. Socioeconomic status modifies the sex difference in spatial skill. *Psychological science* 16, 11 (2005), 841–845.
[6] Richard E Mayer, Jennifer L Dyck, and William Vilberg. 1986. Learning to program and learning to think: what's the connection? *Commun. ACM* 29, 7 (1986), 605–610.
[7] Nora S Newcombe. 2010. Picture this: Increasing math and science learning by improving spatial thinking. *American Educator* 34, 2 (2010), 29.
[8] Robert J Sternberg and Elena L Grigorenko. 1997. Are cognitive styles still in style? *American psychologist* 52, 7 (1997), 700.
[9] Jonathan Wai, David Lubinski, and Camilla P Benbow. 2009. Spatial ability for STEM domains: Aligning over 50 years of cumulative psychological knowledge solidifies its importance. *Journal of Educational Psychology* 101, 4 (2009), 817.

Tools to Support Data-driven Reflective Learning

Stephen MacNeil
University of North Carolina at Charlotte
Charlotte, NC
smacnei2@uncc.edu

ABSTRACT

Reflection is a process of "critical review" of previous experiences to inform future action. Reflection has its origins in design and engineering but has gained traction in education as well. Reflective learning affords students the opportunity to reflect critically on their learning and develop metacognitive skills. Scaffolding is necessary as students adopt a reflective practice, but few tools support this process. Our prior work with teams suggests that students have difficulty estimating their turn-taking behaviors during peer learning activities and reflecting on such misconceptions might be detrimental to the development of social and metacognitive skills. I propose two tools that support data-driven student reflection: BloomMatrix and IneqDetect. BloomMatrix allows students to encode their perceived cognitive processes in an interactive version of Bloom's Taxonomy Matrix. This supports individual reflection, and an aggregated peer heatmap shows other students' perceptions. IneqDetect uses lapel microphones and signal processing to encode live conversations into turn-taking behaviors. In each case, students can reflect about themselves and also about others.

KEYWORDS

Reflective Learning; Data-driven Reflection; Reflection

ACM Reference format:
Stephen MacNeil. 2017. Tools to Support Data-driven Reflective Learning. In *Proceedings of ICER '17, Tacoma, WA, USA, August 18-20, 2017,* 2 pages.
https://doi.org/10.1145/3105726.3105745

1 PROGRAM CONTEXT

I am a Ph.D. student in the College of Computing & Informatics (CCI) at UNC Charlotte. I have completed my coursework and passed my qualifying exams. The remaining requirements are to propose and defend my dissertation. I have begun the proposal writing process and I plan to defend my proposal at the end of the summer (October 2017). This summer, I am finishing the implementation of IneqDetect and studying how a prototype of BloomMatrix supports student reflection. In the Fall, I will evaluate these tools in classroom environments. I will write my dissertation in Spring 2018 and then defend my dissertation during Summer 2018.

2 CONTEXT AND MOTIVATION

Computer science is a domain that is evolving. Concepts, technology, and frameworks are constantly changing and computer scientists are expected to keep up. They are also expected to understand the application domains in which they deliver solutions despite not having a formal background in those domains. Learning how to learn is a sustainable way to adapt to this evolving multi-disciplinary industry. Piaget suggested that an awareness of one's own cognition is essential for learning. Vygotsky builds on this idea by introducing a sociocultural aspect. Ultimately, developing these metacognitive skills is a sustainable way to support life-long learning. Metacognitive skills are developed by reflecting on learning experiences and adapting.

3 BACKGROUND & RELATED WORK

Reflective practice was introduced by Donald Schön in the context of design research, but it has been widely adopted in educational settings. Reflective learning often focuses on reviewing specific experiences through the perspective of a generated artifact such as in e-portfolios. E-portfolios support reflection at micro-level (single artifact) and macro-level (multiple artifacts over time). To our knowledge, few computational tools exist that support reflection, especially from a data-driven perspective. Our data-driven tools may address this gap and support reflection about students' cognitive processes and social interactions that occur during learning. I propose two tools: BloomMatrix and IneqDetect. Based on Piaget and Vygotsky, these tools support reflecting about cognition and social interactions at a micro-level (about themselves) and macro-level (compared to others).

Jay & Johnson proposed a typology of reflection consisting of descriptive, comparative, and critical reflections [3]. In this work, reflectors describe the matter for reflection, incorporate others' perspectives, and then renew their perspective. Brookfield reiterates the importance of incorporating others' perspectives and challenging assumptions when reflecting but acknowledges that it is challenging to be objective because the reflector is influenced by their lived experiences [2]. Data-driven tools may provide some objectivity through aggregating perceptions of cognition (wisdom-of-the-crowds) and ground truth about students' social interactions, leading students to challenge their assumptions.

IneqDetect builds on prior work in conversation and discourse analysis. A significant amount of work has been done in this area such as power-dynamics, politeness, and speech acts theory. One approach for analyzing conversations is to segment them into turns that may contain overlaps (timing-problems, interruptions, and back-channeling). Though semantics and pragmatics are useful for analyzing this turn-taking behavior, prior work has leveraged the number and duration of turns as a way to identify sociocultural inequities that arise during pair programming and online synchronous video discussions [5, 7]. Only one of these approaches analyzes turn-taking automatically, but it is not used by students for reflection. Furthermore, it only detects turns in online environments by leveraging online video affordances.

BloomMatrix builds on prior work that maps cognitive processes to learning outcomes. Bloom's Taxonomy [1] and others support this process, but a thorough review is beyond the scope of this abstract. BloomMatrix is an interactive tool based on the Revised Bloom's Taxonomy [4]. BloomMatrix supports reflecting on individual and aggregated perceptions in a peer heatmap. Prior work has also suggested ways that Bloom's Taxonomy might support reflection [8].

4 STATEMENT OF THESIS/PROBLEM

Providing data-driven tools that allow students to reflect on experiences from cognitive and social perspectives will improve the quality of reflection, ground it in a shared reality, and scaffold the development of metacognitive skills.

Q1. Does descriptive reflection differ from data-driven reflection, such as aggregated peer heat-maps of perceived cognition or visualizations of social interactions?

Q2. How do students interpret data-driven measures of cognition and social interactions?

Q3. Do data-driven tools for reflection induce cognitive dissonance between data and individual perception? If so, does this lead to deeper reflection?

Q4. Does the ability to reflect individually and about others encourage more comparative reflections?

Q5. How long do students spend reflecting on the BloomMatrix and IneqDetect as measured by activity logs?

5 RESEARCH GOALS & METHODS

To evaluate these research questions, students will use these tools in the classroom this Fall. Students will do written reflections for the first 3-4 weeks and then they will start using the tools. Instructors will give bonus points to students who use the tools and provide additional bonus opportunities for students who decide not to use the tools so that students don't feel obligated to participate.

After each learning activity, students use BloomMatrix to indicate along the cognitive and knowledge dimensions of the Bloom's Taxonomy Matrix how they perceived the activity. Then, they reflect on a heatmap of the matrix that aggregates student responses. IneqDetect will be used only during peer instruction clicker quizzes. During these quizzes, stronger students often dominate the conversational floor. Students can reflect on a visualization dashboard of their social interactions to see how many turns were taken, the duration of these turns, and a timeline of turns taken with overlapping turns highlighted. The interaction logs from both tools, focus groups, and surveys will help to answer the research questions enumerated above.

6 DISSERTATION STATUS

I have conducted numerous preliminary studies that situate my dissertation work (e.g. [6]). Three user studies have investigated how students learn in lightweight teams across learning environments.

I've studied turn-taking behaviors in these teams by coding transcripts of the interaction. Students were often unable to estimate their turn-taking behaviors. I've also explored potential sociocultural inequities that might arise within these teams. I have created the Design Space Explorer (DSE) that supports reflection in the context of design about conceptual spaces. I've implemented BloomMatrix, which supports student reflection about perceived cognitive processes. This summer, I am working with three undergraduate students to complete the implementation of IneqDetect which uses lapel microphones to detect turn-taking behaviors automatically. After my proposal, I'll continue collecting and evaluating interaction logs and conduct focus groups to see whether and how these tools support reflection in the classroom. I think the ICER doctoral consortium can help me finalize a model for data-driven reflective learning and workshop ways to mitigate concept shifting in the BloomMatrix tool. Concept shifting is problematic for BloomMatrix because the heatmap ideally captures students' perceptions of the same concept and activity. If students are reflecting on different aspects of the same activity this could lead to less useful heatmaps of aggregated perceptions.

7 EXPECTED CONTRIBUTIONS

Interactive data-driven tools for reflection may prompt students to reflect in novel ways, based on perceived cognition and social interactions. Data-driven reflection, rooted in wisdom-of-the-crowds peer heatmaps and ground truth about social interactions may also provide more objective perspectives that challenge students' subjective experiences and assumptions. Students reflect both about themselves, but also about themselves in the context of others. These novel ways of supporting reflection may lead to more equitable social interactions, a better understanding of one's own cognition, and the development of metacognitive skills that will support life-long learning. Finally, such tools may be used by the instructor as well. Having data about students may lead instructors to create learning activities that better target intended cognitive processes and encourage more equitable social interactions between students.

REFERENCES

[1] BS Bloom, DR Krathwohl, and BB Masia. 1984. *Bloom taxonomy of educational objectives.* Allyn and Bacon, Boston, MA.

[2] Stephen Brookfield. 1987. *Developing critical thinkers.* Open University Press Milton Keynes.

[3] Joelle K Jay and Kerri L Johnson. 2002. Capturing complexity: A typology of reflective practice for teacher education. *Teaching and teacher education* 18, 1 (2002), 73–85.

[4] David R Krathwohl. 2002. A revision of Bloom's taxonomy: An overview. *Theory into practice* 41, 4 (2002), 212–218.

[5] Colleen M Lewis and Niral Shah. 2015. How Equity and Inequity Can Emerge in Pair Programming. In *Proceedings of the eleventh annual International Conference on International Computing Education Research.* ACM, 41–50.

[6] Stephen MacNeil, Celine Latulipe, Bruce Long, and Aman Yadav. 2016. Exploring Lightweight Teams in a Distributed Learning Environment. In *Proceedings of the 47th ACM Technical Symposium on Computing Science Education (SIGCSE '16).* ACM, New York, NY, USA, 193–198.

[7] Adam Stankiewicz and Chinmay Kulkarni. 2016. $1 Conversational Turn Detector: Measuring How Video Conversations Affect Student Learning in Online Classes. In *Proceedings of the Third (2016) ACM Conference on Learning at Scale.* ACM, 81–88.

[8] Martin Valcke, Bram De Wever, Chang Zhu, and Craig Deed. 2009. Supporting active cognitive processing in collaborative groups: The potential of Bloom's taxonomy as a labeling tool. *The Internet and Higher Education* 12, 3 (2009), 165–172.

The Effect of Sketching and Tracing on Instructors' Understanding of Student Misconceptions

Kathryn Cunningham
School of Interactive Computing
Georgia Institute of Technology
85 5th St NW
Atlanta, Georgia 30332, USA
kcunningham@gatech.edu

ABSTRACT

The operation of the notional machine presents a hidden but crucial process in students' understanding of introductory programming. When students *trace* though code, simulating the operation of the notional machine, this hidden operation becomes evident. When students *sketch* this trace by physically drawing it, the operation is also visible to peers, tutors, and teachers as well as to the students themselves. Increased accuracy on code reading problems has already been found for students who sketch and trace. I want to explore whether sketching and tracing helps others better understand what a student knows about the notional machine.

CCS CONCEPTS

•**Social and professional topics** → **Computing education;** *CS1;*

KEYWORDS

CS1; novice programmers; tracing; sketching; notional machine

1 PROGRAM CONTEXT

I am entering the second year of the Human-Centered Computing PhD program at Georgia Tech. This program builds on my undergraduate degree in computer science with training in social science and computing topics that range from ethnography to artificial intelligence. I have emphasized cognitive science and learning science and technology, and have completed a directed reading with an educational psychology professor at Georgia State University. I plan to complete my qualifying exams in Spring 2018, propose by Fall 2019, and graduate by Spring 2021.

I have begun work in my thesis direction with an initial study that replicates and extends prior work [5] on the relationship between student sketching and tracing in CS1 problems involving reading of arrays, loops, and conditionals and success on those problems.

2 CONTEXT AND MOTIVATION

At a time when computing skills are in high demand in an increasingly automated economy, programming remains difficult to learn. Studies suggest that many students reach the end of CS1 without being able to read and understand short pieces of code [3]. Introductory programming also remains difficult to teach. New computing teachers point to a lack of pedagogical techniques as a clear challenge [8].

Researchers believe a major difficulty for novice programmers is building a correct mental model of the *notional machine* [6], a theoretical construct representing the process through which a computer executes code of a particular language or paradigm. Accurate understanding of the notional machine is central to students' ability to read and write code, since they must run code through their mental model of the notional machine in order to predict the outcome of that code's execution. A wide variety of misconceptions about the notional machine have been documented [6].

The process of the notional machine is not directly represented in code syntax. This poses a challenge for students, who must translate tangible code into invisible notional machine action. This is also a challenge for teachers, who cannot directly observe their students' understanding of the notional machine when looking at their code alone.

Student *sketching* and *tracing* are problem-solving methods for students and pedagogical techniques for teachers that make the hidden action of the notional machine visible. When tracing, students track the process of the notional machine for a given problem, typically noting variable states. When sketching, students physically draw this trace, perhaps on paper or on a whiteboard. Sketching a trace requires that the student take an active role as they describe a computational process with their pen.

3 BACKGROUND & RELATED WORK

The Leeds Working Group categorized and analyzed the sketched annotations that students wrote on exam sheets of code reading problems about arrays, conditionals, and loops. They found that students who wrote code traces performed highly, while students who did not write anything at all performed poorly [5]. Sketching and tracing are correlated with positive outcomes in this context, although it is unclear whether they cause the positive outcomes. Students who do not sketch and trace may not have sufficient understanding of the notional machine to complete a trace.

While the Leeds Working Group examined sketched traces "in the wild", sketched traces are also presented in a systematic way in some classrooms (e.g "memory diagrams" described by Hertz and Jump [2]). Tracing is also sometimes experienced by students through program visualization systems, software that displays the action of the notional machine [7].

ICER'17, August 18-20, 2017, Tacoma, WA, USA.
© 2017 Copyright held by the owner/author(s). 978-1-4503-4968-0/17/08.
DOI: http://dx.doi.org/10.1145/3105726.3105746

Sketching has a rich history of use in evaluating misconceptions. Prior work by Ma used student drawings to identify misconceptions about variable assignment [4]. In work by Chi *et al.* [1], sketching was used to evaluate tutors' understandings of student knowledge. At regular intervals during a tutoring session about the human circulatory system, students were asked to sketch their understanding of the path of blood flow and tutors were asked to sketch their tutees' understanding of the same. Tutors overestimated how often their tutees had a correct mental model and had great difficulty diagnosing students' misconceptions.

4 STATEMENT OF THESIS/PROBLEM

While sketching is used in some computing classrooms, the effects of sketching on student learning and teacher or peer interaction with students are largely unknown.

I propose the following research question:

- *Does the use of sketched tracing techniques by students increase instructors' ability to identify student misconceptions about the notional machine?*

5 RESEARCH GOALS & METHODS

First, I need to rigorously define types of sketched traces, and choose the most promising techniques for further study. Types of sketched traces can be found by examining student work, relevant experience reports, and attempts to create new sketched tracing techniques (for instance, most sketched traces focus on tracking memory states, but sketched traces could also focus more on annotating existing code to indicate execution order).

I plan to evaluate a variety of sketching traces on two criteria:

- Are sketched traces **accurate** to the true process of the notional machine?
- Are sketched traces easily **adoptable** by novices?

These two characteristics may be in conflict, since more detailed and more accurate sketches may be more burdensome for students to use. Adoptability can be measured in focus groups and at scale by presenting a variety of sketched tracing methods, and seeing which methods students actually use on subsequent problems. Accuracy can be measured by the ability of students to perform well on challenging questions designed to activate common misconceptions about the notional machine.

Once a variety of sketched traces are identified and evaluated, I plan to select the 2-3 most promising techniques and evaluate them in the classroom and in learner-instructor dyads.

- Are sketches **communicative** of the understanding or misunderstanding of the notional machine of the sketcher?

I plan to use a quasi-experimental design where different TA-led recitation sections of a CS1 course use a randomly assigned sketched trace technique with students. This will produce rich data on the use of the techniques in practice.

Finally, shared knowledge about sketching techniques will allow TA-student dyads to use that technique during experimental tutoring sessions. Similar to the protocol by Chi et al. [1], I plan to record TA-student dyads as they work through coding problems designed to activate common misconceptions about the notional machine.

Periodically, I will pause the tutoring session to ask students to solve an isomorphic problem and ask TAs to predict the response of their tutee on that problem. TAs' accuracy will be compared between different sketching techniques, and also correlated with the amount of sketched traces used in the session.

6 DISSERTATION STATUS

I have begun the process of evaluating the effectiveness and ease of adoption of sketching techniques in my current work replicating and extending earlier findings about sketching by the Leeds Working Group [5]. I identified five sketched tracing techniques used by students and instructors in CS1, and evaluated the accuracy of each method on an exam question. I also worked with a small number of CS1 students to gain initial insight on why some sketched traces may be preferred over others.

At the doctoral consortium, I hope to receive feedback on how I can narrow my research focus and refine my ambitions in order to create a feasible research proposal. I want to explore research directions related to how sketched traces can communicate understanding of the notional machine with others, which I believe is the most promising aspect of sketched traces.

7 EXPECTED CONTRIBUTIONS

This research will develop and evaluate an intervention that may improve introductory programming learning and instruction. This work may help computing education researchers better understand how students make sense of the notional machine, in a way that isn't possible though analysis of their code alone.

My results can also influence other areas of computing education research, such as program visualization systems. If a certain type of sketched trace is favored by students (e.g. a trace where past values of variables are crossed out yet still visible), then it is worth exploring whether program visualization systems should adopt this approach.

REFERENCES

[1] Michelene TH Chi, Stephanie A Siler, and Heisawn Jeong. 2004. Can tutors monitor students' understanding accurately? *Cognition and instruction* 22, 3 (2004), 363–387.

[2] Matthew Hertz and Maria Jump. 2013. Trace-Based Teaching in Early Programming Courses. *Proceedings of the 44th ACM Technical Symposium on Computer Science Education* (2013), 561–566. DOI:http://dx.doi.org/10.1145/2445196.2445364

[3] Raymond Lister, Otto Seppälä, Beth Simon, Lynda Thomas, Elizabeth S. Adams, Sue Fitzgerald, William Fone, John Hamer, Morten Lindholm, Robert McCartney, Jan Erik Moström, and Kate Sanders. 2004. A multi-national study of reading and tracing skills in novice programmers. In *ACM SIGCSE Bulletin*, Vol. 36. 119–150. DOI:http://dx.doi.org/10.1145/1041624.1041673

[4] Linxiao Ma. 2007. *Investigating and improving novice programmers' mental models of programming concepts.* Ph.D. Dissertation. University of Strathclyde.

[5] Robert McCartney, Jan Erik Mostrm, Kate Sanders, and Otto Seppl. 2005. Take note: the effectiveness of novice programmers annotations on examinations. *Informatics in Education* 4, 1 (2005), 69–86.

[6] Juha Sorva. 2013. Notional Machines and Introductory Programming Education. *Trans. Comput. Educ.* 13, 2, Article 8 (July 2013), 31 pages. DOI:http://dx.doi.org/10.1145/2483710.2483713

[7] Juha Sorva, Ville Karavirta, and Lauri Malmi. 2013. A Review of Generic Program Visualization Systems for Introductory Programming Education. *ACM Transactions on Computing Education* 13, 4 (2013), 15.1 – 15.64. DOI:http://dx.doi.org/10.1145/2490822

[8] Aman Yadav, Sarah Gretter, Susanne Hambrusch, and Phil Sands. 2017. Expanding computer science education in schools: understanding teacher experiences and challenges. *Computer Science Education* 26, 4 (2017), 235–254. DOI:http://dx.doi.org/10.1080/08993408.2016.1257418

Author Index

NOTES

www.ingramcontent.com/pod-product-compliance
Lightning Source LLC
Chambersburg PA
CBHW080931220326
41598CB00034B/5748